PATTERNS
OF ADJUSTMENT

McGRAW-HILL SERIES IN PSYCHOLOGY

Consulting Editors **Norman Garmezy** and **Lyle V. Jones**

Adams *Human Memory*

Berkowitz *Aggression: A Social Psychological Analysis*

Berlyne *Conflict, Arousal, and Curiosity*

Blum *Psychoanalytic Theories of Personality*

Bock *Multivariate Statistical Methods in Behavioral Research*

Brown *The Motivation of Behavior*

Butcher *MMPI: Research Developments and Clinical Applications*

Campbell, Dunnette, Lawler, and Weick *Managerial Behavior, Performance, and Effectiveness*

Cofer *Verbal Learning and Verbal Behavior*

Crites *Vocational Psychology*

D'Amato *Experimental Psychology: Methodology, Psychophysics, and Learning*

Dollard and Miller *Personality and Psychotherapy*

Edgington *Statistical Inference: The Distribution-free Approach*

Ellis *Handbook of Mental Deficiency*

Ferguson *Statistical Analysis in Psychology and Education*

Fodor, Bever, and Garrett *The Psychology of Language: An Introduction to Psycholinguistics and Generative Grammar*

Forgus and Melamed *Perception: A Cognitive-Stage Approach*

Franks *Behavior Therapy: Appraisal and Status*

Ghiselli *Theory of Psychological Measurement*

Gilmer *Industrial and Organizational Psychology*

Guilford *Psychometric Methods*

Guilford *The Nature of Human Intelligence*

Guilford and Fruchter *Fundamental Statistics in Psychology and Education*

Guilford and Hoepfner *The Analysis of Intelligence*

Guion *Personnel Testing*

Hetherington and Parke *Child Psychology: A Contemporary Viewpoint*

Hirsh *The Measurement of Hearing*

Hjelle and Ziegler *Personality Theories: Basic Assumptions, Research, and Applications*

Horowitz *Elements of Statistics for Psychology and Education*

Hulse, Deese, and Egeth *The Psychology of Learning*

Hurlock *Adolescent Development*

Hurlock *Child Development*

Hurlock *Developmental Psychology*

Jackson and Messick *Problems in Human Assessment*

Krech, Crutchfield, and Ballachey *Individual in Society*

Lakin *Interpersonal Encounter: Theory and Practice in Sensitivity Training*

Lawler *Pay and Organizational Effectiveness: A Psychological View*

Lazarus, A. *Behavior Therapy and Beyond*

Lazarus, R. *Patterns of Adjustment*

Lewin *A Dynamic Theory of Personality*

Maher *Principles of Psychopathology*

Marascuilo *Statistical Methods for Behavioral Science Research*

Marx and Hillix *Systems and Theories in Psychology*

Miller *Language and Communication*

Morgan *Physiological Psychology*

Mulaik *The Foundations of Factor Analysis*

Novick and Jackson *Statistical Methods for Educational and Psychological Research*

Nunnally *Introduction to Statistics for Psychology and Education*

Nunnally *Psychometric Theory*

Overall and Klett *Applied Multivariate Analysis*

Porter, Lawler, and Hackman *Behavior in Organizations*

Restle *Learning: Animal Behavior and Human Cognition*

Robinson and Robinson *The Mentally Retarded Child*

Rosenthal *Genetic Theory and Abnormal Behavior*

Ross *Psychological Disorders of Children: A Behavioral Approach to Theory, Research, and Therapy*

Schwitzgebel and Kolb *Changing Human Behavior: Principles of Planned Intervention*

Shaw *Group Dynamics: The Psychology of Small Group Behavior*

Shaw and Costanzo *Theories of Social Psychology*

Shaw and Wright *Scales for the Measurement of Attitudes*

Sidowski *Experimental Methods and Instrumentation in Psychology*

Siegel *Nonparametric Statistics for the Behavioral Sciences*

Spencer and Kass *Perspectives in Child Psychology*

Stagner *Psychology of Personality*

Steers and Porter *Motivation and Work Behavior*

Vinacke *The Psychology of Thinking*

Wallen *Clinical Psychology: The Study of Persons*

Warren and Akert *Frontal Granular Cortex and Behavior*

Winer *Statistical Principles in Experimental Design*

PATTERNS OF ADJUSTMENT

RICHARD S. LAZARUS

Professor of Psychology
University of California, Berkeley

THIRD EDITION

McGRAW-HILL BOOK COMPANY

New York   St. Louis   San Francisco   Auckland   Düsseldorf   Johannesburg   Kuala Lumpur   London
Mexico   Montreal   New Delhi   Panama   Paris   São Paulo   Singapore   Sydney   Tokyo   Toronto

To Bunny,
Dave and Mary,
Nancy and Rick,
and my acquired families.

PATTERNS OF ADJUSTMENT

4 5 6 7 8 9 0   D O D O   7 9

Library of Congress Cataloging in Publication Data
Lazarus, Richard S
    Patterns of adjustment.

    (McGraw-Hill series in psychology)
    Published in 1961 under title: Adjustment and personality, and in 1968 under title: Patterns of adjustment and human effectiveness.
        Bibliography: p.
        Includes index.
1. Adjustment (Psychology)   2.   Stress (Psychology)
3. Psychology, Pathological.   4. Psychotherapy.
I. Title. [DNLM: 1. Adapation, Psychological.
2. Social adjustment.   BR335 L431p]
BF335.L34 1976   155.2′4   75-29486
ISBN 0-07-036802-3

This book was set in Optima by Black Dot, Inc.
The editors were Richard R. Wright,
Jean Smith, and James R. Belser;
the designer was J. E. O'Connor;
the production supervisor was Sam Ratkewitch.
The photo editor was Inge King.
The printer was The Murray Printing Company;
the binder, Book Press.

See acknowledgments on pages 391–395.
Copyrights included on this page by reference.

The cover design is a mandala, a mystic symbol of the universe used in Eastern religions and meditation. Each version of the mandala is said to be built up by an individual through active imagination. Although each is different, the overall form is constrained by tradition: Typically a mandala takes the form of a circle enclosing a square. C. G. Jung, the famous colleague of Sigmund Freud, was greatly interested in mandala symbols and their unconscious meanings as expressed in dreams.

CONTENTS

PREFACE

In the preface to the second edition, I expressed the view that the field of adjustment was too important in psychology and human affairs and too rich in theoretical, research, and practical implications to be relegated to "Mickey Mouse" courses that are anti-intellectual or nonintellectual—courses that cheat students of solid understanding of themselves and the world. Indeed, adjustment overlaps many other central topics of psychology, including the psychology of personality, and social, developmental, and clinical psychology, and it has very close relations with all the health sciences. I believe too that there is presently a great growth of interest in topics that are part of the subject of adjustment, such as the stress of life, stress as it relates to illness and health, and the ways in which different people cope with the inevitable problems and crises of living. Both the academic and the practical sides of the psychology of adjustment should be well represented in any text. This value orientation has not changed in the third edition.

Nevertheless, I have made very major changes in the format and content of the book. First of all, by deleting tangential topics—which sometimes made the earlier editions seem like general psychology texts—and by making a more economical presentation, I have shortened it considerably. Thus, although personality is still well represented, I have deleted chapters on personality theory and assessment and have modified greatly the presentation of biological and social factors to make them center more closely on adjustmental processes and outcomes. There is much more emphasis on stress and coping, as well as stress and illness, and I have given substantial attention to the various models of adjustive success and failure, attempting more fully to evaluate the medical-biological, sociogenic, and psychogenic approaches and to help integrate these divergent yet complementary viewpoints in the mind of the reader. Although I have not written a totally new book, it is a substantially altered one.

The purpose of these changes has been to narrow the focus; to make the book less ponderous and formidable for students, more interesting and meaningful, and more teachable; and to bring it up to date with new developments in a rapidly changing field. At the same time, I have been at pains to retain a high quality of thought and depth of treatment (too often texts in this area are superficial) and to present the essential meat of an exciting area of research, thought, and application that is highly relevant for our daily lives. In doing this I have drawn upon my own direct experience with the earlier editions, as well as feedback from students and instructors in diverse types of educational institutions.

If these intentions have been successfully translated into reality, students should be challenged by this new edition, involved in it, truly educated by it, but not overwhelmed. And to the extent that I have succeeded, instructors should be pleased with the high academic standards without feeling that impossible or unreasonable demands are being made on the students' abilities. I have been assisted in this effort by interaction over the years with many graduate and undergraduate students at Berkeley who, unknowingly I suppose, have helped guide my thinking through their honest and thoughtful reactions in lecture courses, seminars, and informal contacts in my office.

My family deserves a share of the pride I take in this work, including my two married children, David and Nancy, and their fine spouses, who have lifted my spirits and also made me worry about the condition of humanity and its future. Above all, in addition to her constant, loving presence, my wife, Bernice, warrants my gratitude for her extensive help with so many of the less joyful management and clerical tasks connected with writing books, thus allowing me more fully to indulge myself in the pleasurable aspects of creative writing. Finally, I express thanks to the publishers, authors, reviewers, and artists on whose material I have drawn in this manuscript and to the editorial personnel of McGraw-Hill whose efforts and talents have helped create the final product.

Richard S. Lazarus

PART I
INTRODUCTION

PART I
INTRODUCTION

Although humans live and adapt as do other biological creatures, one of our truly unique qualities is that we are also aware of ourselves and what we do, and we view ourselves as having a past, present, and future. Like other species, humans are interdependent with the external world and profit from how it works, but our capacity to be aware of ourselves as beings makes us, probably alone among living species, try to understand what we are like as biological, social, and psychological creatures.

The most primitive humans were greatly preoccupied with the need to survive physically in a world of constant hazard. In technologically advanced societies, we have succeeded to a remarkable degree in controlling our physical environment. Now, however, we are beginning to understand that we cannot control nature except at a price—we are interdependent with the natural world, not in full control of it. The more successful we have been in overcoming natural catastrophes, predators, hunger, and disease, the more we have turned our attention toward the problems of social existence. And although we may no longer see nature as a great danger, we still tend to view other persons or groups as threatening and have not yet found effective ways of living together on our

Stephen Shames, from Magnum

1

planet. So today we are preoccupied with the search for serviceable interpersonal relations and inner harmony in an uncertain outer world. We want to understand ourselves and, if possible, use this understanding in piloting our own lives.

Attempts at such understanding make up the subject matter of the psychology of adjustment. In Chapter 1 we inquire about the subject matter of adjustment itself, and because individual variations in the way we adjust are part of the psychology of personality, we explore personality and adjustment in Chapter 2.

CHAPTER 1 LIVING AND ADJUSTING

The concept of *adaptation* originated in biology and was a cornerstone in Darwin's (1859) theory of evolution. There, however, it referred to the biological structures and processes that facilitated the survival of *species*: biological properties of organisms would persist in nature only if they aided in survival by permitting the species to reproduce sufficient numbers to replace themselves and even to increase in numbers. The key biological law was "natural selection" (Fig. 1-1) or, more simply put, survival of the fittest. Thus, in the evolution of species on earth, many new types of organisms perished (became extinct) because they could not adapt successfully to the demands of living, while others survived and multiplied because they could adapt. Throughout evolutionary history there has been constant pressure for the evolution of new, more complex, and adaptable forms, for example, the primates, of which the human is one version. Notice that in this definition of adaptation, the fate of the individual is far less important than the fate of the species, and the quality of life is of no great consequence. All that counts is that sufficient numbers survive and reproduce themselves so that the species does not become extinct.

The biological concept of adaptation has been borrowed and changed somewhat by the psychologist and renamed "adjustment" to emphasize the *individual's* struggle to get along or survive in his or her social and physical environments. The trouble with this word is that over the years it has come to signify making oneself fit the demands of the external world, when actually adjustment consists of two kinds of processes: fitting oneself into given circumstances *and* changing the circumstances to fit one's needs. As we shall see in Chapter 7, dealing with the healthy personality, psychologists who are reluctant to consider psychological health as merely

FIGURE 1-1 Until the middle of the nineteenth century, light moths were far more common in Britain than dark moths, the latter being quite rare. On the top tree trunk the light moth is nearly invisible while the dark one stands out. The light moth is thus protected against being easily seen against the light-colored tree trunks. However, with growing air pollution from industrial factories, which blackened the tree trunks, the light-colored moths were exposed to danger. At the present time the dark forms of moth have replaced the light ones in polluted areas, while moths in the countryside far from pollution are still predominantly light in coloration. Thus, mainly the dark ones survive in polluted areas, while the light ones are more favored in nonpolluted areas, an example of the continuing process of natural selection. (H. B. Kettlewell, University of Oxford.)

getting along or fitting into the external environment whatever its characteristics, and who regard the effective person as one who changes things as well as himself or herself, sometimes want to discard the term "adjustment" because of this one-sided connotation of fitting in with things. However, a change in wording does not solve the problem; for example, "adaptation" can also have this undesirable connotation. What we need to do is recognize that *fitting in* is only one side of adjustment, the other side being *changing the environment* to suit one's needs or values. "Adjustment" remains a highly serviceable word in psychology, and although its roots lie in biology, in psychology it concerns the many ways in which an individual, as distinguished from the species or group, manages his or her affairs.

Adjustment represents a "functional" perspective for viewing and understanding human and animal behavior. That is, behavior has the function of mastering demands made upon a person by the environment, and human and animal action can be understood as an adjustment to such demands. For example, people's clothing varies with the climate in which they live; it represents an adjustment or adaptation to the weather and has the functions of helping to maintain a relatively constant body temperature and making people feel more comfortable. Architectural forms also depend upon climatological and topographical factors, and people have shown great ingenuity in adapting the raw materials of their environment to the need for shelter and warmth. This is illustrated by the Eskimos, who build houses out of ice and snow in adapting to the rigors of life in the Arctic. Different cultures also build houses in distinctive ways even within similar environments, reflecting diverse cultural meanings and the ways in which different peoples view "the good life." Thus, the Japanese house provides little internal privacy within the family but erects a closed wall to the outside, while American houses provide maximum privacy within and remain somewhat open to the neighborhood outside (Rapoport, 1969) (Fig. 1-2).

HOW ADJUSTMENT IS STUDIED

There are two main sources of information about the ways in which individuals adjust and the effects of different life conditions: field studies and laboratory experimentation.

Field study involves the observation of humans and animals adapting to their natural settings. For example, animals in herds or people in social groups or societies may be the objects of field study. Field studies are not confined to the ordinary and familiar settings of life but are also carried out in the unusual settings of extreme emergency or demand.

A striking example consists of observations of the behavior of inmates of German concentration camps during the 1930s and 1940s. One of the best known of these was made by a psychoanalytically oriented psychologist, Bruno Bettelheim (1960), who provided vivid accounts and psychological analyses of the extraordinary physical and psychological hardships to which the prisoners were exposed and of the adaptations they made. Himself a prisoner, Bettelheim attempted to achieve some detachment from the experience in order to analyze what was happening to him and to the other prisoners. His observations provide excellent empirical accounts of what happens to people living under certain extreme conditions of life.

The concentration camp is only one example of many settings of extreme psychological stress that have been studied by social scientists. Sociologists and psychologists have also studied human reactions to unexpected public disasters such as fires, tornadoes, explosions, and floods (cf. Baker and Chapman, 1962) (Fig. 1-3). The panic following the famous Orson Welles radio broadcast simulating an invasion from Mars has also been analyzed and is another example of human reaction to stress (Cantril, 1947).

Field studies have also been made of personal crises such as those in which an individual or individuals face major surgery, military combat, a terminal disease, and the loss of loved relatives

FIGURE 1-2 Japanese- and American-style houses reveal contrasts in conceptions of the good or proper life style. (Top: Frederic Olson, from Black Star; bottom: Elliott Erwitt, from Magnum.)

(Lazarus, 1966). Field investigations by psychologists, psychiatrists, sociologists, and physiologists will be illustrated concretely in later chapters.

The *experimental study* of adjustment differs from field study in that the demands or stresses are produced in the laboratory. Because they are created by the experimenter, the psychological stresses of this type must, of necessity, be milder. The main advantages of the experimental approach over field study lie in (1) the better opportunity to make more precise measurements and (2) the opportunity to isolate important causal factors. The chief disadvantage is the artificiality or contrived nature of a situation that is necessarily simpler than the event would be in nature; the event cannot be duplicated exactly. This "unnaturalness" creates some degree of uncertainty about the extent to which the rules found in the laboratory necessarily apply in real life.

Very dramatic effects may be obtained in laboratory experimentation, however. For example, Campbell, Sanderson, and Laverty (1964) succeeded in producing a strong fear response in human subjects by injecting them with a drug (scoline) that results in rapid, short-lived paralysis of the respiratory and skeletal musculature without pain, anesthetic effects, or unconsciousness. The subjects were volunteers who had been previously informed about the nature of the experience and reassured that there was no actual danger to themselves. The subject suddenly finds himself unable to move or breathe for approximately 100 seconds. The subjects studied reported that they thought they were dying. If a tone is presented through earphones while these effects are occurring, then subsequent presentations of the tone without the drug repeatedly result in the strong emotional reaction of fear produced by the drug itself. In short, the fear reaction was "conditioned" to occur at the tone, illustrating one way fears may be learned.

Disturbed emotional reactions have also been produced in the laboratory by showing stressful

FIGURE 1-3 Victims of Hurricane Fifi, this Honduran mother and child react with grief. (Wide World Photos.)

films (Lazarus, Speisman, Mordkoff, and Davison, 1962); by making subjects believe that they have pathologically misperceived reality (Korchin and Herz, 1960); by making subjects think they have failed at a task that measures intelligence (Lazarus and Eriksen, 1952); and by requiring subjects to lie in a lie-detection situation (Block, 1957). One of the problems in laboratory research on adjustment in humans is the ethical dilemmas that such manipulations pose. Such research cannot be permitted to produce serious or permanent harm to persons or to violate their rights as individuals. All research psychologists would agree with this viewpoint. However, there is much ongoing debate over which types of laboratory manipulations are damaging or not damaging, or violate an individual's rights. For example, many social psychological experiments require that the subject be deceived about what is happening, and there are differences of opinion among psychologists over whether such research—which may be harmless to the individual subject and yet create the widespread impression that research psychologists cannot be trusted in anything they say—is ethical and should be permitted. In any event, because of such ethical dilemmas, it is often necessary to employ infrahuman animals in experiments on adjustive processes.

In a dramatic study with animals, Brady, Porter, Conrad, and Mason (1958; see also Brady, 1958; Porter, Brady, Conrad, Mason, Galambos, and Rioch, 1958) produced severe ulceration of the gastrointestinal tract by giving the animal subjects the "executive" responsibility of avoiding an electric shock through making an appropriate response. Four pairs of Rhesus monkeys were placed in cages and gently restrained throughout the entire day for periods up to six or seven weeks. The physical arrangement of the monkey pair is shown in Figure 1-4. Alternating six-hour periods on and six-hour periods off, the monkeys were subjected to an avoidance-shock condition. The experimental or "executive" animals could control and avoid the shock, which was administered to their feet (and to the feet of the control animals), by learning to press a certain lever. If the lever were pressed within the twenty-second period between shocks, no shock would be administered. Thus, to avoid the shock a monkey had to repeatedly press the lever at a sufficiently frequent rate.

Within a short time the animals had learned to avoid the shock by pressing the lever at an average of about fifteen to twenty times a minute. The most conspicuous result of this situation was the death of every experimental animal as a result of extensive gastrointestinal ulceration. One animal died nine days after the experiment began, another after twenty-three days, and a third after twenty-five days; the fourth was near death after forty-eight days. The paired control animals—in a similar situation but with no *responsibility* for avoiding the shocks—showed no indications of such gastrointestinal ulceration. Although it is not certain which of many factors in the situation was crucial, we can be confident that the stressful experiences of the experimental monkeys caused the severe somatic damage that led to their death. Similar "psychosomatic" disorders can be found in human beings, and some of the causal conditions can be studied with animals in this experimental fashion.

One perplexing feature of this research was some evidence that the intermittent nature of the stress, that is, the fact that it occurred on a six-hour-on and six-hour-off schedule, was an important factor in the production of gastrointestinal ulceration. Brady (1958) has described additional experiments in which the avoidance and rest periods were made to alternate on different schedules, for example, eighteen hours for avoidance and six hours for rest or, at the other extreme, thirty minutes of avoidance and thirty minutes of rest. When schedules were thus var-

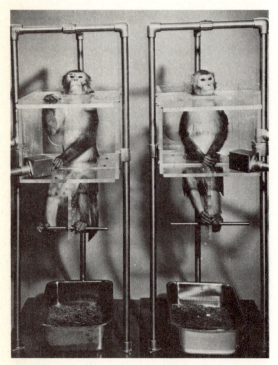

FIGURE 1-4 The physical arrangement in the "executive monkey" experiment. The monkey on the left can control the shock by lever pressing. (Medical Audio Visual Department, Walter Reed Army Institute of Research.)

ied, no gastrointestinal changes occurred in the experimental animals; only the six-hour-on and six-hour-off schedule seemed to produce ulcers. Brady has also reported that the stomach secretions of the executive monkeys became more acid following (that is, during the rest period) rather than during the avoidance period, being greatest in the six-hour cycle and less as the length of the cycle was reduced or increased. This suggests a close relationship between the formation of ulcers and the cyclic character of the stress experience. Brady thinks it has to do with some natural rhythm of the gastrointestinal system with which the six-hour-on and six-hour-off cycle must coincide in order for the stress to produce ulceration.

It should be noted here that other researchers in this field have obtained results contradictory to those reported by Brady, Porter, and their associates, leaving somewhat unsettled the question of precisely what psychological conditions produce the gastrointestinal ulcers. For example, a similar experiment was performed with rats showing that the animals which, like the "executive monkeys," had control of the opportunity to avoid shocks were *less* stressed by the experience than those receiving the same shock without control over its occurrence (Weiss, 1967). There were some differences in the two experimental approaches that could possibly account for the contradiction. Perhaps too, the stress effects work differently in rats and monkeys. At the moment, the issue is not yet resolved, but the research cited nonetheless illustrates well the use of animal experimentation to study problems of stress and adjustment that could not be carried out with people for practical and ethical reasons.

The field-study and the experimental approach to research on adjustment supplement each other, and the advantages of one tend to compensate for the disadvantages of the other. Both are indispensable means of obtaining knowledge. Typically, the ideas generated from field-study observation in the natural setting are tested more

precisely in the laboratory experiment, which allows researchers to isolate the many cause-and-effect variables that are usually mixed together in nature. Some of the exciting field and experimental research that was merely touched upon here will be discussed more fully in later chapters dealing with the stressful life conditions demanding adjustment and the ways in which people cope with them.

WHY STUDY ADJUSTMENT?

Although the reasons for studying adjustment may seem obvious to the professional person, it is important to make explicit for the lay reader the scope of the problem of adjustment and the form that the problem assumes for the society and for the individual person. Aside from intellectual curiosity about people and their problems, the study of adjustment is motivated by practical problems of enormous scope and significance. The most pressing and dramatic problem is the high incidence, in most societies, of mild and severe maladjustment or, as it is oftened termed, mental illness or psychopathology—frequently considered the number one health problem of our era.

Something seems to have been added to our ordinary problems of adjustment with the growing apocalyptic concerns over the fate of the world and of humanity today. We are beset continually by reasoned claims of the dangers of war and of nuclear holocaust; of eventual famine and pestilence resulting from exploding populations worldwide; of imminent destruction of the earth's environment caused by pollution; of corruption and dissolution of the stable social system under which we have lived; of economic chaos and lowered living standards, crime and a breakdown of law and order, and so on. Every age has had its prophets of gloom, but now many sober and informed persons seem willing to take these frightening visions seriously. Such a mood of doom, whether it is related to the near future or to upcoming generations, cannot help but have important implications for the ways people live and react to their normal problems of living, though it remains an intangible factor whose impact is very difficult to assess.

Disturbances of adjustment have been known in all civilized societies. History has observed such aberrations in kings, generals, religious leaders, and other notable persons since ancient times. Undoubtedly the common folk suffered from the same difficulties, but in their case there are no records. In the last century, however, the public has become far more aware of mental illness as one of society's most serious problems.

It is impossible to know for sure how many people are in fairly serious emotional trouble or are failing adequately to manage their lives because only a small percentage of them come to the attention of record-keeping agencies. According to recent U.S. Public Health Service data (1969, 1970) and other like analyses (Yolles, 1967), there were roughly 560,000 patients in state and county mental hospitals in 1955, out of a total United States population of 166 million. In 1970, with the United States population at 205 million, the number of patients in state and county mental hospitals had dropped, but was still about 350,000. The reasons for the decline are complex, among the most important factors being the widespread use of tranquilizing and antidepressant drugs in mental hospitals and the rise in alternate care facilities for the aged, who used to make up a sizable part of the mental hospital population. Since drug treatment is palliative rather than curative, this decrease probably does not mean a real drop in the incidence of people in trouble; it indicates that many such persons are being cared for in different centers than before (for example, community mental health centers) or perhaps have disappeared back into the community without necessarily being capable of managing independently or well. In any case, the hospitalized mentally ill still represent an enormous number of persons experiencing personal tragedy and serving as social burdens, and we have yet to make a real dent in the problem of adjustive failure, though we seem to be doing somewhat better, perhaps, than in the past.

Figures such as those above conceal large numbers of other people who are in some sort of major psychological difficulty and many less seriously disturbed who would profit from psychological help if it were available to them, or if they were able to bring themselves to seek help. Persons in mental hospitals represent only the most severely disturbed. To these figures we must add the roughly half-million Americans in federal, state, and local penal institutions or in the hands of juvenile authorities, as well as the approximately 10 million who come into contact with criminal justice for having committed (or under suspicion of having committed) serious crimes. By conservative estimates, more than 2 million Americans have made suicide attempts in their lives, over 25,000 succeeding annually. Most of these cases are associated with severe depression, and many with alcoholism. The best current estimates (by the National Council on Alcoholism, Inc.) are that roughly 9 million Americans are alcoholic and about 100 million use alcohol. Drug usage without addiction is very difficult to estimate, but the number of addicts in the United States is judged to be between 250,000 and 300,000 (cf. *Newsweek*, 1971). Psychosomatic symptoms also send people by the millions to their physicians. In other countries, or in parts of this country where facilities are poor and public attitudes negative, the incidence of adjustive disturbance may appear lower than it actually is because a higher proportion of such problems go unnoticed and unreported. Therefore, considering that all these statistics are probably the tip of the iceberg, the social significance of the problem of adjustive failure, by any estimate, is staggering. We study maladjustment because it is there, as it were, and because it is a social and personal problem of great magnitude.

Another side to the problem is subjective—the attitudes of people toward their mental health and the ways in which people of different social groups think about their problems. In recent years, systematic surveys by social scientists studying these problems have become more common. One such survey of American attitudes toward mental health problems was sponsored by the Joint Commission on Mental Illness and Health of the United States government and provided a somewhat different perspective than could be obtained from institutional data (Gurin, Veroff, and Feld, 1960). A representative sample of Americans were asked about the sources of their feelings of happiness and unhappiness. Some 35 percent of those interviewed referred to themselves as "very happy," while 54 percent said that they were "pretty happy," and 11 percent called themselves "not too happy." When questioned concerning the sources of unhappiness, 27 percent indicated economic and material difficulties; 11 percent cited their jobs; and 13 percent indicated personal characteristics and problems. When asked the question "Have you ever felt that you were going to have a nervous breakdown?" 19 percent answered "yes," and 23 percent indicated that at some time they had had a personal problem for which professional help might have been useful. The problems that were mentioned in relation to this feeling of impending nervous breakdown included the death or illness of a loved one, tension related to work or financial difficulties, physical illness or disability, personality problems, interpersonal difficulties, and menopause.

There is still a further side to the incidence of adjustive failures. In the effort to promote public awareness of the seriousness of the problem of mental health, professionals have also tended to make us all too aware of our own vulnerability, and one may easily get the false idea that he or she is likely to fall prey to serious mental disturbances. I can recall from my own college experience an overzealous professor who

reported that one out of every ten persons would fall victim to serious mental illness, and we were enjoined to look around the class and mentally pick out those who would probably succumb.

Not only was there something accusatory about this exercise, but it left many of us with unnecessary dread about our chances of having an effective and rewarding life unblemished by mental disorder. Putting it this way emphasized the hazards rather than just the opposite truth, that for most of us the chances were extremely good that we would escape major psychological illness. Moreover, as we shall see later, the bulk of persons exposed to all sorts of personal disasters, such as incapacitating illness, natural catastrophe, family troubles, and so on, manage to adjust remarkably well (Visotsky et al., 1961; Hamburg and Adams, 1967). While we should not understate the extent and importance of the human suffering and ineffectiveness associated with adjustive failure, we must also retain a high respect for the adaptability with which people manage the most demanding and distressing circumstances of life, and for the fact that many come out of such circumstances intact and even psychologically strengthened. The study of patterns of adjustment and human effectiveness includes both sides of the coin, effective coping and mastery as well as ineffective coping and adjustive failure (Fig. 1-5).

The widespread existing fear and ignorance about mental health matters are nicely reflected in an emotionally powerful political event of the United States presidental election of 1972. Senator Thomas Eagleton was nominated in that year as the candidate for vice-president by the Democratic party, with Senator McGovern as the presidential nominee. Shortly after his nomination, it was publicly acknowledged that Senator Eagleton had been treated in the past with electric shock for episodes of depression. The news created a great furor. McGovern at first supported his candidate, and there were many who argued that his psychiatric history had nothing to do with

FIGURE 1-5 The polio patient in an "iron lung" is virtually helpless without someone to attend to his or her needs and probably would not survive without the help of the mechanical breathing apparatus. (March of Dimes.)

Eagleton's present capacities to assume office and conduct his responsibilities competently. Others, far more numerous, worried that the election of Eagleton would put in a high political office a man with demonstrated emotional instabilities. So great was the distress about this possibility that McGovern finally forced Eagleton to resign, which he did, though he remains at this writing a respected figure in the U.S. Senate. You might ask yourself at this juncture how you might have felt concerning the fitness for high office of a man with a previous psychiatric history. If your honest response is to doubt that he is qualified, it illustrates a most general kind of prejudice few of us escape, namely, that anyone who has previously had emotional troubles or sought psychiat-

ric assistance bears a stigma forever after. This prejudice persists despite the fact that people who have never received professional mental health assistance have as much a chance of experiencing emotional troubles during the course of their lives as those who have been treated. In fact, seeking treatment can be itself regarded as a positive indicator of good judgment and maturity in an individual otherwise emotionally troubled, as anyone is apt to be occasionally. We shall examine more closely the problems of labeling and the stigma associated with adjustive disturbances in Chapter 12.

PERIODS OF ADJUSTIVE CRISIS

Young people in our society are apt to go through an especially stormy period of life before they achieve full adulthood. When adolescents are seen in assessment research, psychologists commonly overestimate how "sick" they are or underestimate their capacity to recover from the immediate crisis and achieve stability. One reason for such misjudgments is that standards of mental health are formulated for adults. Fifteen- to twenty-five-year-olds are often still rather remote from the established adult world of responsibility and privilege. Their personality is still forming, and they are still apt to be struggling to determine who they are and how they should live. In comparison with the stable adult personality, the storm and stress of the adolescent period may seem pathological to the observer as well as to the young person. Moreover, the professional who works in a clinic or hospital sees mainly disturbed rather than well-functioning people and may not have much experience, for example, with the adolescent who is going to turn into a reasonably healthy adult.

In any case, young readers of this book have a high probability of feeling psychologically troubled at this stage of life, and this feeling may falsely suggest that they are in deep and lasting difficulty. They may sometimes feel in conflict, anxious, alienated, helpless, and yet at other times able, powerful, and underestimated. They may be confused about their role in life and about the societal values to be accepted or rejected. This is not surprising; in facing the containment and expression of biological urges, the choice of career, marriage, and so on, adolescents do have real and difficult problems that must be dealt with on the basis of limited experience and often limited social support. The presence of these problems and an intense emotional response to them does not, in itself, betoken failure, although it does indicate the presence of a period of adjustive crisis common to this age. If the same crisis is still in force five or ten years later, there may be more legitimate cause for concern.

Similar misapprehensions about the significance of many actions or reactions are extremely common and often fostered by well-meaning parents or by social mores. A classic example is masturbation, although this seems to be less of a problem now than it was in the days when parents and doctors warned vigorously that the practice would produce terrible physical and psychological damage. Another example is the homosexual experience. A young person who has had erotic experiences with someone of the same sex sometimes becomes terrified that he or she may be "gay," although such fears are usually unwarranted. Fear of public exposure also restricts communication about such topics with peers, and thus the person may never learn how common such erotic experiences are.

At the very first sign of deviation or disturbance, people must not "push the panic button" and assume they are in psychological trouble. It should be possible for people to get professional consultation if they are worried about such things without the assumption being made that they should have to enter a lengthy course of treatment. As yet, such consultation is usually not readily available, except perhaps with the family doctor or minister. Unfortunately, the latter are often unable to judge properly whether or not

the person requires merely reassurance or extensive professional treatment.

Although an adaptive crisis can occur at any time in a person's life as a result of events, there are periods when such disturbances are more common because human beings experience a similar course of biological and psychological development. One such period, as we noted, comprises the storm and stress of adolescence in our culture. In this connection, it is known that the mental disorder schizophrenia can apparently arise at any time of life but is most common in late adolescence and early adulthood. This timing is probably no accident, for this is the period when the struggle for personal identity is at its height. This struggle has been discussed at great length, but perhaps the most influential present-day treatment of the "crisis of identity" has been presented by Erikson (1950; also in Lazarus and Opton, 1967; and Erikson, 1963). Knowing about such periods of crisis is useful to parents, relatives, friends, and professional workers, and such knowledge helps a person keep difficulties in perspective.

Another common crisis period occurs in middle age. The most frequent symptom of this crisis if and when it occurs is depression. Children

FIGURE 1-6 When the children leave, the house feels very empty. (Michael Hanulak, from Magnum.)

growing up and leaving the home, physical changes (gradual ending of menstruation in women and loss of potency in men), and the weakening of career commitments are evidence that life is waning (Fig. 1-6).

Certain events in life that produce adjustive crises are experienced in common by many people. Therefore, these events constitute signal occasions either for temporary breakdown or for the appearance or intensification of symptoms of emotional disturbance. Near-universal stressful experiences in living include military combat or invasion, the death of a loved one, separation, sickness or injury, marriage, divorce, loss of job and other economic catastrophes, and major social changes that uproot people and require severe dislocations in social relations (see Chapter 3).

In connection with the fact that adjustive crises occur with greater regularity and frequency at certain times of life, three additional points are important. First, the very act of living inevitably entails difficulties and perhaps tragedy that no one can escape. Everyone must strike out on his or her own when adult, often leaving a highly protective environment; everyone grows old and dies; if one lives long enough, he or she must inevitably face separation from loved ones. Although particular tragedies strike some and not others, no one escapes all of them, and everyone can expect to have to cope with major crises at some times in life.

Second, severe adjustment crises bring on psychological disturbances in most people. If they did not, if one remained untouched by them, this in itself might be a sign of psychological difficulty. In one's lifetime, one can usually expect to falter from time to time, to succumb to weakness and to the overflow of negative emotion, and to display the signs of psychological stress—the irrational thought and the maladjusted behavior. Such disturbances raise doubts about the person's mental health *only* when they are extreme or represent the usual state of mind, when they are protracted over an inordinate period, or

when they endanger one's functioning and sense of identity.

An excellent example of the last point is the danger of suicide in a transient depression. Depressions are not uncommon reactions to severe personal losses. However, they are also usually not lasting mental states. The tragedy of depression is not the temporary distress the person feels; this usually passes. It is when the person successfully commits suicide while in the depressed state. It is tragic because the depression would probably have ended, and the person once again could have participated fully in living. As suicide expert Edwin Shneidman (1963) has pointed out, most people who attempt suicide and are prevented from accomplishing it, either by luck or by professional intervention, are later grateful to be saved from death, even though when they attempted it they may have wanted very much to die.

Third, disturbances of living result probably only in part from psychological deficiencies that reduce the person's capacity to withstand destructive conditions of life; personal inadequacies are only half the story at most. Such disturbances stem also from the stressful social conditions of living. In personal tragedies, such as death of a loved one, separation, sickness, or injury, we are considering some of the near-universal sources of crises. People cannot be faulted for problems that are not of their own making. Too often others behave intolerantly toward them, however, as a means of affirming their own strengths or superior morality.

The mental health disciplines and the mass media have traditionally emphasized that *personal failure* is involved in maladjustment. This is a natural consequence of a culturally based value system idealizing the effective individual, the one who triumphs against adversity. Our heroes have been those who, in spite of damaging life circumstances or lack of advantages, manage to achieve success or distinction. In the 1930s, stories by the American author Horatio Alger served as the motivating fables of a whole generation. Alger's books employed challenging titles such as *Survive or Perish*, *Sink or Swim*, *Success Against Odds*. Such literary heroes have not altogether disappeared, although they have become more sophisticated or perhaps more realistic. Admiration is reserved still for the person who triumphs in spite of personal handicaps, and although it is perhaps tempered or inhibited in humanistic circles, contempt is still directed at the complainer, the abject failure, the weakling and coward. The concept of tragedy is generally focused on the person of heroic proportions, the person who is respected or is an object of sympathy but who cannot overcome inevitable personal disaster (Fig. 1-7).

This is not to suggest that our values are unsound, or that one should not admire those who do triumph over life's insults. Quite the contrary. However, it should be recognized that a large part of adjustive failure concerns destructive social conditions of life. When a person fails, especially if the failure is a temporary condition, additional strengths may be derived from such regressive moments. The notion that the ideal life adjustment is characterized by calm and controlled efficiency and detachment is entirely an inappropriate and dangerous fiction.

FIGURE 1-7 A modern-day Horatio Alger type: Frank Robinson hits a home run in his debut as the first black manager in major league baseball. (Wide World Photos.)

ADJUSTMENT AS ACHIEVEMENT OR PROCESS

There are two important ways of thinking about adjustment. The first has to do with its adequacy. As such, adjustment is regarded as an *achievement* that is accomplished either badly or well. This is a practical way of looking at the matter because it permits us to turn to such questions as how unsatisfactory adjustment can be prevented and how it can be improved. The second perspective is adjustment as a *process*. We ask, "How does an individual, or how do people in general, adjust under different circumstances, and what influences this adjustment?"

In essence, the two aspects of adjustment reflect different purposes. The first is emphasized when we are evaluating or attempting to do something about adjustment. The second is emphasized when we want to understand adjustment for its own sake. Nevertheless, practical purposes require sound knowledge, and in turn, practical efforts also teach us about the processes themselves. Therefore, although the stated purposes of these two points of view are different, they are really quite interdependent.

SUMMING UP

The concept of *adaptation* originated in biology, where it meant species survival, but was borrowed by psychology, where it is centered more on the individual person and how he or she manages living. In psychology it is called *adjust-*

ment and is studied both in field settings and experimentally in the laboratory. It is a particularly important area of research and professional concern because maladjustment is so widespread and costly in terms of human resources and human misery.

Problems of adjustment are universal in that all people must face difficult and troubling circumstances of living. The nature of our problems often changes from one period of life to another. For example, a key problem for adolescents and young adults is the determination of their psychological and social identity, that is, who one is and what one's role is in the social scheme. Later in life other problems will have to be managed, such as bereavement, threats to career or livelihood, aging, and changing commitments in life.

The test of effective adjustment is not the absence of crisis but the manner in which the normally expected stresses of living are handled. No one can remain untouched by adjustive struggles.

As a subject for study, adjustment can be treated in two ways: first as an *achievement* to be evaluated, that is, as something we do well or poorly; second, as something we all do, a process that we need to understand without necessarily evaluating. Although these perspectives on adjustment are different, they also overlap, since only if we can understand the rules about how persons adjust can we deal constructively with adjustive failure by helping parents raise more effective children or helping a troubled individual adjust to life better.

CHAPTER 2 PERSONALITY AND ADJUSTMENT

Personality consists of the stable psychological characteristics of the individual that dispose him or her to deal with situations in certain distinctive ways. Thus, adjustment and personality are inextricably bound together in two ways. First, in the same situation two people often show different kinds of adjustive processes. When exposed to social pressure, for example, one individual conforms or accommodates to it, while another acts independently. There must be some personality quality making them react differently to the same kind of situation. Consequently, in order to understand individual differences in the adjustive process, it is necessary to turn also to differences in biological makeup and in the life history of the person from which personality traits are derived and which, in turn, shape the individual's reactions.

Second, personality refers to *stable* variations in the techniques or processes of adjustment. Stable forms of adjustment can be regarded as traits of personality, in other words, characteristics of a person that make it possible to differentiate that person and his or her behavior from others in a variety of situations and occasions. We say, for example, that one individual tends to persist in striving even after suffering defeat, while another gives up. In short, personality and adjustment are totally interrelated subjects of study. They are two sides of the same coin, and it is really impossible to speak of one without the other.

THE CONCEPT OF PERSONALITY

To the lay person, personality usually means the stimulus value of another individual, that is, how one reacts to that individual. Does the other person have a "good personality" or a "bad personality"? Is he a "nice" guy? Do we like her? Does she impress us? The concern is not what the other person is objectively like, but how he or she meets our personal needs. Since one individual's reaction to a given person may be quite different from another's, in this sense a person might be said to have as many personalities as there are different reactions to him or her.

Although a person's effect on others is an interesting issue, it is not, per se, the way psychologists define personality. Professional interest in personality has to do with the way a person is constructed, so to speak, the psychological properties or traits that influence actions in various situations and how these develop and work. The emphasis is not on how others react to the person, but rather on the consistent ways in which *the person* reacts. The distinction is analogous to the way a geologist, as compared with an artist, looks at rocks. The artist wants to convey the rocks' esthetic impressions; the geologist is interested in their chemical or molecular structure, the variations in this structure, and the conditions creating them. The personality psychologist is concerned with the (psychological) structure of persons, the way this structure develops, variations among different individuals, and the conditions producing these variations.

On the basis of the common-sense relation between the stimulus and behavior, it would be natural to seek an understanding of a person's actions in the transitory milieu in which that person is always embedded. Changes in personal behavior would be attributed to changes in stimuli. The external stimuli are extremely important in guiding a person's reactions, but they are only part of the story. The fact is that we cannot understand behavior simply by reference to the external circumstances in which it occurs. There is also a remarkable degree of consistency to a person. We seem to carry around with us *dispositions* to think or act in certain ways that are to some extent independent of the situation. For example, one individual may practically never evidence anger, even under extremely provoking circumstances, while another carries a "chip on his shoulder," as it were, becoming angry and hostile for the slightest reason.

In the first illustration, the absence of hostile behavior cannot be attributed to the external circumstances, because such circumstances appear to provoke hostility in most other persons. In the second instance, the individual's anger cannot be blamed on the situation alone, because it occurs frequently and somewhat independently of circumstances. In both cases, the hostile behavior or its absence shows consistency from situation to situation. It probably should be attributed to *characteristics within the person.*

Although it is correct to say that without understanding the nature of an individual's personality we cannot fully understand that person's behavior, it is equally true that a knowledge of personality without reference to the circumstances in which a person behaves also provides only limited understanding. For this reason the basis of an analysis of personality structure alone is difficult; the future external conditions to which the person will be subjected are rarely known. The personality of an individual makes certain behaviors highly probable and others improbable, and predictions are essentially statements about these probabilities. However, the actual future behavior of a person is determined by the *interaction* of both personality structure and the social and physical circumstances to which he or she is exposed.

How then is personality defined? One of the best historical discussions of this question is Gordon Allport's (1937), which, although far from recent, is still worth reading today. Allport points out that the word "personality" has its origins in the Latin term *persona*, which denoted the mask first used in Greek drama and later by Roman actors. The mask defined the character in terms of the role that the actor was playing. He identified fifty distinctly different meanings of the concept of personality, beginning with the persona or mask and including many other diverse ideas.

Allport distinguished five different *types of psychological definitions* of personality:

1 *Omnibus* definitions usually begin with the phrase "Personality is the sum total of . . ." Such a definition expresses an aggregate or collection of properties or qualities. An example is the definition that "Personality is the sum-total of all the biological innate dispositions, impulses, tendencies, appetites, and instincts of the individual, and the acquired dispositions and tendencies acquired by experience." Allport has criticized such omnibus definitions because the mere listing of characteristics leaves out the most important aspect of mental life as Allport saw it (p. 44)—"the presence of *orderly arrangement*. The mere cataloguing of ingredients defines personality no better than the alphabet defines lyric poetry."

2 *Integrative and configural definitions* stress the organization of personal attributes, as in the definition of personality as "the entire organization of a human being at any stage of his development."

3 *Hierarchical definitions* involve the specification of various levels of organization, usually with an innermost image or self that dominates. An example is the definition of William James (1890), which is expressed in terms of four selves: the material self, the social self, the spiritual self, and a core category, a pure ego or self of selves.

4 *Definitions of personality in terms of adjustment* have often been preferred by psychologists and biologists whose view of man emphasizes survival and evolution, as in the definition of personality as "the integration of those systems of habits that represent an individual's characteristic adjustments to his environment."

5 Finally *definitions in terms of distinctiveness* are illustrated by the statement that "Personality is the organized system, the functioning whole or unity of habits, dispositions and sentiments that mark off any one member of a group as being different from any other member of the same group."

Allport himself prefers definitions of personality that emphasize three main elements: an *organization* of properties that refer to general styles of life and modes of *adjustment* to one's sur-

roundings and reflect the idea of the progressive growth and development of individuality or *distinctiveness*. He presents a definition that includes each of these within it. Since the publication of his book in 1937—an event which established personality as a systematic psychological discipline—Allport's definition (p. 48) has probably been more widely cited than any other: "*Personality is the dynamic organization within the individual of those psychophysical systems that determine his unique adjustments to his environment.*" The word "psychophysical" is used by Allport to remind us that "personality is neither exclusively mental nor exclusively neural." This definition, which stresses organization, adjustment, and distinctiveness or uniqueness, has never really been improved upon, and it is offered here as the most satisfactory statement of what is meant in the abstract by personality. Of the utmost importance is the idea contained in this definition that personality traits determine the individual's behavior, along with the situations to which he or she is exposed. In effect, personality is what the philosophers of science call a "dispositional concept"; that is, it involves *dispositions to act* in certain ways which a person carries around.

It should be noted that in a recent revision Allport (1961) has changed his definition of personality slightly, to read "*Personality is the dynamic organization within the individual of those psychophysical systems that determine his characteristic behavior and thought.*" Left out of this newer definition is the idea of uniqueness, perhaps because Allport was concerned that such an emphasis might seem to exclude personality from scientific study that deals with generalizations about people. Added is the term "characteristic," presumably to emphasize the idea of stability. And the earlier focus on adjustment has been deleted and replaced with the broader concepts of behavior and thought. For example, Allport suggests that we not only adjust to the environment, but we also reflect on it. Both these definitions, the earlier one and the more recent one, seem quite comparable, and the newer version seems to offer only slight fundamental improvement over the original, especially when one realizes that Allport is still concerned with uniqueness and adjustment, although he would also prefer to encompass this idea of uniqueness within the realm of scientific analysis.

SCIENTIFIC PRINCIPLES AND THE INDIVIDUAL

What, fundamentally, does research in personality consist of? The first problem of such research is to describe the personality. This description is done by observing what people do and by speculating about the properties in people that might account for their behavior. The properties are known from observations of behavior either in the laboratory or in the field. The personality researcher also tries to identify the past conditions that have caused or influenced the observed behaviors. These causal conditions, and the behavioral effects of these conditions, are considered the "empirical variables" of personality research. The unseen properties within the person that are presumably created by the causal variables, and that, in turn, influence the behavioral outcome, are referred to as the "personality variables"—in effect, these latter are treated as *the personality*. More will be said later about the way this strategy of analysis works.

Science advances by formulating general principles about the events in the world. All sciences systematize the multiplicity of known facts by including many events under a relatively small number of concepts. Without such systematization, there would remain a chaotic and unmanageable collection of data. The problem for the personality theorist is to provide a manageably small number of rules that can be applied to persons in general and that enable comprehension of their varying behaviors.

There are millions of persons in the United States and several billions of persons in the world. Each is unique and different from every other person, although they are also similar to each other in certain basic respects. To have separate principles for each person would require too many to be manageable. Thus, scientists try to determine the general principles that can apply to the universe of cases. Such abstract or general principles will necessarily tend to overlook or obscure minor variations among persons, and an apparent gap between the general "model" and the individual specimen will always exist.

This gap can be illustrated by considering the development of social motives, such as approval or achievement. There are general principles about motivation that apply to all people regardless of the particular individuals involved. All people, presumably, acquire motives through the same rules, for example, on the basis of given physiological needs and drives, of the values important to families and peers, and of social experiences, some of which all people share because of common developmental histories (such as inevitably being children or facing frustrations and threats) and some of which vary from individual to individual. A theory of general motivation is a statement about the mechanisms and life conditions by which motives are acquired in all people. The nature of these mechanisms is essentially the same for everyone; thus they constitute general principles of personality development.

The question arises, however, whether or not these *general* principles of motivation can be applied to an *individual* person. To a certain extent they can, indeed, but they cannot be accurately applied to predict the motivational pattern of an individual unless very detailed information about the particular individual and his or her conditions of life is provided. Parental values vary, and even physiological needs and drives are probably not completely identical from individual to individual. For example, one individual lives in a society that emphasizes achievement (for example, the United States), another in a society that emphasizes social approval (for example, Japan). One individual is physically robust, another sickly. In short, the conditions of life relevant to the learning of motives to which one individual is exposed are not the same as those of another. Thus, the specific characteristics of motivational acquisition will vary with the unique combination of relevant events in each particular case. The same point is applicable to any characteristic of personality, whether it be the pattern and strengths of motives, the characteristics of conscience, or the preferred ways of dealing with internal and external demands. The development of a given quality of personality is always lawful and describable in general terms. But application to an individual case presents a complicated problem requiring a large number of specific bits of information from which to predict the particular event.

The scientist of personality is interested, fundamentally, in general laws about behavior and its underlying structure. There are times, however, when understanding and predicting the behavior of an individual case is of paramount practical importance. For example, in our family there may be a disturbed or mentally retarded individual. In this instance, a knowledge of the general principles of pathology will not content us if they cannot be applied to the individual person about whom we are concerned.

This gap between general laws and their practical application to an individual poses a dilemma for the applied scientist or practitioner, both of whom have practical stakes in the operation of the world. The same distinction is manifest between the primary interests of the biologist and the physician, the physicist and the engineer, the theoretical psychologist and the clinical practitioner faced with the task of helping a person in trouble. The problem of the individual case is keenest in the human context where individual variation is great and where the welfare of the individual person is so important. The gap is

often felt keenly also by people who, as citizens, are anxious to find rational solutions to the problems besetting their society and the human race in general.

A key problem in applying general laws to a particular case has to do with the availability of the necessary information. It may be possible to make precise predictions in some applied scientific fields on the basis of knowledge of the important factors, but the measurements that would make such prediction possible are sometimes not readily available. Consider the example of the meteorologist trying to forecast the movements of a dangerous hurricane. If all the relevant conditions for its movement were known, such as the path of the jet stream far above the earth's surface and the pressures and air currents along the course of the storm, the forecaster might be far more accurate. Often, however, such information is not available (Fig. 2-1).

Though the meteorologist may have a well-documented theory about weather, we are acutely aware of practical failures in forecasting because weather is so important to us personally. The same problem exists in psychology, where psychological illness, the activities of political leaders, or the actions of various interest groups are so vital to national and personal welfare. Precise application of scientific laws is often less important in other fields, and fewer emotional demands are made on their theories. For example, no one would ask the physicist to predict the exact course of a falling snowflake. The problem of the individual case exists in physics, but it does not bother us as much. The following was written about the magnetic properties of metals by de Klerk (1953, p. 4):

Some substances, for example, iron and nickel, show a rather complicated magnetic behavior at room temperature. When placed in a magnetic field, they show a magnetic moment which not only is a function of field and temperature, but which also depends on the histo-

FIGURE 2-1 All hurricanes have certain properties in common, but each is also distinctive as well. (United Press International Photos, NASA.)

ry of the specimen; that is, it depends on the fields and temperatures in which the substance has been before.

In other words, to predict exactly the magnetic behavior of an individual specimen of metal, it is necessary to have precise information about the

nature of the specimen, including its history. Although the general laws of magnetics are known, each specimen is unique in terms of the conditions to which it has been exposed, and it has to be studied as such. The same can be said about personality. To consider the personality of an individual, that person's *unique* history must be examined in the light of the general principles about personality organization and development.

Psychologists have developed two contrasting strategies or frames of reference for the study of personality. One of these emphasizes the search for *general* laws about personality, and the other the unique organization of the *particular* individual specimen. The former has been called the "nomothetic" approach (referring to norms of behavior characterizing the average or typical person, or a class of persons); the latter is the "idiographic" approach (specifying the whole idea, the distinctive organization of the individual person).

In *nomothetic* personality research a number of different people are treated as a *type* on the basis of a single trait (or several traits) of personality that they share. The researchers are seeking a *general rule* about the way this trait shapes their behavior. Each individual, however, while sharing one characteristic in common with all the others, undoubtedly differs on numerous other characteristics. What these other characteristics are and how they might affect the reaction is not the focus of concern.

However, a given personality is not made up of a single trait, or even a few traits, but a complex assortment of traits that are *organized* together in accordance with certain rules, traits that interact with each other to determine how the person behaves and feels in many different situations. The normative approach is *analytic* in that it breaks down the organized system of personality into separate components. The danger is that the unified system acts differently from any of its component parts or the mere sum of these parts; that is, strong approval needs in a person who also feels that independence and individuality are important values will influence behavior differently from strong approval needs in a person who feels that people should subordinate their individuality to the welfare of the social group. Thus, in analyzing a single trait or a few traits for study, there is the danger that these separate components cannot be put back together again to *synthesize* the unified system which in its natural state is called "the personality."

A proposed antidote for this difficulty is the "idiographic" approach, which seeks to overcome the defect by the intensive study of *single cases* as they exist in nature. The value of this approach is that it allows the observer to see how the various elements in the personality system are actually organized in that particular individual, a unique specimen never actually duplicated in nature. By studying intensively how an individual reacts over a period of time or in many situations, the researcher can learn how that person is put together, so to speak.

One of the assumptions sometimes made in the idiographic approach is that a single case can permit generalizations or laws about personality that apply to other cases. From such study some notion can be gained about the way an individual personality is organized, but there is often serious question about whether or not anything can be said about how other personalities are organized. William F. Dukes (1965) has selected some important research examples from the history of psychology in which only a single subject was employed, observing that in these cases pivotal generalizations about people were revealed. One example is the classic work of Ebbinghaus (1885) in which the author himself committed to memory approximately 2,000 lists of nonsense syllables and 42 stanzas of poetry in order to make generalizations about rote learning and memory. These generalizations have withstood the test of time and subsequent research. Other examples include the observations of Morton Prince (1905, 1920) on Sally Beauchamp, a woman with a case

of multiple personality (see Chapter 6), and of Breuer and Freud (1895) on the case of Anna O., a woman suffering from a hysterical neurosis from whose treatment the method of psychoanalysis appears to have evolved.

Dukes points out that the intensive study of a single case is particularly appropriate and likely to lead to significant generalizations when variations among individuals are low with respect to the property being studied. In such an instance, the processes studied in the particular case may be quite representative and will lead to duplicated findings when subsequent cases are studied. In other words, to the extent that one individual case is like other cases, an idiographic strategy of personality study can be employed to make general laws. However, the extent to which the generalization is justified can be determined only by comparing one individual with another, which is essentially the nomothetic approach. One case is not enough to firmly establish a generalization. Thus, only when the idiographic approach is *supplemented* by the nomothetic can we move with confidence toward general laws.

A further disadvantage of the idiographic approach is that it provides no opportunity to make controlled analysis of the variables of personality, the separate components or traits. There is no way of being certain that the things assumed to be present in the personality actually have the role in behavior that is attributed to them. The same effects could conceivably result from qualities other than those inferred by the observer. Idiographic study of personalities requires a creative theoretical act that cannot be readily tested by further idiographic study, because there cannot again be found a combination of events (another person) quite like the original one. Only by experiments in which given properties of individuals are shown, repeatedly and under controlled conditions, to have a particular cause or effect can there be an evaluation of the principles that emerge from idiographic study. Without scientific control of the causal conditions and their consequences in behavior, dependable rules can never be achieved.

Psychologists interested in personality have debated the advantages and disadvantages of the nomothetic and idiographic orientations, often making it seem as though they are inimical to each other, rather than supplementary, as has been suggested. One of the best and most sophisticated dialogs on this issue may be found in two articles by proponents of each strategy, idiographically centered Gordon Allport (1962) and nomothetically oriented Robert Holt (1962). The interested reader should investigate these. There is no doubt that some will prefer to study personality idiographically and others nomothetically, but it is equally clear that neither strategy, by itself, is ideal or sufficient. Understanding of personality is best achieved by capitalizing on the distinctive advantages of both approaches.

PERSONALITY: AN INFERENCE FROM BEHAVIOR

Many answers might be given to the question "What are people like?" The answers might be based on physical appearance, emphasizing the similarities and the variations in physical structure. Some descriptive terms would be needed, and these terms would depend on the nature of the physical attributes that were considered important or worthy of description. Such dimensions as height, weight, bodily proportions, and skin color might be included as aspects of anatomy (physical structure). Instead of anatomy, the physical functions that persons can perform might be emphasized. Thus, instead of describing the muscle and bone structure, one could talk about the postures and movements of which this muscle and bone structure is capable. *Structure* always represents the more or less permanent arrangement of things, whereas *process* refers to what they do and how they interact, develop, or change.

Suppose the same question were asked in the psychological sense. A surface description could be given of the characteristic behavior of a person, that is, how he or she acts in most situations—for example, the person may be dominant, aggressive, shy, uncertain, or optimistic. There is some difficulty, however, in talking about the psychological structures and processes underlying this behavior. Physical functions such as walking, digesting, and speaking must have a physical anatomy or structure, and it is comparatively straightforward to observe this anatomy because definite organs can be identified (bones, muscles, nerves, chemical compounds). Observation becomes more difficult when the structure of individual cells, molecules, or atoms is involved. It is also more difficult to recognize the psychological structures and processes underlying behavior, although such structures must exist: like atomic structures, the nature of the underlying structure must be imagined because it is not directly observable. Rather, the structures and processes consist of hypothetical entities such as motives, habits, and defenses. The attempt to go beyond the description of behavior to the underlying psychological structures and processes constitutes the theoretical area of psychology.

Personality is not simply *how* the person acts. If we say that a person is aggressive, we refer to an observation that he or she behaves aggressively. By saying that someone is aggressive, we are merely describing or interpreting superficial acts without reference to the situational and personality determinants that produce them. These determinants are what we are trying to describe and comprehend. Because personality involves the stable psychological characteristics that determine action, the problem is to describe these characteristics adequately and state how they work. The problem is the same for the physicist concerned with the nature of matter. The wood of a chair appears stationary and solid enough, and it seems fanciful to propose that this solid object is made up of atoms and subatomic structures that are in constant motion. These atomic structures cannot be observed yet they are considered to be the basic building blocks for all matter and are conceived to function in certain ways. Theorizing about these structures has been of practical value—has resulted in the construction of atomic and hydrogen bombs and in the creation of industrial power plants. These are practical consequences of speculations about hypothetical structures that have never been directly seen.

In a similar way, human behavior can be understood by postulating the existence of certain hypothetical structures which can never be seen directly but which power and direct action. An obvious example is the concept of motive. No one can observe a motive directly. It is not a chemical condition of the body or a neural element in the brain, although it may depend on chemical and neural activity. It is a conception, an imaginary structure. But even though it is not seen directly, it is known from the *observable* antecedent conditions that cause it or signify its presence and from its *observable* effects. For example, an animal is conceived or inferred to be hungry if it has gone without food for a given period, or if its behavior is evidently directed toward food and eating. The presence of the hunger motive is not an unscientific idea simply because hunger cannot be directly observed. It is known by inference from its antecedents (causes) and consequences (effects). Just as the concept of the atom has been useful to the physicist in explaining matter and energy and in controlling the physical world, psychological concepts and theories of personality aid in understanding human behavior (Fig. 2-2).

HOW WE FIND OUT ABOUT PERSONALITY

Because personality can be known only from its directly observable behavioral effects in given

FIGURE 2-2 Look at this picture and try to infer what the two boys are thinking and feeling on the basis of the situation portrayed and the expressions on their faces. The actual story is printed upside down, below. See whether you have sized up the situation correctly. (Wide World Photos.)

"Please, Spade, don't sit down now." The boy at the left burst into tears as his huge collie decides to stage a sitdown strike while being judged in a school pet show. The boy on the right observes sympathetically.

situational contexts, behavior must somehow be observed in order to study an individual's personality. Such behavior arises naturally out of the ordinary circumstances of living. If it has occurred in the past, one can attempt to find out about it from informants or by asking the person. Or the attempt can be made to arouse behavior experimentally in selected laboratory situations in order to create a basis of inference about the personality. It is sufficient here to note the main varieties of behavior that serve as sources of information concerning the personality.

There are three main sources of behavioral information that can be used to infer characteristics of personality. These are *verbal reports*, *behavioral reactions*, and *bodily reactions*.

VERBAL REPORTS

If one wishes to know whether a person is angry or sad, feels affection or dislike, has a particular motive or desire, or follows a particular procedure to solve problems, the person can be asked. The unique attribute of humans that facilitates the study of unseen psychological processes is their capacity to communicate verbally and to introspect or look inward concerning their mental activity. The use of introspection is limited to humans; no other animal can use verbal language to report on inner experience.

It has been repeatedly pointed out that introspective verbal reports are not always valid indicators of internal states. If a report is taken literally to express inner psychological processes, it is sometimes misleading, either because the person *cannot tell* what is really taking place or, for some reason, *will not tell*. Either the processes that are actually occurring are not available to introspective analysis, or the person may wish to portray his or her experience so as to appear socially in a particular light. Thus, the use of verbal report must be tempered with the recognition that it does not always provide a valid indication of inner conditions, and it must be supplemented with other data that can help in the process of making more accurate inferences.

For example, consider a young man who has been out on a date and who returns to his room unusually early the same evening. A roommate, noting his crestfallen appearance and the early hour of his arrival, questions him about the evening. The young man offers the information that he has been jilted.

"Oh," says the roommate, "that's too bad. You must feel awful."

"Not at all," says his friend. "I didn't care about her one bit. It doesn't bother me at all." And for the next two hours, to his roommate's dismay, the jilted man protests how indifferent he is to the young woman who rejected him.

What can be learned about the underlying feelings and motivation of this man from his reported introspections and his other behavior? If the verbal report is taken at face value, it suggests that he does not care about the broken date. But such an interpretation fails to ring true in the face of his crestfallen appearance and lengthy denial of distress. He protests too much. In spite of maintaining the contrary, he is evidently quite shattered by the rejection but wishes his roommate to think otherwise. As will be seen in Chapter 4, this defensive pattern is often referred to as "reaction formation." The combination of manifestations of strong emotion and overprotestation, including denial of concern, leads to a different interpretation about the feelings than would be obtained by simply asking him how he felt and taking his report at face value. Moreover, distress is the reaction that might reasonably be expected under these circumstances.

Illustrated in this particular example is a contradiction between two sources of information, the verbal report and behavioral evidence about the person's inner state. The content of his words suggests that the person is indifferent; the behavioral reaction suggests that he is quite upset. It is from just such contradictions that inferences about hypothetical processes such as *defense mechanisms* are made. In the defense mechanism the person is thought to deceive himself about some impulse or danger by one of a number of devices. Such self-deceptions will be discussed more fully later in Chapter 4. For now it is important to recognize that denial of distress and reaction formation make up the sorts of unseen, hypothetical processes referred to in the earlier section in the discussion of personality as an inference from behavior.

As a result of observations and interpretations such as these, introspective or verbal report is regarded by the modern psychologist with some skepticism, as a form of behavior rather than as the literally accepted truth about inner states. If the content of verbal report is accepted as literally true, then the person being studied is, in effect, being employed as the *observer*. This subject-observer reports on how he or she thinks, feels, and so on. When such reports are only a guide to inference along with other data, then the person being studied is not being employed as the observer but, rather, as the *object of study* who can be observed acting and reporting about an inner state. Introspection used in this way is a form of behavior like any other.

Despite its vulnerability to errors of the sort identified above, introspection provides data about the person that cannot readily be obtained in any other way and is thus virtually indispensable in personality study, especially when the concern is with affective states such as anger, fear, guilt, shame, joy, and love. If one takes these terms seriously as reflecting qualitatively different states within the person, then there is no way of differentiating these affective states accurately by other methods. To eliminate verbal report altogether as a source of information about personality processes would be to reduce the person to a nearly inarticulate, infrahuman animal and thus to lose an enormous wealth of information about his or her inner experience and psychological activity.

BEHAVIORAL REACTIONS

If one wishes to infer the existence of an emotion or motive state in an animal such as a dog, it is obvious that the animal cannot be asked to report verbally about it. All one can do is to watch its actions and the situations in which they occur. As was noted in an earlier example, the animal is known to be hungry partly because it has been without food for a certain period of time and partly because it is time to eat.

The animal's *actions* also suggest hunger. For example, it is more restless than usual, paws its owner, shows excitement when the refrigerator door is opened, and so on. When it has eaten, the pattern of behavior signifying hunger ceases. If an animal is frightened, it will crouch and seem to withdraw from the danger and, if sufficiently disturbed, may urinate or defecate. Anger is expressed somewhat differently, with snarling, growling, and postural patterns that are quite unique. It is not certain whether lower animals experience other emotional states such as guilt, shame, or depression. However, it is quite clear that the repertoire of psychological processes characteristic of infrahuman forms of life is quite restricted compared with humans. Such complex concepts as defense mechanisms and motives to achieve are not usually applied in studying dogs, cats, or monkeys. Therefore, the task of inferring internal states is somewhat simpler for infrahuman species than for people.

Just as behavioral reactions are the main sources of inference about psychological states in infrahuman animals, they are used for this also in humans. Psychologists speak of two qualities of behavioral reactions: instrumental and gestural-expressive. *Instrumental* qualities refer to intentional behaviors that are oriented toward some goal. For example, if we are frightened by an object, we may act to avoid or escape it. If angry, we may attack the source of frustration. If hungry, we direct ourselves to food; if thirsty, to water, and so on. In other words, the goal direction of behavior is itself a basis of inference about the underlying psychological process. Even if an acquaintance says he would like to see us socially, the fact that he makes no effort to do so, or even appears to avoid us at a party, is instrumental evidence of the opposite meaning from what the spoken words appear to signify.

Expressive qualities of acts consist of the unintended styles with which something is done. The gestures one uses when speaking are an example. The tempo or force with which something is done is another. The same statement can be made emphatically, hesitantly, angrily, or sweetly. Voice quality in depression has a characteristic lifelessness which, when analyzed, shows an absence of the high tones and a loss of normal overtones (Hargreaves, Starkweather, and Blacker, 1965).

Expressive qualities can thus be used to infer internal states and sometimes even to correct an impression derived from the content of speech. A person may claim not to be angry while at the same time pounding on the table and glaring with clenched teeth. The expressive qualities of an act can represent *nonverbal communication*. Often the act's meaning (the inner state communicated by it) is understood even when it is counter to the meaning implied by words, because expression may communicate the inner state without the person intending to do so (see, for example, Ekman, 1965) (Fig. 2-3).

BODILY REACTIONS

When human beings and animals experience emotions, bodily changes occur that can also be used to infer the concomitant inner state. Sometimes the physiological change can be readily observed, as when a person blushes, flushes in anger, or turns pale or when his or her hands become extremely sweaty or tremulous. Consider the distress of public speakers who experience stage fright, discover their hands trembling as they hold the page, or enunciate their words badly because their normal salivary flow is severely inhibited and the tongue is too dry to talk clearly. These are the outward signs that an emotional state is taking place, although the signs could also occur for reasons unrelated to psychological processes, as when, for example, we sweat because of high heat and humidity or flush because of a circulatory disease and not because of emotion.

Many end-organ and hormonal changes occur in disturbed emotional states, and not only can these sometimes be observed because of the visible reactions they may produce, but modern electrophysiological instruments also make possible rather accurate measurements of many of these changes. These physiological reactions will be discussed more fully in Chapter 5.

In any event, in the same sense that behavioral reactions can be used to infer psychological activities, physiological reactions also index emotional states, and these reactions are being studied with increasing frequency by psychologists as sources of information about personality.

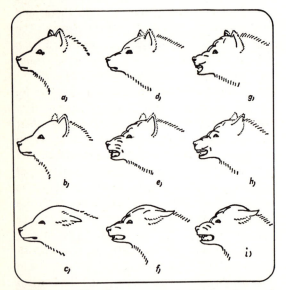

FIGURE 2-3 The dog expresses in his face fear and anger in certain characteristic ways: (a–c) readiness to flee; (a–g) increasing aggression; (e, f, h, i) various combinations revealing ambiguity of intention (after Lorenz, 1963). People probably do also.

PERSONALITY AND CONSISTENCY

Consistency is a very important idea for the science of personality, because lack of it would mean that behavior is entirely determined by the situation rather than by any stable property of the person. If such were the case, a person would not be psychologically recognizable from time to time. As pointed out earlier, when we say "personality" we mean the stable or consistent properties of the person that continue to operate to some extent regardless of the circumstances.

Consistency of personality has been of interest for a long time and in many contexts. For example, the procedure employed by law enforcement authorities of describing an M.O., or *modus operandi* (style of working), to identify the criminal responsible for a series of crimes makes use of individual styles. Such styles (as well as the type of crime itself) are often highly consistent "trademarks" of a particular criminal; a bank will always be robbed in a special way, with particular tools, in characteristic sequences, at a specific time of day, and so on. Such a consistent style is apt to give the criminal away and lead to capture.

In psychology, consistency can be capitalized on to study the structure of the personality, that is, the properties that are constant enough to reveal themselves from time to time and over many different situations. However, one must ask, "What is it that is consistent?" Is it meant that the person performs the same or similar acts under different conditions? Or can the actions be quite dissimilar and still reflect some constant underlying structure?

CONSISTENCY OF BEHAVIOR

The question of personality consistency was first asked systematically about specific actions (a behavioristic or surface approach to personality). It is easier to study the consistency of acts than that of inferred structures or processes, since acts can be directly observed without any further inferential steps. Partly for this reason, the problem was first studied in a strictly behavioral sense of how consistently did the individual perform the same kind of act in various types of situations. In 1928, 1929, and 1930, for example, Hartshorne, May, Maller, and Shuttleworth reported extensive studies of *consistency of moral behavior*. Among the questions that Hartshorne and May and their colleagues sought to answer were whether persons behaved honestly or dishonestly in response to specific situations and, therefore, whether there was such a thing as moral character residing within a person independently of the circumstances.

A large number of preadolescent children were studied under a variety of circumstances. Tests were constructed that permitted the children to act honestly or dishonestly. In one such test, cheating was measured by giving the children a school examination, returning it to them, and asking them to grade their own papers. The teacher read aloud the correct answer to each question, and each child indicated on his or her own paper whether the answer was right or wrong. Because most of the children saw no obvious external danger of being caught, they had an excellent opportunity to change their answers and improve their grade. Unknown to the children, however, a wax impression had been ingeniously made of their original set of answers, and any changes could be identified by comparing a child's corrected paper with the original. In some instances children could take their examinations home to grade. By comparing behavior in different circumstances, it was possible to tell whether a child who acted honestly in one situation was also likely to act honestly in another.

Hartshorne and May found only slight consistency (an average correlation of about .30 on a scale of zero to 1) in children's moral behavior from one situation to another. This degree of correlation is higher than should have occurred merely by chance and therefore could actually be regarded as evidence of consistency. However, the relationship is so small that it provides little encouragement for one who is seeking to emphasize stability in human behavior. With so small a relationship, there is a very high probability that the child who acts honestly in one context or moment will not do so in another. Knowing what the child did in one situation will then not add much accuracy in guessing what he or she will do in another. Arguing from these results, the authors propounded the *doctrine of specificity*, which stipulated that honesty was not a character trait of the individual but, rather, that there were only honest acts in response to particular situations.

The Hartshorne and May studies were models of experimental ingenuity, but they were severely criticized for missing many of the crucial points in the problem of personality consistency. For one thing, the use of preadolescent children imposes limitations, because such a population has not yet developed a stable personality organization to the same degree as adults. Character is still forming in pre- and early adolescence, and behavioral consistency is less likely to be found then than at a later age. The doctrine of specificity also ignores the fact that there were some tendencies, albeit small, to act consistently from one situation to another. In fact, a small proportion of children acted either honestly or dishonestly in most of the experimental situations. Furthermore, such factors as religious training, intelligence, and socioeconomic status played some role in determining whether a child would behave honestly or not, suggesting that some underlying factors arising out of a child's experience were important in determining behavioral honesty.

Of greatest importance, however, is the fact that Hartshorne and May defined consistency in a behavioral sense only. That is, they asked whether honest or dishonest *behavior* would be repeat-

ed from situation to situation. They did not, however, consider the *underlying reasons* that determined the behavior. For example, it was found that brighter children cheated less than duller children. One might say that the brighter children had less reason to cheat because they knew their work and were more confident of doing well. The test probably resulted in differential motivations on the part of the children to succeed, and no doubt they provoked a great deal of fear of doing poorly. Thus, although a child may have behaved inconsistently from situation to situation, the underlying reasons for the behavior were probably characteristic of the child's personality—and therefore consistent. A child who was highly motivated to succeed and knew the material well in one test situation might not cheat but, when given a test that threatened failure, might behave dishonestly. Thus, the superficial behavior might be different from situation to situation, but the underlying structure—say, the child's pattern of motivation—might be very stable in spite of changes in the external conditions. This underlying personality structure would lead to different behavior as a function of the nature of the external conditions. The Hartshorne and May studies demonstrated a degree of inconsistency in *behavior*, but they failed to address the problem of the possible constancy of personality structure.

CONSISTENCY OF STYLE

Psychologists have observed another form of behavioral consistency involving *expression* or *style*. As we saw earlier, in contrast to purposeful or intentional acts, style represents the form that any intentional act can take. Such a concept is only one short step removed from the level of acts; expression or style consists of acts interpreted in a particular way. We can easily recognize a popular vocalist by the style that characterizes him or her, apart from the song or the circumstances in which it is sung. These styles are often so characteristic and unique that they can be imitated and recognized by others. In the same way, acts like lighting a cigarette, walking, or driving a car can be performed in qualitatively different ways by different persons, and one way may be recognizable as characteristic of a particular person. The act itself does not differentiate the two individuals, or one person under different conditions, but the style or form of expression may do so.

Expressive movements The concept of style or expression can involve many types of behavior, including, as we shall see, ways of thinking and perceiving that are called "cognitive styles." However, some of the most common forms of expression, known as "expressive movements," were first studied in a well-known investigation by Allport and Vernon (1933). These psychologists were interested in the tempo of acts, their degree of emphasis, and their expansiveness. For example, in handwriting, letters can be written either large or small and cramped; one can write or walk slowly or at a brisk pace. One can bear down heavily or lightly with a pencil; one can make gestures that are definite or uncertain. Allport and Vernon called these styles in which ordinary acts are performed "expressive movements." In their research on the consistency of such styles, subjects performed a variety of ordinary motor tasks such as reading aloud, walking, drawing circles, estimating distances, finger tapping, and writing. Expressive qualities such as speed of performance, writing pressure, and length of the stride in walking were carefully observed and correlated with each other.

Some degree of consistency was found in the way in which these acts were performed. For example, the amount of space taken up in walking was correlated with the amount of space taken up in writing. There was also some consistency in the amount of emphasis in performing different tasks and in tempo. The consistency was greatest within the same type of task—for exam-

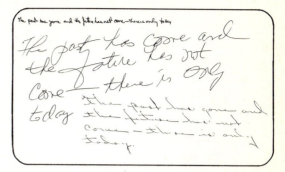

FIGURE 2-4 Expressive qualities of handwriting style are consistent for each individual but show great variety between individuals.

ple, in walking or writing—and less when the comparison was made across such diverse functions. Thus, there was neither complete consistency nor complete inconsistency, and certain activities went together more than others. Allport and Vernon made no attempt to speculate on the psychological structures that account for the surface consistencies they observed, although others have done so (Fig. 2-4).

It has often been proposed that such expressive gestures or styles may actually be powered by motives that are not evident to the person or even to the observer. Consider, for example, the tendency of some individuals to smile a great deal compared with others or to frequently gesture with a positive nod of the head. Do these have any instrumental value, that is, do they have the function of producing some interpersonal reward for the individual using them? This question has been studied using eighteen female students (Rosenfeld, 1966). Half of them were instructed to seek approval and half of them were told to avoid approval in a social interchange with another individual who was seated in the same room with the subject. Observations were made of the gestures used by both groups of subjects, the *approval seekers* and the *approval avoiders*. Two gestures especially were found to be higher among the subjects seeking approval than among those avoiding it: smiles and gesticulations (any notice-able movement of the arm, hand, or finger, indicating attention and involvement). Evidently, expressive movements or gestures can be moti-vated by interpersonal goals. By the same token, people who characteristically are concerned with gaining approval may have acquired, and tend to use, such gestures more than others as part of their permanent styles of behaving.

A related theme is found in a series of articles by Albert Mehrabian (Mehrabian and Wiener, 1966; Mehrabian, 1966), who studied what is referred to as "immediacy" or "nonimmediacy" in one's form of communication to another per-son. For example, a person who says *"those people need help"* as opposed to *"these* people need help" is expressing the same basic thought, but the former expression is less immediate or more distant than the latter. To take another example, the statement "X came to visit *us*" in contrast with "X came to visit *me*" is less intimate or immediate; similarly, "I am concerned about X's *future*" is more distant than "I am concerned about *X*." The authors maintained that whenever the individual's verbal style of interpersonal ex-pression is more distant or less immediate, he or she is expressing subtly a more negative feeling tone or attitude toward the other than if the style is more immediate.

In a typical experiment, a negative experience was compared with a positive experience in its tendency to evoke nonimmediacy in verbal ex-pression. After such experiences, the subject wrote some sentences using either or both of the pronouns "I" and "they." Sometimes the task involved writing such sentences about a person who was liked compared with a person who was disliked. Mehrabian and Wiener showed that verbal styles involving nonimmediacy of refer-ence toward other individuals (or greater psycho-logical distance) increased in frequency as a re-sult of negative experiences or attitudes. The negative attitude is revealed by the subtle manner in which the person refers to the other, by a

slightly less direct style. Thus, even when a per-son does not intend to reveal a hostile attitude, he or she may do so expressively, and such stylistic changes may serve as subtle cues to an observer about interpersonal attitudes. Stylistic variations may be motivated by interpersonal motives or attitudes.

Cognitive and defensive styles Research on cognitive styles is an offspring of the earlier Allport-Vernon work on expressive movements. Instead of motor-expressive variables such as speed of writing, tempo of walking, and expan-siveness in writing and gesture, "cognitive style" refers to stable ways in which the person thinks, perceives, and looks at the world and his or her relationship to it. Implied here is that there are individual differences in the ways these cognitive functions are carried out and that these are stable over many different activities and situations. In other words, it is not the intellectual task or situation alone that determines the form of per-ception and thought, but stable properties of the personality.

One group of personality researchers headed by George Klein (Gardner, Holzman, Klein, Lin-ton, and Spence, 1959) has isolated a number of cognitive styles. Their method is to have subjects perform a variety of cognitive tasks, determining correlations in the performance across these tasks. These correlations show that the person who approaches one of the tasks in a particular way will tend to do the same with other tasks. Generalized styles of thinking are thus defined and can be shown to extend to many other types of tasks. What is common to the performances of individuals across these various tasks is a style of thinking or perceiving, a style that the individual tends to employ in all transactions with the envi-ronment.

The various styles that have been postulated by Klein and his associates cannot be detailed here. However, one concrete illustration will help to make clear what is meant by a cognitive style.

One study dealt with a cognitive style called "leveling and sharpening" (Holzman and Gardner, 1959). *Leveling* consists of the tendency to overlook or "level" perceptual differences among objects; the individual sees things in terms of their sameness or similarity rather than in terms of distinctions between them. In contrast, *sharpening* is the way of looking at things in terms of their differences. The experimenters assumed also that levelers would be prone to use repression as a preferred defense mechanism, because the tendency to overlook differences is a form of thinking ideally suited to reducing threat by not recognizing or seeing the dangerous impulse or thought. They performed a study to determine whether levelers would also show the characteristics of the repressive personality.

Indeed, the levelers showed a pattern of reaction considered characteristic of the defense mechanism of repression on a clinical diagnostic test. These findings strongly suggest that there is some consistency in the way an individual deals mentally with the objects of the world.

There are two reasons for the importance for adjustment of this cognitive-style research. The first concerns merely the problem of *consistency*, the finding that there are stable individual differences in the styles with which people think about stimulus objects. The second reason for its significance is that such styles may also reveal people's ways of defending themselves against threat, in effect, of adjusting to threat. In short, an important psychological process is being tapped that is associated with a cognitive style, namely, the process of *defense*. Speculations are thus made about the dynamics of the personality from consistencies in surface acts. These acts serve as a basis for "diagnosing" or assessing psychological processes relevant to adjustment.

This point has also been forcefully demonstrated by another major contributor to research and theory on cognitive style, Herman A. Witkin (1965). Witkin believes that consistent ways of perceiving and thinking are determined by, or at

least associated with, important traits of personality. As such, they can be used to infer these traits, including defenses and the symptoms of psychopathology that an individual will show.

Witkin's research approach to cognitive style has been quite different from that of Klein and his followers. In an early work (Witkin, Lewis, Machover, Meissner, and Wapner, 1954), a laboratory situation was devised to differentiate those tending to be perceptually dependent on cues from the outside from those tending to depend on cues based on one's own body position. Subjects sat in a chair in a completely darkened room and had the task of judging the tilt of a luminous vertical rod set in a luminous frame. The chair was also tilted in various positions and degrees, sometimes in the same direction as the tilt of the rod, sometimes in a different direction. Since the room was pitch black, the subject was forced to depend to some extent either on bodily kinesthetic cues concerning the upright (the subject seated in a tilted chair might feel the muscles acting against gravity) or on visual cues that indicated the luminous rod was not upright. The extent of either influence could be determined by examining how the rod was adjusted to make it appear vertical to the subject under various conditions of chair tilt and rod tilt.

Witkin et al. found that subjects differed greatly in the extent to which they were dependent on visual or kinesthetic cues. The former (those dependent on visual cues) were called "field-dependent," the latter (those dependent on kinesthetic cues) "body-dependent." These tendencies were rather stable and related to other sorts of perceptual-cognitive tendencies, for example, how rapidly the subject could identify perceptually a figure that was embedded and hidden within a larger and more complex figure. Such perceptual-cognitive styles appeared to be correlated with many personality variables. Women were found to be more field-dependent, generally, than men. In more recent writings, Witkin, Dyk, Faterson, Goodenough, and Karp (1962) have referred to this cognitive-style dimension as "psychological differentiation," thus suggesting that the basic process was the tendency of an individual to be analytical as opposed to global in the perception of objects and situations. Such cognitive styles, however they are analyzed and conceptualized, represent partly stabilized dispositions to react to or deal with the world in certain consistent ways. In short, one's way of thinking and perceiving is a property of personality that distinguishes one individual from another.

CONSISTENCY OF COPING

An experiment by Lazarus and Longo (1953) illustrates a shift of emphasis from surface acts and styles to the consistency or stability of underlying defensive processes. A group of students was given the task of unscrambling a number of sentences, the words of which were all mixed up. Half of these scrambled sentences could not be solved at all; the words could not be put together to form a meaningful sentence. The other half could be readily solved. The students were told that this was a test to measure their intellectual competence and that it should indicate their potentiality for academic and vocational success. The subjects were unaware that some of the sentences could not be unscrambled. A time limit was set for each sentence. Some students who were allied with the experimenter were mixed in with the group of regular subjects. When a scrambled sentence that was impossible to solve was presented, these false subjects put their pencils down to convey the impression that they had completed the sentence, while the experimental subjects continued trying unsuccessfully to find the answer.

At the end of this part of the experiment, the subjects were asked to recall as many of the solvable and unsolvable sentences as they could. Some of them remembered predominantly the sentences on which they had been successful, and others recalled predominantly those sen-

tences on which they had presumably failed. It was assumed that this *selective forgetting* was the way in which the subjects had protected their self-esteem. For some subjects, self-esteem was best protected by forgetting all about the unpleasant experiences of failure. For others, the defense of self-esteem was accomplished through rumination about the failures—perhaps via the symbolic repetition of the threatening experiences over and over again so that they could be overcome. This "rehearsing" presumably resulted in better recall of the failures than of the successes.

The crucial research question was now whether or not this differential recall of successes and failures represented a consistent type of defense that would also be employed under other conditions of psychological threat. Those subjects who had shown an extreme tendency to recall their successes and another group of subjects who showed an extreme tendency to recall their failures were selected for a further experiment. They were presented a list of nonsense words to learn. Each word was paired with another word so that when the first word was presented, the other word had to be remembered. Half of these nonsense words were followed by the presentation of a painful electric shock regardless of whether the subject gave a correct response or not. Only these latter word pairs ever led to the shock. Subjects were never shocked on the other word pairs. At the end of this experiment, the subjects were asked to recall as many of the shocked word pairs and nonshocked word pairs as they could.

It was found that those who had previously protected their self-esteem by recalling their successes rather than failures tended to recall predominantly the words without shock. On the other hand, those who had recalled mostly failures remembered the shocked words best during the second experiment. Subjects presumably carried with them the tendency to remember selectively either threatening or nonthreatening experiences. Perhaps we could also call them optimists and pessimists, avoiders and vigilant types, or whatever. In any case, such an adjustive process was evidently operating in the two threatening experimental situations and could be said to be a consistent aspect of the subject's personality.

PERSONALITY AND CHANGE

Up to this point I have emphasized the idea of consistency of the person from situation to situation. If there really were a very high degree of consistency in a person's actions, we would have to consider his or her behavior as rigid and mechanical. The person would be at the mercy of certain underlying structures and would have difficulty conceiving of rising above these to adjust to the environment. *Total* consistency of acts would entail a view of human behavior similar to the tropistic concepts once employed in biology. In such a view, human behavior would be like that of the moth which is irresistibly attracted to the light of the candle flame and can destroy itself as a consequence of its mechanical, phototropic response. If we expected very great consistency from people, we would of necessity have to expect considerable restriction in their capacity to control their lives. Such control or direction calls for *flexibility* as well as consistency.

Although a certain degree of stability in personality structure must be assumed, there must be room as well for variation, progression, and change. Psychotherapy assumes that personality structure can somehow be altered; otherwise, one would have to be quite fatalistic about the possibility of treating maladjustment. If it were assumed that personality structure is so rigid as to be impervious to change, there could be little hope of doing much for a person whose personality had developed in pathological or deviant directions.

We generally assume that the development of personality structure involves a progressive increase in stability and organization with age. The child is most susceptible to influence. With advancing age, the structure becomes increasingly rigid, and an older person is less capable of change.

The older person is to some extent less able than the young person to survive personal and social change or upheaval.

Some personality theorists emphasize the early age at which personality structure has been formed and stabilized, and others stress the continuing development and change that can take place throughout most of life. Reality probably exists somewhere between these two extremes. In adult life the personality structure is generally quite stable and somewhat resistant to change. However, this stability need not be rigidly or totally unchangeable, particularly in the most mature person or under conditions of great stress. Even the most cherished systems of values, patterns of motivation, and forms of control exerted over behavior can be subject to some modification. If this were not so, then social change, which is always a characteristic of our society, would leave most of us in a totally maladjusted state. The real question is not whether there is complete stability or complete changeability but, rather, *which* structures are stable, how resistant are these to change, and when do they reach a given level of stability? We do not yet have well-established answers to these questions.

SURFACE, DEPTH, AND THE UNCONSCIOUS

The concept of personality, it is clear, is not equivalent to the observable patterns of action of the person; rather it has to do with unobservable (hypothetical) constructs that are inferred from that behavior. It is still possible to offer a description of a person that is relatively behavioral and nontheoretical, that is, what he or she does or says in a variety of contexts. This type of description has been referred to as a "surface" definition of personality. In contrast, the "depth" interpretation has been emphasized here.

Actually, there are two connotations to the concept of depth. In one, the underlying structure of the personality—that is, the aspects of it that are deep, inner, or central—concerns those qualities that are not accessible to direct observation. They cannot be known directly. Implied in this usage of depth is only that the personality structure is hidden from view; it is a constructed or theoretical entity that can be known to *anyone* only by inference from observed behavior.

There is another connotation, however, to the concept of depth as it is used by personality theorists and by clinical psychologists. In this case, the underlying structure is also regarded as inaccessible; however, the inaccessibility is to the *subject*, rather than to the observer. Thus, the personality structure—the forces that energize and direct the individual's behavior—are *unconscious*. One cannot then ask the person about it because it is inaccessible to him or her.

These two meanings are often both embedded in the term "depth," with one or another sometimes being emphasized. Generally, when the latter connotation is emphasized, it is the quality of unconsciousness or the absence of awareness that is being emphasized; in the former connotation, constructs or inferences about the inaccessible mechanisms or dynamics of behavior are being emphasized.

It is methodologically very difficult to test the notion of unconscious determination of behavior (especially when one's view of unconsciousness implies, as in Freudian theory, that material is being actively prevented from attaining consciousness). One of the critical difficulties is to differentiate between the simple reluctance or refusal of a person to communicate real feelings to someone else and actual instances of self-deception.

The most common way the problem is dealt with empirically is to find situations in which there appears to be no reason for the subject consciously to withhold information; even here there can be no absolute proof, because judgment about what is conscious always depends upon the subject's report, usually verbal. What can be said is that there are many instances, especially in the clinical situation dealing with neurotic patterns of behavior, where an individual *appears* to be totally or partially unaware of influences directing his or her behavior. It is theoretically reasonable, then, to infer the existence of processes of which an individual is unconscious. It is often postulated that awareness of these processes is highly disturbing and is avoided by the person.

The therapeutic situation provides some evidence of unconscious processes. States of amnesia and hypnosis and many neurotic manifestations are consistent with the interpretation of unconscious processes, although alternative interpretations are always possible. The notion of unconscious processes is a theoretical one, and personality theorists, especially those working in the clinical setting, have continued to find it most useful in accounting for many of the phenomena they observe. For this reason, the notion, which was originally elaborated by Freud, although controversial and rejected by many, has survived for many decades.

PERSONALITY THEORY

Theoretical concepts are the abstract efforts of any science to make the observable events of the world understandable. They bring order to chaotic facts and enable us to account for as many of them as possible. Commonly they involve imaginary constructs (like electricity or the atom and its working particles in physics, neural mechanisms in physiology, the operation of genes and their chemical effects on cell differentiation in biology, and the makeup of the social system in which we live, including the social roles that all of us play, which are concepts of sociology and social psychology).

We cannot evaluate such constructs directly, since they involve things or processes we cannot see, but we can ask how well such constructs help us make sense of our observations, and we can test their adequacy indirectly by the logical process of deduction. That is, we make "if . . . then" statements. In theory, we reason that *if* the system of constructs operates as we say it does, *then* certain directly observable consequences ought to be found. We then arrange to make observations, either naturalistically or by setting up experiments, to see whether the observable consequences really hold true in nature. If the observations do not accord with our deductions from theory, and assuming that we have made the observations adequately and reasoned soundly, then the theory is thrown into doubt, or it must be discarded or modified to conform better to the facts.

Unfortunately, personality is such a complex idea and concerns such diverse psychological arenas of observation that theories about it are still mainly general ways of thinking about the problem or establishing some rather general assumptions about the way things work, rather than consisting of tightly knit and carefully specified statements that are readily tested by observation. Yet these first and halting efforts are important because they specify potentially useful strategies for looking at personality and adjustment, and they focus our attention on certain kinds of conditions within and outside people that might influence how they feel, think, and act.

Present-day theories of personality, and there are many, direct themselves toward four basic questions or rubrics, namely, description, development, dynamics, and determinants—the four Ds of personality, as it were. One asks first about how the personality can be *described*—"What are the basic units of the personality, the most important structures or elements?"—in the same sense that one might ask about an automobile "What are its major parts?" and come up with familiar terms such as pistons, drive shaft, or generator.

One of the issues of description that divides personality theories concerns the extent to which we react to objective stimuli in the environment or, conversely, to stimuli not as they are but as they are perceived subjectively by the individual. Thus, when we observe someone reacting, say with strong emotion, to another individual and ask about these reactions, the person may tell us that this other individual (the immediate stimulus) has been acting in an insulting and disparaging manner. On the other hand, other observers do not see the behavior in this way. In describing what is going on, the fascinating question remains as to whether we should focus on the objective stimulus event or take the position that we can learn more by describing things in terms of how the individual construed these stimulus events subjectively. Some theories emphasize the former and others the latter. Their perspectives differ about the units for describing human reactions and the personality system, and each has certain advantages and disadvantages. The approach that emphasizes the subjective world of the individual as the cause of feelings and actions is commonly called phenomenology, in contrast to the S-R (stimulus-response) approach.

Personality *development* concerns the emergence and evolution of the personality system and its changes over time, say from birth to death and through the various stages and crises of development. Development requires a time-oriented perspective, and the diverse theories of personality have somewhat different ways of addressing development. For example, Freudian psychoanalysis tends to focus on the emergence of biologically based erotic impulses and the several stages through which they go in their transformation from infancy to adulthood. Freud assumed that everyone must go through certain psychosexual stages, and how adequately and in what way we adjust to the problems of living are reflections not only of the difficulties we encounter in later life but of how these universal stages were dealt with in childhood and adolescence. Other theorists have thought that Freud overemphasized the sexual origins of personality development and underemphasized other things. For example, Robert White (1959) has argued that more important even than getting erotic oral pleasure from sucking and eating was the child's emerging need to have an effect on the environment and to develop competence in dealing with the world. Furthermore, some developmental theories (e.g., Freud's and his followers) have focused on motivational and emotional development, that is, the acquisition of goals and patterns of feeling in relation to certain experiences, while others (e.g., Piaget, 1952) have emphasized cognitive development, that is, how one comes to think and reason about oneself and the world.

The *dynamics* of personality have to do with how the system works, with the processes of adjustment. We cannot understand an automobile merely by knowing its parts; we must also have an understanding of the way the parts move and function in relation to each other—for example, exploding a compressed mixture of gas and air in a cylinder and converting the upward and downward cycling of the pistons into the turning of the driveshaft and ultimately the turning of the wheels. In the same sense, theories of personality must offer some notions about how the personality system works and the rules by which its functions are accomplished.

Here, too, there are differences in some of the basic assumptions about dynamics employed by different theoretical systems. For example, several theories of personality make the assumption that the fundamental rule underlying human behavior is that everything we do and learn is based on an effort to reduce tension or pain resulting from unsatisfied biological needs or external demands that endanger us. The alternative assumptions, on which other personality theories are based, is that people, and even infrahuman animals, often seek stimulation or tension when its level is too low, and that throughout our lives we move toward growth and self-actualization even when such growth is threatening or painful. Thus, the adolescent seeks independence or autonomy in spite of the fact that it is frightening to leave the protective custody of the parental home. This latter view has sometimes been labeled the "force-for-growth" view of human behavior, in contrast with the tension-reduction viewpoint. In any case, these contrasting systems of thought present somewhat different dynamic principles to explain how the personality system operates and underlies the actions and reactions we see on the surface.

Finally, two main classes of *determinants* are considered by all personality theories, though these are differently emphasized and detailed in different theoretical systems. On the one hand, biological factors in the form of genetic influences and constitutional differences among people help shape personality development. Personality theories speculate about human nature, or, put differently, the biological properties of humans and the varying biological characteristics with which different humans start life. On the other hand, our social experiences, affecting us through learning, are also powerful determinants of the personalities we become. As I suggested earlier, Freud was strongly oriented toward a biological view of people, and those who seek to understand adjustive disorders by reference to the biological inheritance of traits that dispose persons to such disorder represent another example of this perspective. Certain theorists after Freud were critical of this biological emphasis and argued from the frame of reference that variations in personality reflect more the patterns of culture into which we are born and the social experiences that are distinctive to each of us in some degree.

As can be seen, personality theories are not

unconcerned with issues of human adjustment and effectiveness, and they include within their scope many of the same concerns as the latter. This interest is especially evident in the personality theory concern with dynamics, which has to do with the principles with which people struggle to manage their lives, to gratify the motives that drive them throughout parts or much of their lives, and to cope with the demands and dangers to the integrity of themselves and their commitments. This interest in adjustment can also be seen in the aspect of personality theory that deals with personality development and its determinants, because how we adjust depends in large measure on the history of that development and the social and biological forces on which it depends.

The focus of personality psychology is on those psychological properties of people that are relatively enduring and stable, including the consistent ways the person handles stress and copes with life crises at various stages of development. Recall in this connection Allport's definition, in which he refers to the "psychophysical systems that determine his unique *adjustments* to his environment." This reference clearly places personality in the functional framework of adjustment.

Finally, the personality psychologist emphasizes the integration of many diverse trends within the person, in short, pointing to the manner in which the normal person gets things together, as it were, and the idea that adjustment is not merely a particular response of a part of the personality system but is a reaction of the whole person to demands upon him or her. It is a total person in his or her world that we are studying, whose diverse components hang together in the organized aims and styles with which he or she directs thoughts, feelings, and actions in the management of his or her life. We can no more speak of personality without reference to patterns of adjustment and to effectiveness than we can speak of adjustment and its effectiveness

without reference to the personality of the individual who comes to terms with the world in which he or she lives.

With this in mind, we are ready to venture in subsequent chapters into an examination of the stresses and ways of coping with such stresses on which effective and ineffective adjustment depend.

SUMMING UP

Personality deals with the stable or consistent ways an individual acts and reacts and with the human characteristics that shape these reactions. One of the most useful ways of thinking about personality is to consider it as "the dynamic organization within the individual of those psychophysical systems that determine his unique adjustments to his environment" (Allport). The science of personality seeks general principles about how the personality is constructed and functions, but the application of such principles to any individual person is always complicated by the need to know all the relevant conditions, internal and external, which make the person tick, since these always vary from individual to individual and from situation to situation.

Personality is also a theoretical *inference* from observed behavior, there being three main sources of information: the person's *verbal reports*, *behavioral reactions*, and *bodily reactions*. Although verbal reports or introspections are highly valuable, they are also subject to errors based partly on lack of knowledge on the part of the person and partly on the reluctance to present oneself candidly. Similarly, behavioral reactions (even expressive body movements) and somatic reactions, while important sources of information about psychological states and processes, have their own sources of error. Ultimately we use a combination of all three sources when trying to develop a picture of what is happening psychologically.

Consistency, the basic theme of personality, can be examined at several levels: surface behavior; style and expression; and modes of thinking, coping, and self-defense. Although there is consistency, there is also variation and change, because the circumstances of life are constantly changing and effective adjustment requires flexible shifts in reaction that are in tune with the changing demands. When our analysis centers upon deeper-lying levels of personality structure and process, we are dealing with events of which the person may well be *unconscious* or unaware. One view of such a lack of awareness is the view of Freudian theory, which holds that important features of the mental life may be prevented by defenses (for example, repression) from becoming conscious.

Personality theory systematically seeks not only to describe personality structure but also to understand the processes by which it works (dynamics), how it got that way over the life span (development), and the biological and social influences (or determinants) that have shaped it. The psychology of personality and of adjustment are intertwined areas of research and thought because the ways in which the person thinks, feels, and acts are mostly oriented to the problems of adjusting to the demands of living. Personality, then, deals with the stable ways in which persons adjust.

PART II
STRESS AND COPING

PART II
STRESS AND COPING

In order to survive and flourish, humans and animals must deal effectively with a variety of physical and social demands. The word "demand" implies some pressure that cannot be ignored lest there be damaging consequence.

In the case of the most primitive animals such as fowl or fish, adjustive reactions to the environment are wired into the nervous system to a high degree and are almost automatically elicited by given environmental stimulus conditions. An example is the tendency of turkeys and other fowl to react with alarm instinctively at the sight of a hawk, while showing no distress in the presence of a goose. This was beautifully demonstrated by the distinguished ethologist (a scientist who studies animals in their natural settings) Nikko Tinbergen (1951). He made up a cardboard silhouette which looked somewhat like a goose when moved in one direction but resembled a hawk when moved in the opposite direction. If the silhouette was moved within sight of the turkeys so that the gooselike neck seemed to be in front, no distress was evident; if, on the other hand, it was moved so that the hawklike neck was in front, the turkeys reacted with evident fright. This difference in the capacity of the cardboard figure to elicit fear was found even in the case of baby fowl that had never previously seen a hawk. In

Constantine Manos, from Monkmeyer

effect, the adjustive emotional reaction to dangerous predators was built into the nervous system of the species and did not seem to depend on learning.

Humans too seem to have certain built-in reactions to environmental stimuli. One example is the inborn tendency of infants around six to eight months of age to become fearful of any stranger who approaches the crib. However, such built-in adjustive reactions are far less important in adult humans than in lower animals. Most of our reactions to the environment, including what is benign and what is hazardous, are developed through our experience with the world, and so to preserve life and well-being the growing child must learn how to react to and to deal with the environment.

Part II will describe the demands of living calling for adjustive behavior in people, especially those demands that we might call stressful—in that they are recognized by the person as important for his or her existence, safety, or well-being and hence carry the potential for generating stress emotions. We shall consider the stresses of life in Chapter 3, the ways in which these are coped with in the course of living in Chapter 4, and the relations between stress and bodily illness in Chapter 5.

CHAPTER 3 THE STRESSES OF LIFE

In the psychological study of adjustment, we usually focus on two kinds of demands. One is primarily *internal*, arising from the biological makeup of the person. This makeup requires that certain conditions be met for survival and comfort. We must be protected against injury, and have sufficient food and water, be able to keep warm, and so on. The other kind of basic demand is *external*, that is, it arises from the external physical and social environment.

Of these, the *social demands* are generally considered by psychologists to be the most important for explaining our emotional life, both the positively toned emotions (such as love, joy, exhilaration, and feelings of ease) and the negatively toned ones (such as fear, anxiety, anger, depression, guilt). This is because we live interdependently with other persons in a social context from the moment of birth, and our relationships with other persons become as important to us as life itself. Moreover, social demands that

start out as external—that is, real or imagined pressures from adults to act in certain ways, expectations about how we should think and feel—later become internal as we begin to take on these pressures as part of ourselves. For example, the desire to achieve high social esteem may have begun as parental or social values or pressures, but later on in life such pressures may have become very deep-rooted features of the individual's personality, acting as internal demands as powerful as the biological urges on which life and limb depend.

At first these social demands concern relatively simple and primitive actions. For example, we must learn to feed ourselves with the utensils (fingers, chopsticks, or fork and knife) used in the society we happen to live in, making the important transition from the breast or bottle. If we live in a modern, industrialized society, it is necessary to learn to use whatever type of toilet facility is deemed appropriate, learning to regulate bladder and bowel activities as befits the social custom. There are further social demands not to damage valuable objects or injure others. As people grow more mature, social demands become more complex and subtle, suited, of course, to the older child's increased intellectual grasp. In highly developed cultures, people must go to school to learn to read and write and to become familiar with the history of their society, its technology and value system, and the acceptable ways of interacting with others in different social contexts and under different social roles and statuses.

The precise pattern of what must be learned varies with the culture, and even from family to family. The Japanese child must learn a language different from that of the American child. Japanese social gestures and expressive reactions are also different. For example, a child is taught to bow to another person rather than shaking hands, and he or she learns that the depth of bow reflects one's social relationship to that person. The American child learns to shake hands in greeting. Handshaking for boys may have a different importance and quality than for girls. In all these matters, and an infinite variety more, the individual is exposed to an extensive and complex set of social demands that have been institutionalized in the society and handed down over many generations.

Failure to comply with these social demands results typically in distressing consequences. Depending on the cultural importance accorded them, failure to comply may lead to punishment by ostracism or rejection, withholding of an expected reward, a physical beating, or the expression of disapproval. Usually, though not always, compliance with social demands leads to reward, either the attainment of some valued objective such as a good grade, a promotion, or the evidence of social approval. Since most satisfactions in life, even in adulthood, arise from a social climate of positive regard, and most negative conditions of life stem from negative regard, the approval of others is a most important social objective. Approval itself may become a vital goal to some persons because it symbolizes being safe from harm. However, the excessive seeking of approval can be destructive of creativity and effectiveness and can result in a bland, conforming individual, as well as leading to continuing personal tension and distress; other personal needs are bound to be frustrated by it, and universal approval is all but impossible to achieve. In any case, the expectations of others serve as pressing social demands because favorable personal outcomes are in some degree tied to compliance.

The fact that makes an environmental condition a demand, whether physical or social, is that we are vulnerable in many ways because of the way we are constructed. Our tissues can be punctured, burned, poisoned, and otherwise injured or destroyed. Without food and water we die. As members of the same species, we share certain tissue needs in common. A sharp object is dangerous to thin-skinned animals, but hardly so for thick-skinned animals, such as the rhinoceros, except perhaps in certain unprotected body areas.

Similarly, as members of the same species and as people sharing a common culture, failure to receive certain social rewards or to maintain certain kinds of social relationships can also be damaging in a psychological sense. This endows the social environment with power over us. However, external social demands endanger us only if they communicate with internal motivating forces or needs of importance to our well-being.

One cannot speak meaningfully about environmental demands without reference also to the properties of persons which make them vulnerable to environmentally induced harm. We all share certain common areas of vulnerability by virtue of our common biological and social heritage, but there are also variations from species to species, culture to culture, and individual to individual in respect to what constitutes an environmental demand and in the ways we adjust to such demands. This means that our focus of attention must be centered on the adjustive *commerce* between the person and the environment, rather than on either alone.

In addition to making adjustive demands, the environment also serves us as a *resource*. We hunt animals for food, use the soil to grow things, make use of the rains and snow, build shelter with the substances found in nature such as wood, clay, stones, and metal, and modify or combine these substances to make tools, using paper, cement, brick, steel, and so on. We join together with other people to strengthen our puny individual physical powers, live in families and societies having complex divisions of labor, learn from others how to do things, make use of others' labor and skills to get rich or powerful, influence others to join in the same cause. Thus adjustment does not mean merely bending to the requirements of the physical and social world, but it consists also of using that world and changing it in accordance with our needs. The environment thus serves as a resource to be exploited in adjusting, and how well we use it is a measure of our adjustive capacity.

STRESS AND ADJUSTMENT

Thus far, in speaking of environmental demands and resources, adjustment appears to be essentially a matter of problem solving. The person must discover the characteristics of his or her environment and how it can be dealt with in living; such learning begins at the moment of birth and remains a continuing process throughout life. However, if adjustment were simply problem solving, it would entail only intellectual processes such as perception, learning, memory, and acquisition of skills for getting along and effectively utilizing environmental resources and opportunities. This is not the whole story. In adjustive activity, strong emotions, particularly the stress emotions such as anger, fear, anxiety, guilt, and shame, are also generated. These result when the environmental demands and opportun-

ities involve high stakes and entail frustration, threat, and conflict. Therefore, in addition to problem solving adjustive activities can involve the products of stress, including ineffective solutions to problems of living, seemingly irrational and disturbed patterns of behavior, subjective distress, and bodily disease. To understand effective and ineffective adjustment, we must therefore give attention to the stresses of living, the conditions that bring stress about, and their consequences.

THE NATURE OF STRESS

What is stress? In the simplest and most general sense, stress occurs when there are *demands on the person which tax or exceed his adjustive resources.* Certain environmental conditions are noxious to the tissues of the body or to the normal integrated functions of these tissues. These are physical stressors, including extreme cold, heat, the invasion of microorganisms, and physical injuries, to mention a few examples. Certain environmental social conditions, on the other hand, can also be damaging, now or in the future. These are called psychosocial stressors. With respect to physical stressors, the defenses of the body must be mobilized to overcome the physical harm, as in the changes required to heal wounds or to maintain a critical balance in the internal environment. Thus, under conditions of cold or heat the body temperature must nevertheless be maintained at a level necessary to sustain life and well-being. When bacterial or viral infections occur, these must be rooted out by blood cells whose function it is to prevent infection from destroying the living biological system. In the case of psychosocial stressors, individuals sense danger or recognize damage and must act to protect themselves against this or to overcome the damage.

Stress is not simply "out there" in the environment, though it may originate there. Stress depends not only on the external conditions, but also on the vulnerabilities of the individual and the adequacy of his or her system of defenses—in effect, on the way the person or animal is constructed, psychologically or physiologically. Some conditions are nearly universal stressors. Examples include military combat, imprisonment, natural disasters such as floods, tornadoes, fires, and explosions, disabling injuries, incapacitating diseases, terminal illness such as advanced cancer, or the loss of a loved one. Many environmental situations, however, are not stressful for everyone, the reaction depending on the kind of person we are. For example, being evaluated in an important examination, being rejected or disapproved by someone we regard highly or love, or anticipating major surgery are more stressful for some than for others.

Moreover, people react to the same stressor in diverse ways. Even in severe disasters in which many are killed or left homeless and in which the whole structure of the community is disrupted or destroyed, there are still some individuals who appear comparatively undisturbed and who act in an effective fashion in spite of everything. In contrast, others become disorganized, dazed, and panicky, generally displaying the signs of severe emotional disturbance. For these former persons, the situation cannot easily be defined as a stressor. Conversely, situations which seem benign to most persons may severely disturb other individuals. For these latter only, the situation can be viewed as a stress stimulus.

Individual differences in reaction to the same stress situation may be observed in every study of wartime stress or human disaster. In World War II, the Korean war, the Vietnam war, and the Arab-Israeli war of 1973, a certain percentage of men broke down and showed incapacitating emotional symptoms requiring that they be withdrawn from combat, either temporarily or permanently. Yet the great majority do not develop such symptoms of combat neurosis. And of those who did, in some cases severe emotional reactions appeared following objectively very stressful experiences, such as seeing a buddy blown to

bits or being engaged in a long battle action in which a high percentage of one's comrades became casualties. In other cases, however, such symptoms developed even before the men had been exposed to any actual conditions of battle—for example, in comparatively benign training situations or in transit to a combat zone. They reacted as though they had been exposed to severe stress conditions. For these men, the training situation was stressful, or they were terrified of anticipated combat, even though it was not particularly so for others. It has been observed too (Janis, 1962) that people respond very differently to a "near miss," that is, a disaster experience in which they came close to death but were not injured. Imagine, for example, being in a car that is in a traffic accident and is virtually demolished, but you survive without injury. Some people react to this with extreme fear of automobiles thereafter, while others develop no such concern or distress. It has been suggested that the former interpret the "near miss" as evidence that they are more vulnerable to death than they had previously believed, since they could easily have been killed. In contrast, others take the experience as further evidence of their invulnerability, since they miraculously survived. Such variations nicely illustrate the central problem in defining any situation as a stressor. It makes little sense to speak of a stressor without reference to the individuals exposed to it and the psychological reactions it produces in them.

Most stress research focuses on the reactions of individuals as well as on the stress situation itself. An example is a study in a medical setting by Wolff, Friedman, Hofer, and Mason (1964). The investigators examined the reactions of parents with a child dying of leukemia, including how the parents coped with this tragic experience. The subjects had agreed to live at the hospital where their child was being treated and to expose themselves to intensive scrutiny. The bereavement experience was actually made somewhat easier for them to deal with as a result of being part of the research study and sharing their problems and distress with others similarly afflicted.

In the course of their observations, the investigators noted that some of the parents utilized the defense of denial, a tactic that appeared highly successful in reducing their distress. Such denial was manifested by the expressed conviction that their child was not going to die, by making unrealistic future plans for the child's schooling, by becoming angry at anyone who suggested that leukemia is fatal, by assuming that new drugs would be found in time to cure their child, or by believing false stories about other cases that had been cured of the disease.

Selecting a group of parents who exhibited such denial, the investigators compared evidence of the physiological stress level in these subjects with another sample of parents who did not deny the realities of the situation. The amount of hydrocortisone (a hormone secreted by the cortex or outer portion of the adrenal glands in situations of stress) in both groups was measured. The greater the stress, the higher the blood level of hydrocortisone should be. It was found that parents who coped with the stress situation by denying the terminal nature of their child's illness showed considerably lower levels of hydrocortisone in the blood than the comparison group. Evidently, because they successfully deceived themselves about the situation, their stress reaction was reduced compared with that found in the parents who realistically faced the tragedy. Here, in essentially the *same* situation of stress, one group showed more stress reaction than the other because of the mode of coping employed.

FRUSTRATION AND THREAT

We must draw a distinction here between harm that has already occurred to the person and harm that has not yet happened but might in the near future. Psychologists have long had a word for the former, namely *frustration*, which refers to the thwarting or delaying of some ongoing course of action or of goal gratification. We speak of someone being frustrated if he or she wants or needs something that is unattainable or must wait for it. As you can see, frustration is a broad term having a number of related meanings: it can refer to the situation which produced thwarting or to the psychological effects of this situation, as when someone is frustrated and reacts with anger, withdrawal, depression, or other forms of distress.

Frustration is an important component of psychological stress, since virtually any seriously harmful condition will thwart important needs and goals and will require some adjustive activity to repair the damage if possible or to get along in spite of it. Consider, for example, what happens when a person loses a loved one (say, a spouse) through illness or death. The stress is apt to be severe because much of the person's life has been closely tied to the spouse and now he or she is no longer there. Huge changes in the life pattern of the survivor are necessitated by the loss. Since the person's normal social role is no longer viable, he or she must find new ways of living and relating to others. Bereaved husbands or wives have lost an integral part of their social and perhaps even personal identity, as in losing an arm or a leg. The old identity and way of life must be given up and replaced with another. Grief is the complex emotional reaction arising from such loss, and the attendant difficulties and distress are apt to be very great (cf. Lindemann, 1944; Parkes, 1972). Bereavement is, of course, only one of the major sources of frustration in life, but because of its frequency and major impact on the victim, it points up the major tasks of adjustment called for by harms to which we are all in some measure vulnerable.

Threat may be defined as the anticipation of harm, whether that harm involves tissue needs as in the pain of injury, or learned social motives, as in loss of the positive regard of another person. The greater the anticipated harm, the greater the threat, the more intense the consequent stress emotion, and the stronger the effort to cope or adjust.

There is good evidence that psychologically produced stress is often worse while a harmful event is merely anticipated than when the actual dreaded event is finally confronted. One group of researchers (Nomikos, Opton, Averill, and Lazarus, 1968) were interested in whether surprise or suspense results in the greater stress reaction. Will it be more or less stressful if a dentist, say, gives an injection with little warning to the patient, compared with giving him some time in which to anticipate it? The researchers showed two versions of the same movie in which three distressing wood-shop accident scenes are viewed, namely, one in which a man accidentally lacerates the tips of his fingers, a second in which a man loses his fingers in a milling machine, and a third in which a board is thrust from a circular saw and kills an innocent passerby. In the standard version of the movie (suspense), approximately twenty to thirty seconds pass during which the viewer expects each of the several accidents to happen; in the other version (surprise), the anticipatory scenes of two of the accidents are cut out and only a few seconds of anticipation are permitted, barely enough to sense what is about to happen. No alteration of the third accident was made. It was found that increases in heart rate and sweat-gland activity (measured by the electrical conductivity of the skin) of the viewer were far greater in the situation of relatively long anticipation than when it was shorter. This is shown in Figure 3-1 for the measurement of skin conductance. Furthermore, as can be seen in the figure, most of the rise in stress reaction occurred while the subjects were anticipating the accident scene, not during the actual scene itself (impact). That is, while the blood is spurting from the severed finger and the victim looks at it in distress, there is little further increase of stress reaction. In fact, the bodily disturbance seems to be ending at this point (impact), even declining while the distressing scene is taking place. It is the anticipation of that scene more than the actual event itself that accounts for most of the stress reaction.

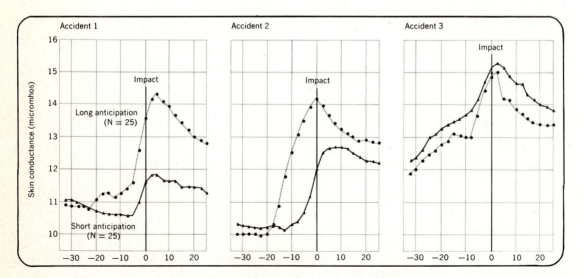

FIGURE 3-1 Skin conductance before and during accident scenes under conditions of long and short anticipation. (From Nomikos, Opton, Averill, and Lazarus, 1968.)

TABLE 3–1 RELATION BETWEEN ACTUAL DANGER AND INCIDENCE OF NEUROSIS AMONG COMBAT FLYERS

DUTY	RELATIVE INCIDENCE OF NEUROSIS	RELATIVE FLYING HOURS PER CASUALTY IN THESE DUTIES
Night bombing	12.0	160
Day fighting	6.0	188
Night fighting	3.4	231
Coastal reconnaissance	3.3	360
Training	1.1	1,960

SOURCE: Tompkins, 1959, p. 76.

The concept of threat as an anticipation of future harm implies an evaluation by the person, an appraisal of what the present situation portends. By and large, situations that in the individuals' experience, have never previously been connected with harm will not result in the appraisal of threat; and conversely, events previously linked to harm tend to be threatening. This does not mean that the experience of harm must be direct. One can learn from the experience of others, a process sometimes called "vicarious learning." It is not necessary to have been killed in an airplane to believe that airplanes may be dangerous. Reading about airplane crashes in the newspaper can suffice to connect flying with danger. The appraisal of threat is an inference about the danger implications of a situation based on experience, either real or imagined, vicarious or direct.

Learning through experience is an important basis of threat in the analysis made by Grinker and Spiegel (1945) of combat stress in air crews. They point out that the crews came to anticipate harm from flak bursts (antiaircraft shells that explode near the plane and spew dangerous fragments in all directions) only after the experience of seeing the damage they can do. The authors write (p. 127):

This is an actual learning process. The situation may appear at first to be innocuous, and the primary reaction to combat is usually detach-

ment and objective interest. The antiaircraft fire may look like a spectacular but harmless Fourth of July celebration, entertaining but not dangerous. This attitude is soon changed by the repeated demonstration of the destructive effectiveness of flak bursts. Other possible dangers are only appreciated after some objective demonstration has alerted the ego. After a crash due to motor failure, the most vigorous attention may be paid to the sound of the motors, a sound which was never given any special emphasis before. . . .

The appraisal of threat is thus usually related to actual, realistic, or *objective dangers* of being harmed. Observations in the military setting by a British psychologist (Tompkins, 1959) suggest that the greater the actual danger, the greater the severity of the stress reactions. He used as an index of threat the incidence of neurotic breakdowns associated with different flight duties in which the number of battle casualties varied. For example, night bombing was more dangerous than day fighting because more planes were shot down at night than during the day. Table 3-1 gives Tompkins's data on the incidence of neurotic breakdown in different types of flying jobs and the number of actual flying hours in each job before an actual battle casualty occurred. As we would expect, the shorter the number of hours, the more hazardous the duty. The table shows that the relative incidence of neurotic breakdowns increases dramatically with the hazardous-ness of the duty.

Nevertheless, the objective danger of the situation does not alone account for all stress reactions. A lack of precise correspondence between objective danger and the appraisal of threat can often be observed, especially where the realities of the situation are difficult to assess. A fascinating example of this comes from a study by Irving Janis (1958) of patients facing surgery. He found little relationship between the objective seriousness of the operation, as judged by surgeons, and the degree of fear that was reported by the patient. The trained and knowledgeable surgeon had a different basis from the untrained patient for judging how serious the surgery was. For example, a patient having a suspicious lump removed experiences little physical discomfort; he or she may also not have been told of the possibility of cancer and may not be aware of this danger, or may deny or overlook these dangers. In contrast, the patient with gall bladder disease experiences great discomfort and strange, frightening symptoms he may not understand, all of which makes him very apprehensive. However, the physician knows that gall bladder operations are relatively minor and have an excellent medical outlook in contrast with a potential cancer. Threat depends on what the person knows or believes about the situation, and this knowledge need not correspond with objective reality. Information from the situation as well as the capacities and dispositions of the person to assimilate it are thus important in determining whether or not the situation appears threatening, and if so, how severe the threat will be.

Another example of failure to evaluate danger correctly comes from research on natural disasters (Withey, 1962, p. 116) such as floods and hurricanes.

An amazing number of people refused to believe that the flood could hit them, that it could come anywhere near to the previous severe flood of 1903. The result was that they would not move themselves and their belongings out of their houses. Many others piled furniture up in the center of the room, even though the warning had been issued that the flood water would destroy their possessions left at that level. The result was that many had to be rescued out of the second stories of their homes. Of 10,000 homeless people, nearly 3,000 had to be rescued by boat.

And of another instance, Withey (1962, p. 116) writes:

An element which seems to influence people's behavior during the threat of crisis is the commonly found myth or legend that "It can't happen to me." This legend often seems to serve the function of minimizing the feeling of danger. More than half of the respondents claimed that Ocean City would never have a tidal wave or be washed away because "the sand bar was building up all the time." The fact that a portion of Ocean City had been washed away in a 1933 hurricane was used to rationalize and emphasize the "no-danger" theme. Because the 1933 hurricane "had widened the inlet to the bay, there was even less danger from high tides."

These illustrations point up the principle that appraisal of threat, while certainly influenced by the objective circumstances of the danger, depends also on the particular interpretation that individuals place upon what they know or what is communicated to them about the situation. It may even be illogical, as in the immediately preceding quotation.

In sum, when a harm is anticipated but has not yet occurred, we speak of threat. When the harm has already taken place, we often speak of frustration. Threat is a *future-oriented* psychological state, and frustration is *present-* or *past-oriented*. When threatened, people usually attempt to take some sort of preventive action. For example, if a person is threatened by the prospect of failure in an important examination, he or she usually makes some effort to prevent the failure, perhaps by a plan of study; but there are some individuals who might try to deceive themselves about the actual prospects, thus controlling the distressing anxiety associated with the threat. On the other hand, when the harm is occurring or has already occurred, as in the situation in which the examination has already been failed, what is now required is not *preventive action* (the previous damage, i.e., failure, can no longer be prevented); rather, *corrective action* designed to overcome, remove, mitigate, or tolerate the harm is in order, if it is possible. Perhaps a revision in goals would be appropriate, or a change in the route by which the same ultimate goal might still be attained. Coping with threat involves different strategies from those used in coping with frustration or harm.

A moment's reflection will reveal that most psychological stressors contain elements of both frustration *and* threat. Harm that has already been experienced may have future damaging consequences that can be anticipated. Both threat and frustration are thus typically mixed together in life situations. This point is nicely illustrated in comments by psychiatric researchers Hamburg, Hamburg, and deGoza (1953), who have studied intensively the reactions of individuals who were hospitalized for severe burns. Even though the harmful occurrence, the burns, had already happened, there was to be a long period of incapacitation and painful treatment, and there remained possibilities of death, permanent disfigurement, and disruption of long-established interpersonal relationships. Each patient considered the significance of the injury in the light of his own expectations and motives. They write (pp. 2–4):

> When a psychiatric observer enters a ward in which there are a number of severely burned patients, all in the acute phase (covered with bandages, receiving transfusions, and so on), he is likely to be impressed by the varieties of behavior evident. One patient is crying, moaning, complaining, demanding that more be done for him; another appears completely comfortable and unconcerned; another appears intensely preoccupied and seems to make very little contact with the observer; still another appears sad and troubled but friendly, responding with a weak smile to any approach made to him; and so it goes, from one bed to the next. Thus, the observer quickly gains the impression that although the injuries are quite comparable, the experience must have somewhat different meanings for each of the patients. As he talks with them, he sees that each one is struggling with his own personal problems, involving not only the injury itself, but his own interpretation of it. These problems are often dramatically highlighted by the extreme life-threatening nature of the situation, complicated by pain, uncertainty, toxicity, sedation, analgesia, and the like. . . . Sooner or later every patient had to consider such questions as "How badly am I hurt?", "How much damage will remain after I am well?", "Will I be disfigured?", "Will I have to change my plans?"

CONFLICT

Conflict is the presence, simultaneously, of two incompatible action tendencies or goals. They are incompatible because the behavior and attitudes necessary to accomplish one are countermanded by those required by the other. Conflict can arise (1) because internal needs or motives are in opposition, (2) because external demands are incompatible, or (3) because an internal need or motive opposes an external demand. Conflict is an especially important concept in adjustment because it makes threat or frustration *inevitable* precisely because the actions designed to satisfy one goal necessarily threaten or frustrate the other.

There is no completely satisfactory solution to conflict as long as the person remains committed to both goals. He or she can try somehow to

FIGURE 3-2 The power of self-sacrificing motives, in this case, maternal feeling: Vietnamese women attempt to shelter their children as they huddle in a rice paddy during fighting in their sector. (Wide World Photos.)

tolerate the frustration; give up or modify one or both goals; or engage in self-deception in which the goal or its frustration is denied. Conflict poses no great problem when the needs, motives, or external demands involved are weak. When they are strong, however, threat or frustration is great. Since conflict is a universal problem, how it is handled is of the utmost importance for adjustment. Successful and unsuccessful adaptation depend on the way in which threat and frustration, resulting from conflict, are handled. Our effectiveness in living is closely tied to our success in mastering the threats and frustrations produced by conflicts occurring throughout life.

An interesting example of combat stress viewed as a result of conflict is a discussion by

Grinker and Spiegel (1945) about the forces that kept air crew members in the battle situation in World War II in spite of severe danger to life and limb. (Although this illustration comes from World War II and may seem dated, the observations and analysis are just as applicable to battle situations of today as well as many other situations of grave physical danger other than war that require the willingness to remain on the spot in order to carry out one's social responsibility.) The basic conflict is between several *internal demands*, most important of which are the airman's need to survive, on the one hand, and the need to be respected by others and to live up to his own standards of conduct on the other. If one refused to go on a combat mission in order to avoid being killed or injured, he would have endangered these two other equally powerful motives. He would have had to face the shame of being condemned by his peers and superiors and the guilt connected with such a cowardly and selfish action while his buddies risked their lives and died. Such a conflict is largely ''internal'' because all the demands can be seen as forces within the personality, namely, the need to survive, the need to be esteemed by others, and the need to maintain a given standard of conduct. Such a standard of conduct, for example, may have once been external, but it is now an integral part of the person; we say it has been internalized.

A reasonable solution for the airman studied by Grinker and Spiegel was to live up to his personal standards and those of the social group by completing his combat tour of duty in spite of the continued threat of death and the fear connected with it. Sometimes the unresolvable conflict and the persistent emotion associated with it resulted in severe neurotic symptoms, and hospitalization or treatment became necessary. In such cases the airman was, perforce, removed from the conflict without his realizing what was happening, seemingly against his will. Such a solution was felt, by and large, to be an honorable one in that the airman could not be blamed (or blame himself) as much for his "weakness" as he might be for voluntarily withdrawing and leaving his comrades in the lurch.

An example of conflict between *external demands* is when parents disagree with each other about a child's life goals and impose on him or her powerful and contradictory pressures to accommodate to their wishes. The child is caught between these pressures: accommodation to one automatically means the thwarting of the other. A father may encourage his son to be masculine and aggressive, perhaps a professional athlete. The mother may be offended or frightened by this goal, and with equal vigor she urges the boy toward artistic or intellectual directions. Fearing he will be injured in sports, she places pressure on him to avoid competitive sports activities. It is obviously difficult or impossible for the boy to satisfy both sets of demands. The external conflict can be further complicated if the boy has internalized some of the father's or the mother's standards. For example, he may feel that he will be feminine and inadequate if he does not succeed in sports. Since his self-esteem is therefore tied to the outcome, and if he lacks the necessary skills, he is bound to experience serious personal defeat. Thus, in addition to being unable to successfully manage both of the conflicting external demands, a third internal force is added to the conflict, adding greatly to the boy's adjustive dilemma.

This type of situation has been discussed extensively by Karen Horney (1937), a psychoanalytic writer who has described many conflicts between the explicit and implicit values of Western culture. For example, although our culture explicitly admonishes people to live by the golden rule, love their neighbor, exhibit kindness to others less fortunate, and reject material things, at the same time the person who is most admired is the one who, by aggressiveness, initiative, and acquisitiveness, achieves a wealthy and powerful social position. Gentleness is both admired and condemned, as is aggressiveness. Or, to consider another example, adolescents are commonly urged by their parents and by society to be grown-up and self-sufficient. Simultaneously, however, they are not fully allowed the privilege and responsibility of self-determination. They are constantly being guided, pushed, and controlled in dating, dress and speech, staying out late, keeping suitable company, choosing an occupation, and so on. On the one hand, cultural standards urge the individual toward a certain type of value and behavior pattern, and at the same time they place a value on other incompatible ones. These contradictory values are often built into the culture and make conflict all but inevitable. When the culture is changing rapidly, as seems to be the case today (see Toffler, 1970), this sort of conflict is even more likely.

One of the simplest and commonest types of conflict occurs between an *internal need or motive* and an *external demand*. Many impulses cannot be gratified readily because they are dangerous or disapproved by society or by the people who count. Many important impulses have to be constrained with respect to form, place, and time. For example, although the early adolescent is mature sexually, inhibition of sexual activity until marriage is encouraged, creating major frustration. There are, as everyone recognizes, some marked changes in outlook on this subject occurring today compared with earlier decades, although this is a major source of public contention. However, even if this problem did not exist, the sexual impulse must find a willing partner and a suitable setting, another source of conflict between impulse and external conditions. Every society has its own rules of conduct, its own values, and its own sanctions about and opportunities for the gratification of common social motives and psychological needs. This means that every person will, to some extent, experience conflict between needs and impulses and external demands. Mastering life involves the handling of such conflicts.

People differ greatly in the skills required to find suitable, and socially acceptable, ways of gratifying internal and external demands with severe frustration and threat, that is, in the management of conflicts between them. Moreover, although societies differ in the type of impulse expression they allow and in the degree to which suitable opportunities are provided for this expression, they usually have institutionalized ways of channeling needs and motives. An excellent example is provided by aggressive or destructive impulses. Obviously, no society can allow unrestricted aggression or assault on people or property. In our own, such assault is condemned except under narrowly defined circumstances. Thus, an angry person must often suppress his or her anger, or in any event keep it within bounds. However, there are socially acceptable fashions and settings for the expression of aggression.

One such setting is competitive and body contact sports, such as boxing and wrestling, where (up to a point) participant and spectator alike can warm up to injuring the other fellow. The crowd at a boxing match usually likes the fight best if one or both of the participants is badly beaten up. The announcer gives the juicy details of the

FIGURE 3-3 "Go get him, Champ." This photo was snapped at a boxing match in New York City. The young man stands up and punches the air as he vicariously experiences the fight, thus expressing aggressive impulses safely and in a socially acceptable manner. (Wide World Photos.)

damage to the hungrily awaiting radio or television audience, describing blood oozing from a wound, perhaps, or a cut or swelling over the eye. And best of all, this aggressive discharge is socially acceptable, even approved (as long as it doesn't go too far), and shared as an experience with many others. For the audience, it is a vicarious experience of venting anger; for the participants, it is direct. The photograph in Figure 3-3 illustrates the behavior of one boxing fan who is so carried away by the vicarious experience of aggression that he acts it out at ringside to the amusement of one spectator in the background, although he is ignored by most of the others.

CONDITIONS LEADING TO THREAT APPRAISAL

Some of the conditions that lead a person to be threatened, harmed psychologically, or in conflict have their source in the external environment, while others arise from the personality of the individual. Let us examine each of these in turn.

Environmental conditions No single aspect of a complex environmental stimulus itself produces stress—rather it is the total arrangement of its elements. For example, a complimentary statement may at one moment or in one context be reassuring, and at another the same statement can be highly threatening. Accompanied by a tone of sarcasm, it can indicate contempt, but without the sarcastic tone it can signify positive regard. Tiny changes in the stimulus pattern can drastically alter the significance of any stimulus event, as when a small gesture or facial expression contradicts the actual content of what is being said. Praise after a poor performance may be judged as a sign of hostility or as an admission by someone who is trying to make one feel better that one's performance was inadequate. It may even have a condescending ring, implying "You'll do it right eventually, I suppose." How this statement is judged depends on the total constellation of cues, the tone, the context, past relationships with the other person, and, of course, the personality of the individual and his or her capacity to recognize meanings that are sometimes rather subtle. A stress stimulus is usually a complex event rather than a simple one.

Many aspects of a life event are important in pushing a person to appraise a situation as threatening or harmful, or as involving conflict. We will look at two, namely *helplessness* on the part of the person to influence the outcome of a harmful event and the *imminence* of the anticipated harm.

In discussing threat, Mechanic (1962, p. 10) writes: "To the extent that an individual acquires the tools capable of dealing with difficult life situations, that which in some circumstances might be a threatening situation can become routine and ordinary." Threat depends on the extent to which a person feels *capable* of mastering danger. When he or she feels fully capable of preventing the harm, threat is absent or minimal. When the person feels *helpless* or too weak to prevent it, threat is increased, its severity, of course, depending on the seriousness of the anticipated harm.

In most life settings we tend to avoid placing ourselves in a situation where we are helpless to control danger. In the early stages of learning to drive an automobile, when our command over the vehicle is shaky, we practice on safe streets and at slow speeds. Only when we believe we have reasonable mastery do we enter crowded metropolitan areas or drive at high speeds. As the conviction grows that one is in command of the situation, situations that were once frightening now can be met with pleasure and security. A little risk may titillate, but real danger is threatening.

The importance of competence and its opposite, helplessness, is widely observed in stress research. This theme is expressed by Visotsky and his associates (1961) in the context of their

FIGURE 3-4 The unemployment line is an unexpected shock for many. The situation is apt to increase one's sense of helplessness and threaten one's good opinion of oneself. "What is wrong with me that this should have happened? What is wrong with the social system? How am I and my family going to manage?" (Alex Webb, Magnum.)

observations of the reactions of patients hospitalized for paralytic polio. During the early stages of the illness when the patient is still in critical condition and is entirely dependent on others, the authors note (p. 431) that:

At this stage of the illness, interaction with other patients seems useful chiefly in the sense that there are other human beings around at all times. For most patients, a sense of isolation is quite threatening. . . . The patient in a private room is bound to have a good deal of time alone, since staff members cannot ordinarily be with him constantly. In his extremely helpless and vulnerable state, ordinary loneliness can become much more frightening than it would be in better circumstances. The mere physical proximity of other patients with its accompanying sense of shared difficulties serves a useful purpose.

Seriously life-threatened patients with low vital capacities were placed next to patients with good vocal ability, who could call for a nurse or aid when a sicker patient needed help.

This favored the development of a sense of security in the helpless patient and a sense of competence for the vocal patient.

The more people have a sense of power over the potentially harmful agent, the less vulnerable they are to threat. Personal resources based on the individual's skills, knowledge, history of success in previous crises, and generally positive beliefs about his or her fate, all contribute to a sense of security and reduce the likelihood of threat. Resources reducing the impact of potential harm can be found in the environment itself, especially other people who have proved themselves to be dependable. Evidence that other competent people can be called upon tends to be reassuring.

The response to the death of a loved one also varies from culture to culture depending on the institutionalized supports that are available to the bereaved person (Lindemann, 1960). In the United States, for example, the isolation of the small family consisting of husband, wife, and children imposes a severe burden on each family member in the event of a death, since supporting relationships on which the bereaved person can depend for aid in the crisis, and which can tide him or her over the process of establishing new roles and relationships, are less likely to be available. In Italy, in contrast, severe mourning reactions are less common because the extended and organized kinship system there offers important supports during such a critical period.

The mere presence of apparent external social supports does not in itself guarantee an increase in the person's sense of mastery of potential harm. Others on whom one wishes to depend, or from whom one hopes to gain assistance, may act in such a way as to make the situation even *more* threatening. This point is made effectively by Mechanic (1962) in his observations of graduate students facing a crucial upcoming examination. He offers an interesting and insightful comment about the sort of behavior in the spouse of the graduate student that either provides support or creates added burdens for the person already beset by self-doubts and apprehensions over the chances for success. Mechanic writes (p. 158):

> In general, spouses do not provide blind support. They perceive the kinds of support the student wants and then they provide it. The wife who becomes worried about examinations also may provide more support than the spouse who says, "I'm not worried. You will surely pass." Indeed, since there is a chance that the student will not pass, the person who is supportive in a meaningful sense will not give blind assurance. Rather she will seek to find the realistic limits of the situation, the weaknesses of the spouse, and the anxieties and tensions that are being experienced; and then she will attempt to help reduce these. Often a statement to the effect, "Do the best you can," is more supportive than, "I am sure you are going to do well." The latter statement adds to the student's burden, for not only must he feel the disappointment of not passing, but also the loss of respect in the eyes of his spouse.

In a moving clinical description of the dilemma of parents facing the imminent loss of a child suffering from cancer, Friedman and his colleagues (1963) have also described how relatives can increase the threat rather than decrease it by their behavior (pp. 618–619):

> Typically, the children's grandparents tended to be less accepting of the diagnosis than the parents, with more distant relatives and friends challenging reality even more frequently. The tendency for the degree of reality-distortion to increase with the remoteness of its source from the immediate family almost made it appear that some of the parents were surrounded by "concentric circles of disbelief." Friends and relatives would question the parents as to

whether the doctors were *sure* of the diagnosis and prognosis, and might suggest that the parents seek additional medical opinion. Comments would be made that the ill child, especially if he was in remission, could not possibly have leukemia as he looked too well or did not have the "right symptoms." Individuals cured of "leukemia" would be cited, and in a few cases faith healers and pseudo medical practitioners were recommended.

Although parents generally perceived most of these statements and suggestions as attempts to "cheer us up and give us hope," they found themselves in the uncomfortable position of having to "defend" their child's diagnosis and prognosis, sometimes experiencing the feeling that others thought they were therefore "condemning" their own child. Thus, the parents were not allowed to express any feelings of hopelessness, yet . . . they were paradoxically expected to appear grief-stricken.

Grandparents not only displayed more denial than the parents, but often appeared more vulnerable to the threatened loss of a loved child. Therefore, many of the parents felt that they had to give emotional support to the grandparents, at a time when it was most difficult for them to assume this supportive role. . . .

An additional problem was that friends and relatives often besieged the parents with requests for information about their child. Parents would have to repeatedly describe each new development, listening by the hour to repetitive expressions of encouragement and sympathy, and occasionally having to reassure others that the disease was not contagious. This arduous task was ameliorated in the cases where a semiformal system evolved where some one individual, often a close friend or minister, would be kept up to date so that he in turn could answer the multitude of questions.

Although it was clear that friends and rela-

tives sometimes aggravated the parents' distress, they also provided significant emotional support in the form of tactful and sympathetic listening and by offering to be of service. . . . The major source of emotional support for most parents during the period of hospitalization appeared to be the other parents of similarly afflicted children, with the feeling that "we are all in it together" and with concern with the distress experienced by the other parents. . . . The parents learned from each other, and could profit by observing the coping behavior manifested by others in the group. Thus, the common fear of "going to pieces" when their child would become terminally ill was greatly alleviated by watching others successfully, albeit painfully, go through the experience.

In short, environmental resources act in the same way as personal resources. Their presence in positive terms assists the person to feel capable of meeting harms and thus reduces threat. Their absence or inadequacy intensifies the threat by communicating weakness on the part of the person in the struggle with dangers to his or her well-being, thereby increasing feelings of vulnerability.

If the advent of harm is distant in time, degree of threat will be reduced. As the harm grows nearer in time, threat increases. The limiting factor, of course, is the harm's severity, since an imminent harm that is minor will produce less threat than an imminent one that is more serious. In short, the *imminence* of a harmful event is highly relevant to the degree of threat one is apt to experience.

A common-sense example is the threat of death. Fear of death is a widespread phenomenon, though it is also widely denied (Feifel and Branscomb, 1973). However, the degree of this fear seems to be closely related to its subjective imminence. Certain situations provide impressive cues or indications that death may be imminent—for example, when an individual suffers

FIGURE 3-5 "Final approach?" (Ziggy, Tom Wilson, Universal Press Syndicate, 1975.)

from certain types of diseases or enters a situation where there is great mortal danger.

An anecdotal example may be seen in the common experience of flying. People who ordinarily regard death as remote may become extremely fearful in situations they regard as dangerous, such as in an airplane. When aboard a plane, especially during landing and takeoff, which they recognize as particularly hazardous, such people become markedly apprehensive. At these moments, sudden sounds and sharp changes in movement occur frequently. The ground appears close, and it seems that in an instant they could be easily destroyed. Apprehension is enhanced by recalling stories of disasters in similar aircraft. Some of the apprehension may be eased by the steady, dependable noise of the engines in normal flight. However, any cue that is difficult to interpret (say, an unusual noise or movement or the sudden loss of altitude) can intensify the threat because it again seems to

bring death closer (Figure 3-5). The widespread nature of this passenger reaction, which is so little verbalized during flight, is attested to by the extent to which flight insurance is purchased and by the frequency with which comedians play upon the theme of the frightened airplane passenger. Humorist Shelley Berman once referred to the instruction to fasten seat belts as "an ominous sign"!

We have comparatively little systematic observation about the role of imminence in the intensification of threat. A most provocative and interesting study of sport parachute jumpers has been made by Epstein (1962). He and his colleagues assessed threat by a series of self-ratings of positive versus negative or "avoidance" feelings made by the parachutists. Avoidance feelings included wanting to turn back or to call the jump off, feelings of fear, and self-questioning about why the parachutist had ever allowed himself to get into the jumping situation. In this way, Epstein was able to assess the amount of threat connected with various temporal periods during the jumping cycle—for example, the points at which the threat was greatest or least.

Twenty-eight parachutists were studied. After each had made his jump, he was interviewed and asked to make the ratings for the following periods before and during the jump: the night preceding the jump, the morning of the jump, upon reaching the airfield, during the training period immediately preceding the jump, at the time they were strapped to the equipment, while boarding the aircraft, during the plane's ascent, at the ready signal, upon stepping toward the jumping stand, upon waiting to be tapped to jump, during the free fall immediately after the jump, after the chute had opened, and immediately after landing. Subjects estimated on a 10-point scale the extent of positive or approach feelings, rating their avoidance feelings separately in the same way. A naive expectation would be that threat should increase as the period just before the opening of the chute neared, since that is the point of greatest danger. The curves of approach and avoidance made by these twenty-eight men at different points in the jump sequence are shown in Figure 3-6. The two kinds of feelings provide mirror images of each other; that is, they give essentially the same information because when feelings of approach are strong, feelings of avoidance are weak, and vice versa.

The data show that up to the moment of the *ready signal for jumping*, approach feelings declined and avoidance feelings increased. Following the jump signal, the pattern is reversed. Threat has evidently increased from a low point the preceding night to a high point at the moment of the ready signal. By the time the aircraft is boarded, the degree of threat has become intense, and the avoidance feelings exceed approach feelings. While the jumper is waiting to be tapped, waiting for the chute to open, making his landing, and so on, he is actually beginning to have more positive feelings, and threat is lessening.

At first this seems surprising. However, as Epstein points out, in spite of the fear and the predominance of negative feelings, the parachutists do, after all, jump. This requires explanation. Why should they jump if, at the point of boarding the aircraft, their desire to withdraw from the situation is so strong? Epstein suggests that they are jumping on a kind of psychological momentum. In a sense they have been committed much earlier, and it is difficult to reverse this decision once they are in the aircraft. It should be added that their self-image and the esteem of their colleagues makes withdrawal itself a highly threatening prospect. They are in a real conflict

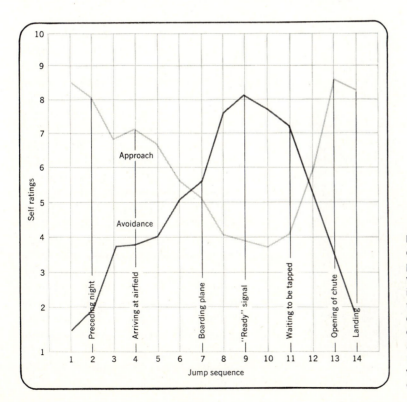

FIGURE 3-6 Ratings by parachutists of feelings of approach and avoidance (fear) at various points before and during a parachute jump. (From the measurement of drive and conflict in humans: theory and experiment by S. Epstein. In *Nebraska symposium on motivation*. M. R. Jones [Ed.], University of Nebraska Press, Lincoln, Nebr., 1962, p. 179.)

situation, and many forces, both external and internal, push them to go through with what they have started even though they experience considerable fear.

The peak of threat occurs not at the moment of jumping but at the point of *final commitment* to jump—where jumping can no longer be avoided, where the parachutist can no longer turn back. When the parachutist is in free fall, which is actually the most critical moment of objective danger, the threat has already markedly receded, and approach feelings at this point actually exceed avoidance feelings. Apparently it is the moment of decision which subjectively carries the most threat. The internal struggle is greatest when the parachutist can still physically withdraw. After committing himself irrevocably to

FIGURE 3-7 The commitment to jump: Attached to the rig, there is no turning back now. (Wide World Photos.)

jump, or after he has actually jumped, there is nothing more he can do. American military paratroop organizations appear intuitively to recognize this in their policy of relieving the jumpers of the last-minute responsibility for making the decision (Figure 3-7). The jumper is hooked to a device and pushed out of the plane once he is near the target. At this point, were a man to have the option and refuse, there would be physical obstruction to others waiting to jump, and great confusion would occur, endangering the entire mission.

Some caution must be exercised in accepting without qualification the precise details of the temporal sequence of approach and avoidance feelings as reflected in Epstein's data. They are derived entirely from retrospective reports made by the parachute jumpers. That is, they are obtained after the entire experience is over rather than at the various moments that are specified during the experience. Thus, they depend in part on the subjects' memory of these highly threatening moments. Moreover, there is a feeling of elation after the successful jump which may make the previous fearful experience appear different in retrospect. One cannot easily say to what extent there may be distortion in the reported sequence of reactions.

Fortunately, however, further studies (Fenz and Epstein, 1967) using physiological recordings of the parachutists' levels of arousal have shown them to be consistent with this verbally reported picture. For experienced parachutists, during ascent in the aircraft there was a continuous increase in reactivity early in the jump sequence followed by a decline, so that at the moment of the jump the level of bodily arousal was nearly normal. In effect, the knowledgeable parachutist shows his greatest distress and highest level of stress reaction long before the moment of jump, and as the moment of jump arrives he has already coped successfully with the threat and is almost in a relaxed state. Thus, the temporal picture of relaxation-distress portrayed in Figure 3-6 appears to be a sound guess about the experienced parachutist's psychological reactions. Such data provide an excellent illustration of the role of *imminence of danger* in determining the degree of appraised threat and stress reaction. It must be remembered that the essential harm potentially involved in the jump, violent loss of life, is a constant factor at all times. In spite of this constancy, as the critical moment of commitment nears, threat increases. Thereafter it declines.

Another illustration of the role of imminence of danger of harm in threat appraisal is found in the studies of Mechanic (1962) that have been referred to several times previously (studies of students facing a crucial examination). Mechanic shows two things: (1) that the degree of stress reaction increases as the date of the examination nears, and (2) that the kinds of behaviors used to cope with the threat change as the danger grows nearer. Mechanic writes (p. 142):

As the examination approached and as student anxieties increased, various changes occurred in behavior. Joking increased, and, while students still sought social support and talked a great deal about examinations, they began specifically to avoid certain people who aroused their anxiety. Stomach aches, asthma, and a general feeling of weariness became common complaints, other psychosomatic symptoms appeared, the use of tranquilizers and sleeping pills became more frequent.

And further (p. 144):

When the examinations are nearly upon the student, anxiety is very high, even for those rated as low-anxiety persons, although students do fluctuate between confidence and anxiety. Since studying is difficult, the student questions his motivation, interest, and ability in the field. He reassures himself that he does not care how well he does—that all he really wants out of the process is the Ph.D. degree. Even four weeks prior to the examination 82 percent of the students reported that they had said to themselves, "All I really want from this process is the Ph.D. degree." They attempted to defend themselves against their feelings by behaving in a silly, manic way, and avoidance joking became very prominent. Expectation levels were set lower and lower, and many of the students jokingly talked about what they were going to do after they failed or how they were going to prepare for the examinations the next time they took them. It appears that for the student supreme confidence at this point was considered not only presumptuous, but sacrilegious. Under these conditions the group became very cohesive, and individuals became supportive of one another and exclusive of the younger students in the department.

Among other things, one sees here the steady progression of signs of threat and stress reactions with greater imminence of the examination. In contrast with the parachute situation studied by Epstein, conflict about whether or not to commit oneself was not a prominent feature. However, although the potential harm itself remained roughly constant throughout this period, there were marked changes in the amount of stress reaction as the date grew near.

Personality factors The more extreme a stressor is, the more uniform will be its capacity to produce threat in most people. This is because extreme stress situations such as death, imprisonment, torture, destruction of the social order, incapacitation, etc., deprive (or threaten to deprive) people of their most cherished life goals, including their very survival (Figure 3-8). This is not to say that the reactions to these situations will be all the same, but rather that severe threat and frustration are made more likely in all the victims of such extreme situations. As we move away from the massive and complex physical and social disasters to the milder situations of stress,

FIGURE 3-8 The noose is tightened around the neck of a captured Viet Cong soldier to induce him to talk. (United Press International Photo.)

The degree of harm signified by any life event depends on the needs and motives of the person. If the anticipated outcome appears irrelevant to the person's goals (that is, has no power to frustrate their achievement) or if it seems to facilitate achievement of the goals, threat will not occur. Furthermore, the stronger the motive that is endangered, the greater will be the threat.

Some relevant research observations on this principle have been made by Mahl (1949), who was studying the psychological and physiological bases of ulcer formation. Mahl assumed that a critical factor in the production of ulcers was excessive secretion of hydrochloric acid (HCl) in the stomach under conditions of chronic psychological stress. Selecting eight student volunteers, he taught them to swallow a stomach tube without distress, the end of which could absorb and measure the fluid contents of the stomach. He then made a number of measurements of the quantity of HCl in the stomachs of these students during control days on which there was no special occasion for stress. The same measurements were made in the period just before an important examination that would determine whether or not they would gain admission to medical school. Comparing the HCl levels during the "benign" control periods with those obtained just prior to the exam, he found a substantial increase for the group as a whole because of the examination threat.

Close inspection of the data further revealed, however, that two of the eight students showed a slight decrease in HCl secretion before the exam rather than an increase. This required some explanation. Fortunately, Mahl had interviewed each subject during the stomach-tubing session prior to the examination and had obtained some evidence about the attitudes of the two student subjects that might explain their paradoxical reaction. In both cases, the students seemed not to regard the examination as a threat, although for slightly different reasons. One of them had already been accepted by a medical school of his

far greater individual differences will be found in the resulting degree of threat or frustration. Variations in the personalities of the individuals affected begin to play a much greater role. Thus, motivational variables, as well as differences in belief systems and coping abilities, will be more important in determining threat appraisal when the stressful conditions are mild than when they are severe.

A number of personality traits are probably important influences on threat appraisal. Two will be considered here, namely, the pattern of motivation of the individual and general beliefs about the environment and one's capacity to control it.

choice on the basis of an outstanding academic record. From his point of view, the examination in no way endangered his status. The other student appeared content to obtain "the gentleman's grade" of C and had little motivation for advanced study anyway. With only weak motives to achieve academically, the pre-med examination did not pose any great degree of threat. In this latter case, especially, *lack of motivation* to do well seems to account for the *absence of threat* in a situation that threatened others.

One might say, then, that people will react with stress in like fashion and degree to a given situation only when they share certain needs and motives that are threatened. To the degree that motives vary among different individuals, what is threatening to them will also vary. Even universal psychological stressors, such as the threat of dying, produce individual differences in reaction that seem to be linked to varying personal goals. Feifel (1959) has given a somewhat poetic expression to this theme of individual differences. He writes (pp. 126–127):

The research . . . reinforces the thinking that death can mean different things to different people. Death is a multifaceted symbol, the specific import of which depends on the nature and fortunes of the individual's development and his cultural context. To many, death represents the teacher of transcendental truth incomprehensible during life. For others, death is a friend who brings an end to pain through peaceful sleep. . . . Then there are those who see it as the great destroyer who is to be fought to the bitter end. . . . Death may be seen as a means of vengeance to force others to give more affection to us than they are otherwise willing to give us in life; escape from an unbearable situation through a new life without any of the difficulties of our present life; a final narcissistic perception granting lasting and unchallenged importance to the individual; a means of punishment and atonement—a grati-

fication of masochistic tendencies in the idea of perpetual self-punishment, etc. One leitmotiv that is continually coming to the fore in work in this area is that the crisis is often not the fact of oncoming death, per se, of man's insurmountable finiteness, but rather the *waste of limited years, the unassayed tasks, the locked opportunities, the talents withering in disuse, the avoidable evils which have* done. . . . [Italics added.]

Motivational factors that account for the individual differences in reaction to death are suggested by Feifel in the italicized clauses at the end of the quotation. More explicitly even than Feifel, and based directly on empirical study, Diggory and Rothman (1961) have attempted to answer the question of what it is about death that is feared by different individuals (p. 205). They prepared a list of "consequences of one's own death" and gave a group of research subjects the task of indicating which of these consequences were most distasteful to them. The consequences in the list were: (1) "I could no longer have any experiences," (2) "I am uncertain as to what might happen to me if there is a life after death," (3) "I am afraid of what might happen to my body after death," (4) "I could no longer care for my dependents," (5) "My death would cause grief to my relatives and friends," (6) "All my plans and projects would come to an end," and (7) "The process of dying might be painful."

It was found that the social backgrounds of the subjects and the goals stimulated by this background were important determinants of what it was about death that was feared. Their findings and conclusions, which they summarize as follows (p. 209), back up the comment of Feifel:

Our hypothesis, that a person fears death because it eliminates his opportunity to pursue goals important to his self-esteem, is supported by the following: Fear that one can no longer care for dependents varies systematically with roles defined by marital status, sex, and age; the purpose of items of having experiences and completing one's own projects are consistently near the high end of the scale, except for people who may be assumed to believe that death is not the end of experience.

In short, death is feared in different degrees and for different reasons depending on the *motivational pattern* of the individual. Its psychological effects on people can only be fully understood by considering the impact of death on their most important personal goals or commitments.

Some relevant clinical observations have also been made by Hamburg, Hamburg, and deGoza (1953), whose observations about severely burned patients have been previously cited. What is threatening about the injury depends, according to these researchers, on the individual's pattern of motivation. They state (p. 19):

> Our observations suggest that the severe injury may present serious problems to a patient over and above the question of functional recovery or partial disfigurement, for the patient with such an injury may readily interpret it as threatening those functions which are most important to him, and this involves many more spheres in his life than simply his bodily integrity. It appears that, as a critical estimate, the intensity of threat is directly proportional to the need which the patient has for the function that he feels is jeopardized. Or, put another way, *the more important the function is to him psychologically, the more readily it is threatened by his injury,* even though the injury may appear to another person to have only a small connection with that function. [Italics added.]

In the studies thus far cited, one is dealing with variations in motive patterns stemming from different life experiences within the same culture. These variations arise presumably from different familial values and child-rearing practices. Cultural anthropologists have also studied such vari-

ations as a prime subject of interest and have observed that different culturally based motives make some situations threatening and others benign. For example, Benedict (1946) has suggested that the Japanese have an unusually intense desire for approval and acceptance and a great sensitivity to criticism. She writes (pp. 287–288):

> One striking continuity connects the earlier and later periods of the child's life: the great importance of being accepted by his fellows. This, and not an absolute standard of virtue, is what is inculcated in him. In early childhood his mother took him into her bed when he was old enough to ask, he counted the candies he and his brother and sister were given as a sign of how he ranked in his mother's affection, he was quick to notice when he was passed over and he asked even his older sister, "Do you love me *best*?" In the later period he is asked to forgo more and more personal satisfactions, but the promised reward is that he will be approved and accepted by "the world." The punishment is that "the world" will laugh at him. This is, of course, a sanction invoked in child training in most cultures, but is exceptionally heavy in Japan.

It has also been suggested (Caudill and Doi, 1963; Doi, 1963) that dependence on the approval and support of others is a favorably accepted attitude among the Japanese. Unlike the American, whose self-esteem is at least outwardly tied to individuality, the Japanese are not threatened by manifesting the wish to lean on others. Such a motive is compatible with the cultural values they have learned from childhood, and it is accepted as a legitimate aspect of themselves which is not embarrassing. To the extent that these analyses of the differences between the Japanese and American character are sound, concern with approval and support of others should be highly threatening for the average American, but not at all for the

Japanese. Motivational differences arising from cultural patterns should affect what is threatening and produce variations from culture to culture.

Our *beliefs* about ourselves and the world are also a personality factor affecting the appraisal of threat. In a personality scale which he created to measure a trait called "dogmatism," Rokeach (1960) has, for example, included a number of questions that point to the conception of oneself as alone, isolated, and helpless in the face of an environment which is hostile and dangerous. Some examples of such items from the dogmatism scale are: "Man on his own is a helpless and miserable creature"; "Fundamentally, the world we live in is a pretty lonesome place"; "Most people just don't give a 'damn' for others"; and "I am afraid of people who want to find out what I am really like for fear they will be disappointed in me." Answers of "yes" to these and other items probably reveal a belief system disposing the individual to see threat in many social contexts. With such a system of beliefs, a person might be expected to view many physical and social situations as threatening that others would not regard as such because of a habitual sense of helplessness to cope with a hostile world. Such individuals have a greater tendency to feel vulnerable than those with a more positive and secure outlook.

Davids (1955) has developed a similar questionnaire, with items roughly parallel in content to those found in Rokeach's scale of dogmatism in that they convey a sense of helplessness in the face of a hostile environment. Davids called the trait in which he was interested "alienation." He defined it as the disposition to egocentricity, distrust, pessimism, anxiety, and resentment. The attitudes or beliefs represented by this trait are illustrated in some of the items on his scale. The person taking this questionnaire must indicate his extent of agreement or disagreement with each item on a 6-point scale from strong agreement to strong disagreement. Some examples of items from this scale are (p. 22):

No longer can a young man build his character and his hopes on solid grounds; civilization is crumbling, the future is dreadfully uncertain, and his life hangs by a thread.

There are days when one wakes from sleep without a care in the world, full of zest and eagerness for whatever lies ahead of him.

Beneath the polite and smiling surface of man's nature is a bottomless pit of evil.

The real substance of life consists of a procession of disillusionments, with but few goals that are worth the effort spent in reaching them.

Davids describes the people with high alienation scores (1955, p. 27) as "lone wolves with grievances, distrustful of their fellow man, apprehensive and gloomy in their anticipations of the future." These are people, for example, who tend to answer the first item above as "strongly agree," the second item as "strongly disagree," the third and fourth items as "strongly agree," as well as many more in the same gloomy direction. They differ from individuals low in alienation in that they are characterized by an apprehensive outlook much of the time. Davids found that the trait of alienation was a consistent quality of many individuals he tested and that their perception of the situation in a great many settings was consistent with the interpretation of the environment as hostile and dangerous and of themselves as helpless to significantly alter their fate.

An interesting experiment illustrating the tendency of some people to be made anxious by situations that do not ordinarily threaten others has also been reported by Glickstein and his colleagues (1957). They tested a number of hospital patients during a series of days before and after a stress interview and during a stressful situation in which blood was drawn for diagnostic purposes.

Heart rate was measured as an index of degree of stress reaction. By plotting the heart rate during the prestress, stress, and poststress periods, they observed two kinds of heart-rate patterns. In the "A" pattern, a high level of heart rate was found most of the time, even during presumably benign periods when no specific stress condition was introduced. Such patients did not seem to display any marked rise in heart rate during the stressful interview or the drawing of blood. In the "B" pattern, the level of heart rate during benign periods was generally lower, with distinct rises in response to the stressful interview and to the drawing of blood. Both patterns of heart rate are illustrated in Figure 3-9.

Examination of the figure shows the comparatively low heart rate for the group displaying the B pattern. One can see the marked elevation during the two stress periods. These variations are more modest in the group showing the A pattern. The latter subjects also exhibit a generally higher level throughout. Judges independently rated each patient in regard to the level of anxiety they usually displayed. It was found that patients characterized as being highly "anxiety prone" displayed mainly the A-type pattern, and patients

rated as low in anxiety proneness showed predominantly the B pattern. These heart-rate–stress response patterns suggested that *anxiety-prone individuals* reacted as though the entire strange situation in which they were placed was threatening, even the procedures that, in themselves, were not designed to produce stress, as in the preexperimental sessions. The patients not prone to be readily threatened and low in the trait of anxiety responded comfortably and securely during the specifically nonstressful periods but reacted sharply to the situations designed to be threatening. Glickstein and his colleagues state their interpretation in the following way (1957, p. 106):

The more disturbed subject, we might suppose, starts each experimental day with a distinctly greater amount of anticipatory anxiety. Taken from familiar surroundings and people with whom he has worked out some mode of adjustment, he is acutely aware of the potential threats in a strange laboratory, with its imposing wires and machinery and the business-like,

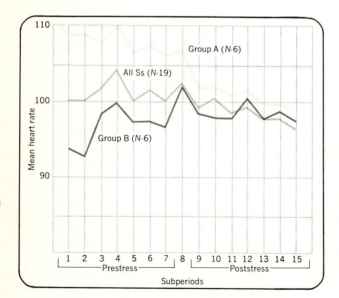

FIGURE 3-9 Heart rates before and after situational stress among anxiety-prone (Group A) and nonprone (Group B) patients. (From Glickstein, Chevalier, Korchin, Basowitz, Sabshin, Hamburg, and Grinker, 1957.)

somewhat cold, experimenters. . . . To be in an experiment in the first place is a stress. . . . With somewhat less anxiety a patient becomes somewhat less sensitive to the more implicit threats of a situation in general and, simultaneously, is more capable of distinguishing and reacting to the more explicitly disturbing events.

The findings of Glickstein et al. and similar research by others support the interpretation of anxiety as a disposition to react with threat appraisal to situations not explicitly threatening. Such individuals make the general assumption (or have the belief) that the *environment is hostile and dangerous*, that they will be victimized by it and unable to cope successfully. Those without much chronic anxiety tend to assume a benign environment or their positive ability to master it, at least until some situation arises which is explicitly harmful. At such times, they also experience anxiety. One of the important open questions is how these different *belief systems* originate and what the life experiences are on which they are based.

ANXIETY AS A STRESS EMOTION

Common sense tells us that there are many different emotions. Psychologists tend to distinguish between two main kinds—(1) positively toned emotions such as love, joy, and exhilaration and (2) the stress emotions such as anger, jealousy, fear, anxiety, guilt, depression, grief, and shame. These latter emotions are products of disturbed or stressful relationships with the environment and are, therefore, particularly important in maladjustment and illness.

Each specific emotion probably reflects a different kind of adjustive commerce the person is having with his or her environment and the way this commerce is evaluated or appraised by the person. Thus, if the commerce is judged to be conducive to well-being, the person will experience a positive emotional state, while if it is seen as harmful or threatening, a stress emotion will be generated.

The stress emotions are complex disturbances that include three main components: (1) a subjective affect (such as feeling angry or afraid); (2) action, or impulses to act in particular ways to resolve the difficulty—for example, to attack the agent of harm, to flee or avoid it, to restore the lost person, as in grief; and (3) physiological changes produced as part of the body's mobilization for the action. In any emotional state, the impulse to act may be inhibited, as in the case noted earlier of aggression that may be held back or expressed depending on what seems safe or socially accepted. In such a situation of inhibition, the person is stirred up but there is no simple way to dissipate the disturbance rapidly; the bodily disturbance is left to dissipate slowly, the person remaining upset for a while, perhaps trying to find some way to "cool off."

Some of the above ideas can be illustrated by a brief discussion of one of the most important stress emotions, *anxiety*. The concept of anxiety has long played a key role in theories of adjustment and maladjustment. No state of mind has been more widely held to be at the root of human misery and adjustive failure than anxiety. The present era has often been called the "age of anxiety."

Psychologists and philosophers have tried to distinguish between anxiety and fear. The latter appears to be a relatively concrete and stimulus-bound state in which a concrete and immediate danger is present. This might better be referred to as fright. Rats show signs of fright when placed in a strange open space; young turkeys are frightened by the silhouette of a hawk; monkeys and human infants appear to show fright at a particular age if confronted with a stranger. The stimuli in these examples portend immediate danger, and the animal seems to react as if it is the stimulus itself (the hawk silhouette or the stranger) that is frightening. As we go up the phylogenetic scale from lower animals to human beings, we see that the situations resulting in fright become more diversified and less immediate, ultimately reaching the point in humans where "fears" become highly symbolic and future-oriented rather than immediate. As this shift occurs, some psychologists tend more and more to speak of anxiety rather than fear.

The key features of anxiety seem to be: (1) It is anticipatory, that is, it refers to something harmful in the future, not necessarily physical harm but psychological harm, as in threat to one's key identity or being; this is in contrast to fright, which is immediate and concrete. (2) It concerns highly symbolic dangers; thus, the existential psychologists speak of existential anxiety, which is the dread of nonbeing, or loss of self. (3) It concerns dangers and potential adjustments the nature of which is highly ambiguous; the person does not seem to know clearly what the danger is, what will happen, when it will happen, or how it might be dealt with. Thus, the experience of anxiety is reported to be a vague feeling of apprehension or unease which can even become quite severe, or of foreboding, whereas fright is quite specific and always has a clear external reference to which the person can point. We might say that anxiety is a predominantly human emotion, since the lack of symbolic capacity in lower animals, their relative inability to anticipate the future, and their lack of self-consciousness make them respond more to the concrete here and now rather than to the vague and symbolic future.

Freud viewed fear (or fright) as a normal emotional reaction to external dangers. He saw anxiety, on the other hand, as a neurotic reaction having its origins in dangers arising from within; that is, it was the result of a forbidden impulse that, if expressed, would either be at odds with one's conscience or would bring down on one's head the danger of retaliation from the environment. This is consistent with the vague uneasiness characteristic of anxiety; the person does

not know what is causing the trouble, since the impulse is repressed and unconscious. In any case, the neurotic version is probably a special sort of anxiety reaction since its origins in part lie within the person as forbidden impulses rather than in the environment. Nevertheless, as is always the case with anxiety, it reflects the sensing of danger, and it probably also involves the action impulse to escape or avoid the danger. Yet to the extent that its origins are unclear (ambiguous) to the person, there is nothing concrete for him or her to escape or avoid, hence anxiety is experienced as both vague and accompanied by a sense of helplessness and uncertainty about what to do.

The state of mind called anxiety is different from that in the other stress emotions such as anger or depression, although several such emotions can occur in combination. Though all three emotions have in common a troubled psychological commerce with the environment and the appraisal of harm or potential harm, the factors contributing to anger or depression are also different from those involved in anxiety. For different stress emotions to be experienced, the person must be interpreting that harm, its implications, and possible adjustive solutions somewhat differently in each case.

Thus, in *anger* there is a clearly definable external source of the harm (for example, an enemy to attack), and the person feels perhaps unjustifiably injured, attacked, or demeaned; or the anger could reflect the need to justify oneself for doing something shameful that contributed to the injury (as in "righteous anger"). Having identified an external source or provocation, the natural impulse is to demolish it (the enemy) by attack. When attack is inhibited because the person lacks sufficient power to overcome the external provoking agent, or because such aggression violates strong internal standards of feeling and conduct, we speak of "aggression anxiety."

In *depression*, the person appears to feel that

the situation is hopeless and perhaps that he or she is unworthy and even responsible for the trouble. There is a feeling of despair. There seems no way to overcome the trouble, and the person can no longer face life with verve and enthusiasm. When someone reacts to injuries or losses with such despair or hopelessness, he or she is apt also to make little or no effort to cope and to withdraw from all involvements. There is then the danger of suicide, which may come to be regarded by the person as the only remaining solution to a hopeless situation. Usually, such a state of mind, whether in mild or severe form, is transitory, and the feelings of depression pass.

STRESS AND MALADJUSTMENT

At the beginning of this chapter I pointed out that stress has a very special importance in adjustment because it implies a change from simple problem solving to a situation having emotional overtones. Strong emotional situations often result in seemingly irrational rather than effective ways of coping with adaptive problems. Why is it that stress increases the potential for maladjustment in the handling of the problems of living?

Stress does not, of course, always produce maladjusted behavior. Sometimes it mobilizes unusually strong and effective modes of adjustment, motivated by the importance for the person's welfare of what is happening. As we shall see in a later chapter, stress is therefore often a force for growth in an individual who is in trouble but has sufficient resources available to meet the problem. Ordinarily these resources would not be drawn upon, but they are called up under very demanding conditions. However, stress also can be traumatic, that is, destructive of effective adjustment. When a person is overwhelmed by demands because he or she cannot find suitable means to cope with the problem, impairment in the person's adjustive functioning rather than growth is apt to take place. One of the most

challenging questions for those seeking knowledge of adjustment concerns predicting the conditions of life under which stress will enhance or impair the person's handling of life tasks.

Aside from producing bodily disease, which is one of the costs of stress (dealt with later in a separate chapter), stress can damage adjustive effectiveness for two main reasons. First, stress emotions are very demanding of the person's attention; as such they serve as distractions that interfere with productive thinking and skilled behavior. Consider the experience of a student who is extremely anxious about an important examination. As he picks up the test to read it, he is tremulous and feels jittery. He starts to read the questions, and after a quick glance his distress grows because he doesn't understand them or because the questions seem to tap knowledge areas in which he feels inadequate. Worse still, he is reading the sentences, but their meaning eludes him. His attention is centered on his troubles, say, the prospects of failure or traumatic experiences with evaluations in the past, and he is convinced he never should have tried to compete academically. Thoughts do not come; facts seem to have been forgotten. Perhaps prior to the exam he has had sleepless nights and a disturbed gut. Again and again he tries to settle down, and much effort must be mobilized to shut out the irrelevant and debilitating thoughts and emotions about what might happen. The thinking process, normally directed at comprehending the questions and digging up the necessary facts and issues, has been interfered with by the stress emotion generated by the threat of being evaluated and of being inadequate. The problem is so extensive in the school setting that several major research programs have been organized to study ways of attacking it (Sarason, 1972; Phillips et al., 1972).

Second, the stress emotions, or rather the conditions that bring them about, mobilize desperate and often unrealistic efforts to get the individual out of jeopardy. These efforts can create further troubles for the person over and above the problems that caused them. A good example is provided by someone who, when threatened, avoids thinking about what is happening and therefore fails to do anything constructive about the threats. If we can convince ourselves prior to an exam that there is nothing to worry about, or turn our thoughts away from preparation for the examination because such preparation focuses attention on the source of anxiety, we may feel temporarily more at ease. Like the parents of a child dying of leukemia, denial and avoidance of the problem can serve for a time to limit the distressing emotion, but ultimately the threat must be faced if the person is going to master the situation. By not thinking about the exam, or by fooling himself about its significance, the anxious student may also fail to take the adjustive steps of preparing, steps that might be necessary for him to be successful.

Maladjusted behavior in the face of life stresses, then, is often the result of attempts to regulate distressing emotions by means of avoidance or defense mechanisms such as denial; these mechanisms are motivated in part by the wish to prevent confrontation with a harmful or threatening event and to regulate the distress produced by thinking about it. The behavior is maladjusted because it prevents the individual from taking effective steps to master the problem. The more stressful an event is, the more likely that the person will resort to solutions that are at best temporary palliatives, rather than taking rational and effective steps to cope. Desperate situations seduce the person into desperate actions that fail to help resolve the situation. Thus, stress is an important factor in maladjustment, though not the only one.

When all is said and done, the adequacy of the efforts to master stressful commerce with the environment bears the chief responsibility for the adequacy of adjustment. This takes us directly to the problem of coping with stress in Chapter 4.

SUMMING UP

Adjustive effort is required because of the constant presence of multiple internal and environmental demands, some arising from the physical environment and others from social living. (The environment serves as a resource for the person, too.) The psychological impact of external demands depends on the biological and psychological properties of the person and the nature of the *adjustive commerce* that the person is having with the environment.

Stress arises when demands tax or exceed the resources of the person; there are marked variations in what is stressful and in how the person or a social group responds to stress. In some life stresses, the person is already harmed, in which instance we tend to speak of *frustration*— a need has been thwarted, or progress toward some goal has been delayed. In other life stresses, the harm has not yet occurred but is anticipated, in which case we speak of *threat*. Most stressful life events include both harm or frustration and threat. Although, on the average, stress is aroused when there are objective dangers or harms, it is how the person evaluates or appraises the significance of the event for his or her well-being that determines whether he or she will experience stress and in what degree. *Conflict*, in which two action tendencies or goals are incompatible, is important because it makes stress more or less inevitable—gratifying one goal means the thwarting of the other.

Some of the conditions leading to threat appraisal can be found in the external environment while others arise from the personality of the individual. Examples of the former include circumstances that the person is *helpless* to master, and the *imminence* of an anticipated harm. Generally, the more helpless the person is and the more imminent the harm, the greater the threat. Personality factors contributing to threat appraisal include strong *motivation* or commitment to some goal or outcome and the general *belief* that one is inadequate to master an environment characterized as dangerous or hostile. Persons with such an outlook or belief are likely to feel threatened and anxious by merely being in a new or unfamiliar situation. *Anxiety* is a particularly important stress emotion arising when harm is anticipated, when the harm (or the coping required by it) is ambiguous, and when that harm tends to be symbolic rather than concrete (as in fright) and concerns a central feature of the person's identity or self.

Life stress can result in maladjusted behavior, but it sometimes also mobilizes highly effective forms of adjustment. One of the basic, as yet unresolved questions of psychology concerns the conditions under which these divergent outcomes will occur.

CHAPTER 4 HOW WE COPE WITH STRESS

If we think back to the definition of a stressor as a demand that taxes or overpowers the person's resources, we can see that persons facing such a demand will remain in trouble unless and until they do something to neutralize it. Whether the problem is appraised as a challenge, an injury or loss, or a threat, they must deal with it in some way, and what an individual does to master the situation is most commonly called *coping*.

Coping is best considered as a form of problem solving in which the stakes are the person's well-being and the person is not entirely clear about what to do. In a sense, coping is a synonym for adjustment, except that adjustment is an even broader concept referring to all reactions to environmental and internal demands; "coping" specifically refers to what the person does to handle stressful or emotionally charged demands. When we meet a person on a narrow street, we move sideways automatically to avoid bumping into him or her. Normally, this is a simple and automatic adjustment, and we would not use the term coping to refer to it. If, on the other hand, we were threatened by the prospect of bumping into the person (perhaps he or she is suffering from a communicable disease), or we had some uncertainty about whether we could succeed in doing so, or no ready response was available to do so, we might speak of coping with the threat.

In their studies of the ways young children manage new and demanding experiences, Lois Murphy and her colleagues (1962, pp. 1–2) have written about coping as follows:

It is possible that by watching them [children], we may learn something about how all of us deal with new demands and stressful experiences, newness which cannot be met by well-established habits or ready-made answers. When responses are not automatic, when we do not know just what to do, we have to cope with the situation as best we can, trying to arrive at a solution that will enable us to get along. Much of what we call "getting experience" consists of just this, and out of these efforts to cope with new situations eventually develops a certain know-how, patterned ways of dealing with newness itself.

The new situations Murphy refers to are rather ordinary experiences such as going to nursery school for the first time, moving to a new home, or having to deal with the demands of strange laboratory tests. They also include more severe stressors, for example, an episode in which one of the three-year-old children nearly lost the tip of his finger because a door was closed on it and it had to be sewed on, or another in which a child contracted polio and experienced a lengthy period of learning to deal with his resulting physical limitations. Many of the children's experiences contained elements of gratification, challenge, frustration, and threat, and often several of these occurred simultaneously, as in a psychiatric examination that was sometimes threatening and sometimes challenging to the child.

"Coping" too is a very general word, and we must narrow down its meaning somewhat and consider several kinds. All coping can be divided into two main categories, direct actions and palliative forms. *Direct actions* refer to any behavioral effort by the person to deal with harm, threat, or challenge by altering his or her troubled relationship with the environment. *Palliation* is directed at reducing, eliminating, or tolerating the distressing bodily, motor, or affective (subjective distress) features of a stress emotion once it has been aroused by troubled commerce with the environment. Taking palliative action means to soften or moderate distress, in short, to seek comfort.

DIRECT ACTION

We shall focus on four varieties of direct action, all aimed at modifying the person's troubled relationship with the environment, namely, preparing against harm, aggression or attack, avoidance, and inaction or apathy. These illustrate some of the main things people do when threatened, harmed, or challenged.

PREPARING AGAINST HARM

If the danger is external, persons can often take active steps to eliminate or reduce it by addressing themselves directly to the threatening circumstances and taking an action that is suitable to meet the danger. If the action succeeds, the signs of danger may recede, so that threat is eliminated or reduced. Positive emotional reactions such as joy or relief may be experienced in its stead. However, if it becomes clear that these attempts have failed or produce additional threats, stress emotions (depression, shame, guilt, anger, anxiety, or fear) are likely to result.

Coping action tendencies are as varied as the nature of the danger itself. Against the danger of tornado, storm shelters or escape from the area are alternatives. Against the possibility of flood, dams offer protection. Against the possibility of failing an examination, programs of study are appropriate. Against harm from social criticism or rejection, conforming to social norms and expectations offers a solution. Against the possibility of appearing foolish or inadequate in giving a report in class, careful preparation will be valuable. Against the danger of epidemic disease, immunization is possible. For every threat situation, different specific forms of action present themselves, some realistic, others inappropriate, some tried and true, others experimental; some safe, others dangerous because they violate social or internal standards; some simple and capable of instantaneous activation, others requiring extensive knowledge, or a sequence of planned steps.

The following newspaper story illustrates a woman's desperate efforts to cope with a situation that was acutely stressful:

On July 17, 1974, Mrs. Ortiz' 3-year-old son Rolando, became seriously ill. Over a three hour period, the mother kept calling the doctor assigned to her. . . . She got no answer. She called the . . . emergency number and was told to continue phoning her doctor. Her son's "fever was about 105 degrees. [He] went into convulsions.

Mrs. Ortiz then called San Francisco General Hospital. She was told it did not accept [her health plan] and that she should call St. Luke's Hospital, which accepted plan members.

[According to Mrs. Ortiz] St. Luke's informed her they could not treat Rolando without her doctor's authorization. Mrs. Ortiz then took her son to Harbor Emergency Hospital. There the doctors said she should get treatment for the child at San Francisco General. They gave her a referral slip.

That evening, Mrs. Ortiz went to S.F. General where a nurse administered medication to Rolando and tried to reach the Ortiz doctor and the emergency number. . . . She got no answer. The hospital then called St. Luke's and asked if they would admit the child who still had a temperature of 104. When Mrs. Ortiz reached St. Luke's with the help of people waiting outside the hospital, she was told they still could not care for her son without authorization from the assigned doctor. Mrs. Ortiz broke down and . . . "began weeping and begging the hospital personnel to treat her son."

St. Luke's also tried without success to contact the assigned doctor. Mrs. Ortiz was then told she could get medical help if she went to Golden Gate Hospital. She had no money to get there. Her son went into convulsions in the waiting room.

After several phone calls, San Francisco police agreed to transport Mrs. Ortiz and her son to Golden Gate Hospital. There, the police persuaded the doctors to help. Finally between 11 p.m. and midnight, Rolando got medical attention.

Preceding the decision to act, a *search* may be instituted by the person to learn what he must face and to select the most adequate alternative, especially if the danger is preceded by sufficient warning. Such a search in itself constitutes a form of direct action. The cues about what to do may be ambiguous or crystal clear. The person may or may not possess the resources necessary for coping adequately with the threat or for comprehending the nature of the danger. In the absence of sufficient information, the person may remain vigilant so as to anticipate the arrival of the danger and to be alert for new information about it or about what might be done; or he or she may turn away from inputs about it to prevent the distress that it brings.

In many instances of threat, some specific kind of preparatory action designed to strengthen the person's resources against the harm is possible. An illustration of such preparatory coping behavior comes from a previously cited field study by Mechanic (1962) of the reactions of graduate students to a crucial examination. The stakes connected with passing or failing were generally very high. Many of the students had the responsibility of marriage and family. For many, failure meant elimination from the educational program and the end of a long commitment toward obtaining the Ph.D. Passing the examination virtually assured the student of completing the requirements for the doctorate. Thus, the threat imposed by failure was very great, and the potential gratification connected with passing correspondingly high.

Since the examination date could be anticipated many months in advance, there was a long warning period, and coping activities could begin far ahead of the exam. Mechanic made numerous observations of how the students prepared themselves and reacted to the continuing threat. As was noted earlier, when they have the opportunity people usually *search* for evidence about how to cope with danger in order to base their reactions on realistic grounds. The students in Mechanic's study were extremely sensitive to any cue that might help them decide how to prepare. This sensitivity is illustrated in the following episode described by the author in which a rumor about a useful textbook spread among students (p. 37):

> A number of months previous to the examination, one of the students ordered a newly published statistics text. . . . Students are very sensitive to the reading of other students. The book was described as clear and lucid, and was aimed at the non-mathematically sophisticated reader. Some of these students noticed this text on the desk of an individual who had purchased it. And, as the student who had bought the book spoke of it enthusiastically, information about it soon began to diffuse throughout the student communication structure. It was reported that this evaluation had been legitimatized by a remark made by an important member of the department to the effect that this was an excellent statistics text. One student described why he decided to read this text: "A couple of people started talking about it and I looked at it. [An influential faculty member] mentioned one day that it was a great book. And it's just a book that's easy to read and yet it seems fairly complete."
>
> Approximately three weeks prior to examinations, students were asked to indicate the three books or articles that they thought most important in each of their areas. In the central building where there was a large chain of communicators, including 11 persons, all 11 indicated the statistics text as one of the three listings in the statistics area. . . .

We need not concern ourselves about whether the statistics text chosen by the students was a good one. The question of the adequacy of this choice is a complex and difficult one, and, while relevant, it is not of primary importance here. The important point is that the choice of book stemmed from a chance comment supported by rather limited evidence. In the absence of clear evidence, as in the present illustration, the coping action had to be based on extremely tenuous grounds. It resulted from a highly motivated search for information that might help to strengthen the students' resources against the threat of failure. And in spite of the inadequacy of the evidence, doing *something* was better than nothing.

A careful study has also been made (Moore, 1958) of the reactions of people to the experience of a tornado. In 1951 the people of Waco and San Angelo, Texas, had seen their communities severely ravaged by a tornado that struck unexpectedly. During the year following the tornado, one-third of the families of the Lakeview section of San Angelo constructed storm cellars. Although storm cellars are common in this area, prior to the tornado less than 10 percent of the homes in Lakeview had them. Thus, the awakened sense of danger resulting from the previous experience led to a widespread effort to cope with the prospect of yet another storm. Interviews with the people who had built storm cellars revealed that, during subsequent storms, fear was much reduced when the families went into the shelter. Friends and neighbors would gather together in the cellar, and these occasions were reported as pleasant rather than terrifying. As in the case of Mechanic's study, one sees specific actions designed to prepare against harm, actions which reduce both the actual danger and its psychological threat value (Fig. 4-1).

FIGURE 4-1 Two examples of preparing against harm: (Top) for college students, study is future-oriented. Study involves preparing positively for citizenship, richer intellectual lives, and future careers, as well as preparing negatively against the threat of failure imposed by examinations or the threat of ineptitude in facing the tasks of later life. (Bill Anderson, from Monkmeyer.) (Bottom) training in preparation against the threat of gas warfare in Bombay, India. (Wide World Photos.)

In still another example, a mine disaster provided an excellent opportunity to study coping behavior in a situation where what seemed to be the best coping action turned out to be inadequate. (Lucas, 1969). Two groups of men were trapped in an unexpected "bump," a sudden underground bursting of the coal or of the strata in contact with it. A number of men were killed, and one who later died had been severely injured

and partially buried in the disaster. The six survivors of one group first reacted by fanning out and searching painstakingly for a way out, which, on the basis of stories of previous such disasters, they assumed would be found. In the heat, dust, and exertion of the vain search for an exit, most of the available water was rapidly used up, so that when it became evident that they were truly trapped, a new danger emerged, namely, that the water supply would not last long enough for the rescue parties to reach them in time. Rationing was finally instituted. Ultimately they had to resort to drinking urine to stay alive, an act that was for most of the men very distressing and difficult. To do so required considerable self-control over the initial distress and tendency to gag.

After eight-and-a-half days in the mine, the six were rescued and interviewed in considerable depth concerning their efforts to survive, the ways in which as a group they coped with fear and hopelessness, how they handled outbursts of emotion, how they managed to accept the drinking of urine, and other related forms of coping. The factors in their community history which led them to handle the situation as they did were also explored. One interesting, perplexing, and unresolved question concerns their failure to conserve water until it was nearly all used up. Rationing was introduced only when it finally became evident to the group that they might remain trapped for a long period and might succumb to thirst, coal gas, or another explosion.

AGGRESSION

Attack on the agent that is judged to be harmful is another common method of self-protection. To destroy, injure, remove, or restrict the person, animal, or object considered responsible for a threat might take the endangered person out of jeopardy. Because of its significance in human welfare, *aggression* is a topic of much concern among psychologists. Probably no other subject in personality and social psychology has produced more empirical research aimed at discovering the rules under which it occurs.

The sources and functions of aggression in man and animals are very complex. There are good grounds for viewing aggression as the result of our biological makeup as well as a reaction to frustrations or social assaults on our identity (Fig. 4-2). However, it is not relevant here to discuss how biological and social scientists have approached this. What is relevant is that aggression is often a useful way of handling danger when such danger is the result of an external enemy of some kind, such as a predator or someone who wishes us harm. In this sense, aggression or attack on whomever wrongs or endangers us can be a way of *coping* with threat or frustration as well as an emotional state.

This side of aggression is reflected in analysis (Smelser, 1963) of the factors involved in riot. A hostile outbreak (such as a riot) can be seen functionally as a collective effort to overcome the harm or threat by means of hostile action. Smelser states (p. 101): "The modification is to be effected by destroying, injuring, removing, or restricting a person or class of persons considered responsible for the evils at hand."

Attack may be overtly expressed and accompanied by evidence of anger—that is, *aggression with anger.* Sometimes there are only indirect signs of anger; the impulse to attack is present, but because direct attack, either verbal or physical, does not occur, one infers that the behavioral expression of attack has been inhibited—and that is *anger without aggression.* Finally, *attack* can occur *without anger.*

In each of these three forms of attack, the precise pattern of the observed reaction differs in important respects, and these differences provide the bases of inferences about the actual internal psychological state of the person. The individual may report that he or she is not angry in order to appear to the observer in a particular light. Nevertheless, redness of the face and unwitting gestures such as a clenched fist lead the observer to sense anger in spite of what was said. Or the individual may claim not to be angry even though he or she attacks someone, and the observer may be inclined to accept this statement because the context calls for the attack as part of the "rules of the game." The presence of the emotion *anger* suggests that the person is threatened or frustrated in some way and has the impulse to injure the agency held responsible. The more threatened or frustrated the person is, the more intense is the anger.

Notice that for anger and attack to occur together, some *agent of harm* must be identified by the individual. If the individual cannot identify such an agent, then there is no person or object to be attacked. The agent blamed may, of course, not represent the objective or actual source of harm, which may be unknown or ambiguous. The harmful agent may be manufactured, so to speak,

FIGURE 4-2 An up-to-date version of human savagery in Vietnam—the actual aftermath of a Viet Cong attack. The particular source of the attack is irrelevant to the point, since savagery is obviously not an exclusive possession of any one people. (United States Army Photograph.)

by the person, or the responsibility may be shifted from the real source of harm to another object that is a convenient scapegoat. This process of shifting the blame from the real object of harm to another one is known as *displacement.* Displacement is generally regarded as a type of defense mechanism, generated when the agent of harm is so powerful that retaliation from it is a greater danger than the original threat itself, or when retaliation threatens some deeply ingrained personal value. Such a process will be discussed in greater detail below.

When *attack* is observed in connection *with* the affect of *anger,* general agreement is found among the response indicators from which the internal state is inferred. The verbal, physiological, and motor aspects of the reaction all will be in accord, signifying the presence of the inner pattern of anger or rage expressed directly in attack. If a man is angry, it will be manifested in the physiological changes specifically associated with that emotional state. He also displays the external actions appropriate to this emotion; for example, his words may express destructive connotations, or there may be assaultive actions toward the object of his anger. His gestures and body postures accord with this inner state: his face will express anger, and his bodily stance will be that of attack. When the emotion is especially strong and uninhibited, the observer is unlikely to be misled about it (Fig. 4-3).

FIGURE 4-3 Attack with and without anger: Anger is an evident component of the aggressiveness of a male lion defending his territory but is not displayed by this female lion stalking prey. (Top: Leonard Lee Rue III, from Bruce Coleman, Inc.; bottom: Masud Quraishy, from Bruce Coleman, Inc.)

When an action tendency to attack is aroused, however, the person may also anticipate harmful consequences of this action. The individual who acts aggressively in such a context risks social censure or perhaps explicit punishment. The expression of aggression or the consequences of aggression may also conflict with the other important *internal values*. The expression of aggression itself, therefore, will be threatening. These social constraints and internal values concerning aggression often result in the *inhibition of aggression,* even though the impulse to attack is aroused and the emotion of anger is experienced. Some implicit psychological cost accounting of the relative strengths of the original threat and the new threat imposed by the coping action of attack probably determines whether the aggression will be expressed or inhibited. Individuals vary considerably in the degree of control they are capable of exerting over impulses, and impulsive individuals may fail to inhibit the impulse to attack even though it may be dangerous or socially taboo.

When there has been an impulse to attack and *anger is inhibited,* that is, experienced but not expressed, we have a pattern of coping whose observable reactions differ importantly from instances in which there is an uninhibited expression of anger. In the case of inhibited anger and attack, the person may report that he or she is not angry, or even feels positively toward the threatening or frustrating agent. In effect, there will be disagreement among the various behaviors signifying the internal state; in the above instance, the individual's reported feelings, the motor-behavioral evidence, and the physiological reaction pattern are at odds. Nevertheless, there can be unintended expressive activity suggesting the anger, as in slips of the tongue or subtle gestures.

In short, the observed *pattern* of reaction reveals the internal state, and when the emotional state is inhibited from expression, there are apt to be seeming contradictions between the various response indicators. The verbal report will sug-

FIGURE 4-4 Society sanctions and applauds the aggressiveness of the football lineman. (Studio 41.)

gest one psychological process, while the gestural or physiological reaction suggests another.

Attack behavior can also occur *without anger.* Examples of this include the aggressive behavior found in competitive sports, such as boxing and wrestling. They also include situations where the goal of the person is to injure or destroy the other only because such destruction is necessary to achieve some other goal, as in business competition or war, where the object of aggression may not even be known personally. It has been pointed out (Sargent, 1948) that attack may be the socially sanctioned way of acting in some communities or groups—for example, in primitive warlike societies or in a tough slum area where mutual respect is based on attitudes and behavior indicating toughness and disregard of the social rules of the larger society (see also Toch, 1969). The aggressive behavior in these cases need not reflect threat or frustration; rather, the nature of the game requires attack (Figs. 4-3 and 4-4).

An excellent illustration of this is the situation of military combat, especially the impersonal type of battle condition that often exists in modern warfare. The individual soldier fires his weapons without necessarily experiencing hatred toward the enemy, and he may attack without any clear understanding of the reasons for the warfare in the first place. He is there, and he is required to fight, albeit reluctantly. In short, the distinction between anger expressed directly in behavioral attack and attack without anger is exemplified by the soldier who fights because it is his duty, but who later, after the enemy has killed his best buddy, fights with real anger. Commanders regard lack of anger toward the enemy as a handicap to vigorous fighting; that is, anger is presumed to facilitate attack. In order to produce anger, propaganda paints the enemy as menacing, savage, brutal in its treatment of prisoners, reprehensible in all particulars, an evil that must be wiped out. It is also important to convince the soldier that he need not fear the enemy as much as hate him. The reaction that is desired is not flight from battle, but vigorous attack. If the soldier is merely frightened, there is more chance he will flee, conceal himself, and fail to fire his weapons. Effective, disciplined military units have confidence in their ability to fight and in the tools they employ. The reasons for elaborate war propaganda stem partly from the fact that a person *can* fight without anger but will probably fight more vigorously when angry. Anger based on threat presumably helps justify and mobilize the reaction.

AVOIDANCE

Like attack, avoidance and escape as a form of coping with threat are found in all animals, including humans. It is probably a basic form of coping in all sensate beings when they are threatened by an agent that is overwhelmingly powerful and dangerous. The same three basic patterns of reaction can be found in avoidance as were described for attack. Avoidance reactions may be accompanied by the emotional state of *fear;* the fear may occur, but the *avoidance behavior* appropriate to it may be *inhibited;* finally, *avoidance* may occur *without fear.* The reasons for

these various avoidance patterns are parallel with those involved in attack patterns.

For example, a soldier in battle may be frightened and give behavioral expression to this fear by deserting or by running from the battle scene. There is fear along with *avoidance* or escape. On the other hand, the person may be unwilling to admit either to himself or to others that he is frightened; he therefore takes no avoidant action. This is *fear with its behavioral expression inhibited.* The person may fear the potential loss of social or self-esteem for cowardice more than the danger to his life. Thus, his behavior may appear to contradict how he actually feels.

Finally, *avoidance without fear* occurs in special situations which demand avoidance behavior as "part of the game," where there is no actual threat or frustration, or where the person feels in complete command of the danger. A common example is the child's game of hide-and-seek, in which the person who is "it" must locate and confront others who are hiding. The rest of the players have the task of avoiding such a confrontation, and they engage in this avoidant behavior without fear. Only if the immature child takes the game too seriously, that is, if the distinction between the benign game and real threat fails, will real fear occur. Although this sometimes happens, the game will not be played, as a rule, unless the sense of threat is absent or minimal.

The same rules of inference must be utilized with the avoidance patterns as are employed with attack patterns. The total pattern of reaction, including motor behavior, reports of affective state, and physiological changes, provides the clues to differentiate between fear with avoidance, avoidance with its behavioral expression inhibited, and avoidance without fear. In observation of the pattern, recourse to only one source of information, say, what the person says or does, can result in an erroneous inference about the intervening psychological activity. Consistencies and inconsistencies in the observable pattern of responses of the person form the basis of judgments, both lay and professional, about the psychological states of other persons.

INACTION OR APATHY: A PATTERN OF HOPELESSNESS OR DESPAIR

Certain situations of threat offer absolutely no grounds for hope that the harm can be prevented or overcome. In such a situation, regarded as hopeless, there is probably no impulse to attack or avoid the harm. *Inaction* means the complete absence of any impulse to cope with the threat because of the absence of alternatives. *Apathy, depression, and despair* refer to the affect or attitude associated with this inaction in a hopeless situation.

The situations in which a person is totally accepting or resigned to the harm that must be faced are probably comparatively rare, and they are certainly not well understood. They are rare because, in spite of the evidence, people tend to "grasp at straws" or find even small grounds for

FIGURE 4-5 A child usually experiences no strong fear while playing hide-and-seek. (Erika Stone, from Peter Arnold.)

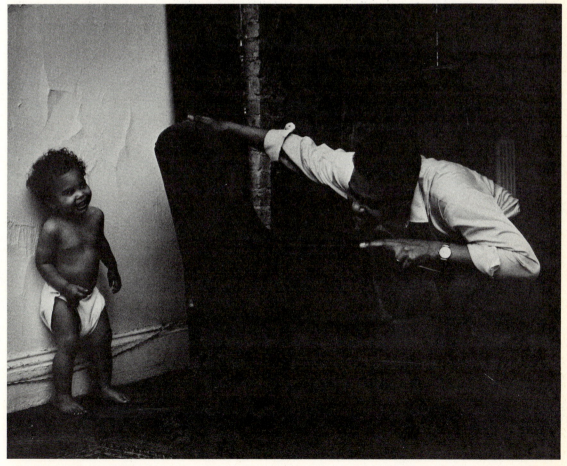

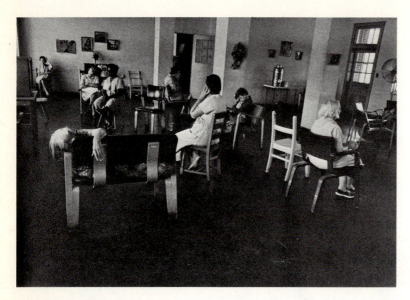

FIGURE 4-6 The apathy, despair, and idleness of patients in a state mental hospital. (Roy Zalesky, from Black Star.)

retaining hope that the worst will not happen. It is also difficult to distinguish between the calm acceptance or resignation of hopelessness and the defensively maintained feeling that there is no real danger in the first place.

The notion that inaction is the coping consequence of hopelessness is consistent with the observations that in a situation of danger where there are no avenues of escape, there appears to be no struggle or panic. According to Mintz (1951, pp. 157-158), "There seems to be no panic when people are trapped so that there can be no struggle for an exit, e.g., at submarine and mine disasters." A similar apathy has been observed among soldiers trapped in Korea after an amphibious landing, facing the sea on the one hand and enemy fire on the other (Marshall, 1947). There was no place to go, and they were described as sitting mute and immobile in the line of fire until captured.

A sense of hopelessness about improving the situation has also been suggested as an explanation of clinical depression. In severe depression, the patient expresses feelings of hopelessness

and often displays what is called "psychomotor retardation," a form of comparative inactivity which is evident in the extremely slow, retarded, apathetic response to any kind of stimulation. When either attack or flight is conceived of as a possible reaction, it arises as an impulse even though it may be inhibited from expression, and the emotional accompaniments are those of anger or fear, respectively. However, when there are no possibilities for such direct action, when the situation appears hopeless, inaction and apathy or depression may be the most likely consequence (Fig. 4-6).

Studies of the hormonal stress reactions of clinically depressed patients have produced some seemingly contradictory findings. Some studies show that depressed patients exhibit heightened physiological (hormonal) evidence of stress, a finding consistent with the idea that the depressed person is, indeed, reacting to a stressful personal loss of some kind. However, other studies show no difference between depressed patients and normals in their physiological stress levels, a finding that seems out of keeping with the stress interpretation of depression. Recent research and analysis of the problem (e.g., Sachar et al., 1968) has suggested, however, that there are different phases to psychological depressions. In one phase, for example, a woman might feel her situation was hopeless, and thus she would make no effort at all to cope with her problem. At other times, however, she might struggle with the loss, attempting to overcome it, to redefine her place in the world and to achieve a new identity. One sees this very clearly in grief reactions in which the person is highly mobilized and even agitated in the early phases but may become depressed and withdrawn later on. Struggle is associated with much physiological stress, in contrast with periods of hopelessness, inaction, or apathy, where there is little physiological evidence of stress. Thus, to speak of psychological depression as a state of hopelessness is only partly correct because such a state is often transitory. The person can sometimes be jolted into actively striving to cope with his or her problem, in which case the dominant pattern is no longer one of hopelessness and inaction or apathy.

PALLIATIVE MODES OF COPING: THE DEFENSE MECHANISM

In contrast with direct actions, palliation, as I noted earlier, is devoted to moderating distress rather than changing the troubled commerce with the environment. There are two main subtypes of palliation, *symptom-directed modes* and *intrapsychic modes.* The former include the use of alcohol to reduce stress and distress, tranquilizers and sedatives, training in muscle relaxation, or any other body-centered ways of reducing the disturbances connected with stress emotions. Drugs must be widely used in our society, judging from the extremely large numbers of medical prescriptions for Valium and Librium, two major tranquilizers, and from the sales of alcohol. Their

aim is to help the person to feel better or to function effectively or relatively comfortably in the face of emotionally disturbing conditions of life and work. Although we are often quite moralistic about the use of such symptom-directed modes of palliation, we know little about how well they work, about the cost to an individual who uses them, and about the conditions under which they are used. Clearly these methods of achieving a degree of comfort are an important part of the coping activity of a very large number of persons, and it is difficult to understand fully the patterns of coping in the population and in given individuals without taking them into account.

Similarly oriented to obtaining relief from the stresses of living are the intrapsychic modes of coping, or, to refer to them in their more traditional terminology, *the defense mechanisms.* These are so important in the management of stress that they have been given great attention in the literature of clinical psychology, personality, and abnormal psychology, and we shall spend considerable time here in examining their forms and functions in the process of adjusting to conditions of stress.

As employed by Freud (1943), the concept of a defense mechanism referred to an *unconscious* psychological maneuver or device by means of which persons deceived themselves about the presence of threatening impulses or external dangers. The person is said to be unaware of the self-deception, or else it doesn't work in lowering stress. Implied in "defense," of course, is that the threat is reduced *only in the mind of the individual* and not in reality. Hence it is intrapsychic, that is, a process taking place only in the person's mind. Each form of defense involves mental acts designed to eliminate threat in specific ways.

Sometimes another connotation is given to the term "defense," namely, as a deliberate, conscious presentation of the self to others in order to create a particular social impression. We say the person is being "defensive." Such a process need not be unconscious but can exist in full awareness and can be communicated if the person is willing. Psychologically oriented writers have long been aware of these latter kinds of social maneuvers, as in the expressions "presentation of the self" (Goffman, 1959) and "the games people play" (Berne, 1964). This, however, is not what Freud meant by defense. This matter of *awareness* is one of the unresolved issues about defense that is extremely difficult to deal with scientifically, because self-awareness is hard to evaluate except by asking the person—who may be unwilling or unable to tell us. Direct questioning often telegraphs the intent of the questioner and may increase the likelihood that he or she will provide misleading answers.

The discussion of defense that follows is predicated on the assumption that the person is deceiving himself or herself and is thus unaware or at best only dimly aware of the process. As used here, then, the term "defense" implies a *self-deception,* although social manipulations (or defensiveness) of which the person is aware remain difficult to distinguish from defenses.

DESCRIPTION OF THE DEFENSES

Theories of defense are in the main loose and descriptive. Certain classes of defensive strategies are described and given names, such as denial, projection, and so on. However, these theories usually do not tell us precisely the conditions under which each defense will occur or when a defense of any kind will occur as opposed to direct actions (such as avoidance or attack). Thus, one identifies defenses after they have occurred, rather than being able to predict their occurrence. All defenses have the same primary function of protecting the person against threat regardless of the source of the threat or the form of the defense.

There is no universally accepted or completely satisfactory classification of defenses. Disagree-

ment exists over the basic mental acts involved in each defense, as well as over which defenses belong together and which do not. For example, Freud considered identification and sublimation (or displacement) as the only two *healthy* defenses. Other defenses, such as repression and projection, were regarded as *pathological.* In contrast, others (Miller and Swanson, 1960) group defenses into two different families, simple or *primitive* ones (such as denial) and *complex* ones (such as projection and displacement). The former are thought to involve maximum distortion of reality and are not specific to a particular threat or conflict; the latter are more specific to a given type of threat or conflict and involve less distortion of reality. A final listing and classification of defenses requires more agreement and knowledge than is now available, so in the treatment here no attempt is made to bring them all together into groups or families.

Presented below is a fairly traditional list of defense concepts described in more or less accepted fashion, including those frequently mentioned in the psychological and lay literature. Although these concepts have become rather general in clinical usage and meaning and no longer specifically psychoanalytic, it is helpful to remember their theoretical origins in Freudian psychoanalytic theory (Freud, 1943; see also A. Freud, 1946).

Identification   The process of *identification* was considered by Freud to be of the utmost importance in the healthy development of the personality and in the socialization process by which people adopt the ways of their culture (Freud, 1961). By means of identification the child takes on or internalizes characteristics of other people, especially the parents. There is much debate over the exact way this mechanism works—for example, whether it is through imitation of models, through direct or vicarious learning, or through fear of the powerful adult. Freud wanted to emphasize in the concept the idea of relatively permanent, unconscious acquisitions to the personality, as opposed to superficial imitation (Fig. 4-7).

The connotation that identification is a defense against threat is specifically Freudian and is expressed in the term "identification with the aggressor." This concept is used to explain *why* the boy, for example, takes on the values of the parent. He does so in part as a defense against the threat of castration resulting from his hostile impulses toward his father, who is a competitor in his relationship to the mother (Oedipus complex). By identifying with the aggressor, the father, the boy rids himself of the offending impulse (hostility) and shows himself to be deserving of affection rather than retaliatory anger. He becomes, in short, what his father wants him to be. Such a concept has also been employed by others (for example, Bruno Bettelheim, 1960) to explain the perplexing phenomenon in which inmates of the German concentration camps during World War II came to act and even think like their oppressors. Writers have sometimes spoken of this as "brainwashing." A psychoanalytically oriented clinical psychologist, Bettelheim was himself a concentration camp prisoner and wrote about it retrospectively. About this process of identification with the aggressor, he wrote (p. 171):

> From copying SS verbal aggressions to copying their form of bodily aggression was one more step, but it took several years to reach that. It was not unusual, when prisoners were in charge of others, to find old prisoners (and not only former criminals) behaving worse than the SS. Sometimes they were trying to find favor with the guards, but more often it was because they considered it the best way to treat prisoners in the camp.
>
> Old prisoners tended to identify with the SS not only in their goals and values, but even in appearance. . . . The lengths prisoners would go to were sometimes hard to believe, particularly since they were sometimes punished for trying to look like the SS. . . .

Bettelheim saw an analogy between the helpless child with his powerful father and the helpless prisoner and the powerful SS guards. In time, the prisoner coped with the continuing threat of annihilation by identifying with these guards. He reduced the threat of castration (symbolic castration, that is) by repressing his own identity, which was unacceptable to the SS, in favor of a new identity with their standards of value.

This same concept has also been used (Elkins, 1961) in explaining the modal personality of the American black, manifest during the years between original slavery and the present. Stereotyped as docile but irresponsible, loyal but lazy, humble but addicted to lying and stealing, full of infantile silliness and childish exaggeration, this "Sambo" image came about as a result of the early slavers' systematic attempts to eliminate the black's link with his past culture. The first nightmare of capture and travel through the jungle and

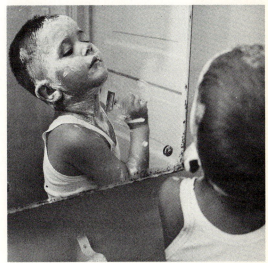

FIGURE 4-7 "Little shaver"—an example of the process of identification. (Robert J. Smith, from Black Star.)

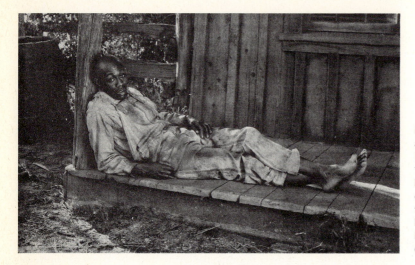

FIGURE 4-8 "Boy, I'se ti-ahed!" A photo of Stepin Fetchit, a movie actor of the 1930s who typified the "Sambo" stereotype of the American Negro and led audiences to roar in appreciation, perhaps often without even clearly realizing at whose expense. (Culver Pictures, Inc.)

across the ocean caused approximately two-thirds of the Negroes to expire due to extreme hardships. The subsequent absolute authority of the white owner permitted little to emerge but the role and personality of the dependent slave. The same process of "identification with the aggressor" and the consequent transformation of the personality occurred, according to this view, in both the concentration camp and the Southern American plantation as a result of the absolute authority manifested in both. Both systems demanded a "childlike" conformity from their victims (Fig. 4-8).

Whether this concept of defensive identification provides an accurate or complete picture of the process of socialization in the child is a controversial issue. Nonetheless, the concept has been an influential one in psychological thought, and it represents a fascinating attempt to understand the ways in which certain extreme conditions of life deeply influence the personalities of people exposed to them.

Displacement   Often human needs and motives cannot be gratified because of the physical and social conditions of life. One way to cope with

this frustration is to direct the expression of the motivational force into new channels permitting gratification in a different form, a process referred to as *displacement*. In Freud's concept, the instinctual need cannot be changed, but the object which permits its gratification can. For instance, heterosexual impulses toward the mother or father cannot be gratified without disapproval and danger; but these same impulses can be gratified by the selection of another love object. The person ultimately finds a mate external to the immediate family. When this has occurred, one love object, the parent, is *displaced* by another in order to gratify the need.

One form of displacement is called "sublimation." This term is specifically Freudian in origin and meaning and refers mainly to the transformation of sexual and aggressive impulses into other socially acceptable forms. Erotic energies, for example, which cannot find expression directly, are expressed indirectly in creative activities such as painting, music, literature, or scientific curiosity. The fundamental type of satisfaction of the erotic impulse is displaced in favor of desexualized forms.

In Freud's view, the process of displacement is

essential to the development and maintenance of civilization because it permits the diversion of dangerous, primitive impulses—sex and aggression—into safe channels. It is the means by which humans can live in harmony and productivity in contrast with the more primitive herd animal. Moreover, it makes possible the complex pattern of interests and attachments that characterizes the human adult. This flexibility of object choice is lacking or more restricted in lower animals, which act in a far more mechanical fashion, driven to perform certain fixed patterns of behavior by relatively unmodifiable urges and built-in behavior sequences. Human beings, in contrast, show more versatility in adapting to circumstances and readily altering the forms and objects of their gratification.

Displacement is a mechanism that has been much studied by psychologists in the laboratory, especially the displacement of aggression from

FIGURE 4-9 Displacement of aggression, but this time with a just ending. © Punch, London.

one object to another. In the typical situation, a person is frustrated by another who is more powerful. Under these conditions, the frustrated individual may inhibit the expression of aggression toward the powerful adversary but display it toward another, less powerful one.

An analogous process has been observed among infrahuman animals, which suggests an evolutionary origin to displacement in humans. For example. baboons and chimpanzees displace aggression from a more dominant animal to one lower down in the dominance hierarchy. Often that animal, in turn, attacks one lower in the hierarchy, and so on down the line (Fig. 4-9).

Repression   This is usually considered to be the most important defense mechanism described by Freud. In *repression,* an urge or impulse is said to be blocked from expression so that it cannot be experienced consciously or directly expressed in behavior. It is blocked because its expression is threatening, either violating an internal proscription or provoking punishment from an external danger. In Freud's earliest use of the term, "repression" was the fundamental defense under which all others were subsumed. Recent writers on this subject appear to treat repression as one of many equally important strategies of coping with threat. However, its status in relation to other defenses still remains somewhat unclear.

Freud spoke of two kinds of repression, depending on what it is that is kept out of consciousness. *Primal repression* denies entry into consciousness of the ideational (thought) representation of the impulse, in effect, the wish. However, the content of the impulse can sometimes be slipped past the censorship into consciousness in disguised, symbolic forms, as in a dream, or in expressive gestures the meaning of which the person does not know. For example, certain dream contents were regarded by Freud as disguised representations of the sex act, as in dreams of a man and woman dining together. In effect, the charged idea of heterosexual activity

has been expressed in the superficially bland form of dining in place of copulation.

One of the most important and undeveloped areas of inquiry concerning this Freudian conception is the study of symbols. Controversy revolves around whether some symbols are universal expressions of socially taboo drives or, instead, have idiosyncratic meanings specific to the individual. If the former is true, then we could "read" the meanings of the dream contents of other persons without great effort, because these reflect universal symbolic representations. If the latter is true, the specific meanings of symbols for each individual would have to be made known in order to evaluate the primitive, repressed thought that is being communicated. In all probability, some symbols are widely used because of the shared experiences of all mankind (cf. Jung, 1965), and some are idiosyncratic to the individual because of his own unique history.

Repression proper involves blocking from consciousness not the original impulse representation or wish itself, but derivatives of these, material which has been connected with the repressed urge. For example, ideas such as love, sex, excitement, woman, and beauty can become associated with the repressed impulse so that these too command repression. Clinical psychologists think that individuals given to repression as a defense will often show marked evidence of repression proper because a wide spectrum of related ideas are kept out of their awareness. Such individuals may be described as unusually naive for their age and intelligence. So much extended associative material has been repressed that the person is, in consequence, surprisingly uninformed in areas of human experience about which he or she should be well versed. Excessive naiveté thus becomes a clinical sign of the process of repression.

Repression must be distinguished from *suppression.* Repression refers to an unconscious process. The person is unaware not only of the impulse itself, but also of the process by which it is blocked from expression. In suppression, however, there is a conscious or volitional inhibition of an impulse or of certain ideas connected with it. For example, since death is a painful topic, a person or a group of people may decide not to talk or think about it. Or, one feels angry but resolves not to express the anger in any way or let anyone know about it. The impulse is suppressed. For those theorists who emphasize unconscious mental processes, who assume that there can be many levels of awareness, and who believe that variations in the level of awareness make a significant psychological and behavioral difference, the distinction between suppression and repression is a real and important one. The distinction is a specific example of the one made earlier between a defense in the psychoanalytic sense and defensiveness, the explicit, conscious effort to present oneself socially in a particular light. Suppression is the conscious, socially oriented maneuver, and repression is the parallel, unconscious, self-deceptive process.

Denial This process is usually thought to be closely related to repression. For some writers (A. Freud, 1946), it is parallel with repression, *denial* being directed toward external dangers while repression deals with impulses arising from within the person. Not everyone agrees with this distinction. In denial, the person copes with threat by denying that it exists. "I am not angry," and "I am not dying of cancer," are verbal illustrations of denial. In general, the bad thing is said not to happen, or not to be bad. More detailed examples of this defensive process were discussed in Chapter 2.

Reaction formation Here the threatening impulse is expressed in speech and action by its opposite. The impulse is, in effect, *reversed* from its normally threatening character to an opposite one, usually benign. For example, instead of expressing hostility to the other person, a person expresses love. Presumably, the stronger the hostility, the more intense is the positive expression of love.

The idea of *reaction formation* is expressed in literary form by the statement of Hamlet's mother, "The lady protests too much, me thinks." In the play within a play, which is used by Hamlet to trap his uncle into revealing his secret murder of Hamlet's father, the wife of the king also treacherously deceives her husband into believing she is loyal. Her protestations are designed to conceal from him her real feelings. Reaction formation is usually inferred on the basis of excessiveness of the affirmation, the tactic perceived by Hamlet's mother, when watching the play; she senses that the other woman's claim is excessive and says, "The lady protests too much." Genuine expressions of an impulse are not usually so extreme and compulsive. This is why we intuitively tend to mistrust individuals who praise us too much or profess affection for us in extravagant terms. In reaction formation the person is obliged, even when it is unnecessary, to manifest the opposite feeling from the threatening one.

Projection Instead of accepting an impulse as one's own, it can be dealt with by attributing it to someone else. For example, hatred in oneself can be projected onto someone else. *Projection* was conceived by Freud to be the prime mechanism of defense of paranoid individuals, who believe that others are seeking to injure them. Actually, it is inferred that the paranoid person has injurious thoughts toward the supposed enemies. Freud maintained that displacement as well as projection was involved in paranoia. The impulse threatening the paranoid was thought to be homosexuality. In his famous analysis of the Schreber case, Freud (1933) argued that the homosexual impulse was first transformed into that of aggression (from sexual assault to physical attack) and then projected onto the person toward whom the patient had the homosexual impulse. Thus, the paranoid's own homosexual impulse is transformed in his mind into the idea that the object of his erotic impulse is actually seeking to attack him.

An ingenious experiment involving *projection* was accomplished by exposing heterosexual male subjects to a homosexual threat and giving them the opportunity to employ projection as a defense against it (Bramel, 1962). The subjects were each assigned to a partner and allowed to have a brief social interaction with him. They were also attached to a fake physiological indicator of sexual arousal. The indicator needle was supposed to communicate to the subject and the experimenter the subject's degree of sexual arousal while looking at pictures. Actually, the experimenter himself, unknown to the subject, made the needle rise whenever a homosexual picture was observed. The clear (and in our culture, threatening) implication was thus given that the experimental subjects (the threatened ones) had homosexual tendencies; to other control (nonthreatened) subjects no homosexual implication was provided in the procedures.

Following this experience, both experimental and control subjects were asked to rate their partner's degree of homosexuality. Under the experimental, homosexual-threat condition, subjects gave higher ratings of homosexuality to the partner than were given under the nonthreat control condition. In effect, if an individual had himself been threatened with having the trait, he attributed more homosexuality to the other person. It was argued that outright denial of the homosexuality was not possible in this situation, since the evidence of the needle movement (indicating erotic arousal) was striking, and there was no evident reason to doubt the validity of the measurement. Being unable to deny the threatening impulse, subjects resorted to another common method of coping with the threat, namely, by *projecting* it onto another person, thus divesting themselves of the onus of the trait.

Intellectualization   A different kind of defensive maneuver is illustrated in the mechanism of *intel-*

lectualization, in which the person gains detachment from a threatening event in order to remain untouched by it emotionally. It is closely related to the mechanism of *isolation,* in which two ideas are kept apart (isolated) in the person's thoughts because bringing them together would be threatening. In intellectualization, an emotional event is dealt with in analytic, detached terms, as though it were something to study or be merely curious about rather than emotionally involved in. Such a mechanism is often found in professional individuals whose job it is to deal with ordinarily disturbing experiences. For example, a pathologist examines diseased tissue as though it were merely a neutral object of study rather than part of a suffering, dying fellow human. Or a nurse in an emergency or intensive-care medical unit keeps his or her level of distress under control by not identifying too closely with the patient's suffering (Hay and Oken, 1972). By this detachment, the nurse or pathologist can retain a useful objectivity rather than becoming too involved in painful experiences. Sometimes such a process of detachment is impossible to achieve. A professional person dealing with life-and-death matters, however competent, will not usually bring his or her skills to bear on a close relative, because the intellectualized detachment that ordinarily gives protection on the job cannot be readily maintained when the problem is so "close to home."

Intellectualization is thus a common way of dealing with potentially threatening experiences. Sometimes, as above, it helps in dealing with life problems. The attitude of detachment or intellectualization is, for example, an ideal of science, since rational study of any problem is difficult under conditions of intense emotional involvement. However, were this protective attitude to become a pervasive part of the lifestyle, the person might then be deprived of the opportunity to have positive emotional experiences or form healthy attachments to other persons. A loving relationship with another person might be forsworn because it made one vulnerable to being "hurt." Often such a person is perceived to be distant, even excessively rational and unemotional, someone who has withdrawn from the usual emotional aspects of participation in life. Nearly all defenses, intellectualization included, have their harmful uses as well as virtues in coping with life's problems (Fig. 4-10).

PROBLEMS WITH THE DEFENSE CONCEPT

There are two particularly sticky problems in connection with the list of defenses presented above. The first concerns the issue of *self-deception*, the second the *adequacy of the system of classification*. Let us consider these issues in more detail.

It seems to many theoreticians and observers that people often utilize threat-reducing devices which are not, strictly speaking, distortions of reality or *self-deceptions*. Such devices represent particular ways in which people deploy their attention or selectively emphasize the benign rather than the disturbing aspects of relatively ambiguous events. That is, they may not really be distortions of reality, but rather self-protective interpretations of ambiguous situations. The person may be fully aware of such deployment of attention.

An example comes from research on smoking. There has been a major propaganda assault directed at getting smokers to stop smoking because of its hazards to health. One group of researchers (Pervin and Yatko, 1965) were interested in investigating how smokers dealt with the threatening contradiction between the behavior of smoking and the information about the health hazards connected with it. They studied fifty smokers and fifty nonsmokers in a college student population, getting them to display their mode of thinking about the issue by responding to a lengthy questionnaire. The questionnaire provided the opportunity for smokers to show how they dealt with the matter by indicating in

their answers the extent to which they knew the facts linking smoking with cancer. Some of the strategies that might be employed included not knowing the threatening facts, knowing the threatening facts but considering them personally irrelevant, minimizing the dangers of smoking compared with other dangers, and minimizing the negative consequences of smoking, such as its impairment of taste and its effects on the smoker's breath, while emphasizing its pleasures. The authors found that the most common strategy employed by the smokers was to minimize the validity of the smoking-cancer findings and the personal danger to themselves of smoking. They did not know less about the facts, but rather interpreted these facts as minimally threat-

FIGURE 4-10 We are frequently bombarded by pathetic pictures of other people in tragic circumstances. These can be viewed without distress by the process of intellectualization or detachment, by distancing ourselves from the disturbing emotions inherent in their plight. Some writers have referred to this as dehumanization, that is, by viewing such persons as nonpersons, as less than human, and hence not warranting our empathic feeling. This is both a valuable device protecting us from being overwhelmed by distressing feelings and a dangerous one making us callous about other's problems. (Werner Bischof, from Magnum.)

ening. In short, they reduced threat by *selectively deploying their attention to the benign rather than the harmful aspects of the situation.*

Is this a defense in the sense we have been using it here? The behavior *appears* like denial, but is there self-deception or distortion of reality? Only if one can say that the interpretation is unequivocally unwarranted can one argue that distortion of reality is involved. But the facts are not denied, only their significance, and that significance is, indeed, somewhat controversial. The smoker appears to be saying, "Yes, smoking does constitute a potential health hazard, but not an important one to me personally." It is like realizing that to be bitten by a black widow spider could be fatal, but concluding that the prospects of such an accident happening are so small as to be not worth worrying about. The smoker also appears to be deemphasizing, rather than denying, the disturbing facts and paying attention mainly to those things about smoking that please him or her. Somehow this pattern looks superficially like denial, but cannot be precisely categorized as such; it fits the "defense" concept only if one squeezes and extends the concept of defense so greatly that it no longer resembles its original meaning. Perhaps the original meaning of the concept of defense in psychoanalytic theory has already become eroded and overextended. Or perhaps the original concept is unsound, and the above offers a better analytic model.

The second problem concerns the adequacy of the existing categories in describing all the varieties of threat-reducing psychological mechanisms employed by people. Not all the defenses that are sometimes postulated by professional writers have been listed here. For example, rationalization, regression, and undoing were omitted. Moreover, it is difficult to find two lists which are identical. But more important, even if every concept that has ever been seriously proposed is listed, certain behaviors that appear to have

threat-reducing properties would be difficult to fit into the existing, traditional categories. This is illustrated in Mechanic's (1962) study of graduate students coping with the problem of a critical examination in the near future. Table 4-1 provides a list of what Mechanic called "comforting cognitions," ways of thinking about the examinations that are threat-reducing. These statements came from interviews in which the students discussed their reactions to the threat.

An examination of Table 4-1 reveals the problem of classifying the thoughts of the students within the traditional rubrics of defense. It is difficult to know from the information given, for example, whether the statement "I've handled test situations in the past—there's no good reason why not now" is a realistic appraisal or a defensive one, to some extent out of touch with reality. Is the statement "I've already demonstrated my competence in past work, so they will pass me" a denial of the threat? Should any of these statements be regarded as "defenses" against threat, and if so, which defenses? These questions illustrate some of the special difficulties in the analysis of methods by which people cope with threat or frustration by intrapsychic processes as opposed to direct actions.

HOW DEFENSES ARE RECOGNIZED

The crucial requirement in using the defense concept clinically is being able to say whether or not a given behavior represents a defense. This can be illustrated with denial. Suppose a woman is asked whether or not a situation made her angry, and she answers "no." To speak of this response as a denial, there must be evidence that she is, in reality, angry. Otherwise, the "no" is not a defense at all but merely an accurate subjective report of her emotional state. Suppose a man interprets a situation that others think is anger-provoking as not calling for anger at all. The observed person may have not perceived an

TABLE 4-1 STUDENTS' REPORTED USE OF COMFORTING COGNITIONS

COMFORTING COGNITIONS	PERCENT OF STUDENTS	
	Who report using this cognition very or fairly often	Who report using these cognitions with any frequency
I'm as bright and knowledgeable as other students who have passed these examinations.	64	91
I've handled test situations in the past— there's no good reason why not now.	59	86
I am doing all I can to prepare—the rest is not up to me.	50	86
I wouldn't have gotten this far unless I knew something.	50	86
I'm well liked in this department.	45	77
I've already demonstrated my competence in past work, they will pass me.	26	77
You can't fail these examinations unless you really mess up.	23	73
They wouldn't fail me—they've already decided I'm going to pass.	18	30
This is a test of stress; I can deal with that.	14	59
If I'm not cut out for the field, it's best that I know it now.	14	55

SOURCE: Mechanic, 1962, p. 121

insult, either because he is naive or dull-witted or because he failed to interpret it as such, and thus he experiences no anger. To the extent this is so, one cannot speak of a defense. Some trait of personality may have caused the misperception, but this is not precisely what is meant by a defense.

Let us assume, however, that the latter individual is utilizing a defense such as denial. He really feels angry, but he is unaware or not fully aware of this. Then it should be possible to observe evidence of anger, either in bodily gestures, in what Freud called "slips of the tongue" in which some unintended expression of the anger breaks through to the amusement of the observer and consternation of the doer, or in physiological evidence that an emotional state of anger exists.

Actually, the inference of an active defense is usually made from a variety of bits of evidence at the same time. First, it is made with considerable risk of error when a *situation* which seems to call for one reaction actually results in another. That is, in a situation in which most people are anxious, the subject reports no uneasiness. Second, the inference may be made on the basis of *inconsistencies* in the statements of the person. For example, at one moment a woman says she was not frightened, but at another moment she admits she was. Third, the verbal statements of the person *contradict* what appears to be the import of her actions, gestures, or physiological reactions (e.g., blushing, flushing, paling). A boy says he likes some other person, but appears always to take steps to avoid contact with that person; or he reports the absence of fear in a given situation, but turns ashen in color. There are always hazards to inferring defense mechanisms, since other possibilities exist which could account for the observed pattern of reaction, and these must be ruled out before the inference can be confidently believed in. These are the same hazards seen earlier in inferences about the internal states of anger and fear.

SUCCESSFUL DEFENSE

One of the things not much emphasized in the usual treatment of defense is that defenses can vary in degree of success. Theoretically, the defensive self-deception can sometimes be fully accepted or believed by the person engaged in defensive effort, and sometimes only partly accepted. It may succeed some of the time but fail at other times. An example will make this clearer.

Occasionally a girl may say, "I tried to tell myself that everything would be okay." She might have added, but didn't need to, "But I didn't really believe it." The observer may hear the words of denial, but it is also evident that the speaker has really been unsuccessful in convincing herself that there is no danger, that things will turn out all right. Under these circumstances, stress reactions (physiological, subjective, or behavioral) will be evident because the person is still threatened in spite of the effort at denial. In contrast, when the defense is completely successful, such disturbances of reaction should be absent because the individual is thoroughly convinced that he or she is under no threat. The clinician sometimes refers to such a successful defense as "well consolidated," meaning that there appear to be no gaps, no occasions when there are doubts, no evidence of emotional disturbances which point to a breaking through of the threatening impulse or of signals from the environment that there is danger. In sum, the more successful the defense, the less evidence there will be of stress reactions.

POSITIVE VERSUS NEGATIVE CONSEQUENCES OF A DEFENSE

The adjustive consequences of a defense must be distinguished from its success. A defense may be successful yet be considered maladjustive or negative. These are different dimensions of analysis. While success refers to whether or not the self-deception is convincing to the person, its "positive or negative consequences" refer to whether it aids or harms him or her in transactions with the environment. Psychological comfort, which is one of the products of a successful defense, may be purchased at the expense of other failures in getting along which are sometimes evident only later on.

By definition a defense is a distortion of reality, but it does not usually succeed in altering the actual external circumstances. Only the person's appraisal of reality is changed by a defense. If, as in real disaster situations, the harm is from an external source, then a defense will do nothing to avert the harm. Thus, the parents of the children suffering from cancer who denied the terminal nature of the illness ultimately had to face the inevitable death of the child (Wolff et al., 1964). There is some evidence that those parents who used denial, though less stressed during the child's illness, were more stressed afterward (Hofer et al., 1972) than those who faced the anticipated grief beforehand. There are also observations of men who greatly endangered their lives during and after a heart attack by denying the significance of their symptoms and hence delaying seeking medical attention (von Kugelgen, 1975). And in still another instance reflecting the possible maladjustive consequences of defenses, women have been observed who denied the potential seriousness of a lump in their breast, thereby allowing the cancer to become a deadly illness (Katz et al., 1970).

Whether it is better to "know the truth" and suffer psychologically as a consequence or to deceive oneself about it and be comfortable is partly a matter of values, and even professional persons differ somewhat in their views about this. The issue cannot be easily settled in the abstract, although one can certainly determine in specific instances the harmful and the positive consequences of defensive self-deception and weigh their value. The best rule of thumb is probably this: When a defense gets in the way of direct action that can change the situation for the better, it is negative or maladjustive; when nothing constructive could be done anyway, it probably doesn't matter and might at least help the person feel better and cope with other problems.

If defenses can have positive as well as negative consequences, why is it that they are so commonly regarded as pathological or maladjustive, especially since all people appear sometimes to use defenses? The solution has usually been to assert that psychological ill health is in direct proportion to the frequency with which a person employs defensive as opposed to nondefensive solutions to threat. But equating defense mechanisms and psychopathology is oversimple because defenses can at times have positive consequences and therefore, by implication, be healthy. Rather than a blanket rule, what is required is the independent evaluation of this quality of a coping process, regardless of whether it is defensive or not. Psychopathology, so-called, should be linked to the maladjustive *consequences* of the defense, when there are any.

Why has it become traditional to regard the defense mechanisms, per se, as pathological— that is, as evidence of maladjustment? For one thing, one of our strong cultural values is that knowing the truth about reality is a virtue; to know and to be aware, even if it makes us miserable, is considered better than gaining comfort from ignorance. In our society, which is focused on mastering one's environment, we have identified blissful ignorance as somehow bad or immoral.

Nevertheless, the main professional reason why defenses are so commonly considered to be pathological concerns some of their undesirable consequences, consequences that were first emphasized by Freud in his conception of the neuroses. Defenses are said to be *costly* to the person; he or she is presumed to pay in one way or another for the psychological comfort attained by means of defense.

There are at least three ways in which defenses might exact a price from the user:

1 The term "cost" often refers to the mobilization of energy or effort required to maintain a self-deception in the face of contradictory objective cues. Otto Fenichel (1945) used the expression "silent internal tasks" to refer to the *loss of productive energy* which is expended to maintain a defense. He created the image of the person who is too tired to meet the ordinary tasks of life with verve because internal struggles have depleted so much energy that they interfere with satisfaction-giving activities. Aside from anecdotal observation, no very clear evidence has been amassed that one of the costs of defense is the depletion of energy. Yet the concept remains an intriguing one to many professionals and has a considerable degree of plausibility.

2 The second possible cost of defense is far less controversial. It concerns the distortion of reality inherent in a defense and the fact that the resulting misperceptions may lead to faulty life decisions. For example, a student protecting his self-esteem by attributing academic failure to inadequate teachers may be covering up his own inadequacies or lack of motivation. Of what harm is such a self-deception? Were he to recognize the truth, he might wisely decide to quit college and take up a vocation more suited to his talents and interest. However, by convincing himself that failure is not the result of personal inadequacies or limited commitment, he continues to make maladjustive choices in using his time and energy, choices that will probably lead to further threat and frustration.

3 The third cost of defense consists of the increased and continuing vulnerability to threat and the failure of the person to seek more adjustive alternatives. The defense, by definition, is imposed against contrary evidence. However, situations are never static. They are always changing, and sometimes the evidence against the defensive interpretation may grow stronger and more insistent. This makes the defense less tenable and reinstates the threat unless the person can intensify the defensive effort or give up the defense in favor of a more positive solution.

One of the cornerstones of the theory of defense mechanisms is that individuals who defend against threat are vulnerable to any cue which might intensify the impulse or the recognition of danger that is being defended against. Stress emotions (such as anxiety) appear to be related to the successfulness of the defense. That is, as evidence contradictory to the defense mounts, stress reactions also increase. Thus, the individual employing a defense is apt to be continually vulnerable. He or she is excessively sensitive to changes in the situation, overreactive to experiences that would not touch other individuals, and likely to experience fluctuations of mood without understanding the changing conditions that bring these fluctuations about. And in concealing the true state of affairs, the defense inhibits the adoption of other coping processes that would provide more adjustive solutions.

Thus, defenses are typically regarded as pathological because they so commonly produce harmful consequences or symptoms. A degree of psychological comfort may be purchased by the sacrifice of effectiveness. Energy needed for such effectiveness may be sacrificed; the distortion of reality is likely to result in maladjustive life decisions; the absence of reality testing may make the person continually vulnerable to threat resulting from contradictory evidence that makes the de-

fensive fiction even more difficult to maintain. In effect, the psychological comfort initially produced by the self-deception may, ironically, give way to new misery created by the defense itself.

SUMMING UP

Effective adjustment depends on how a person *copes* with the stresses of life. There are two broad classes of coping, direct action and palliation. *Direct actions* involve behavioral attempts to alter the troubled commerce between a person and the environment. They include preparing against an anticipated harm, aggression toward a harmful agent, and avoidance of that agent. When an individual views the situation as hopeless, he or she becomes paralyzed by despair and ceases actively to cope, a psychological state usually described as apathy and depression. Normally, such apathy eventually gives way to renewed efforts to cope.

Palliative modes of coping include somatic-oriented efforts to ease bodily and subjective distress, say by alcohol or other drugs, and intrapsychic modes of coping typically referred to as *defense mechanisms.* Some of the main defenses are identification, displacement, repression, denial, reaction formation, projection, and intellectualization. Although each involves a specific mental process, they all have the same function of changing a negative appraisal of harm or threat into a benign one, although the objective harms and dangers remain the same. Thus, defenses are self-deceptions in which a painful reality is reinterpreted in positive or benign terms.

The concept of defense is descriptive rather than predictive, and we are not yet sure which defenses tend to go together in the same individual or in the same situation of harm or threat. Moreover, the key idea that defensive processes are unconscious is difficult or impossible to test scientifically, and so it remains controversial in psychological theory. Defenses are recognized by noting contradictions between what the person says at one time and another, between verbal statements and actions, or between situational demands and the way the person responds to them. They are inferences from the total pattern of behavior (including bodily reactions) of the person in a given situation. Sometimes the self-deception of a defense is successful, and at other times the defense fails when the person is not convinced by the benign fiction he or she has generated. Defenses can have positive consequences, as when the person gains a measure of comfort that does not cause interference with actions available to change the situation, or because such action would be futile. They can also have negative or harmful consequences by demanding otherwise needed energy (thus leading to inaction or inappropriate coping actions predicated on the self-deception) and by increasing the person's vulnerability to threat.

73253

CHAPTER 5 STRESS AND BODILY ILLNESS

One reason stress is so important in the health sciences is that it can lead to bodily illness as well as disturbances in the ways people manage the tasks of living (maladjustment). A high percentage (estimated variously at from half to more than two-thirds) of medical patients display symptoms that are partly or entirely psychological in origin: they are, in effect, stress-connected. The field that is concerned with the link between psychological problems and bodily illness is called *psychosomatic disorders*, though some common alternative terms include "stress disorders," "diseases of adaptation," and "psychophysiological disorders." These expressions imply that a problem which begins at the psychological level may ultimately produce disturbances in the normal operation of the organs of the body, and even permanent damage to tissues.

To say that the mind affects bodily states is to make a partly unjustified separation between the mind and the body. The relations between mind and body, and the wisdom of thinking of them as separate, have been debated for thousands of years. The very language implying that mind affects body, or vice versa, is a vestige of a philosophical view that they are separate and discrete, though they may interact in certain ways. Mind and body can also be viewed as two distinguishable facets of one organic process, two sides to the same coin, as it were, not really independent except for logical convenience and ease of speaking. What happens at one level must be closely tied to what happens on the other level, though this is described and understood in different terms and concepts. For example, when we think, feel, or act, parallel biochemical and neural processes are also occuring, so both mind and body are in that sense one: there would be no mental activity without bodily (tissue) activity, and by the same token organic disease also involves disturbances in psychological activity. The reader should not get too concerned about grasping this complex and difficult philosophical issue. It is sufficient to recognize that when we speak of psychosomatics or of psychological stress as producing bodily disease, we are using language that merely distinguishes two facets of the same biological process, mind and body, without intending to suggest that they are biologically separate sets of events.

Psychosomatic illness refers to certain bodily disorders such as stomach ulcers, intestinal colitis (diarrhea), hypertension (high blood pressure), and migraine headache, to mention some of the most important. However, there are other forms of illness which psychological stress is probably capable of inducing or aggravating, including chronic indigestion, hives, allergies, susceptibility to infection, accident proneness, and many others less familiar as psychosomatic ailments. Moreover, many thoughtful professionals think that all illnesses have psychosomatic overtones or, put differently, that most illness is not merely the result of an attack by microorganisms or other noxious conditions external to the body, but that illness arises in part because the person's resistance to it has been impaired by stress or other factors. Infections develop, for example, because there has been a disturbance to the smooth, integrated functioning of the various tissues of the body, making the person more vulnerable or creating strain on certain organs, say the heart or the lungs, that bear the brunt of the adjustive requirements of living. Later we shall see some examples of research that adopts this view and seeks to demonstrate a relationship between stress and bodily disease of any kind.

EMOTIONS AND BODILY CHANGES

Emotional disturbance lies at the core of the causation of psychosomatic illness, and it is important to see in at least a rudimentary way how emotions affect the body. Emotions are controlled by the brain and other portions of the nervous system and by various glandular hormones (powerful chemicals) that course through the body in emotional states.

At this point the author's teaching experience tells him that a large proportion of students taking a course in adjustment dread the subject of physiology and would prefer just to "skip it." However, except for a strange new terminology, the limited quantity of physiology in this chapter is not difficult or mystifying, and even just a rudimentary understanding of what is presented should make the problem of stress and bodily disease infinitely easier to grasp. The basic questions that must be addressed concern why it is that we feel as we do when we experience emotion and why the physiological changes involved in these feelings can create bodily illness. It will be well worthwhile to master the material which follows, because the physiology of the problem cannot be divorced from the psychological issues of stress and illness without destroying understanding.

NEURAL CONTROL OF EMOTION

The neural systems and mechanisms in emotions are, as one might guess, quite complex, and knowledge about them is too highly specialized to allow more than a cursory examination here. In accordance with present knowledge, the main areas of neural control of emotion are to be found in the reticular formation of the brain stem, the hypothalamus, the limbic system, and the cerebral cortex. A schematic diagram of these areas, and some of the other nearby systems, can be seen in Figure 5-1.

The cerebral cortex In the discussions of threat, frustration, and challenge and of the stress emotions in Chapters 3 and 4, emphasis was placed on the cognitive appraisal or evaluation of the significance of a situation for the person's well being. Thus, threat involves anticipation of harm. The cognitive processes involved in this—for example, evaluating the significance of events, anticipation of the future, or choosing between coping alternatives—are the functions of the cerebral cortex, the portion of the brain that is most

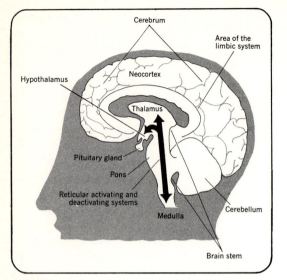

FIGURE 5-1 Diagram of the human brain, within the skull. Besides the cortex the areas particularly important in emotion include the reticular systems, the hypothalamus, and the limbic system.

advanced in the evolution of species. This is where most higher mental processes take place in primates such as human beings.

FIGURE 5-2 The cerebral cortex.

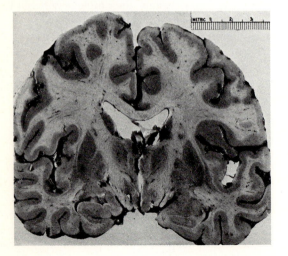

The cerebral cortex is the outer layer of brain cells that covers the lower portions of the brain just as an orange rind covers the meat of an orange (see Figure 5-2). The word cortex is in fact derived from the Latin word for rind or shell. In contrast, the reticular formation, autonomic nervous system, hypothalamus, and limbic system, which will be discussed shortly, are located more deeply within the brain and concern primitive functions (engaged in by all animals) necessary to the maintenance of life itself.

Physiological psychologists know relatively little about the cortex and its role in emotion compared with more primitive areas. Nevertheless, to the extent that higher thought processes are basic to our stress emotions, guiding our appraisals of various life events and triggering emotional processes (including the somatic changes in which we are interested here), we must ultimately discover the physiological steps by which appraisal of threat or challenge leads to the mobilization of the person's physiological resources; and we must learn how the bodily states generated under the stress emotions are controlled. Till now, studies of the neurophysiology of emotion have paid much more attention to the lower centers in arousal states and to the humoral (hormonal) influences that create and control the bodily reactions associated with strong emotional states.

The reticular formation To respond to and deal with external stimulation requires an alert or aroused organism. One portion of the brain stem that has been of great recent interest, the portion intimately involved in states of activation and quiescence, is the *reticular formation* or, as it is often called, the "reticular activating (and deactivating) system" (see Figure 5-3). This central core of the stem of the brain comprises pathways to and from the peripheral nerves and the higher portions of the brain, like way stations in between. Sensory impulses (involving touch, smell. hearing, etc.) from all over the body travel to the cortex, and branches from these pathways join (synapse) with other neurons or nerve cells within the reticular formation; these in turn stimulate the cortex among other things, alerting or activating the animal. Cortical messages are shunted downward too, via the reticular formation, regulating (activating and deactivating) peripheral nerve activity and the viscera (the internal organs). The pathways from the sensory nerves at the periphery of the body which pass through and join at the reticular formation, whence they go to higher centers, are referred to as the "ascending reticular activating system" (ARAS), while those which pass from the cortex downward comprise the descending portion.

The reticular system along with the hypothalamus is involved in the control of many visceral functions. For example, reticular-hypothalamic influences operate in the secretion of hydrochloric acid in the stomach: one hypothesis advanced for the gastrointestinal ulceration in the "executive" monkeys, which was reported in Chapter 1 (Brady et al., 1958), is that the stress caused excessive HCl secretion via such reticular-hypothalamic activation. In any case, the reticular system is heavily involved in endocrine and visceral regulation and thus plays a major role in the physiological changes in emotional and other activated states.

Many psychophysiological researchers (for example, Lindsley, 1951; Malmo, 1959; Duffy, 1962) have emphasized the activating functions of the reticular formation, conceiving of emotions essentially as a state of heightened general activation. Physiologically, an activated person or animal is known from such bodily changes as increased heart rate and blood pressure and increases in the electrical conductivity of the skin. Such visceral changes are mediated by activity of the autonomic nervous system (this system will be discussed later). Activation also produces changes in the electrical activity of the brain as recorded by means of the electroencephalogram (EEG). Behaviorally, an activated animal is alert or

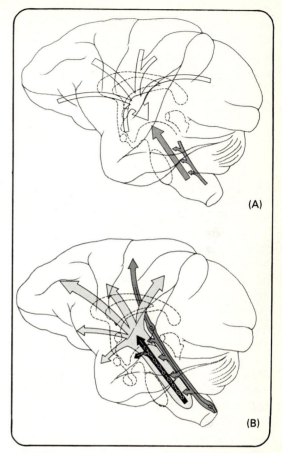

(A)

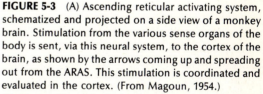

(B)

FIGURE 5-3 (A) Ascending reticular activating system, schematized and projected on a side view of a monkey brain. Stimulation from the various sense organs of the body is sent, via this neural system, to the cortex of the brain, as shown by the arrows coming up and spreading out from the ARAS. This stimulation is coordinated and evaluated in the cortex. (From Magoun, 1954.)
(B) Descending reticular activating system, also schematized and projected on a side view of a monkey brain. Shown here are both incoming stimulation (arrows going up) and descending neural influences (arrows going down) from higher brain centers, mainly the cortex. (From French, Hernández-Péon, and Livingston, 1955.)

excited. One can readily appreciate the adjustive importance of a system of nerves and nerve connections in the brain which activate or alert the animal or person in a general sense, and which appear also to have specific alerting functions in which the individual's attention may be focused on inner bodily states or directed toward the external cues on which successful adjustments might depend.

The limbic system The management of emotional behavior is of the utmost importance for the survival of an animal, and one of the functions that the brain must perform is the regulation of emotional reactions in accordance with feedback from the environment. This is evidently a major function of the *limbic system.* Much of the limbic system lies in the evolutionarily older or earlier portion of the cortex; some of it, however, also includes certain subcortical (below the outer shell) structures with neural links to the hypothalamus (see Figure 5-1). In fact, "limbic" means border, or borderline system; it overlaps somewhat with other portions of the brain which have already been mentioned. Although the particular neural structures of the limbic system that might be implicated in particular emotions have not been clarified, it is now widely held that the entire, complex limbic system may be involved in the regulation of emotional and motivational states. If the emotions connected with adjustive activities such as feeding, fighting, fleeing, and mating are not made appropriate to the environmental conditions, adjustment would be most inadequate indeed. As Magoun (1963, p. 54) has put it:

> The life- and race-preserving pursuits of innate behavior relate closely to the basic appetites and drives, as to emotion. Their obtrusive presence throughout the animal series implies management at neural levels established early in phylogeny. Considerable evidence implicates structures called limbic. . . .

The essential point is that while the hypothalamus appears to be mainly involved in the integration of emotional expression, portions of the limbic system are believed to be critically involved in the experience of emotion and in its integration with environmental input (Papez, 1937; MacLean, 1949, 1958).

The hypothalamus One of the portions of the brain which was recognized very early as being important in emotion is the hypothalamus (Goltz, 1892), which is located in the forebrain below the thalamus (see Figure 5-1). It had been observed that dogs whose cerebrums (containing the highest brain centers) had been removed surgically showed great readiness to display rage by growling, barking at, and attacking stimuli which never before surgery had elicited such a reaction. Many years later, one of the major figures in the physiology of emotion, Walter B. Cannon (1927, 1928), made similar observations with cats. The emotionlike reaction of decerebrate (cerebrum cut out) and decorticate (cerebral cortex cut out) animals was called "sham rage" because it looked like rage or anger but was not well coordinated or adjustive; it was produced by any stimulus rather than appropriate ones, and it terminated as soon as the stimulus was removed. Cannon's experiments, and those of others during this period, led to the discovery of the importance of subcortical areas such as the thalamus and hypothalamus in emotional and motivational states.

The hypothalamus has continued to receive great attention from physiologists interested in motivational and emotional processes. It is generally believed that it integrates the various autonomic and somatic reactions that are noted in emotional states; thus, the hypothalamus is an important neural way station in the process of emotion and is sometimes referred to as the "head ganglion" (key, overriding way station or switchboard) of the autonomic nervous system. But this integration is far from complete, and further integration at the level of the limbic system and cortex is required for normal emotional activity.

The autonomic nervous system The earliest physiological work on emotions stressed what happened to the visceral organs of the body, probably because this was one of emotion's most obvious features. We all recognize that when we are aroused many bodily changes occur. The heart races and pounds, sweat begins to flow, especially on the palms of the hands and in the armpits and groin, and there are peculiar sensations in the stomach region, to mention a few commonly experienced features. To a large extent, these bodily changes are products of the activity of the *autonomic nervous system.*

The organs and tissues of the body may be divided into integrated groups or systems based on certain anatomical and physiological similarities—for example, the skeletal system (for bones), the muscular system, the endocrine gland system, and the nervous system. The nervous system itself is further differentiated into the central nervous system and the peripheral nervous system. The former consists of the brain, the brain stem (or stalk), and the spinal cord. The latter is made up of the nerve fibers that enter and leave the brain stem and the spinal cord going to and from the rest of the body. The autonomic nervous system (in contradistinction to the peripheral somatic nervous system, which controls the striped muscles with which we locomote) is thus one part of the peripheral nervous system, and it innervates (stimulates) all the internal organs such as the heart, lungs, and gastrointestinal tract, some of the glands of the body (such as the sweat glands), the small blood vessels, and the hair follicles.

The autonomic nervous system is itself divided into the sympathetic and parasympathetic branches. The former consists of a network of nerves which depart from the middle portion of the spinal cord, while the parasympathetic nerves join the central nervous system above and below the sympathetic, at the brain stem, and in the tail area. A schematic diagram of the autonomic nervous system with its sympathetic and parasympathetic branches and the visceral organs they innervate is given in Figure 5-4.

One of the important things to remember about the sympathetic and parasympathetic nervous systems is that they often, though not always, work *antagonistically;* that is, most of the visceral organs are innervated by both sympathetic and parasympathetic nerve fibers, and these two sets of fibers produce opposite effects. Thus, for example, the sympathetic nerve to the heart produces acceleration of heart rate, while the parasympathetic nerve makes it slow down; and sympathetic nerves inhibit the rhythmic muscular contraction (peristalsis) of the stomach and intestines necessary for digestion, while parasympathetic nerves increase peristaltic activity. Psychophysiologists have provided a useful list of the various bodily reactions that are stimulated by the sympathetic and parasympathetic nervous systems, respectively. This is nicely summarized in Table 5-1 showing facilitative and inhibitory autonomic functions.

There are anatomical differences between the sympathetic and parasympathetic systems which help us understand their respective roles in emotion. In the *sympathetic nervous system,* fibers coming from the spinal cord are usually very short. In order to reach the visceral organs, they join with other neurons (nerve cells) in *ganglia* (groups of cell bodies) just outside the spinal cord. There is a chain of such way stations (switchboards) or ganglia, and each preganglionic sympathetic neuron has contact with many postganglionic neurons. This anatomical arrangement, which is illustrated in Figure 5-4, means that sympathetic nervous system activity is likely to be rather *diffuse.* That is, stimulation of one sympathetic center or nerve will result in widespread changes all over the body—not just in one organ, but in many. In contrast, in the *parasympathetic system* there is little communication among the nerve fibers going to the various organs. Each preganglionic fiber is very long and synapses (connects with other fibers) very

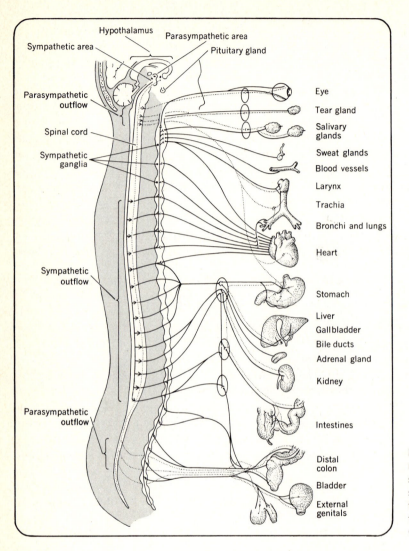

FIGURE 5-4 The autonomic nervous system presented in schematic fashion, with the sympathetic and parasympathetic branches and the organs they control. (From Krech and Crutchfield, 1958.)

close to a visceral organ, thus tending to stimulate only that one.

"You can think of the SNS [sympathetic nervous system] as having a mass-action shotgun approach, while the PNS [parasympathetic nervous system]—like a rifleman—selects its target organs quite specifically" (Sternbach, 1966, p. 21). Thus, when we are stirred up emotionally, the reaction is not specific to particular bodily

organs but tends to spread all over the body, involving the cardiovascular system, the digestive system, the lungs, the mucous and sweat glands, the genitourinary tract, and the endocrine glands. Precisely this diffuseness of effect accounts for the name "sympathetic" which was coined by Galen, the Roman physician, to suggest cooperation or "sympathy" among the various parts.

This concept of the sympathetic nervous system as engaging in "mass action" is, of course, something of an oversimplification. However, it helps us understand some of the subjectively more obvious qualities of emotion. Nevertheless, it is also likely, as will be seen shortly, that there is some patterning as well as diffuseness to the physiological responses during emotion. For example, there may be a different pattern of organ reactions in fear as opposed to anger, both of which are sympathetic nervous system reactions, and such patterning could not occur if the innervations of the system produced only widely diffused, unspecified changes in the visceral organs. Thus, the sympathetic nervous system shares the same principles of neural functioning as the parasympathetic or somatic nervous systems, but it has the important special feature of a considerable degree of diffusion of its effects over many organs, which tends to give it more widespread and massive effects than is true of other neural systems.

The often antagonistic action of the sympathetic and parasympathetic nervous systems on each visceral organ makes possible a rather precise *regulation* of the internal milieu of the body. In this regulation an optimal set of internal conditions is usually maintained in spite of various external or internal demands. Body temperature, blood pressure, blood sugar, blood acid-alkaline

TABLE 5-1 SOME PROMINENT FACILITATIVE AND INHIBITORY AUTONOMIC FUNCTIONS

STRUCTURE	PNS EFFECT	FUNCTION	SNS EFFECT
Eyes Iris	+	Constriction	−
Eyes Lens	+	Accommodation	−
Lacrymal glands	+	Tears	−(?)
Nasal mucosa	+	Secretion, dilation	−
Salivary glands	+	Salivation	−(?)
Gastrointestinal tract	+	Peristalsis	−
Stomach glands	+	HCl, pepsin, and mucus	0
Pancreas (islet cells)	+	Insulin	0
Heart (rate)	−	Acceleration	+
Lungs (bronchia)	−	Dilation	+
Adrenal medulla	0	Adrenaline	+
Peripheral blood vessels	?	Vasoconstriction	+
Sweat glands	0	Sweating	+
Pilomotor cells	0	Piloerection	+
Internal sphincters Bladder Intestine	−	Contraction	+
Bladder wall Lower bowel	+	Contraction	−
Genitalia	+	Erection	−

NOTE: In the table (+) indicates a facilitative effect and (−) an inhibitory effect. Note that the upper portion of the table emphasizes facilitative effects of the cranial parasympathetics, that the bottom portion separates the sacral parasympathetic effects, and that the central portion emphasizes sympathetic facilitative effects.

SOURCE: Wenger, Jones, and Jones, 1956. Courtesy of the authors and publisher.

level, and so on are kept within certain "normal" or healthy limits, and any prolonged or severe deviation from this optimal level is an indication of pathology. The balance, or rather the process of maintaining the balance, is usually called *homeostasis.*

The homeostatic function of the autonomic nervous system is obviously extremely important for adjustment. The balance is necessary to life, but it also can be temporarily thrown out of order by unusual demands. (This is the reason why stress can produce somatic disease, as was noted at the beginning of the chapter.) Demands arising from acute dangers, for example, require special mobilization of energy to deal with them. The autonomic nervous system helps make this energy available and also compensates for it. Sternbach has stated this as follows in an instructive passage (1966, pp. 23–24):

A person could live all right without an autonomic system, but to make up for the lack of internal compensators he would require a very constant and benign external environment, with moderate temperature, minimal threats, etc.

The SNS in general serves to provide "emergency" responses, and strong SNS activity has been called a "flight or fight" reaction. This is what happens. The heart beats faster, and increases the amount of blood pumped out with each beat. Superficial blood vessels and those going to the gastrointestinal tract constrict and blood pressure increases. The arteries serving the large muscles dilate and so their blood supply is increased. The pupils of the eyes dilate, increasing the amount of light impinging on the retina and thus improving visual acuity. The adrenal medulla secretes adrenaline which, besides reinforcing the other SNS effects as it circulates in the blood, also causes the liberation of blood sugar from the liver, thus making available a larger energy source for the muscles. Breathing becomes faster and deeper, the bronchioles of the lungs dilate, the secretion of mucus in the air passages decreases, and so more oxygen is available for the metabolism of the increased carbohydrates going to the muscles.

These effects, the breakdown of stored supplies and the rapid increase of metabolism, are called catabolism, and SNS functions are therefore sometimes called catabolic. The opposite effect, the restoration of supplies and slowing of metabolism, is called anabolism, and when PNS functions dominate, this anabolic process is said to occur. There is no specific emotion, like fear or rage, which clearly demonstrates this, but what happens during sleep is close enough.

During sleep the cardiovascular functions are reduced. The heart beats slower, and the volume of blood pumped with each stroke is less. The blood flow to the periphery of the body is minimal, but that supplying the gastrointestinal tract and the other abdominal organs is greater. Blood sugar is stored in the liver as glycogen. The production of mucus is increased in the eyes and nose, mouth and throat, lungs and alimentary canal. Digestive processes are likewise increased, both in the movement of the gastrointestinal tract and the flow of digestive juices. Altogether the picture is one of rebuilding, or restoring, and is quite the opposite of the massive expenditures of energy seen in catabolic (SNS-dominated) states.

We know a person is emotionally excited from some of the visible signs of sympathetic nervous system activity. But these visible signs are inaccurate because they are incomplete, hence psychophysiologists have made extensive use of more precise and reliable electrical measurements of the end-organ effects of this activity. For example, because the sweat glands are innervated by the sympathetic nervous system and their activity in turn alters the electrical resistance of the skin, it is possible to make precise measurements of sweat-gland activity by an electrophysical instrument called a psychogalvanometer. One method of doing this is to pass a tiny amount of constant current (too small for the person to feel) through the skin. The voltage necessary to create such a current will change as the electrical resistance of the skin changes because of sweat-gland activity. The change in electrical resistance of the skin is called the "galvanic skin response," or GSR. By measuring the voltage changes needed to maintain the constant current, a continuous measure of sweat-gland activity is provided. In turn, this sweat-gland activity reflects sympathetic nervous system activity, which increases in an emotional state. The same type of thing. using different electrophysiological techniques, can be done for many of the other end-organ effects of autonomic nervous system activity. For example, heart rate, skin temperature, blood pressure, or respiration can be measured and recorded by sensitive instruments.

It should be noted that one of the consequences of the antagonistic action of the sympathetic and parasympathetic nervous system on the visceral organs is that we cannot always tell whether the effect is the result of an *increase of sympathetic activity* or a *decrease of parasympathetic activity*. Both will produce the same effects. In special cases, such as skin resistance, the effect is strictly sympathetic; but this is because the sweat glands are among the few internal organs which are innervated only by sympathetic nerve endings. In most cases, when autonomically induced changes in end organs are being measured without knowing the stimulus conditions which produced them, one tends to speak generally about autonomic rather than sympathetic activity per se, because whether the effect is sympathetic or parasympathetic is not known.

A practical medical application of this equivalence of effects may be seen in the use of atropine by an ophthalmologist wishing to dilate the pupils of the eyes in order to take a good look at the retinas in an eye examination. The pupils are dilated by sympathetic nervous system fibers, while the antagonistic parasympathetic fibers, if left to their own devices, would normally act to constrict the pupils. A few drops of atropine block the action of parasympathetic fibers, thus freeing the sympathetic fibers, which are now unopposed, to dilate the pupils. The treatment of an asthmatic attack is in marked contrast. The patient's windpipe and lungs have become congested with mucus, presumably as a result of parasympathetic activity. The problem is to counteract the parasympathetic innervation. This can be done with adrenaline, a sympathetic nervous system activator. An injection of adrenaline quickly dries up the mucus and reduces its secretion, and the patient can breathe freely again. The trouble with this, however, is that sympathetic activity, in contrast with parasympathetic activity, tends to be very diffuse. Thus the patient must experience not only the pleasure of a return to free breathing, but also many other sympathetically innervated unpleasant reactions, for example, palpitations and pounding of the heart and a disturbed feeling. It is often necessary to counteract these effects by giving a barbiturate sedative at the same time the adrenaline is taken.

One of the modern applications of electrophysiological measurement of autonomic nervous system activity is *lie detection* as sometimes practiced in police work or military interrogation. Several end-organ reactions, such as changes in skin resistance, heart rate, blood pressure, and breathing, are recorded simultaneously in response to questions that are put to the person. The assumption is that autonomic reactions indexing emotion will give away the liar. A key problem is to differentiate between the guilty individual and the innocent one who is merely frightened. The lie-detection procedure attempts to handle this by contrasting the person's reactions to innocent or neutral questions with those to incriminating ones that are specifically relevant to his or her possible guilt.

Although the logic of the lie-detection proce-

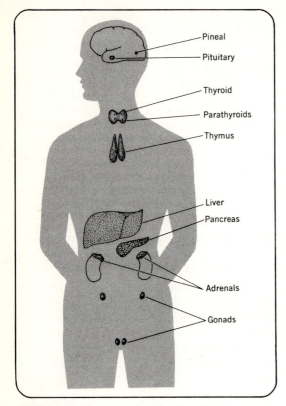

- Pineal
- Pituitary
- Thyroid
- Parathyroids
- Thymus
- Liver
- Pancreas
- Adrenals
- Gonads

FIGURE 5-5 The endocrine glands and their approximate locations.

dure is sound, lie detection by means of electrophysiological measurements is far from dependable. Individuals sophisticated in the technique will often know enough to confuse the examiner, for example, by engaging in emotional thoughts during innocent questions, or creating autonomic effects by physical means such as deep breathing which result in an uninterpretable record. Extremely labile individuals may show marked reactions to all or most questions. Nonresponsive individuals may reveal nothing. There are also ethical and legal arguments against the use of lie detection which need not concern us here.

The autonomic reactions being discussed here, such as changes in skin resistance, heart rate, or blood pressure, are not associated with emotional states alone but can be created by any condition in which homeostasis or the internal balance of the body is disturbed, for whatever reason. During strenuous exercise, for example, many of the same autonomic changes will take place as when we are angry or afraid. Although emotions will normally always activate the autonomic nervous system and the end organs it serves, such bodily changes should not be automatically accepted as signs of emotion, unless it has been possible to rule out the other causes which can also produce them.

BIOCHEMICAL CONTROL OF EMOTION

The nervous system is not the only basis of the regulation and control of adjustive behavior; there is *biochemical* control as well. A variety of biochemical substances act within the nervous system itself, influencing, for example, the speed and direction of nerve impulses at synapses. Moreover, biochemical substances secreted at nerve endings are the means by which nerves activate the organs and glands of the viscera. Thus, the nervous system itself cannot function without a host of biochemical substances which affect cellular neuronal activities and the communication between them. Some of the most obvious instances of the biochemical control of adjustive behavior are reflected in the hormones secreted by the *endocrine glands*. These are particularly relevant in emotional states. Thus, discussion of the endocrine glands follows readily from the discussion of the autonomic nervous system.

The *endocrine glands* include the pituitary, thyroid, adrenals, gonads, pineal, parathyroid, liver, and pancreas. (See Figure 5-5.) Their chemical secretions, called "hormones," are secreted directly into the bloodstream whence they are circulated to the various organs of the body.

The endocrine glands form an integrated system, one gland influencing the other. Perhaps the gland that has the most important role in the regulation of the system is the pituitary, sometimes nicknamed the "master gland." The pituitary secretes many hormonal substances each of which activates other glands in the system, for example, a thyrotropic hormone and an adrenocorticotropic hormone, substances that stimulate each of these respective glands. All of the endocrine glands are important, and though they have mutual influences, each performs some specialized function; more is known about some than about others. The glands which have received the most attention in the study of emotion are the adrenals.

There are two main portions to the *adrenal gland,* both factories for different types of hormones which have different functions. The outer portion of the gland, known as the cortex, produces several hormones called corticosteroids that serve to regulate metabolic activities (such as protein breakdown and fat and carbohydrate metabolism) and to permit maintenance of suitable water and salt balances. The corticosteroids serve an essential metabolic role in enabling the animal to remain mobilized over long periods against chronic stresses when sustained coping activity is required. These hormones have been emphasized by Hans Selye (1956) in his research on physiological stress to be described shortly. As a result of his work, psychophysiologists often assess stress reactions by measuring the amount of a corticosteroid, hydrocortisone, and other related hormones secreted in the blood or excreted in the urine.

The other main portion of the adrenal is the medulla, or inner part. Originally, the biochemical substance *adrenaline* was regarded as the prime chemical factor in emotional states such as fear and anger. Later on another hormonal substance secreted by the adrenal medulla was discovered and called "noradrenaline." These substances are known as "catecholamines," which refers to their chemical composition. This greatly complicated matters, for there was the clear implication that these two substances had over-

lapping but also different functions, perhaps associated with different emotional reactions.

What these diverse functions of adrenaline and noradrenaline are is not yet clear. It was once widely believed that adrenaline secretion was most important in states of fear, while noradrenaline was associated mainly with anger (for example, Ax, 1953; Funkenstein et al., 1957; Wolf and Wolff, 1947). More recent research (that of Levi, 1965, and Frankenhauser, 1975, among others) throws doubt on this simple formulation. Moreover, there is much overlap between the effects of autonomic nervous system activity and those of the hormones of the adrenal medulla. The two systems seem to work hand in hand in emotional states. Hormones like adrenaline seem to prolong many of the reactions set in motion by autonomic nerves. This may be one reason, for example, for the common experience that even after an adjustive crisis, the disturbed bodily state seems to continue for a while; after a near-accident in an automobile, even when the danger has passed we may find ourselves too tremulous and excited to continue driving until we "calm down." It takes a while for the hormones coursing in the blood to dissipate, and so their effects seem to last long after the situation that precipitated their secretion.

In the light of what has been said thus far about the relationship between emotions and bodily changes and their link to illness, we might examine the diagram in Figure 5-6 provided by John Mason (1970), who refers to his field of research as psychoendocrinology. In the diagram, Mason begins with a schematic drawing of the brain from which emanate neural influences on two interrelated systems, the endocrine (hormones) and the autonomic nervous system. The internal environment, that is, the operation of our visceral organs such as the heart or digestive tract, is regulated by the endocrine and autonomic nervous system, maintaining a condition of homeostasis (a steady state of the sort required to preserve life and health). When these are thrown

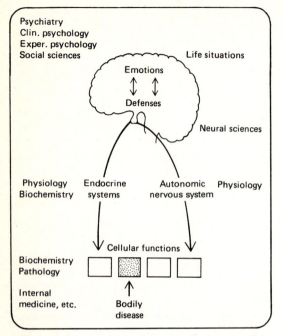

Psychiatry
Clin. psychology
Exper. psychology
Social sciences

Life situations

Emotions

Defenses

Neural sciences

Physiology
Biochemistry

Endocrine
systems

Autonomic
nervous system

Physiology

Cellular functions

Biochemistry
Pathology

Internal
medicine, etc.

Bodily
disease

FIGURE 5-6 Disciplines that must be integrated in psychosomatic research. (From Mason, 1970.)

out of kilter, illness appears to be a consequence. A third system, the skeletal muscular, is brought into play in the adjustments called for by the external environment, as when we escape or attack danger, or eat and drink to maintain life. Mason's diagram also points up the interdisciplinary nature of the professional study of stress and adjustment. For example, you will see that psychology, psychiatry, and other social sciences deal with (1) the mental processes taking place in the brain which govern emotions and our adjustments to them and (2) the relationships between these and the bodily changes they induce. On the other hand, the neural sciences are concerned with the functions of neural tissues in the brain, and physiology and biochemistry are concerned with the various neurohumoral regulatory activities linking every cell of the body. Finally, pathology and internal medicine deal with disturbances

in the cellular functions in disease. We can see that the stress emotions are not the province of one discipline but involve many, each specializing in various parts of the whole. For full understanding, each must draw on knowledge obtained by the others.

PSYCHOSOMATIC MECHANISMS

Having briefly discussed what happens to the body in emotion, let us now examine how it is that such changes might lead to bodily illness. The overall process is illustrated in Figure 5-7, which deals with one emotion, anger. In illness the tissues are temporarily disturbed but may also be seriously damaged. Thus, an ulcer not only produces pain and distress but may also eventuate in a hole in the stomach wall that can lead to death unless repaired by surgery.

How does it happen that some people develop psychosomatic symptoms while others do not, or that some people have ulcers while others suffer from high blood pressure or migraine headache? The best way to tackle such questions is to look first at the classic work of physiologist Hans Selye and then at alternatives to Selye's analysis.

SELYE'S GENERAL ADAPTATION SYNDROME

Until the time of Selye, the predominant assumption was that the reaction of a person or animal to stress depended on the specific type of stressor (say, severe cold, heat, bacterial invasion, starvation, physical injury. or psychological harms and threats) and on the physiological reactions such stressor conditions produced in a particular individual. Early in his research Selye began to notice that the physiological reactions of the stressed organism seemed to be universal and consisted of an orchestrated pattern of defense against the assault. He called this defensive pattern the *general adaptation syndrome* (Selye, 1956).

Selye (1956, pp. 15–16, 26, parenthetical statement added) writes both charmingly and personally about this discovery, beginning with his own medical school experience:

> What impressed me, the novice, much more [than the specific characteristics of illnesses] was that apparently only a few signs and symp-

toms are actually characteristic of any one disease; most of the disturbances are apparently common to many, or perhaps even to all, diseases.

Why is it, I asked myself, that such widely different disease-producing agents as those which cause measles, scarlet fever, or the flu

FIGURE 5-7 Illustration showing the neural and humoral elements in anger and some of their interrelationships (somewhat oversimplified). (Adapted from Netter, 1958.)

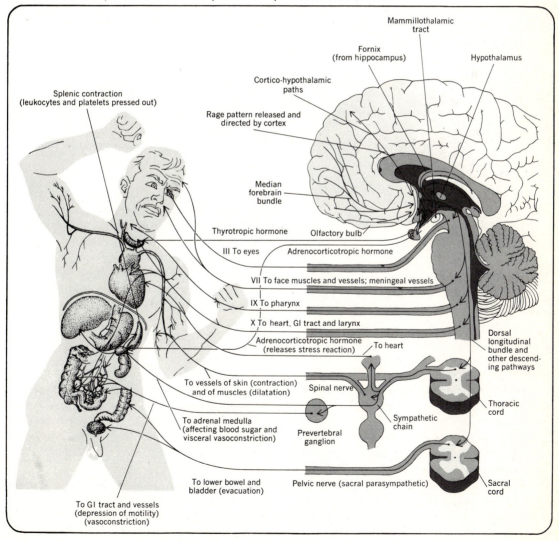

share with a number of drugs, allergens, etc., the property of evoking the nonspecific manifestations . . . ?

Yet evidently they do share them; indeed, they share them to such an extent that, at an early stage, it might be quite impossible to distinguish between various diseases because they all look alike. . . .

Surely, if it is important to find remedies which help against one disease or another, it would be even more important to learn something about the mechanism of being sick and the means of treating this "general syndrome of sickness," which is apparently superimposed upon all individual diseases!! . . .

It had long been learned by sheer experience that certain curative measures were nonspecific, that is, useful to patients suffering from almost any disease. Indeed, such measures had been in use for centuries. One advises the patient to go to bed and take it easy; one tells him to eat only very digestible food and to protect himself against drafts or great variations in temperature and humidity.

In very general terms, there are two basic ideas in Selye's concept of the general adaptation syndrome. First, he believed that the defensive physiological reaction did not depend on the stressor agent but was a universal pattern of reaction serving to protect the organism and preserve its integrity. In other words, the source of stress did not matter, and the nonspecific defensive reaction pattern was essentially the same for all animals. Physiological changes could be observed in

FIGURE 5-8 The typical triad of the alarm reaction. From top to bottom: adrenals, thymus, a group of three lymph nodes, and inner surface of the stomach. The organs on the left are those of a normal rat, those on the right of one exposed to the frustrating psychological stress of being forcefully immobilized. Note marked enlargement and dark discoloration of the adrenals (due to congestion and discharge of fatty-secretion granules), the intense shrinkage of the thymus and the lymph nodes, as well as the numerous blood-covered stomach ulcers in the alarmed rat. (After Selye, *The Story of the Adaptation Syndrome*, Courtesy Acta, Inc.)

a stressed animal. induced through use of an activating hormone secreted by the pituitary gland and referred to as ACTH (adrenocorticotrophic hormone) because its action was to release other hormones (steroids) produced in the cortex or outer layer of the adrenal glands. These latter hormones produced three key physiological changes (see Figure 5-8): (1) enlargement of the adrenal cortex associated with the production of its hormones; (2) shrinkage of the thymus gland, spleen, and lymph nodes and the consequent disappearance of eosinophiles, which are a type of white blood cell needed to fight infection: and (3) the production of ulcers in the stomach, duodenum, and intestines. These changes helped the animal to cope physiologically with the stressor agent. Moreover, one of the adrenal cortical hormones (mineral corticoids) promotes inflammation of the tissues—an important defense against infection helping to segregate the affected tissues, as in the swelling that occurs around a wound—and the other (glucorticosteroids) inhibits inflammation, so that it does not get out of hand, and raises blood sugar.

The second idea is that these very defenses, if severe and prolonged, result in "diseases of adaptation." In effect, other illness can be a cost of defense. Selye argues that effective defenses are commensurate with the seriousness of the assault. Occasionally, however, the resources of the physiological system are overextended, or, as in the case of allergy, the defense is excessive in relation to the seriousness of the assault (irritating substances in the environment), and the cure is worse than the disease, as it were. Selye postulated three stages (see Figure 5-9) of the G.A.S., the initial *alarm* stage involving very widespread physiological mobilization, the stage of *resistance* in which in the ideal case limited organ systems best able to deal with the problem become involved, and finally a stage of *exhaustion* in which the mobilized organ systems break down and lead to breakdown of the defense and

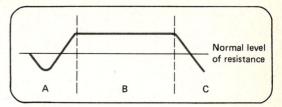

FIGURE 5-9 The three phases of the general adaptation syndrome. (From Selye, 1974.)

A. Alarm reaction. The body shows the changes characteristic of the first exposure to a stressor; at the same time, its resistance is diminished and, if the stressor is sufficiently strong (severe burns, extremes of temperature), death may result.

B. Stage of resistance. Resistance ensues if continued exposure to the stressor is compatible with adaptation. The bodily signs characteristic of the alarm reaction have virtually disappeared, and resistance rises above normal.

C. Stage of exhaustion. Following long-continued exposure to the same stressor, to which the body had become adjusted, eventually adaptation energy is exhausted. The signs of the alarm reaction reappear, but now they are irreversible, and the individual dies.

even death. Anaphylactic shock is an example of a severe and sometimes fatal reaction to foreign substances to which the person is allergic, and ulcers of the stomach or intestines which bleed and perforate also illustrate the destructive course of the G.A.S. if not corrected in time.

Some of the adaptive (in the species sense) biological processes of population control in lower animals also reflect the costs of physiological adaptation to the individual. These occur in the highly competitive and stressful struggle occurring when population density increases beyond the capacity of the environment to support it. It has been shown, for example, that the death rate among rats increases as a result of excessive adrenal cortical secretion, which in turn increases the susceptibility to disease and induces more miscarriages among pregnant females (Christian and Davis, 1964). This is good for the species because it forces the population size down to the point where life can be adequately sustained by the environmental resources. However, many individuals must die to accomplish this end.

Thus, even in ourselves chronic stress produces enlarged adrenals, as Selye shows, and this will lead to greater susceptibility to disease on the part of vulnerable individuals. Ironically, the very existence of protective or defensive physiological mechanisms against stress, when carried too far, produces its own cost in bodily illness. The term "diseases of adaptation" conveys the important idea that such defenses are a double-edged sword—aiding in defense of the physiological integrity of the person and at the same time contributing to illness.

SPECIFICITY IN ILLNESS

Although Selye's general approach to the diseases of adaptation has been enormously important and influential, there is a growing body of opinion holding that it has been overstated and that there is more specificity in the bodily response to stressors than is implied in the general adaptation syndrome. In effect, some theorists are reviving the older idea which Selye had attacked. Moreover, Selye did not pay much attention to the psychological processes that determine when adjustive commerce will be stressful (threatening, say) and when it will not. The focus of his attention was on what happens biochemically after the body's defenses have been aroused, not on the physiological and psychological signaling system that "recognizes" the noxious potentials and effects and distinguishes them from benign events. Recent writers (for example, Lazarus, 1966, 1974; Mason, 1971) have suggested that the hormonal changes comprising Selye's G.A.S. may be the result of the psychological impact on the person or animal. Thus, when an animal is injured, it is apt to sense that is is in trouble, and this psychological process may be what triggers the hormonal defensive reaction rather than the physical injury itself.

The evidence that the nature of the stressor conditon does not matter in inducing the G.A.S. is mixed at best. Mason has observed, for example, that some noxious physical conditions such as exercise, fasting, and heat do not produce the G.A.S., while others do. If a patient is dying from injury or disease and is unconscious during this death process, in autopsy the adrenals are not shown to be enlarged; however, they are enlarged if the patient was conscious during the terminal phases of the injury or disease (cf. Symington et al., 1955). What might have been left out of Selye's analysis is the crucial role of psychological factors in affecting the secretions of the pituitary and adrenal glands.

In an interesting demonstration (Shannon and Isbell, 1963), military subjects were exposed to various experimental conditions related to dentistry. In some instances the men were actually given a hypodermic needle injection. In other instances they were made to expect the injection, but the tissues were never actually touched. As anyone who has been a dental patient will understand, it was found that merely anticipating the injection resulted in as much stress reaction, as measured by an adrenal hormone (namely, hydrocortisone) in the blood, as actually experiencing the physically noxious stimulus of the needle puncture itself. Clearly, physiological changes associated with the G.A.S. can be brought about entirely by the anticipation of a painful or harmful experience, and the physical harm seems not to add any more physiological changes not already produced by this anticipation (see Figure 5-10). Whether or not this psychological process of recognizing harm or danger is crucial is still an open question.

Many researchers have also shown in recent years that the pattern of physiological reaction in stress situations is greatly affected by the specific stimulating conditions or the type of psychological reaction to them. This point has been brought home by studies of the heart rate response, which is under autonomic nervous system and adrenal medulla control. The heart rate response seems to be bidirectional, rising when a person is oriented to shut out or ignore environmental input but dropping when he or she is expecting or looking for a stimulus whose appearance can be anticipated (Lacey, 1967). Even when the anticipated stimulus is highly stressful, as, for example, just before the instant when a painful electric shock is administrered, the heart rate falls sharply (Folkins, 1970). The implication is that the physiological reaction pattern is in some degree selective and depends on the nature of the stressor.

Another example comes from biofeedback research on the self-regulation of bodily states. There proves to be a surprising degree of specificity even among autonomic nervous system end-organ reactions that are normally interdependent in the regulation of the bodily state. For example, research subjects were given pictorial feedback about their blood pressure and instructed to alter it if they could. They were rewarded if they increased their blood pressure in one condition, or if they decreased it in another. They were able to raise or lower their blood pressure although their actual heart rate remained unchanged, in spite of the fact that heart rate and blood pressure are normally closely related. Moreover, when the procedure was reversed so that only changes in heart rate were rewarded, blood pressure remained the same while heart rate could be raised or lowered (Shapiro, Tursky, and Schwartz, 1970). Again we see an example of how the physiological reaction pattern can be manipulated in a rather specific fashion.

GENERALITY VERSUS SPECIFICITY IN THE EXPLANATION OF ILLNESS

Given that there is a certain amount of both generality and specificity in the body's response to stressful conditions, how can we understand variations in the susceptibility of different individuals to psychosomatic illness and in the types of illness from which different individuals suffer? From the point of view of *generality* (á la Selye) the nature of the stressor shouldn't much matter. What then accounts for the individual variation in illness pattern? The most obvious answer is that genetic-constitutional variations among individuals result in different organ-system vulnerabilities. Therefore, when an individual is exposed to severe or chronic stress regardless of the psychological reasons, he or she is apt to develop ailments reflecting the ravages of the G.A.S. on the most vulnerable organs. If the stomach is one

FIGURE 5-10 "What next?" (Wayne Miller/Magnum.)

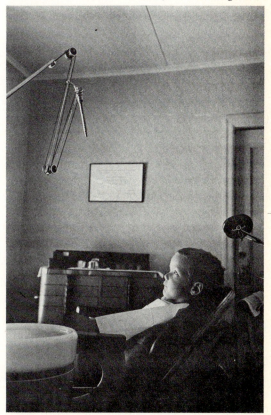

of these, for example (perhaps the lining of the stomach in that person lacks adequate buffering against chemical digestive substances such as pepsinogen), an ulcer is likely to form; or if the area of vulnerability for that person lies in the physiological mechanisms controlling blood pressure, then he or she will suffer from hypertension (high blood pressure).

What about psychosomatic illness from the point of view of *specificity*? Here the options seem to be more varied, including at least three factors related to the production of a stress emotion. First, the *formal characteristics* of the environmental or stressful demands appear to be relevant. Some time ago it was demonstrated (Mahl, 1952, 1953) that hydrochloric acid secretion in the stomach did not increase under acute stress, that is, stress that was short-lived, but was markedly affected under chronic stress. Presumably, therefore, we would not be likely to suffer from ulcers if exposed to abrupt stress episodes, but only if our stress experience was long and drawn out.

Second, the *quality of the emotional reaction* could be very important. These reactions surely depend not only on the nature of the environmental demand to which the person is reacting but also on the personality, both of which influence whether the person feels helpless and depressed, uneasy, guilty, angry, or whatever. It must also be acknowleged that Selye, in a book entitled *Stress Without Distress,* seems to have recently shifted his position somewhat about the importance of different kinds of life stress and their positive and negative impact on one's state of health. He suggests that the G.A.S. does not occur, or is at least not destructive, in all kinds of stress but only in certain ones, stating (1974, pp. 133–134): "A better understanding of the natural basis of motivation and behavior . . . should lead to choices most likely to provide us with the pleasant stress of fulfillment and victory, thereby avoiding the self-destructive distress of failure, frustration, hatred, and the passion for revenge."

There is only weak evidence at best that the body's total reaction does indeed differ among these emotional states, but the expectation that it should seems reasonable enough.

This idea is illustrated in research on the relationship between people's attitude toward certain troubling events and their bodily reaction or psychosomatic illness (Graham, 1962). In one study, for example, patients were interviewed by psychiatrists, and from recordings of these interviews judges rated the attitudes expressed by patients suffering from different psychosomatic illnesses. The psychiatrists and judges did not know which illness a patient had when doing the interviews or judging the attitudes, but there was above-chance agreement between the attitudes selected and the psychosomatic illness from which patients suffered. For example, the attitude best matching ulcerative colitis was feeling injured and degraded (being humiliated or damaged) and wishing to get rid of the responsible agent. The attitude linked to high blood pressure was feeling threatened with harm and having to be ready for anything. From observations such as these it has been suggested that each psychosomatic disease is associated with its own specific attitude, and that each attitude has its own specific physiological concomitants. And as noted earlier, such attitudes toward stressful encounters are probably dependent both on the troubling situation or environmental demand and on the personality of the individual.

Third, variations in coping processes are also likely candidates to help explain individual differences in psychosomatic illness. A person who successfully denies that he or she is in some kind of danger or has suffered some sort of harm or loss will display a diminished stress emotion (e.g., Wolff et al., 1964). If the person copes effectively by eliminating the danger, the stress emotion will also be done away with. However, if an individual constantly feels angry or anxious in some repeated or chronic interpersonal context, but is only able to bottle up the anger or anxiety by inhibiting or disguising his or her words and actions, the underlying stress emotion nevertheless should remain along with its bodily concomitants. To the extent that such continuing mobilization is physiologically destructive, we have the makings of a psychosomatic illness, the particular kind, perhaps, depending on the nature of the stress emotion itself. We have already seen in earlier discussions the important role of coping processes in the self-regulation of stress emotions.

CURRENT RESEARCH LINKING STRESS AND BODILY ILLNESS

Can a causal relationship really be demonstrated between life stress and bodily illness? Clearly, the logical and theoretical arguments for such a relationship are quite strong, and most professional workers believe that adjustive struggles and stress emotions are important in the production of illness. Yet, ironically, in spite of much psychosomatic research over many years, the scientific case for this very reasonable idea remains weak and inferential. There are many reasons why, some of the most important being the difficulty of measuring stress intensity and quality, problems of separating out the many different components of stress and coping, and the fact that in field research with humans, causal inferences depend entirely on correlational analysis, an approach not ideally suited to proving a cause and effect relationship. With humans, for example, ethical considerations prevent experiments to prove causation, so we must look to animal research, such as that of Brady and his colleagues (1958) cited in Chapter 1, in which massive gastrointestinal ulceration was produced by laboratory stress procedures. Moreover, demonstrating a general causal relationship between stress and illness is only part of the problem. What is equally important is the kind of stress (in terms of quality and intensity) capable of producing illness, and the

conditions (in the situation and the person) under which illness will or will not occur when stress is present. These more subtle and detailed issues and answers are yet to be resolved.

There has been a resurgence of research interest in the psychosomatic problem in recent years after a period of discouragement and loss of interest. This can be illustrated by two influential research programs which have also probably contributed importantly to the resurgence. One involves attempts to measure life stress in a more sophisticated fashion, and the other is a programmatic attempt to pinpoint the personality basis of individual differences in vulnerability to heart disease.

THE STRESS OF DEMANDING LIFE CHANGES

Beginning in the late 1960s, several investigators at the medical school of the University of Seattle (e.g., Holmes and Rahe, 1967; Casey, Masuda, and Holmes, 1967) began a research program on life changes and illness. This research has continued under Rahe with another group (e.g., Pugh, Erickson, Rubin, Gunderson, and Rahe, 1971) at the naval base in San Diego. One key feature of this research is the development of a questionnaire to measure common life changes that could be stressful, such as the death of a spouse, getting married, a job promotion, foreclosure of a loan or mortgage, a change of residence, and minor violations of the law, to mention a few examples. Subjects in this research had to identify their life changes over a prior period of a year or so. A second key feature was the creation and use of a scale representing the amount of readjustment presumably required by each of the life change events. That is, people were asked to evaluate the extent of social readjustment required by each of the life changes on a scale of 0 to 100, starting with marriage, which was given an arbitrary value of 50 by the investigators. What emerged, then, was a scale identifying how most people viewed the readjustment demands of many common life changes. There was considerable agreement about this for the scale as a whole among individuals and even across cultures, such as that of Japan and the United States (cf. Masuda and Holmes, 1967). Thus, death of a spouse was rated very high at 100 life change units, marriage 50 (as arbitrarily set by the investigators), foreclosure of a mortgage or loan 30, change of residence 20, and a minor violation of the law a low 11 points, and so on (see Table 5-2).

A number of separate studies were conducted to evaluate the relationship between the amount of life change units (LCU) of readjustment required of the person, say over the past year, and the likelihood that he would display some sort of illness or psychiatric difficulty. A consistently positive relationship was found. That is, the probability of later illness was greater if the person had a high life change unit score, say greater than 150, with the probability of illness increasing as the score increased from mild stress (150–199 LCU), to moderate (200–299 LCU), to major stress (300+ LCU).

One of the controversial features of the Rahe and Holmes approach to life stress and illness is the working assumption that any life change, a positive one as well as a negative one, is capable of increasing the risk of illness depending on its power to require major social readjustments. For example, included in the list of life change events are marriage, marital reconciliation, pregnancy, gain of a new family member, change in financial state, outstanding personal achievement, vacation, Christmas, and so on, any of which could be quite positive (or negative) experiences for any given individual. In short, Rahe and Holmes assumed that it is the fact of change, or, more precisely, the *adjustment required by change*, not whether the change is perceived positively or negatively, that is important in illness. Research is now being done to evaluate whether or not the kind of change and how it is appraised and coped with makes a difference, with as yet inconclusive answers.

The research cited above suffers from certain methodological difficulties that limit one's confidence in the conclusion that there is a causal link between life stress and illness. For example, many (though not all) of the studies depend entirely on retrospective verbal reports; persons making the reports, having once said that they have some illness problem, may tend to justify this by also reporting more severe stress in their recent past. People who see their health as a problem may also tend to see their lives as turbulent. Because the evidence is correlational, other equally plausible explanations could easily be advanced. Moreover, the illnesses referred to in the research are very varied, including infections, accidents leading to broken bones, surgery, and a host of psychological complaints, and little if any theory has been offered to connect such diverse forms of "illness" or to relate them all to life stresses in a consistent way. Finally, important life changes for many groups of persons such as children, adolescents, the aged, or ethnic minorities are left out of the list. To the extent the list is incomplete, there is a degree of bias in the assessment of live change units for different kinds of groups and persons. Nevertheless, the creation of a way of scaling stressful life changes is an important contribution, and further refinements of the scale and in the methodology of its use should make it possible to strengthen the observations linking life stress and illness and to facilitate more dependable and detailed analyses of the adjustmental factors contributing to illness and health.

STRESS AND HEART DISEASE

In a time when heart attacks have become a frequent cause of death and incapacity at an early age, it is not surprising to find great interest in the psychological factors that predispose a person to suffer heart disease. What makes the research program of Friedman and Rosenman (1974) distinctive is its focus on personality and life style

TABLE 5–2   SOCIAL READJUSTMENT RATING SCALE

RANK	LIFE EVENT	MEAN VALUE
1	Death of spouse	100
2	Divorce	73
3	Marital separation	65
4	Jail term	63
5	Death of close family member	63
6	Personal injury or illness	53
7	Marriage	50
8	Fired at work	47
9	Marital reconciliation	45
10	Retirement	45
11	Change in health of family member	44
12	Pregnancy	40
13	Sex difficulties	39
14	Gain of new family member	39
15	Business readjustment	39
16	Change in financial state	38
17	Death of close friend	37
18	Change to different line of work	36
19	Change in number of arguments with spouse	35
20	Mortgage over $10,000	31
21	Foreclosure of mortgage or loan	30
22	Change in responsibilities at work	29
23	Son or daughter leaving home	29
24	Trouble with in-laws	29
25	Outstanding personal achievement	28
26	Wife begins or stops work	26
27	Begin or end school	26
28	Change in living conditions	25
29	Revision of personal habits	24
30	Trouble with boss	23
31	Change in work hours or conditions	20
32	Change in residence	20
33	Change in schools	20
34	Change in recreation	19
35	Change in church activities	19
36	Change in social activities	18
37	Mortgage or loan less than $10,000	17
38	Change in sleeping habits	16
39	Change in number of family get-togethers	15
40	Change in eating habits	15
41	Vacation	13
42	Christmas	12
43	Minor violations of the law	11

SOURCE: Holmes and Rahe, 1967.

characteristics as a possible determinant of susceptibility to heart attacks.

These researchers have attempted to demonstrate that type A persons, who are hard-driving, ambitious, time-oriented (having the feeling that there never is enough time to do what they are committed to do), are more vulnerable to heart disease than type B persons, who are more relaxed, more easy-going, and less dedicated to occupational striving. They have presented data suggesting that coronary attacks are far more frequent among the former, who therefore have a much higher mortality rate. To the extent that this is true, encouraging the vulnerable type A person to ease off could have a significant effect on the incidence of coronary heart disease and premature deaths, although not surprisingly it appears to be quite difficult to change such deeply ingrained attitudinal and life-style patterns.

As in the Holmes and Rahe research, the link between heart attacks and the hard-driving—hence stressful—style of life is correlational, and the extent to which personality or life style is a causal factor in heart disease is difficult to establish firmly. Nor is the relative importance of this style in producing heart disease clear. Heart attacks are caused by many things, not one. It is possible, for example, that factors other than stress itself are linked with the hard-driving personality, such as smoking or carelessness with habits of physical hygiene, and that these latter are the factors accounting for the relationship. Or perhaps those who are typically tense from the start, perhaps for constitutional reasons, are also likely to be the hard-driving persons and to have vulnerable cardiovascular systems as a result of genetic factors. If the relationship is causal in the way Friedman and Rosenman argue, it is also not yet clear what in the type A life style accounts for the cardiovascular damage. The physiological mechanisms could depend in part on cholesterol production, which is thought to increase the rate of arteriosclerosis; deposits of fatty substances along the arterial walls narrow the coronary artery passageway and increase the chance of a blood clot and damage to the heart muscles (infarction). This could be one factor among many. Still other mechanisms involving the way blood platelets react to physical demands in type A persons have been implicated in recent research (Simpson et al., 1974). In any case, the work of Friedman and Rosenman, and others as well, is certainly strongly suggestive of a personality, stress, and heart disease link, pointing to increasingly concrete ties between the way a person lives and copes and cardiovascular disease.

CONCLUDING COMMENT

In this chapter, a number of theoretical bases have been examined for the general psychosomatic hypothesis that stress and bodily illness are linked, and we have studied some of the mechanisms of this linkage that are being proposed by those concerned with the problem. Most professionals believe that such links are important in helping us to understand a large assortment of common bodily ills. There remain a number of unresolved issues, however.

First, it is not clear to what extent all illness has psychosomatic or stress implications, or whether only certain illnesses have this tendency.

Second, it is not clear to what extent illness arises from the pattern of stressful conditions to which a person is exposed or how much of it derives from his constitutional or personality makeup, or both. This issue applies especially to the marked individual differences in vulnerability to illness in general, and to particular illnesses.

Third, there is debate about whether the relationship between stress and illness has been adequately demonstrated, and especially whether the relationship is causal. If it is causal, the specific mechanisms that translate stressful commerce with the environment into the bodily illnesses remain to be spelled out more clearly.

Finally, we are as yet quite unclear about how much stress is damaging. Some stress is clearly necessary and even advantageous. Distinctions must be drawn between the severity of the external demands on the person, as judged by others, and the ways in which the individual person appraises the troubled commerce he or she is having with the environment. From this standpoint, the measurement of severity of stress cannot depend entirely on what is happening outside the person, but must also take into account factors within the person which determine whether he or she will feel injured, threatened, challenged, or enhanced, say, by that commerce. We still do not know whether it makes any difference for the development of the diseases of adaptation if a person feels, say, challenged rather than threatened. Perhaps all that is important, as Holmes and Rahe suggest, is how much the person must mobilize in order to cope, regardless of whether his or her adjustive commerce is perceived positively or negatively. In any case, such issues are of great import for our mental and bodily health and for human adjustment in general. Perhaps future research will provide the necessary answers.

SUMMING UP

One of the most striking things about emotion is that it is accompanied by changes in one's bodily state; the more intense the emotion, the more massive the changes. This fact forms the main basis for the connection between stress (or stress emotions) and bodily illness.

Emotions and the bodily changes that accompany them are regulated by a number of areas of the brain. The perception and appraisal of danger or harm is the function of the *cerebral cortex.* The maintenance of alertness or relaxation involves the *reticular formation.* Integration of the various response systems and facets of an emotional reaction takes place in the *hypothalamus* and the

limbic system, the latter also providing that the emotional reaction is in tune with the environmental situation. Finally, regulation of the activity of the organs of the viscera, such as heart rate, vascular blood pressure, or the digestive processes, is accomplished through the antagonistic operation of the two branches of the autonomic nervous system, the sympathetic and the parasympathetic.

There is also powerful hormonal or biochemical control of the body's response in emotional states. This involves all of the ductless glands, but to stress physiologists the most important are the *adrenals.* The inner or medullary portion of this gland secretes adrenaline and noradrenaline, both extremely powerful substances (catecholamines) that are known to be involved in fear and anger, and in adjustive activity in general. The outer or cortical portion secretes a number of steroids that play an important role in metabolic functioning (say, the utilization of sugar) under noxious stimulating conditions.

The most influential work on adrenal stress physiology is that of Hans Selye, whose *general adaptation syndrome* describes a universal, orchestrated defensive reaction of the body to any kind of assault or noxious stimulation. If maintained too long or too intensely, the G.A.S. also results in *diseases of adaptation* or stress disorders; in effect, the defense or the "cure" also becomes the basis of another disease, resulting eventually in bodily exhaustion and death. Thus, for Selye a stress disorder comes about because of the severity of the body's defensive response to noxious stimulation. From this standpoint, individual differences in stress disorders arise from genetic constitutional differences in organ vulnerability to the ravages of the G.A.S.

Others have questioned the extreme generalist position of Selye, which focuses on universal features of the body's response regardless of the nature of the stressor. It has been argued, for example, that the neural and endocrine gland response to stress might depend on recognition by the person or animal that he or she is in trouble. Moreover, this response can be quite specific to the formal nature of the assault (for example, acute versus chronic), the quality of the emotional reaction (say, fear versus anger), and the type of coping process. The outlook of specificity gives a far greater role to personality in contrast with physical constitution in accounting for individual differences in stress disorders.

Two examples of current research on stress and bodily illness were also reviewed in the chapter, namely (1) the impact on illness of life changes and the adjustments they require and (2) the possible role of a hard-driving, impatient, ambitious life style (type A person) in the production of heart disease.

PART III
OUTCOMES OF THE STRUGGLE TO ADJUST

PART III
OUTCOMES
OF THE STRUGGLE
TO ADJUST

In Chapter 1 two different orientations toward adjustment were distinguished; that is, it may be viewed as a process or as an achievement that is accomplished either well or badly. Till now attention has been centered mainly on the *processes of adjustment*—on the demands or stressors to which people must adjust and the ways they cope with these stressors.

In Part III we turn to the *achievement* side of adjustment and consider how well or badly adjustment is accomplished. In Chapter 6, which deals with adjustive failure (the usual subject matter of abnormal psychology), we shall see the many clinical forms that such failure takes. In Chapter 7, The Healthy Personality, we deal with the opposite side of the coin, namely, successful living. There we shall review various attempts to conceive of psychological health and some of the main issues about which professional workers debate in their attempts to define what is healthy and what is pathological.

Sam Falk, from Monkmeyer

CHAPTER 6 FAILURES OF ADJUSTMENT

In this chapter we explore some of the psychological outcomes of a person's struggle to adjust to the stresses of living when these stresses are beyond his or her coping resources. Traditionally, adjustive failure falls within the topic of abnormal psychology or psychopathology (mental disorder), and the reader may wonder why the usual language has not been used here.

There has been a growing debate among professional workers about the suitability of medical terms implying illness and health. In view of this, it is important to avoid casual use of the traditional health/disease language pattern in the titles and headings of this chapter. Later on, in Part IV, we shall closely examine this debate about language and models of adjustive success and failure.

Aside from the bodily illnesses discussed in the previous chapter, we can say that persons are having adjustive troubles, or are in some measure failing to handle adequately the demands of living, from three telltale bits of evidence:

1 They may display behavioral "peculiarities," in effect *deviating* from societal standards or requirements. We say their actions are strange, offensive, or crazy in more extreme instances, and as such they may arouse distrust, fear, or annoyance in others. They may alarm the people around them or, at the very least, be a nuisance in social contexts. Such negative reactions are often expressed verbally in remarks like: "He's a nut," "She's neurotic," "She's sick," or "He's psychotic or insane." The burden of living with such a person is one of the primary reasons why other people feel they need to institutionalize their mentally troubled relatives or coworkers, thus putting them out of the way, though this decision is usually rationalized as providing help or treatment. Such a rationalization often has elements of truth, but much of the time treatment is absent or inadequate in our large mental institutions.

2 An observer (and sometimes the affected person) can recognize the individual in question is in trouble from impairment of effectiveness at handling environmental demands or attaining personal goals. Fearfulness about social relationships may lead troubled people to avoid otherwise desired social interaction; evaluative situations (such as school exams) may result in marked anxiety and interfere with their performance; chronic or readily aroused anger may lead them to act ineptly with a supervisor or other person whose good offices are important to their welfare; they may deeply want others to think highly of them, yet constantly alienate others by boasting or excessive humility; they may have valuable knowledge, but clam up or block in the presence of others. Whether in minor or major ways, adjustment troubles and inadequacies are typically reflected in *impairment of effectiveness* in the person's day-to-day adjustive commerce with the environment.

3 Another major reason why people seek therapeutic help for their problems is frequent or chronic *subjective distress*. The person in trouble may feel almost continually anxious, perhaps even to the point of panic; perhaps he or she is often depressed, or guilty, or angry, without having a clear understanding of where the misery is coming from. Such disturbed states of affect are, of course, products of troubled adjustive commerce with the environment.

All of us at times will experience any or all of these dysphoric states of mind. There is no clear line of demarcation between the effectively functioning and comfortable person and the one who suffers from adjustive difficulties and affective distress. The difference is a matter of degree. Moreover, an individual may do better at some times or in one setting than he or she does in another. Thus, a person who has normally functioned well and generally experiences feelings of well-being may, during periods of personal crisis, begin to display one or all of the signs of adjustive difficulty or failure.

The classic signs of adjustive difficulty or failure are, in a sense, the temporary or long-term costs a person pays for not managing life successfully. To be isolated because of "peculiar" behavior, to function ineffectively or below one's capacity, or to feel frequent or chronic distress are clearly undesirable reactions to one's life situation. The society also pays a price when such psychological disturbances are widespread in that it is deprived of human resources that might otherwise be of social value. Society flourishes when its members are well integrated into it, function effectively, and feel positively about their lives; it flounders when maladjustment is rampant.

Traditionally, the clinical professions (psychiatry, clinical psychology, and social work) have described adjustive failure by means of a system of classification that was first devised by the German psychiatrist Emil Kraepelin (1907) and subsequently revised several times. The classification system was based largely on the patterns of "symptoms" troubled people displayed. Although there has been much criticism of it and, in fact, of the entire idea of classifying mental disorders, this basic system of classification remains with us today and does have some utility. Although we will look carefully at some of the criticisms later in Part IV, we should first examine some of the major varieties of mental disorder as traditionally described.

A major distinction is made between *organic* and *functional* mental disorders. Let us examine it in some detail.

ORGANIC DISORDERS

These refer to impairments in adjustment that are clearly the result of injury to the tissues of the brain or of malfunctioning of the biochemical substances on whose operation these tissues depend. It should come as no surprise that brain damage resulting from injury, infection, syphilis, alcohol and other poisons, aging, or hereditary defects produces disturbances in adjustive behavior, especially if such conditions affect important portions of the brain—the organ that regulates all human functioning. As might be guessed, there are many forms of *organic mental disorder,* depending on the extent of injury or malfunction and its location.

When brain damage is extensive, the primary symptoms include disturbance of orientation and of intellectual functions such as memory, learning and comprehension, and judgment. A classic set of medical questions are used to test whether the patient is suffering from an organic brain disorder: Does the patient know who he is, where he is, and what day it is? Sometimes the disorientation of memory is so severe that if the patient is merely put on another floor in the same hospital wing, he or she may be unable to find the way back unaided to the original room. When disorientation is as severe as this, there are good grounds for assuming an organic disorder of the brain.

The diagnosis of an organic disorder in milder cases is not always so simple. Remember that its essential character is defined by damage to the brain. This damage may not always be readily apparent in a living person. Neurological tests aid in making the diagnosis and are effective in the most severe cases. But the brain cannot be directly seen without opening the skull, and the pattern of symptoms is not always clear enough to rule out nonorganic disturbances. Sometimes the history of the case provides clues—for example, an accident involving injury to the head or a history of alcoholism or syphilis. In the borderline case, where the neurological signs are not so clear and the history ambiguous or negative with respect to possible specific causes, diagnosis is difficult but of great importance, since the entire line of treatment hinges on whether the condition is understood to be functional or the result of brain damage.

To some extent the degree of behavioral disturbance is related to the amount of brain damage. However, the relationship between the specific damage and the symptoms is not entirely clear.

This is especially true of the personality changes resulting from the impairment of brain tissue. Some patients become irritable and even paranoid in attitude and behavior; others become docile, affable, and dependent. Some are depressed and apprehensive; others are excited and euphoric. There is by no means a simple, one-to-one relation between the suspected or known brain damage and the observed disturbances of behavior. The basic research challenge of relating brain structure and function to behavior still remains for physiology and medicine. Until the way in which the brain controls behavior is more fully known, the diagnosis of types and degrees of brain damage from behavioral disturbances will remain far from exact.

Below is an example of an organic mental disorder (Colman, 1972, p. 550) in a man who had been a successful engineer and had retired about seven years prior to his being hospitalized for the disorder:

During the past five years he had shown a progressive loss of interest in his surroundings and during the last year had become increasingly childish. His wife and eldest son had brought him to the hospital because they felt they could no longer care for him in their home, particularly because of the grandchildren. They stated that the patient had become careless in his eating and other personal habits, was restless and prone to wandering about at night, and couldn't seem to remember anything that had happened during the day but was garrulous concerning events of his childhood and middle years. After admission to the hospital, the patient seemed to deteriorate rapidly. He could rarely remember what happened a few minutes before, although his memory for remote events of his childhood remained good. When he was visited by his wife and children he did not recognize them, but mistook them for old friends, nor could he recall anything about the visit a few minutes after they had departed. The following brief conversation with the patient, which took place after he had been in the hospital for nine months, and about three months prior to his death, shows his disorientation for time and person:

DR. How are you today, Mr. _____?

PT. Oh . . . hello . . . (looks at doctor in rather puzzled way as if trying to make out who he is).

DR. Do you know where you are now?

PT. Why yes . . . I am at home. I must paint the house this summer. It has needed painting for a long time but it seems like I just keep putting it off.

DR. Can you tell me the day today?

PT. Isn't today Sunday . . . why yes, the children are coming over for dinner today. We always have dinner for the whole family on Sunday. My wife was here just a minute ago but I guess she has gone back into the kitchen.

Interest on the part of psychologists and psychiatrists in the organic disorders is considerably more limited than in the functional disorders. Perhaps one reason for this is that there is no way to get brain tissue to regenerate once it is damaged. Thus, the organic disorders appear especially hopeless and refractory to treatment. However, with the increasing percentage of our population entering the aged category because of increased longevity, organic brain disorders are becoming a major social problem. For example, it has been observed (Malzberg, 1959) that first admissions to New York State hospitals for senile disorders rose from 6.6 percent of all admissions in 1910 to 16.3 percent in 1950. A similar picture is found for cerebro-arteriosclerosis, a widespread disease of the circulatory system which can result in brain damage as well as heart attacks. Increasingly our hospitals are filled with the elderly suffering from behavioral disturbances that result from brain damage. How to assist such individuals to use their competencies and live out the rest of their years with comparative satisfaction is a social problem of serious and challenging proportions, as well as a major medical and psychological problem.

FUNCTIONAL DISORDERS

These refer to disturbances of adjustment that have not been traced to diseases of the brain. To some biologically oriented professional workers and theoreticians, this does not mean that physical pathology does not or could not be involved causally, but only that such physical pathology has not yet been definitely implicated. On the other hand, to social science–oriented professionals and theoreticians, the *functional disorders* are disorders of social living stemming from faulty learning, or *failures* to have acquired adequate patterns of coping with life stresses.

Within this large and diverse group of disorders, further distinctions are traditionally made among a number of subtypes, namely, the psychoses, neuroses, personality disorders, psychosomatic disorders, and temporary episodes of life crisis. We have already reviewed the psychosomatic disorders involving bodily illnesses in the previous chapter, and life crises and the transient psychological disturbances they may bring on have been touched upon in previous chapters dealing with stress. Here we shall concentrate on the psychoses, neuroses, and the personality disorders.

THE PSYCHOSES

Psychosis is a technical word replacing the lay term insanity; it signifies a profound disorganization of the mind. Three main classes of functional psychoses are usually distinguished: the affective disorders, the schizophrenias, and paranoia. There is a great deal of overlap between the classes, many cases showing combinations of

FIGURE 6-1 Dejection in a depressed patient. (Esther Bubley.)

symptoms which cut across categories. However, some brief descriptions of the idealized psychotic patterns will be useful here.

Affective psychoses The *affective psychoses* involve primarily disturbances of mood or emotion. Such disturbances of mood are not necessarily qualitatively different from the normal mood fluctuations that take place in most of us—periods of euphoria or gaiety, agitation, periods of depression—but they are so severe as to make a person a problem to himself or herself or to others, a public nuisance, and perhaps even a public charge.

There are two major forms, manic-depressive reactions and psychotic-depressive reactions. The *manic-depressive* reactions are marked by severe mood swings, from extreme mania to severe depression. In the manic state, the patient is elated or irritable, overtalkative, with so-called "flight of ideas" in which one idea is superseded by another at an extremely rapid rate and the person seems out of touch with the external situational events. There is also apt to be greatly increased motor activity. In the *depressive* reac-

tion, the mood is one of overwhelming sadness, hopelessness, and self-recrimination or guilt. There may be great inhibition of mental and motor activity.

Psychotic depressions externally resemble the depressed state noted above in the manic-depressive reactions. Moreover, there is often an environmental event which could have precipitated the depression, for example, a severe personal loss. This diagnostic category used to be referred to as "reactive depression," in order to differentiate it from those depressions that appear not to have been precipitated by an environmental factor. When a condition is said to be reactive, we mean that the depression is a reasonable reaction to some known event in the person's life. What makes this a psychotic reaction as opposed to neurotic is mainly the severity of the disturbance, which may perhaps involve suicidal efforts, delusions, or hallucinations. More typically, however, the patient with a depression is in fairly good contact with reality and shows no serious disorientation of thinking.

The traditional diagnostic classification system also includes another form of affective disorder, *involutional psychoses*. The separate classification is based on the timing of the disorder at the involutional period of life, for example, the menopause in women. A relationship is implied between the climacteric (change of life) and the occurrence of the disorder; this may be hormonal, or based on the psychological effect of the loss of certain physical and mental powers. The symptoms are the same as those seen in psychotic depressions. In fact, the one cannot be differentiated from the other, symptomatically. Only the connection of the affective disturbance with the involutional period of life distinguishes it as possibly a separate disorder. There is considerable doubt among socially oriented professionals that involutional depressions are in any fundamental way different from the psychotic depressions.

Some psychotic and involutional depressions are of the stuporous variety; that is, the predominant pattern is that of mental and motor retardation. Patients with this disorder are inactive and appear dejected and slow to react. They isolate themselves from other patients and are not likely to initiate conversation unless spoken to. Other depressions are of the agitated type. Patients cry, wring their hands, and cannot sleep or relax. In both cases, the predominant mood is that of depression (Fig. 6-1).

Schizophrenia There is no more puzzling or serious group of mental disturbances than the *schizophrenic disorders*. They account for about 50 percent of all hospitalized psychiatric patients and about 25 percent of the hospital beds utilized for any reason in the United States. The condition has been identified since ancient times, although knowledge about it increased rapidly in the late nineteenth and early twentieth centuries.

One of the earlier terms for schizophrenia was *dementia praecox*. It was popularized by the German psychiatrist Kraepelin, who borrowed it from a Belgian psychiatrist, Morel; the latter first introduced the term (*démence précoce*) in 1860. The

term, meaning mental deterioration (dementia) beginning early in life (praecox), was employed on the presumption that the disorder was essentially limited to youth or, rather, that it began early in life. Some years later, in 1911, Bleuler (1950) introduced the modern term *schizophrenia*, partly because he viewed the disturbance as the splitting or separation of emotional processes from thought processes. The term schizophrenia has been retained even today, although the conception of the disorder introduced by Bleuler has been much modified, and the concept "splitting of the personality" is no longer in common usage except among lay persons.

The term schizophrenia now applies to a rather wide variety of disorders that have in common disturbances of thought processes, the severe distortion of reality, frequently bizarre behavior patterns and ideas (including delusions and hallucinations), and the loss of integrated and controlled behavior. It is the most serious of the functional disturbances, the most devastating to the total personality, and the most baffling, and it has the poorest outlook for treatment of all the functional disorders. It can result in long periods of hospitalization and, in many cases, continual psychological deterioration in hospitals over a long period of years.

The most typical subclassification of schizophrenic disorders is descriptive, that is, it is based on symptom complexes of four types: simple, catatonic, hebephrenic, and paranoid. In *simple schizophrenia* there is a gradual narrowing and loss of interest, emotional flatness, and social withdrawal. There may be periods of moodiness or irritability, and overall there is increasing indifference and deterioration of personal appearance. The simple schizophrenic displays an unreadiness to assume normal obligations and often appears content to lead an irresponsible and dependent existence. Many such patients get along outside of the hospital mainly because of the good will of others; for example, their families may conceal and support them. They may also manage to get along marginally as vagrants, although such persons occasionally run afoul of the law because of sexual assaults and other antisocial activity. The simple schizophrenic seems to belong to a large general class of inadequate personalities, commonly showing a long history of inadequacy and irresponsibility. He or she commonly lacks the more colorful symptoms of other schizophrenics (delusional systems, hallucinatory experiences, and bizarre qualities of thinking).

The *catatonic schizophrenic* usually shows one of two dramatic patterns: stupor or excitement. In stupor there is a loss of animation and a tendency to remain motionless in certain stereotyped positions or postures, which are sometimes maintained for hours or days. There is minimal contact with anyone and frequently mutism (the refusal to speak), which can continue in some cases for months or even years.

There are many varieties of patterns of stupor. For example, the patient may automatically obey commands, imitate the actions of others, repeat phrases in a stereotyped way. "Waxy flexibility" can be observed; when the patient's arm is raised to an awkward position, it is maintained this way for long periods or until the position is changed. Often such a patient displays great resistance to

FIGURE 6-2 (Top) Stuporous catatonic patient on hospital ward, showing evident disregard of his physical and social surroundings, and perhaps some posturing: notice his left arm awkwardly stretched out with his hand holding something. He seems to be asleep but is probably not. (Bottom) Catatonic patient showing "wavy flexibility." (Esther Bubley.)

any effort further to change position or posture. He or she may refuse to eat, pay no attention to bowel and bladder controls, and have to be washed, dressed, and cared for as an infant. Although apparently out of contact with other persons, such a patient can notice a great deal of what is going on, demonstrating this after recovery from the stuporous condition (Fig. 6-2).

In the catatonic excitement, the patient seems to be under great pressure of activity. He or she may talk excitedly and incoherently, pace back and forth rapidly, masturbate publicly, indulge in self-mutilation, attack others, and in general exhibit a frenzy of activity that encourages restraint. This excitement can last hours, days, or weeks and even alternate between periods of stupor.

The *hebephrenic schizophrenic* shows perhaps the most severe disintegration of personality. Progressive emotional indifference and infantilism in his or her reactions are characteristic. The patient is silly and incoherent in thought, speech, and action. There is little connection between expressions of emotion, such as laughter and crying, and the circumstances under which they occur. As with the catatonic, hallucinations and delusions are common. The deterioration of behavior is so severe that the patient must be cared for like an infant (feeding, cleanliness, toileting, dress, etc.).

Cases of *paranoid schizophrenia* shade off in various degrees into the disturbance called paranoia. The extent to which paranoid or schizophrenic qualities predominate varies. The most common symptoms are delusional systems, usually involving the idea of persecution, in which the patient is suspicious of being watched, followed, poisoned, or influenced in some way. Delusions of grandeur can also be found, in which, for example, a man may believe he is some famous historical or current figure such as Napoleon, Jesus Christ, or a recent president.

If the schizophrenic pattern predominates, these delusions are bizarre, illogical, and changeable, now taking one form, now another. There

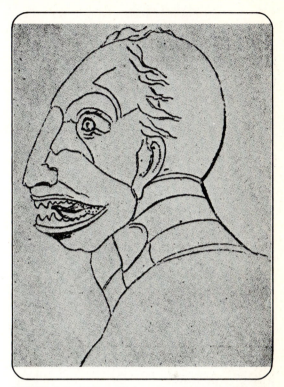

FIGURE 6-3 William Blake, who during his life displayed many symptoms of schizophrenia, portrayed one hallucination in his drawing "Ghost of a Flea." This flea, according to Blake, told him that fleas contained the damned souls of bloodthirsty men. (Born, 1946.)

will often be hallucinatory experiences, loss of contact with reality, deterioration of the personality in general, and disorders of thought. When the paranoid elements predominate, the delusional system is more logical and encapsulated in the sense that other forms of thinking and reality testing are not disturbed, and thought disorder is less prominent. The more unpredictable and changeable is the delusional system, the more clearly is there a schizophrenic process involved. In such cases the behavior and appearance of the patient are more likely to deteriorate (Fig. 6-3).

The brief conversation between a doctor and a patient below illustrates very well the paranoid style of thinking in a patient who is also diagnosed as schizophrenic because the delusional thinking is fleeting and inconsistent (Coleman, 1972, p. 276):

DR. What's your name?

PT. Who are you?

DR. I'm a doctor. Who are you?

PT. I can't tell you who I am.

DR. Why can't you tell me?

PT. You wouldn't believe me.

DR. What are you doing here?

PT. Well, I've been sent here to thwart the Russians. I'm the only one in the world who knows how to deal with them. They got their spies all around here though to get me, but I'm smarter than any of them.

DR. What are you going to do to thwart the Russians?

PT. I'm organizing.

DR. Whom are you going to organize?

PT. Everybody. I'm the only man in the world who can do that, but they're trying to get me. But I'm going to use my atomic bomb media to blow them up.

DR. You must be a terribly important person then.

PT. Well, of course.

DR. What do you call yourself?

PT. You used to know me as Franklin D. Roosevelt.

DR. Isn't he dead?

PT. Sure he's dead, but I'm alive.

DR. But you're Franklin D. Roosevelt?

PT. His Spirit. He, God, and I figured this out. And now I'm going to make a race of healthy people. My agents are lining them up. Say, who are you?

DR. I'm a doctor here.

PT. You don't look like a doctor. You look like a Russian to me.

DR. How can you tell a Russian from one of your agents?

PT. I read eyes. I get all my signs from eyes. I look into your eyes and get all my signs from them.

DR. Do you sometimes hear voices telling you someone is a Russian?

PT. No, I just look into eyes. I got a mirror here to look into my own eyes. I know everything that's going on. I can tell by the color, by the way it's shaped.

DR. Did you have any trouble with people before you came here?

PT. Well, only the Russians. They were trying to surround me in my neighborhood. One day they tried to drop a bomb on me from the fire escape.

DR. How did you know it was a bomb?

PT. I just knew.

Paranoia   The main distinguishing characteristic of *paranoia* is the delusional system, usually persecutory or grandoise. The word "paranoid" itself refers to a quality to thinking, an intellectualized system of defenses characterized predominantly by delusions which can shade off in less disturbed paranoid personalities into a general sense of grandiosity or suspiciousness. These latter patterns of behavior are not uncommon among persons functioning within relatively normal limits. Such persons can be hypersensitive and readily assume that others are talking about or plotting against them, but in the paranoid personality the delusional system never takes complete hold, and it can usually be kept under sufficient control to prevent serious trouble. It is a frequent characteristic of paranoids that they have sufficient judgment and self-control both to avoid hospitalization and to maintain limited social functioning. The suspicious or exploited inventors, the persecuted businessmen, extreme reformers and prophets, and crank letter writers are often cases of paranoid personalities, troubled but not psychotic. Their deviations do not necessarily lead to hospitalization unless they create a serious public disturbance or danger.

In the true and more rare paranoia the intellectual defense system has been elaborated to such a degree that a highly systematized delusional system is created. This often makes paranoid individuals a serious homicidal risk, and they must be hospitalized. Aside from their delusional system, their general functioning is apt to be normal. Such persons are logical and coherent, and the delusional system may not appear in casual contact, asserting itself only when they begin to feel secure in a relationship.

The delusional system itself tends to be logical, but it is built on some false premise. If one could accept the premise as sound, then frequently everything else the paranoid says follows in a reasonable way. The paranoid may call upon considerable intellectual and educational resources in constructing the delusional system, sometimes making superficial use of physical or electronic concepts; for example, a woman may believe that her mind is being influenced by some new invention, say, which sends out invisible waves on the same wavelength as her own nervous system. She is completely convinced of her delusional system and cannot be dissuaded from it. The delusional system itself is an extremely well-entrenched ego-defense mechanism, but the paranoid frequently has sufficient contact with reality to recognize that others do not accept it. When hospitalized he or she may inhibit expression of it, being aware that attempting to convince others is futile and, in fact, leads to punishment.

THE NEUROSES

The classification of neuroses in general use today includes six main forms: anxiety reaction, dissociative reaction, conversion reaction, phobic reaction, obsessive-compulsive reaction, and neurotic depression.

FIGURE 6-4 The anxiety neurotic frequently experiences muscular tension, emotional strain, and insomnia. (Charles Gatewood.)

Anxiety reaction   The term *anxiety reaction* describes one of the most common of the neurotic syndromes. It is used when the primary symptom is anxiety and when other more specific symptom patterns do not predominate. The person with an anxiety reaction describes himself as continually uneasy or "nervous," and there may be secondary complaints, usually insomnia, inability to concentrate, and various autonomic nervous system signs of disturbance (Fig. 6-4).

An interesting feature of the anxiety is that although it can be directed at specific objects or situations, the patient often cannot identify an objective source for the apprehension, or it shifts frequently from one kind of object or event to another. This kind of anxiety is usually called "free floating" because it is not attached to a single situation. The usual theoretical reason given for this is that such persons are using some defense mechanism that conceals from themselves the real source of apprehension. Anxiety can be chronic or acute. In the acute anxiety reaction or panic state, a person senses an impending catastrophe without being able to specify its nature; his or her distress can be so severe as to require sedation or considerable reassurance before the anxiety attack subsides. Panic states are usually brief, lasting anywhere from a matter of minutes to days, but they usually come to an end in a fairly short while. Occasionally such panic reactions are precursors of a more severe disturbance, such as a psychosis.

One common conception of the psychological mechanism of the more acute and severe states of panic is that strong, conflict-laden impulses have been aroused in the person which previously had been weak enough to be subdued. The person's reaction is one of panic lest these dangerous impulses break through to consciousness or into overt behavior. When previously existing neurotic defenses are unable any longer to master the stimulation, they tend momentarily to dissolve, placing the person in an acute state of panic. This state continues until he or she is able

to restore the original defenses, gets out of the situation that was too tough to handle, seeks therapeutic help, or "regresses" to a psychotic level of personality organization.

A brief description from a person (in my own clinical experience) suffering from attacks of anxiety will serve as illustration:

An eighteen-year-old male university student, in his first year, arrived at the campus psychological clinic a week before Christmas holiday with the complaint that he was extremely jittery and uneasy, but he had no idea why. He could not sleep, yet he felt exhausted. He could not study; when he started to read, his attention would wander. He had no appetite, and ate very little. His stomach hurt, and he trembled a great deal. He also had frightening dreams in which his mother appeared as a terrifying specter, with large protruding eyes, and he would usually wake up in terror and soaked with sweat.

He had been on the campus for about three months, and had been fine until just before the Thanksgiving holiday, at which time he felt very much as he did now. Saturday during the Thanksgiving weekend he decided against going home and the distress disappeared, only to reappear now just before Christmas. He was desperate, and felt that something terrible was going to happen.

When he was questioned about his plans for the holiday, he spoke warmly about his anticipated visit home, and brought out a letter from his mother on which there was a postscript from his father. The postscript seemed to this writer to be very hostile, but the student characterized his relationship at home as pleasant and rewarding, and he extolled his closeness with his father. But as the time for going home neared, the anxiety seemed to grow worse, becoming almost unbearable. When he returned to the clinic after the holiday, he was again relaxed and no longer troubled by the previous distress. Later that spring, the same symptoms again appeared, this time evidently in connection with the end of the semester and his anticipated return home.

In the course of further discussions, it began to appear that in spite of his protestations to the contrary, the anxiety was generated by the expectation of going home and having interchange with his family. There began to emerge a picture of bitter conflict between himself and his father, in spite of the earlier statement of a benign home life. He seems to have constructed in his mind a distorted (defensive) picture of his family relationship. There was no problem in maintaining this picture while he was away at school, but as holiday time came around, the realities of the tumultuous and threatening interchanges with his father and mother to which he would soon be exposed began to crowd in on him, making the maintenance of the benign fiction increasingly difficult. Each time he struggled with what was reality in contrast to the myth he had constructed, and as he faced the ambivalence about whether to go home or stay on campus for the holiday, the anxiety whose cause he did not recognize mounted virtually to panic. At Thanksgiving the firm decision by Saturday of that weekend not to make the visit home temporarily ended the threat and calmed him. But before Christmas, and again before summer when he knew he would have to go home, the conflict again surfaced along with the anxiety. Only with the later discovery of his real feelings was he able to begin to face and cope with the problem. Ultimately the next fall he was able to make further progress, although he continued to have much anxiety in connection with visits home; his subsequent attacks were comparatively mild and more manageable.

A disturbance once classified separately, but presently regarded as a variant of an anxiety reaction, is *hypochondriasis.* In this case the anxiety has been focused on the person's state of bodily health. Anxiety is the main symptom, but it is anxiety about peculiar organic symptoms or sensations. Such persons are often fearful that they may die or be seriously ill. From a psychodynamic point of view the hypochondriacal reaction is based on defenses that protect the person from a recognition of his or her inadequacies, offering excuses for failures and permitting escape from painful situations. The real source of anxiety tends to be displaced toward a preoccupation with the body and its functioning. Hypochondriacal persons are said to be using their symptoms to manipulate others by obtaining sympathy or support.

Dissociative reactions   This remarkable group of neurotic disturbances, called *dissociative reactions,* includes amnesias, fugues, multiple personalities, and somnambulisms. The common quality is a dissociation of disturbing memories or thoughts from the rest of the personality. In a sense the disturbing thoughts or impulses are simply not recognized, or forgotten, or treated as alien because they cannot be successfully integrated with the rest of the personality.

In *amnesia,* a person cannot recall certain past experiences of his life. Some amnesias are based upon brain damage, but "functional" amnesia involves no such injury. The forgotten material remains inaccessible to the patient, although it can often be restored after a time or with treatment. Because the patient cannot cope with this threatening material, it is thought to be eliminated from consciousness by repressive mechanisms. *Fugue* states are basically amnesias in which the person has a fugue (or flight), and a new life is undertaken without the forgotten memories being restored. There have been cases where persons have lived away from their original home for ten or more years, starting a new occupation, building a family, only to "reawaken" later, missing their old, "forgotten" place of origin.

Multiple personalities are relatively rare, but

the problem has recently been brought to the attention of lay people because of the successful book by Thigpen and Cleckley (1957), *The Three Faces of Eve,* which was also made into a movie. Like classic descriptions of multiple personalities (e.g., Prince, 1905, 1920), this book describes a case of a young woman who alternates between several personalities, some of them seemingly unaware of the existence of the others. It is as if several sections or systems of the personality have become separated or *dissociated* from each other, the person shifting abruptly from one to the other. Each system has distinct emotional and thought processes, each dramatically different from the other. Commonly, one personality is free and impulsive, and another is extremely inhibited or overcontrolled. (Perhaps present-generation readers who are unfamiliar with *The Three Faces of Eve* will have run across a more recent, popular book, *Sybil* (Schreiber, 1974), which describes a multiple personality apparently fractionated into sixteen temporarily separated selves before reorganizing in therapy into "the new Sybil.")

Eve White was a young woman of twenty-five who began therapy complaining of severe headaches often followed by "blackouts." She had recently been divorced following marital trouble. She seemed to be a conventional and somewhat retiring, inhibited woman. In the course of therapy, she seemed suddenly to be seized by pain, bringing her hands to her head, and then abruptly appeared to undergo a remarkable transformation to an entirely different sort of person. Thigpen and Cleckley (1957, p. 137) write about this new personality as follows: "There was in the newcomer a childishly daredevil air, an erotically mischievous glance, a face marvelously free from the habitual signs of care, seriousness, and underlying distress, so long familiar in her predecessor. This new and apparently carefree girl spoke casually of Eve White and her problems, always using *she* or *her* in every reference, always respecting the strict bounds of a separate identi-

ty. When asked her own name she immediately replied, "Oh, I'm Eve Black."

The two contrasting personalities, Eve White and Eve Black, can be distinguished in the following ways:

Eve White gave an appearance of quiet sweetness, sadness, carefulness, and dignity. She spoke in a gentle and controlled voice and dressed neatly, conservatively, and inconspicuously. She was a good and hard-working housekeeper, with a taste for serious literature, unspontaneous, honest, with a strong character that was admired by others. One had the impression that she was highly controlled, somewhat passive, a bit pathetic, and likely to be abused.

Eve Black could hardly be more different. She was mischievous, seductive, carefree, and inclined to tease, especially her counterpart Eve White, whom she saw as prissy. She dressed somewhat provocatively and expensively. She behaved in an unthinking way, was attractive and likable, but not too responsible. She had a quick and ready wit, and always seemed ready for anything, including fun. Rather than exuding pathos, she appeared joyful and exuberant, secure from stress and sadness.

After approximately eight months of therapy, a third personality suddenly emerged (Jane), apparently more mature and capable than Eve White, but with a stronger personality. Jane knew of the existence of the two Eves. She seemed to be a distillate of the other two, but yet unstable, since later on, after speaking of a traumatic experience of her childhood, Jane gave way to still another different personality, more like Jane than the other two, yet a more complete integration of Eve White and Eve Black. At the beginning of her troubles, it was as if the impulses and outlook of an Eve Black had been present in Eve White but inhibited (repressed) and submerged. Now, however, the separate, opposing identities, Jekyll and Hyde–like, had been put together again in the form of a new and more adequate person whom she decided to call Evlyn, her full legal name. Evlyn remarried and was later reported to have achieved a stable family life (Lancaster and Poling, 1958).

Still another type of dissociative reaction is called *somnambulism.* Here, systems of ideas that are thought normally to be kept out of consciousness are so strong during sleep that they determine the patient's behavior. The sufferer rises from bed and carries out some act which sometimes can be rather complex. In many respects somnambulism is similar to multiple personality in that there is a dissociation of some subsystem from the rest of the personality, and it gains expression during sleep. As in amnesias, there is usually no memory during the waking state.

Conversion reaction *Conversion reaction* is another dramatic neurotic manifestation, traditionally classified under the term "hysteria" although in many ways it is like the dissociative reactions. It is dramatic because the patient suffers from physical symptoms that have no organic basis. For example, there can be anesthesia (the loss of sensitivity of some part of the body) with the patient being unable to feel pain or any sensation in that part. Hysterical blindness, deafness, convulsions, or the inability to talk or to swallow are other examples of conversion symptoms. The patient appears to be quite unable to see, hear, or feel, but there is no structural (organic) basis for the disturbance.

Experimental proof that such disorders had a basis in psychological processes rather than neurological defects was provided decades ago (Cohen, Hilgard, and Wendt, 1933; and Hilgard and Wendt, 1933) in patients with hysterical blindness. It was also evident from the early observations (of Charcot) with hypnosis. Very commonly the conversion symptom takes a form inconsistent with the actual physical patterning of the nervous system. For example, in the classic "glove anesthesia" the entire hand up to the wrist loses all sensitivity, as though covered completely by a glove. Such an anesthesia is a neurological impossibility, but the person nonetheless feels nothing when cut or stuck by a pin or touched by an examiner. At times the conversion symptom disappears for a period or changes its locus; the anesthesia or paralysis may occur in one part of the body today and another tomorrow.

Conversion reactions were first discovered by neurologists because the pattern of symptoms suggested a neurological disturbance. The disorder played a large part in the development of Freud's psychoanalytic theory. It is interesting to note that the word "hysteria" comes from the Greek word that means "uterus." Hippocrates and other ancient Greeks thought that this disturbance occurred only in women (it is more common) and was caused by the wandering of the uterus (which had been deprived of children) to various parts of the body. Hysterical conditons were thus linked in Greek thought to sexual difficulties. Freud elaborated this concept, believing that conversion reactions originated in an unresolved oedipal sexual conflict and that the energy of the repressed sexual impulse was converted into the physical symptom. The symptom was thought to reflect or symbolize the particular nature of the conflict.

One sometimes finds in conversion patients what has been called *la belle indifférence* (beautiful indifference). They show relatively little overt concern or anxiety to indicate that they are indeed under stress. Conversion patients may report that all is well psychologically, that they are simply suffering from some mysterious symptom that they wish could be cured. The symptom frequently gives them so-called *secondary gains* such as sympathy and escape from unpleasant situations. Primarily, however, it is assumed to reflect stresses that such persons cannot face directly—stresses that are expressed as a physical symptom.

True conversion hysterias appear to be less common today than they were years ago, possibly because through education we have become more sophisticated about neurology and about the psychogenic aspects of somatic symptoms. If it is true that the conversion reaction has a heterosexual basis, it may also be that changes in our views toward sex and changes in the family structure since the late 1800s and early 1900s have reduced somewhat the potentiality of sexual conflicts as a source of psychological stress. There is little objective evidence, however, to support this impression.

The *dissociative and conversion reactions* are believed by psychoanalytically oriented theorists to involve the defense mechanism of repression. A system of impulses or ideas that is dangerous or unacceptable to the person is repressed or segmented off from the rest of the personality. It remains unconscious (is repressed) but gains expression in some special way, say through amnesias, fugues, multiple personalities, somnambulistic actions, or hysterical symptoms. The repressive defense inhibits discharge of these ideas or impulses, which can then be expressed by dissociation from the rest of the personality. Why the repressed material is expressed in one or another particular symptom pattern is not understood.

Phobias A *phobic reaction* is a chronic fear of something, often a very intense fear that seems irrational in the light of the actual situational reality. A phobia often interferes with everyday activities. A patient with a phobia about, say, balloons can be perfectly comfortable in most situations but is never able to go to a party comfortably because of the possibility that balloons will be used as decorations; the mere sight of them will elicit the fear.

Phobias can involve a wide variety of objects and situations, and fancy names have been given to such phobic reactions, some of which are very well known. For example, claustrophobia involves the fear of enclosed places; acrophobia, the fear of high places; zoophobia, the fear of animals or some particular animal. The person recognizes the irrationality of the fear but can deal with it seemingly in no other way than to avoid or flee from situations that elicit it.

An example of a phobic reaction is provided below (Maher, 1966, p. 3) in an individual whose job was threatened by his disorder:

A forty-five-year-old married man came for out-patient psychiatric treatment to a private psychiatrist. He referred himself, but under some pressure from his employer, after having taken several months of sick leave. The patient was a regional sales manager for a large investment trust company, and his duties required much traveling. Some months previously he had developed strong fears of all kinds of transportation, finding it impossible to go to an airport or railroad station or get into a car without becoming anxious and nauseous. There had been no obvious incident or accident which had been related to this fear, but its onset seemed to date shortly after he had been informed that he was being considered for the position of national sales manager in the company. As his services were valued by his employers, he was given sick leave "to get over" his fears, on the presumption that they were due to overwork. As time passed with no improvement, he was asked to seek psychiatric help or be relegated to a position of less responsibility which would not require traveling. Apart from these fears, the patient had no other complaints at the time of the initial interview.

Psychoanalytic theory treats phobias as having been acquired from a shameful impulse or act occurring early in the life of the person. If he or she is too frightened or ashamed to talk about the experience, it may be repressed, and any object or situation connected with it may become a source of subsequent fear. Psychoanalytic workers assume that the feared object or situation is really a displacement of the original anxiety to some object or idea that symbolizes the feared impulse but that, itself, is neutral. The patient remains completely unaware of the real source of anxiety. In effect, the phobia permits the person to shift his or her attention to a relatively innocuous object or circumstance, thus avoiding recognition of the real impulses and threats associated with the repression. In addition to a strong fear experience early in life, there is presumably some reason why the person refuses to verbalize or label the original experience, so a phobic person usually cannot say why such a strong irrational fear exists. This psychoanalytic explanation is rejected, however, by behavior theorists, as we shall see later in the chapter on psychotherapy.

Obsessive-compulsive reaction Patients with an *obsessive-compulsive reaction* seem to be forced against their will to think about something (obsession) or to engage in unwanted actions (compulsions). They usually recognize the irrationality of their reaction but feel they can't help themselves. This tendency to have obsessional thoughts or engage in compulsive acts is not unusual and need not reflect a serious neurosis. A tune keeps repeating in the mind; a person cannot seem to stop thinking about something that recently happened; we feel impelled to engage in some ritualistic act like regularly straightening up our desk, or we drum our fingers on the table in some symmetrical or rhythmical pattern. Children commonly engage in various compulsive rituals, like stepping over the cracks on sidewalks, doing things by twos, or walking around a ladder instead of under it.

Patients with a severe compulsion neurosis have been known to wash their hands needlessly dozens of time a day. The compulsive act seems to reduce anxiety to some degree, but there is an insatiable need to persist in the ritual. In *Macbeth,* Shakespeare captured the essence of an obsessive-compulsive reaction with great vividness and insight; after the murder of the king, Lady Macbeth is obsessed with the idea that she still has blood on her hands and cannot wash it off, trying over and over nevertheless and crying, "Out, out, damned spot." In the neurotic instances of obsessive or compulsive behaviors, the thoughts or acts involved are more difficult to get rid of or control than in the more ordinary versions, though they probably have a similar significance. They serve no useful purpose and are regarded as silly and unwanted by the person, seriously disrupting everyday behavior yet seemingly impossible to prevent without causing the person to be overcome with intense anxiety.

The obsessive-compulsive reaction, like the phobia, theoretically involves the transformation of certain unacceptable or threatening impulses to another form. In the case of obsessions, the thinking of certain thoughts keeps other, more terrible, thoughts from having to be faced. In psychoanalytic theory, such thoughts involve dangerous hostile or sexual impulses, but the threatening aspects of these thoughts have been disguised. Below is an instance of a patient who defended himself against repressed aggressive impulses toward his family by developing exaggerated fears concerning their safety (Masserman, 1949, p. 43):

A successful executive who for various reasons hated the responsibility of marriage and fatherhood was obsessed many times a day with the idea that his two children were "somehow in danger," although he knew them to be safe in a well-run private day school to which he himself brought them every morning. As a result, he felt impelled to interrupt his office routine twice daily by personal calls to the school principal who, incidentally, after several months began to question the sincerity of the patient's fatherly solicitude. Similarly, the patient could not return home at night without misgivings unless he brought some small present to his wife and children, although, significantly, it was almost always something they did not want.

Compulsions, in a sense, represent attempts to deal with danger by ordering everything in such a way that the person will be safe. Compulsions can also represent attempts to undo unacceptable impulses—for example, washing one's hands because they are somehow unclean, metaphorically speaking, or because of immoral acts, as in the case of Lady Macbeth. For the neurotic person, having the wish or impulse is as threatening and reprehensible as having actually performed the tabooed act. The compulsions are thought to represent defensive reactions against impulses and the continual undoing of the situation in order to make things right. Sometimes the actions are direct representations of the guilty impulse or act, or they can be disguised or symbolic representations of it. The compulsion tends to establish controls which protect the patient from the impulses he or she fears. We frequently speak, for example, of someone who works compulsively. That person may follow an exhaustive schedule of daily activities, thus making other, perhaps threatening, activities impossible.

Neurotic depression *Depressive reactions* may range from mild to extremely severe. The latter are usually defined as psychotic, the former neurotic. They can occur without any evident basis in the external circumstances of the person's life, or they may be clearly reactive to specific circumstances of loss. The symptoms of both types include dejection (even hopelessness), discouragement, sadness, feelings of worthlessness, and guilt. In the reactive depression there is usually a precipitating cause, and when this cause has been removed, the depressive reaction eventually disappears.

Neurotic depressives are evidently predisposed to develop depressed feelings in situations to which others are not apt to react so strongly. Because of unconscious feelings of hostility, for example, such persons could be especially prone to react with guilt when there has been a loss or death of someone close. The depression is overdetermined and excessive; that is, it is not a normal response to a personal loss, but appears to be unreasonably extreme and generally complicated by the person's guilt feelings (Lindemann, 1944).

DISTINCTIONS BETWEEN NEUROSES AND PSYCHOSES

The American Psychiatric Association (APA) diagnostic manual of 1952 states (p. 31): "In contrast to those with psychoses, patients with psychoneurotic disorders do not exhibit gross distortion or falsification of external reality (delusions, hallucinations, illusions) and they do not present gross disorganization of the personality . . ."

Thus, in the psychoneuroses, not only is the extent of personality disorganization presumed to be less extreme and involve less reality distortion, but there is less likelihood that the person will be hospitalized because the deviancy does not threaten the decorum or safety of the community. The psychoneurotic patient suffers, but the suffering is less likely to involve those nearby. Psychoneurotic patients may lack insight into the causes of their difficulty, but they usually know that something is wrong. Psychotics, however, typically will not even recognize their behavior as deviant. Psychoneurotic patients do not usually lose control over their impulses and, thus, rarely appear dangerous; psychotics may act quite primitively with respect to impulse expression, thus frightening and offending greatly those around them.

One of the fascinating and unsettled questions about psychoneuroses and psychoses has to do with the theoretical relations between them. It has been suggested that the neuroses, while appearing quite different in many respects from the psychoses, nonetheless represent earlier, milder stages in the disorganization of the personality under stress (Menninger, 1954). That is, neuroses are more integrated ways of dealing with stress, while psychosis is more severe and involves more primitive forms of coping; it is, in short, a "regression" to a more primitive level of functioning. The neurotic ego is weaker and less adequate than that of the healthy person, but more capable indeed than that of the psychotic who cannot even maintain the most tenuous neurotic forms of adjustment. Presumably, if the neurotic person fails to maintain his shaky integrity under stress, the situation might become overwhelming and cause further regression into psychosis (Fig. 6-5).

There is some research and observational support for the above idea, although the evidence is in no way conclusive. One bit of evidence comes from anecdotal observations of patients initially displaying clearly neurotic types of disturbances and defense who later develop temporary psychotic episodes during which the neurosis appears to break down into a more disorganized psychotic pattern. If such patients recover from the psychotic episode, they sometimes appear to return to the original neurotic defensive pattern.

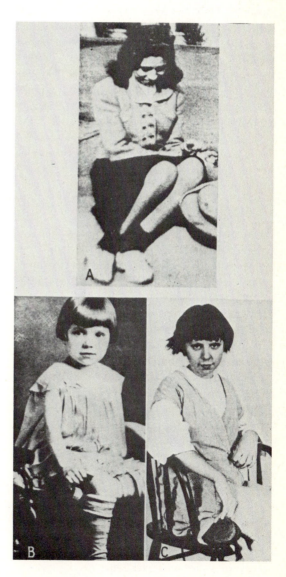

FIGURE 6-5 An example of regression. (A) Photo of young woman of 17 who came from a very troubled family background. She had first showed symptoms of disturbance at the age of 4, when her parents began to quarrel violently. When she was 7 her mother refused further sexual relations with her father, but the girl continued to sleep in his bed until she was 13. Suspecting that the girl was being incestuously seduced, the mother obtained legal custody of her and moved with her to a separate home. The girl resented the separation from her father, quarreled with her mother, and became a disciplinary problem at school. When she was 17, she insisted on visiting her father and found him living with a girl "in questionable circumstances." A violent scene ensued, and again her mother took her home against her wishes. After this she refused to attend school and became sullen and withdrawn. In her mother's absence she went on destructive rampages in the house, and on one of these forays found the photograph (B) of herself at the age of 5. Using this as a model, she cut her hair to a baby bob and began to affect the facial expression and posture of the pictured child, as shown in photo (C). She became infantile and untidy and no longer controlled her urine. She "appeared to have regressed to a relatively desirable period in her life antedating disruptive jealousies and other conflicts; moreover she acted out this aggression in [probably] unconsciously determined but strikingly symbolic patterns. . . ." (From Jules H. Masserman, *Principles of Dynamic Psychiatry*, Plate I. Philadelphia: Saunders, 1961. Photos and data courtesy of Dr. John Romano and Dr. Richard Renneker.)

Although this does not prove a functional relationship between neurosis and psychosis, it is consistent with the idea that psychotic defenses arise only if neurotic solutions fail.

Furthermore, studies of the formal characteristics of the perception and thought patterns of normal persons, neurotics, and psychotics (Hemmendinger, 1960) suggest that the thought patterns of schizophrenics appear similar to those of young children. The severely disturbed individual is thus said to regress (go backwards) to more primitive, earlier-developed styles of thinking and adjusting. While the psychotic's style of thinking appears to resemble formally that of the young child, the neurotic's is more advanced and similar to the older child or adolescent, and the normal is still more advanced. Thus, it seems plausible to suggest a developmental link in psychological functioning in the psychoses and the psychoneuroses.

PERSONALITY DISORDERS

These disturbances, sometimes referred to as "character disorders," differ theoretically from the psychoneuroses and psychoses in very fundamental ways. With the psychoneuroses, unresolvable internal conflicts are thought to threaten the person and to be dealt with by various ego-defensive processes each of which defines the particular subcategory of neurosis. In the psychoses there is said to be a breakdown of defenses, a regression to a more primitive and disorganized mode of functioning. In contrast, the *personality disorders* are characterized by a general failure to acquire effective habits of adjustment and adequate social relationships. Instead of suffering from internal struggles or conflicts, the individual seems to display a developmental ineptness in dealing with the environment. Whereas the predominant features of neurosis are anxiety and self-deceptive defense, the personality disorders give evidence of little anxiety or personal conflict; rather, such persons display a lifelong pattern of disturbed social behavior.

Let us examine a few diverse examples of personality disorder. As we saw earlier, the *paranoid personality* shows the style of thinking of the true paranoiac but in milder form and without any full-blown delusional system. A man with this personality characteristically behaves toward others with suspiciousness, envy, jealousy, and stubbornness. He is ready to believe that others have taken advantage of him, or will do so, that his work has not received ample recognition, or that others have profited at his expense. It is not at all clear whether the sensitivity to insult and the suspiciousness seen in the paranoid personality have the same origin (that is, reflect the same defensive process, say, projection) as in the paranoid psychotic, although this seems to be the usual assumption.

The *passive-aggressive personality* shows extensive inability to deal with interpersonal relations, expressing itself in one of three patterns, passive-dependent, passive-aggressive, and aggressive. The passive-dependent pattern involves helplessness, indecisiveness, and the tendency constantly to manipulate relationships with others so that the person will be taken care of or given emotional support and direction. The passive-aggressive pattern shows continuing hostility, not so much in direct opposition, but in passive, indirect ways, such as pouting, stubbornness, procrastination, inefficiency, and indirect obstructionism. Instead of opposing a suggestion, such a person may appear to follow it, while characteristically obstructing its completion in the ways mentioned. Finally, the aggressive personality typically reacts to frustrating situations with irritability, temper tantrums, and destructive behavior. Said to underlie all three patterns is a basic core of dependency or passivity, sometimes disguised broadly, as in the aggressive pattern.

Persons with *antisocial patterns* are usually in continuous social or legal trouble. Such persons appear to profit little from punishment and maintain no deep loyalties to other persons or groups. They seem callous and concerned only with their own immediate satisfaction; they are often said to be lacking in conscience. Other terms which have often been used to describe this personality pattern are "psychopath" and "sociopath."

Addictions to drugs and alcohol are also classified psychiatrically under the general category of personality disorders, specifically within the group of "sociopathic disturbances," although there is a movement away from this kind of labeling in recent years. The latter term, applied to any consistent antisocial behavior, implies a lack of conformity to the social norms or values of the society in which the person grows up. Although a chronic pattern of drinking may result in damage to the brain and the production of a chronic brain disorder (Korsakoff psychosis), problem drinking itself as a behavior is typically classified as a personality disorder (Fig. 6-6).

There is by no means a clear definition of what constitutes alcoholism. How much drinking it refers to, or for how long a period, cannot be readily specified. Many people drink heavily without apparent impairment of their functioning, or without ever coming to the attention of a clinic or hospital, the law, or a medical specialist. Others who drink heavily cannot hold a job or manage the usual social tasks of life.

Alcoholism is not usually regarded as a physiological disorder but is classified as a disorder of personality. Drug addiction is similarly classified, even though the person who is physiologically addicted suffers extreme physiological disturbances when deprived of the drug. In both instances the assumption is made that the person is escaping difficult-to-solve interpersonal problems by the use of alcohol or drugs. Such a statement might seem strange to the reader in view of the public clamor aimed at the addicting substance itself, as if its presence were the problem. The focus of attention is often directed at making alcohol unavailable to teenagers (about half of the young people in the United States have tried alcohol by the time they are fourteen, and that figure rises to 80–85 percent by eighteen years of age—see Hornick and Myles, 1975, p. 12)

FIGURE 6-6 The alcoholic experiences a mental obsession and a physical compulsion to drink as the disease progresses. (Ingeborg Tallarek, from Nancy Palmer Photo Agency.)

or controlling the supply of heroin, for example. On the other hand, the statement above places the responsibility on the person rather than on the substance, which is the way professional workers tend to see the problem. This can be illustrated in the following extract from Ottenberg (1975, pp. 7–8):

We appear to be focusing intently on alcohol, the substance being abused, rather than on the abusers, their environment and the manner and meaning of their drinking—just as a few years ago when, under the shaping influence of governmental authorities and the media, public interest was riveted on marijuana, on LSD and heroin, on crime, on "pushers," on the poppy fields of Turkey, and on every part of the complex network of interacting forces involved in the addictive problems; and least of all, and last of all, on the addicts, on the alcoholics, on the abusers, and on the culture medium in which the problems generated and flourished: our society.

For too long we have been trapped in the fallacy of thinking alcoholism, narcotic addiction, drug abuse, polydrug abuse and now teenage alcohol abuse as separate and distinct problems, when we ought to perceive them as different aspects of the same generic problem—substance abuse. Of the three interacting variables (the person, the environment and the substance) that determine whether and how a person will abuse a substance, the least important for understanding the problem and doing something useful about it, though usually the most talked about, is the substance. . . .

Consider the following brief account of a teenage drinker from Hornick and Myles (1975, pp. 13–14):

Don is black, an eighteen-year-old senior in high school. His mother migrated to New York from the South before he was born. The youngest of three children, he is not an alcoholic, although alcoholism is more commonly found in only children and youngest children. He started sipping alcohol at ten and was drinking regularly at fourteen. He likes blackberry wine best, smokes pot often, and sniffs cocaine on occasion. He has experimented with "dope" (heroin) and LSD, but he has never been a habitual user of either. He drinks a pint or more of wine a day—every day—and has been drunk only twice in his life.

Don likens school to a plantation where the masters are eager to flunk students and reluctant to teach the course material. His life apart from school works fairly well for him. He has delivered papers in the morning since he was fifteen, and with the proceeds he has been

dealing pot. This nets him enough money to buy clothes, to drink, and to date. His parents are separated, and he lives with his mother who is a churchgoer and a teetotaler. She disapproves of his drinking, but he is discreet and she is ignorant of his conduct. He has never been arrested.

We became acquainted with Don in a rap group which he used to "clean up" what he called his "mess." He realized that, despite his hatred of the school and the teachers, he might as well be graduated. So he organized his course work to finish this year, and he is considering college. Don is a typical "drinker" in our neighborhood; he is not considered an alcoholic by us or by himself.

Now let us look at a second account, in which the progression of alcoholism has reached the stage of interfering seriously with a person's life (McNeil, 1967, pp. 185–186).

Norm R. would get a little high at parties and live it up too much but this was harmless and most often went no further than boisteriousness, talking too loud, telling dirty jokes, and slopping his drink on other people. When he did get totally drunk, it was usually the aftermath of being nagged by his wife who felt he always acted like a fool when he got a little liquor in him.

The superego or conscience is one part of the human psyche that can be dissolved by alcohol. This is what happened to Norm R. His usually temperate, reserved, polite, cautious self faded away, and the "other" Norm would leap vigorously onto the scene. When Norm was drunk, he could never judge accurately if he was being hilariously funny or just plain repulsive. If his judgment about people could be described as substantially diminished when he drank, then his judgment about his perceptual skills under the influence of alcohol could only be called disastrous. From friends' reports, he really believed he could drive as well drunk as he could sober. It is more probable that he was convinced he could drive drunk better than most other drunks. He had once gotten home by driving the car with the wheels on its right side rubbing against the curb. When he came to an intersection, the car would lurch to the right and prod him to alertness again for another block. He made progress in this fashion for about two miles till his car stalled and he fell asleep on the front seat. He was more than a little startled when he was awakened rudely by the homeowner whose driveway he blocked when he fell asleep.

Tonight it was happening again. He was trying to hug somebody's wife when a shoving match began with the aggrieved husband. That tore it as far as Norm's wife was concerned and she made the mistake of chewing him out in front of the others. Norm slammed out of the party filled with righteous indignation and a gnawing sense of guilt. He took the wheel of his station wagon, fumbled with the keys for a minute, and roared out of the driveway.

It had gotten much colder, but Norm's thinking was disconnected and focused mostly on the indignities he had just suffered. He was talking out loud to himself as he drove and swearing fruitlessly at everything that was wrong with his wife and the world in general. The damn windshields were filthy, he thought. He missed his first pass at the windshield-washer button and when the wipers finally started to sweep the windshield it took him a few seconds to realize that the water on the windshield had frozen cutting off his forward vision completely. Norm glanced out his left hand window at the curb to keep from driving out of his lane and began, slowly, to apply the brakes. The street was icy so he eased off the brake pedal for a second when the car started to skid. This was the last Norm could remem-

ber. Norm's wife told me the rest of what happened.

I was in a blind rage when he left the party and tried lamely to explain to everybody that Norm had been sick lately and shouldn't have had so much to drink. Boy, was I going to get him when I got home. I finally arranged to ride home with a girlfriend and he still wasn't there when I got there. That didn't bother me too much because I was mad and knew he usually went someplace to drink and sulk for a while and then would sneak home and sleep it off on the couch. He's really a good man if he doesn't drink and he doesn't act like a fool very often. Well, I was tired so I went to sleep. Then about seven o'clock in the morning the police called and said he had had an accident and was in Receiving Hospital. They wouldn't tell me how badly he was hurt so I got the kids off to school and got a taxi to take me to the hospital. The police were there and they told me he hit the steering wheel with his face and then hit the windshield with his head. He never would wear his seat belt unless I yelled at him about it and this was exactly what I thought might happen some time. His windshield was all iced over and there's a pedestrian island right there on Jefferson Avenue and a lamppost so people can see it. The police said he hit the lamppost head on and never knew what happened when he flew into the windshield. I don't know what we are going to do now. He can't work and we've got bills piling up.

An alternative conception, proposed by organically oriented professional workers, is that the alcoholic (the person who cannot any longer seem to control the impulse to drink) suffers from a biochemical anomaly which presents itself as an abnormal tissue need for alcohol, making it impossible for him (or her) to prevent further drink-

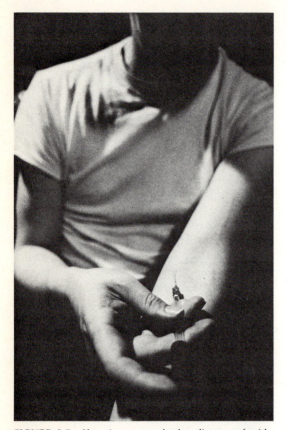

FIGURE 6-7 Shooting up ends the distress of withdrawal from heroin. (Steve Rose, from Nancy Palmer Photo Agency.)

A.A. is estimated by the National Council on Alcoholism, Inc., to have a membership of 400,000 persons.

Alcohol can be taken in mild or moderate doses by many persons throughout their lives without the development of addiction or later brain damage, but the steady use of any narcotic drugs derived from opium, such as morphine and heroin or cocaine, will usually lead to addiction within a relatively short time, especially if it is taken by direct injection into the bloodstream. The problem of drug addiction is a serious one because in our society it usually leads to a severe deterioration of behavior; the drug must somehow be obtained to prevent serious withdrawal symptoms. It is difficult to treat because, like alcohol, the drug produces an escape from severe problems, and the cessation of its use produces symptoms which are so painful and terrifying that an addict, unless hospitalized, will commit criminal acts to prevent them.

The first symptoms of *withdrawal* (which is the true sign of physiological addiction) are yawning, sneezing, sweating, loss of appetite, and a growing desire for the drug. There follow increasing restlessness, depression, feelings of impending doom, and irritability. There may be chills alternating with excessive sweating, vomiting, diarrhea, abdominal cramps, pains, and tremors. In severe cases there may even be cardiovascular collapse, which can result in the death of the patient. The administration of the drug at any point during the withdrawal syndrome shortly ends the distress, but then the patient must continue to have more and more of the drug to prevent the recurrence of the withdrawal syndrome. The withdrawal syndrome itself usually lasts about a week or more, with its peak around three to five days. The tolerance that the patient has built up for the drug during the addicted period disappears after the withdrawal symptoms have ceased, and if the patient becomes addicted again, he or she must begin with smaller dosages all over again (Fig. 6-7).

As in the case of alcohol, there is a deteriora-

ing if he once allows himself to take the first drink. More will be said about such conceptions in Part IV.

Popular treatments of the subject of alcoholism have helped familiarize the lay person with the problem. Most professional approaches to the treatment of alcoholism have been conspicuously unsuccessful. This has been a factor in facilitating the work of the therapeutic fellowship known as Alcoholics Anonymous, whose efforts focus on keeping the member from taking the first drink, making him or her feel a welcomed part of a group which shares the problem, and devotedly assisting the person who slips back into drinking.

tion of behavior, a reduction in health, ostracism by society, and frequent criminal behavior in an effort to obtain the expensive doses of the drugs. If the drug addict could maintain a well-balanced diet and an adequate supply of drugs (this is, of course, difficult because in the United States narcotics are illegal), he or she might remain in this addicted state indefinitely. This type of approach has been followed in Great Britain by physicians, who are legally able to administer such drugs routinely. The success of the English approach is a subject of some current disagreement, especially its use in the United States.

The treatment of drug addiction is difficult because, even after the immediate addiction has been eliminated by withdrawal of the drug, the same "characterological" problems push the person to return to the habit. If a person after treatment is still unable to face the old problems, the drug pattern will, in all likelihood, begin all over again. Recently in the United States the use of methadone has come into considerable favor in the search for a successful treatment method against such opiate drugs as heroin, cocaine, and morphine. Methadone is also a narcotic; with proper use it does not seem to create the "high" characteristic of heroin, though if injected it can also apparently do so. Yet many users seem able to manage their life and work successfully on it. The long-term value of methadone remains controversial. It is not clear, for example, whether the methadone addiction and dependence can be any more easily broken than addiction to other opiate drugs, and much research on this problem is being conducted throughout the country.

In describing the various forms of adjustive failure, I have been using the main outlines of a system of clinical classification that has been in use for roughly three-quarters of a century, one that despite its advantages has also been subject to much criticism along many diverse lines. It is important to discuss the bases of this criticism and the issues that are inherent in it, but it is best to defer this until we have examined what is

meant by psychological health or successful living and have reviewed in Chapters 8 through 11 the various ways professional workers have tried to explain success and failure. Later on, in Chapter 12, we shall examine problems of classification along with the explanatory models in use both in the past and currently. Therefore, let us proceed directly to successful adjustment in Chapter 7.

SUMMING UP

Over and above bodily illness, a person may display adjustive failure in any or all of three ways, namely (1) actions that seem peculiar or strange because they deviate from societal standards and may even disturb or alarm others, (2) impairment of effectiveness in managing the adjustment tasks of living, and (3) frequent or continuing subjective distress including, say, anxiety, depression, anger, guilt, and the like. Adjustive failure manifests itself in a wide variety of types and degrees, and this is reflected in the traditional system of classification that has been used clinically with slight variations for roughly seventy-odd years.

In this system, a key distinction is made between organic disorders and functional disorders. The *organic disorders* involve damage to the tissues of the brain as a result of injury, hormonal or toxic disturbances, infectious disease, and so on. The patient's disturbed and disoriented behavior is attributed to this organic damage. Typically, such patients show disturbances of memory, perception, and thought, sometimes mild, sometimes severe and incapacitating, as in the organic psychoses.

Functional disorders involve no such brain damage, though physiologically oriented clinicians tend to assume that brain damage or malfunctions as yet undiscovered are implicated causally in all or some forms, for example, the psychoses such as schizophrenia. The main classes of functional disorder include the psychoses, the neuroses, and the personality disorders.

The *psychoses* (in lay language, insanity) are the most severe forms of adjustive failure and involve profound disorganization of the personality. There are three main subcategories, the affective disorders, the schizophrenias, and paranoia. *Affective disorders* are primarily severe disturbances of mood, for example, depression and mania or manic excitement. *Schizophrenia* is the most common form of severe mental disorder, or psychosis. There are apt to be disturbances of thought, severe distortion of reality, bizarre patterns of behavior and ideas, delusions and hallucinations, and the loss of integrated and controlled behavior. *Paranoia* is a mental condition in which the person displays delusions of grandeur or of persecution. In true paranoia, the delusional system is highly organized and logically integrated, though the basic premise is unreal or lacks adequate foundation. Paranoia can shade off into paranoid schizophrenia, in which delusional thinking is a prominent symptom, but it is changeable and less systematic. Mildly paranoid persons may remain in pretty sound control of themselves and the world in which they live yet be repeatedly suspicious of others or believe that they are being taken advantage of or exploited. In an indifferent and often competitive and hostile world, one can see how difficult it might be to distinguish between the hypersensitivity of a person who with justification feels abused or exploited, as in a member of a minority with a history of persecution or exclusion, and one who is expressing a paranoid mentality without evident external provocation.

Neuroses reflect generally less severe types of adjustive disturbance than psychoses, but nonetheless represent a troubled, conflict-laden adjustment characterized by chronic use of one of a number of ego-defense mechanisms, such as repression, reaction formation, intellectualization, and so on, in situations of stress. Six forms of neurosis are typically distinguished, depending on the symptoms that predominate. These include anxiety reaction, dissociative reactions, conversion reaction, phobias, obsessive-compulsive reaction, and neurotic depression.

Personality disorders are characterized by the failure to acquire effective habits of social adjustment and adequate social relationships, as contrasted with the neurotic and psychotic pattern of internal struggles, subjective distress, and defense or regression to primitive modes of functioning. The person with personality disorder has grown up without acquiring the skills needed to manage his or her affairs and get along with others in society, or without adequate socialization.

There are serious defects in the traditional clinical system of describing and classifying patterns of adjustive failure, and there has been of late considerable criticism too of psychological classification in general. But discussion of this is best left until a later chapter, after explanations of adjustive success and failure have been dealt with.

CHAPTER 7 THE HEALTHY PERSONALITY

It would seem to be obvious that successful living must be just the opposite of adjustive failure. Therefore, all we need to do to understand successful living and its psychological features is to invert the analysis of failure. We might then emerge with the plausible but inadequate idea that successful living is equivalent to the absence of stress-related bodily illness, unimpaired adjustive functioning, behavioral normalcy, and subjective comfort. Indeed, this is the way mental health professionals tended to view the matter up until roughly the 1950s. You were mentally "healthy" if you fitted nicely into the world in which you lived with minimal signs of stress and discontentment—if you resembled, so to speak, a contented cow.

The events in Germany before and during World War II, among other things, raised serious questions about such an outlook. Did mental health mean, for example, that if you were a German in the mid-1930s you should conform to the Nazi social pattern and accept the values and conduct of the Hitler regime? What if you could not adjust to such an evil social system or if you fought it? To do so would surely lead to being treated as a pariah or worse, with the inevitable stress and distress that this would bring about. Would such signs of conflict identify you as an adjustive failure? On the basis of the above definition of mental health as the opposite of pathology, the answer is "yes." Yet something is clearly wrong, or at least something is incomplete, with this traditional outlook in which successful living is synonymous with being in comfortable conformity to the requirements of the social environment. Indeed, this very value-laden issue spawned a widespread questioning in American clinical and social science of the traditional psychiatric outlook. Some of the questioners ultimately identified with the expression "positive mental health" and began to seek alternative definitions of successful living.

FIGURE 7-1 The Nazi "final solution" for the Jews: endless piles of incredibly thin corpses awaiting burial in a common grave at Belsen, Germany, 1945. (United Press International Photo.)

ATTEMPTS TO STUDY HEALTHY PERSONALITIES

Because the concepts of mental health and psychopathology are so closely connected, and because those who have taken the greatest interest in them were mostly practicing clinicians treating people in trouble, systematic observations of persons managing their lives reasonably well are very scarce. Thus the observational data base for such concepts was and still is quite inadequate. We know very little about the day-to-day emotional lives of ordinary people in the community. Yet in the wake of renewed interest in positive mental health, several studies were made during the 1960s which sharpen our understanding even though, as we shall see, they also raise as many questions as they resolve. Let us begin our exploration with some observations that point up the diverse ways in which mental health professionals have defined successful living.

GRINKER'S "HOMOCLITES"

One of the earliest to see the need to study "normal" or "healthy" persons was Roy Grinker (1962), a distinguished research psychiatrist whose major life work had been the study of stress and coping with life crisis. He coined the term "homoclite" to capture his idea of the average person, explaining it as follows (p. 405):

Because such terms as "normal" and "healthy" are so heavily loaded with value judgments, a neutral word was sought but not found in the English language. Even the Greeks did not have a word for the condition I am describing. Dr. Percival Bailey made the suggestion that, since *heteroclite* means a person deviating from the common rule, the opposite or *homoclite* would designate a person following the common rule. The reader will soon discover that the population to be described is composed of "normal," "healthy," "ordinary," "just plain guys," in fact *homoclites.*

Grinker provided rich and extensive descriptions of a population of male college students obtained from George Williams College in Chicago. Thirty-one of the students displaying no evidence of maladjustment on psychological tests were further interviewed to determine their suitability for study as ordinary or healthy persons and then studied more closely through additional interviews. Later, thirty-four additional male students who entered the college were added to the sample. Thus, the report is based on a study of sixty-five subjects. The discussion by Grinker of how he came to do the research in the first place is interesting in that it highlights the traditional psychiatric outlook and Grinker's challenge to it (1962, pp. 405–406):

> The impact of these interviews on me was startling! Here was a type of young man I had not met before in my role as a psychiatrist and rarely in my personal life. On the surface they were free from psychotic, neurotic, or disabling personality traits. It seemed that I had encountered some mentally "healthy" men who presented a unique opportunity for study.
>
> Perhaps this experience could serve as a tentative definition of "mental health"—its startling impact on a psychiatrist who has devoted most of his professional life to working with people who complain unhappily, suffer from disabling symptoms, and behave self-destructively. Three years after my preliminary shock and after this peculiar population was systematically studied, I came across the following reassuring sentence written by Henry Murray. . . . "Were an analyst to be confronted by that much-heralded but still missing specimen—the normal man—he would be struck dumb, for one, through lack of appropriate ideas."

The subjects studied by Grinker came from families whose fathers worked in laborer, semi-skilled, or white-collar groups; these included the occupations of janitor, truck driver, street repairer, watchman, farmer, and schoolteacher. Their fathers' incomes ranged from $4,500 per year to over $10,000, with an average of $6,000; only six fathers earned around $10,000. They came from all over the United States and Canada, with the highest representation in the Midwest. Their verbal intelligence test scores ranged from an IQ of 88 to 133, with an average of 110. One year later most either still remained in school or had graduated, although two had resigned for financial reasons, and two had been dropped because of poor grades. The grade point average of the sample for the first year was slightly better than C, as compared with the school average of C+.

Grinker described his sample (1962, p. 445) as showing, in general, "little evidence of crippling, disabling, or severely handicapping illness." Generally, they were not the types likely to be seen by psychiatrists. Psychopathology was not completely absent, and some of the individuals were suspicious, unhappy, withdrawn, fearful, compulsive, for example. Nonetheless, the average member of the group was able to work effectively at his job. In spite of procrastination and cramming for exams (according to Grinker, this is typical among the American student), he passed his exams and graduated with a C average. He enjoyed play and could manage emotional experiences with adequate and realistic control. He knew who he was, felt generally favorable about himself, and had positive hopes for the future. His relationships with others, such as parents, teachers, or friends, were warm.

The people whom Grinker studied were not particularly visible in the society in which they lived, making no splash and not achieving notoriety. They had little ambition for social or economic gains, striving mainly to do their jobs well. Their aspirations were mainly *"to do well, to do good, and to be liked."* They lived simply and comfortably, raised families, and retired ultimately on modest pensions and social security.

Grinker was strongly impressed by the evident differences between this population of "healthy homoclites" and the patient typically seen in the psychiatrist's office. The homoclites were goal-directed in the sense of wanting to do the best they could, taking school and work seriously. But the ambition to rise and to live better than their parents was lacking, and this surprised Grinker. There appeared to be little dissatisfaction with their home environments. He quoted them (p. 446) as saying, "We lived in a nice house, our clothes were good, we always had enough to eat. True we had an old car, but it ran. Why would we want to earn more? A job you like is better than one you don't, even if it pays more." Commenting on this bland and satisfied set of attitudes, Grinker noted (p. 446):

> I often described my subject population to various local and professional groups characterized by driving social upward-mobile or prestige-seeking people who, although outwardly serene, were consumed with never-satisfied ambitions. The invariable comment was "those boys are sick, they have no ambition." In the broadest sense, to "do the best I can" seems to be a true ambition.

One problem in a study of this kind is the representativeness of the population being studied. In Grinker's study, the students interviewed and tested came from a school that might not be considered altogether representative of other colleges, in that it was a YMCA training school. Perhaps some of the characteristics Grinker observed as typical in these students arise from the decision to attend this type of institution and perhaps train for a well-defined, secure, and respectable job, one in which there were comparatively limited prospects for advancement or for conflict. This special nature of the college may have played an important role in determining the

predominant personality pattern of the subjects Grinker studied. In any event, Grinker's homoclites are one version of the healthy personality, albeit an old-style, contented-cow version with its accent on the benign and *accommodated* individual rather than the exceptional or creative individual.

THE MERCURY ASTRONAUTS

Several studies have also been performed (by Sheldon J. Korchin and George E. Ruff, 1964, and by Ruff and Korchin, 1964) on the psychological reactions of the seven Mercury astronauts to space-flight training. These were the first American astronauts in the early days of the space program. Since these men appeared to many to be prototypes of unusually competent and psychologically healthy men, assessments were also attempted of their personalities. The researchers appear to have conceived of the healthy person as one who is able to *function effectively* and without impairment *under conditions of stress.* Indeed, the public was highly impressed with the astronauts' highly controlled and effective behavior under stress. In the first such ventures, video audiences watched in awe and suspense as the rockets were launched with their human cargo, and they were thrilled by each new exploit. The flights seemed to require tremendous courage and stability, and the astronauts became modern-day heroes. As individuals they were described in magazine articles and were glimpsed accepting awards and making public statements. One even ran for public office. What manner of men were these? Were they truly prototypes of optimal functioning, of healthy personality? This is what Korchin and Ruff set out to explore.

Studies were first made of the astronauts' efficiency in perceptual and motor skills as well as changes in their mood at various times—that is, under normal, nonstressful conditions, at moments just prior to simulated flights when anticipatory anxiety might be expected to be greatest, and again after the simulated flight itself. Little difference in performance was found on these occasions, suggesting that they coped exceedingly well with the stresses involved in the simulated flight situation. With respect to mood, the astronauts generally described themselves more in terms of positive rather than negative emotional states, that is, as friendly, energetic, and clear-thinking, as opposed to aggressive, jittery, and depressed. After simulated flight, there was a tendency for them to feel less energetic and clear-thinking, more anxious, and more friendly toward people, but such changes were very slight.

In the main, stressful episodes produced extremely little evidence of mood disturbance as reported by the men and observed in their behavior. The most difficult problem for them to deal with seemed to be that of not being chosen for the first flight. Upon selection, the astronauts' energies were directed mainly at achieving a sense of readiness for it. Anticipatory anxiety was mild and experienced as a feeling of tension or of being on edge. The anxiety seemed more related to concern over the flight's success than over fear of injury or death. Such a task-oriented as opposed to a fear-oriented outlook has also been described as applying to successful sports parachute jumpers (Fenz, 1975).

Korchin and Ruff have suggested that the astronauts exhibited a high degree of control over emotion. Although each man was aware of the many possible malfunctions which could have ended his life, this knowledge did not disrupt his functioning. The astronauts appeared to have great confidence in their mastery of stress and in their ability, through training and technological sophistication, to deal with critical situations. In interviews they would often comment about the necessity in tight situations to stop and take stock of the situation, to decide what must be done and go ahead and do it. They felt that it was better to keep busy rather than to worry. Not being able to do anything was the worst problem.

FIGURE 7-2 Group photograph of the seven Mercury astronauts in space clothing. (NASA.)

Korchin and Ruff have described the seven astronauts in considerable detail. They were selected from sixty-nine candidates, all of them experienced military jet test pilots. When selected they were between thirty-two and thirty-seven years of age, all married and with children. Five had two children, one had four, and one had one. They came from families of the middle-middle or middle-upper class and were generally well off during childhood. All grew up in small towns or on farms. All were Protestant, although they varied in the extent of participation in church activities. All enjoyed sports and outdoor living. They had been educated in public schools and had graduated from colleges. All had majored in engineering. All were described by Korchin and Ruff as highly ambitious, concerned with success and sensitive to failure, highly able and intelligent, free from consuming self-doubts, capable of dealing with stress without undue disturbance, persevering, and having accurate testing of reality and a high degree of control over their feelings and emotions.

Korchin and Ruff (1964) have also speculated about some of the psychodynamic forces at work in the astronauts' personalities as follows (pp. 206–207):

In the main, these are men with firm identities. They know who they are and where they are going. This, in turn, has derived from development in a well-organized family with considerable solidarity. They grew up in stable communities, usually smaller ones, where the family's position was socially secure if not very influential. Within the family, there was usually strong identification with a competent father or surrogate. It is noteworthy that four of the seven men are "junior." A common theme in many of the interviews is the happy memory of outdoor activities shared with the father—hiking, fishing, or hunting.

From childhood on, their lives flowed in relatively smooth progressions. There were relatively few crises or turning points, as each phase led naturally into the next. Rarely were there overwhelming numbers of competing alternate possibilities to choose among, but rather one predominant choice. Development seemed to flow from stage to stage, rather than to involve successive crises and the mastery of these crises before progression could continue. . . .

The high order of innate intellectual and physical abilities of these men should not be overlooked. They started with considerable ability and have been exposed to situations which could be mastered within the repertory of their capacities. This has led to success, and from success to heightened self-esteem. One might picture life histories that start with fine abilities and a favoring childhood environment, providing basic emotional security and firm identification. Thereafter follow recycling progressions, consisting of appropriate aspiration, success, increasing self-esteem, increased aspiration, and so forth. Examination of the professional careers indicates smooth progressions without major setbacks. Their development, conceived in this way, seems congruent with the astronauts' present personal competence and stress resistance.

Are any reservations warranted in this picture of the healthy personality? One is that the astronauts represent only one version of healthy personality. The main value expressed here seems to be resistance to stress or, more precisely, the ability to perform effectively and without impairment under certain kinds of stress. Nothing is said about such things as altruism and love, spontaneity, spiritual experience, intimacy, creativity, and resistance to conformity, the latter being some of the qualities emphasized by other writers (e.g., Maslow, 1954). We are not told how the astronauts fare on these counts; indeed, their selection for the space program was not predicated on such qualities but on estimates by the space chiefs about the qualities important to carrying out of the space missions themselves. Perhaps the astronauts do fulfill Maslow's criteria as well as those emphasized by the space program. But there is no way of knowing this from the observations of Korchin and Ruff, since the interests of these authors tended to reflect also the values of the space program itself.

A second reservation concerns the absence of anything but an implicit comparison between the astronauts and other men. Without an attempt to study other men in other contexts, it is difficult to know how typical or atypical these seven men are. Are their qualities rare or common? How would those men who were rejected for the program on one ground or another have fared? One might guess, along with Korchin and Ruff, that the astronauts were uncommonly adequate in their work spheres; but one cannot be sure about this without additional and extensive comparisons.

A third reservation concerns the degree of threat to which the astronauts were actually exposed: or, put another way, the stressors to which they were exposed were of a very special sort, perhaps not at all like the more usual kinds of life stress. To the layman, flying in a spacecraft, being catapulted by rocket engines over one hundred miles above the earth into the hostile vacuum of space, would be a terrifying experience. Anyone who can volunteer for this, look forward to it, and tolerate it is likely to be thought of by most of us as remarkably stress-resistant. But this experience may not have been subjectively very threatening to the astronauts. Because of their unique training and experience as test pilots, what might have been strange and frightening to the ordinary person, might be almost routine to them. One must remember that the astronauts had survived for many years as skilled test pilots, engaged in an occupation that is usually regarded as extremely dangerous. As a result of this experience, these men knew their resources in this special sphere.

The astronauts were also assigned to a program in which no stone was left unturned to array enormous technical competence and careful preparation against the possibility of failure. Procedures were tested and retested. Equipment was scrutinized in the most minute detail to prevent accidents. Significantly, not one astronaut has had a fatal accident in space flight, which most laymen tend to regard as the dangerous period; however, three died in two separate and ordinary airplane crashes when no extraordinary danger was assumed to exist, and three perished in an accident on the ground during a test and simulated lift-off.

This is not to belittle the astronauts' extraordinary accomplishments, but merely to suggest that a truly complete picture of their command over various life stresses is lacking. The stresses involved in the Mercury program were limited primarily to one type, a type with which they had been extremely familiar much of their lives. There are no published observations about how these men might have handled other types of stressors,

for example, failure, lost social esteem, bereavement, or degrading experiences such as the concentration-camp prisoner had to undergo. Interestingly, however, one of the later astronauts published an autobiography in which he describes a severe adjustmental crisis some years after his participation in the space program (Aldrin and Warga, 1973). This is consistent with the speculation that far more is probably involved in the psychological makeup of the astronauts than is revealed in these limited studies. Korchin and Ruff speak of the astronauts as having high degrees of stress tolerance, seeming to generalize from the space program to all kinds of other life stresses. Perhaps this generalization is sound, but without relevant evidence it is a speculation rather than a demonstrated fact. Additional information on this would be most valuable in extending and sharpening our picture of the healthy personality.

COMPETENT YOUTH

Two major programs of overlapping research on psychologically healthy adolescents have been reported in recent years. In one, high school students of outstanding competence were first studied as they prepared to go to college, and in the other a similar group of such students were studied after a period in college. This research performed by Silber and his associates (1961) and by Coelho and his associates (1963) represents one large integrated effort, oriented toward understanding the ways in which so-called healthy young people cope with new threats and challenges. The conceptual orientation of the authors is expressed in the concept of *competence*. Comments by Silber and his colleagues about the purposes of their research efforts are instructive (1961, p. 355):

The usual source material for describing adolescence comes from studies of clinically disturbed people, either from reconstructions through adult analysis or from analyses conducted during adolescence. However, we wished to study a group of effective adolescents and to use a naturally occurring life situation as an extended laboratory through which the adolescent's adaptive behavior could also be studied. We were interested in exploring a life situation which offered an opportunity for examining adolescent behavior patterns in response to the potential challenges of new specific life tasks.

The situation which the authors selected was the transition from high school to college, a transition which they regarded as a "revealing sample of the larger transition from adolescence to early adulthood" (p. 355). Certain tasks are prominent in the process of making this transition from adolescence to adulthood, particularly as the youngster moves from high school to college. These tasks include separation from parents, siblings, and friends, development of autonomy in making decisions, assuming responsibility for and regulation of one's behavior, establishing new friendships, dealing with sexual intimacy, and handling new intellectual challenges.

The first study (Silber et al., 1961) was performed with a group of high school seniors planning to go to college. The general personality attributes of these healthy adolescent personalities and their strategies for coping with new experiences were revealed by extensive interviews over more than a year's time.

The subjects were selected from volunteers who were in the top half of their class academically. These students were then rated by eight teachers with respect to motivation, industry, initiative, influence and leadership, concern for others, and responsibility and emotional stability; those receiving the most favorable ratings were interviewed further. Students who seemed overtly troubled, who reported neurotic symptoms, or with whom the interviewer had difficulty

establishing rapport were dropped. There remained finally fifteen students (six boys and nine girls) who were subsequently interviewed weekly during the last part of their senior school year. The findings reported by the authors stem from these interviews made prior to the students' departure for college.

What were the *psychosocial characteristics* of these young people as noted by Silber et. al.? They displayed satisfaction about scholastic achievement and no evidence of anxiety about their intellectual ability; they exhibited varied interests and had as a central value to be "well rounded"; they had close friends toward whom they indicated a warm regard; mutuality rather than exploitiveness was the predominant form of social relation, though they were not necessarily the most popular students; finally, they found social groups, such as religious or social organizations, in which they could participate actively.

Certain *modes of coping* were common to these fifteen students. For example, they expressed positive attitudes toward new experiences, which were seen not as threatening but as desirable, exciting, rewarding; they saw going off to college as requiring new contacts and friendships, and they did not wish to block themselves from these by clinging to old ones; they exhibited self-reliance and positive action in corresponding with colleges, in preparing their clothes, in working out financial arrangments; and they enjoyed the experience of mastering problems and figuring out what had to be done.

Characteristic of these students also was the *self-image* of being *adequate* and capable. It comforted them as they thought ahead to college, and it was sustained in a variety of ways: for example, by remembering past occasions in which they had coped successfully; by making efforts to learn about the new situation they would have to face in advance through catalogs, talks with college students, visiting the campus, and so on; and by anticipating and rehearsing in fantasy and action patterns of behavior that they would be called upon to perform. An adequate self-image was also sustained by identifying with the high school group that shared a reputation for being well prepared for college, by lowering their level of aspiration about the grades they might achieve in college (where competition would be greater) so as not to experience a loss of self-esteem, and by selectively perceiving and attending to positive things they heard about the new environment and deemphasizing the negative aspects (Fig. 7-3).

The authors also observed a number of effective techniques of *managing disappointments and anxiety* in these adolescents. For example, they recognized that their problems were shared with others rather than being unique, and they gained some support from this realization. They did a certain amount of worrying, but generally had a positive rather than a negative attitude toward this. Worry was viewed as a means of keeping down overconfidence and preparing as best as possible for anticipated threats or challenges. They also often used the technique of working through future concerns by *preparatory activities* in the present. For example, one of the students was concerned about the fate of his

mother, who was widowed. Without his assistance he feared the household duties would prove excessive for her. Before he left for college, he attempted to get everything done about the house that was needed, a valuable form of anticipatory planning to deal with the guilt the student would probably experience in leaving, and a way to protect the mother against unnecessary problems that might arise in his absence.

In the second study (Coelho et al., 1963), fourteen high school seniors (nine female and five male) were chosen by the research group in essentially the same fashion as before, but whereas the first study had examined the ways the new experience would be prepared for, the focus of this study was on the major *coping strategies* found in these adolescents when actually facing the demands of the new college environment. A number of strategies were found in the college situation that were consistent with what had been observed also in the earlier sample in the high school setting. For example, the selected adolescents appeared able to look ahead and see what was expected of them and to organize their time appropriately, distinguishing

FIGURE 7-3 High school seniors visiting the college they are planning to attend as part of the preparation for life and study in the new environment. (John Briggs.)

important from unimportant demands; they could study for long stretches of time without becoming bored or resentful and could concentrate under difficult conditions; since some goals were more important than others, they could tolerate relatively poor grades in subjects outside their major commitments, but set a floor below which they would not fall in those subjects that were vital—in this way, they could experiment with new courses and experiences without jeopardizing their main objectives; they freely used upperclassmen in seeking information; they could also identify positively with the faculty

FIGURE 7-4 The sometimes apprehensive-hopeful search for posted grades through which success or failure is indicated. *Columbia Daily Spectator,* Editorial Photocolor Archives.)

without relating to them excessively at the expense of peer groups (Fig. 7-4).

Of special interest are the ways in which these competent young persons appeared to handle academic disappointments and dissatisfactions, *preserving their self-esteem* in spite of these. One student dealt with poor performance in an essential subject by making added and systematic efforts to strengthen his grasp of the material. Disappointments with the quality of the entire educational experience were compensated for in another case by more satisfying outside activities. Failure in one career direction was dealt with in still another case by *giving up the goal and substituting another* without serious damage to self-esteem. Supports through friendships and from effective utilization of the many diverse resources of the college environment provided further strength against threatening and disappointing experiences.

The authors see competence as an outgrowth of successive *experiences of mastery* that help young children strengthen their sense of identity and gain control over their environment. In their view, it is the successful experiences of mastery rather than the damaging ones that strengthen the ego. One is reminded here of Korchin and Ruff's (1964) observation that the highly competent astronauts had a previous life history unmarred by important failure, their present high level of functioning seeming to be continuous with that of earlier stages in their development. You will recall that very little is known about when an experience will be damaging and when it will be a constructive influence. This is a prime research question concerning personality development. Nor is a great deal known about the extent to which the strengths necessary for high competence are already fully formed by adolescence or are still being acquired.

Despite their general value, a number of serious defects in these studies with competent youth reduce their effectiveness in providing understanding of healthy adjustment. The most serious defect lies in the selection of the so-called competent adolescents: (1) By using volunteers, then having them rated by teachers and finally eliminating by means of psychiatric interview those who seemed troubled or reported neurotic symptoms, the authors have managed to thoroughly bias the kinds of personality characteristics which might have been found in the effective student. Eliminated from the sample studied were many adolescents who were thought effective by their teachers but might have displayed quite different modes of adaptation to the transition to college, and possibly even greater pathology. (2) There is also no adequate comparison group with which the studies might be compared. For example, as in the astronaut sample, we do not know anything about the distribution in the population of the traits being studied, and whether such traits could also be found in highly troubled youths. (3) Moreover, the data were obtained anecdotally, from impressionistic self-reports of the students, rather than from direct observations of their functioning. It is possible that direct observations might have revealed patterns of behavior contradictory to those the students reported. Thus, the conclusions from these studies cannot be fully accepted without support from further, more carefully designed research.

The early pioneering studies cited above are beginning to seem a bit dated, though they have stimulated other researchers to further explore the tasks of adjustment characteristic of the transition to college and adulthood. A somewhat more recent approach, for example, is that of Madison (1969, 1971), though it is different from the earlier ones in that instead of attempting to preselect students who were free of emotional difficulties and distinctively competent, Madison studied several hundred students at Swarthmore, Princeton, Stanford, and the University of Arizona to identify the "core experiences" that might foster or impede personality development. He too looked carefully at the tasks of adjustment which adolescents in college had to face and master. Madison sees these adjustmental tasks as part of the larger psychological process of personality growth and maturation. The subjects were volunteers from courses on personality development who supplied journals about their experiences and reactions. Although it is impossible to say how typical these students were of the average college student, the research does not suffer from some of the difficulties inherent in working with a group preselected by psychiatric and personality test criteria, and so Madison's subjects are apt to be more typical of the average student than those of Grinker, Coelho et al., and Silber et al.

One of the immediate problems facing many students consisted of conflict between their expectations of success based on past performance and the discovery that they were having trouble understanding some of their work. Such difficulties contributed to the need for making a meaningful vocational choice based on realistic information about their abilities and alternative life values such as materialism and humanism. In the process of growth and self-discovery, personal crises and anxiety are common phenomena; these should not be regarded as necessarily pathological, since they are characteristic of rapid and normal growth. Such growth involves change, and change is unsettling and demanding. Madison suggests, in fact, that "in the college system an adolescent who is not to some degree anxious and who does not experience crisis is an adolescent who is developmentally on the shelf" (1971, p. 104).

Much has been written about the adolescent problem of dealing with biological urges such as sex, and Madison's data confirms this to be a major adjustmental task at this time of life. Few of the adolescents studied arrived at puberty with a clear and mature understanding of this aspect of themselves or with a well-crystalized, adult sexual pattern of drives. Ignorance of sexuality and how to deal with it is common as a result of growing up in a world of deception about such matters. Fear is also added to ignorance, and often shock is the reaction to the first explanations of intercourse. Misconceptions abound, with frightening childhood sexual experiences being far more common than adults usually suppose, and confusion is engendered by presentations of sex in the mass media. However, left to themselves, many adolescents "heal" themselves of such misconceptions which beset children of our culture, often through the acquisition of a deep, positive relationship between a girl and boy. Madison cites a not atypical journal by a young woman named Florence to illustrate this developmental process (1969, pp. 217, 219, 220):

Questions . . . about sex were answered by my mother in a twisted, euphemistic fashion. When I did become aware of the truth from other people, my trust and faith in my mother was lost. Now, as then, I simply am unable to talk with her frankly about sex. Thus, when I went into high school, I thought about sex with feelings of guilt and shame. . . . During my freshman year in high school I got to know boys four and five years older than me. . . . I became fascinated by and interested in these older boys. Of course, their ideas were quite different from mine. It was during this time that I first became aware of sex as personally involving me. Once I engaged in necking and petting with John, the biggest, strongest guy in the group. This was the first time anything like this had happened to me, and I was very naive and absolutely too young mentally for this. After this happened my next monthly period did not occur. I knew better, but guilt plus naiveté and imagination made me think that God had performed a miracle to punish me, and I was now pregnant. For about six weeks I lived in fear, guilt, anxiety and uncertainty. I feel that the episode with John added a great feeling of fear to my already existing shame-guilt complex

about sex. The fear was in part due to my ignorance, for which I blame my mother.

I spent the summer following my freshman year in college in Bermuda, and it proved to be the most educational few months I have ever experienced. . . . I met Ray. . . . His fight for independence from his parents was really causing him trouble. . . . Immediately, I was full of feelings for him. . . . I sensed that he needed somebody, and I wanted very much to be the object of his dependence. . . .

We went everywhere together, and a mutual understanding grew. I loved all of the adventures we had—surfing, shopping, sleeping on the beach, skin diving, or climbing to a mountain pool to swim. Soon it turned out to be quite convenient if I would sign out for weekends and merely stay with him. We worked and lived together. As before, affection and sex entered into the situation. He did not push me, and I began to lose that ugly fear. Our relationship was really turning into something wonderful. Then he began to expect more and more. I wanted to be able to give and love him. Yet this idea of morals that had plagued me and always been there arose. We had many arguments about it but I just couldn't. Once we came very close to intercourse, but I suddenly felt great fear and began sobbing and crying. Ray . . . would sit down and try to explain and make me understand how he felt and how he thought. . . . Ray was the first person to make me understand that morals are a personal, circumstantial type of thing rather than blind, hard-and-fast rules. It changed me a great deal. . . . I ended up staying an extra month in Bermuda.

Along with Erikson (see pp. 172–173), Madison regards a primary task of growing up to be the establishment of a sense of self-identity, which includes the establishment of occupational and social goals. About this Madison writes (1971, p. 108):

For the male in our society, competence in a vocational role is as important as is masculinity in his sex role. Again, the male is held to a more sharply defined criterion. The condition of the late-adolescent boy is much more complex and drastic than we realize. Consider his situation: he is in transition from the personality supports of family and high school and peer groups to the still-distant adult world. Typically, he is still hung-up on unrealistic, childhood-determined vocational goals. Further, the college curriculum tells him very little about whether he will either like a projected field of work or do well in it. The college faculty, too, are poor models for all but the few future professors in the student body. Yet by the end of the student's sophomore year, the registrar insists that he commit himself to a department and an implied career—a commitment that he has neither the experience nor the facts at hand to make; he can only guess.

In all, Madison's research seeks to describe and understand the adjustmental tasks characteristic of college youth and how these are managed. The focus is not on specific coping tasks or skills but on the major requirements of moving from adolescent to adult: finding a place in the world for oneself; dealing with the problems of sex and intimacy; taking one's own measure in the world and learning about oneself as a person; coping with conflict, frustration, and challenge; and, above all, achieving an effective synthesis of external pressures and internal demands in the course of growing and maturing, in effect becoming an adult person who is in command of life. Again and again Madison points to the normality of such struggle and its symptoms in the process of growth, and to the likelihood that the demands involved in such personality development and change will ultimately be managed successfully by most youths. Although the emphasis is not on health and pathology per se, such accounts provide an important picture of the adjustment process in a wide representation of young persons in the present college world of the United States, young persons presumably much like the readers of this text.

When all is said and done, the young persons studied by Coelho, Silber, Grinker and Madison above show a basic pattern of conventionality, of *accommodation* to the standards and values of their society, and of substantial assimilation of those standards into their own personal sense of identity. They are all in some degree work-oriented and will take their expected place within the society as it exists, rather than being alienated from that society or struggling to change it. Although Silber and Coelho tend to emphasize competence in mastering environmental demands and the conventional tasks of life, the definition of mental health implicit in all these studies, as well as that of Korchin and Ruff, has much in common with the traditional psychiatric concept of minimal stress, illness, and distress—it is a variant of the "contented cow" metaphor. In contrast, one could emphasize struggle and rebellion as a valid lifestyle, as will be seen below.

REBELLIOUS YOUTH

During the 1960s, a number of researchers have suggested a very different image of healthy adaptation in which the central theme is not harmony and a work identity within the society as it exists, but turmoil and struggle and even rebelliousness against injustice and dehumanizing social conditions. Such a view is truly at variance with the traditional outlook; in a sense it is anachronistic in that it tends to view stress and conflict as a positive (and perhaps inevitable) feature of successful living, rather than an irredeemably negative one.

This latter idea is exemplified by some of the youths who participated in the civil rights movement during the early 1960s or who fought the

FIGURE 7-5 "The War is Over." Folk Singer Joan Baez leading a celebration of peace in New York City's Central Park, May 25, 1975. (*New York Post* photograph by Frank Leonardo © 1975, New York Post Corporation.)

United States participation in the Vietnam war. They chanced injury, ostracism, and even death in challenging the Jim Crow laws of the deep South and in helping blacks to register to vote. They endured exile and imprisonment by refusing to be inducted into military service during the height of the Indochina War. Some of them, such as the singer Joan Baez and her husband, became highly visible on the national level because of their political activism, while many others remain obscure to the public though they too suffered punishment for such actions as refusing to fly bombing missions or to train medics in the Green Berets because of the belief that this group was using and withholding medicine immorally in Indochina as a military tactic (Fig. 7-5).

In considering such protest and activism in the context of mental health, we should probably distinguish between *alienated* and despairing youth (such as the dropouts from society) and those having a *principled commitment* to a high set of human values leading them to espouse unpopular efforts to change what they perceived to be societal evils. Motives for protest and rebellion can be highly varied. In some cases,

they could reflect boredom and a juvenile search for excitement—these could be considered as analogous to panty raids and other forms of adolescent mischief for the sake of thrills. In other instances, they could reflect mainly hatred of parental authority, a deeply troubled or disturbed personality, or a means of achieving notoriety. However, in many instances they also express sensitivity to injustice and the desire to improve the world and make it live up to the highest social ideals. It is often difficult to disentangle the complex reasons that underlie rebellious behavior in young persons, or, for that matter, in older individuals too, but the distinction seems important if we are to treat such rebelliousness as a sign of mental health or, at least, as compatible with personal health or soundness.

In widely influential books, for example, two kinds of rebellious youth—one identified as "uncommitted" or alienated (Kenniston, 1965), the other as "committed" or dedicated to social reform (Kenniston, 1968)—have been studied. Available evidence suggests that the former have poor relationships with their parents and reject parental values. They are truly alienated from the society, rootless, and convinced that the world is unreliable and unresponsive. They believe that the normal social roles people play have no salience or holding power for them. They have been referred to as "obsolete youth" (Bettelheim, 1969) and as disillusioned, despairing, without a social identity (Adler, 1968, 1970). On the other hand, the committed, rebellious youths maintain positive relationships with their parents and respect their values, which also express a rejection of social injustice and an idealism about improving the lot of mankind.

Barron (1963, p. 144) has written a forceful defense of rebelliousness as a vital aspect of mental health:

The first and most obvious consideration in the relationship of rebelliousness to morality and psychological health is one which by now has passed from iconoclastic protest to virtual stereotype. Nonetheless, it should not be disregarded. It is simply this: rebellion-resistance to acculturation, refusal to "adjust," adamant insistence on the importance of the self and of individuality is very often the mark of a healthy character. If the rules deprive you of some part of yourself, then it is better to be unruly. The socially disapproved expression of this is delinquency, and most delinquency certainly is just plain confusion or blind and harmful striking out at the wrong enemy; but some delinquency has affirmation behind it, and we should not be too hasty in giving a bad name to what gives us a bad time. The great givers to humanity often have proud refusal in their souls, and they are aroused to wrath at the shoddy, the meretricious, and the unjust, which society seems to produce in appalling volume. Society is tough in its way, and it's no wonder that those who fight it tooth and nail are "tough guys." I think that much of the research and of the social action in relation to delinquency would be wiser if it recognized the potential value of the wayward characters who make its business for it. A person who is neither shy nor rebellious in his youth is not likely to be worth a farthing to himself or to anyone else in the years of his physical maturity.

The virtues of rebellion can clearly be overstated. The nub of the problem concerns how morality is to be judged and who is to decide. Youthful rebels often greatly oversimplify issues and are thereby led to use criminal means to achieve the things they believe in. A tragic example is Camilla Hall, the twenty-nine-year-old daughter of a Midwestern Lutheran minister who died in the spring of 1974 along with five other members of the Symbionese Liberation Army. Her belief in violent revolutionary change led her to participate, or at least concur, in the murder of Marcus Foster, black Superintendent of Schools in Oakland, and in the kidnaping of Patricia Hearst, daughter of a wealthy newspaper executive, acts which in themselves are highly immoral and reprehensible. One is reminded too of the fact that most wars, massacres, and oppressions of one people by another over the ages have been justified by their protagonists on the highest religious and moral principles. A letter from Camilla Hall to her parents, partly reprinted below, portrays the remarkable story of love, dedication, justification of evil, and rebellion which eventuated in murder and kidnap and ultimately in early death for herself.

Dear Mom and Dad,

How are you? I've been thinking about you a lot, hoping that all is well with you. I get a lot of strength from our love. It really helps keep me going. . . . I know you are probably being watched very carefully now.

My name has been in the papers, TV, etc. (the FBI missed me by a matter of days in Berkeley) but we're staying several jumps ahead of them at all times by using our own creativity, determination to survive, and to carry on the business of the revolution. . . .

. . . so-called radical leaders . . . scared witless because we have put them in a situation that calls for action to fulfill the courage of their convictions.

Our support is from the people, and will continue to grow with each victory as we prove to the people that the revolution can indeed be successful. We intend to be around for quite a while to live to see the victories.

I know you trust my sincerity even if you haven't come to agree with the course of action I have committed myself to. I am young and strong and willing to dedicate my courage, intelligence, and love to the work.

I feel really good about what I am doing—want you to also. . . .

There are lots of other parents and friends and lovers going through the same thing. I hope for your courage to understand these things and keep them in your heart. . . .

I sent _____ $5 and a note with this, saying I was on the road and hadn't been able to get anything together for your birthday, Mom, and would they please buy you some pretty flowers and hand deliver them with this letter to you.

I'm sorry I can't promise to be able to do this on our special family days, but know that I remember them and send my love on many, many more days than just those. Be strong.

Love, Camilla

Barron clearly distrusts the conventional conceptions of "psychological health." He expresses this in a brief case history of a troubled but original and creative graduate student whom Barron calls, significantly, "an odd fellow," pointing up the idea that bland conformity to social standards is not what he means by psychological health. This student arrived at the Institute of Personality Assessment and Research at the University of California at Berkeley (where Barron was a research scientist) in response to an advertisement for subjects, and he immediately marked himself by his behavior as a rather deviant and extraordinary person. He appeared facetious, unsociable, and argumentative. His intellectual performance ranged from the mediocre (perhaps on tasks he cared nothing about) to brilliant and original.

Barron presents in some detail evidence that this student is a highly creative person, in accurate touch with reality. At the same time there is ample evidence of personal alienation, as well as a life history filled with pathogenic experiences. He had been identified by the chairman of his department as being within a year of his Ph.D. However, he did not complete the degree on schedule following criticism of his dissertation, which he had submitted in rough draft. Rather than make extensive revisions he dropped out of school. Two years after the assessment program, a psychologist on the institute's staff accidentally met him prospecting for silver and gold in Death Valley, California. The following year, however, he returned to graduate work with a new thesis plan which involved considerable mathematical work done during his absence from the university, and this unusual student finally obtained his Ph.D. Barron presented this case of "an odd fellow" to show the multiple faces of creativity and mental health and to get the reader used to the idea that the common social virtues are not necessarily synonymous with personal soundness.

In keeping with his emphasis on struggle, vitality, and creativity rather than benignness, Barron makes the following comment (1963, pp. 64–65) about psychological soundness:

The conclusion to which the assessment staff has come is that psychopathology is always with us, and that soundness is *a way of reacting to problems, not an absence of them.* The transformation of pathological trends into distinctive character assets and the minimization of their effects through compensatory overdevelopment of other traits are both marks of "sound" reaction to personal difficulties. At times, indeed, the handling of psychopathology may be so skillful and the masking of pathological motivations so subtle that the individual's soundness may be considerably overrated. There is no doubt that some of our apparently "balanced" subjects were balanced quite precariously, and that their stability was more semblance than fact. It is possible to mistake for soundness what is actually rigidity based on a sort of paralysis of affect engendered by a fear of instinctual drives. These cases of pseudo-soundness were probably few, however. . . .

The existence of psychopathology in even the quite sound individuals has been emphasized here partly by way of counteracting the sort of trite determinism with which so many clinical studies seem to conclude: broken homes leading to delinquency; psychosis in the parents being passed on, through whatever mechanism, to the offspring; unloving mothers rearing hateful children; catastrophe breeding catastrophe. Undoubtedly such correlations exist in nature, and they were, indeed, found in our own investigation; but considerable variance remains unaccounted for. What we should like to suggest here is that within the population of subjects of ordinary physical and psychological integrity, soundness is by no means exclusively determined by circumstances but may be considered in the nature of an unintended—and perhaps largely unconscious—personal achievement. Our high-soundness subjects are beset, like all other persons, by fears, unrealizable desires, self-condemned hates, and tensions difficult to resolve. They are *sound* largely because they bear with their anxieties, hew to a stable course, and maintain some sense of the ultimate worthwhileness of their lives.

ISSUES CONCERNING "WHAT IS HEALTHY?"

In the large and rich literature about mental health, there are many diverse themes, of which

we have observed here only a small sample. Even in this limited sample, however, we can begin to see some of the varying emphases in the definitions of mental health. We have, for example, (1) benign, relatively conflict-free, or bland accommodation to environment pressures and personal needs, both of these being somehow in harmony or balance; (2) resistance to stress, autonomy, or competence in mastering difficult life tasks and demands; (3) willingness to struggle with life and even rebel; (4) creativity, zest, and exuberance, with meaningful commitment to desirable social work and responsibility; and (5) cognitive values such as accurate or realistic perception of the world and of oneself. Commenting on this diversity of themes, Smith (1961, p. 299) states:

The various lists of criteria that have been proposed for positive mental health reshuffle overlapping conceptions of desirable functioning without attaining agreement or giving much promise that agreement can be reached. The inventories repeat themselves, and indeed it is inevitable that they should, since each successive list is proposed by a wise psychologist who scrutinizes previous proposals and introduces variations and emphasis to fit his own values and preferences. Some give greater weight to the cognitive values of accurate perception and self-knowledge (e.g., Jahoda, 1955); some to moral values, to meaningful commitment, to social responsibility (e.g., Allport, 1960; Shoben, 1957); some to working effectiveness (e.g., Ginsburg, 1955); some to the blander social virtues (e.g., aspects of Foote and Cottrell, 1955); some to zest, exuberance, and creativity (e.g., Maslow, 1954). Their terms recur, but in different combinations and with connotations that slant in divergent directions. . . .

In thinking about these diverse ways of viewing successful living or mental health, it will help at this point to raise three central issues that lie at the core of any attempt to choose the most compatible or serviceable approaches. These issues do not provide us with an answer, since, as we shall see, any answer is apt to be embedded in our personal value system. Nevertheless, unless we understand them we will be in a very poor position to address the problem and to understand the several ways in which professional workers have tried to conceptualize adjustive success and failure, the topics of Part IV. The three central issues are: (1) Should mental health be considered as an integrated system or as a collection of unrelated traits? (2) What values should we use in defining health? (3) What is the role of the environment in fostering or denying mental health in an individual?

PSYCHOLOGICAL INTEGRATION AND HEALTH

One way of viewing mental health is to see it as a collection of unrelated traits. Writers such as Jahoda (1958) have suggested that healthy personalities have certain distinguishing characteristics. For example, they view the world objectively, see themselves accurately, are accepting of themselves, continue to expand and grow as persons, are competent in handling their environments, and are autonomous or independent rather than conforming and dependent, to mention the main criteria she lists.

Does this mean that if you have one of these attributes, you also have the others? Is a woman who is objective in perceiving the environment also, of necessity, objective in perceiving herself? And if a man perceives himself accurately, does this mean that he will also be accepting of what he finds in himself? If the answer is "no," such traits must be independent or unrelated. Even more to the point, does being healthy imply having all the requisite attributes, or could a reasonably healthy person fail in one or several departments?

In thinking about this issue, one might draw an analogy to somatic health and illness. An otherwise physically healthy person can have a minor skin disease (say, psoriasis) and suffer from poor eyesight for which glasses are needed without these defects having any serious implications for longevity or bodily integrity. After a medical examination, a physician would undoubtedly pronounce the person as healthy, perhaps even unusually so. On the other hand, if the skin disease is cancer, the question of health is now in grave doubt, since cancer—if inoperable or advanced too far—can invade and destroy the operation of the rest of the system. When one organ system invades or interacts with the functioning of another in an integrated system, then damage to one could have serious implications for the viability of the remainder. In short, it is possible to think of each attribute of mental health either as separate and unrelated or as part of an *integrated system* such that defects in one make adequate functioning in the other difficult or impossible.

The resolution of this issue seems to vary somewhat among writers. Some (for example, Smith, 1961) argue that each trait is best considered as evolving separately and independently. This means that mental health should not be studied as an entity, but as a rubric, a topic heading within which there are a number of desirable and undesirable traits each of which contributes to successful living. Each trait should be studied on its own, for example, as to how it developed and what role it plays in the adjustive activities of the person. Thus, creativity as a trait, say, might have its own developmental history and characteristics, and likewise with objectivity in perceiving the environment, the ability to control one's impulses, one's self-acceptance, or one's competence in mastering the environment. A person may be competent yet unaccepting of self, objective yet incompetent, and so on.

In contrast, others such as Erikson (1963) emphasize the integration of all elements into an interdependent system. Erikson is generally called a neo-Freudian (new or latter-day Freudian) because he has elaborated and modified Freud's theory. Freud (1943) saw psychological development as proceeding inexorably through a series of psychosexual stages from oral to anal to genital. In early infancy and childhood, argued Freud, erotic pleasure first is centered on the mouth and is derived from sucking; the mouth is the main organ of gratification and exploration. Later, the locus of erotic activity shifts to the anus and involves the retention of feces and their expulsion. Ultimately, the locus of erotic activity shifts to the genital organs (penis in the boy, clitoris and vagina in the girl), and this is when the "family triangle" (Oedipus complex) emerges, with the boy in competition with the father over the affections of his mother and the girl in competition with the mother over the affections of her father. Ultimately, this triangle is resolved in favor of another love object, and in the healthy person mature genital love then emerges.

In his extensions of Freud's ideas, Erikson did two things; First, he explicitly linked each of the psychosexual stages of development discussed by Freud to the acquisition of the social attitudes and behavior patterns of the person, in effect, relating the biological properties of oral, anal, and genital activity to the developing child's psychological makeup. Second, he enlarged Freud's list of stages from three to eight, extending the analysis of psychological development into adulthood, rather than stopping it as Freud did at the juncture of adolescence and young adulthood. We can get an idea of how this was done with two illustrations, the anal stage (roughly two years of age) and a later stage for which Erikson is famous, that of "ego identity." With respect to the anal stage of development, Erikson writes (1963, p. 251):

> Muscular maturation sets the stage for experimentation with two simultaneous sets of social modalities: holding on and letting go. As is the case with all of these modalities, their basic conflicts can lead in the end to either hostile or

FIGURE 7-6 Erik Erikson. (Courtesy of W. W. Norton & Co.)

> benign expectations and attitudes. Thus, to hold can become a destructive and cruel retaining or restraining, and it can become a pattern of care: to have and to hold. To let go, too, can turn into an inimical letting loose of destructive forces, or it can become a relaxed "to let pass" and "to let be."

What Erikson is saying seems to be this: The early struggles of the child are biological, first revolving around oral activity and concerning what to take in and expel, and then anal activity and concerning whether to hold or expel fecal matter. These impulses and the manner in which they are handled also involve the world of other people. For example, it is the mother who gives nourishment orally, thus stimulating the oral cavity; and more broadly, it is the mother who cares for and protects the dependent infant. It is also the parent who expresses the cultural attitude toward feces and toileting, and who demands that the child obediently hold the sphincter muscles of the anus closed until the fecal matter is deposited in the specified place, and perhaps even at the specified time. Thus, in managing erotic impulses that derive from the oral and anal stages, a constellation of social relationships necessarily become involved. The issue of anal retention becomes, of necessity, the issue of discipline or social control and its conflict with the independent or autonomous desires of the child.

Erikson thus expanded the Freudian description of the psychosexual stages to include what is implicit in Freud but not always fully clarified, the psychosocial meanings that accompany each stage and shape the impact of each stage on the personality. Each stage must be seen as a developmental crisis that the child must resolve. The social conflict that characterizes the oral stage in Erikson's analysis is that of *trust versus mistrust.* The manner in which the mother responds to the biological needs of the infant during the oral stage, sensitively responding to it or failing to do so, determines the trust or mistrust the child will acquire concerning the social environment. The social issue associated with the anal stage is *autonomy versus shame and doubt.* At the phallic stage it is *initiative versus guilt.* During the latency period when the child is struggling with the preparatory phases of establishing a work role in the society, *industry versus inferiority* are the conflicting polarities. In puberty, with the return of the oedipal urges and the evolution of psychosexual maturity, the basic psychosocial issue is first the establishment of an *ego identity versus role confusion*, and then of *intimacy versus isolation.* And in later life the person must struggle between what Erikson calls *generativity* and *stag-*

nation: either we become capable of investing ourselves in the next generation, our offspring, for whom we accept responsibility, or we remain egocentric about our commitments. Finally, we must be able ultimately to accept our own life cycle as a positive event and its termination in death. The positive resolution of this life task or stage is called *ego integrity* as opposed to *despair.*

The best-known and most widely discussed quality of mental health as conceived by Erikson is that of *ego identity.* One's sense of identity begins to become established as childhood comes to an end during puberty and as youth begins. During this time adolescents are "primarily concerned with attempts at consolidating their social roles" (1950, p. 134), finding themselves as biological and social beings.

What does Erikson mean by the concept of ego identity? According to his own writings (1951, p. 9):

The central problem of the period is the establishment of a sense of identity. The identity the adolescent seeks to clarify is *who he is,* what his role in society is to be. Is he a child or is he an adult? Does he have it in him to be some day a husband and father? What is he to be as a worker and an earner of money? Can he feel self-confident in spite of the fact that his race or religious or national background makes him a person some people look down upon? Overall, will he be a success or a failure? By reason of these questions, adolescents are sometimes morbidly preoccupied with how they appear in the eyes of others as compared with their own conception of themselves, and with how they can make the rules and skills learned earlier jibe with what is currently in style. . . .

The danger of this developmental period is self-diffusion. As Biff puts it in *Death of a Salesman,* "I just can't take hold. I can't take hold of some kind of a life." A boy or girl can scarcely help feeling somewhat diffuse when the body changes in size and shape so rapidly, when genital maturity floods body and imagination with forbidden desires, when adult life lies ahead with such a diversity of conflicting possibilities and choices. [Italics added.]

Thus, Erikson's concept of ego identity, the prime requisite of mental health, can be summed up by saying that individuals with a well-developed ego identity know who they are and where they are going and have an inner assurance that they will be recognized and accepted by those who count.

This is a unified or *integrated system* of mental health because Erikson regards the resolution of each earlier stage as crucial to the healthy resolution of the later ones. Each stage builds on the previous ones. Only the person who has emerged positively from each developmental crisis (that is, the problems at each psychosexual stage) can develop a healthy ego identity. The state of health for Erikson, then, includes a unified set of traits each hammered out of a different developmental crisis or battleground, and each necessary to the healthy condition. For example, he wrote (1950, p. 137):

The emerging ego-identity, then, bridges the early childhood stages, when the body and the parent images were given their specific meanings, and the later stages, when a variety of social roles become available and increasingly coercive. A lasting ego-identity cannot begin to exist without the trust of the first oral stage; it cannot be completed without a promise of fulfillment which from the dominant image of adulthood reaches down into the baby's beginnings and which creates at every step an accruing sense of ego strength.

This is not the same concept of mental health as merely listing a series of traits that are to be regarded as signs or attributes of good functioning. This is an approach in which each separate component is an integral part of a total working system. Such a view is probably the dominant one in the thinking of mental health professionals, although that does not make it necessarily the correct one or the most useful. Still, if we take as a parallel the notion of bodily health and illness, most often we see illness as lack of integration or lack of harmony among the various organ systems of the body, and health as harmonious integration. As pointed out in the discussion of stress and illness in Chapter 5, a basic theme in psychosomatic medicine is that stress disrupts this harmony by generating powerful hormones to protect the system against assault, but the price paid for such emergency reactions is increased vulnerability to bodily illness. Later, in Chapter 12, we shall study the debate about whether the analogy between psychological health and physical health is warranted. Nevertheless, to many people mental health equals harmonious integration of the various component parts or subsystems of the personality and between the personality and the external world, while mental illness equals disintegration or dissociation of the component parts. Only further study will help us determine which of these two outlooks will prove more fruitful.

VALUES ABOUT HEALTH AND ILLNESS

Although the words illness and health suggest a scientific or biological standard, there is a large component of valuation embedded in them and more than a little disagreement about the standards of good and bad which should be applied. This is more obvious in judgments of positive mental health, but it also applies to the matter of illness or psychopathology too. For one thing, the values we adopt are always embedded in the culture in which we live, and these tend to vary from culture to culture and from era to era. Such variation concerning what is good or bad in adjustment has been referred to as "cultural relativism." What is considered bad or abnormal

FIGURE 7-7 Himalayan girls' custom (nose ring), which is "normal" for these people but which probably appears bizarre or pathological to Westerners. (Jean Lyon, from Black Star.)

also changes with the circumstances. Wile (1940, p. 232) has commented, for example:

Cotton Mather was regarded as normal in his acceptance of witchcraft and as abnormal in his espousal of vaccination. Protecting against the evil eye, the wearing of amulets, the use of flagellation, the exhibition of hysteria, the mob spirit in action, the jitterbug, social hypocrisy, the pursuit of power, pressures for social reform, the intolerant totalitarian states, the urged reform of marriage and divorce, are behaviors concerning which one might ask, "Are they essentially morbid?" Are they sufficiently pathological to require treatment? Does normal behavior always present the wholesome and the beneficial: if not, should it be regarded as normal? Clearly the norm is not

static—the same behavior may be normal today or abnormal tomorrow. A dry mouth is not normal under many conditions, but it is in a state of fear or fever. Lying is differentiated from pathological lying, fantasy and imagination are not far apart. The normal style of today is abnormal tomorrow and the absolutes of yesterday appear to be the relatives of today.

In some ancient societies, the person displaying psychotic (insane) behavior and having hallucinations was revered as a god. In other societies, especially in the Middle Ages, such a person was thought to be possessed by devils. The devils were "exorcised" by ritual or by cutting a hole in the skull to let them out. In some eras and settings, the person was punished or destroyed, as in the witch burnings in Europe and seventeenth-century America. In some societies, homosexual behavior was regarded as perfectly natural and acceptable, while in others homosexual behavior is a sign of illness or evil and regarded with fear or distaste (Fig. 7-7).

These examples highlight the problem of values in judging failure of adjustment. From the perspective of one criterion a person may be regarded as sound, but from another the same individual may be considered in trouble. The person who inhibits chronic anger toward friends, relatives, and neighbors may develop in consequence a physical symptom such as a headache, ulcers, or high blood pressure. People who know him or her are not offended by the somatic symptom, but might regard the person as disturbed if he or she frequently expressed anger in actions. Which reaction is more maladjusted? The answer clearly depends on how one evaluates the "badness" of each consequence. The same issue was found earlier in Chapter 4 in the discussion of the defense mechanisms.

Positive and negative terms In a discussion of the topic of positive mental health, Andie L. Knutson (1963, p. 300) stated the theme that a practical approach to adjustment, whether the emphasis is on psychopathology or health, requires value judgments:

> Man, perhaps more than any other creature, is a valuing animal. A subtle network of values, chiefly acquired in infancy, guide both the direction and mode of his thought and action, and give meaning and significance to his efforts. The intensity with which these values are held may at once impart fervor to his strivings and blind him to other possible, even more fruitful alternatives. Unless shaken up by some unusual situation or value conflict, he may be unaware of their guiding—and restricting—influence.

Knutson also pointed out that the modern preference for a positive mental health perspective leads to a more benign and hopeful feeling tone compared with the focus on illness. The term "mental illness," for example, was once probably less threatening and more attractive than other terms that had been previously in use, such as "lunacy" or "insanity." By the same token, to say that one is seeking help from a mental *health* clinic seems less frightening, less damaging to one's ego, and more hopeful-sounding than to say that one is consulting a specialist in mental *illness* at a clinic for mental *disorders.*

Thus, "mental health" as a term appears to have two meanings: (1) It is an attempt to replace a term that has negative connotations ("illness") with a term that has positive connotations ("health"), without really altering the meaning; and (2) it connotes a set of values about what is desirable in human beings. Furthermore, noted Knutson (1963, p. 303), "Health, no matter how many qualifying adjectives we place in front of it, conjures up the image of illness."

The high-minded attempt to replace negative words with positive words runs counter to the characteristic emphasis in our language. Knutson has made the interesting point that our language is more richly geared to the negative terms (p. 304):

> I have been surprised to discover what may have been obvious to others, that our language, on the whole, seems to be a language of hardship. We have rich vocabularies filled with vitality and meaning to describe personal aches, pains, and illness, and for expressing sympathy, empathy, and support. We possess a wealth of simple, cogent, expressive terms for noting the ills of society, the poverty, suffering, vice, crime, human wastage, and other social maladies which cry for attention and reform. Yet we seem to have a paucity of terms for describing horizons and vistas beyond the absence of these restricting conditions.
>
> Like the Aztecs, whose experiences have led them to acquire many words to describe the climate most familiar to them, but only one word for snow, ice, and cold (Whorf, 1947), our hardship experiences seem to have left us wallowing in terms to deal with suffering and dismay but linguistically impoverished when we seek to describe a positive potential in other than escapist terms. Even the visionaries of Western society have tended to describe their utopias in terms of the absence of restrictive or demoralizing conditions of society rather than in terms of vistas. The five freedoms of which Roosevelt and Churchill spoke are more freedoms *from* than freedoms *for.*

Health versus virtue   The truly central and most momentous question in an analysis of the values underlying the concepts of mental health is whether "health" means anything different from "good" or "virtuous." By alluding to *health* (or disease) rather than *human goodness* (or badness), one is reminded that people of ancient and medieval times would have understood the question "Is he a good or virtuous man?", although the question "Is he a well-adjusted man?" or "Is she a healthy woman?" would have made no sense. Is there a difference between the two? The answer that is implicitly encouraged is usually "yes." But on what grounds? All the writers in this field appear to be acting as philosophers in scientists' clothing. They appear to use the concept of *health* just as the religious fundamentalist uses Genesis—to buttress their personal philosophies by the chapter and verse of scientific pronouncement.

It is useful to remember that nineteenth-century Chinese and Europeans regarded one another as barbarians, each correctly from their own point of view. This mutual disrespect was

FIGURE 7-8 Women's liberation demonstrators on the steps of New York's St. Patrick's Cathedral during Women's Equality Week. (Cary Herz, from Nancy Palmer Photo Agency.)

not merely a matter of nationalism but stemmed from basic differences in values. For example, for the Westerner, loyalty to one's nation or ideology was among the highest virtues, while to the Chinese, loyalty to one's clan was more important. Hence the Chinese who would sell out his country for personal (family) advantage was properly despised by his Western bribe givers on the basis of the latter's value system, but by Chinese standards he was merely doing his filial duty.

One of the interesting current examples of how values can, without our recognizing it, enter into our conceptions of what is healthy or unhealthy concerns the way traditional sex roles in our own society have been viewed. Deviations from the norms of masculine and feminine were, until recently, regarded as unhealthy or undesirable for the person's well-being. For example, it has generally been considered good for girls to inhibit aggression and for boys to be aggressive but to inhibit dependency; moreover, little girls should be concerned with attractiveness while little boys should be concerned with achievement. Bem (1972) points out that one common assumption in this is that ". . . children will somehow be 'better off' if their behavior conforms to society's stereotypes of sex-appropriate behavior." She notes that highly influential books on child development often explicitly state this, thus making the traditional sex roles in effect a prescriptive code for the cultivation of mental health through child-rearing practices. Bem challenges the existence of any evidence that girls who conform to this stereotype are better adjusted (or healthier) than those who grow up with traits normally thought of as masculine, or that boys are better adjusted if their personalities do not include traits normally considered as feminine. Here too one sees how, without their being identified as such, values connected with a culture's sex role requirements enter into the definitions of health and illness (Fig. 7-8).

Another example concerns the matter of the "work ethic." Freud spoke of mental health as

FIGURE 7-9 "Satisfying work" on the assembly line, as satirized by Charlie Chaplin in the movie *Modern Times.* (Culver Picture, Inc.)

consisting of the capacity for love and work, the former altruistic rather than purely erotic love, the latter involving contributing something of value to the society through one's efforts. The unhealthy person, psychologically speaking, is one whose capacity for love and work has been inhibited, warped, or distorted. We have already seen that Erikson's conception of ego identity also includes having a constructive place in the world of work. All this seems predicated, however, on a work ethic that may well be disappearing in the increasingly automated technological society, where work for most people is becoming increasingly meaningless except as a means of obtaining a livelihood. What would happen to Freud's and Erikson's conception of mental health if the work ethic as a cultural value were replaced, as Etzioni (1974) suggests is happening, by an ethic of hedonism, that is, by a value system in which the accepted prime mover in human affairs is the desire to minimize pain and maximize pleasure? There do appear to be cultures in which work is considered to be an evil to be avoided except when absolutely necessary. Clearly, the notion that integrating oneself productively into the working world is an essential feature of mental health is not only value-laden but stems from values that have been dominant in a particular culture in a particular era. When and if the dominant cultural values change, will the definition of mental health also change? Very probably (Fig. 7-9).

There are relatively few *basic* differences in the criteria of mental health employed by various writers, though there are great differences in emphasis. In all probability, a behavior considered to be healthy by one writer would not be regarded as unhealthy by another. Thus, the differences often appear to be more verbal than fundamental. In fact, all writers on mental health might be considered to share a common cultural heritage, that of the upwardly mobile American middle class of Western European descent. Perhaps this is the reason why their views of what is healthy (or virtuous) are similar, give or take a few adjectives or slight variations of emphasis. Writers about positive mental health are generalizing their own culture's values to the whole world. Some of us may like or share these values; however, they are clearly values about *goodness* or *virtue,* and to clothe them in the scientific terminology of *health* and *disease* does not alter this basic fact.

Social class differences in outlook.   That the dominant conception of mental health is culturally determined and has a middle-class basis has been vigorously claimed by Robert Reiff (1966). He, like others, has noted that the popular point of view concerning mental health and mental illness is quite different from that of the mental health professional. Popular thinking begins with normal behavior as its point of reference, emphasizing the human qualities of rationality and the exercise of self-control. Mental illness, in which rationality is impaired, is seen as the opposite of normality; the person has presumably lost control of his or her behavior and is no longer responsible. Most working-class people see mental illness in terms of psychosis or insanity and, hence, as a very threatening thing. It is the ultimate catastrophe. Considering mental illness in the extreme terms of psychosis, the lower-class worker thus views mental health and mental illness not as on a continuum but as discontinuous or separate phenomena.

This is quite different from the psychiatric point of view, which is also the educated viewpoint. The educated position starts with abnormal behavior as its point of reference and extrapolates from that to the normal. In the view of the mental health professional, mental health and mental illness are on a continuum, differing only in degree. There is virtually no such thing as normal, and distrust of the absolute concept of normality is implied in the tendency of the professional to refer instead to the "so-called normal." Behavior is not assumed to be entirely under rational control at all, but is seen as in large part determined by unconscious, emotional forces.

Thus the educated middle-class person may be reassured by the idea that the psychological mechanisms characteristic of sick people are little different from those of anyone else; but the lower-class, uneducated person is unable to accept such an idea, since he or she holds that mental illness is the opposite extreme of normalcy. Furthermore, working-class people accept that mental illness (equated with severe psychosis) exists, but they have difficulty accepting the idea of neurotic disturbances as illness. The term "neurotic" confuses them. It is understandable to consider a raving psychotic as emotionally upset, since the normal behavior is out of control; but it seems incomprehensible that a fellow with a lame back or a girl who is particularly passive and permits everyone to take advantage of her can be ill or emotionally disturbed.

According to Reiff, the basic aim and justification of most psychotherapy is that the person should actualize him- or herself, realize his or her full potential, discover better and more satisfying ways of living. Such an aim makes good sense to educated middle-class or upper-class persons, who see themselves as capable of playing many roles in society, of selecting the most fitting role, and of achieving self-actualization. Lower-class persons see themselves as powerless to do this. Reiff puts it as follows (1966, pp. 53–54):

The view that one can realize his full potential presupposes a view of society in which there are many possibilities and opportunities and that one need only remove the internal difficulties to make a rich, full life possible. For the most part, disturbed middle-class patients see themselves as *victims of their own selves.* Low-income people, on the other hand, are not future-oriented. They are task-oriented, concrete, and concerned primarily with the here and now. They live in a world of limited or no opportunities. There is little or no role flexibility. They see themselves as *victims of circumstances.* Self-actualization under these conditions is meaningless to them. Before they can become interested in self-actualization, they have got to believe that they can play a role in determining what happens to them. Thus, *self-determination,* rather than self-actualization, is a more realistic and more meaningful goal for them.

If Reiff is correct about the different meanings of mental health and illness as a function of social class, and there is ample reason to think he is, then it follows that the opportunities to realize one's human potentialities are quite different in lower-class populations compared with middle- and upper-class populations. To the middle-class individual, the widely accepted professional view may be quite meaningful; to the lower-class person, it may make absolutely no sense at all. The latter cannot usually realize his or her human potentials to the full; it is not just that some unfortunate people are unable to. Rather, lots of people think it is senseless or meaningless under the conditions of their lives.

The value differences cited above between middle- and lower-class societies within the United States are actually minor compared with the huge differences that exist across grossly different cultures, say between many Oriental and Western societies, or between industrialized and relatively primitive societies. Curiously, differences among people that are viewed as having to do with good and evil, when considered in the cross-cultural context, may be viewed as manifestations of mental illness when they involve a deviant within one's own society. Incest, various forms of cannibalism, or the use of drugs for their effects on the mind (other than alcohol and tobacco) when observed in other cultures were all judged as "barbaric," "savage," or "uncivilized" by nineteenth-century America, while the same behavior occurring at home was viewed as evidence of "moral depravity," a concept which is a mixture of ideas about mental health and meanings of good and evil.

There is probably no concept of positive mental health that is valid across all cultures, though many have tried to find one. Thus, the ability to form intimate interpersonal ties, creativeness, sense of individuality, self-actualization, or what have you, are *all* irrelevant to what it means to be "healthy" or "good" in many societies; moreover, such qualities are probably considered evil, sick, and/or maladjustive in some societies. In Japan, for instance, individuality should be subordinated to the welfare of one's society or social group. This sort of *conflict of values,* rather than being a mere surface problem, is undoubtedly at the root of much intercultural conflict.

Are some societies healthier than others? We might touch upon one further question here, namely, whether some societies are "healthier" than others. It might be better to ask whether some cultures are better to live in than others from some given point of view, since the prior question implies a culture-free standard of health, and doubts about this have been expressed above. Still, there are writers who strongly maintain that societies do vary in their capacity to promote and permit "healthy" psychological functioning (for example, Fromm, 1955). Given the assumption of some basic human needs, it is possible to ask whether any given society fully permits or encourages their gratification.

There are two aspects to the question of whether some societies are healthier than others. First, do some subcultures have such *different ideals* about mental health or virtue that they are prevented from supplying the conditions for personality development which favor healthy outcomes? Or do most subcultures share basically the same ideals but vary in their *capacity to meet these ideals?* If the former is true, then certain subgroups in our culture will develop patterns of behavior which are classed as unhealthy by the uncomprehending majority. For example, perhaps people within our society largely agree, say, that a job is essential for one's self-respect, that a man must support his family, or that one's home is one's castle. However, poverty-stricken subcultures cannot as readily meet these ideals, even

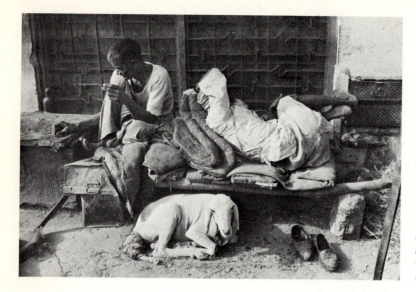

FIGURE 7-10 Cultures and subcultures may share the same ideals of mental health but vary in their capacity to meet these ideals. The people living here in socially induced squalor could have culturally based concepts of the good life that are indistinguishable from those of the middle-class reader—for example, self-realization, independence, autonomy, and growth—but their chances of meeting such ideals are severely curtailed. (Henri Cartier-Bresson, from Magnum.)

though they share them with the rest of the society. It is probable that both of these alternatives are partly correct, but it is not clear whether or not both are equally important (Fig. 7-10).

Second, are there some societies whose ideals are so much in conflict with biological capabilities that many individuals growing up within them cannot meet the ideals and are thus doomed to be "unhealthy" by their own society's definition? This point of view asserts that there must be a matching of the society's values with those most naturally arising from human biological makeup. The difficulty lies in establishing what these biological dispositions are and the extent to which they can be modified without creating, of necessity, emotional disturbances in people. At this stage of knowledge about human beings and the capacity of society to transform them without psychological harm, it is only possible to raise the issue. It is a fascinating question.

Finally, although the tendency of scientists to conceal, perhaps inadvertently, their culturally based values under the guise of such science-centered terms as "health" and "illness" has been criticized, this does not imply that there is no room for science in attacking value-laden

questions. Once we have recognized that definitions of positive mental health are based not on scientific proof, but on acceptance of the cultural norms that surround us, or on philosophical considerations, we can then proceed to bring the science of psychology back into the picture. It is possible, and important, to assess empirically how well a person has achieved the positive goals he or she has accepted from society or chosen from his or her philosophy and to determine the childhood antecedents of the achievement of these goals. It is only the *definition* of positive mental health that is tangled up with values. The study of the causes and effects of achieving or not achieving the criteria of positive mental health, however defined, is not only possible by scientific methods but is a matter of the greatest scientific importance.

To sum up by restating the answer to the question about whether "healthy" is different from "good" or "virtuous," *mental illness*—at least in its most severe and common forms (for example, schizophrenia and depression)—evidently occurs and is branded as abnormal in most societies. Similar forms of reaction can also be observed in monkeys and other primates.

However, *positive mental health* probably has limited meaning apart from the cultural context. If one tries to define values common to all societies, one appears to end up with values so vague and few in number as to be quite unsatisfactory for a working definition of positive mental health. Alternatively, if one takes a single society as the base for investigation, the definition of positive mental health which is derived will usually be exactly coterminous with that society's values. And those who would propose mental health values which differ from those recommended by the society in which they live (for example, Fromm, 1955) are in fact extracting the values of a *subculture* and saying that everyone should really think as they do.

Thus, the position of the author is that there is *no difference* between positive mental health and what used to be called "good," "right," and "virtuous." The reason people refer to positive mental health in place of virtuousness is that doing so appears to give these ideas the support of scientific authority. The values then take on the quality of being "eternal verities" supported by science, as opposed to evanescent historical fads which will come and go. One can believe in love, creativity, and honesty without having to have scientific support. However, by basing these values on medicine or science and identifying them as "healthy" rather than merely virtuous, we are reassured about their truthfulness in the face of alternative values in cultures just a few jet hours away. But we should not be misled into thinking that the concepts of mental health as conceived today are fundamentally different from the concepts of virtue as it might be conceived today.

The author is not opposed to the acceptance of values in the definition of health or virtue. Such acceptance cannot be avoided, and therefore professional workers should go about choosing values in as sophisticated a fashion as possible. No one should be fooled, however, into believing that values are not involved in concepts of mental health; yet they should not be clothed in the guise of science. Once a value has been chosen, it can be studied with all the scientific acumen at one's disposal. This point has been effectively expressed by Smith (1961, pp. 302–303):

> The psychologist has *as much right* to posit values as anyone else, in some important respects more. It is time to dispel the shopworn bromide that the humanist (or moralist or philosopher) has a corner on pronouncements about values, while the psychologist (or sociologist or scientist generally) must restrict himself to facts.
>
> The old myth had it that man lost his precultural innocence when, biting the fruit of the Tree of Knowledge, he became aware of Good and Evil. In becoming modern, man has taken a second portentous bite of the same fruit. There are alternative versions of Good and Evil, he discovers to his discomfiture, and it is up to him to choose the commitments he is to live by. From this emerging view that can no longer turn to authoritative interpretations of tradition or divine revelation to resolve questions of value, it makes no sense at all for us to encyst ourselves behind a pass-the-buck notion that we can leave value judgments to some other discipline that specializes in them. There is no discipline that has this mythical competence: the humanist and the theologian speak with no greater authority than we. We are all in it together.

MENTAL HEALTH AND THE ENVIRONMENT

The recognition that the opportunities for full realization of human potentialities differ from one social class to another merges with the third issue, namely, whether we can speak of health or illness without reference to the conditions under which people live.

The concept of mental health tends to favor the image of the person who, regardless of circumstances, is effective, accepting, altruistic, secure, loving, sexually adequate, and so forth. But there are many circumstances under which these idealized traits have no chance to emerge, or are unlikely to. Circumstances have a great deal to do with how one feels and behaves. As Scott (1958, p. 37) has put it, "Attempted adjustment does not necessarily result in success, for success is dependent on the environment. The best mode of adjustment only maximizes the chances of success. It is mentally healthy behavior even if the environment does not permit a solution of the problem."

This has most interesting implications. It says that mental health cannot be defined without reference to the conditions to which a person must adjust. Even a person who displayed symptoms of psychopathology could be regarded, nevertheless, as "doing pretty well" if he or she lived under relatively poor circumstances which made suffering and failure almost certain. Such a person may be doing as well as—or better than—one might expect, or is at least employing adjustive processes that resonate with the overwhelming difficulties being faced.

What should we say about the emotional disturbances we observe in persons who have grown up under conditions of severe environmental deprivation? About those who have lived for a time in a concentration camp? About those exposed to continuing natural disaster or to military combat? About persons with drastic physical handicaps? About children who have suffered repeated, severe physical beatings at the hands of their parents? Can we expect them to transcend these handicaps which are not of their making as easily as those of us who have lived under highly favorable circumstances of life? Many of the most effective and creative persons have started life under damaging environmental conditions, and the drive to acquire competence and to grow was, in some degree, probably strengthened by the stresses of their lives. Yet in other instances, instead of being helped to grow, persons have been severely traumatized. And we have said nothing of the continuing price in neuroticism

that some of the most competent individuals have paid for the struggle to transcend a destructive early life environment. For those who have succeeded magnificently in spite of environmental handicaps yet have paid the price of a perpetually troubled mind, and for those who were not altogether beaten down by adversity but who bear deep scars, one must say that they have done as well as or better than might have been expected in the light of the environmental conditions they had to face.

It should be easier to meet the criteria of positive mental health if the circumstances of one's life have been favorable than if they have been unfavorable. If one defines mental health without reference to the conditions of life, past as well as present, one of its major components—the environmental situation—is being ignored. This makes the establishment of a standard of health highly inequitable, and perhaps of little meaning. The existence of the problem makes the attainment of *absolute* standards of mental health quite difficult, if not impossible. What is needed also is a *relative standard* for considering the person's functioning in the light of the circumstances of his or her life.

People and social groups seem to vary greatly in the extent of stress in their lives, and hence in their chances to achieve positive mental health. However, it is also true that some major stresses are inevitable for all people. And to some degree, variations in the adequacy of adjustment in living depend on the extent to which the person has learned how to cope with such stresses. This is not merely a matter of luck, but it constitutes an achievement that some people accomplish well and others poorly, given even roughly similar conditions of living. There are countless examples of persons who manage surprisingly well despite extremely traumatizing conditions of life, and we must not detract from such accomplishment. Thus, many individuals cope successfully with, for example, severe and crippling spinal cord injuries, constant pain, blindness or deafness (witness the impressive life of Helen Keller, both blind and deaf), a death sentence, loss of their whole family in an accident, uprooting and transplantation late in life, or misshapen bodies or ugly scars to which others react with revulsion. Added to these may be the more ordinary stresses that others must face, such as separation from or loss of parents, displacement by siblings, parental rejection in childhood, transition to independent adulthood, puberty, competitive failure in school or work, marriage, pregnancy, menopause, constant moves from one community to another, retirement, rapid social change, or wars and threats of wars.

When can we say that a person is doing or coping well despite being exposed to damaging conditions of life? There are at least four things he or she should be doing, or (to put it differently) there are four major coping tasks in the face of stressful conditions:

1 Tolerating or relieving all or some of the attendant distress.
2 Maintaining a sense of personal worth despite defeats.
3 Maintaining rewarding interpersonal relationships.
4 Meeting the specific requirements of the stressful tasks that are being faced, or utilizing the opportunities available for accomplishing any of the above (see, for example, Hamburg and Adams, 1967).

The most successful persons (in adjustment) are somehow able to do these things in the face of stressful life conditions, searching for information needed to meet the stress situation, preparing or planning for problems that can be anticipated, distinguishing between that which can be changed and that which must be endured, taking whatever actions must be taken, and, overall, sustaining a mainly positive or hopeful rather than a negative outlook and an active engagement in the tasks of life over the long term.

From the above standpoint, it is possible to end our discussion of the healthy personality, or successful living, on a positive though realistic note—namely, that many or perhaps most people do rather well in coping with severe stresses of life. This is nowhere better stated than in the comments by Hamburg and Adams below (1967, p. 278) about coping by patients with severe injuries:

It is clear enough that severe physical disability, coming on quite suddenly, is an extreme test of coping resources. Indeed, a plausible case can be made for expecting uniformly devastating results. One might suppose that the vast majority of severely damaged patients would be psychologically overwhelmed and left with lasting disturbances.

Yet clinical experience indicates that the outcome is sometimes surprisingly favorable. A few systematic studies on outcome indicate that a substantial proportion of severely injured patients make impressive psychosocial recovery.

We must come to understand better through psychological research on stress and coping the way this comes about and the factors in the person's past and present which contribute to successful living even under highly damaging life experiences.

SUMMING UP

Various attempts have been made to conceptualize positive mental health and to study healthy personalities. Some of the major efforts were reviewed in this chapter. For example, in one group of average or ordinary persons (called homoclites) characterized by *benign*, relatively *un-conflict-laden attitudes* and the absence of strong ambition and dissatisfaction were studied. Researchers examining the personalities of the

Mercury astronauts regarded mental health as the ability to *function effectively* under certain kinds of *stress.* The concept of *competence* as health was central to studies of the adjustive efforts of effective youths anticipating and handling the transition from high school to college. Finally, recent studies of youthful rebellion offer still another view of mental health, not as benign conformity and the absence of struggle but as *creative striving* and even *rebelliousness* against societal evils. Each of these attempts began with a somewhat different idea about what is healthy as a starting point for investigation.

Three difficult-to-resolve issues are inherent in any attempt to conceive of and study mental health. First, should we conceive of health as a collection of relatively *independent spheres* or traits, with success in one sphere having little or no relationship to success in another? Or is mental health best thought of, à la Erikson, as an *integrated system* in which each of a series of early life transitions or crises has been successfully passed through, producing a harmonious integration of diverse psychological tendencies?

Second, a large component of valuation exists in whatever way we ultimately view health and illness. *Values* are reflected in the fact that what we usually mean by healthy tends to be coextensive with the culturally based outlook on the nature of human goodness. To speak of virtue as health or illness is an attempt to buttress our value biases with the authority of scientific pronouncement, or by the dictates of a biological law.

There are also major *social class differences in outlook* toward health and psychopathology, with middle-class persons and professionals treating health and illness as a continuum and lower-class persons thinking of health as the opposite of being crazy or insane. The latter group, therefore, is apt to be frightened by the idea of mental illness and to avoid seeking help in psychotherapy for their troubles, which they tend to blame on the external environment rather than on remedial defects within themselves. People often ask whether some societies are healthier or sicker than others. This breaks down into two basic issues: First, cultures can have different ideas about what is healthy or virtuous, in which case the attributes that are healthy in one may seem unhealthy in another; second, cultures may share common ideals about mental health but provide unequal opportunities to their members for achieving it. Professionals frequently assume that there must be a good *match between human biological makeup and the values and demands of the society* in order to maximize healthy personality development.

Any adequate treatment of mental health and illness must also take into account the *environmental conditions* under which people live. Because of severely negative environments, some persons may be having considerable difficulties in adjusting yet be doing as well as could be expected with the resources available to them. Thus, the opportunities for mental health are not equal in all societies or all social segments, and health cannot be properly defined without reference to the conditions to which the person must adjust. We need a *relative standard of health* as well as an absolute or ideal standard. Nevertheless, it is not uncommon for people to *transcend extremely traumatizing or stressful conditions* of life and to manage to live very successfully despite them. Clinical evidence points to the fact that many people manage to perform the major coping tasks in a highly successful fashion, namely, by tolerating or relieving personal distress, maintaining a sense of personal worth, maintaining rewarding interpersonal relationships, and meeting the specific requirements of stressful tasks or utilizing environmental resources, despite highly damaging conditions of life. It is encouraging to realize that most human beings turn out to be highly *resourceful* and *resilient* in the face of life stress.

PART IV
MODELS OF SUCCESS AND FAILURE OF ADJUSTMENT

PART IV
MODELS OF SUCCESS
AND FAILURE
OF ADJUSTMENT

Understanding requires far more than mere description and classification. We need to seek explanations of adjustive success and failure, and we can do this in two interdependent ways: First, we try to conceive or theorize about the mechanisms or processes involved in the diverse patterns of adjustment; second, we need to identify the causal factors or conditions in people's lives that account for such patterns.

In Chapter 8 we survey how men and women in the past understood failure and success in adjustment and how modern thought has evolved from this past. The three main theoretical models of failure and success in use today are then explored. Chapter 9 discusses the medical-biological explanation, which seeks to pin adjustive failure on constitutional factors arising from genetic influences or acquired neuro-humoral defects. The sociogenic model is reviewed in Chapter 10. This focuses on the impact of culture and social institutions which impair the ability of a people or subgroup to adjust successfully or prevent the development of the skills and resources necessary to function well. Chapter 11 turns to the psychogenic model, which focuses on the individual and his particular social history.

In Chapter 12, the problems of classification inherent in the clinical material presented earlier in Chapter 6 are examined, and a critique is offered of the

Dorothea Lange, from Magnum

individual models—especially the medical-biological or illness model, which today is under serious attack from many professional quarters. Finally, Chapter 12 ends with an effort to synthesize the various explanatory positions examined in Part IV and to show that each of the individual approaches is insufficient by itself: rather, all are needed, with one supplementing the other.

CHAPTER 8 ANCIENT AND MODERN OUTLOOKS TOWARD MENTAL ILLNESS

The topic of human adjustment is a very modern one. In earlier eras, the virtuous life—however this was defined by a particular society—was the primary standard or norm against which individual persons could be judged. People who deviated from the norm were assumed to do so because of inherent evil or stupidity, or because they were afflicted or possessed by demons, devils, or other supernatural forces. Statements such as "He is a good person" or "She is a bad person" would have been readily understood by an Athenian or a Roman, someone in the Middle Ages, or a citizen of Europe during the Renaissance. However, to say "She is adjusting successfully (or unsuccessfully)" or "He is mentally healthy (or ill)" would have made no sense to these peoples. The concept of adjustment is a product of the modern naturalistic era of science; it is an idea derived from Darwin's concepts of biological evolution which became influential only in the mid-nineteenth century.

To speak thus of "modern" implies an evolution of thought over the ages, and indeed there have been major changes over historical time in the way society has viewed mental illness and health. It will be instructive to examine briefly the ways in which adjustive failure has been viewed in ancient civilizations and in primitive ones still in existence today, as well as to look at the evolution of later thought. In doing so, we shall draw upon accounts of this history that have been written by Zilboorg and Henry (1941), Jerome Frank (1963), and Alexander and Selesnick (1966). In examining how primitive humans, the Greeks, or Europeans during the Middle Ages viewed mental illness, or how we do so today, we must bear in mind that we are engaging in a degree of oversimplification. Such statements refer to the dominant views of that time or place as judged from historical accounts and other writings, and no doubt not everyone at that time thought in the same way. Thus, although the dominant view of the Middle Ages was one of superstition and magic, there were dissident voices who (no doubt vainly) adopted or pressed for a more rational and scientific view or a more humanistic one.

THE PRIMITIVE OUTLOOK

Frank (1963) portrays the attitude of *primitive man* toward illness as a misfortune encompassing the whole person and stemming from the person's relationship with the supernatural world. Primitive societies do not distinguish sharply between mental illness and bodily illness. Any illness may be seen as the result of the patient's loss of his or her soul, of being possessed by an evil spirit, of being harmed by something inserted into the body by a sorcerer, or of being the victim of an ancestral ghost who feels malicious toward the victim or has been offended by him or her. Most often the patient is assumed to be partly responsible for the misfortune by having performed some witting or unwitting transgression against the supernatural or by in some way incurring the hostility of someone who is employing a sorcerer for revenge. Sometimes it is the transgression of a relative of the patient that has created the difficulty and not that of the patient. In many primitive societies natural causes as well as the supernatural are recognized—a bone may be broken because of a fall—but the root cause of the fall is nonetheless considered to be the offended spirit or sorcerer.

Frank describes the case of a sixty-three-year-old Guatemalan Indian woman (first published by Gillin in 1948). Frank's account illustrates aptly the viewpoint of modern primitive people toward

illness. As we shall see, those of ancient and medieval times had essentially the same viewpoint. The woman involved was evidently suffering from what a modern American psychiatrist would refer to as an "agitated depression." Depression involves deep feelings of hopelessness and worthlessness; in agitated depression, these feelings are also associated with much evident distress, crying, wringing of the hands, and sleeplessness. The Guatemalan Indians explain such disturbances as the loss of the person's soul, and the condition cannot be relieved until the soul is retrieved. The present episode of depression was the eighth suffered by this woman. Frank's account of the treatment conducted by the local shaman or healer goes as follows (1963, pp. 46–49; quotes from Gillin, 1948, pp. 389, 391, 394):

> The treatment began with a diagnostic session attended not only by the patient but by her husband, a male friend, and two anthropologists. The healer felt her pulse for a while, while looking her in the eye, then confirmed that she was suffering from "espanto." He then told her in a calm authoritative manner that it had happened near the river when she saw her husband foolishly lose her money to a loose woman, and he urged her to tell the whole story. After a brief period of reluctance, the patient "loosed a flood of words telling of her life frustrations and anxieties. . . . During the recital . . . the curer . . . nodded noncommittally, but permissively, keeping his eyes fixed on her face. Then he said that it was good that she should tell him of her life." Finally they went over the precipitating incident of the present attack in detail. In essence, she and her husband were passing near the spot where he had been deceived by the loose woman. She upbraided him, and he struck her with a rock.
>
> The curer then told her he was confident she could be cured and outlined in detail the

preparations that she would have to make for the curing session four days later. She was responsible for these preparations, which involved procuring and preparing certain medications, preparing a feast, persuading a woman friend or kinsman to be her "servant" during the preparatory period and healing session, and persuading one of the six chiefs of the village to participate with the medicine man in the ceremony.

The ceremony itself began at four in the afternoon and lasted until five the next morning. Before the healer arrived, the house and the house altar had been decorated with pine boughs, and numerous invited guests and participants had assembled. After they were all present, the healer made his entrance, shook hands all around, and checked the preparations carefully. Then there was a period of light refreshment and social chitchat, which apparently helped to organize a social group around the patient and to relax tension.

After dusk, the healer, chief, and others of the group went off to church, apparently to appease the Christian deities in advance, since "recovery of the soul involves dealing with renegade saints and familiar spirits certainly not approved of by God Almighty." When they returned, a large meal was served. The patient did not eat, but was complimented by all present on her food. Then the healer carried out a long series of rituals involving such activities as making wax dolls of the chief of evil spirits and his wife, to whom the healer appealed for return of the patient's soul, and elaborate massage of the patient with whole eggs, which were believed to absorb some of the sickness from the patient's body. The curer, the chief, two male helpers, and the ever-present anthropologists next took the eggs and a variety of paraphernalia, including gifts for the evil spirits, to the place where the patient had lost her soul, and the healer pleaded with various spirits to restore her soul to her.

On their return they were met at the door by the patient, who showed an intense desire to know whether the mission had been successful. The curer spoke noncommittal but comforting words. This was followed by much praying by the healer and the chief before the house altar and a special ground altar set up outside, and by rites to purify and sanctify the house. Some of these activities were devoted to explaining to the household patron saint why it was necessary to deal with evil spirits. All this took until about 2 A.M., at which time the ceremony came to a climax. The patient, naked except for a small loin cloth, went outside. Before the audience, the healer sprayed her entire body with a magic fluid that had been prepared during the ritual and that had a high alcoholic content. Then she had to sit, naked and shivering, in the cold air for about ten minutes. Finally she drank about a pint of the fluid. Then they returned indoors, the patient lay down in front of the altar, and the healer massaged her vigorously and systematically with the eggs, then with one of his sandals. She then arose, put on her clothes, lay down on the rustic platform bed, and was covered with blankets. By this time she was thoroughly relaxed.

Finally, the healer broke the six eggs used in the massage into a bowl of water one by one, and as he watched their swirling whites he reviewed the history of the patient's eight "espantos," pointing out the "proofs" in the eggs. The sinking of the eggs to the bottom of the bowl showed that all the previous "espantos" had been cured and that the present symptoms would shortly disappear. The healer "pronounced the cure finished. The patient roused herself briefly on the bed and shouted hoarsely, that is right." This ended the ceremony and everyone left but the patient's immediate family.

The patient had a high fever for the following few days. This did not concern the healer, whose position was that everyone died sooner or later anyway, and if the patient died, it was better for her to die with her soul than without it. He refused to see her again, as his work was done. The anthropologist treated her with antibiotics, and she made a good recovery from the fever and the depression. The author [Gillin] notes that for the four weeks he was able to observe her "she seemed to have developed a

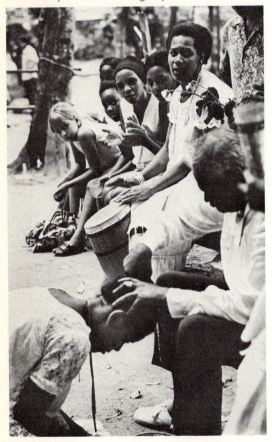

FIGURE 8-1 Brazilian *macumba*, or voodoo ceremony—a baptismlike rite during which the "saint" prays over the woman, marks her head with chalk, then pours beer over her, while the other participants chant and clap to the rhythm of a drum. (Werner Muckenhirn, from Nancy Palmer Photo Agency.)

new personality. . . . The hypochondriacal complaints, nagging of her husband and relatives, withdrawal from her social contacts, and anxiety symptoms all disappeared."

Frank also discusses "cures" taking place at the religious shrine at Lourdes, France, making it clear that fully documented cures of unquestionable and gross organic diseases are extremely rare, with about the same frequency as is found in secular settings. Therefore, these are probably not cures of organic diseases, but rather of *psychological* or *psychosomatic disorders*. They depend on suggestion, on the relationship with the healer, on evidence of concern and support on the part of the family and friends, on the hopes and expectations of the individual for relief, and on the emotionally charged atmosphere of the healing ceremony. Those that are helped are generally rather simple-minded and uncritical individuals who become highly aroused by the healing ceremony.

THE VIEW OF ANCIENT CIVILIZATIONS

The above case demonstrates the reliance of modern primitive people on magic and religion and the importance given to evil spirits, sorcerers, and gods in the conception of illness. This is precisely the way the ancients conceived of illness also, that is, in terms of a mixture of *magic and religion*. One sometimes finds these magical-religious concepts suffused with astute psychological insights that have a surprisingly modern quality. For example, the modern concepts of the defense of projection, and other psychological mechanisms, are anticipated in ancient Hebrew writings. A story is told of an antivice crusader who accused the people of Jerusalem of crimes which he himself had committed, an evident instance of projection. Elsewhere in ancient Hebrew writings it is observed that good men have wicked dreams, thus anticipating the Freudian idea that dreams express wishes which are morally proscribed. Hebrew writings also recommend that the mentally troubled patient should talk freely about his or her worries as a form of treatment.

The Hebrew view was that God or demons (who were the precipitating agents) represented the source of both health and illness. In Exodus, for example, it is said, "For I am the Lord that healeth thee." In Deuteronomy are the statements "I will kill and make alive; I wound and I heal" and "The Lord will smite thee with madness." Thus, God is the primary cause of disease, which was one way for Him to punish men and women for their sins.

There are also examples in the Hebrew literature of accurate, naturalistic observations of mental illness even before the period of the classical Greek civilization. The biblical description of Saul's mental illness is a case in point. Evidently severely depressed, Saul attempted to persuade a servant to kill him. The servant refused, upon which Saul committed suicide. Catatonic excitements and epileptic fits were also described, and the famous king Nebuchadnezzar (605–562 B.C.) was portrayed as having the delusion that he was a wolf.

The dominant viewpoint toward illness found in Mesopotamia, Egypt, Persia, and the Far East can also be characterized as religious and magical, and the ill person was thought to be possessed by demons. Gradually, however, beginning with ancient Greek civilization and gaining momentum very rapidly in the nineteenth and twentieth centuries, many people (at least the scholars and thinkers) began to assign to natural causes the forces they had earlier thought to be controlled by divine will, magic, or providence. This is the overriding importance of the Greek influence, that is, its emphasis on *rational, biological* approaches to an understanding of man, nature, and society. Its scholars believed that natural phenomena must have natural explanations.

This emphasis on rational explanation, on *natural causes,* is illustrated by the writings of Hippocrates (460–377 B.C.), who is often referred to as "the father of medicine." Hippocrates argued that those who considered the disorder of epilepsy to be a divine or sacred malady were merely concealing their ignorance of its real nature. He viewed the brain as the organ of intellectual activity and thought that mental illness was due to brain pathology. He introduced the first apparent classification of mental life, attempting to describe personality in terms of four types based on bodily humors—yellow bile, black bile, phlegm, and blood. The types of temperament he described included the choleric, melancholic, phlegmatic, and sanguine. Although the humoral (hormonal) concept on which these are based is no longer accepted (yet it presages the modern concept of the relations between glandular secretions and behavior), the terms describing people's temperaments have permeated our language and are still used colloquially and in literature.

The remarkable Greek period is filled with many brilliant and well-known names, including Pythagoras, Socrates, Plato, and Aristotle, all of whom enlarged the rational tradition of classical Greece and contributed much to psychological thought. This tradition was followed and extended by the Romans, whose best-known contributor to medical psychology was the physician Galen, a staunch advocate of the Hippocratic viewpoint.

MEDIEVAL HORRORS

During the medieval period of European history the Greco-Roman tradition of rationalism and naturalism was virtually buried for over a thousand years. This appears to have been brought about in part by the collapse of the Roman civilization. The Romans had assimilated the intellectual heritage of Greece, had fashioned stable social and legal institutions, and had made technological advances which were compatible with this heritage. These had been protected by military might. Eventually, however, the empire declined and the Roman institutions disintegrated. This disintegration resulted in a regression of most of the existing world to belief in magic and demonology, which the Greek period seven centuries earlier had begun to challenge and dispel.

One illustration of the return to a magical-religious outlook toward illness during the Middle Ages comes from a document referred to as "Code of Jewish Law," the Schulchan Aruch, first printed in Venice in 1565. The code was written by Joseph Karo (1488–1575), a Jewish scholar and legalist from Spain who undertook the document in order to unify Jewry. The Jews had been widely scattered throughout the world and were following customs that varied with the local community in which they lived. Karo wanted to provide a universal handbook of Jewish life. In an English translation published in the United States (Ganzfried, 1928, pp. cxxii, 85), the following passage reflects the medieval Jewish attitude toward illness:

> Rabbi Phineas, the son of Chama, preached saying, "Whosoever has any one sick in his house should go to a wise man and ask him to plead for mercy on his behalf, as it is said: 'The wrath of a King is as a messenger of death, but a wise man will pacify it'" (Prov. xvi:14). It is customary to give alms to the poor on behalf of the sick person for, "Repentance, Prayer, and Charity avert the evil decree." It is also customary to bless the sick person in the synagogue, and if he be dangerously ill, he is blessed even on the Sabbath, and a Festival. At times, the name of the sick person is changed, as this may avert the judgment decreed against him.

Here, as in the primitive world, the sick one is said to be punished by the wrath of God and must repent his or her sins in order to expect relief.

Such an outlook has been carried down to the present and may be found among many current religious groups throughout the world. For example, among Christian Scientists evil or sacrilegious thoughts are said to underlie all somatic illness, and sick persons are enjoined to purify their thoughts if they are to get well. Health is a badge of virtue and sickness a sign that the individual has allowed bad thoughts to "take possession" of him or her.

Christian fervor and ethics during the troubled Middle Ages simultaneously provided two important social influences: solace for the people who lived in these troubled centuries and intolerance toward the scientific approach which relied on observation and reason and which was seen as competitive with religious dogma for people's minds. If scientific thought took positions which conflicted with Church doctrine, it could not be tolerated. Thus, rationalism went underground for many centuries, and the traditions of Greco-Roman empiricism, skepticism, and scholarship were preserved only in monastic libraries and by the Arabs. Although some of the writings of scholars in this rational tradition were in part preserved, their thinking was not permitted to flourish or develop further. The organized Church was a political force with enormous power in Europe, and its power was used to stifle or control the way people thought in every sphere of life. Throughout Europe there was a revival of the magical, nonrational pattern of thought, and this pattern became dominant after the sixth century B.C.

It is generally assumed that the medieval period was associated with the most diabolical and inhumane treatment of the mentally ill. Actually this is only partly correct. The torture and killing of the mentally ill prevailed rather late in the medieval period, from about 1300s or 1400s until modern times. In spite of the fact that mental illness was considered to be the result of demoniacal possession, during the early medieval period mental patients were often treated with concern, and the community accepted responsibility for their care. The physical care of the "insane" was far better in the early Middle Ages than during the seventeenth and eighteenth centuries. Alexander and Selesnick (1966, p. 53) have the following to say about the mental patient of the early Middle Ages:

> When they were able to leave the hospital in the care of their relatives, they were given arm badges to wear so that they could be returned to the hospital if their symptoms should recur. These patients received so much attention and sympathy from the community that vagrants often counterfeited badges so that they would be taken for former patients [of Bethlehem Hospital in London, later to be named Bedlam].

Elsewhere (than in Europe) in the early Middle Ages, for example in the Moslem World, relatively civilized behavior toward the mentally ill could also be found. Humane asylums for the mentally ill were built at Fez, Morocco, and in Baghdad, Cairo, Damascus, and Aleppo. The Arabs evidently did not consider the mentally ill victims of demons, but as somehow divinely inspired. The hospital care which was given mental patients appears to have been benevolent.

However, the humanitarian atmosphere of the early Middle Ages underwent a severe deterioration during the thirteenth century in what was a dismal and tragic development. It was a period of growing demoralization, inquisition, and witch hunting (see Trevor-Roper, 1967). The witch hunts arose as a desperate attempt to invoke a magical solution for a growing crisis of fear and uncertainty. There were several influences accounting for the cataclysm. First, severe plagues had occurred which cut the population of Europe in half. Also important, the existing social order, feudalism, was beginning to crumble. The discovery of gunpowder and the invention of the printing press contributed to its demise. The stirrings of the Renaissance were also creating

uneasiness. The Church was being attacked for its corruption and abuses by early reformers foreshadowing the Reformation. The response of the political Church was to attempt to suppress the dangerous ideas and influences which were threatening the existing order.

The most impressive symbol of the growing mood of witch hunting in the late Middle Ages was a frightful book written by two German Dominican monks, Johann Sprenger and Heinrich Kraemer. In 1484, Pope Innocent VIII had issued a papal bulletin exhorting the clergy to detect and exterminate the evil witches who were to be blamed for the manifest evils and disasters of the period. The two monks undertook the task of preparing a manual for this "search and destroy" operation, and in the same year they obtained approval from the Pope to publish their "textbook of the Inquisition" entitled *Malleus Maleficarum,* or The Witches' Hammer (translated into English in 1928). The document was approved also by Maximilian I, the king of Rome, and shortly afterwards by the faculty of theology at the University of Cologne. Thus, the Church sanctified the document of inquisition; an important university approved it; and the monarch of Rome authorized it in the name of the state. It became official policy, and although it did not cause the ignorance and superstition of the times, it clearly contributed importantly to them.

The *Malleus Maleficarum* is divided into three parts. The first part sets about the task of proving that devils and witches exist and indicates that readers who are not convinced by the arguments must themselves be victims of witchcraft or heresy; in short, dissent is forbidden and marks the individual as a witch, worthy of extermination. The second part provides information about how to identify the witch from his or her behavior. The third part discusses legal procedures for examining and sentencing a witch.

The best way to destroy the devil, says the *Malleus,* is to burn his host, the witch in whose

FIGURE 8-2 Medieval woodcut by Loefller of the burning of witches. (The Bettmann Archive, Inc.)

body he lodges. If a doctor cannot find a reason for a disease, or "if the patient can be relieved by no drugs, but rather, seems to be aggravated by them, then the disease is caused by the devil" (1928, p. 87). The *Malleus* also states that "All witchcraft comes from carnal lust which is in women insatiable. . . . Therefore, they are more inclined towards witchcraft who more than others are given to these vices. . . . Women being insatiable it follows that those among ambitious women are more deeply infected who are more hot to satisfy their filthy lusts" (1928, p. 47). This attack was justified by Sprenger and Kraemer with the statement that women were imperfect in body and soul since they came from the inferior rib of Adam. The *Malleus* is also a treasury of pornography, with vivid passages describing sexual orgies that occurred between demons and their human hosts. The judging inquisitors are, in effect, granted voyeuristic pleasure in the recommendation of the *Malleus* that prior to her being sentenced, the witch should be stripped naked

and her pubic hair shaved so that the devil would not be able to hide there.

This manual resulted in the burning of hundreds of thousands of women and children. Presumably directed against heretics, the worst victims were the mentally ill who could not protect themselves and who often played into the hands of the inquisitors by confessing to or manifesting the very sexual sins which the *Malleus* concluded were the province of the witch (Fig. 8-2).

Historians Alexander and Selesnick provide an excellent summary and overview of the long, bleak period during the late Middle Ages. Because of its clarity and excellence, it is quoted here at some length (1966, pp. 68–70):

In seeking to evaluate the cultural developments of the Middle Ages, the historian faces the difficult task of appraising complex and heterogeneous trends. Contradictory movements such as the underground trickle of Greco-Roman tradition, the original pure Christian spirit, regression toward supernatural demonology, and growing Oriental influences were all involved. One's evaluation may well come to depend upon one's selection of the trend he prefers. One can readily admire the charitable accomplishments of the monasteries, the erection of the first hospitals in Europe, the foundation of the first universities, the psychological genius of St. Augustine, the encyclopedic scholarship and deductive finesse of St. Thomas Aquinas, and the enlightened outlook of Avicenna and Maimonides, which stands out sharply against a background of prevailing obscurantism. But one can also deplore the intellectual sterility of the scholastics, the return to prehistoric demonology, and the institutionalization of the vital principles of Christian ethics that led in time to unparalleled excesses of intolerance and injury committed in the name of those principles.

Some clarity can be discovered if one recognizes behind these contradictions the eternal conflict between man's two fundamental psychological principles of attempting to master his insecurity—knowledge and faith. With the failure of the rationalist Greco-Roman experiment, man returned to the security of faith in the supernatural, to an infantile state of helplessness and dependence on something stronger than himself to lead him from panic and confusion. The first five hundred years of the Middle Ages were chaotic, confused, and fearful, made so by wars, famines, and plagues. The Church, with its promise that "the disinherited will inherit the world," offered security to the civil body, and out of this trust came a humane hospital system. Still while some forms of human suffering might respond to faith, organic calamities might not. Monastic medicine could not stem the tide of empirical knowledge in Western Europe any more than the medicine man could have in antiquity.

The Romans had preserved Greek thought in Constantinople. The Nestorian physicians brought the Grecian manuscripts to Syria and Persia, where the Arabians discovered them. In the twelfth and thirteenth centuries the crusaders brought Arabic contributions back to Western Europe; Constantinus Africanus translated the Arabic works into Latin, and the lay school at Salerno began to flourish. Having come to devote themselves exclusively to philosophical speculations, the monks retained their involvement with the problems of the mind but defaulted medicine to lay physicians, with whom they now vied. The devil was exorcised to cure the mind, and empirical methods began to alleviate organic suffering. The practical psychotherapeutic measures of Avicenna and Rhazes were lost as the scholastics speculated. The great universities in the middle centuries of the Middle Ages contributed information but not ingenuity. The scholastics venerated Aristotelian logic, and the lay physicians re-

vered Hippocrates and Galen. And man's outlook had not moved forward.

By the thirteenth century the trickle of Greek manuscripts became a powerful stream. The influence of Aristotle began to challenge the Christian influence, and the old struggle between faith and reason began to recrudesce. Dogma went into defensive action on the theoretical level. Aristotle was adapted to Christianity through the exclusion of the realistic spirit of his views and the retention of only his deanimated words. Under the attentions of the scholastics, Aristotle's views were deduced from Christian dogma. In the light of such revealed truth, further exploration—the inductive approach to knowledge—appeared superfluous. However, the theoretical defensive against free inquiry was insufficient.

Another counterforce to Renaissance enlightenment was the recrudescence of exorcist practices over the next three hundred years. Paradoxically, that period of renewed enlightenment was marked in part by a violent regression toward supernaturalism, which, in the face of the strengthening rebirth of knowledge and exploration, turned to repression of heresies by the sword. The mentally ill were caught up in the witch hunt. Theological rationalizations and magical explanations served as foundations for burning at the stake thousands of the mentally ill as well as many other unfortunates. Those who had written about the mind now wrote death warrants as the tradition of scholastic reasoning in defense of dogma gave way to bloody persecution.

RENAISSANCE ENLIGHTENMENT AND MODERN BEGINNINGS

Two forces were at work during the period between the *Malleus Maleficarum* and today. One force was a return to demonology and the evolu-

FIGURE 8-3 A seventeenth-century engraving of the treatment (probably of an epileptic woman) in which St. Clara is portrayed as "casting out the devil." (The Bettmann Archive, Inc.)

tion of witch hunts; the methods of treatment of human deviation were burning, primitive exorcism in which the devil was expunged from the sufferer by magical rituals, flogging, starving, chaining, and other forms of torture. The second force was the recovery of scientific rationalism and empirical exploration during the *Renaissance,* culminating in the tremendous spurt of science and technology during the nineteenth and twentieth centuries. The Renaissance involved a reawakening of the inquiring human mind and of human artistry, directed at understanding people and the world.

This return was by no means smooth and steady, and remnants of the regressive demonology and cruelty based on fear remained, and still do today. Witches were burned in Europe as late

as the eighteenth century, and they were burned and hanged in seventeenth-century America. Yet as early as 1565, Johann Weyer, a physician, published a book pointing out that many of the people imprisoned, tortured, and burned were really "mentally ill," and that great wrongs were being committed against innocent people whose only crime was being "insane."

In Europe in 1798, Immanuel Kant proposed a taxonomy of mental disturbances, including the categories of "senselessness," "madness," "absurdity," and "frenzy." Despite the archaic language, some of Kant's descriptions are quite recognizable today. For example, he wrote (1964, p. 13):

The hypochondriac is . . . determined not to let himself be dissuaded from his imagining, forever going for help to the doctor, who has no end of trouble with him pacifying him no differently than a child (with pills made of bread crumbs, instead of medicine). And if this patient, who, for all of his continual ailments, can never become sick, consults medical books for advice, he becomes altogether insufferable, since he now believes that he feels in his body all the ailments of which he reads in the books.

Yet Kant's understanding and his ideas of the causes of mental disturbances were actually very far from modern. For example, he wrote that frenzy can sometimes be induced in the beholder "merely from the staring gaze of a madman" (1964, p. 4).

On the positive side, the French psychiatrist Philippe Pinel, when placed in charge of the hospitals for the insane at Bicêtre and later Salpêtrière in the late eighteenth century, removed the chains from the inmates, provided sunny rooms instead of dungeons, and substituted kindness for abuse. Similarly in England during the same period, William Tuke under the Quaker movement established the York Retreat for mental patients, a pleasant country house where the patients could live and work in an atmosphere of kindness. In the United States in the late 1700s and early 1800s, Benjamin Rush made efforts to organize the training of psychiatrists and introduced humane treatment in institutions under his direction. It is interesting too to realize that he also failed to escape completely from the primitive and magical past, since his medical concepts were substantially tainted with astrology, and his principal treatment methods were bloodletting and purgatives.

In the nineteenth-century United States, the mental health movement was first organized by an energetic New England schoolteacher, Dorothea Dix, who suffered from tuberculosis. As a result she quit her regular teaching job and subsequently began to teach Sunday school for female prisoners. Discovering the deplorable conditions under which prisoners and mental patients lived, she undertook a vigorous campaign to arouse people, obtain reform legislation, and acquire funds for hospitals for the mentally ill. Some historians, ironically, believe that Dorothea Dix—who is usually celebrated for helping to found mental hospitals all over the United States—thereby helped create the huge, modern, bleak custodial institution which isolated the patient from the community and made effective treatment and rehabilitation even more difficult. By filling the same hospitals indiscriminately with criminals, the aged, the psychotic, the outcast in any form, the selective and humanitarian treatment of disturbed individuals was probably impaired crucially.

At any rate, the mental health movement initiated by Dorothea Dix was further stimulated by publication in 1908 of a book entitled *A Mind That*

FIGURE 8-4 An engraving by Hogarth portraying the asylum of St. Mary of Bethlehem in London, also called "Bedlam." It shows two fashionable women making a visit. The modern English term "bedlam," meaning chaos, comes from the disorderly conditions that characterized this institution. (The Metropolitan Museum of Art, Harris Brisbane Dick Fund, 1935)

FIGURE 8-5 Pinel depicted as removing the chains that typically restrained patients in a French mental hospital. (New York Public Library Picture Collection.)

Found Itself, written by a former mental patient, Clifford Beers. Beers, a graduate of Yale University, wrote about his own mental collapse and of the terrible treatment he had experienced. He observed that in place of chains straitjackets were now being used to restrain excited patients. His book aroused much interest and sympathy and helped to gain greater respect for the mental patient. It was an important factor in the improvement of conditions in the mental hospitals. Beers also founded the Society for Mental Hygiene, which later became the National Committee for Mental Hygiene, and, still later, the worldwide International Committee for Mental Hygiene.

One must not assume that the mental health reforms and the movements cited here wiped out the older demeaning attitudes and customs toward the mentally ill and the miserable conditions of institutional life, although they did alleviate the problems. As recently as 1946, scandalous conditions in state mental hospitals were exposed through a series of photographs taken at

Byberry Hospital in Philadelphia, Pennsylvania, by Jerry Cooke of Life Magazine.

Commenting on the exposure reproduced here, *U.S. Camera,* 1947 (edited by Tom Maloney, p. 138) stated:

America looked again in 1946 at one of her worst sore spots—apparently with an eye to healing. Investigations were made by journalists and the raw facts given by picture and word in the news magazines and papers. Coming in for excessive scrutiny were the state institutions in Philadelphia and Detroit, which were known respectively as Byberry and Bedlam.

The pictures taken by Jerry Cooke for *Life* were as stark and self-assertive as those taken of the German concentration camps. (They left no room for doubt.) Corroborating these eyewitness accounts of the neglect and brutality that the states allowed to be visited upon their mentally ill were excerpts from the verified reports of the National Mental Health Foundation. This organization was made up of over 3000 conscientious objectors who had been relegated to work in various mental institutions for the duration of the war. These young men, religiously Methodists, Quakers, Mennonites, and Brethren, have now presented a report covering about one-third of all the state hospitals in 20 states.

Also in 1946, Mary Jane Ward wrote the distressing book *The Snake Pit* (later made into a popular movie), whose title became the perennial bitter expression for the mental hospital "pesthole," and later, in 1948, Albert Deutsch used the expression "the shame of the states" as the title of another book attacking the treatment of the mentally ill in the United States. Deutsch printed a photo of a ward of Byberry Hospital which, along with its caption, produced much revulsion among his readers. The caption read (1948, p. 49):

The male "incontinent ward" was like a scene out of Dante's *Inferno.* Three hundred nude men stood, squatted and sprawled in this bare room, amid shrieks, groans, and unearthly laughter. Winter or Summer, these creatures never were given any clothing at all. Some lay about on the bare floor in their own excreta. The filth-covered walls and floor were rotting away. Could a truly civilized community permit humans to be reduced to such an animal-like level?

One must remember that this statement was written, not in the seventeenth or eighteenth century, but only about three decades ago concerning a hospital in a major American city. However, although the overall message that we are still neglecting the mentally ill is surely sound, Deutsch's photo caption borders on sensationalism rather than an attempt accurately to portray the situation as it is. For example, "male incontinent wards" are apt to be filled with profoundly

mentally retarded persons more than psychotics, and one reason these patients are not given any clothes is that they generally tear them off or soil them as soon as they are put on. Attention is gained more readily by appealing to the emotions than by presenting a reasoned analysis. We should be upset by such pictures, but resolving such matters depends on correct assessment of their causes. The situation is certainly not everywhere the same today, although it is in many communities of the United States. We cannot realistically assume that the institutional horrors of the Middle Ages were merely expressions of a frightful, decayed society which no longer exists today, nor can we be much reassured that such inhumanity is safely in the distant past and that modern society is doing that much better.

Furthermore, in portraying the viewpoint of ancient and primitive man toward illness and maladjustment as magical and religious while regarding that of our own as akin to the Greco-

FIGURE 8-6 A 1946 *Life* photo by Jerry Cooke entitled "All Day Long," showing patients sitting idly and in starkly bare circumstances at Byberry Hospital in Philadelphia. (Jerry Cooke/Photo Researchers, Inc.)

Roman tradition of rationalism and empiricism, we somewhat inflate the status of these latter virtues in both the classical and modern societies. It is appropriate to recognize that to the masses of people even in our society, superstition and magic remain important modes of thought. One cannot legitimately picture modern thought as ideally rational and respectful of evidence and ancient and primitive thought as the antithesis of this. Rather, these represent, at best, dominant themes of these times. The gap between an epoch's highest intellectual reach and that expressed in the daily life of its people is, in reality, often disappointingly large, though we have made great strides forward since World War II. Thus one sees today the same two contradictory forces observed during the Middle Ages: on the one hand, superstition and fear of deviant individuals and the tendency to punish them both for their transgressions of our mores and for the nuisance they create and, on the other hand, the rational search for understanding and the humanitarian sense of responsibility and sympathy.

Possibly because of the prevailing earlier belief that the human mind was sacred (that is, supernatural and beyond the ken of natural science), it was among the last of the natural phenomena to become a matter of systematic scientific interest. The first important writers of the Renaissance on psychological and sociological subjects were actually theologians and philosophers—for example, Descartes, Kant, Berkeley, Hume. The concept of human behavior as a subject worthy of scientific study in its own right hardly flowered until later in the nineteenth century. Psychology in this country did not fully emerge as an independent, science-oriented academic discipline until after World War I.

The emphasis on *natural causes* eventually evolved into the psychologists' present working position that behavior is caused by both biological and social factors. As we shall see in the next chapter, however, many professionals today stress mainly human biological makeup in their clinical work and in their research on the causes of maladjustment. In Chapter 9 this is referred to as the medical-biological model. Still other models emphasize the role of social factors in the environment (cf. Chapters 10 and 11). Regardless of the divergent theoretical emphases of these models, the philosophy of natural science—that any speculation about how the "mind" works must be in accord with what can be observed by watching people in their natural setting—has been fundamental to the growth of modern psychology as a scientific discipline.

SUMMING UP

The outlook of ancient and modern civilized peoples toward mental illness has greatly changed. Ancient peoples, and some primitive ones living today, interpreted illness as the result of possession by demons, devils, or other supernatural forces, in effect, through a mixture of magic and religion. The classical Greeks introduced the then new idea that natural phenomena must have natural causes, an outlook usually referred to as rationalism. Biological determinants such as pathology of the brain were sought to explain mental illness. The Romans continued this rationalistic tradition and added to it.

During the Middle Ages, however, with the collapse of the Roman Empire, there was a regression once again to magic and demonism—although at the beginning of the period the mentally ill were treated with humanitarian consideration. With threats to the power of the Roman Catholic church in Europe, and in view of widespread social demoralization and death at the hands of the plague, systematic efforts were made to blame human troubles and the collapsing social institutions on witches, who were systematically sought out by the "Inquisition" and burned at the stake. The principal victims were the mentally ill, who often were too confused to defend themselves adequately against the new persecution. This reached a peak of intensity in the fifteenth century and actually continued into eighteenth-century Europe, in spite of a growing number of dissident and rational voices that were evident as early as the sixteenth century. Gradually, such medieval horrors were replaced by more humanitarian approaches as science and medicine began to flourish, though there is ample and widespread evidence of indifferent and often vicious treatment of mental patients even up to the present.

With the rise of modern science and a return to rationalism, mental illness was once again approached naturalistically. The working position of psychology in the late nineteenth century came to be a search for the biological and social causation of mental illness. Using the guiding philosophy of natural science, psychology began to explore how the "mind" works through observations of people in their natural settings.

CHAPTER 9 THE MEDICAL-BIOLOGICAL MODEL

Historically, the medical model, which ties adjustive failure to bodily illness or disease, is an outgrowth of the rational-scientific approach to understanding the world. As learned men and women moved away from magic and demonology as explanations of the natural world, medical scientists also began to examine the tissues of the body to understand human functioning, including maladjustment. As we saw in Chapter 8, Greek physicians [for example, Hippocrates (460-377 B.C.)] were the first to view the brain as the governing site of human activity. In the sixteenth century and thereafter, anatomists and physiologists studying the way tissues worked made very substantial progress in exploring the construction and mode of operation of the brain. If one believes that natural explanations can be sought for everything, it is an obvious step to assume that something must be wrong with the brain of a person who acts crazy.

Aside from the reasonableness and utility of such a view, the idea that adjustive failure resulted from a disease of the body had a very important professional and social consequence. It meant that "crazy" people should not be seen as inherently evil or possessed by the devil, but as "sick" in the same sense as a person who has an infection or who breaks a bone. The treatment then would not be to punish the person for his transgressions or exorcise the devil within, but to find out in what way he or she was sick and to locate a natural cure.

This became the medical approach to mental illness and represented an important scientific and humanitarian advance over earlier approaches. As it turns out, in spite of the spread of this view among professionals and educated persons, most of the public never completely assimilated it. "Crazy" people are still regarded widely with fear and loathing, often with the implied criticism that their disturbed behavior is the result of moral weakness or evil.

The medical-biological model states, then, that all forms of adjustive failure are products of disease in the tissues of the body, especially the brain. Such disease can be brought about through heredity or by damage acquired during the person's life course—by injury, infection, or hormonal disruption produced by stress, among other things. When, for example, the neural tissues fail to function properly, disturbances in the bodily and behavioral functions follow. By the same reasoning, psychological disorders result from physiological disorders, and their successful treatment requires correction or amelioration of the tissue defect through physical therapies such as drugs, surgery, and the like.

The medical-biological model gets its best support in the case of the organic disorders, an example of which was give in Chapter 6. Such disorders are produced by brain injuries, toxic conditions, or senility, in which case the brain tissues are destroyed by circulatory ailments in the aging person that impair the blood supply. There is no debate about the validity of this view of causation in the organic psychoses, although relatively little is still known about which tissues are essential to normal adjustment, or about precisely how the tissue damage leads to the ensuing disordered behavior. Research on the physiology of the brain remains an essential key to unlock the remaining mysteries about the neural control of adjustive behavior.

On the other hand, in the most common "garden" varieties of adjustive failure, such as the neuroses, personality disorders, and the so-called functional psychoses such as schizophrenia and depressions, the tissue defects or malfunctions presumed by the medical-biological model to cause them remain unknown. That tissue defects are operating to produce the behavioral and psychological difficulties in such cases remains an article of faith. What then is the evidence that nourishes this article of faith? The

most important evidence comes from research on genetics (heredity) and adaptation, and we shall explore this in this chapter.

GENETIC FACTORS IN ADJUSTMENT

Because children physically resemble their parents, often even in gesture, manner, temperament, and attitude, these characteristics appeared to early thinkers to be somehow transmitted biologically from parent to child. Charles Darwin vigorously supported the concept of the inheritance of mental characteristics. Darwin believed that mental as well as physical characteristics evolved in species from the struggle for survival. In 1873 he published a book comparing the mental powers and moral sense of animals and humans and attempting to demonstrate that the differences between humans and infrahuman animals were a matter of degree, not of kind. The flavor of Darwin's views on the inheritance of psychological characteristics can be illustrated by one of his pronouncements on the subject (1873, vol. 1, pp. 106–107):

So, in regard to mental qualities, their transmission is manifest in our dogs, horses, and other domestic animals. Besides, special tastes and habits, general intelligence, courage, bad and good temper, etc., are certainly transmitted. With man, we see similar facts in almost every family; and we now know through the admirable labors of Mr. Galton that genius, which implies a wonderfully complex combination of high faculties, tends to be inherited; and, on the other hand, it is too certain that insanity and deteriorated mental powers likewise run in the same families. [See Fig. 9-1.]

The "Mr. Galton" referred to in Darwin's statement was Francis Galton, his half cousin. Galton's main contributions to psychology include the innovation of modern statistical methods for han-

FIGURE 9-1 The German shepherd is easily trained to attack, a temperament quality that seems to be characteristic of the breed. The Saint Bernard, in contrast, is known for its gentle and docile qualities. (Top: H. Armstrong Roberts; bottom: Myron Wood/Photo Researchers, Inc.)

dling psychological data, the development of mental testing, and a major research effort on the inheritance of genius (1869). It is this latter work to which Darwin alluded and which is of concern to us here.

Greatly influenced by Darwin's *Origin of Species,* Galton turned to the problem that was to occupy his central interest, the inheritance of mental capacity. He published a number of major research treatises on this problem, all of them presenting evidence for the inheritance of intelligence. His main argument was based on the finding that among relatives of intellectually highly endowed persons, there is a much greater number of extremely able persons than might be expected by chance. There is, of course, an objection to this line of reasoning: the relatives of eminent persons often have educational, social, and economic advantages in common. Galton recognized this criticism and tried to refute it, noting further that the closer the family relationship, the higher was the incidence of superior persons.

Although the specific mechanisms of heredity had not yet been worked out, biological scientists were very receptive to the notion of inheritance at the time of Galton's writings, largely as a result of Darwin's views, and Galton's work was very influential in advancing the case for the inheritance of behavior. However, there was also a great need for a workable theory concerning the mechanism of hereditary transmission. The research of Gregor Mendel in the garden of a monastery at Brünn, Moravia, filled this need with a set of systematic observations about the inheritance of simple characteristics in pea plants. Mendel's original publication remained overlooked for thirty-four years until 1900. However, after it was discovered and its significance recognized, there was a very rapid development of the science of genetics. Thus, at the turn of the century, key hereditary notions such as the gene, dominance and recessiveness, hybrid, genotype, and phenotype were already established. During the next several decades, advances were made concerning the anatomy of genes and chromosomes, mutations and the changes produced by irradiation, the complex interplay of genetic structures, and the biochemistry of their action.

We shall not be concerned here with the biological mechanisms of heredity, but only with some of their implications for the causation of mental illness. The interested reader will find in Lerner (1968) a highly readable account of evolution, heredity, and its social implications (see also Dobzhansky, 1962, 1967 *a* and *b*).

VARIABILITY AND HERITABILITY

The interest of early researchers on heredity was initiated by the recognition (1) that people and infrahuman animals showed much within-species variation in their physical and psychological traits and (2) that the physical and psychological traits seemed to show some continuity from generation to generation. It was a reasonable conclusion that something in the structure of the organism was passed on or "inherited" from generation to generation to account for this continuity.

The question was posed whether a given trait is inherited or is, instead, the result of experience with the environment. Put in this fashion, the question gave rise to fruitless controversy over which was more important, heredity or environment. We now realize that *every* trait, physical or psychological, is the result of the interplay of both hereditary *and* environmental influences. Therefore, the problem must be reformulated, the fundamental question being not whether a characteristic is inherited, but rather what proportion of the variation in a given trait can be accounted for by heredity and what proportion can be attributed to environment.

Notice that when one speaks about variation in a characteristic, an image is created of a distribution of that characteristic in some given population. A good example is intelligence, which obviously varies greatly from person to person. Accu-

rately surveying such variation requires measuring devices, and a whole field of psychology, namely, tests and measurements (Tyler, 1971), is devoted to the assessment of individual differences in psychological traits. Moreover, it is necessary to understand that heritability involves, first, variation among a population of individuals in some measureable characteristic and, second, the fact that some proportion of that variation can be attributed to genetic processes.

Under a given set of environmental circumstances, some traits are more influenced by hereditary factors than others. That is, under the particular conditions of development of that trait, environmental influences have far less impact than hereditary influences. Comparatively simple physical traits (such as the color of the skin, eyes, or hair, and skeletal size) show a very strong hereditary component, while others, such as aggressiveness or achievement motivation, probably show less heritability. This does not mean that any trait can be considered a product of *only* heredity or *only* environment, but that traits vary in the *extent* of heritability under any given conditions. The question of importance concerns to what extent the variation in any given behavioral trait of interest to psychologists is influenced by hereditary factors and, further, what are the relevant genetic and environmental conditions. We shall return in greater detail to the interplay of hereditary and environmental influences a little later, where it will be illustrated that the heritability of a trait does not represent a constant value but rather is a function of the variability among the relevant environmental and genetic influences.

INHERITANCE OF MENTAL DISORDER

Newer methods of behavior genetics have been developed over the past thirty years to identify the influence of heredity and of environmental variables on adjustive traits. Some are only partially successful in isolating the hereditary and

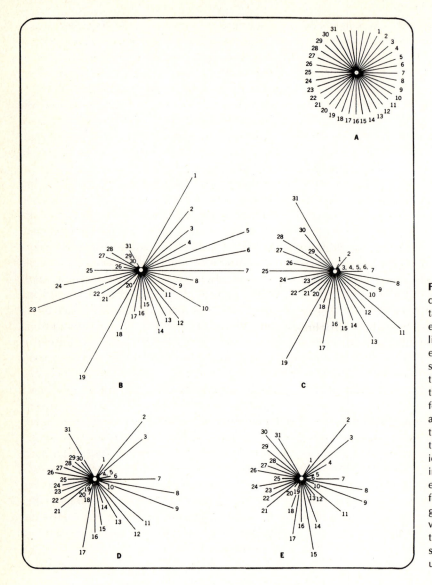

FIGURE 9-2 Biochemical individuality as expressed by taste sensitivity to 31 different substances. The length of lines under A represents average sensitivity of all persons tested. Deviations from the average are indicated by the relative length of lines for four individuals, of which D and E are identical twins. Notice that the pattern of sensitivity is very similar in the identical twins (D and E); but in B and C, who are unrelated, the patterns are quite different, an illustration of how genetic factors create quite variable physical constitutions affecting how the same substances taste to each of us. (From R. J. Williams.)

environmental components fairly. One effective method consists of examining the degree of correlation of a specific trait such as intelligence among people with *different genetic relationships.* For example, one examines the extent to which high intelligence (as measured by a test) is correlated among biological parents and their children, or among identical twins (with the same genes and hence the same hereditary influences) compared with fraternal twins. As the genetic relationship gets closer, higher correlations are usually found, which, for that sample and set of environmental conditions, suggests a greater hereditary influence on that trait (Fig. 9-2).

EVIDENCE OF GENETIC INFLUENCE

A special variation of the method described has been utilized by Franz Kallmann (1952, 1953, 1956) and called the "concordance" method. Concordance means the percentage of times, in a large population of pairs, that one of the pairs has a particular illness when it is known that the other member of the pair has it. The pairs are identical twins, fraternal twins, or siblings. This is analogous to examining the correlation of a trait such as intelligence test scores among identical and fraternal twins. If hereditary influences are involved in that trait, the correspondence or *concordance* of the trait should be greater in identical twins since they share the same genes; likewise, the concordance rates for schizophrenia, or for any other disorder presumed to have a hereditary basis, should be higher among identical twins than among other pairs who are less closely related.

Kallmann has claimed to have demonstrated a strong genetic influence in mental illnesses such as schizophrenia, manic-depressive psychoses, and involutional depressions. Table 9-1 portrays some of these data which seem to offer dramatic confirmation of the role of inheritance in these disorders. For example, over 86 percent of the identical twins of schizophrenic patients gave evidence of the disorder, while only a little more

than 14 percent of the fraternal twins were similarly afflicted. These findings are frequently cited as providing strong support for the existence of a genetic factor in various mental disorders.

In spite of these findings, the genetic basis of psychopathology remains a somewhat controversial issue. There are methodological flaws in Kallmann's research which throw doubt on the findings, and these flaws have resulted in the rejection by many authorities of the genetic interpretation. Chief among the criticisms are three considerations: (1) Kallmann did not make the judgment of whether or not the twin was mentally ill with a particular disorder independently of his knowledge of the twin's relationship to the disturbed relative. Thus, his own biases in the matter may well have influenced the data. (2) The diagnosis of the disorder itself is open to serious question. As will be seen later, the classification and diagnosis of mental disorder is, in general, a somewhat unreliable affair, and the criteria for placement of a patient or his relative in one or another category vary greatly with different institutions and among different professional workers. (3) It is likely that identical twins are exposed to more similar environments than fraternal twins or siblings. Families, and the twins themselves, tend to "play up" the identicalness, dressing alike, and so on. Even when they are "reared apart," in many studies this means living apart from about fifteen years of age (Jackson, 1960), so that they have experienced a very similar environment for most of their formative years, and this

TABLE 9-1   KALLMANN'S DATA ON CONCORDANCE RATES FOR VARIOUS DISORDERS

TYPES OF PSYCHOSIS	HALF SIBS	FULL SIBS	FRATERNAL TWINS	IDENTICAL TWINS
Schizophrenia	7.1	14.2	14.5	86.2
Manic depressive	16.7	23.0	26.3	95.7
Involutional	4.5	6.9	6.9	60.9

The table entries give the percentage of types of pairs of relatives having the disorder during their lifetime depending upon degree of genetic relationship to the disturbed persons.

SOURCE: Kallmann, 1953, p. 124, Fig. 36.

TABLE 9-2 EXPECTANCY OF SCHIZOPHRENIA AND MANIC-DEPRESSION
IN (MZ) MONOZYGOTIC (I.E., ONE ZYGOTE OR EGG)* AND (DZ)
DIZYGOTIC (I.E., TWO ZYGOTES OR EGGS)† TWIN HUMAN BEINGS

INVESTIGATORS	SCHIZOPHRENIA, % EXPECTANCY		MANIC-DEPRESSION, % EXPECTANCY	
	MZ	DZ	MZ	DZ
Luxemburger (Germany)	66.6	3.3		
Rosanoff et al. (United States)	68.3	14.9	69.6	16.4
Essen-Moller (Denmark)	71.4	16.7		
Slater (United Kingdom)	76.0	14.0	66.7	23.3
Kallmann (U.S. and Germany)	86.2	14.5	92.6	23.6

*Identical twins
†Fraternal twins

SOURCE: W. R. Thompson, 1965.

environment is very likely to be produced by one or two highly disturbed parents. (4) Finally, the percentage of twins is only 1 in about 85 births, and only about one-third of all twins are identical. Thus, generalizing about the inheritance of schizophrenia, for example, on the basis of so infrequent a phenomenon (twinning) appears somewhat risky (Jackson, 1960).

Table 9-2 summarizes the results of six different investigations using the concordance method, including that of Kallmann, and performed in different countries (Thompson, 1965). Although it will be seen that there are some differences in the concordance rates reported by different investigators, the findings in general seem to agree rather well. Thompson writes (1965, p. 34) that these studies ". . . have established beyond a doubt a strong correlation between expectancy of contracting one of these illnesses and degree of genetic relationship to an already affected individual. This relationship appears to be independent of socioeconomic factors and hence supports a genetic hypothesis."

Thompson notes critically, however (p. 34):

On the negative side, in many of the studies, methodology has been weak, diagnosis of the disease imprecise, and environmental influences not directly controlled. Furthermore, expectancy rates in the general population and in kinship groups do not fit closely to known models of genetic transmission, though several have been hypothesized by various investigators. . . . It is highly probable that genes play a crucial part in determining a disposition to abnormal behavior of many varieties, but their exact mode of operation, their transmission, and the manner in which they are given full expression by environment have still to be worked out.

Some of the most carefully controlled and more recent research (for example, that of Gottesman and Shields, 1966) has overcome or at least reduced some of the methodological flaws of the research cited by Thompson, and a strong relationship between hereditary influences and adjustive failure is still found (see also Rosenthal, 1970). The concordance rates in this research are somewhat lower, about 42 percent for identical twins compared with 9 percent for fraternal twins in cases of severe disorder. Where the disorder is mild, the concordance rates are smaller still, but they still suggest a genetic component. In the light of such data, it becomes difficult not to take seriously the assertion that the disposition to develop severe mental disorders such as schizo-phrenia has some hereditary basis, though the extent of this and (as we shall see below) the way in which it operates remain uncertain.

WHAT IS INHERITED

Many biologically oriented psychologists and behavior geneticists (including, for example, Kallmann) do not believe that mental illness is directly inherited as one inherits eye color, but rather that some factor is inherited which predisposes an individual to be particularly vulnerable to damaging life experiences. If this factor is present, along with the appropriate environmental conditions, the person will develop a particular set of reactions (symptoms) such as schizophrenia, anxiety neurosis, depressive psychosis, or whatever. Without the precipitating life experiences an individual would not be expected to develop the disorder, even if he had the pathogenic genes (cf. Meehl, 1962). Such a model represents an analogy to what we know about tuberculosis. Evidently, one inherits a physical constitution which provides either good or poor resistance to the disease. Thus, one must make contact with the tubercle bacillus in order to suffer the illness. If one is fortunate enough to be born with high resistance to tuberculosis, or to live where the germ does not exist, the disease will never appear. If the person has the genetically determined disposition, whatever precisely this turns out to be, then he or she will be vulnerable to the disease if exposed to the germs. In the case of mental illness, the argument is the same. If the person has inherited the genetic factor, unfavorable life experiences (severe stress, limited coping resources, or whatever) will precipitate the disorder. Thus, the genetic and environmental positions are not mutually exclusive in this model, since both influences interact to eventuate in mental health or illness.

As stated earlier, there is no scarcity of hypotheses and research seeking to pin down the inher-

ited biochemical or neurological defect that might differentiate schizophrenics, say, from nonschizophrenic persons. The hypotheses that have been taken seriously include factors of human physique, biochemical defects of several kinds, disturbing biochemical consequences of severe stress, and direct pathology of the brain. A few of these theories will be examined briefly here, specifically those concerning the role of physique and of biochemical defects. For a fuller discussion of these and related biologically oriented formulations, the interested reader might consult an excellent and readable account by Maher (1966).

Physique, personality, and mental illness   One of the earliest notions about mental illness (and about personality in general) was based on the fact that people differ greatly in physique or body type. It was proposed that these differences were associated not only with differing personality characteristics, but also differing vulnerability to certain types of mental disorder. The general idea is illustrated in the comment of Shakespeare's Julius Caesar: "Let me have men about me that are fat; sleek-headed men and such as sleep o' nights: Yond Cassius has a lean and hungry look; he thinks too much: such men are dangerous" (Act I, Scene ii). The idea that physique influences personality and mental illness was elaborated and studied by the German psychiatrist Kretschmer (1925, 1926), who described several main variations in body build, for example, the round and fat ("pyknic") type, the muscular ("athletic") type, and the thin and angular ("asthenic") type. Pyknics were supposed to be good-natured and relaxed; athletics were driving and energetic; and asthenics were introversive and intellectual. Kretschmer claimed that a pyknic would be more likely to be a manic-depressive, while asthenics had a greater likelihood of becoming schizophrenic.

A carefully delineated and measured elaboration of this idea was later developed by Sheldon and his associates (1942, 1954), though Sheldon used a different terminology: "endomorphic" for the soft, round (fat) type, "mesomorphic" for the muscular, athletic person, and "ectomorphic" for the slender, fragile type. Sheldon greatly improved the definitions and measurements of these body builds, which made possible more systematic research on the relations between physical types, personality, and psychopathology. Much of this research, including some fairly recently, has supported the hypothesized relationship (for example, Sheldon et al., 1954; Davidson et al., 1957; Glueck and Glueck, 1962; Damon and Polednak, 1967; Cortés and Gatti, 1970).

Although there does indeed seem to be evidence for a moderately significant connection between physique, personality, and type of mental illness, a direct cause and effect relationship, as suggested by Sheldon and Kretschmer, is not widely accepted. Sheldon's terms (endomorphic, etc.) are based on notions about the embryological tissue-development process whereby body build is laid down in the uterus of the mother. Sheldon assumed that somatic characteristics directly led to temperamental characteristics and hence mental illness. However, most psychologists tend to assume that body build affects adjustment only indirectly because of its social implications rather than directly by creating personality traits or mental illness patterns. For example, soft, round children are apt to be inept and hence rejected in sports, and they are less often regarded as attractive physically; this social response probably leads endomorphs to develop a particular sort of personality—cheerful and accommodating rather than aggressive, let us say. On the other hand, the social reaction to the strong, muscular type will be quite different, and their arenas of success in social living as well as their concepts of themselves are likely to follow from this. The slender, fragile type (ectomorph) is apt to be sensitive, intellectual, and introverted because he or she too cultivates those things in childhood and youth that lead to a functional way

of adjusting to others' reactions; such persons will deemphasize those activities that do not fit with their bodily resources and social impact. Thus, the usually assumed causal route from body build to personality and illness pattern is via the social impact of one's physique rather than through direct constitutional or tissue processes. If so, this would be an example of interaction between biology and environment in shaping adjustment, and we shall learn more about this topic later. Perhaps psychologists should take such interactions more seriously, but up to now they have not.

Biochemical-defect hypotheses Of all the current approaches to inherited constitutional factors in mental illness, especially schizophrenia, none has stirred more interest than the search for a biochemical defect. When no gross anatomical differences were found between schizophrenics and normals, for example, in obvious brain structure, size, or in the presence of tissue damage, one of the next logical possibilities seemed to be in the complex metabolic chains by which biochemical substances are broken down in the brain tissues and metabolized. Such research was hardly possible before modern advances had occurred in the understanding of cellular biochemistry and in the technical ability to measure the presence and amounts of such substances in the body. Most readers (along with the author) will not feel at home with the neural biochemistry essential to this research and theory. However, the purpose of the following brief account is not to spell out the precise neurophysiology but to provide a rough grasp of the thinking involved. Do not be intimidated by the technical terms and mechanisms encountered, but try only to get a general idea of the three hypotheses that are outlined below.

1 One of the best-known hypotheses has been developed by Heath (1960). This researcher assumes that the schizophrenic patient suffers from a genetic disorder in which a protein substance called *taraxein* is present in the body. This substance can react with other bodily chemicals to form chemical compounds that are toxic and disturb the functioning of the brain. The disturbing consequences of this defect are particularly pronounced when the person is experiencing stress. The patient's pleasure-pain mechanism is thereby disturbed; he (if the patient is male) discovers early in development that he does not feel as other people do. As a result, he feels increasingly alienated and troubled about his identity and his perception of reality, adding the distress of anxiety to his already major interpersonal troubles. For Heath, and those preceding him in this line of thought (for example, Rado et al., 1956), these two symptoms—the inability to feel as others do and the anxiety over one's identity and ability to judge what is real—are the primary characteristics of what he calls *schizotypes*; the more familiar schizophrenic symptoms are said to be secondary complications of these basic symptoms of the disease.

Evidence concerning this hypothesis has been more or less positive. For example, Heath and his colleagues administered taraxein to normal volunteers and reported alterations in electrical activity of the brain similar to those recorded from psychotic patients. This seems to implicate the limbic system of the brain, which (as explained in Chapter 5) plays a major role in the regulation of emotional behavior. In one study along these lines, for example, Heath and his associates (1957) gave taraxein to prison volunteers and observed a variety of psychotic-like symptoms such as blocking and fragmentation of thought, impairment of concentration, decreased attention, and marked apprehension. Subjects commonly reported, "I never felt like this in my life before." Maher (1966, p. 332) has provided a handy summary of the tarxein hypothesis (see Figure 9-3).

There are some problems with the taraxein hypothesis, although as yet much of the evidence is favorable. The chief difficulty may be logical:

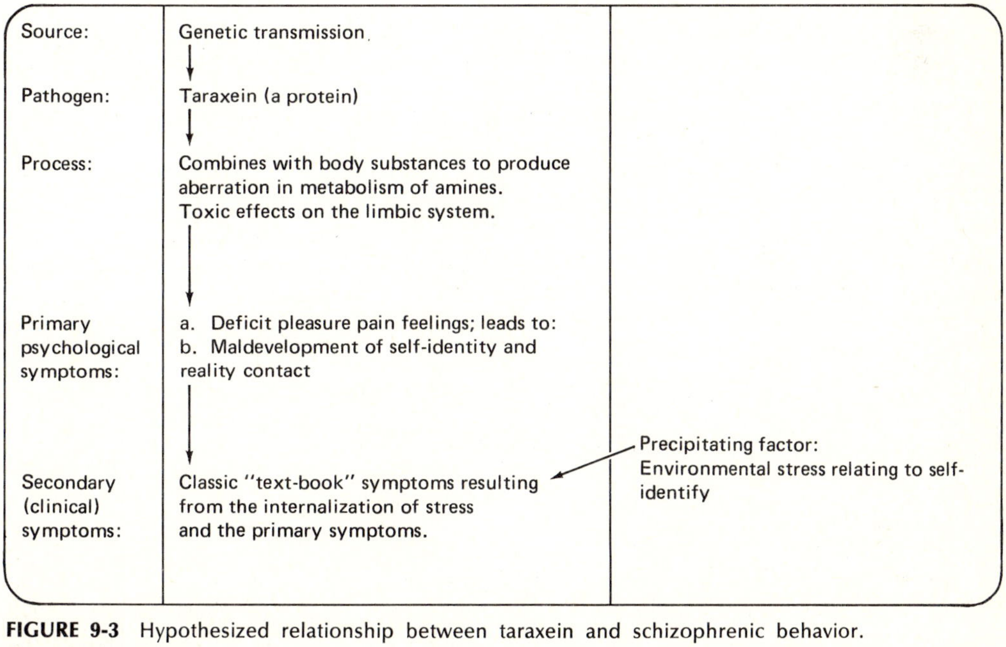

Source:	Genetic transmission	
Pathogen:	Taraxein (a protein)	
Process:	Combines with body substances to produce aberration in metabolism of amines. Toxic effects on the limbic system.	
Primary psychological symptoms:	a. Deficit pleasure pain feelings; leads to: b. Maldevelopment of self-identity and reality contact	
Secondary (clinical) symptoms:	Classic "text-book" symptoms resulting from the internalization of stress and the primary symptoms.	Precipitating factor: Environmental stress relating to self-identify

FIGURE 9-3 Hypothesized relationship between taraxein and schizophrenic behavior. (From Maher, 1966.)

How could the mechanism, which presumably produces disturbances in the person's sense of identity over a long developmental period and only then results in the secondary symptoms of schizophrenia, work so quickly in normal volunteers when they are administered taraxein? Moreover, the assumption that the limbic system contains a pleasure-pain system, whose function is presumably impaired by taraxein, is as yet unproved, though not at all unreasonable in the light of what is known. Lastly, there is no evidence as yet that taraxein or the basis of its production is genetically transmitted. At this stage, however, the taraxein hypothesis must be taken seriously as a possible genetic-biochemical explanation for schizophrenia, though much must be done before it can be regarded as likely or proved.

2 Still another biochemical hypothesis revolves around a substance known as *adrenochrome.* It had been observed that mescaline, a psychedelic drug that is derived from Mexican peyote and has profound psychological effects, especially in perception, is similar chemically to adrenaline (Osmond and Smithies, 1952). Adrenaline is always present in the human body and is itself a powerful hormone, but it has been suggested further that it could be improperly metabolized into a substance with the same properties as mescaline and, therefore, could produce the schizophrenic's mental disturbances. Adrenochrome is suggested as this substance.

From a research standpoint, however, there is a serious problem: adrenochrome is very unstable chemically. Some research workers believe that it is converted in the body into two other compounds, one of which, *adrenolutin,* is said to be toxic and to produce the schizophrenic symptoms. Some investigators have reported that adrenolutin impaired complex and recently acquired skills (Braines, 1959), the effects lasting for a week or more, and others (Schwarz et al., 1956) have shown that monkeys injected with adrenochrome were made drowsy and had higher

thresholds for pain. Since adrenochrome reduces histamine production in the body, another researcher (Lea, 1955) argued that schizophrenics should be more resistant to allergy than non-schizophrenics, and supporting evidence for this deduction was indeed found. There has also been negative evidence, including the inability of some researchers to detect adrenochrome in either schizophrenics or normals (Szara et al., 1958); and in another study (Holland et al., 1958) differences in the way adrenaline was utilized by schizophrenics and normals could not be detected. All in all, the case for the adrenochrome-adrenolutin hypothesis is as yet fairly weak.

3 The discovery of a substance called *serotonin* in the limbic system of the brain and other parts of the body has prompted still a different biochemical hypothesis. There is a structural similarity between serotonin and both LSD and adrenochrome, as well as certain tranquilizers such as reserpine. This similarity of structure makes it possible for one such substance to occupy a brain site, and by virtue of being a pharmacological antagonist of other substances with the same structure, it is capable of blocking the action of the others. Serotonin and LSD, for example, can block each other's actions on the neural tissues. Moreover, serotonin plays an important role in the brain in the normal transmission of nerve impulses. Too much serotonin could result in reduction of the transmission along certain nerves, while too little could increase transmission. For normal behavior, there should be a stable balance in transmission levels, a balance that could be disrupted by a deficiency or an excess of serotonin.

Research shows that LSD can either diminish or increase the effects of serotonin (Shaw and Woolley, 1956; Costa, 1956). There is also evidence that a chemical substance that produces serotonin in the body is secreted by schizophrenics less than by normals (Lauer et al., 1958), though negative results on this have also been reported (Bannerjee and Agarwal, 1958; Kopin, 1959).

Other research has also shown that acute schizophrenics show a lower level of serotonin than chronic schizophrenics. However, this evidence must be balanced against the confusing finding that brain-damaged patients, and patients who were disturbed but not psychotic, show deviant levels of serotonin, but the direction of the deviation is not consistent with the serotonin hypothesis. The most serious problem with the serotonin hypothesis, one that also troubles the adrenochrome explanation, is that psychedelic drugs such as mescaline and LSD do not really produce symptoms of schizophrenia, though they do have profound mental effects. The pattern of reactions reported under LSD is too different from the behavior patterns exhibited and the mental states reported by recovered schizophrenics to allow us to draw an analogy between them with any assurance. Still, the idea that disturbances in serotonin activity in the brain affect behavior remains alive in the search for the biochemical defect presumably underlying schizophrenic disorders.

Present confidence in the research outlined above is seriously weakened because of the tremendous methodological obstacles facing the worker in this field (see Kety, 1959). Much of the research has been flawed because of (1) failure to control relevant variables such as the atypical diets served in hospitals in which the patient population was studied; (2) failure to define accurately the patient population itself, which in such research is often a very heterogeneous mixture of troubled persons rather than schizophrenics in any precise sense; (3) failure to control for different types of treatment (including shock and drug therapies) accorded the patients sampled in a research study; and (4) the bias of the researchers, who have often approached their work with a polemical rather than a detached, inquiring stance.

Lest the reader get the impression that serious efforts to implicate biochemical or physiological defects have been limited only to severe adjustive failure such as schizophrenia, considerable research along these lines has also been done with persons suffering from anxiety reactions (or anxiety neuroses). Here the most common type of hypothesis is that such persons lack the normal capacity adequately to control or regulate their physiological arousal when placed under stress; hence they react excessively and in a fashion that impairs their ability to function properly. We have already seen in Chapter 5 how the body reacts under stress, and it is known that very high levels of arousal can interfere with productive thinking and problem solving.

There is substantial evidence that anxiety neurotics do, indeed, show greater physiological disturbance under stress than persons not so afflicted and that such persons do not recover from stress-induced physiological arousal as rapidly as others (for example, see Martin, 1971, chap. 3, for a review and discussion). Moreover, anxious patients seem not to be very discriminating about the situations to which they react with anxiety, so that they are likely to maintain high levels of physiological disturbance in a wide variety of life situations (see also Glickstein et al., 1957, as discussed in Chapter 3). It has been suggested (Gellhorn, 1967) that in cases of pathological anxiety the inhibiting mechanisms of the hypothalamus of the brain fail to function normally, and alternatively that there is some defect in the inhibitory mechanisms of the reticular activating system of the brain stem (Malmo, 1966).

The main problem with this type of formulation is demonstrating the asserted cause and effect relationship; that is, it is difficult to determine whether anxiety neurotics overrespond as they do because of some defective neurohumoral regulatory mechanism (either inherited or acquired) or because of faulty social learning leading to inadequate coping with stress at the psychological level. The writers cited above, and others favoring a physiological explanation, state or imply that such a neurohumoral defect exists, though the exact nature of this defect (if it does) remains still to be demonstrated. In any event, there is no shortage of enthusiasm for an essentially physiological explanation for the adjustive difficulties encountered by persons suffering from anxiety reactions.

What then is the answer to the question posed in the heading earlier, namely, "What is inherited?" As yet, there is no answer. Biologically oriented research workers are busy trying to discover the constitutional defect, "the twisted molecule" (to borrow a famous phrase), that makes a person become schizophrenic under any or some special conditions of life, just as psychosocially oriented research workers are trying to locate the social conditions and experiences responsible for severe adjustive disturbances. The repeated findings of genetic research showing that heredity makes a significant contribution to severe mental illness forces us to seek the specific inherited constitutional characteristic or characteristics that are part of the causal chain. Heredity can operate on behavior only through some physical trait or traits, some constitutional element (or elements) that is passed on from one generation to another and affects psychological development and adjustment. This is what powers the continuing search by biologically oriented workers, despite the minimal encouragement thus far obtained from the research results.

INHERITANCE OF MENTAL RETARDATION

If we go outside the traditional categories of adjustive failure such as the psychoses, we can find other important illustrations of the role of heredity and constitutional defects which support the premises of the medical-biological model. The most frequently cited example is a fascinating "detective story" about a defect known as phenylketonuria (PKU), sometimes called "Fölling's disease." It is a rare biochemical disor-

der in which the afflicted individual is mentally retarded. In 1934 Fölling had shown that the mental defect was associated with the abnormal excretion of large amounts of phenylpyruvic acid in the urine. Shortly after, it was demonstrated (Penrose, 1935; Jervis, 1937) that the defect was inherited.

Jervis's work especially is a fine illustration of careful scientific reasoning on this topic. In coming to his conclusion, he studied the family biographies of victims of the disorder, supplementing these data with a statistical analysis of the frequency of the defect's appearance in the families studied. The defect seemed to be inherited because the frequency with which it appeared in the offspring followed so closely the ratios for recessive traits found by Mendel in his work with the pea plant.

Jervis's data left little doubt that phenylketonuria is determined by a specific genetic factor. Later all doubt was dispelled when the defect was shown to be a reduced metabolic ability to convert phenylalanine, an essential amino acid, into tyrosine (Jervis, 1947, 1953). This failure resulted from the lack of an appropriate enzyme in the victim, phenylalanine hydroxylase. The resulting mental retardation is now believed to stem from the toxic neural effect of the accumulated phenylalanine or its derivatives. Diets free of phenylalanine begun early in life can materially improve the condition, illustrating the importance of environmental factors even in the case of a trait that has heredity as the prime cause. The details of the biochemistry of the defect are too complex to go into here, but the essential point is that phenylketonuria is a striking example of an important disorder of adjustment that has been shown to be *directly inherited.*

Because the causes of most cases of mental retardation are still unknown, phenylketonuria has sometimes taken on the role of a *prototypic genetic disease* in mental retardation. The argument goes as follows: Once upon a time phenylketonuria (like general paresis) was of unknown origin. In fact, it was undifferentiated from any other instance of mental retardation; one could not tell them apart. Now, thanks to Jervis and Penrose, we know it is a specific, inherited disease, and we can differentiate it from other forms of mental retardation through the presence in the urine of phenylpyruvic acid. Is it not possible that these other forms of mental retardation are also the result of some genetically based biochemical anomaly? The history of research with phenylketonuria thus encourages the assumption that many disorders whose causes are as yet unknown will ultimately succumb to similar genetic and physiological discoveries. This analogy helps give phenylketonuria its importance, since statistically it accounts for only a tiny fraction of cases of mental retardation. As a rare disorder without this prototypic feature, it would hardly warrant the extensive treatment it has been given here.

There is, naturally, an opposing argument to this presumed analogy between phenylketonuria and other forms of mental retardation. The counterargument states that the finding of a genetic cause for a *tiny* number of cases of severe mental retardation (phenylketonuria) does not necessarily presage the discovery of genetic causes for the large number of remaining cases. Severe mental retardation is rare, occurring only in a small percentage of retardates, most of whom have mild intellectual limitations (IQs, for example, of 55 to 70). Thus, there is reason to think that the truly severe forms of retardation are in a class by themselves and are not representative of the same causal conditions associated with mild retardation (Zigler, 1967).

Moreover, severe retardation, of which PKU is one cause, appears fairly evenly distributed among all social classes, while the highest percentage of mild retardation seems to come from the lowest socioeconomic class. This suggests that many, if not most, such cases are at least partly the result of growing up under conditions of environmental deprivation, involving, for example, inadequate social and intellectual stimula-

tion, language, nutrition, and hope. Still, the reason people of low measured intelligence are more numerous among the lower socioeconomic classes could nonetheless be that low intelligence limits their achievements. Notice two things here: (1) The arguments and counterarguments are not mutually exclusive; both could apply, since adaptive intelligence grows out of the interplay of genetic and environmental conditions; (2) the impossibility of resolving the debate in general terms illustrates nicely the fallacy of attempting to infer causation from a correlation. That is, there may indeed be a correlation between social class and intelligence, but by itself this cannot prove a causal relation between them, nor can it be resolved without other evidence about which factor might be the cause and which the effect. In any event, there is good reason to believe that PKU is simply not a prototypic case, as has sometimes been claimed. The question of the relative importance of genetic and environmental factors in "normal" mental retardation (in the context of present socioeconomic conditions) is still an open one, just as it is with the high or exceptionally gifted end of the intelligence distribution.

THE INTERACTION OF HEREDITY AND ENVIRONMENT

It would be unthinkable to leave the question of heredity in adjustment and maladjustment without somewhat more fully addressing an issue that has been a constant source of confusion in psychological thought, namely, the relative roles of heredity and environment. The reader has probably come across this issue in other forms. For example, it has sometimes been referred to as the "nature-nurture" controversy, nature meaning genetic factors and nurture the process of learning from experience. The layperson has a far more simple notion of genetics than is held by the specialist, who knows that many complex factors combine to make a given trait appear in an offspring. It has been pointed out (McClearn, 1962), for example, that the simple phrase "is inherited" is really a convenient expression for a very complex idea. An individual who possesses a given gene pair or pairs will develop measurably different attributes than some other individual as a result of the interaction of biochemical processes and environmental influences. Moreover, even such an involved statement as this is incomplete in suggesting the complexity of the relationships which are involved in inheritance.

Some traits may, of course, be inherited in the traditional, simple sense of stemming directly from the factor in the parents, as in hair or eye color. This factor appears in a certain percentage of the offspring in accordance with statistical laws originally worked out by Mendel. However, for a great many physical characteristics, such as height, the Mendelian laws are not applicable, and it is more suitable to think of *many* genetic factors combining to produce the effect. There are no single genes, for example, that control the shape of the nose, although this shape is undoubtedly influenced by many genes, how many and by what mechanism being as yet unknown. As one moves into the inheritance of complex psychological properties, the situation becomes still more complicated, and it is necessary to recognize that the same genetic factor may have many different end results, proceeding in a long and involved causal chain.

An example is given by McClearn (1962, 1964) of some old research on a genetic disorder in mice. It shows that many diverse symptoms can be related through a "pedigree of causes" to a single genetically produced defect. The genetic trait is a defect in cartilage formation which is, in turn, expressed in various skeletal, respiratory, and circulatory disorders; the latter are not themselves inherited directly. From the cartilage defect there may develop thickened ribs, abnormal positions of the chest organs, alterations of the nasal passage, and so on. These bodily defects, in

turn, can lead to emphysema or hemorrhages of the lung, to difficulties of eating, and to heart failure. The directly inherited trait is the defect in the animal's cartilage, nothing more. The thickened ribs or alterations of the nasal passages, for example, are not inherited. Yet in a very real sense, the subsequent untimely death of the animals from heart failure, hemorrhages of the lung, and starvation are all linked indirectly to the inherited cartilaginous defect, through a "pedigree of causes." Let us build on this case an example of some of the many ways in which heredity and environment can interact:

Suppose half of a group of mice afflicted with the cartilaginous defect are put in a damp, cold room and the other half are fed a marginal diet. It is then likely that most of the former will die of respiratory illness and most of the others will die of starvation. Presumably, if given ideal, supportive environments, fewer might have succumbed. In contrast, suppose also that a group of genetically normal mice (without the cartilaginous defect) are exposed to the same environmental stresses and most of them survive. Is the demise of the abnormal mice the result of poor environment or defective heredity? Obviously the appropriate answer is that *both* poor environment and defective heredity were crucial factors.

Hereditary and environmental contributions can never be completely separated because they are in continuous interplay in the production of every physical or psychological trait. The relative contribution of one depends on the specific context of the other, and this contribution will appear larger or smaller depending on whether the circumstances permit each one to vary greatly or little. For example, in a culture where all the people have an adequate diet, the heritability of traits such as weight or height will be very high because little of the variation can be the result of nutritional differences; however, where distribution of food among the population differs widely, the heritability of the same trait will probably be much lower because there is the possibility for the environment to exert a strong influence. This is why there are no absolute answers to the nature-nurture question. Heritability refers to a particular trait, in a given population, at a certain time, and under specific environmental conditions (see also Hirsch, 1967). Such relativity in the proportional contribution of environmental or hereditary factors may be illustrated by two extreme and opposite hypothetical situations. Imagine, for example, what would happen if an inbred, homogeneous population, with all the individuals having identical genes, were placed in a very diversified environment. In such a case, all the trait variations among the individuals would result from the environment, since this is the only influence allowed to vary. The heritability would be zero. Imagine, in contrast, a genetically heterogeneous population which was placed in a homogeneous environment. In this case, any variations among the individuals would be due entirely to the genetic factors, since these are the only ones which are allowed to vary. Here the heritability would be unity. Finally, if this population were allowed to develop in this diversified environment, its variability would be the result of both sources of variance, and the amount of heritability would be somewhere between zero and one.

THE EMOTIONAL HANGUP ABOUT HEREDITY AND ENVIRONMENT

One would think that the evidence and analysis offered above would have settled the matter and convinced everyone of the banal conclusion that *both* heredity and environment are important in all human functioning. As will be seen, such a conclusion is only banal because of its vagueness, and the problem really gets interesting when stated about particular traits in particular contexts.

The issue of heredity versus environment, in spite of its fruitlessness when raised outside of a specific context, has been the subject of endless discussion and writing, much of it diatribe. It turns out that the issue of how much heredity and environment contribute to adjustment is an *emotionally loaded* one. This contributes to the failure of the public, and of many scientists not familiar with modern genetics, to understand the problem; as a result, the intellectual climate on which the emotional hangup flourishes is created.

THE NOTION OF SUPERIOR AND INFERIOR PEOPLES

People seem to need a sense of pride and continuity with their immediate ancestral past. A sense of continuity is gained when we recognize features we share in common with parents and grandparents. There are qualities in our children, in our parents, and in ourselves that we would like to own or disown, and this is where the sense of pride comes in. Typically, the blame for undesirable traits, or the pride over desirable ones, is heaped on inheritance, although oddly enough there might be more grounds for pride or shame concerning our actions and social impact rather than about our genes, since we have little control over the latter and much more control over the former. Anyway, for better or worse, and for right or wrong reasons, there is usually a strong emotional identification with the genetic past.

The emotional problem in the field of genetics also stems in part from the fact that a considerable portion of the research deals with the variable of IQ. This is particularly important because intelligence seems to be so crucial to adequate and inadequate functioning in the modern world and to our self-esteem. The emotional side of things is also aggravated by the unresolved problem of race relations and by the existence of marginal members of the community who live in slum ghettos and on social welfare. From a hereditary point of view, marginality is the result of defective genes. From an environmentalist point

FIGURE 9-4   The status quo of some peoples has been fixed by force. (Fred Ward, from Black Star.)

plishments are not actually the products of the prideful individual but, rather, were achieved by others in the historical past. Nevertheless, through a process of identification, the person of modest pretensions gains a sense of pride and superiority, taking credit implicitly for the desirable attributes of the group with which identification is made, thus reducing his or her individual sense of inadequacy or helplessness.

THE HEREDITARIAN AND ENVIRONMENTALIST IDEOLOGIES

There are grave social dangers inherent in the extreme hereditarian's doctrine. Obvious examples include the racism of whites toward blacks, which is often justified on the assumption of the latter's supposed genetic inferiority. Another version of this was the Nazi characterization of so-called Aryans and non-Aryans during the Hitler era. The conception that intellectual or other behavioral defects can be stamped out by the sterilization of such individuals so they cannot breed is another distortion derived from an extreme hereditarian position. So is the view that special training for the mentally retarded would have no value in helping them to adjust more successfully, since the problem stems strictly from an inherited defect which is unmodifiable. Hereditarians are particularly prone to rigidly fix the status quo of peoples in social hierarchies on the assumption that these strictly reflect the inherited endowments or attributes of individuals and groups (Fig. 9-4).

of view, it is the result of inadequate or damaging social experiences. Thus, a number of emotional social issues converge on the problem of heredity and environment, and the argument tends to be cast incorrectly, in an either/or sense, in terms of heredity *versus* environment, in spite of positive knowledge that adjustive functioning involves the complex and continuing interplay of both.

The wish on the part of people to feel superior to others, and the tendency to think of "good" and "bad" peoples, is perhaps the major element in the emotionality of the nature-nurture issue, usually expressed in connection with membership in a particular family, class, nation, ethnic group, or race. Whether one ought to feel this way or not, such feelings of superiority and inferiority connected with membership in different social groups (tribalism) have existed and been encouraged seemingly as long as human beings have lived. Often this ethnocentrism is justified by citations of the unique accomplishments of one's group or country, and it is evidently irrelevant to this feeling that these accom-

The opposite extreme of the environmentalist position also carries with it social dangers. One example comes from the treatment of Soviet geneticists during the period of Lysenko, when the official state position emphasized environmental factors at the expense of the hereditary. Those who espoused the hereditary argument were discredited, and even imprisoned. The tying of this issue to official state policy not only impaired scientific research in the Soviet Union during this period and had a harmful effect on the scientists themselves, but it evidently also produced incalculable damage to Soviet farm productivity because of the environmentalist distortion of principles of plant growth and animal husbandry (Fig. 9-5).

Another potential social harm would be to conclude from extreme environmentalism that all children should be treated alike in school. If one argued that there were no important and perhaps irreversible effects of genetic endowment, then differences among children's abilities would be attributed to the way they were raised, and individual differences in capacity might not be recognized at all, except as a mistake of the culture. Variations in intelligence due largely to genetic factors would not then lead to the appropriate application of selective educational methods— for example, separate programs for gifted and for retarded individuals. Both emotional extremes

concerning the nature-nurture issue can have socially harmful consequences because they represent distortions of the facts and of logical analysis.

SCIENTISTS ARE NO EXCEPTION

It is not fanciful to suggest that the nature-nurture issue has sociopolitical overtones or that scientists as well as informed lay persons sometimes deal with it on the basis of emotional bias; at least one empirical research study has shown that a connection does indeed exist between personal ideology and the response to that issue. Pastore (1949) has pointed out that the nature-nurture controversy is a very old one and has demonstrated that political conservatives tend to take a hereditarian position, while political liberals and radicals adopt an environmentalist position (as in Soviet communism). Pastore selected

FIGURE 9-5 Four views of Western genetics from the pen of the famed Soviet caricaturist Boris Efimov, which appeared in the 1949 *Ogonyok*, a popular journal, to illustrate an article entitled "Flylovers—Manhaters." The inscription on the flag reads "The banner of pure science." Clearly the Soviets rejected genetics entirely as the vicious lie of capitalist monsters and fascists. (From Lerner, 1968.)

twenty-four well-known scientists who had been prominent in the nature-nurture controversy during the period from 1900 to 1940 and who had expressed themselves clearly in their writings in favor of either heredity or environment as the important determinant of human functioning. Pastore also made a study of writings by these same scientists which were expressive of their socioeconomic points of view. On the basis of their published statements, twelve of the scientists were classified as liberals or radicals and twelve as conservatives. The list included distinguished biologists, psychologists, and sociologists. Among the psychologists were Francis Galton, William McDougall, Edward Lee Thorndike, Henry H. Goddard, Lewis M. Terman, James McKeen Cattell, and John B. Watson; some of the geneticists included William Bateson, J. B. S. Haldane, and Herman J. Muller; the list also included other distinguished names in the biological and social sciences, such as Karl Pearson, Paul Popenoe, Charles H. Cooley, and Franz Boas.

Relating position on the nature-nurture issue to political ideology, Pastore found that eleven of the twelve liberal-radicals took an environmentalist stand, while eleven out of twelve conservatives were hereditarians. Not all these scientists could be regarded with certainty as well-informed in the field of genetics, so one must be cautious about excessive generalizations about scientists in that field. Moreover, the field of genetics in those years was not as advanced as it is today; in all likelihood, the sort of relationship found by Pastore holds more strongly on the scientific frontiers, where the definition of problems is more ambiguous and the evidence adduced more limited. Nevertheless, the evidence points to a strong link between political ideology and the emphasis on nature or nurture in explaining human behavior.

One should not distrust the scientist's efforts to deal with the world, but rather recognize that in many areas of intellectual exploration, including

that of genetics and behavior, ideology substantially colors investigation. Scientists are not necessarily different from other people; they too become emotionally involved in the burning issues of our times. Questions of race relations, poverty, the education of our children, and liberal as opposed to conservative sociopolitical ideology are very apt to touch a raw nerve. Nothing can be said about hereditary as opposed to environmental influences on human adjustment in general, abstract terms, except that they are both highly important. Only when a particular trait— under specified environmental conditions and in a particular species of animal—is studied with respect to its heritability can we hope to rise above the emotional hangups that surround the issue.

Before we leave the question of heredity and environment and close the discussion of the medical-biological model, some mention should be made of the continuing argument about racial differences in intelligence and its emotional and polemical overtones.

The allegation that blacks have a genetically based inferior IQ compared with whites would seem to be impossible to support for several reasons. First, although blacks in the United States do score lower than whites on intelligence tests, there are many sociological or environmental reasons why this might be so, including the fact that such tests are standardized mainly with reference to whites and reflect middle-class culture and values; moreover, cultural factors also result in unequal opportunities to learn or to acquire the motivation to learn and perform many of the things on which intelligence test scores are based. Thus, such findings fail to follow the basic rule of heritability we saw earlier, namely, that the impact of heredity cannot be assessed without equating the impact of environment. Second, although it is perfectly reasonable to argue on the basis of the evidence that intelligence in individuals has a strong genetic component, such an argument cannot be applied to an entire social group that is not even homogeneous with respect to racial characteristics or IQ performance. Most blacks in the United States are racially mixed with whites and many other strains, and anthropologists cannot even agree about how many human races there are, since so many diverse and overlapping characteristics are involved.

Concerning the cultural differences in opportunity and motivation, Pettigrew has observed (1964, p. 132):

Intelligence (and virtually every other adaptive quality of man) is a plastic product of inherited structure developed by environmental stimulation and opportunity, an alloy of endowment and experience. It can be measured and studied only by inference, through observing behavior defined as "intelligent" in terms of particular cultural content and values. Thus, the severely deprived surroundings of the average Negro child can lower his measured I.Q. in two basic ways. First, it can act to deter his actual intellectual development by presenting him with such a constricted encounter with the world that his innate potential is barely tapped. And, second, it can act to mask his actual functioning intelligence in the test situation by not preparing him culturally and motivationally for such a middle-class task.

Yet although there is no way of adequately comparing whites and blacks (or any other racial groups) on the extent of their innate intelligence, since there is no completely adequate way to equate their cultural experiences some scientists and lay persons keep fighting with each other publicly about inadequate data. The present controversy has been kept alive partly by popular prejudices on both sides of the matter, partly by media irresponsibility, and partly because of the vigorous public espousal by individual scientists of one or the other position, despite the fact that neither side can be demonstrated.

One of the scientists who has been at the center of recent debate is Arthur Jensen, an educational psychologist who took up on request the difficult problem of whether remedial education had any significant effect on IQ and scholastic achievement. Jensen believes, as do others, that heredity accounts for about 80 percent of the IQ differences among individuals. Not only is this impossible to demonstrate and hence misleading, especially when stated in such general terms without specifying the environmental conditions and the population involved, but, in the author's view, if an answer is ultimately given, such an estimate is much too high in light of what we know about the important role environment plays in performance and achievement, the criteria on which IQ estimates are based. Jensen intimated in his article, however, that innate differences may exist between blacks and whites.

Unfortunately, although it was not the primary theme of the Jensen analysis in 1969, his apparent support of the idea that racial differences in IQ exist was instantly taken up in the mass media. Jensen added fuel to the fire by appearing to opt for innate racial differences in intelligence (a shift from "may exist" to "probably does exist"), while exuding an air of being scholarly, scientific, and unbiased about the outcome of the issue of racial differences in ability. He thus has become, at least in the minds of his readers and audiences, a major spokesman for the old idea of racial superiority and inferiority, clothing this idea in apparent scientific respectability of sorts. One of the most respected American behavior geneticists has recently argued that either Jensen has displayed scholarly incompetence in his writings by selectively distorting the facts and issues, or he is dishonest and fundamentally racist in his aims and outlook (Hirsch, 1975).

In addition, a Nobel laureate in engineering and physics (for the discovery of the transistor), who knew little of the biological and social science problems inherent in racial comparisons of intellectual ability, William B. Shockley, loudly insisted that blacks were indeed genetically inferior to whites, and demanded repeatedly that the National Science Foundation confirm his prejudices by undertaking systematic studies of the matter.

The problem was further compounded by frequent refusals on the part of liberal and radical students and faculty to allow Shockley to speak on their campuses, thus adding to an already unfortunate situation the further spectacle of attacks on free speech taking place in educational institutions dedicated to free speech and inquiry even when the views expressed are highly displeasing. The publicity attendant upon this polemical debate did little to educate the public on the real scientific issues and only created the impression that scientists were lining up on either side of the issue. In reality, several major scientific associations, including the American Psychological Association, the American Sociological Association, and the American Anthropological Society went on record that the allegation of black genetic inferiority in intelligence was without foundation. Most major figures in American genetics (for example, Stern, 1960; Dobzhansky, 1962; Lerner, 1968) had been making it clear all along that racial comparisons of this sort were totally inappropriate scientifically on the basis of methodological limitations for addressing the question. Jensen himself should have known that the existing data could not demonstrate his conclusion and that such a demonstration was probably impossible to make in light of the technical difficulties of separating out the genetic contribution from the environmental. This is why so much of the influential work in this field has depended on the use of identical twins, whose genetic makeup is the same.

In this distressing story, which has no doubt not yet ended, one sees clearly the impact of the emotional hangup that has been discussed in the preceding pages. Despite the fact that the existing information does not permit any conclusion whatsoever, some scientists have willingly or reluctantly allowed themselves to be placed in the position of advocating the existence of group superiority and inferiority. And because of the newsworthy and emotional nature of the issue, the mass media have contributed to the confusion, often without the slightest sense of responsibility for educating the public on a matter of such great social importance. It is one of the truly dismal episodes of our time.

SUMMING UP

The medical model sees the root cause of adjustive failure as *disease of the body's tissues, especially the brain.* Such disease can be the result of injury, infection, or stress-induced disruption of hormonal activities, which can impair the functioning of the brain in adjustive behavior. There is no debate about the capacity of organic brain damage (as in senile psychosis) to produce disorders of adjustment. Arguments about the adequacy of the medical-biological model center mainly on the so-called functional psychoses such as schizophrenia and depression, the neuroses, and the personality disorders. Here the case for organic disease or defect is very weak.

One of the most important assumptions of the medical-biological model is that hereditary or *genetic factors* are implicated in many or most mental illnesses; this chapter focuses on some of the evidence for this, on the way this might work, and on the comparative roles of heredity and environment. A key essential for the science of behavior genetics is the fact of *variability* among persons in physical and psychological traits; this variability makes it possible to ask to what extent the trait variation is the result of hereditary influence. The proportion of the variation that is attributable to heredity as opposed to environmental influences is called *heritability.*

There has long been evidence that mental illness has, to some extent, a hereditary basis. The research of Kallmann using a method called "concordance" studied the incidence of mental disorder in one member of a pair of twins when it was known that the other member was disturbed. By varying the degree of genetic relationship— say, from identical twins to fraternal twins and ordinary siblings—he was able to show that the stronger the genetic relationship the more likely would the one member of the pair be disturbed if the other was mentally ill. The findings of Kallmann, however, have proved highly controversial because of serious methodological difficulties. A number of other similar studies have been done in various countries which support Kallmann's thesis, though these too are subject to some of the same methodological criticisms. More recent and sounder research continues to demonstrate a genetic factor in serious mental illnesses such as schizophrenia, though the strength of this factor is probably lower than earlier claimed.

It is not usually claimed that mental illness is inherited directly, but that some physical characteristic is inherited which predisposes the person to such illness if the appropriate life conditions (such as severe stress) are encountered. The argument draws an analogy between mental illness and diseases like tuberculosis. One is apt to develop the illness if he or she has poor constitutional resistance to the germ, but if the germ is never encountered, one does not get sick.

The evidence that there is probably a genetic contribution to mental illness requires a search for the constitutional defect or quality that predisposes some people to suffer such illness. One long-standing hypothesis about this is that *physique* or body build may be involved in whether or not a person develops a particular kind of mental disorder. There does seem to be a relationship, endomorphic (soft, round) types having greater likelihood of becoming manic-depressive and ectomorphic (thin, angular) types developing schizophrenia, but most psychologists assume that the relationship is not causally direct, but comes about because of the social impact of one's body build. A second kind of hypothesis

implicates one or another *biochemical substance* which acts toxically in the brain and accounts for the symptoms of severe mental illness (for example, schizophrenia). Examples of substances that have gained considerable research attention are taraxein, adrenochrome, and serotonin. What is presumably inherited is a genetic defect in metabolism that results in the production of the toxic substance, or in deviant amounts of ordinary substances that are normally present in everyone. The evidence of such genetic biochemical defects is as yet too meager to conclude that a biochemical explanation for severe mental disorder has been found.

Mental retardation is cited as another example of an adjustive problem which in certain limited instances can occur through an inherited constitutional defect. For example, phenylketonuria (PKU), a disorder involving a metabolic defect that produces toxic chemicals that damage the brain, is clearly inherited, and it results in severe mental retardation if not treated in early childhood. For those adopting the medical-biological model, this type of disorder is a prototypic genetic disease. It suggests that comparable inherited defects might be found for other kinds of mental retardation and for many or all mental illnesses.

It is unfortunate that the issue of heredity and environment is so often phrased in either/or terms rather than as a matter of constant interaction of both in the development of any trait. Moreover, genetic influences prove to be far more complex than most people realize, involving many genes for most traits; such influences are clearly dependent on environmental factors at all stages of development.

Failure to think clearly about heredity and environment, including their mutual role in personality and mental illness, is facilitated by emotional hangups peculiar to this issue. The key basis of the emotional hangup is a sense of pride and superiority which people seem to need and the corresponding tendency to denigrate other individuals or groups. The wish for people to feel superior often leads them to seize upon the hereditary argument in explaining and at the same time denigrating groups that are economically and socially marginal or unattractive. The most common example is the assertion that blacks are genetically less intelligent than whites. Such ideologically based prejudice even finds its way into the writings of famous geneticists, biologists, and psychologists taking either an extreme hereditarian or environmentalist position about individual and group differences in social adequacy.

The emotional hangup about heredity and environment can never be dispelled until it is realized that one can never say anything about heritability in the abstract, but only for a given trait, in a particular species, and under specified environmental conditions. Individual variation is the primary reality. The legitimate study of genetic factors in mental illness and other variations in adjustment is clouded by the logical and empirical errors that are encouraged by hangups in this emotionally charged and ideologically loaded area.

CHAPTER 10 THE SOCIOGENIC MODEL

In contrast with the medical-biological approach, the social science approach looks to the social history of the person and his or her current life stress in order to understand the pattern of adjustment. In the social science approach, which includes both sociology and psychology, attention can be focused either (1) on the ways social institutions operate and on the social pressures that a whole culture or a large cultural subgroup experience in common, or (2) on the sociocultural history of the individual. The former is often referred to as the *sociogenic* model, the first half ("socio") referring to the society and the other half ("genic") meaning causal origin.

Let us begin with the broad idea that culture influences the extent and pattern of adjustive failure. The basic theme here is that the frequency and the form of psychopathology vary from culture to culture or among various subgroups within a culture. There are three main reasons for this: First, varying cultural contexts engender greater or lesser opportunities for satisfaction,

frustration, or threat, thus influencing how widespread emotional disturbances are in a given society; second, the belief systems and motivational patterns characteristic of a culture, and its ways of coping with the crisis experiences which are an inevitable part of living, ought to shape the kinds of emotional disorders that people develop, that is, the *pattern* of maladjustment. Third, cultures also promote diverse ways of explaining and managing emotional disorders once they have occurred.

These points are made effectively by Spiro (1959, p. 142):

It is my guess—hopefully, educated—that each culture creates stresses and strains—some of them universal, some unique—with which the personality must cope; that the cultural heritage provides, to a greater or lesser degree, institutional techniques for their reduction, if not resolution; that the incidence of psychopathology in any society is a function, not merely of the strains produced by its culture, but also of the institutional means which its cultural heritage provides for the resolution of strain; that those individuals who, for whatever the reasons, cannot resolve the culturally created strains by means of the culturally provided instruments of resolution resolve them in idiosyncratic ways (neuroses and psychoses); and that to the extent that different cultures create different types of strain, idiosyncratic resolutions of strain (neuroses and psychoses) will reveal cultural variability.

In order to understand patterns of adjustment in a given society, it is also necessary to understand that society's modes of thinking and believing. What is reality in one society may appear to be nonsense in another. Without some knowledge of the cultural background of individuals, the psychological significance of their dreams, their ideals and dreads, and their forms of individual **deviance**, for example, cannot be adequately **understood**. This has been effectively expressed **long** ago (Hallowell, 1936, p. 1294) as follows:

It is chiefly in reference to the beliefs regarding the nature of the external world and the normality of interpersonal relationships that are engendered by certain traditions in our culture that the belief systems of primitive peoples appear to be "flights from reality," comparable with the delusional systems of psychotic individuals in our society. But can the concept of "reality" itself be regarded as having any absolute content? Just as the psychotic person acts as if his delusional system constituted reality (as it truly does for him), so the individuals inculcated with the belief systems of primitive societies act as if such beliefs were true. But whereas the psychotic reifies a specific personal version of reality, the normal individual of a primitive society reifies the generic beliefs typical of the cultural heritage to which he has

been subjected. . . . The delusional system of an individual of a primitive society must be evaluated with reference to the definition of "reality" characteristic of his culture and not that of some other.

CULTURE AND ADJUSTIVE VARIATION

The incidence of emotional disturbance in different cultures can be estimated in two ways: first, on the basis of study of a sample population which is assumed to be representative of the whole and, second, on the basis of the hospital admission statistics for that region. There are serious difficulties in making such estimates, including the problem of defining what is pathological, the problems of sampling, the dependency on the cooperation of the local population, and the problem of working in a language other than one's own (Wittkower and Fried, 1958). Estimates based on hospital statistics are especially subject to error because of great differences in facilities, patterns of patient admission, and variations in the willingness to care for the mentally ill within the home. Therefore, there are no existing statistics about the incidence of mental illness in different cultures that are free from serious methodological errors. Experts must make estimates that are subject to much qualification.

Some of the observed differences may not be the result of the particular culture but instead may stem from certain factors that are common to all cultures and merely particularly evident in that one. For example, many observers have noted that schizophrenics in primitive cultures show greater limitation in the richness of the mental content displayed, more marked shallowness of affect, and greater dilapidation of behavior compared with advanced cultures. However, the richness of the clinical symptomatology depends greatly on the intellectual and cultural resources of the patient, and these same differences can be found between educated and uneducated individuals within any culture. Thus, what may appear to be a cultural difference may have little or nothing to do with the culture as such, and much more to do with its complexity and educational level. In spite of these difficulties, Wittkower and Fried (p. 25) conclude that:

Suggestive evidence has been submitted to substantiate the hypothesis that cultures differ significantly in the incidence and symptomatology of mental illness. The available evidence strongly suggests that cultures differ a) in the amount of aggression, guilt, and anxiety generated within the structure of the life situations faced, and b) in the techniques used by the members of these cultures in dealing with aggression, guilt and anxiety. These areas require further elaboration. Such sociocultural variables as family and community organization, rapid sociocultural changes, migration, population pressure, and political events are undoubtedly related to the etiology of mental illness.

ATTITUDES TOWARD ALCOHOL

The thesis that emotional problems vary with cultural factors is well illustrated in an anecdote reported by Caudill (1959, pp. 215–216) concerning the Japanese attitude toward alcohol:

It is striking that there is much drinking by men in Japan, and a great deal of male dependency and passivity, but there is little alcoholism as this would be defined in the United States. Some aspects of this question may be illustrated by a simple thing like a whiskey advertisement in *Bungeishunju* (a popular monthly magazine) which says a great deal about attitudes in Japanese culture when it shows a pleasant old gentleman smilingly anticipating the pleasure of drinking the six bottles he saved up, while his gray-haired elderly wife kneels on the floor and counts her money. The caption reads, "To

each his own happiness." Further understanding is provided by the fact that the wife in the Japanese family manages the money, and circumstances permitting, gives her husband an allowance on which to go out and do his drinking. It is not likely that such an ad, nor the cultural circumstances represented in it, would occur in the United States, and from this example it is possible to gain some appreciation of the influence of the cultural context on the patterning of instinctual gratification.

One might say reasonably enough of the above example that it is merely an ad in a popular magazine, although the ad gains a certain validity from the fact that it would not be likely to appear unless it were acceptable in the culture and useful in selling whiskey. That such an ad, however, had its counterpart in behavior was brought home to me in the experience of several of my friends in Japan. I had one friend with whom I spent many evenings drinking and talking. He had a habit on one night each week of taking the allowance provided for the purpose by his wife in the family budget and going out to drink with his cronies. When he arrived home late in the evening his wife would meet him at the door, help him off with his shoes, prepare a snack for him in the kitchen, and then assist him to bed. Equally, I had another friend whose job entailed great responsibility and power. He liked to drink American whisky, and I would occasionally bring him a bottle as a gift. He saved these bottles and others, until his store amounted to several dozen. His plan was to wait until a suitable vacation period permitted him the leisure to drink them up. This vacation became a reality in the interim between one important job and another, and he was able to put his plan into effect.

These examples would seem to indicate that the Japanese man does not anticipate rejection from others because of his drinking and is less likely, at least through stimulation from this outside source, to feel guilty about his drinking.

Such observations provide important clues about the possible variations among cultures in mental illness and the handling of it by those cultures. These observations gain further significance in the light of known differences in the rates of alcoholism among national and ethnic groups. Opler (1959b) cites, for example, a number of studies which show that alcoholism is a common accompaniment of personality disorder in the Irish; however, certain other groups, for example the Chinese in New York, are free of this symptom, and Italian and Jewish populations also have exceedingly low rates of alcoholism.

MENTAL ILLNESS IN IRISH AND ITALIAN-AMERICANS

Many other examples of cultural variation in the incidence and type of mental illness can be found (Opler, 1959b) among such populations as the American Indian and the people of the South Pacific, Asia, Africa, and Western countries. One particularly interesting example comes from a study by Singer and Opler (1956; also Opler, 1959a) with Irish and Italian schizophrenic patients. The study was based on the assumption that the cultural conditioning of Irish and Italians would lead to divergent interpersonal orientations and ways of thinking which would determine the *symptoms* in the event of serious emotional disturbances.

Irish and Italian Americans were chosen for the study because anthropological evidence had indicated marked differences in their respective family constellations, including the social and sexual role of the male and female. In the Irish family, for example, the mother plays a dominant and controlling role in contrast with the Italian mother, who defers authority to the father. Moreover, in the Irish family sexual courtship is

mild and protracted, with marriage being long delayed and celibacy emphasized; sexuality is subordinated to procreation, and sexual feelings are apt to be regarded as sinful and guilt-producing. In contrast, in the Italian setting sexuality is generally regarded as a normal part of emotional life and is accepted as an assertion of healthy maleness. The Irish family with its relatively powerful mother and female siblings emphasizes inhibition and delay of gratification, while the Italian family is characterized by a powerful father, important male siblings, and the expressive acting out of feelings. These differences in family pattern led the authors to anticipate culturally based variations in modes of thought and expressiveness among the Irish and Italian schizophrenic patients. The Irish patient should be more inhibited, beset with fear and guilt, and marked by a controlled hostility to female figures; the Italian patient should be more expressive and given more to overtly hostile and destructive urges aimed chiefly at male parental images.

Singer and Opler tested sixty male schizophrenic patients, half from Irish-American stock and half Italian-American. All the patients ranged from first- to third-generation Irish or Italian, with residence in New York City. Their ages ranged from eighteen to forty-five. Both ethnic groups were of comparable education and socioeconomic status and were hospitalized at about the same time. All were Roman Catholics. Thus the two groups were quite comparable in most background factors except for their Irish or Italian ethnic origins. The patients were given a battery of psychological tests, and observations of their ward behavior were also made in order to permit evaluation of the central question about the role of culture in shaping the expressions of psychopathology.

Major differences were found in the symptomatic patterns displayed by the two populations, as anticipated. Opler (1959a, pp. 434–437) has summarized some of the impressions derived from the study as follows:

> The majority of Irish patients struggled with sin and guilt preoccupations concerning sexuality, whereas Italians had no sin or guilt preoccupations in this area. Instead, the Italian case histories and current ward behavior showed behavior disorders in the realm of poorly controlled impulses, weak personal attachments, and widely fluctuating or flighty emotional affects. The attitudes toward authority in the two groups diverged in parallel fashion, Italians having been verbally rejecting or actively flouting of authority in tests or case history, while Irish were . . . compliant for the most part, with only the most passive forms of outward resistance in evidence. . . .
>
> Practically no Italians proved to have the highly systematized and elaborated delusions found frequently in the Irish patients, as we had hypothesized. . . .

> Chronic alcoholism was found in the histories of nineteen of the Irish patients and only one of the Italian patients. In two-thirds of the Irish cases, anxiety was directed toward female figures, while in only three cases did the father appear more central.

> In sharp contrast, Italian cultural values set greater store on male parental or eldest sibling dominance while at the same time reinforcing more direct expressions of the resultant hostile emotions. This acting-out of feelings brought more hostility to the fore in poorly repressed conflicts with fathers or elder male siblings. One Italian patient, for example, entered the acute phases of illness at the time of his elder brother's wedding and expressed himself, with floridly violent accusations, against his father. In practically all cases there was a strong repulsion from the father, elder brother, and even surrogate authority figures. The Italian mothers, in such instances, were often subtly rejecting and preferred the eldest son. In some cases, the mother, playing a subordinate role in the family, had compensated by assuming a mildly seductive and pampering role in relationships with the son. One could trace the effects of a harsh and punitive or domineering father. The mother compensated for her own feelings of neglect at the father's hands by building up hostile forms of impulsiveness in these sons, along with features of poor emotional control. Italian patients, even when labeled like Irish as schizophrenics with paranoid reaction, had more prominent problems of emotional overflow (schizoaffective features) which took the form of elated overtalkativeness, curious mannerisms, grinning and laughing hyperactivity, or even assaultiveness. Even hostility directed toward oneself came into evidence when elated excitements gave way to inept suicidal attempts. One-third of the Italian sample showed such periodic excitements with confusion and emotional lability (catatonic excitements) while the other two-thirds were subject to extreme mood swings in which the depressed and quiescent periods gave way to destructive outbursts, elation, suicidal behavior, or curious mannerisms. In brief, all Italian patients had so much affective coloring, aimed primarily at male figures and images, that the paranoid schizophrenic label seemed to fit them poorly.

In this research, cultural shaping of the symptomatology of mental illness is very clearly in evidence in the types of delusions and fantasies about male and female figures Irish and Italian patients display, as well as in their overall ward behavior. The force of the argument is strengthened further by the sensible fit that was found between the symptom patterns and what is

FIGURE 10-1 The formal accouterments of dining are distinctive features of the upper class. (Elliott Erwitt, from Magnum.)

known about the family structure in both cultures.

ATTITUDES TOWARD PAIN AND ILLNESS

Another example of the role of culture in mental health comes from observations of Jewish and non-Jewish attitudes toward illness in children

and the frequency with which they consult a physician. For example, in a study of reactions to pain it has been observed from interviews that Jewish and Italian mothers were both overprotective and overconcerned about the child's health compared with "old Americans" (those whose families had lived in the United States for many generations, and were thus fully assimilated). Jewish and Italian patients responded to pain emotionally and tended to exaggerate it. In contrast, "old Americans" were more stoical and "objective" in their reaction to pain (Zborowski, 1958).

Similarly, American Jews have a much higher tendency to visit a doctor and to take medication than either American Protestants or Catholics, regardless of their educational or economic levels (Mechanic, 1963). One possible explanation for this lies in the great importance of "health and illness" within the traditional religious ideology of Jews. In any event, such findings illustrate that behaviors relevant to mental health vary among different cultural groups.

More recent studies than those of Singer and Opler devoted to Italian and Irish symptoms of psychopathology have shown that there are variations among these ethnic groupings in the physical complaints they present to medical clinics, as well as in their attitudes toward the symptoms of disease (Zola, 1966). Physical disorders are commonly considered to be comparatively objective events. Yet medical abnormalities in a population are really the rule rather than the exception, although for a variety of reasons they are reported to medical specialists rather infrequently. This makes it possible for cultural factors to play a strong role in determining the symptoms which are acknowledged and selected for attention when people present medical complaints.

Even when the diagnosed disorder for which the patients sought aid was held constant, it was observed that the presenting complaints of eighty-one Irish-Americans and sixty-three Italian-Americans were strikingly different. The chief complaint of the Irish patients was much more commonly centered on the eye, ear, nose, or throat, while the most common Italian complaints were centered on other parts of the body. Significantly, when both groups were asked to identify the most important part of their body, more Irish than Italians emphasized the eye, ear, nose, or throat. Thus, the symptoms which gave the Irish-American sample the most concern occurred predominantly in those organs which were felt to be most important. The Italian sample also complained more of pain than did the Irish. Furthermore, problems complained about by the Italian-Americans tended to be more often of a diffuse and multiple nature, while those of the Irish-Americans tended to be highly specific and more often a single symptom.

In all these data one sees a pattern of behavior and concern about matters of health which distinguishes ethnic groupings. Such findings nicely illustrate the relationship between culture and illness-centered behavior, and they can be duplicated with many other groups of different cultural backgrounds (see also Mechanic, 1968, and Smelser and Smelser, 1970). The complete details of the relationship between culture and adjustment are not yet well known. However, there appears to be little doubt, either logically or empirically, that an intimate relationship does indeed exist between them. The relationship sketched here provides prime instances of the general importance of the society and its culture in shaping adjustive patterns.

SOCIAL CLASS AND ADJUSTMENT

Within the larger culture, there are many social divisions. A major kind of social division is that of social class. Much sociological research beginning in the 1930s was directed at describing social class patterns in the United States and the ways these affected various facets of the person's life, attitudes, beliefs, and patterns of conduct.

This research clearly portrayed a strong social class orientation in our society (and most other societies) which produced barriers in communication and social interaction among the population and markedly affected living patterns and psychological characteristics. As Roger Brown (1965, pp. 132–133) put it charmingly:

The life-style differences arborealize into the flimsiest trivia. Upper-class Americans like martinis before dinner, wine with dinner, and brandy after dinner; beer is a working-class beverage. The upper class likes a leafy green salad with oil and vinegar, while the lower class likes a chopped salad or head of lettuce with bottled dressing. If you are middle-class you say *tuxedo,* where the upper-class says *dinner jacket;* in England you say *mirror* where the aristocracy says *looking-glass.* If you, like me, give your trousers a little hitch when you sit down so that they will not bag at the knee, then you are quite irredeemably middle class.

Far more important than these trivia, of course, are the major attitudinal variations connected with social class which, especially before the age of television (which seems to have reduced such variation), influenced child-rearing practices with respect to permissiveness versus a more disciplinarian style. There are also important differences in the ways "mental illness" is viewed by the various social classes, the likelihood of seeking and getting professional help for personal problems, and the environmental stresses to which one is exposed. Let us consider particularly the latter issues since these are closely related to the patterns of adjustment and maladjustment.

THE FARIS AND DUNHAM STUDY

One of the earliest attempts to relate social class to maladjustment was made in the late 1930s in Chicago (Faris and Dunham, 1939). These researchers began with the observation that greater and mental hospital admission rates were tabulated for each zone. The rates of schizophrenic patients were highest in the center of the city and diminished as one went toward the outlying areas.

HOLLINGSHEAD AND REDLICH'S RESEARCH

Following up on this arresting set of observations, Hollingshead and Redlich (1958) later reported a further study that greatly stimulated interest in the relationship between social class and mental illness. Hollingshead was a sociologist and Redlich a research-oriented psychiatrist. Their research in New Haven, Connecticut, provoked much discussion and subsequent research. They found a definite association between social class and mental illness, with lower-class patients predominating in mental institutions catering to the psychotic patient. Higher-class members of the community tended more to use private psychiatric facilities and practitioners, and they had a more favorable view of psychiatry as a solution to emotional problems. In turn, psychiatrists tended to have a preference for treating higher-class individuals, with whom they are generally more compatible. Members of a higher social class tended to be treated more for neurotic disorders, while those of lower social classes were more often treated for psychotic disorders.

FIGURE 10-2 Urban stress. The padlocks and iron gate graphically suggest the underlying fear of vandalism and being ripped off in the city. (Charles Gatewood.)

SUSCEPTIBILITY TO ILLNESS OR ACCESS TO TREATMENT?

The data of Hollingshead and Redlich and of Faris and Dunham raised the question about whether the apparent differences among the social classes were the result of different susceptibilities to mental illness or different ways in which the society deals with people of different education and means. The former explanation says that lower-class individuals experience greater life stress than upper-class individuals, or are less

amounts of social disorganization could be found in the city ghettos of Chicago, which displayed high rates of broken homes, unemployment, and delinquency. If social disorganization were important in adjustment, higher rates of "mental disorder" should be found in these urban areas than in communities or neighborhoods characterized by social and economic stability. The city of Chicago was divided into concentric rings or zones from the downtown area to the suburbs, adequate biologically; they are therefore more vulnerable to severe disorders. In other words, social class is said to bear a causal relationship to disorder. This kind of explanation is preferred by a number of modern writers in this field (for example, Srole et al., 1962; Langner and Michael, 1963)(see Fig. 10-2).

On the other hand, the latter explanation involving different access to treatment among the social classes seems to be more widely favored by social scientists. It states that when a member of the lower classes becomes ill, the illness is not essentially different from that experienced by someone of a higher social class. However, lack of economic means and an unfavorable attitude toward psychiatry conspire to force the individual of a low social class into a publicly supported hospital, to be treated mainly with drugs and other physical therapies (see Chapter 15). Higher-class patients, in contrast, are more apt to be privately treated with psychotherapy. Thus, there may be social class-related treatment patterns too. And in the hospital itself, the psychiatrist is likely to give more of his attention to patients with whom he can strike up a relationship than to those with whom rapport is difficult. Psychotherapy itself is favored by the verbal, introspective values and attitudes that are more common among the highly educated than the uneducated person. Furthermore, lower-class individuals may fear and avoid psychiatry in part because their experiences with it are apt to be quite negative. For example, in many state hospitals which may allot a few dollars per day for each patient and have one physician (often not a psychiatrist) per 250 patients, the resulting atmosphere can only be one of minimal custodial care, electric shock, and tranquilizing drugs, rather than attentive psychiatric treatment. In short, social class differences between therapists and patients influence attitudes, thus serving as barriers to communication between them, and, in turn, they influence the *degree of attention* and the *form of treatment* given.

ATTITUDES TOWARD ONE'S PROBLEMS

A survey by Gurin, Veroff, and Feld (1960) of American attitudes and practices concerning mental health is also relevant here. This nationwide interview survey provides observations clearly supportive of those by Hollingshead and Redlich concerning social class, mental health, and adjustment. The purpose of the study was to obtain systematic national information about mental health problems and how they were being dealt with. A careful selection of 2,460 people had been made to provide a representative sample of American adults. These subjects were interviewed carefully about their life situation, happiness, personal problems, efforts to deal with these problems, knowledge and use of therapeutic resources, and so on.

One of the themes which appeared throughout

FIGURE 10-3 The external environment within which lower-class people tend to define their problems. (Bruce Davidson, from Magnum.)

the report was that the manner in which people define their problems is related to their social class. Lower-class people (those low in income and education) tended to define their problems *externally,* that is, in terms of economic deprivation, the material aspects of their marriage, parenthood, or job, and with an emphasis on physical rather than psychological symptoms. Members of the higher classes tended to see their difficulties more psychologically, that is, as related to *interpersonal* and *intrapersonal defects.* As Gurin, Veroff, and Feld (1960, p. 223) point out, "Interpersonal and personal sources of satisfaction assume prominence only when the basic material requisites for living are no longer in doubt, as in the economically comfortable groups." Furthermore, the tendency to see one's problems as deriving from external sources (the lower-class attitude) was less likely to lead to the seeking of professional help. In contrast, those who were introspectively inclined and who defined their problems psychologically were more likely to solicit professional assistance for these problems. As phrased by the authors (p. 298):

The relationships between the subjective adjustment indices and self-referral supported our assumption that people who seek help for a personal problem tend to be those who have a more psychological orientation toward life and the problem it presents, who are more introspective and self-questioning. The tendency to turn to professional help when faced with personal problems was found to be associated with introspection, with a structuring of distress in personal and interpersonal rather than external terms, with a self-questioning more than a dissatisfied or unhappy reaction toward life roles, with psychological rather than physical symptoms.

The recent concerns among American social scientists with the problems of poverty lead in a similar direction. Poverty poses a special problem when it is associated with what Oscar Lewis (1966) has called "the culture of poverty." Lewis suggests that some (though not all) victims of poverty also suffer from a set of cultural and personality handicaps which tend to perpetuate their bleak circumstances of life, even when opportunities to escape appear (pp. 19–21):

The culture of poverty is not just a matter of deprivation or disorganization, a term signifying the absence of something. It is a culture in the traditional anthropological sense in that it provides human beings with a design for living, with a ready-made set of solutions for human problems, and so serves a significant adaptive function. . . .

Once the culture of poverty has come into existence it tends to perpetuate itself. By the time slum children are six or seven they have usually absorbed the basic attitudes and values of their subculture. Thereafter they are psychologically unready to take full advantage of changing conditions of improving opportunities that may develop in their lifetime.

What is wrong with this culture, and the type of adjustment it engenders, is that persons grow up in it with a strong feeling of fatalism and a sense of helplessness, dependency, and inferiority. They are present time-oriented rather than future-oriented and will usually not make any effort to defer gratification and plan for the future. There is little social organization and little historical perspective or awareness of things beyond the local setting. It is characterized not only by economic poverty but also by a "poverty of culture." Lewis likens the culture to that of the "jet set" or "café society," with its orientation to gratification and the immediate discharge of impulses and its emphasis on spontaneity, which tends to be blunted in the middle-class future-oriented person (Fig. 10-3).

Of particular interest, Lewis argues (1966, p. 19)

FIGURE 10-4 It would seem that for poor Woodstock, the locus of control is decidedly external. (Drawing by Charles Schulz; © 1970 United Feature Syndicate, Inc.)

that the culture of poverty is basically similar in whatever society it is found. "This style of life transcends national boundaries and regional and rural-urban differences within nations. Wherever it occurs, its practitioners exhibit remarkable similarity in the structure of their families, in interpersonal relations, in spending habits, in their value systems and in their orientation in time." Lewis (p. 21) thinks that it is particularly a subculture of Western industrial society with its "class-stratified, highly individuated value system. It represents an effort to cope with feelings of hopelessness and despair that arise from the realization by the members of the marginal com-

munities in these societies of the improbability of their achieving success in terms of the prevailing values and goals."

Lewis's analysis clearly relates to the earlier observation that lower-class Americans externalize their problems and are not as likely as higher classes to see themselves as capable of giving a direction to their lives. The analysis adds a psychological dimension to the findings of class variations in patterns of adjustment. Its general arguments are also consistent with experimental effects of a reward or a punishment depend on whether the person perceives the reinforcement as *contingent on his or her own behavior* or as independent of it. That is, rewards and punishments will not necessarily have much effect on subsequent behavior if there appears to be nothing that the person can do to make them happen or not happen. With respect to those who belong to the "culture of poverty," or to the lower classes as studied by Gurin, Veroff, and Feld, attitudes of helplessness or powerlessness are probably central to their common failure to capitalize on opportunities when they do occur to alter for the better their circumstances of life.

The controversy over whether social class position is causal in mental illness or is an effect of it has been succinctly summarized by Dohrenwend et al. (1970, p. 197):

> Is low social status more a cause or is it more a consequence of psychiatric disorder? On the basis of research to date, it has been impossible to tell: for this relationship can be explained with equal plausibility as evidence of social causation, with the environmental pressures associated with low social status causing psychopathology; or by contrast, it can be explained as evidence of social selection with preexisting psychiatric disorder leading to low social status. The latter interpretation is compatible with the position that genetic factors are more important than social environmental factors in etiology.

So we do not have a definitive answer about the nature of the complex relationship between social class membership and adjustment. It is quite possible that both the social causation hypothesis and the social selection hypothesis are potentially correct and help to explain the relationship between social class and adjustive failure. As we shall see later, many modern studies have shown that one's chances of becoming seriously disturbed as an adult are greatly increased if one grows up with parents who are themselves seriously disturbed.

WEAKNESS OF THE SOCIOGENIC MODEL

Despite the substantial relationship observed between cultural factors, social class, and maladjustment, the sociogenic model is actually a rather weak one because it does not clearly specify the ways in which lower-class membership might serve to increase the risk that an individual will display serious maladjustment (Garmezy, 1974*a*). Such a model makes the implicit assumption that all lower-class individuals experience conditions that make for maladjustment. Yet there is ample evidence that a substantial proportion of ghetto dwellers, for instance, develop important adjustive strengths and, indeed, may have higher competence in handling the kinds of social conditions to which they are accustomed. As Kohn (1968, p. 164) has put it:

> Social class indexes and is correlated with so many phenomena that might be relevant to the etiology of schizophrenia. Since it measures status, it implies a great deal about how the individual is treated by others—with respect or perhaps degradingly; since it is measured by occupational rank, it suggests much about the conditions that make up the individual's daily work, how closely supervised he is, whether he works primarily with things, with data, or with people; since it reflects the individual's educational level, it connotes a great deal about his style of thinking, his use or non-use of abstractions, even his perceptions of physical reality and certainly of social reality; furthermore, the individual's class position influences his social values and colors his evaluations of the world about him; it affects the family experiences he is likely to have had as a child and the ways he is likely to raise his own children; and it certainly matters greatly for the type and amount of stress he is likely to encounter in a lifetime. In short, social class pervades so much of life that it is difficult to guess which of its correlates

are most relevant for understanding schizophrenia. Moreover, none of these phenomena is so highly correlated with class (nor class so highly correlated with schizophrenia) that any one of these facets is obviously more promising than the others.

In other words, even if social class is related to the tendency to develop adjustmental disturbances of a particular kind, we must still determine the manner in which this works psychologically for any given individual. The sociogenic model focuses on social or institutional factors, and these probably affect people differently. Such a model is therefore insufficient by itself without knowledge of the psychological processes shaped by social class which, in turn, influence an individual's adjustive success of failure. We must therefore turn to a psychogenic analysis, that is, to a concern with the individual's personal history (as opposed to a group's) and how this history might increase or decrease the risk of his or her growing up with problems of adjustment.

SUMMING UP

The sociogenic approach focuses on the significance for adjustment of the ways in which social institutions and culture affect large groups. Many observations have been made of the relationship between *culture* and patterns of adjustment; a prime instance is the difference in attitude toward alcohol found among Japanese and Americans. Another involves an extensive comparison of the clinical symptoms of Italian-Americans and Irish-Americans hospitalized for psychosis. Differences were found which appear to arise from the two distinctive patterns of family life and attitude in these ethnic groups. Attitudes toward pain and illness are also found to differ among ethnic groups within the United States. These in turn lead to divergences in illness behavior, for example, in the degree of readiness to seek medical assistance, in apprehension over symptoms, and in the type of medical complaints made.

Social class is another sociogenic variable affecting adjustment. An early study by Faris and Dunham revealed a strong relationship between social class, urban environment, and the incidence of severe mental illness; the latter was much higher in the central city, where lower-class neighborhoods abound. This research was followed up by Hollingshead and Redlich, who showed that psychosis seemed to be more prevalent among lower-class persons than among the higher classes. However, their findings raised the possibility that it was mainly access to treatment and the kind of treatment given that differed among the social classes rather than the incidence of severe mental illness. Since then the basis of the relationship between social class and mental illness has been debated widely, the two main positions being that lower-class persons (1) are more susceptible to serious mental illness because of the especially stressful and deprived conditions of their lives and (2) lack the access to treatment enjoyed by those in the upper classes, a factor which might make the former also more vulnerable to serious disturbances because of the lack of preventive treatment in the early stages of emotional difficulty.

Recently a third social class–centered factor has emerged, the *attitude toward one's own problems*. Members of the lower classes tend to define their problems physically and externally and to feel powerless to change the situation; hence they are less likely to seek treatment for psychological difficulties. In contrast, higher-class persons are more likely to blame their problems on personal defects and to see them as psychological; hence they readily seek and obtain professional help. Such differences in outlook resulting from social class have the greatest significance for the types of problems people display, for the likelihood of seeking and obtaining treatment, and for public statistics on the distribution of types of mental illness in institutions and in the larger population.

Although a substantial relationship exists between cultural factors, social class, and maladjustment, the sociogenic model of mental illness is seriously incomplete. Its main lack is that it treats people as members of large social groups and ignores the great individual variation among them—for example, the many persons whose behavior deviates from their position in the social or cultural scheme. Social institutions do not affect people in the same ways. In order to understand adjustment and maladjustment completely, one must also determine the way such factors operate psychologically in any individual. We need to supplement the sociogenic analysis with a psychogenic model.

CHAPTER 11 THE PSYCHOGENIC MODEL

The psychogenic model of adjustive failure centers attention on the *individual*, his or her social history, the way the individual has been reared, the influences to which he or she was subjected in growing up, and the special experiences that have shaped psychological development. It is a very reasonable assumption that this pattern of experiences, especially in early life, contributes to one's relative vulnerability or invulnerability to adjustive failure under the stresses of life and perhaps even to particular forms of maladjustment.

Maladjustment is seen as the result of stresses that retard or impair the development and utilization of the competencies required for successful living. Although there are many alternative ways of conceptualizing how this might happen, the psychogenic model in general emphasizes the nurture side of the classic nature-nurture debate in the form of the proposition that the competencies required for successful living are largely acquired or learned through social experience. Culture and social institutions (as emphasized in the sociogenic model) are important of course, but it is what *individuals* learn from their experiences with institutions and social patterns that determines how they adjust and their adjustive success or failure.

The life experiences which differentiate the maladjusted from the well-adjusted person are investigated in one of three ways: (1) by correlational or experimental studies linking contemporaneous or past patterns of rearing or social experience to how the person is managing his or her affairs; (2) by retrospective analyses of the life histories of such persons; and (3) by longtitudinal or cross-sectional studies of personality development in which persons selected on various bases are observed over brief or long periods of time, sometimes over the entire life course.

CORRELATIONAL AND EXPERIMENTAL RESEARCH

The interests of researchers in the area of family life and child rearing often extend beyond merely determining the patterns that go along with severe adjustive failure. They also involve how child rearing affects personality, and although much of this research does not deal with severe maladjustive patterns such as schizophrenia, it is nevertheless instructive to look at examples of studies relating to milder as well as more severe emotional disturbances. In correlational studies, one selects persons showing different patterns of adjustment and looks for factors in their family environment that might help account for these patterns; or the reverse is attempted, whereby one starts with particular family patterns and assesses the kinds of adjustment that are associated with them.

Usually, what is examined in such research is not chosen at random but reflects the theoretical notions of the investigator about social factors that might be important in shaping personality and adjustment. For example, when a Freudian looks at *specific child-rearing practices,* he or she is likely to emphasize the way the parents handle the three major theoretical stages of the child's psychosexual development—the oral, anal and phallic-genital stages. An example is cross-cultural research (Whiting and Child, 1953) designed to test the idea that frustration and punishment produces anxieties connected with the stage of psychosexual development at which the child happens to be. Data were collected concerning childrearing practices and adult beliefs about the causes of illness from seventy-five societies all over the world. In cultures where the children were frustrated and punished severely with respect to sexuality, for example, it was found that the adults of that culture believed illness was caused by violations of sexual taboos; similarly, in cultures where severe toilet training (anal stage) was imposed, anal explanations of

illness were common. Studies of personality development and child-rearing patterns which focus on such practices as weaning, toilet training, and the handling of genital impulses, have usually been strongly influenced by the Freudian psychosexual theory.

In contrast with the approach which stresses specific child-rearing practices, others (for example, Fromm, 1949) have emphasized the *atmosphere of the parent-child relationship.* For example, even in the case of the mother who is physically neglectful of the child because she must work, the relationship between the two can be secure and supportive because she communicates a sense of being wanted and loved during the periods when they are together. From such a standpoint, the emphasis is placed on the atmosphere of the parent-child relationship rather than on the details of maternal care or the specific child-rearing practices engaged in by the mother. Being wanted and loved is seen as more important for the developing child's personality than how early or harshly the child is weaned or toilet-trained. Thus, while everyone concedes that the personality is influenced comparatively early in life by things the parents do, precisely what elements or qualities are most important in the parent-child relationship, and why, is the subject of considerable controversy.

The atmosphere of the parent-child relationship can be examined in regard to a variety of characteristics. For example, parental attitudes toward the child can be described as neglectful, overprotective, possessive, arbitrary, democratic, accepting, warm, hostile, rejecting, and so on. Research workers at the Fels Research Institute (Baldwin, Kalhorn, and Breese, 1945) have suggested three basic, independent dimensions: (1) *Acceptance-rejection,* which deals mainly with the degree of warmth expressed by the parent toward the child. Cross-cultural studies have shown considerable differences among national and ethnic groups (for example, English and Italian) in expressiveness and warmth on the part of parents. (2) *Possessiveness-detachment,* concerned with the extent to which parent is protective of the youngster; this can range from extreme overprotectiveness to neglect and disregard of dangers and traumatic experiences. (3) *Democracy-autocracy,* that is, the extent to which the child can participate in determining the family's policies. Some children are handled in a dictatorial fashion, while others are permitted considerable self-determination. Differences along these dimensions are found not only within our own society, but also between societies.

MATERNAL OVERPROTECTION

The study of childrearing can be illustrated by a classic work on maternal overprotection (Levy, 1943) which seems quite timely in the light of other more recent studies along related lines. Levy's study dealt with the consequences of *maternal overprotection,* that is, caring for a child as one would a baby far beyond the age at which such care is appropriate, and in ways that prevent the development of independence. Levy observed two different patterns of maternal overprotection. One he called dominating and the other indulgent. Dominating mothers imposed excessive controls on the child; indulgent mothers pampered the child's every whim and made little attempt to control him or her. In both types there was oversolicitude; the child was forced to stay within sight or call. The overprotective mothers were overattentive through even minor illnesses. They bathed and dressed the child even after he or she was old enough to assume such responsibility.

The mother-child atmosphere of overprotection produced some striking behavioral effects, the precise pattern varying with whether it was dominating or indulgent. The overprotected and indulged children showed behavior characterized by disobedience, temper tantrums, and excessive demands on others. They tried to dominate and tyrannize other children of their own

"This will teach you not to hit people."

FIGURE 11-1   Or, don't do what I do, do what I say! (Drawing by Stanley Stamaty; © 1951 The Saturday Review Associates, Inc. Used with permission.)

age. They had difficulty making and keeping friends, and typically they became isolated from everyone except members of their immediate family. They did well in school, since their mothers stressed education and spent much time with their children's schoolwork. For such children intellectual pursuits seemed more rewarding and safer than social relations, about which they felt apprehensive. The main difference between the dominated and the indulged, overprotected children appeared to be that the former were obedient, submissive to authority, and timid and backward with their peers, while the latter were demanding and disobedient.

Both groups of children were anxious and insecure. Both were generally inadequate in social relations. Presumably because of the continual warnings against danger that went along with the overprotection (for example, "don't cross the street, you might get hurt"; "don't run so much, you might get sick"), these children perceived the world as dangerous and frightening. They distrusted others and failed to develop interpersonal skills because there had been little opportunity. The mother had prevented the acquisition of independent social skills and tended herself to be the center of the child's social interest. Dominated children learned to avoid the dangerous world by doing what the mother said and not exercising initiative; indulged children learned that protection and safety are obtained by demand, the protector to be coerced by tantrums and other forms of manipulation.

There are several difficulties with a study such as Levy's, none of which are probably fatal to the conclusions drawn by the investigator. First, studies of this type rarely employ control groups, for example, comparison with a nonoverprotected group. Would such a comparison group be less anxious, insecure, and inadequate in social relations? Probably, but one cannot be perfectly sure. Secondly, if one studies so general a feature as the atmosphere of maternal overprotection and observes certain general effects, it is difficult to say precisely what it is that is causing them. In other words, we cannot say which of the many details of maternal overprotection are really responsible, although a first approximation can probably be obtained.

PATTERNS OF PARENTAL AUTHORITY

More recent research of Baumrind (1975) has focused on parental styles of child rearing differing in *patterns of authority* and on the effects of these patterns on the child's personality. The studies were performed at the Institute of Human Development of the University of California, Berkeley, with the families being studied over a period of eight years. One group of parents was described as *authoritarian,* the type where the "parent values obedience as a virtue and favors punitive, forceful measures to curb self-will at points where the child's actions or beliefs conflict with what he or she thinks is proper conduct. . . . The child should accept the parent's word for what is right." A second group, termed *authoritative,* attempted "to direct the child's activities in a rational, issue-oriented manner. . . . Autonomous self-will and disciplined conformity are valued. . . . He or she exerts firm control at points of parent-child divergence but does not hem the child in with restrictions." Finally, the *permissive* parent behaved in an affirmative, acceptant, and benign manner toward the child's impulses and actions, . . . giving the child as much freedom as is consistent with the child's physical survival. Freedom to the permissive parent means the absence of restraints."

Baumrind found that those parents who were most warm and permissive produced children who lacked self-reliance and self-control. The children of authoritarian parents were discontented, withdrawn, and distrustful. The children of authoritative parents, who were controlling and demanding yet warm, rational, and receptive to the child's needs, were the most self-reliant, self-controlled, inclined to explore and try things out, and content with themselves and their relationships with others.

Notice that the above research of Whiting and Child, Levy, and Baumrind did not begin with severely disturbed persons but rather with parental patterns, and the personality consequences of these patterns were then observed. To balance this, we might also look at correlational research in which the starting point is serious emotional disturbance and a search is then instituted to identify features of the current family atmosphere which could be held responsible for the disturbance. Such research is commonly performed with schizophrenic patients.

FAMILY COMMUNICATION IN THE CASE OF DISTURBED CHILDREN

Around the mid-1950s, a number of research workers began to view schizophrenia as a product of disturbed family life, and with this in mind they started to investigate the family patterns of schizophrenic patients. They looked at the family as a social unit and studied the patterns of interaction and communication among the members, rather than focusing on the schizophrenic patient alone. Among the best-known of these are the ideas and research of Bateson and his colleagues (1956), Lidz et al. (1965), Lidz (1973), and Wynne et al. (1958), the latter eventuating in a program of research by Wynne and Singer that we shall examine more closely below. Although the specific hypotheses about what feature of the disturbed family situation creates a schizophrenic offspring differ somewhat among each of these groups, we can begin to understand their general point of view and the clinical interactions observed in families of schizophrenics by examining a representative research program, in this case that of Singer and Wynne (1964, 1966; Morris and Wynne, 1965; Wynne and Singer, 1963). They have begun to identify some distinctive features of the family atmosphere created by the parents of schizophrenic children and have supported their concepts with substantial clinical data.

The investigators looked for ways in which the parents of the schizophrenic communicate with each other (and with the child) that are different from the families of normals and neurotics. The focus is not on the content of what they think and say, but rather on the styles of their communication and interaction with each other.

Singer and Wynne note that most familiar research on schizophrenia has emphasized the content of parental attitudes and child-rearing practices that might lead the child to withdraw psychologically from contact with others. In communication, two persons usually share the same focus of attention. The parents of schizophrenics, however, according to Singer and Wynne, exhibit thought disturbances which lead them to communicate peculiarly with each other and the child in a fragmented (unorganized, broken apart) fashion. Thus, children in such a family fail to

receive focalized, goal-oriented, clear communications from their parents. Since the parents lack the ability adequately to focus attention, there can be no sharing of ideas or thoughts in the transactions that they have with their offspring. Consequently, the child's own thought processes undergo the same kind of fragmentation.

Singer and Wynne emphasize not merely what the parent does to the child, but also the manner in which the family as a whole interacts. They point out that even if one parent fails in communication, normal interactions might still be possible between the other parent and the child. Thus, the thought and communication processes of both parents are important. Moreover, the influences are not one-directional, but go from the child to parent as well. They write (1964, p. 28):

The family constellation and shared transactions are what seem internalized by the offspring, providing links between patient and family which are not predictable by looking at only an individual parent in relation to an individual patient. Studies of just the mothers of schizophrenics, or just the fathers, are not sufficient. Rather, it is what a pair of parents together provide as a transactional milieu that is the essence of what children seem to internalize. . . .

A transactional view of family life causes research to focus upon processes that go on among family members. It prevents research from focusing on one-way influences or upon just one person. For example, if the question is asked, "What did these parents do that caused this child to be this way?", the search is almost doomed from the beginning. The wording of this question . . . causes the focus to be one-way, in the sense that the child's contributions to family processes are not considered. Such a question may cause the research to focus upon isolated events of long ago, and fail to consider that transactional styles have probably been in

TABLE 11–1   DIAGNOSIS OF OFFSPRING ON THE BASIS OF THE PARENTS' FIRST RESPONSES TO EACH RORSCHACH INKBLOT

DIAGNOSIS OF OFFSPRING	BOTH PARENTS' SCORES OF 4 OR MORE (MEDIAN OR ABOVE)	AT LEAST ONE PARENT, SCORE OF 3 OR LOWER (BELOW MEDIAN)	NUMBER OF PAIRS
Schizophrenic	(17)	2	19
Neurotic	7	(13)	20
Normal	4	(16)	20
	28	31	59

SOURCE: Singer and Wynne, 1966, p. 32.

Note: Numbers in parentheses represent correct predictions of whether a child would be found to be schizophrenic, neurotic, or normal. In other words, 17 of the schizophrenic children were correctly predicted, 13 of the neurotics, and 16 of the normals.

continuous effect but, because of the growing age of the child, had differing influences at different times.

A typical research method of Wynne and Singer is to select three groups of children, one psychotic (schizophrenic), one neurotic, and one normal. Examinations are made of the parental behavior and performance on diagnostic tests. The attention of the authors is directed at the styles (not contents) of the parents' thinking and communication. On the basis of observations and ratings of parents' styles of communication, efforts are then made to predict whether the offspring will be in the schizophrenic, neurotic, or normal groups. Singer and Wynne made far more accurate guesses about this than would ordinarily occur by chance, supporting their analysis of the family determinants of schizophrenia. In one study they showed that when both parents show disturbed styles of communicating, their offspring will almost certainly be schizophrenic. This is illustrated in Table 11-1, which shows the diagnosis of the offspring (schizophrenic, neurotic, or normal) and the frequency of pairs of parents showing schizophrenic-style communication scores that are above or below the medians for all parents.

The best way of illustrating the communication patterns observed by Singer and Wynne among the parents of schizophrenic patients is to present a case example (Morris and Wynne, 1965, pp. 27–29). An excerpt and analysis is given from a therapeutic interview with the Franks family (a pseudonym to protect the identity of the real family), whose communication is described as fragmented. The interview is with the mother and father of the schizophrenic patient. Prior to the point where the excerpt begins, ". . . the therapist had been emphasizing the family's feelings about their difficulties in getting their points of view across, and he began to wonder out loud if they each felt like giving up at times. Until now he had had little success in getting this question across, although Mrs. Franks agreed that her husband had a 'give-up' attitude." The excerpt continues as follows:

Therapist: Well, I'm wondering whether . . .
Mother: (continuing her complaint against her husband): . . . and he's really . . .
Therapist: . . . maybe it's not—unique to any particular person, that this is something we share . . .
Mother: Well, I tell—like you say, some . . .
Therapist (louder): . . . depending on how—

uh—impossible it has seemed to ever get anything across!

The rater thought that the therapist tried to
restate two points, that all of the family members
had difficulty in getting their views across and
that this leads to despair. He now was extending
these points to include all members of the family
group, including himself.

Father: I always reckoned—uh—when you get
married, it's a give and take proposition. (3-
second pause.) And I've given in—uh—lots of
times. To keep peace. (6-second pause.) For
instance, this cuttin' the radio and television
off. I've asked to cut it off—in a nice quiet way.
(Pause.)

Mr. Franks responded in terms of the cliché
"marriage is a give and take proposition" and
added the generality about his giving in to keep
peace. However, the example which he cites
illustrates his asking the other person to give in.
In addition, he redirects the conversation away
from the major emphases of the therapist. His
"give and take" remark seems to be a rejoinder to
his wife's criticism of his "give-up" attitude.
However, the connotation of the word "give" in
these two usages is so different that the shift
almost has the irrelevancy of a clang association.
These shifts are disjunctive and confusing because he speaks as if he were still focusing on the
same points brought up by his wife and the
therapist. Communication sequences which are
unintentionally disjunctive in this way illustrate
what Singer and Wynne have called "transactional thought disorder." It should be noted that
these shifts take place in a context of deadly
seriousness whereas, in a different context, dis-
jointed communication of this kind can be either
intentionally humorous or a sophisticated playing
with ideas.
Two features of this exchange were common
maneuvers of the Franks: pseudo-specific re-

marks which shifted the focus from the preceding
speech but which were stated in a positive manner as if they maintained the same focus, and a
vigilant preoccupation with reacting to one another in terms of a narrow band of feeling-tone.
They brushed aside other feelings and discrepant
ideas, as well as other persons, including the
therapist. Thus, their intensely emotional reactivity to one another was very constricted in range
and had, for this reason, a fragmenting effect
both upon the kind of meanings which could
emerge and upon the overall relatedness in the
therapy group, which included the therapist and
two daughters.

Therapist: The trouble is that—giving in
doesn't really—solve the problem and—and
then there may be peace for a little while, of
a sort, and then the problem—comes up again.
Doesn't it?
Father: You're right there! (Pause.) You're right
there!
Therapist (after a pause): So it—kind of leaves
the problem—you can sort of pull away from it
for a while, but then the problem—is still
there!
Father: It grows still larger the next time.
Therapist: Hmmmm?
Father: The problem gets to be larger the next
time.
Therapist: Yeah.
Father: That's *true.* (3-second pause.) And I've
always heard a man and wife should agree!

The therapist was momentarily led astray by the
father, agreeing on the point that giving in does
not solve problems. Then Mr. Franks disjunctive-
ly said that a man and wife should agree, as if this
exemplified the point of his consensus with the
therapist. However, since the therapist's point
was that false agreement is not useful, the agreement between the therapist and father at this
point was pseudo-mutual, a false consensus in
which the falsity went unrecognized. When there

are such subtle but abrupt changes of context and therefore of meaning, an overfocused response is one way of salvaging a sense of relatedness, even though meaning is fragmented.

The mother then joined in with a pseudo-hostile form of relatedness to the father, taking the form of perpetual bickering that is pseudo-hostile in the sense that it serves to hold the pair in contact with one another:

Mother: Not necessarily.

Father: Even if the man—uh—comes in and—switches the child and he—his wife *knows* maybe that the husband is wrong a little bit. She should *never*—say anything to him right before the child! She should call him off and talk to him.

Mother: Yeah, and what have you said before the children?

Father: The *man* should do the same thing! And—uh . . .

Mother: Some of the—vulgar—language you've used in front of 'em. You—you don't think that makes an imprint, do ya'?

Father (after a pause): I recognize I've used a few curse words—sure.

Mother: Well.

Father (in a low voice): You *tantalize* me and make me use them.

Mother: I (very low) don't tantalize you. (Pause.) You tantalize your *own* self! With your *own* language.

Father: You stand up and stand there and look at me. "You ain't—you're touchin' 'em—you're not *doin'* it—you get out of here."

Mother: Well, you're *not!*

Father: "I brought them two children into the world, and I'm not gonna see you touch 'em!" (4-second pause.)

Mother: Not when you get mad! I'm not (low) gonna have you do it.

The bickering between the Franks continued throughout the rest of the session, with the therapist finally abandoning his early point and asking for clarification of some of their charges and counthercharges, which, by and large, they did not explain to him. Thus, the therapist's original effort to establish a shared focus of attention on their feelings of difficulty in getting things across was lost in their fragmenting reactivity.

This example clearly suggests that Mrs. Frank protected the children from her brutal husband, and one would expect them to see her as their protector. But in another excerpt, she gave a long emotional oration about how sick her daughter was because her daughter saw her as physically threatening. This makes one doubt the effectiveness of Mrs. Frank's role as the protector of her children, suggesting that her role was vacillating or ambivalently uncertain. This illustrates a third characteristic feature of this family, a lack of consistency in their individual stands in addition to the fragmentation produced by their interaction together.

In summary, this ineffectually manipulative father vacillated confusingly between a dogmatic and an excessively humble stand, between an overly optimistic and an unduly pessimistic view, and between a too general and a too literal position. He took each stand with the emotional insistence and verbal looseness of a high-pressure salesman who does not really believe in his own product. Yet his individual statements considered in isolation were explicit, colorful, and quite well differentiated.

His wife was a little less lively and explicit in her responses, being highly tentative or preoccupied with details. She frequently dredged up past grievances as if they were current events. She became absorbed in petty bickering with her husband, becoming inattentive to anyone else.

Their interaction was limited to continual fighting and blaming maneuvers, except when one of them indulged in a monolog which ignored the spouse altogether. Their usual high degree of reactivity to each other was much more marked than that shown by the Abbotts and Allens, two other families studies. Vivid and clear impressions of the Franks and their interaction emerged temporarily, but in contrast to the Allen or Abbott families these impressions soon disintegrated in a bewildering, kaleidoscopic fashion. Particular exchanges were shorn from their general context, or fragmented. Sometimes the Franks narrowed down to one limited piece of experience at a time, stripped of connotation and connection with the rest of their experience.

It is important to keep in mind that the context for these parental exchanges includes the therapist, who is seeking more clarification than the couple talking alone would be likely to seek or find.

The relation of these parents seemed dominated by blaming, controlling maneuvers, and defenses against blame and control, not by efforts at understanding one another or sharing meaning. They left no room for clarification of either agreements or disagreements. The therapist, again, had the difficulty of dealing with their inconstancy. He was likely to become ensnarled by their transient good insights and understanding, which were then promptly demolished into disorganized, incoherent fragments. Thus, the parents repeatedly failed to share in a sustained focus of attention, which would have been a prerequisite to shared meaning and to the emergence of empathic relatedness and genuine mutuality.

Prediction This family's clarity of expression, though transient, their high affective activity, and their intense involvement differentiated them from the previous families. The judge correctly predicted the presence of a fragmented form of thinking and of labile, poorly modulated affect. However, he felt uncertain as to whether the patient would be frankly schizophrenic or have a borderline schizoid reaction, finally predicting the latter.

Independent clinical evaluation Clinically, the daughter was frankly schizophrenic, fragmented in type, with a psychosis of moderate severity. Her thinking was disorganized and bizarrely para-

noid, with colorful, explosive affect, and with interactions ranging from catatonic withdrawal to stormy involvement.

EXPERIMENTAL RESEARCH ON CHILD REARING

Experimental research into child-rearing practices that might prove destructive to adjustive competence is all but impossible to perform with humans for obvious ethical reasons. One cannot take the risk of damaging children and adults by willfully exposing them to life experiences merely to test some notion about the etiology of emotional disturbance. Such experimentation is only possible with animals, and one very famous series of studies having a major impact on our knowledge in this area has been performed with monkeys by Harry Harlow and his colleagues (Harlow, 1958, Harlow and Harlow, 1962, Harlow and Zimmerman, 1959). This research is so fascinating and provocative that it has been written up extensively in popular magazines. Only a very brief account of it can be given here.

Harlow had observed in previous research that monkey mothers, like human mothers, seemed to be quite variable in their handling of their young. It was not unusual for some of the youngsters to be mistreated and to die of neglect. He thought, almost facetiously, that an artificial mother could be created which offered a more dependable source of whatever it is that the good mother provides to the young monkey, and he set about creating such an artificial mother and separating out various components of mothering for experimental study. In one experiment (Harlow and Zimmerman, 1959), for example, newly born monkeys were provided with two kinds of artificial mothers, one made of exposed wire mesh, and the other made of the same wire mesh covered with terry-cloth material. A nipple with an inexhaustible supply of milk protruded from only the wire-mesh "mother," at which the monkey could feed. No milk was provided by the terry-cloth mother. This gave a less than esthetic

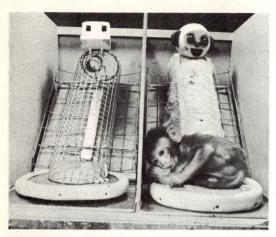

FIGURE 11-2 Wire and terry-cloth mother substitutes used in Harlow's research. (Photo by Sponholz for the University of Wisconsin.)

but very functional arrangement which can be seen in Figure 11-2.

For the person who believes that it is the breast (providing food and oral erotic satisfaction), per se, which is the basis of infant love and affection, it will come as a surprise that the babies, if given the choice, uniformly preferred to spend their time with the terry-cloth "mother." Although they fed at the totally dependable food source on the wire-mesh "mother," they spent the bulk of their time clinging to the barren terry-cloth "mother." When exposed to a frightening wooden spider, the babies would run to the terry-cloth mother as the more effective source of security (see Figure 11-3). When the terry-cloth mother was present, the baby monkey was bolder in exploring the new stimulus than when the wire mother was there. Harlow concluded that the infant monkey, and perhaps the infant human, is innately satisfied by tactile stimulation, which is the basis of the attachment. In any case, it is clear that this tactile quality, and not feeding itself, was the main source of gratification and security for the infant monkeys. In the human counterpart, the sucking of the infant at the breast may

be providing it mainly with the soft, warm, tactile element it needs, and this may be more important psychologically than other elements of the experience such as food or oral stimulation. Thus, the advocate of breast feeding may have misplaced the locus of pleasure and love but accidentally touched upon an important feature of the breast as a source of pleasure, namely, tactile stimulation.

Later on in the research, however, some unexpected observations suggested that very important experiences normally provided by a real monkey mother were not being supplied by the artificial mother. Harlow observed that the monkeys raised on surrogate mothers exhibited abnormal behavior later on. The artificially raised monkeys became very aggressive and unsocial as adults. They were also very inadequate in initiating heterosexual activities. Somehow the ordinary *social contacts* between the mother and baby monkey seem to be essential for the proper development of social behavior later in life. These findings, although inconclusive with respect to which particular social interactions are crucial, are consistent with the findings of a number of observational studies with humans which have shown that the absence of "mothering" has damaging effects on the child's development. For example, children reared in institutional settings (hence missing the normal mother-child interactions) are more retarded intellectually than those given normal maternal attention; they are also more likely to be unresponsive emotionally and more maladjusted. And later work by Harlow and Harlow (1962) also demonstrated that the absence of *peers* may be even more devastating to adult-monkey social and sexual behavior than the absence of real mothers. For example, he found that monkeys raised with real mothers but no monkey peers were less adequate as adults than monkeys raised with artificial mothers but with peer contact.

Harlow's research points up one of the previously mentioned perennial difficulties in research on the atmosphere of parent-child relations and adaptation. When we speak of atmosphere, we are usually referring to a complex but vaguely specified pattern of behaviors on the part of the parent. Although we can reliably distinguish between, say, an atmosphere of rejection and an atmosphere of acceptance, or an atmosphere of overprotection versus one of neglect, they each involve a wide assortment of specific parental acts whose causal role in psychological development is not clear. Although Harlow can state with confidence that the absence of a real mother and peer contacts resulted in abnormal social behavior in the monkeys studied, it has not yet been made clear what exactly are the crucial things that the real mother and peers do or provide for the offspring. Further theorizing and experimentation is required to identify the conditions of early social experience necessary for healthy or pathological social behavior.

RETROSPECTIVE STUDY OF LIFE HISTORIES

It makes a great deal of sense to look for the traumatic past life experiences (for example broken homes or parental rejection) which can distinguish persons who have developed severe adjustive disturbances such as schizophrenia from persons who are functioning adequately or well. Usually one starts with adults who are presently in trouble—for example, patients in a mental hospital—and a comparison group of persons who are not in trouble. Then a search is instituted for evidence of traumatic life events in both groups.

The retrospective data may be derived from life history interviews with the patients and comparison groups, interviews with others who know the person well (usually parents, relatives, and friends), or from societal records. Interview reports have often been shown to produce distorted information because of either lapses of memory, self-defensive distortions, or failure to have

recognized the significance of past events when they occurred, in which case the informant may not report them or may cast them in the wrong perspective. Thus, societal records such as school data, teachers' assessments, and court or child guidance case records provide a more objective source of information than subjective reports from informants.

Such retrospective study also requires that one have a set of notions about what to look for in the past histories of disturbed persons. However, this can lead the researcher to focus on the wrong material merely because he or she has incorrect ideas about what is important. For these and other reasons, retrospective studies have been severely criticized, and in truth they are probably subject to more error than most. In fact, as we shall see, this approach has produced a bewildering and often inconsistent pattern of findings which fail to make a good case for the social causation of adjustive failure.

An excellent illustration of this is a study by Schofield and Balian (1959) using interview data. A comparison was made of the personal histories

FIGURE 11-3 Typical response of infant monkey to terry-cloth mother substitute. Monkey appears to attain security by clinging to it in the presence of the frightening wooden spider in the foreground. (Photo by Sponholz for the University of Wisconsin.)

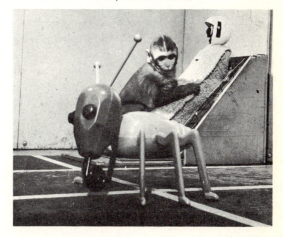

of a group of 178 schizophrenic mental patients and a group of 150 normals. The patients were institutionalized at the University of Minnesota Hospitals. The normals consisted of individuals without prior or present evidence of psychiatric disorder, most of whom had been referred to the hospital for other than psychiatric problems. The two groups, psychiatric and nonpsychiatric, were matched with respect to age, sex, and marital status. Life-history data had been compiled at the hospital for the psychiatric group, and they were similarly obtained from the normals through a comprehensive clinical interview. Both groups were compared with respect to characteristics such as school achievement, home conditions, and parental relationships (for example, how affectionate these relationships were, evidence of rejection by parents, poverty, death of a parent, parental divorce).

The basic assumption of the psychogenic, social-learning viewpoint is that the life histories of schizophrenics should be characterized by a high incidence of unfavorable, traumatic circumstances. Some experts had suggested, for example, that schizophrenic patients are products of a particular kind of mother, called a "schizophrenogenic mother." The following quote from Woolley (1953, pp. 187–188) is illustrative:

> Psychoanalytic students are uniform in the opinion that maternal rejection and domination are regularly found in the histories of those who are found later to have been predisposed to the development of schizophrenia. The mother of the schizophrenic is variously described as cold, dominating, narcissistic, lacking love for the child, having death wishes toward it.

Schofield and Balian actually found little difference between the life-history data of the schizophrenic patients and those of the nonschizophrenics. They summarized their findings as follows (1959, p. 137):

The single most impressive feature of the data . . . is the sizable overlap of the normal Ss and the schizophrenic patients in the distributions of the various personal history variables. Of the 35 separate tests which were run, 13 (or 37%) failed to reveal a reliable difference between the two samples. Further, on 5 of the remaining 22 variables, the distributions showed a reliably greater presence in the normals of negative or undesirable conditions. In those instances where the statistical tests did indicate a reliable characterization of the schizophrenics by prevalence of a pathogenic variable, the normals generally also showed a close approximating degree of the same factor.

With respect to the concept of schizophrenogenic mothers, the authors noted slight tendencies for maternal domination and overprotection to be more common among the schizophrenics. However, this was found in less than one-fourth of the cases in the study. Serious doubt is cast by the study on the significance of certain life factors which are so commonly thought to be central to the development of severe personality disturbance, at least as single, isolated variables.

Representative of retrospective research studies based on societal records is one by Watt and his colleagues (Watt et al., 1970; Watt, 1972; Watt, in press, as described in Garmezy, 1974). First a computer list of every patient between fifteen and thirty-four years old who was first admitted to a public, private, or Veterans Administration hospital in Massachusetts during 1958 through 1965 was obtained. Of this list of 19,179 patients, 15,811 had been initially diagnosed as having a psychosis, neurosis, or personality disorder. Using the files of a public school in Boston, two matched groups were composed, ninety in the patient group and seventy-two in the control high school group whose subjects had not been admitted to any hospitals for psychopathological reasons. These data are still currently being evaluated, but comparisons are presently available for thirty patients who had been diagnosed as schizophrenics as compared with a random group of the nonhospitalized youths. Preliminary results suggest some interesting differences. For example, the male schizophrenic group showed early evidence of more unsocialized aggression, internal conflict, overinhibition, and emotional depression than the nonpatients. Females had been more overinhibited. The schizophrenic boys had also achieved a lower academic performance, had been less cooperative and well behaved, and less pleasant relative to the controls; schizophrenic girls had been more immature and less attention-seeking than the controls. One-half of the preschizophrenics had been socially deviant by adolescence, whereas early childhood revealed few indicators of deviance. There were more parental deaths before finishing high school in the schizophrenic group (19 percent) compared with the control group (8 percent), although this did not seem to apply to those diagnosed as neurotic. Organic handicaps (neurological disorders, cardiac and sensory impairment, obesity, for example) were also more common among the preschizophrenics (39 percent) compared with the controls (21 percent).

In spite of scattered positive results such as those above, Frank (1965) has concluded that findings in retrospective studies of the life histories of persons with severe emotional disturbances have been quite inconsistent and inconclusive. He writes discouragingly about this type of effort to locate the background causative factors as follows (p. 191):

Psychologists generally make the assumption that the experiences to which the individual is exposed over a period of time lead to the development of learned patterns of behavior. From this, psychologists have reasoned that the experiences the individual has in his early life at home, with his family, in general, and his mother, in particular, are major determinants of the learning of the constellation of behaviors subsumed under the rubric, personality, and in particular, the development of psychopatholo-

gy. A review of the research of the past 40 years failed to support this assumption. No factors were found in the parent-child interaction of schizophrenics, neurotics, or those with behavior disorders which could be identified as unique to them or which could distinguish one group from the other, or any of the groups from the families of controls.

To those of us who believe that social factors are important causative agents in adjustive failure, such a conclusion is difficult to accept. Frank is not incorrect in saying that the case has not been made, but yet there must be something very wrong with the approach of much retrospective research, since it has failed to come up with consistent findings implicating early childhood factors. Why should this be the case? (As we shall see below, research employing other approaches and not dependent on retrospective study has had a much better batting average in producing meaningful results.)

The problem is actually extremely complex. For example, an experience at one point in life (when the child has few means to cope at his disposal) may be seriously traumatic, while at another time of life, or in another child, the same experience may result in the acquisition of reliable adaptive skills (Murphy, 1962). In the latter instance the child can use the experience as a means of positive growth. Moreover, the absence of threatening or frustrating experiences, although protecting the child from trauma, can stunt the growth of effective means of coping (see also Chapter 4).

Few writers would actually argue today that a single experience can acccount for pathology. Rather, what is important is a continuing pattern of such experiences and the failure to master them. Moreover, corrective life experiences can to some extent undo the harmful aspects of severe threat and frustration. It is possible that the search for single traumatic events in the development of mental disorder in human beings offers much too limited a perspective. One must

"I've known you since you were a young woman."

FIGURE 11-4 In longitudinal research investigators are likely to be old before the research is completed.

look not for single causes but for multiple causes and the manner in which they interact over the entire life course in the causation of healthy or inadequate adjustment.

LONGITUDINAL RESEARCH

Longitudinal or "follow-up" research, as it is sometimes called, begins with children and reviews their development over time by examining the circumstances of their lives at a later date—perhaps once, perhaps many times. This is the most costly and difficult of the approaches designed to track down the early life influences in adjustive failure and success; if the research is carried out over several decades or more, the original investigators become old, retired, or deceased before the investigation is complete. Often several generations of psychologists must be involved in such research. The assessment methods employed, the psychological attributes observed, the questions asked in the original

study when the child is first seen may go out of date later on because the things considered important at first may no longer seem relevant, and because assessment technology may change.

When the longitudinal approach is applied to the development of severe forms of maladjustment such as schizophrenia, there is a special problem, namely, that the base rate for schizophrenia (base rate means the proportion of schizophrenics in the general population) is quite low. Estimates of the incidence of schizophrenia in the United States range from about 2 to 6 percent of the population (Yolles and Kramer, 1969). Even if the higher figure were accepted, even in a pretty large sample of cases selected in childhood for longitudinal study, very few would end up as schizophrenic, and this would make it difficult to assess causal factors with any confidence. On the other hand, certain background conditions (such as having parents who are schizophrenic or growing up under severely traumatizing or impoverished environmental circumstances) seem greatly to increase the risk of adjustive failure in the developing child, perhaps to as high as 35 to 45 percent (Rosenthal, 1974). Thus, if the longitudinal research program does not select children and families characterized by high risk, it will not end up with much to say about the factors contributing to severe maladjustment.

In spite of the cost and difficulties of longitudinal research on child development, there have been a number of major attempts over the past several decades. One of the best known is a series of projects at the University of California at Berkeley (Jones, 1960; Bayley and Schaefer, 1960; MacFarlane, Allen, and Honzik, 1954), which began in the 1940s and has continued up to the present with several generations of investigators and a few who have remained with the program since its beginning. Some of the research projects started with infants, following them up to middle age, while others started with children at later developmental periods. Another well-known example of longitudinal research of this sort is that of the Fels Research Institute (Kagan and Moss, 1962) which extended over a period of thirty years. In each of these programs, later researchers have made use of data obtained on the children and their families many years earlier by other investigators as well as recent data they themselves obtained in on the same individuals at various adult periods of their lives (e.g., Block, 1971; Maas and Kuypers, 1974; see also Kagan, 1964, for a review).

These longitudinal studies have provided us with much rich material on the development of personality, the consistency of personality traits over time, and some of the family influences linked to such characteristics. However, because they were not specifically directed at children and families at high risk, such studies do not throw much light on the social-developmental factors contributing to serious adjustive failure. They produce findings more analogous in their scope to those of Levy (1943) and Baumrind (1974) which were discussed earlier, although they are certainly relevant to coping and adjustment. For this reason, there has been a rapid growth in recent years of a type of longitudinal or follow-up research comparing children "at high risk" with those "at low risk."

Such research begins with children selected, usually at an early age, because they are growing up with troubled or seriously disturbed parents, or because they have themselves given early evidence of emotional disturbances. The risk may be defined as having a biological or adoptive parent (or two of them) who is severely disturbed; or the risk may refer to a host of theoretically damaging conditions of childhood. Much of this sort of research is of recent vintage, so that findings are as yet limited and incomplete and do not permit us to draw firm conclusions. Yet the data that already exist seem strongly to implicate early-life patterns of influence, as well as genetic-constitutional factors, in the development of adult maladjustment.

One such study, directed at the later adult-life

adjustment or antisocial children (Robins, 1966), will serve as an example. In it 526 (mostly male) patients who had been seen clinically in St. Louis for behavior disturbances were matched with 100 elementary school children in a follow-up about thirty years later. The researchers were able to locate 88 percent of the guidance clinic patients and 98 percent of the matched controls. Out of the total sample 416 were interviewed, and in 75 cases interviews were obtained with relatives. In addition, public records were used as well as an evaluation by two psychiatrists concerning the occurrence of psychiatric illness during the intervening years.

For the patient sample 26 schizophrenics were found, 20 percent of whom had been hospitalized. Among the controls no adults were diagnosed as schizophrenic among the males, but two were found among the female controls. Only 20 percent of the index cases (the patients who had been seen clinically for behavior problems thirty years earlier) were considered free of emotional difficulties, compared with 50 percent of the control group. Moreover, the preschizophrenic's family histories were marked with psychiatric illness, parental inadequacy, and marital disharmony, and psychosis in either of the parents seemed to predict later development of a schizophrenic disorder, especially if the disturbed parent had been the mother.

Of special interest in the Robins study was a continuity between antisocial behavior in childhood and in later adulthood. It appears that antisocial patterns in males in which the child acts out his troubles on the environment, or, to put it differently, externalizes his problems, are more apt to be followed up by schizophrenic symptoms later in life than patterns of being shy and withdrawn; moreover, when antisocial behavior in childhood leads to schizophrenia, it is of a combative and acting-out type. Several other studies confirm this relationship between acting-out childhood problems and later psychosis, as well as suggesting that children with neurotic problems have a higher incidence of good mental health in adulthood than those with delinquent patterns.

This finding concerning antisocial conduct in childhood is interesting because of the widespread traditional belief that children who internalize their problems—who are shy, inhibited, and withdrawn—are indeed showing a behavior pattern that is a precursor of later severe psychological withdrawal. Such withdrawal is regarded as the key process underlying schizophrenia. Yet study after study (see Garmezy, 1974) shows that shyness or introversion in children does not predict the occurrence of later schizophrenia, while acting-out behavior does. This suggests that such shyness in childhood is evidently not analogous to the social withdrawal of schizophrenics as they turn psychologically into their own private world.

Quite an alternative process of becoming schizophrenic is proposed by some researchers. Childhood shyness and introversion are not seen as the beginning of a long withdrawal process; rather, the development of psychosis is said to proceed in stages from protest to despair and finally to apathy and withdrawal. Ricks and Berry (1970, p. 47, as cited in Garmezy, 1974) put it as follows:

> Whether the process moves on from protest or despair to apathy does not seem to depend so much on intolerable feelings as it does on neurological integration and the set of social and vocational capacities that White (1959) sums up in the concept of competence. If one can be active, effective, and successful, protest can work. If one can extrapolate from past solutions to future solutions, so that hope is not lost, then despair need not develop even after extreme losses or disappointments. On the other hand, if one has a long history of failure, then even a minor disappointment can have a subjective meaning of disaster. . . . Our results are consistent . . . in indicating that the determinants of regression or recovery, staying in the hospital or getting out, are not such ephemeral things as feelings, but the clear, hard data of IQ, social and vocational success, and a reasonably receptive environment. When we ask, in turn, what determines competence, then the characteristics of parents, the home environment, and the presence or absence of biological handicap all are relevant.

The above quote sums up rather well the general conclusions one might draw from the preliminary findings of follow-up studies of children at risk. Children with parents who are psychotic seem to be very vulnerable at all ages but especially in early childhood, when so much of the person's competence or lack of it is being laid down in development. Children of psychotic parents show a large variety of adjustive difficulties that can often become manifest within one or two weeks after birth. Such early difficulties are likely to be followed by increasing troubles as the child grows older and the complexity of the parent-child relationship and the tasks of life increase.

What does it mean, actually, to speak of a child "at risk"? Such a child has been exposed to any one of dozens of factors, both biological and social, which impair his or her chances to develop essential competencies and coping skills. Such factors could include a broken home, a domineering mother and a passive father, parents who fail to communicate clearly or consistently what the child should do or feel, and so on. It also means that such children early in life might have shown some symptom, disturbance, or characteristic that increases the chances of subsequent adjustive failure—for example, a reading disability, functioning below potential, seeming to be uncontrollable or running away from home, being hyperactive, being enuretic (wetting the bed), having a low attention span, walking during sleep, taking drugs, or being funny-looking (Rosenthal, 1974). To speak of them as children at risk means that someone thinks (or evidence suggests) their chances are greater than usual for later maladjustment. Research is then designed to reveal which, if any, of these factors actually do contribute to heightened risk of maladjustment.

CONCLUDING COMMENT

When discussing the medical biological model of mental illness in Chapter 9, I suggested that the evidence implicating tissue disease and genetic defects in the "garden variety" of adjustive failures was weak, at best; many biological scientists, however, continue to have faith that conclusive evidence will eventually be found. Similarly, in discussing the sociogenic model I suggested that, despite the evident relationship between cultural and institutional factors and adjustive adequacy and form in social groups, the sociogenic model is also incomplete and requires a better understanding of the psychological factors that determine how the *individual* reacts to his or her social institutions.

In this chapter we have considered some of the evidence and arguments about the psychogenic model, that is, about the role of social experience in affecting the individual personality and, more importantly, in shaping his adjustive approach and adequacy. Here too, however, the findings remain only suggestive and inconclusive, and it must be clear that we are still a long way from possessing dependable knowledge about what makes one individual successful in adjusting and another unsuccessful, and about why individuals vary so greatly in the manner in which they approach the adjustive tasks of living. Thus, despite the social scientist's confidence that maladjustment is a product largely of faulty social learning and the damaging social experiences of one's early life, this confidence too must be regarded as an article of faith. The suggestions from systematic research observations are certainly supportive and indicate that we are on the

right track, but the proof, chapter and verse, of our most cherished assumptions is still missing.

SUMMING UP

This chapter has been devoted to research built on the *psychogenic model* of adjustive failure. In this approach, emphasis is placed on the *individual person's social history*—the special experiences that might have shaped his or her psychological development and contributed to mild or severe emotional difficulties. Three main research approaches to the study of this history were examined.

Correlational and experimental research is designed to find factors in early life, or in the child's present family environment, that are especially important in shaping personality characteristics. These include *specific child-rearing practices* on the one hand and the more general *atmosphere of the parent-child relationship* on the other, the latter including items such as acceptance-rejection, possessiveness-detachment, or democracy-autocracy. Examples include cross-cultural studies of weaning and toilet training, Levy's study of maternal overprotection, and Baumrind's research on parental authority. Also relevant are Singer and Wynne's observations of the formal communication patterns of parents of schizophrenic, neurotic, and normal children. Harlow's research on mothering illustrates experimental laboratory research. Monkeys raised without a real mother or without an opportunity to interact with peers (other young monkeys) were likely to be more maladjusted and emotionally unresponsive than monkeys not so deprived.

Another research approach makes use of *retrospective life-history* data based on interviews and societal records. The studies of Schofield and Balian and of Watt serve as examples. Retrospective studies, taken all together, have generated rather inconsistent and inconclusive findings, probably because single (or a few) negative experiences are rarely sufficient to create adjustive failure. One must examine the mix of life events, negative and positive, and the resources of the person to cope with them at any given stage of life, in order to gain an understanding of healthy and inadequate adjustive outcomes.

A third approach, *longitudinal research,* requires the study of given individuals over time. This is costly and difficult to accomplish, but it offers the best prospects for gaining dependable data on individual life experiences which contribute to personality development and adjustment. When it is used to identify the life-history origins of severe mental disorder such as schizophrenia, longitudinal or follow-up research faces a particularly awkward problem, namely, that the base rate of severe disorder is very low, making it difficult to find enough instances in the chosen sample of persons who will later develop such disorder.

One of the recent antidotes for this difficulty has been the study of children who are "at high risk," meaning that they show a high incidence of unfavorable life circumstances, which greatly increases their chances for adjustive failure compared with children "at low risk." Potential risk factors are many, but a few examples are highly disturbed parents, broken homes, severe poverty, physical handicaps, and showing early signs of emotional difficulty. This type of research is still in its infancy, but it does offer promise that the numerous developmental factors relevant to achieving successful or unsuccessful adjustment might be extracted and evaluated as to their importance. As in the search for genetic components in mental illness, the present state of our knowledge about the social factors contributing to adjustive success and failure permits few dogmatic assertions. Confidence that mental illness is the result of stress-induced failure of social learning remains largely an article of faith.

CHAPTER 12 CRITIQUE AND SYNTHESIS OF THE MODELS

This chapter has two major aims, namely, to provide some criticisms of the traditional ways in which adjustive failure and success have been regarded professionally and to suggest possible directions of future thinking in this area.

First we shall return to a discussion of the classification of adjustive failure or psychopathology that was presented some time ago in Chapter 6, in order to evaluate such classification and its use in professional work. Then we proceed to an evaluative discussion of the various models of adjustive success or failure which were considered in Chapter 9 through 11.

PROBLEMS WITH THE CLASSIFICATION OF MENTAL DISORDERS

There are three main scientific and practical problems which have made the traditional meth-

ods of classification the object of much criticism and dissatisfaction: (1) The system is inadequate in reflecting underlying processes (or dynamics) and causes; (2) There are large variations in diagnostic assessment by different clinicians using this system; and (3) in addition, there are some ethical-ideological criticisms concerning the idea of classifying people at all.

UNDERLYING PROCESS VERSUS DESCRIPTION

Zigler and Phillips (1961) have presented one of the best recent analyses of the problems of clinical diagnosis. They point out that the question of validity is the most important one in judging the adequacy of classification (p. 612):

> The problem of validity lies at the heart of the confusion which surrounds psychiatric diagnosis. When the present diagnostic schema is

assailed, the common complaint is that class membership conveys little information beyond the gross symptomatology of the patient and contributes little to the solution of the pressing problems of etiology (cause), treatment procedures, prognosis, etc. The criticism that class membership does not predict these important aspects of a disorder appears to be a legitimate one. This does not mean that the present system has no validity.

Two different values for evaluating the classificatory scheme are embedded in the above quotation from Zigler and Phillips. One of these is administrative; the other concerns the causes of the disorders and the ways they might be treated. With respect to administrative values, the classificatory scheme appears to have its greatest utility. It is useful, for example, in the legal determination of insanity, in declarations of incompetence, in deciding the type of ward that would be required for custodial care, in compiling census figures and statistical data (e.g., the incidence in the population of different kinds of disturbances such as alcoholism or senile difficulties), and in screening men for the armed services or for other functions. The classificatory scheme seems to have least value in permitting the identification of the causes and differential treatment of the disorders within the system. Actually, Kraepelin's aim was to develop a classification that would identify causes and type of treatment. The present system contains both elements, causal and descriptive, but its most important category, the functional disorders, is mainly descriptive and based on symptom combinations without any necessary causal implications.

For example, you will recall that among the types of schizophrenia, paranoid, hebephrenic, catatonic, and simple schizophrenic reactions are differentiated. The differences among these types have to do with how the patient acts—whether he manifests, for example, delusions of persecution (as in the paranoid forms) or muteness and motor disturbances (as in the catatonic forms). Although the possibility exists that these different forms of schizophrenic disorders could have different causes and mechanisms, the emphasis is placed clearly on the description and grouping of behavior patterns. Distinguishable causes for each type have never been established, although the basic system is over seventy years old. However, other parts of the classificatory scheme are quite intentionally causal in form. For example, the organic disorders (damage to the brain) are classified in accordance with the external cause, that is, whether the disorder is produced by a brain injury, tumor, infectious disease, metabolic defect, and so on. But in these instances, the external cause hardly seems to matter much, since the proximal (more immediate) cause is destruction of brain tissue, and too little is now known about the relations between the particular tissue destroyed and the pattern of symptoms.

The result of this emphasis in the functional disorders on symptoms or patterns of response rather than on underlying processes and causes is that the great majority of diagnostic categories are not very useful in establishing a treatment program for individuals so afflicted. One cannot really say, for example, that the treatment of choice for the schizophrenic patient should be thus and so, while another form of treatment is called for in the depressive patient. Attempts have actually been made to do this, but they have very dubious validity. For example, it is widely held that electric shock treatment should be reserved for the depressive patient and that it is not especially effective with schizophrenic patients. Similarly, certain drugs should be used with one type of disorder and other drugs with different disorders. However, such rules of thumb are highly controversial and without much empirical support; no treatment has clearly demonstrated very great effectiveness with any type of patient, much less selectively.

Consider, in contrast, a clear disease entity such as general paresis, which can be the result of syphilitic infection. For every general paretic a common set of antecedent conditions can be observed, namely, infection by a particular bacillus and ultimate damage to the brain. If one destroys the bacillus by means of penicillin, brain damage is prevented or is arrested from going any further. Each paretic patient shows some similar mental symptoms, for example, loss of orientation concerning who he is, where he is, and when it is—in short, the classic symptoms of the patient with severe brain damage. Of course, there are individual differences too in the details of the symptoms of the disorder. However, this is a disease entity because not only is there a common core of symptoms but there are also clearly identified processes and causes. Such a set of common antecedent factors are not known for the patient who is diagnosed as schizophrenic.

Put another way, disorders such as multiple personality or obsessive-compulsive neurosis are probably not really disease entities at all. The reason cases of obsessive-compulsive reaction are classed together is that they all share some common behavioral qualities. But if these common features have little or nothing to do with the causal conditions of the disorder, the category "obsessive-compulsive neurosis" cannot be fruitfully regarded as a disease entity, at least until a common antecedent or antecedents for it are found and common psychological mechanisms or processes located.

In an excellent review of the sociological issues pertaining to mental disorders, John A. Clausen (1966) has added the thought that the nosology (system of classification) of the American Psychiatric Association fails to be truly international in scope and utility because of its emphasis on symptomatology rather than causes. Psychiatric symptoms are often very difficult to equate from one culture to another. Clausen states the criticism as follows (pp. 30–31):

It must be acknowledged at the outset that modern psychiatry has not been conspicuously successful in the classification of mental illness. Whereas an internationally accepted nomenclature has been achieved for the classification of most other types of disease, national and even local customs and considerations have prevented agreement on all but the most gross categories of mental illness. In the United States the nomenclature—that is, the set of names or classes by which the various disorders are known—was changed shortly after World War II but remains variant from the nomenclature proposed by the World Health Organization (WHO) and adopted, at least in part, by most of the other countries with advanced medical services. This state of affairs exists largely because our knowledge of the etiology of major segments of mental disease is incomplete and because symptom patterns are diverse and overlapping. With symptoms still our primary basis for classification, we are at the same stage of knowledge about mental disease that medicine occupied a century ago with reference to the "fevers." Typhoid, malaria, and a number of other diseases, readily distinguishable now, were all lumped together.

Indeed, the picture for mental disorders is even more confused than was that for "fevers." The symptoms of mental disorder are ideational and behavioral. Therefore, they reflect cultural emphases as well as disease processes. Many symptoms cannot be adequately interpreted without a knowledge of the norms of the subculture to which the individual belongs. For example, certain severe mental disorders are characterized by persisting delusions, such as believing oneself bewitched. In a culture in which most people believe in witches, however, such a belief cannot be considered delusional. It may be lacking in a scientific basis, but the same can be said of all beliefs in the supernatural realm. The culture not only provides the norms for assessing any given pattern of belief or behavior, but also provides the coloring or emphasis to the manifest symptomatology and the characteristic modes for dealing with such behavioral manifestations. Therefore it becomes extremely difficult to equate symptoms from one culture to another or even from one time to another.

VARIATIONS IN DIAGNOSTIC ASSESSMENT

One of the most apparent difficulties with the traditional scheme of classification is the absence of good agreement among professional workers about how to classify any individual patient. Most garden-variety adjustive inadequacies and failures, those you and I may suffer from in the course of our lives, are mixtures of patterns. Rarely do actual psychotic and neurotic difficulties fit nicely into the neat categories we have reviewed earlier. For this reason, one clinician will list the patient as schizophrenic, and another may identify the same patient as a schizoid personality or mental retardate. In spite of the standardization of nomenclature for the different disorders, there are great variations in the way this nomenclature is applied to individual patients, both among different clinicians and in different hospital settings. Some disagreement is probably inevitable in using any classificatory scheme. However, there is controversy over whether the unreliability of diagnostic ratings is too great to be comfortably tolerated.

Many years ago, for example, this reliability for a five-category system was studied, and very poor agreement was found (Ash, 1949). This has remained a vexing problem because one cannot have high confidence that a patient's disorder, classified as simple schizophrenia (or some other type of disorder) by one clinician, will be similarly classified by another.

A second example comes from efforts to diagnose a severe childhood disturbance that is sometimes referred to as childhood autism. The disorder is characterized more or less by withdrawal from the environment, failure to acquire or maintain overt speech, serious impairment in the acquisition of numerous skills, and seemingly senseless and stereotyped movements. Some autists recover, but many later end up in mental

hospitals diagnosed as schizophrenics. The diagnosis given to 445 such children by the doctor who was first consulted has been compared with that of a second doctor later consulted (using the traditional diagnostic categories for severely incompetent children). These categories included concepts such as autism, childhood schizophrenia, emotional disturbance, brain damage, mental retardation, psychosis, and deafness. No correlation between the two medical opinions was found; the two diagnoses were virtually random (Rimland, 1971). As Tinbergen (1974, p. 20) recently put the problem of such disagreement, "What these doctors have been saying to the parents is little more than, 'You are quite right; there is something wrong with your child.'" Everyone can agree upon that, but the question of what is wrong and how to categorize or label it meaningfully remains quite elusive.

On the other hand, some researchers (Schmidt and Fonda, 1956) have obtained more encouraging evidence that classification of patients into only three major categories—organic, psychotic, and personality disorders—resulted in agreement in about four-fifths of the cases. Disagreements were far more common when more narrowly defined diagnostic categories were employed, for example, within the grouping referred to by the term "personality disorder" (such as passive-aggressive or passive-dependent personality) or within the schizophrenic category.

Although there is considerable unreliability in traditional clinical diagnosis, this is not to say that the categories are always totally chaotic. Studies (Wittenborn, 1951; Wittenborn and Holzberg, 1951) have shown that clear symptom clusters among patients can be found in spite of the differences in the judgments of clinicians and between hospitals in which the evaluations are made. Hospital patients were rated by psychiatrists on the basis of observations of symptoms. The organic disorders were excluded from the study. Fifty-five symptom characteristics were included, such as insomnia, refusal to eat, grandi-

TABLE 12-1   SYMPTOM CHARACTERISTICS STUDIED BY WITTENBORN AND HOLZBERG

1	Acute insomnia	29	Organic pathology with emotional basis
2	Ideas change with spontaneous rapidity	30	Rigidly orderly
3	Unjustified sexual beliefs	31	Dramatically attention-demanding
4	Cannot banish obsessive thoughts	32	All overt activity is at a minimum
5	Delusional belief that he or she is evil	33	Grandiose notions
6	Gives in easily to others	34	Does not believe he or she has a problem
7	In almost constant movement	35	Compulsive acts continuous
8	Unaware of the feelings of others	36	Great variation occurs in rate of speech
9	Use made of physical disease symptoms	37	Initiates physical assaults
10	Refuses to eat	38	Delusions of homosexual attacks
11	Deliberately disrupts routines	39	Mood changes very frequent and abrupt
12	Temper tantrums	40	Has made attempts at suicide
13	Avoids people	41	Failures of affective response
14	Shouts, sings, and talks loudly	42	No concern over physical handicaps
15	Behavior disrupted by phobias	43	Cannot make decisions
16	Incontinent because of own negligence	44	Opinions exceptional to physical laws
17	Engrossed in plans	45	Hallucinations
18	Feelings of impending doom	46	Memory faults
19	Exaggeration of ability and well-being	47	Fear of committing an abhorred act
20	Cannot resist compulsive acts	48	Words not relevant to recognizable idea
21	Unable to stick to or carry out any plan	49	Shows failure and blocking
22	Cannot believe that he or she can be helped	50	Repudiates earlier insights
23	Fears others misunderstand him or her	51	Speech is stilted
24	Patient's thinking clearly delusional	52	Overt homosexual demands
25	No organic basis for complaints	53	Lies or steals
26	Feels systematically persecuted	54	Exaggerated affective expressions
27	Believes others influence him or her	55	Characteristically oppositional
28	Desperately distressed by anxiety		

ose notions, hallucinations, lying or stealing, and so on. The list of these symptoms may be seen in Table 12-1.

The method of analysis of these data was statistical, based on a technique of factor analysis in which each of the symptom-rating scales was correlated with the other scales to determine the degree of relationship. Then those scales that seemed to go together and have a similar pattern of relationships (indicated by a further statistical manipulation) were considered to belong to the same family of symptoms, that is, to represent a coherent factor. The question posed by these studies is whether recognizable clusters of symptoms can be observed, not whether there was agreement between observers and individual cases. Six basic symptom patterns appeared which did correspond with some of the diagnostic labels. These were schizophrenics, excited types, manic-depressives, anxious or hysterical patients, and paranoiacs.

In short, in spite of variations among the raters and differences in the location (the two studies were done in different hospitals), certain symptoms as rated by psychiatrists did indeed seem to go together and form stable patterns. Put another way, the categories used to identify mental disorders are descriptive of real consistencies observed in the behavior of mental patients. We must therefore be careful not to suggest that symptomatic behaviors do not fall into meaningful categories or syndromes (groups of symptom that go together) such as those traditionally used. However, this says very little about the problem of agreement or reliability of diagnosis when it comes to individual patients. It does tell us that the descriptive categories are not totally chaotic.

In their general discussion of the problems of classification, Zigler and Phillips (1961, p. 611) have underscored the importance of reliability and commented on the work done on diagnostic classification as follows:

> In evaluating the body of studies concerned with the reliability of psychiatric diagnosis, one must conclude that so long as diagnosis is confined to broad diagnostic categories, it is reasonably reliable, but the reliability diminishes as one proceeds from broad, inclusive class categories to narrower, more specific ones. As finer discriminations are called for, accuracy in diagnosis becomes increasingly difficult. Since this latter characteristic appears to be common in the classificatory efforts in many areas of knowledge, it would appear to be inappropriate to criticize psychiatric diagnosis on the grounds that it is less than perfectly reliable. This should not lead to an underestimation of the importance of reliability. While certain extraclassificatory factors, e.g., proficiency of the clinicians, biases of the particular clinical settings, etc. may influence it, reliability is primarily related to the precision with which classes of a schema are defined. Since the defining characteristic diagnosis is the occurrence of symptoms in particular combinations, the reliability of the system mirrors the specificity with which the various combinations of symptoms (syndromes) have been spelled out. It is mandatory for a classificatory schema to be reliable since reliability refers to the definiteness with which phenomena can be ordered to classes. If a system does not allow for such a division of phenomena, it can make no pretense of being a classificatory schema.

SOME PROBLEMS WITH CLASSIFICATION IN GENERAL

There is a sense in which any broad form of classification is misleading when one is dealing with individuals, because to place them in pigeonholes is, perforce, to compress persons into a small number of categories that emphasize only the few ways in which they are alike and overlook the tremendous complexity and diversity of their behavior. This may be useful in the scientific search for common principles of behavior, but it may get in the way of considering the person as an individual. Thus, if we act on classificatory categories, we run the danger of treating an individual in accordance with certain *stereotypes* inhering in the categories themselves. These can be detrimental to a sense of individuality, just as is the case when we react to individuals as blacks, whites, Jews, Italians, the poor, the rich, and so on. In short, any given class of persons also contains great heterogeneity. Moreover, we run the risk of treating the individual as a "nonperson," to use a term coined by Sarbin (1967; Sarbin and Mancuso, 1970), as when we speak of that individual as a schizophrenic or an alcoholic, or as "sick"; we are saying that we do not have to respect that person or have much regard for what he or she says and does; such people are members of the class of non-persons.

Another negative consequence of classification affects individuals, namely, the self-fulfilling consequences of such labels. By labeling the person as "schizophrenic" or "sick," we often see in his or her behavior precisely what the label suggests even when it is not present. Although this is an old idea, a recent and provocative study on a mental hospital ward by Rosenhan and his colleagues (1973) points up precisely this danger. In Rosenhan's research, eight "sane" persons, including a psychology graduate student, a pediatrician, and a psychiatrist, gained admission to a number of mental hospitals and thereupon acted as normally as possible, attempting to be discharged as quickly as possible. Despite ceasing to complain of and manifest psychiatric symptoms after gaining admission, they were continually treated by the staff as if suffering from mental disorders, and their release from the hospital was much delayed. As Rosenhan puts it, they failed to be detected as normal for some time thereafter, and they continued to be reacted to in accordance with the original label of mentally ill until eventually released. This was the case even though the professional workers in the hospitals were kindly and highly motivated professionals, partly perhaps as a result of severe understaffing but also, at least in part, as a result of the expectations among the staff that had been created by the initial label of mental disorder. Rosenhan (1973, p. 257) writes:

"Mr. Whirp, it isn't that you have an inferiority complex— you are inferior."

FIGURE 12-1 A pigeonhole of diagnosis.

Whenever the ratio of what is known to what needs to be known approaches zero, we tend to invent "knowledge" and assume that we understand more than we actually do. We seem unable to acknowledge that we simply don't know. The needs for diagnosis and remediation of behavioral and emotional problems are enormous. But rather than acknowledge that we are just embarking on understanding, we continue to label patients "schizophrenic," "manic-depressive," and "insane," as if in those words we had captured the essence of understanding. The facts of the matter are that we have known for a long time that diagnoses are often not useful or reliable, but we have nevertheless continued to use them. We now know that we cannot distinguish insanity from sanity. It is depressing to consider how that information will be used.

By labeling we also tend to encourage in the very people whom we wish to help behavior that the label implies, another instance of the opera-

tion of the *self-fulfilling prophecy*, this time on the patient. A sick role for the patient is encouraged by our expectations, in the same way that when a child in school is told that he or she has a low IQ, we may be encouraging him or her to cease trying and to choose limited goals. Educational research has shown that children given low expectations about their potential educational accomplishment do more poorly in school than children with similar abilities who are not discouraged in this way by evaluative labels. Likewise, persons who are labeled as psychotic, lacking in self-control, or whatever are more likely to behave accordingly than if they had not been victimized by the stereotypic label.

Taxonomies (systems of classification) historically have been extremely important in the march of scientific understanding, as in the cases of the classification of elements in physics or of animals and plants in zoology and botany. Behavioral classification systems for individual persons, however, carry with them certain special dangers that should make us wary of their casual use despite their potential importance for science.

PROPOSALS FOR AN ALTERNATIVE APPROACH

Those psychologists who have stressed the control and modification of behavior by environmental manipulation (see, for example, Krasner and Ullmann, 1965) have been among the most critical of the traditional psychiatric classification system. Arguing that behavioral deviance can be understood as socially learned ways of adapting to social rewards and punishments, Ferster (1965, pp. 9–10) believes that such description and classification leaves out crucial information about causative factors and therefore is inevitably doomed to failure:

> A complete moving picture record of "a man running down a corridor" provides enough data for only a minimal classification of behavior. The man could be running because someone is chasing him. The man could be running because the train will leave in ten minutes from a distant station. The man could be running because he has just won a sweepstakes prize.

Ferster then explains that each of these behaviors appears similar, but they are really extremely diverse if one considers their antecedents or causes. They should each be classified differently in accordance with these causes. In the first case, the man could be described as exhibiting avoidance behavior. In the second case, he is displaying a reaction to a fixed environmental schedule of reward and punishment. In the third, the running is based on an emotional reaction. Ferster's suggestion is that the classificatory scheme should be revamped to incorporate the *environmental feature* which shapes or causes the reaction—for example, dangerous or aversive stimuli such as loud noises, criticisms, or fines that people attempt to avoid, punishments that re-

quire complex and sustained performances to prevent, and positive rewards. Instead of the term "abnormal" or "disorder" being applied to maladjustive behavior, the reactions of such individuals should be described as "deviant," which is the reason they are classified as "abnormal."

Such a point of view directs attention toward a different way of classifying adjustive failure, namely, on the basis of presumed causal situational factors. However, it does not yet provide a systematic account and description of behavior deviations which could presently be used in a practical way, nor does it cover historical factors in the development of troubled personalities. It is mainly an expression of hope and intention and of a general direction toward which classification of behavioral deviation might ultimately be turned. It cannot as yet substitute for the traditional classification system, however inadequate that might be. One can agree that the classification system should point to causes and underlying processes. There is no doubt that the present system must ultimately be replaced, or at least much improved or extended as we learn more about the causes of adjustive failure. But for the present, no alternative system of classification has been proved more useful than the traditional one, either descriptively or in the delineation of causes and mechanisms, perhaps because we know so little as yet about such causation. As Zigler and Phillips (1961, p. 616) put it:

> The authors are impressed by the amount of energy that has been expended in both attacking and defending various contemporary systems of classification. We believe that a classificatory system should include any behavior or phenomenon that appears promising in terms of its significant correlates. At this stage of our investigations, the system employed should be an open and expanding one, not one which is closed and defended on conceptual grounds. Systems of classification must be treated as tools for further discovery, not as bases for

polemic disputation . . . a descriptive classificatory system appears far from dead, and if
properly employed, it can lead to a fuller as
well as more conceptually based understanding of the psychopathologies.

In sum, with respect to the classification of
mental disorders, there is general dissatisfaction
with the present scheme and hope that a better
alternative will some day be found. However, this
scheme is sufficiently useful to warrant its retention until a more satisfactory one is developed. At
the very least, it aids us in communicating about
how people act who are in trouble. Without it we
would indeed have had a very difficult time
outlining and graphically portraying the varieties
of adjustive failures that have so long been
known clinically. It remains for future research
and theory to advance knowledge beyond this
point. And it also remains for professionals to be
very wary of using stereotypical labels that can be
detrimental to the welfare of individuals in their
charge.

CRITICISMS OF THE MEDICAL-BIOLOGICAL MODEL

None of the models presented in Chapters 9
through 11 is totally adequate by itself to explain
adjustive success or failure. Each offers part of the
explanation, and each suffers from certain limitations which we should examine briefly and which
require some kind of synthesis, enlarging the
scope and adequacy of our understanding. One
way to approach this is first to offer a critique of
the medical-biological model and then to use this
as a starting point for a broader view.

The main criticisms of the medical-biological
model are as follows:

1 There is really *little evidence* that tissue
defects or "disease" underlie the garden-variety
types of adjustive failure, for example, the so-

called neuroses, functional psychoses, and personality disturbances. This does not mean that
what happens in the brain has no bearing on
adjustment—indeed it does, since the brain is
involved in all adjustive activity—rather, it says
that the person's "trouble" is largely based on
faulty learning about how to master the social
demands of living rather than the result of clear-
cut disease of the brain tissue. Outside the obvious and uncontested instances of organic mental
illnesses, no one has yet made a convincing case
that most of the kinds of adjustive failures described in Chapter 6 have an organic basis.

If we are to think of adjustive failure as a
disease-related problem, such a view cannot now
be a literal one—that every adjustive failure has at
its roots a tissue defect or illness—but must
remain an article of faith, capable of being demonstrated, perhaps, but certainly not on the basis
of what is now known. In the absence of hard
evidence that mental illness operates in the same
fashion as physical illness, when we use the term
"illness" it is merely a metaphor or *analogy* to
other forms of illness. That is, we must continually say about the disturbed person that "it is *as if*
he or she were sick," and we must look to forces
other than tissue defects to explain and treat the
problem. On this point, Sarbin and Juhasz (1966,
p. 3) write:

In (our) own historical search, the first meta-
phorical use of sickness to denote behavior
deviations occurred in the 16th Century. In an
effort to save some hysterical nuns from the
Inquisition—and probably influenced by the recently rediscovered writings of Galen—Teresa
of Avila, one of the significant church figures of
the counter-reformation, declared that the
nuns were not evil, but *como enfermas* (as if
sick). This declaration was made at the time of
the rise of modern science (the science of
physick, from which medicine evolved) and of
humanistic opposition to the excesses of the
Inquisition. The new metaphor ultimately

transferred the task of passing judgment on disordered persons from ecclesiastical authorities to medical practitioners. With the further development of Galenic medicine and the strengthening of the mind-body dualism, Teresa's *as if sick* became shortened to *sick* (from *como enfermas* to *enfermas*). Thus the myth [of mental illness] was born.

And on the same issue, Adams (1964, p. 191) puts the matter as follows:

The concept of functional mental illness is a *verbal analogy*. While it is appropriate to speak of neurological disorders as true organic illnesses of the nervous system, comparable to organic illnesses involving the circulatory or digestive system, it seems questionable to apply the term "illness" to arbitrarily defined patterns of behavior, particularly when there may be no evidence of any physiological malfunctioning. The plain fact is that the term "mental illness" is applied in an indiscriminate way to a motley collection of interpersonal behavior patterns. Often there is no positive evidence whatever of any physiological or organic malfunctioning, as in the so-called "functional disorders." Actually, organic physical illnesses and the functional types of mental illnesses are defined by *different kinds of criteria . . .* and they are modified or ameliorated ["treated" or "cured"] by *fundamentally different procedures.*

Failure to clarify these distinctions has had unfortunate consequences. Efforts toward understanding and effective alleviation have long been hampered by the semantic confusion which results when the word "illness" is used to denote both physical disease entities and maladaptive patterns of interpersonal behavior. This ambiguous usage has perpetuated the glib fallacy that mental and physical illnesses are the same thing. It has interfered with the understanding of fundamental psychological phenomena and made for an ineffectual and often harmful approach to some of the most serious recurring problems in human relationships.

2 As explained in Chapter 6, the grounds are weak for thinking that the traditional diagnostic categories, such as schizophrenia and the several subtypes within it, hysteria, or passive-aggressive personality, truly represent disease entities with a common causation and course of illness, as do tuberculosis and yellow fever. To the extent that the causative factors within a given category such as schizophrenia vary with the particular case, then it becomes extremely difficult to justify treating all those who share a common pattern of disturbed behavior as suffering from the same disorder. Yet the medical model presupposes just this.

3 Despite the presumption of disease, most kinds of psychopathology are, in practice, *defined socially* rather than in terms of tissue diseases. For example, a primary reason for hospitalizing troubled persons is that their behavior is *deviant* in the eyes of the community. The community and family find seriously disturbed persons a nuisance that they cannot tolerate, or they are frightened by their strange behavior. The symptoms themselves are thus socially defined, but the individuals are called "sick." Even in the case of the organic psychoses, the evidence that they are "sick" comes from their social actions and reactions, and not the fact of brain damage; because a live person's brain is difficult to examine, the damage is inferred from certain losses in mental function: the person has difficulty remembering who he is, where he is, and when it is. Moreover, after a time such an individual comes to play the *sick role* as defined by those nearby, who expect him or her to act deviantly. If released from the hospital, he or she carries the *stigma of mental illness,* which is exceedingly hard to shake.

The case of Sen. Thomas Eagleton, mentioned in Chapter 1, illustrates the effect of such stigma. Eagleton, it will be recalled, had to resign as the vice-presidential candidate in the 1972 elections because it was discovered that he had previously been treated for episodes of depression with electric shock. The unspoken dictum is, "Once a mentally ill person, always a mentally ill person." The mentally troubled person is usually looked upon with suspicion as long as this clinical history is known to exist, and in turn the negative public reaction has a tendency to push the person into a pattern of maladjustive behavior that is very difficult to alter. This is referred to as a "self-fulfilling prophecy," and as much or even more than the person's coping inadequacies, this may perpetuate the adjustive failure.

4 Finally, in spite of the persistence of the medical model with its unproved assumptions about implied causation and treatment, much actual treatment of adjustive failure is *behavioral* rather than physiological. Thus, people who seek psychotherapy receive treatment which is most often of two main behavioral types, either a series of conversations with the therapist designed to provide insight on the part of the client into the problem and lead him or her toward more adjustive ways of coping with living (psychodynamic therapy), or efforts to teach the client to adopt alternative ways of coping through forms of conditioning (behavior therapy). We shall examine these approaches to treatment in Part V. The essential point is that despite adherence to the medical model, a high proportion of treatment approaches are not physiological at all but behavioral, implying that the problem is faulty social learning rather than defective physiology.

On the other hand, in the case of the more severe behavioral disturbances such as the psychoses, the most common institutional approach to treatment is, admittedly, the use of drugs. Indeed, as we shall see in Chapter 15, widespread use of drugs has markedly changed

patient behavior on mental hospital wards, dramatically reducing violent and highly disturbed behavior and sharply increasing the rate of patient release. However, most observers, even those highly sympathetic to the drug approach, regard the effects of drugs as a *palliative* rather than a cure. For example, the patient must remain on drugs to stay out of the hospital with the attendant problems of interminable dosage management and side effects. Other physiological modes of treatment, such as electric shock and brain surgery, have generally poor support among mental health professionals, both as to whether they help much and whether they do additional damage. Few regard these treatments as curative, and there is no consensus about why they help if and when they do.

WHY DOES THE MEDICAL-BIOLOGICAL MODEL PERSIST?

In the face of this inconsistent pattern in which even the medical model does not lead to truly disease-centered treatment, one might wonder why the medical model continues to be accepted in mental health circles. There is no difficulty in understanding this in the case of biologically oriented professionals who truly accept the article of faith that mental illness is literally physical disease and who continue to search for evidence of physiological pathology, as well as for drugs or other physical treatments that will cure the assumed disease. Yet the medical-biological model continues to have a following among mental health professionals who do not accept it absolutely literally.

The answer seems to be twofold: first, obvious and outstanding *humanistic gains* were made when adjustive failure ceased to be thought of as the result of human evil or possession by the devil, becoming an illness like any other. Although a large portion of the public has really not taken this to heart and persists in a moral evaluation of maladjustment, it is clearly easier for troubled persons to view themselves as the victims of disease then to accept moral responsibility for their troubles. One arena in which this may be seen very clearly is alcoholism. If the disease model is attacked, the alcoholic is both threatened and apt to respond defensively. Consider the following two responses in a letters-to-the-editor column of a major newspaper after the medical model had been challenged in an earlier letter ["Letters to the Editor," *San Francisco Chronicle,* February 24, 1965, p. 40]:

Editor: I must say Elvyn S. Cowgill's Letter to the Editor, February 16, entitled "Alcoholism" startled me. People working in the field are well aware of the fantastic lack of understanding of an illness rated as the number four major cause of death, an illness affecting some 5,000,000 Americans. But I never thought that ignorance such as displayed in this letter I refer to could exist in this day and age. Let this contributor attempt to "consciously acquire" susceptibility to alcohol. Unless he is an alcoholic he will find it impossible.

The statement attributed to Dr. Menninger proves nothing. Dr. Menninger is knowledgeable in this field; his statement does not confirm your contributor's position. Dr. Jellenek, when asked at a Commonwealth Club luncheon a few years ago, how he would define alcoholism, said, "I don't! There are many alcoholisms."

It might be news to Elvyn Cowgill that the American Medical Association recently reaffirmed its statement that "alcoholism is a disease."

And the following quotes might interest him and others also:

"Alcoholism is at last being recognized for what it is—a medical and public health problem." (Robert M. Felix, M.D., Chief, Mental Hygiene Division, U.S. Public Health Service)

"All drunkenness is not to be forgiven on the basis that alcoholism is an illness—only alcoholism, compulsive drinking, is an illness." (H.

W. Haggard, M.D., Director, Laboratory of Applied Physiology, Yale)

"Happily alcoholism has been graduated from the category of moral and social dereliction, and assumed, now, its rightful position among the growing and more serious medical problems of our time." (Harold N. Lovell, M.D., Professor of Neurology, Flower and Fifth Avenue Hospitals, New York)

"Too much valid medical testimony exists to prove that an uncontrollable appetite for liquor stems amazingly often from a pathological condition rather than moral weakness or human perversity. Research has demonstrated that a confirmed alcoholic is a sick man rather than a sinner." (John J. Wittner, M.D., Asst. Vice-President, Industrial Relations, Consolidated Edison Co. of New York, Inc.)

And we could go on and on. Alcoholism is no respecter of persons. No one can be criticized justly for becoming an alcoholic. But, the alcoholic is subject to criticism if he fails to do something about it. And this is true of any person who is suffering from any other illnesses.

Alcoholics are sick people; alcoholics can be helped; alcoholics are worth helping. This is all that counts. How, when, where, why he became an alcoholic is of little or no importance. Whether he consciously or unconsciously acquired the problem—the fact is, he's got it!

San Francisco   JACK I.
[The writer is Central Secretary of the San Francisco Fellowship of Alcoholics Anonymous.—Editor.]

Editor: Elvyn S. Cowgill displays a familiar disdain and critical attitude toward the disease concept of alcoholism. . . .

The "crutch," as this person calls the impression of illness that the alcoholic is given, does not "salve" their conscience about continued excessive drinking, but in many cases it has been the light of hope to alcoholics who have considered themselves just "plain, lousy

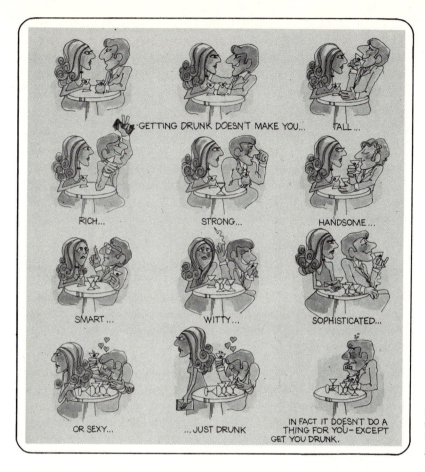

FIGURE 12-2 The glamorous world of alcoholism. (National Institute on Alcohol Abuse and Alcoholism.)

drunks." It has been the first factor in their painstaking effort to alleviate their problems caused by drinking.

The fact that several doctors do not agree with the diagnostic term used is by no means proof that alcoholism is not indeed an illness. Have you ever heard of any medical concept that at least three doctors did not disagree with?

I had the same contemptuous attitude toward the alcoholic until I found to my complete bewilderment that it was happening in my own family. After many agonizing, fruitless months of trying to find some logical reason for this alien behavior, I was fortunate enough to find Al-Anon. This group is affiliated with Alcoholics Anonymous and is for the family of the alcoholic to try to understand the symptoms of this commonplace disease and help each other cope with the problems it creates in the home and try to correct our own character deficiencies.

For the information of Elvyn Cowgill and others who are of the same opinion, let me state unequivocally that alcoholism is a disease. . . .

I hope those who form the great mass of public opinion will take the time to read some of the excellent literature available on the subject of alcoholism and with an open mind and perhaps even a little compassion for the problem of our fellow man, will at least give the title disease, in this case, the benefit of the doubt. It doesn't hurt a bit.

RACHEL OF AL-ANON

One may note also the 1966 decision of the United States Fourth Circuit Court of Appeals in Richmond, Virginia, concerning the arrest of chronic alcoholics. The court's ruling stated that chronic alcoholics cannot be arrested and treated as criminals, although they may be detained for medical treatment. The decision occurred in the case of a man who had been convicted more than 200 times for public intoxication and who estimated that he had spent about two-thirds of his life in jail. The court's ruling stated that alcoholism is "now almost universally accepted medically as a disease. . . . The upshot of our decision is that the state cannot stamp an unpretending chronic alcoholic as a criminal if his public drunken display is *involuntary as the result of disease.*"

Although no medical or research authority has established the nature of this "disease," that is, the physiological agent that drives the alcoholic "against his will" to drink, such an agent is assumed in the court's decision. However, it is notable that alcoholism, until recently, was classified by the American Psychiatric Association as a *functional,* personality disorder, not an organic disorder. It is clear that the disease concept has great social importance, both in terms of the self-respect it preserves in people who transgress social convention and in the treatment the concept requires public authorities to give to such individuals. The disease model has, at least in this social sense, perhaps not yet outlived its usefulness, even though it might not be justified technically.

The second reason for the persistence of the medical model in spite of major logical and empirical challenges to its validity and utility has to be seen in *professional-political terms.* The profession of psychiatry was the first to enter the field of treatment of adjustive failure. Since their origins were in medicine proper, it was not surprising that the early psychiatrists were

"neuropsychiatrists," that is, they assumed a neurological-disease basis for maladjustment. However, as social psychiatry came more and more to see adjustive failure as a product of social experience and treat it as such, departing somewhat from concern with physiology and biochemistry, it became less popular with professional medicine which had spawned it. Psychiatry has had to struggle hard to become an accepted subdiscipline of medicine. It succeeded in this, in part, although it still is widely viewed with distrust and sometimes contempt by other medical specialties. Having at least partly managed to be accepted as a branch of medicine, psychiatry did not relish an attack on the medical model suggesting that psychopathology and its treatment really has little to do with disease as such. Moreover, the hard-pressed claim that the treatment of adjustive failure was the sole business of medicine was a way of reserving the field of mental health to itself and of keeping out other disciplines such as psychology and social work whose stock in trade included social learning and development.

Such a narrow, restrictive, and self-serving view of adjustive failure does not by any means characterize all medically trained psychiatrists. In fact, the most articulate critic of the medical model, the man who first referred to mental illness as a myth, is a psychiatrist named Thomas Szasz (1960, 1961, 1963). Contrariwise, one of the most ardent protagonists of the medical model is a psychologist (Ausubel, 1961). Thus, the lineup of protagonists and antagonists of the medical model does not follow strictly professional lines. As with the two major political parties, within which one may find both liberal and conservative ideology, so there are biologically oriented and socially oriented professionals within psychiatry and psychology.

Still, examining the politics of the professional world of mental health does help us understand why so much emotion is expressed in debates about the medical model—the emotion stems from a degree of understandable professional resentment at the power play mounted by one profession over others. A widely read, spicy, and somewhat extreme comment by Albee (1966, pp. 7–8), made in his address as outgoing president of the Division of Clinical Psychology of the American Psychological Association, illustrates this:

> There is precious little firm evidence to support the *illness* model. Mental disorder is, in truth, a sickness like *no* other, and the scientific support for an explanatory model based on biological defect ("There can be no twisted behavior without a twisted molecule!") is thin indeed. Indeed, if all the evidence supporting the illness model were laid end-to-end it wouldn't fill the space between Kallmann and Heath sitting together at a meeting of the Society of Biological Psychiatry.
>
> Let us be crystal clear about this matter. So long as the illness model prevails—so long as legislative bodies, newspaper editorial writers, and members of the Ladies Aid Society all believe that crazy people are sick, all the laws and regulations will be written with highest priority given to beds and nursing care, and medical direction, diagnosis, and treatment. And available research funds will be spent largely to support the urine-boilers and myelin-pickers looking for the defective hormone or the twisted synapse. . . .
>
> If my crystal ball is not hopelessly cloudy, the model we will develop will be a social-learning model, and the professional users of this model will be bachelor's-level people working in tax-supported institutions more like schools than like hospitals.

A SYNTHESIS OF THE DIVERGENT VIEWPOINTS

We have seen that the social science and biological science approaches to adjustment are both incomplete. The sociogenic model, of necessity,

ignores the meaning for the individual of the social conditions under which he or she lives, and both the sociogenic and psychogenic or social-learning models fail to consider genuine constitutional or biological sources of adjustive success and failure. In turn, the medical-biological model in its most literal form ignores the crucial role of social learning and experience in shaping adjustment, both successful and unsuccessful. A synthesis of the approaches to the problem requires above all that we recognize in some way the *interaction* of both biological and social factors in shaping the psychological development and functioning of the individual in situations demanding adjustment.

THE INTERACTION OF BIOLOGICAL AND SOCIAL FACTORS

When the enormous variety of social influences to which humans are exposed is considered, it is no wonder that every person ultimately comes out differently, even those who share the same geographical region. If to this huge variation is added the large number of hereditary-constitutional variables on which people differ, one cannot fail to be impressed with the complexity of the task of understanding and predicting human adjustive behavior. Rather than be discouraged about what is known, it is really a wonder that so much progress in understanding has been achieved. It must always be remembered that the person is not merely a simple sum of the different influences to which he or she is exposed, but is a complex product of many interacting variables, both social and biological.

Personality develops over the person's lifetime and is a product of *both* biological and social forces. At birth, the main forces influencing this development are biological, since there has been little opportunity as yet for experience with the social world to have occurred. Those physiological dispositions, which are present at birth, or which mature at various points later in life (many inherited dispositions do not appear at once, but await later stages of development), undoubtedly *interact* with the social environment. In other words, a given physiological disposition will probably have a somewhat different effect in one social context than in another, or, conversely, a given social context will probably affect people differently depending on the physiological substrate on which it is imposed. In Chapter 9 we learned in fact that this even applies to genetic mechanisms themselves (Fig. 12-3).

There is some evidence that infants vary greatly in level of activity, some sleeping restlessly, for example, others showing minimal activity (Fries and Lewi, 1938; Irwin, 1930; Wolff, 1959). Infants also differ in the amount of stimulation required to elicit responses and in the rate of adaptation to

new stimuli (Bridger, 1961), some continuing for a long time to respond to the same stimulus on repeated presentations, others rapidly ceasing to respond. Probably there are also differences in sensitivity to touch and pain right from the start of life outside the womb. Variations also seem to exist with respect to the physiological system (which responds to stressful conditions), the gastrointestinal tract, the respiratory apparatus, the skin, or the cardiovascular system.

But what about the *interactions* with social conditions? Assuming that newborn babies start out with many physiological differences, how might the interaction between biological and social variables work? Most probably, the response to these physiological dispositions will be

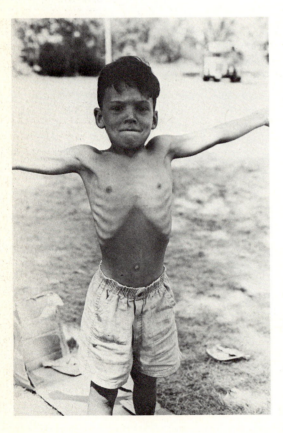

FIGURE 12-3 The environment will undoubtedly respond differently to these two youngsters on the basis of their physical appearance and physical resources. (Left: Eric L. Brown, from Monkmeyer; right: David Herman, from Photo Trends.)

FIGURE 12-4 This child may need to be stimulated to develop adequately; that child may need to be calmed down and protected from too much stimulation. (Left: Erika Stone, from Peter Arnold; right: Harvey Barad, from Monkmeyer.)

determined partly by the attitudes and needs of the parents. The extremely active or irritable child may disturb, annoy, or overburden some parents yet be a tonic to others. Contrariwise, the lethargic infant born into a family where the adults themselves are lethargic may obtain insufficient environmental stimulation; but the same baby born into a family of hyperactive parents may be frequently roused from its lethargy to participate constructively in its surroundings (Fig. 12-4).

The same principle probably applies throughout the life span of the person, although developmental psychologists might be inclined to consider the early life experiences as especially important for personality development. Consider, for example, the probable differences in social experience of the adolescent who is good-looking and physically able compared with one who is unattractive and physically inept. In a culture in which a particular appearance or physical prowess is of great importance, the latter child will feel inadequate and the former will experience considerable success. Each will discover different things about the way the social environment responds. In cultures with different norms and values, the impact on the child's social experience of its physical makeup is apt to be quite different accordingly. Thus, there should be a continual interplay between the social context and the physiological dispositions which characterize the person from birth on. In all probability, one should not say that a given physiological trait at birth has, per se, a specified effect on personality development, or, for that matter, that a given social context, by itself, will have certain outcomes. Rather, to fully understand personality development it is necessary to consider the *interaction* between such physiological traits and the social context in which they appear.

By the same token, it is probably not possible to say that a given pattern of parental behavior toward the child is sound or unsound, or that "good mothering" consists of one or another form of behavior without regard to the type of child. For an infant with a given sort of physiological disposition, say, hypersensitivity to stimuli, good mothering might involve protecting the infant from excessive stimulation which might be overpowering. For an infant with hyposensitivity to stimulation, good mothering might require considerable prodding to give the child sufficient experience with the environment. Furthermore, the same maternal attitudes which have desirable effects at one stage of development, say in infancy, might be harmful at another, say in preadolescence. The problem is undoubtedly complicated, and any statement about what is desirable or undesirable in parental conduct not only depends on the kind of infant or child with which the parent is dealing but also on knowledge which is not yet available about the conditions which shape the developing personality.

In the light of this, let us go back for a moment to the notion of children at risk which was discussed in Chapter 11. Here we can see that the integrative approach to both the biological and social determinants is to include both sets of factors in research on the development of adjustive failure. Some of the risk factors are undoubtedly genetic or constitutional, while others are social. As we know, research already suggests (cf. Rosenthal, 1972) that severe maladjustment occurs more often among the biological relatives of children with major behavior problems than among the biological relatives of control cases, or

among nonbiological relatives as in the case of adopted children. Thus, to get at risk factors means to look at genetic-constitutional characteristics as well as environmental ones.

Anthony (in press) has attempted to work up an overall or composite risk profile which illustrates the meaning of risk and from which a risk score can be derived for any individual. Anthony's profile speaks of each risk factor as a "loading"; that is, the more each factor applies to the individual the more it contributes to the risk of major maladjustment. The higher the total score, the higher the risk of adult adjustive failure is assumed to be. Anthony's risk profile is shown in Table 12-2 as an illustration.

Anthony's risk loading table does not provide a factually well established set of factors contributing to severe maladjustment; rather, it offers a set of likely candidates and thus provides a blueprint for continuing research on the problem. Nor does high risk necessarily mean that a child is doomed to psychosis, for this depends on a host of interacting factors including the success of his or her efforts to overcome or transcend the potential despair inherent in growing up with a parent who is severely troubled or under conditions of extreme pathological deprivation.

Statistics and lists of risk factors fail to capture the poignancy of the experience of a great many childhood worlds. Anthony (1969) gives us a few statements from children of psychotic mothers which portray experiences that few of us can fully appreciate in the light of our own backgrounds. Three of these are presented below (p. 445). Picture yourself in such a setting. The child is speaking:

Child 1 "She is quite a nice mother, really. She doesn't do anything bad. She doesn't hit or anything. She just sits. She is like a kid, mostly. When I give her a lot of candy she just sucks it all up like a vacuum cleaner. She doesn't comb her hair and her dress has spots on it. Some-

TABLE 12-2   ANTHONY'S RISK PROFILE AND TOTAL RISK SCORE

Risk Profile

Name: _____

Age: _____

		GROUP E/C
1 Genetic loading		CHECK
No reported psychosis in family tree	0	___
Reported psychosis at great-grandparent level	1	___
Psychosis in extended family group (grandparent level)	1	___
Psychosis in extended family group (parent level)	1	___
Psychosis in nuclear family group (grandparent level)	1	___
Psychosis in nuclear family group (parent level)	1	___
Psychosis at child level	1	___
TOTAL:		___
2 Reproductive loading		
No apparent reproductive casualty	0	___
Prenatal maternal ill health (vomiting, weight gain, B.P. rise, albuminuria, swelling, etc.)	1	___
Prenatal fetal ill health (threatened abortion, signs of fetal distress, etc.)	1	___
Paranatal difficulties in the mother (delayed labor, contracted pelvis, instrumental delivery, C. section, placenta pr. eclampsia, etc.)	1	___
Paranatal difficulties in the child (abnormal presentation, multiple births, prolapsed cord, signs of fetal distress, etc.)	1	___
Postnatal difficulties (anoxia, cyanosis, jaundice, maturity, low birth weight, excessive molding)	1	___
Neonatal difficulties (evidence of intercranial damage, convulsions, infection, etc.)	1	___
TOTAL:		___
3 "Constitutional" loading		
No apparent constitutional defect	0	
Hyper- or hypoactivity for infancy	1	___
Hyper- or hyposensitivity for infancy	1	___
Hearing or visual handicap	1	___
Poor coordination	1.	___
Dysplastic or linear body build	1	___
Abnormal temperamental traits (schizoid, cycloid, paranoid, fearful, etc.)	1	___
TOTAL:		___
4 Developmental loading		
No apparent developmental stresses	0	___
Infantile "colic" in first year (eating, sleeping problem)	1	___
Marked training crises (battle of B & B, negativism, severe tantrums, etc.)	1	___
Preschool crisis (kindergarten problem, difficulties in leaving home, socializing, phobias, obsessions, etc.)	1	___
Difficulties in grade school (refusal to attend, difficulty in socializing, unable to adjust to routine, lagging behind, reading difficulty, repeating grades, etc.)	1	___
Difficulties in junior school (truanting, learning problem, social problem, peer difficulties, pubertal problems, etc.)	1	___
Difficulties in senior school (dropping out, isolation, goofing off, disciplinary problem, emotional and social maladjustment, etc.)	1	___
TOTAL:		___

TABLE 12-2 (Continued)

5 Physical ill-health loading

No significant physical illness apart from normal childhood complaints	0 ___
Acute gastrointestinal or respiratory illness in the first 2 years of life	1 ___
Chronic infectious illness during childhood (tuberculosis, osteomyelitis, etc.)	1 ___
Allergic illnesses during childhood (eczema, asthma, hay fever, etc.)	1 ___
CNS illness during childhood (meningitis, encephalitis, cerebral abscess, etc.)	1 ___
Chronic serious illness during childhood (diabetes, ulcerative colitis, anemia, etc.)	1 ___
Periodic illness during childhood (epilepsy, migraine, etc.)	1 ___
TOTAL:	___

6 Environmental loading

No apparent environmental deficiency or stress	0 ___
Institutional placement during childhood	1 ___
Foster placement during childhood	1 ___
Marked residential mobility of family	1 ___
Mental disorder or defect in a parent	1 ___
Physical disorder or defect in a parent	1 ___
Socioeconomic handicap (poverty, welfare, ghetto, poor living conditions, poor school, etc.)	1 ___
TOTAL:	___

7 Traumatic loading

No apparent traumatic experience	0 ___
Medical trauma (hospitalization, surgery, burns, physical injury, etc.)	1 ___
Physical assault trauma (battering, bullying, cruelty, attack by animals, physical disasters, etc.)	1 ___
Sexual assault trauma (exposure, molestation, rape, incest, etc.)	1 ___
Loss of family member (through death, divorce, separation, desertion, etc.)	1 ___
Emotional "shock" (frightening encounters, "ghosts," uncanny experiences, etc.)	1 ___
Social trauma (loss of friends, ostracization, victimization, segregation, rejection by group, public humiliation, etc.)	1 ___
TOTAL:	___

Assessment of risk

Low risk   1 2 3 4 5 6   High risk

1 Genetic loading

2 Reproductive loading

3 "Constitutional" loading

4 Developmental loading

5 Physical ill-health loading

6 Environmental loading

TABLE 12-2 (Continued)

7 Traumatic loading	☐☐☐☐☐☐

Total risk score:

High risk (28–42) ——
Moderate risk (14–27) ——
Low risk (0–13) ——

Risk of developing mental disorder during childhood (Check one): High___ Moderate___ Low___
Risk of developing mental disorder during adult life (Check one): High___ Moderate___ Low___

times she laughs at me and I am not making any jokes. I say: 'Mom, why are you laughing at me?' and she just laughs more. I don't like it when she laughs like that. It's not like real laughing. She never used to be like that when I was little. She was just ordinary."

Child 2 "You cannot believe what it's like to wake up one morning and find your mother talking gibberish."

Child 3 "I wake up dreaming or maybe just daydreaming. I don't know what, but her face is coming toward me and she looks good and then suddenly her face begins to change and look mean and horrible like a monster."

CONCLUDING COMMENT

By now the problem has been clearly stated. In Chapter 9 there were two messages: First, the evidence pointed to genetic and constitutional factors as partial determinants of adjustive failure; second, there were nevertheless serious defects in the medical-biological model of adjustive failure. Then in Chapters 10 and 11 we reviewed the evidence in favor of a social-learning model, in which adjustive failure is viewed as a product of inadequate development of skills for coping competently with life stresses. This lack of competence is presumed to arise from destructive or deficient conditions of growing up and

from contemporaneous stresses. Finally, it has been said that the adjustive status of the person is the outcome of continuous interplay or *interaction* between biological and social factors over the entire course of his or her life. In the light of all this, how then should we view the medical-

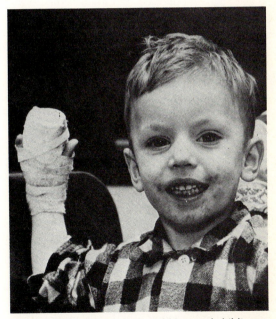

FIGURE 12-5 This three-year-old battered child's parents held his hand over a lighted gas burner "to teach him a lesson." (United Press International Photo.)

biological and social science models? Is there any satisfactory key to integrate them?

The medical-biological model gets us into trouble primarily when literally applied to forms of adjustive failure for which a clear tissue disease cannot be implicated. Literalness means several things: (1) that the adjustive failure is classified as a definite disease or tissue defect, (2) that we can classify or group all instances of the maladjustment (for example, schizophrenia or depression) together because, presumably, they share the same disease process (as do tuberculosis or rabies), and (3) that inasmuch as the adjustive failure is a disease, it should be treated by medical personnel and procedures such as drugs, surgery, diet, or other physical therapies.

There should be no quarrel with the view that many maladjustive patterns are the direct result of brain damage or other tissue defects involving biochemistry. When it comes to other kinds of maladjustment, the case for a medical model gets very fuzzy. Some professionals view the schizophrenic disturbances as diseases or illnesses but exclude most neuroses and personality difficulties from the literal illness category. They make the assumption that severe disturbances such as schizophrenia must have some basis in tissue defects, even though the nature of these defects has not yet been determined. Other professionals put schizophrenia into the nondisease category. In short, one solution is to specify some forms of adjustive failure as medical diseases and others as a product of social development and learning.

While such a solution is helpful, it still leaves us with a partial dilemma because it seems to imply that some adjustmental problems are learned while others are biological in origin, and—as already pointed out—this is an untenable position although the weighting of biological and social factors could vary from case to case. If abandoning the medical-biological model means abandoning also the principle that biological factors are important in adjustive failure, this is a

very bad solution. Both biological and social factors interact in a complex fashion in all individuals regardless of their adjustmental status. Even the most minor forms of maladjustment involve biological handicaps that have made becoming competent and effective in the tasks of living somewhat more difficult. Thus, some of us have larger mental capacities than others, are physically healthier, more resistant to infectious disease, less prone to digestive distress or allergy, and so on. To suggest that such genetic-constitutional differences do not affect how well the person manages his or her life would be absurd, although such factors do not operate alone and can probably have quite opposite effects depending on the social history of the person and the circumstances to which he or she must adapt.

The obvious answer is that "medical" refers only to disease and is not equivalent to biological. Thus, we can reject the medical or disease model as inapplicable in a wide variety of adjustive disturbances such as neurosis and the so-called functional psychoses, without rejecting the idea that these disturbances have biological (hereditary and physical constitution) as well as social roots, and without denying that psychoses produced by brain damage, poisons, hormonal defects, and so on are true diseases requiring largely medical treatment. What has confused us about the problem is that the medical or illness model has been hopelessly overextended. It has been used to cover all types of maladjustment, although this is impossible; to denigrate the important role of societal factors and social learning; and, most pernicious of all, to achieve professional power or control over treatment. It would be better to speak of the medical-disease model only in cases where it applies to organic tissue defects, when proved, and to recognize that most difficulties of human adjustment have both biological and social determinants that interact over the entire course of a person's life. We should drop the hyphenated term "medical-biological" and replace it with "medical-disease," using terms such as biological and social to refer to the direction of interest of professionals in certain classes of determinants.

The same caution applies to the social science model. Here too the enthusiasm of protagonists often results in understating the importance of genetic and constitutional factors in the person's pattern of adjustment. And here too it is something of an article of faith, albeit a very reasonable and research-supported one, to believe that the person forges a way of life out of social experiences, especially in the formative years. But as we saw earlier, the evidence is incomplete, often confusing, and sometimes contradictory. One sees a high percentage of children who are troubled but who emerge as extremely adequate and effective adults. In fact, it has been seriously suggested by some researchers that some degree of early stress is an essential factor in the forging of a "healthy" personality, and that children who have a smooth and secure life are not as effective in adulthood as those who have had a difficult personal struggle.

In sum, even as we recognize the importance of the individual's developmental history in shaping his or her pattern of adjustment later in life, what is important in this history and how it shapes later adjustment is extremely complex, and we cannot yet spell out at all clearly how even the most serious forms of maladjustment are brought about. All this calls for modesty in claiming understanding about the causes of adjustive failure and for a sense of respect vis-a-vis the problem and the scope of the task of understanding. Obtaining viable answers still remains the great challenge for the social and biological sciences and for "mental health" professionals. The problem is multiprofessional, and there is ample room for more than a few disciplines, working together, to be charged with the study and treatment of failures of adjustment and with the task of prevention by means of improving the biological and social conditions of human development.

SUMMING UP

This chapter provides a critique of the traditional approaches to mental disorder and health, beginning with the problems of classification and proceeding through the difficulties inherent in the medical-biological model. It ends with an attempt to synthesize the divergent professional outlooks by emphasizing the principle that human adjustment is the product of both biological and social factors in continuing interaction with one another.

The chief problem with the traditional *classification of mental disorders* is threefold: First, with the exception of the clearly organic disorders, such classification depends largely on the *description of symptoms,* grouped into larger categories or entities without adequate reference to the causes and mechanisms underlying each—on which treatment could be based. Second, the diagnostic categories are, in the main, too *unreliable,* especially when fine distinctions are made, though they are not by any means meaningless in describing the symptom clusters that troubled people display. Third, classification itself introduces several *hazards to the individualistic and humanistic* response to persons: pigeonholing leads to *stereotypes,* which, if we take them too seriously, lead us to respond to those in trouble as "non-persons" rather than as distinctive individuals who may not fit the stereotype in most or many respects. Also, by labeling people we expect them to conform to that label even when they do not; indeed, individuals themselves may come to act according to the way in which they believe they are labeled. We refer to this as the *self-fulfilling prophecy.*

There are four main *difficulties with the medical-biological model* of adjustive failure.

First, there is *little evidence* supporting the belief that most garden-variety forms of maladjustment are truly the result of tissue defects or disease. To speak of "disease" or "sickness" in such cases is to make literal truth out of what is really only an analogy. Second, most of the categories of adjustive failure do not meet the criteria for coherent *entities,* as in clear-cut diseases such as tuberculosis or general paresis. Third, despite the presumption that a given neurosis or psychosis could be the result of tissue disease, the person's problem is in practice *defined socially,* that is, in terms of his or her deviant behavior or difficulties in managing everyday affairs. Fourth, even when the presumption is made that the mental patient is suffering from an organic disease, in the main treatment is usually *behavioral* rather than physiological. Where drugs or other physiological treatments are used rather than psychotherapy, this treatment typically has no relation to a specific causation (as in the use of antibiotics effective with certain germs) and is regarded as *palliative* rather than a cure.

Nevertheless, the medical-biological model continues to hold sway widely, partly because psychologically it has supportive value to the person who would rather believe that he or she is suffering from a disease than from a moral defect or a form of social incompetency, and also because of the professional-political commitment of psychiatry (1) to its place as a medical science and (2) to controlling the processes of treatment and research in mental illness.

None of the biological or social science models of adjustive success and failure is complete or adequate in itself, since adjustment is always a continuing product of the *interaction of biological and social determinants.* The term "disease" should be employed only when there is clearly a tissue-defect basis for a problem of adjustment, not when the problem is heavily laden with factors of social learning. Biologically oriented professionals should not understate the importance of social factors, and likewise socially oriented professionals should not downgrade biological factors in the shaping of human adjustment. Adjustive failure is a multidisciplined problem, and it should be tackled by all disciplines that are involved with any of the major influences bringing it about over the life course of the person in trouble. No single academic discipline or profession can "go it alone" where the study or treatment of troubled human beings is concerned.

PART V
TREATMENT

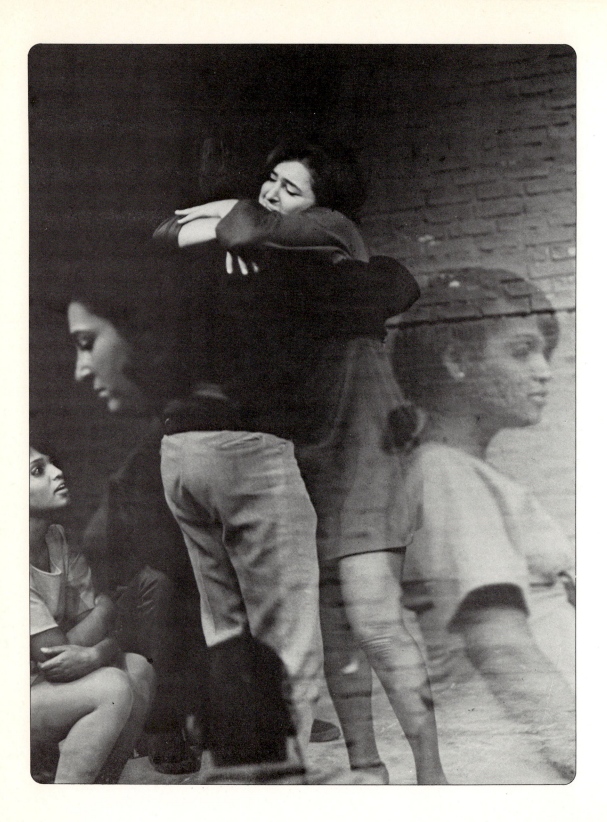

PART V
TREATMENT

This section is about treatment, the professional effort to correct or ameliorate the social and individual problem of adjustive failure once it has developed. We seek here to gain an understanding of the most central issues which the treatment professions must face in trying to provide adequate help to troubled persons.

The earliest treatment programs in the mental health field were directed at the most severely disturbed people, because these severe cases of disorder were more dramatic and socially disruptive than the minor adjustive problems from which most of us suffer. As the psychological "healing arts" developed and evolved into self-conscious professions, therapeutic efforts began to spread from the severe psychoses to the mildly disturbed person. Public acceptance of psychotherapy led more and more people to seek its benefits. The treatment of all kinds of emotional disturbance came to be a major function of psychiatry, clinical psychology, and social work.

The treatment of adjustive failure fulfills two important needs: First, and most obvious, its objective is to alleviate suffering, to eliminate symptoms, to increase adjustive effectiveness and the satisfaction derived from life, and to add to the understanding of oneself; second, it provides for the professional worker a laboratory for the study of personality. In the attempt to produce constructive change in the patient, the person in treatment is also studied intensely. This

Raimondo Borea

285

resulting psychological laboratory has been a most important force in our theories of human personality. The most influential of such theories were created by people who were actively involved with treating problems of adjustment. At the most distinguished level of practice, the psychotherapist is a *scientist,* trying to learn about the human organism he or she is treating, as well as a *humanist* attempting to apply what has been discovered to assist people to live more effectively.

The lay person often fails to differentiate between psychotherapy and *psychoanalysis.* The latter is one of the most widespread formal doctrines or orientations to psychotherapy, although by no means the only one. Thus, people carelessly speak of being psychoanalyzed when, in reality, they mean receiving psychotherapy, since that procedure is not necessarily part of the psychoanalytic orientation. Psychoanalysis involves a specific body of theory and a related form of practice. Even within psychoanalysis itself there are divergent practices and schools of thought. Although most modern forms of psychotherapy overlap a good deal and tend to share some common assumptions originating in psychoanalysis, psychotherapy and psychoanalysis are not equivalent terms, and to use them interchangeably reflects an ignorance of their particular meanings. In short, *psychotherapy* is a more general term than psychoanalysis, and treatment is even more general in that it does not connote a specific approach or strategy.

Another source of confusion is that not one but several professions are involved in the treatment of adjustive failure. In the order of recognition by the public, these are psychiatry, clinical psychology, and social work. However, other responsible persons also engage in psychotherapy, often calling it by a different name. Perry London (1964, p. 30) comments about this confusion as follows:

More confusing perhaps is the fact that psychotherapy is practiced by many more different kinds of professionals who, unlike those above (psychiatrists, psychologists, and social workers), differ in most functions as well as in their titles. Some of these find it impolitic to identify their therapeutic work with this label. Ministers who do psychotherapy call it "pastoral counseling" or "psychoanalysis" or some such term which refers to no formal profession and overlaps in meaning with several other terms all properly equivalent to "psychotherapy."

What distinguishes psychotherapy from any other form of treatment is that it is basically a face-to-face situation in which one person, the psychotherapist, agrees to provide assistance to a patient or a group of patients who have sought help with their problems of living. The assistance is provided in a fashion guided by a systematic doctrine held by the therapist about personality and psychopathology and about how the problem might be professionally understood and relieved. It is this *systematic* approach which distinguishes psychotherapy from ordinary relationships with friends and nonprofessionals. What is crucial is that the therapist acts in accordance with what he or she professionally believes will help patients to manage their lives or problems better, rather than what will make the relationship more comfortable, pleasant, or in conformance with the tit-for-tat rules of friendship.

As we have already seen, there are many different schools of thought about human nature and about mental health, and there are likewise many different ways to conceptualize the patient's problems and deal therapeutically with them. We can conveniently recognize at least three major approaches to the treatment of adjustive failure, the psychodynamic, the behavioral, and the societal and institutional approaches. The next three chapters deal with these in turn. Let us begin in Chapter 13 with the psychodynamic approaches, partly because these were historically earliest and partly because the general public is most familiar with them.

CHAPTER 13 THE PSYCHODYNAMIC THERAPIES

"Psychodynamic therapies" covers a diverse group of approaches emphasizing discovery by the patient of the various psychological processes impairing his or her ability to manage life tasks effectively. Such discovery is called *insight*. One should not be put off by the high-sounding term "psychodynamics"; it merely refers to the forces or influences that account for one's actions and reactions. (*Psycho-* means psychological, and *dynamic* means the motive power that makes the person go, just as a dynamo is the source of energy that makes a machine go.) In most psychological theories these forces include such things as motives or impulses, conflicts, inhibitions, defense mechanisms, feelings of alienation and the absence of meaning in life, or being out of touch with one's own true nature and self. In Freudian theory they are assumed to have arisen in childhood and to be unconscious or relatively inaccessible to the patient. Therefore, the major task of psychotherapy is to help patients discover what has been happening to them, that is, to help them obtain better *insight* into the psychodynamics of their problems and to use this understanding to change their troubled ways of living and reacting.

This general outlook originated with Freudian psychoanalysis, but in the ensuing years it has been modified and shaped into many diverse forms of psychotherapy, each making certain assumptions about the nature of man which reflect a particular theoretical or philosophical influence (for example, existentialism), or the thinking of a professional worker (for example, Carl Jung or Erich Fromm) who regarded Freud's system of thought as wrong, inadequate, or incomplete. Nevertheless these diverse systems share in common the basic theme that psychotherapy must be designed to reveal to the patient what has gone wrong with his or her psychic life; this should enable the patient to strike out in new, more satisfying, and more effective directions. For this reason, these therapies are also often called *insight therapies,* as well as *psychodynamic therapies.*

The psychodynamic therapies share two major unifying and interrelated features: (1) All such approaches employ *talking* as the primary instrument of treatment, and it is the patient mainly who determines what will be talked about. The therapist may influence this choice directly or indirectly, but most insight therapists take pains to minimize their intrusion into the discussion so that the patient rather than the therapist dominates the scene; (2) although there are notable exceptions, in the most traditional psychodynamic approaches, such as psychoanalysis, the therapist tends to adopt a *professional* rather than a personal attitude, concealing from the patient the details of his or her personal life and not acting as a friend or acquaintance might. This professional relationship with the patient is quite different from ordinary social interactions, as Colby (1951, p. 7) observes:

> As the patient talks, the therapist listens and tries in his own mind to sort out, from the mass of thoughts, memories, and feelings the patient presents, an important neurotic conflict or group of conflicts. That is, the therapist attempts to see clearly the wish-defense system involved in a symptom-producing conflict. By various tactics he then brings this area to the attention of the patient in whom up until that time the ingredients of the conflict have been unconscious. As the defense of the conflict is brought to the patient's consciousness through verbalization, the motivation for the defense (affects of anxiety, guilt, shame, disgust regarding the wish) receives attention in terms of the patient's present and past life experience. Thereby the patient's "reasonable adult ego" is given the freedom to judge and relinquish his particular anachronistic defense as its motivation is seen to be of infantile origin.

There are some important tactical differences among the varieties of insight therapy. For example, orthodox psychoanalytic therapy is usually conducted for three to five sessions each week over a period that usually lasts several years; neo-Freudian and most other therapies emphasize a shorter period of treatment, sometimes a brief duration of several weeks or months, with one therapy session per week. The physical position of the patient in Freudian psychotherapy is lying on a couch with the patient unable, without making an effort, to view the therapist; in the neo-Freudian and humanist-existential systems, the patient is typically seated in a chair face to face with the therapist, and the therapist may intrude freely into the relationship or introduce role-playing games and other tasks which reveal the life styles of the patient. Although the Freudian therapist focuses on the current flow of the patient's experiences, he or she also has great interest in early childhood relationships and experiences; the neo-Freudian and humanistic-existential therapists are less concerned with the past. The Freudian makes extensive use of dreams, treating them like any other material offered by the patient; other types of therapists may consider this a waste of time. Yet despite these evident differences, the general form of the psychodynamic therapies is one of placing the responsibility for what is talked about on the patient and of intruding on this process only with reserve in order to guide the content of the interchange.

BASIC PRINCIPLES OF PSYCHODYNAMIC THERAPIES

What are the guiding principles of this form of therapeutic arrangement and dialog between patient and psychotherapist? The key principle is best expressed in the term *insight.* All insight therapies assume that the patient has not been

FIGURE 13-1 A typical therapeutic setting and arrangement. (John Briggs.)

able to follow Socrates' injunction "know thyself" or Polonius' dictum "to thine own self be true." The patient (for convenience, let's assume here that he is male) has one set of goals, attitudes, motives, and self-conceptions which he knows about and consciously strives to realize, but presumably he has another *conflicting* set of which he is not aware, because they threaten him. These latter *unconscious* aspects of the patient's personality are *holdovers from childhood.* Their presence in the adult is usually harmful for two reasons: First, they were appropriate to a life situation (childhood) that no longer exists. They are by definition immature and self-centered. Secondly, being unconscious, they operate silently but effectively in the present; thus, they are largely outside the control of the patient's rational and conscious thought and decision. The patient cannot be the kind of person he wants to be because, without daring to acknowledge it to himself, he simultaneously wants to be a different sort of person, to do different, mutually incompatible things. In short, he is in

continual conflict and is continually threatened and frustrated.

The patient's solutions to this are apt to be inept because they are *defensive* and predicated on an unrealistic assessment of the trouble. The trouble is apt to be expressed in affective distress—for example, anxiety or depression, symptomatic behavior and inadequate functioning, and perhaps even bodily symptoms reflecting the continuing internal struggle. These symptomatic expressions bring him to the therapist for help and, in the patient's eyes, are the "troubles" for which he requires treatment. Insight refers to the discovery of these unconscious, or silently operating, forces which prevent the patient from leading the life of which he should be capable. A procedure is needed which will permit exposure and understanding of these forces within the person, so that more rational solutions and life directions can be chosen.

Notice that the patient has come or has been brought to the therapist because of the symptoms of maladjustment. The insight-therapy view of neurotic disturbances, however, is that the symptoms are less important than the pathological forces that created them. Here lies an evident paradox: The patient comes to the therapist for relief of his painful symptoms, but the therapist considers the symptoms to be secondary, surface manifestations, merely superficial expressions of some more basic, underlying neurotic process. They might be disposed of without insight, but then the underlying problems will break out again in another form. Thus, to attack the symptoms directly is to take the risk that their removal without understanding about how they operate will create new symptoms that are worse than the original. Hence, in this view the most basic difficulties—unhappiness, ineffectualness, and self-defeating behavior of the patient—cannot be eliminated without insight. It is through the latter that adjustive, corrective action can be taken. The patient must discover the nature of his misconceptions about himself and of the faulty beliefs which guide his life course inappropriately (cf. Raimy, 1975). Only the patient, not the therapist, considers the symptom of prime importance.

The insight principle produces three main difficulties: First, the aim of psychodynamic therapies is not the patient's aim but is very much broader and more ambitious, that is, (1) to alter if possible the patient's view of his problem and, in fact, his entire way of life, and (2) to develop a new understanding of himself.

Second, how is one to know that the appropriate insight has been achieved by the patient? Each theorist has a different definition of correct insight, because they all see psychodynamics differently. One answer to this dilemma has been to propose that only the correct insight will produce symptom removal and more satisfactory modes of adjustment, while incorrect insight will not. This, of course, is circular until independent criteria of valid insight are specified. Although Freud did attempt to do this, the patient may return for another analysis; with the Freudian

method, lengthy and repeated treatment is common. An alternative is to argue that insight itself is not the important thing at all—only that the patient believes he or she has the answer.

Third, the requirement of insight makes the task of evaluating the degree of success achieved by a course of therapy more difficult in a practical sense. One has to judge therapeutic success in psychoanalysis by complex and subjective criteria such as self-understanding, increased happiness, and the acquisition of more satisfying and effective interpersonal relationships. In contrast with these more subjective and difficult-to-judge features of therapeutic success, removal of the symptom is a more simple and objective criterion.

Having considered briefly the general similarities of psychodynamic therapies, we should now examine some of the major variations found within this category. The father (or grandfather) of all psychodynamic therapy is Freudian psychoanalysis, since most of the other approaches either are spin-offs from it or arose in opposition to it.

FREUDIAN PSYCHOANALYSIS

The key concepts in Freudian therapy are catharsis, resistance, transference, and reeducation or working through. People have long believed that the expression of feelings has the helpful effect of relieving tensions. This release of feelings is one of the oldest processes recognized in insight therapy. Because Freud referred to this, metaphorically speaking, as a purging, he used the term *catharsis*. Catharsis was once considered the primary agent of therapy, the idea being that the bottling up of deep-lying feelings was responsible for the neurotic symptoms. It is now believed that far more is required for successful therapy than the mere release of feelings. Freud himself deemphasized catharsis as his psychoanalytic approach began to mature. Nonetheless, some elements of catharsis are apt to remain in the treatment process because (1) the therapy cannot proceed if the patient does not express or even relive to some extent the feelings and impulses that lie behind his or her trouble and (2) because this very discharge of feelings is often the means of some relief, thus encouraging the patient to continue treatment.

RESISTANCE

A first and essential step in psychodynamic therapy is that the patient talk about his problems. (Again, for convenience, we'll assume that the hypothetical patient is male.) The patient will usually begin with a story that he is prepared to tell, one that is colored by self-deceptions. It consists often of descriptive, intellectual statements. Or, as in expressive hysterics and depressives, for example, it involves a flood of emotion that can continue indefinitely unless the therapist induces the patient to do some thinking. All these are forms of *resistance,* the basic enemy of insight.

Resistance is considered to be an inevitable process in psychotherapy by which patients protect themselves from painful discoveries about the real nature of their problems (see, for example, Reich, 1949; Hendrick, 1939; or Freud, 1935). Basically, resistance is the operation in the therapeutic context of the varied mechanisms of defense which are fundamental to the neurosis itself. Ironically, although the patient has come voluntarily to the therapist for help, he seems to resist such help by refusing to examine and expose impulses, attitudes, and experiences which are responsible for his problem.

But resistance is not so remarkable if we truly understand what is meant by the idea of a defense mechanism and its role in neurosis. Defenses are aimed at avoiding the recognition and expression of impulses that are dangerous or unacceptable. Yet the therapist is asking the patient to give up the very self-deceptions that

have permitted him to get along, albeit at a neurotic level of functioning. The present structure of his personality, however troubled, has been achieved over a period of many years and with considerable struggle, and it is not easily altered or given up. The patient has come to the therapist for relief from his symptoms, and the therapist, in effect, tells him that such relief can only come about by the even more *painful* process of faithfully examining himself and exposing things he has hitherto not been able to face.

The process of resistance is manifested behaviorally in many ways—for example, by frank protest at a therapist's interpretation, by avoiding talking about certain matters, by disinterest or leaving treatment, or by inability on the part of the patient to freely associate, that is, allow his thoughts to flow into words without censorship, without digressions from painful subjects, without blockage of speech (when the patient can think of nothing to say). The insight therapist usually regards this process of resistance as *unconscious,* that is, it occurs without awareness rather than being a consciously chosen act. If the resistance is stronger than the wish to remain in treatment, the patient may leave the psychotherapeutic situation altogether.

Alexander and French (1946, pp. 76–77) give the following case example of resistance in the form of a frank protest against a therapeutic interpretation following which the patient had a temper tantrum:

. . . An attractive young woman . . . spent the greater part of one analytic interview talking in glowing terms of a minister with whom she was closely associated in church work. She concluded by remarking that it sounded as though she were in love with the minister. The therapist quietly agreed that she must indeed be in love with him, and the rest of the hour was spent in friendly discussion of the problem created by the fact that the minister was married. Two days later this patient had a violent temper tantrum; when she was seen by the analyst (before her anger had subsided), she was quite unaware of the cause of her outburst.

To the therapist, however, it was evident that, although disguised, this was a very natural, and indeed inevitable, reaction to the interpretation that had been made in the previous session. At that time the patient had been able to discuss her feelings for the minister because she had not yet fully sensed the conflict into which they must plunge her. She had thought of her feelings for the minister in terms of her pleasure in working with him professionally. Even after it occurred to her that she was talking as if she were in love with him, she did not take the idea very seriously. She was able to agree with the therapist that she must be in love with the minister because at the time she had no sense of the intensity of her feeling for him nor of the conflict and frustration in which these feelings involved her. Such an attachment to a married man was quite incompatible with her conscience, reinforced as it was by her religious training. Her love for the minister, therefore, faced her with frustration either of her forbidden love or of her devotion to her religious standards—both of which were very strong. Anyone who attempts to intervene in a quarrel between friends is likely to draw the anger of both upon him. Similarly, a therapist who attempts to make a patient aware of a conflict between two strong but incompatible wishes must inevitably stir up the resentment of both sides of the patient's conflict against himself. It was inevitable that this patient should react with anger to an interpretation that involved so much frustration for her.

. . . Frank opposition to an unwelcome interpretation may be a normal reaction in defense of the neurosis and irrational only in the sense that the neurosis is itself irrational. The patient's reaction in the case just cited differs from such a frank protest only in that, instead of being an open refusal of the proffered in-

sight, it is unconsciously disguised as general ill-temper so that the patient is able to avoid full awareness of the conflict exposed by the new insight. A disturbing interpretation is a present reality, an attempt upon the part of the therapist to interfere with defenses necessary to the patient's peace of mind. When a patient reacts with anger to such an interpretation, therefore, his anger is not based upon a misunderstanding of his present situation as a repetition of a memory from the past. His anger is rather a direct reaction to the therapist as a real and present threat to the patient's peace of mind. Such a reaction is obviously a manifestation of the patient's resistance to treatment.

One of the major tasks of Freudian therapy and most other psychodynamic versions is to overcome the patient's resistance, but this usually cannot be done by direct attack. The psychotherapist must be careful not to press the patient too hard. One force that can help to keep the patient in the therapeutic situation is the positive effect of catharsis. Another is the acceptance of the patient's feelings by the therapist and the paternal or maternal interest and support that the therapist provides. These weapons against resistance sustain the patient in his or her arduous and threatening task of gaining self-awareness and understanding. But the most important force in overcoming resistance is the *transference* relationship.

TRANSFERENCE

As the therapy proceeds, particularly in intensive therapies such as Freudian analysis, the patient develops certain emotional attitudes toward the therapist. He or she may show evidence of an emotional attachment, or perhaps of hostility. Patients sometimes express resentment about the time the therapist spends with other patients, solicit affection and approval from the therapist, seek more attention, criticize the therapist for indifference, or give other evidence of a childish emotional reaction. The details of this emotional reaction will vary from patient to patient, but is expected in some form or other by the therapist.

Generally, Freudians view the emotional relationship displayed by the patient toward the therapist as an unconscious reenactment of the emotional relationships of early childhood (Freud, 1921, 1924). The patient is said to *transfer* to the therapist emotions that he or she has experienced as a child toward parents. If the important object relationships of childhood were characterized by affection, the transference relationship will accordingly be *positive;* however, if the predominant childhood relationship was hostile, this too will be reenacted with the therapist as *negative* transference.

Because Freud believed that the seeds of the neurosis are planted in the very earliest years of childhood, he considered it essential that the pathological emotional relationships of childhood be reenacted via the transference in order to be understood and corrected in therapy. In Freud's view, only certain kinds of persons were capable of this kind of relationship, and for this reason he believed that psychoanalysis was suitable only for those neurotic disturbances where the *transference neurosis* was possible. The term transference neurosis tends to have three types of usage: (1) as any neurosis which characterizes the patient capable of establishing transference with the therapist; (2) as the process or phenomenon of transference itself; and (3) as an extreme version of transference in which all of the patient's infantile urges and conflicts focus upon the therapist. In any case, certain types of patients whose problems or developmental histories make them incapable of emotional identifications with others cannot, therefore, experience the transference, hence they are unsuited for therapy. These include persons with personality disorders, such as the psychopath (antisocial personality), and those with acute psychoses, such as the schizophrenic. Others, such as hysterical

and obsessive-compulsive neurotics (see Chapter 6), both capable of such a relationship, offer better prospects for successful psychoanalytic treatment.

The process of transference was believed to take place most readily with the therapist seated behind and out of view of the patient, minimally intruding as a real person. Freud has sometimes been accused, perhaps out of hostility, of arranging things this way because he was too shy and embarrassed to sit face to face with the patient. Whether this is actually true or not is far less important than the logical and psychological reasons given by Freudians. When the therapist is out of sight of the patient and his or her interventions are kept to a minimum, the patient is then free to engage in infantile and unrealistic fantasies about the therapist, being less influenced by the latter's objective characteristics as a stimulus. It is believed that if the therapist is too intrusive, such fantasies might be impeded, which would interfere with the establishment of the transference. This is one reason why psychoanalytic therapists minimize their own intrusions into the conversation, especially in the early stages of therapy.

Colby (1951, pp. 106–107) has summarized the matter in this way:

The patient's feelings toward the therapist are guided and determined in accordance with (a) his reality perception of the therapist's professional role, and (b) his past interpersonal experiences with significant family figures. At any given moment in therapy, the patient's orientation to the therapist represents a compounding of these two determinants with one or the other assuming reigning proportions. Reactions arising from (a) we consider appropriate to the present reality situation. For example, if the therapist openly insults the patient until he becomes angry, then the anger is not a transference but a normal emotional response appropriate to the situation. But if the patient is enraged because the therapist wears bow ties, then the disproportionate and inappropriate response signifies the presence of a transference.

The fact of the tendency toward an emotional relationship of patient toward therapist in intensive psychotherapy is not generally contested, but there is considerable controversy about how this should be understood. Alternative interpretations are quite possible. It could be suggested, for example, that during the course of intensive psychotherapy it is natural for the patient to feel strongly about the therapist merely because the latter appears to hold the key to important rewards and punishments. For example, the therapist gives a sense of promise to the patient that eventually his or her neurotic suffering will be relieved; and when seeming to be critical, the therapist may seem to be denying this promise. Furthermore, the patient has revealed to no one else the most intimate secrets of his or her life. Being thus exposed and now highly vulnerable, is it any wonder that the patient develops these intense feelings, and even shows a childish dependency upon the therapist?

However it is interpreted, the emotional relationship between patient and therapist is a highly complex one, probably determined in part by immature childhood patterns with parent figures and in part by the immediate situation—for example, the demeanor and actions of the therapist as a contemporaneous stimulus. The psychoanalytic interpretation of the transference emphasizes the reenactment of childhood object relationships, in contrast with the contemporaneous influences. In point of fact, there has been little research to evaluate the various influences which are probably at work in producing the charged relationship between patient and therapist which Freud called transference and which is a cornerstone of psychoanalytic therapy.

The following case example shows a manifestation of transference (from Colby, 1951, pp. 113–114):

Jailed for stealing, a tough adolescent boy snarled and wisecracked at all adults. A major event in his past life was the war death of an older brother noted for his kindness toward the patient. On meeting the therapist, the boy showed his usual bored nonchalance. For a few minutes he gave clipped answers to questions about his age, school grade, etc. Then spontaneously he added:

Patient: You know, it was my birthday yesterday.

Therapist: And did anyone remember you?

Suddenly the patient burst into tears and sobbed heavily. From this moving transference reaction the therapist can see beneath the insouciant façade elements which do not appear in a routine psychiatric history.

To the psychoanalytically oriented therapist, the transference relationship is important for two reasons: (1) It can provide important clues concerning the patient's childhood patterns of identification and characteristic relationship with others. Thus, the analyst learns fundamental things about the patient's personality from this reenactment of childhood, and, even more important, the patient can ultimately learn these things too. Transference, therefore, is a learning experience for both therapist and patient. (2) The therapist can take advantage of this strong affective relationship to encourage the patient to overcome resistances. Because the patient's dominant wish at this time may be to please the therapist, and because he or she also obtains a form of protection and support from the relationship, the transference makes it less difficult to bring up material that ordinarily would be too anxiety-producing to tolerate.

The transference relationship ultimately has to be dissolved. That is, the patient must see the relationship for what it is, an instance of past relations with his or her parents. The patient must ultimately give up this childishness in order to function without it when therapy is terminated and to establish mature adult relationships with the important persons (husband, wife, children, friends, employers, parents) in the current life situation.

The variants of psychodynamic therapy treat the emotional relationship of patient to therapist in divergent ways. In Freudian psychoanalytic therapy, for example, the analysis of the transference is considered to be the core of the treatment. Other types of insight therapy (for example, those based on suggestion) use the relationship but do not attempt to analyze it. In short-term insight therapy, the phenomenon of transference is deemphasized and, in fact, discouraged. In most insight therapies, however, the emotional relationship between the therapist and the patient, however it is conceived, is thought to play some role.

It was once believed that the mere bringing up of unconscious memories and feelings, *catharsis,* was the primary therapeutic agent. Later, the *transference* relationship itself was considered to be the important feature of therapy. Still later, the importance of *insight* (Reik, 1948) on the part of the patient was emphasized. In more recent years, *all* these features have been considered important, and insight has come to be thought of as an intermediate, although significant, step toward the resolution of neurotic conflict. Since neurosis is believed by the psychodynamic therapist to involve defensive operations against factors producing anxiety, these defense mechanisms must be given up in order for the patient to comprehend clearly, and to come to grips successfully with, the neurotic problem. Because defenses are unconscious, they must be brought to awareness before the patient can begin to deal with them in a more rational fashion.

REEDUCATION

However, at least one further step must be accomplished in insight therapy, the step of *working through* or, as some writers have termed it, *reeducation.* Persons must also learn new and more adequate ways of dealing with the neurotic

conflicts before they can function successfully. They must apply the insights they have learned in a wide variety of situations. As we shall see, this notion of working through helps to bridge the theoretical gap between psychodynamic therapies and action or behavior therapies, in that both agree that the patient must learn new ways of behaving.

The purpose of Freudian psychoanalysis is not ordinarily to assist a patient to solve a very specific problem, but rather to aid him or her in developing *general* resources with which to solve *any* emotion-producing problem. The patient's general capacity to make satisfactory adjustments to new as well as to old interpersonal problems must be enhanced. This means that whatever insights are gained in the psychotherapeutic situation must be available to the patient for dealing with a wide range of problems throughout life. This is a reeducational process. The Freudians believe this is possible only when patients have examined and understood their reactions and applied what they have learned to new situations. Adequate modes of coping must be substituted for the pathological modes which characterized their adjustment prior to psychotherapy.

We can see more clearly how the Freudian therapy might work by considering an illustration from Colby (1951). This segment or portion of the therapy takes place during what Colby sees as the middle phase of treatment of a female patient. The excerpt contains evidence of resistance, transference, and "working through" over a series of five interviews (Colby, 1951, pp. 121–133):

Our patient is a mannerly woman in her mid-twenties. She comes for help because of generalized feelings of depression and dissatisfaction both with her job and her marriage. Working full time for low pay as a secretary she gloomily sees no chance for a better financial future. This impinges on her relationship to her husband, who also earns little and who cannot keep a steady job. Even more upsetting is his heavy drinking. Two or three nights a week and every weekend he drinks himself into a helpless stupor. All efforts on the part of the patient to help him stop drinking have failed. In fact he claims that it is her attitude toward him that makes him drink all the more. He refuses to consult a psychiatrist about his alcoholism, saying that it is entirely a matter of his own free choice whether he drinks or not. The patient suffers from conflicting thoughts whether to break up the marriage or try to keep it going.

Her background was that of a small-town girl growing up in a farming area in the West. Her parents were hand-working, religious people of the soil concerned with the immediacies of survival. She feels that she and her brother, five years younger, were raised in a fair and kindly spirit, her only criticism being that her father kept himself aloof from the jolly, rough-and-tumble play she saw carried on by other fathers with their children. On graduating from high school, she left home for a job in the city. First a clerk, she studied nights and advanced to a position as secretary in the company she works for at present. Three years ago she met her husband, at that time also employed by this company, and, after six months' courtship, they married. The husband drank only socially when she first knew him, but in the past two years he has become increasingly alcoholic.

Therapy thus far has consisted mainly of an expression of her feelings about the job and her husband, with some clarification of the second problem as being primary. The clinical diagnosis is a reactive depression complicating a character neurosis. The working dynamic diagnosis concerns the patient's orientation toward men, her husband in particular, and her participant role in a symbiosis with an alcoholic. Up to this point in therapy the therapist's remarks have consisted mainly of interpositions with an occasional comment to the effect that she feels protective as well as resentful toward her husband. The next five interviews are given in some detail.

Interview 15

Today the patient is talking about many of the little habits and mannerisms her husband (John) has which irritate her. He never can sit still, he is always making some kind of noise with his mouth or nose, and he is inattentive about his clothes.

Pt.: His clothes are a sore spot with us. He never cleans or brushes them. If I'd let him, he would wear the same suit for days. I have to get after him constantly to change his underwear. And he never likes to buy a new suit. We are going down tomorrow to get him a new suit. He hasn't had one in years.

Ther.: You go with him when he buys his clothes?

Pt.: Yes. I don't trust him. He'd pick out something horrible. That's why I always buy his socks and ties. He has no taste in clothes. He likes bright colors, like yellow ties and green socks. He tries to look flashy, but he's not the flashy type at all.

Ther.: Does he object to your picking out his clothes?

Pt.: No. He seems to like it. Once in a while he used to squawk, but now he accepts it. Other things that I do annoy him, though. Like meals. He doesn't eat much, and he likes things that are bad for him—hot dogs and pie. I try to see that he has a balanced diet, fruit and vegetables. Yesterday we planned to have dinner at six. About four-thirty we went past a hot-dog stand and he wanted one. I told him it would spoil his appetite for dinner. He blew up, said I never let him have his own way. He's right as far as eating goes. But I do it for his own good.

Her concern over the husband's clothes and food and the way she dominates him "for his own good" point to her concept of him as a child requiring her motherly care. The therapist makes a clarification interpretation in the form of a question.

Ther.: It seems you are very worried about his diet. Are you afraid he will get sick?

Pt.: Yes, I am. John is quite thin and gets colds easily. And his drinking. I've read that if you drink a lot and don't eat the right things you're liable to get liver cirrhosis or a vitamin deficiency. God, we had a terrible time the other night. He came home drunk and kept on drinking. I didn't say anything to him about it because I'm beginning to see that it's hopeless. I can't do anything about it. He kept on drinking bourbon and stumbling around. I went to bed. About three o'clock I woke up and he still hadn't come to bed. So I went into the kitchen and he was lying there out cold. I tried to drag him but he's too heavy. He came to a little and pushed me away. He wanted to walk by himself. Now I know what they mean by "blind drunk." He just couldn't see things. He'd crash right into a table, fall down, get up again and smack into the door. Finally he let me put him to bed. When he gets that bad he's just like a helpless baby.

Ther.: Maybe that gets close to your feeling about him when he's sober, too. Buying clothes for him, looking after what he eats, protecting him from sickness—those are all things that mothers do for their children.

Pt. (*hesitantly*): Yes. I suppose so. Although I don't want to be a mother to him. Another thing that happens is, he gets so drunk that he's still drunk in the morning and can't go to work. That's why he can't hold a job. He doesn't show up regularly and they fire him.

The initial confrontation apparently does not sink in. She is hesitant to accept it and moves away from it in another direction. However, such understandings develop slowly and in small steps. The opportunity will arise again to show her this aspect of her marital relationship. The therapist's next question keeps her close to the general mother-child area.

Ther.: Do you get breakfast for him when he's drunk in the morning?

Pt.: Sometimes I leave orange juice for him to drink. Usually I'm so furious when he doesn't get up for work that I just leave. What burns me up is that I have to get up to go to work so that we'll have enough money to get by on.

She then continues to speak of their financial problems and his irresponsibility in money matters. She doesn't trust him to run a checking account and pays all the bills herself. More and more a picture of this marriage develops in which, while he appears as the weak and submissive child bitterly taking refuge in the infantile oblivion of alcohol, she is the strong, managing, and domineering mother-figure. The interaction of the personality configurations of this couple illustrates how neurotic processes are shared. The problem for therapy is showing her her contribution to the symbiotic drama without accusingly attacking her self-esteem. Of greatest value will be her involvement of the therapist in a transference similar to the relationship with her husband.

Interview 16

Pt.: What you said last time about being a mother to John struck me. I was thinking about it afterwards . . .

Testimony that the seemingly dismissed interpretation of the last interview had an impact and echo.

Pt.: . . . how that works. I do treat him like a child. Then I was thinking about other men I knew before I was married. Something of the same happened there. For instance, I went with a fellow for about two years. My girl friend said he was a mouse and that I led him around by the nose. At the time I couldn't see it, but I can now. He used to like to go fishing, but I hated it, so we always did what I wanted to do on weekends. I had to teach him how to dance and how to act in a restaurant.

She continues to describe this relationship, which in many ways parallels the present one to her husband. The man was passive, submissive, and eager to please her. She finally sent him away because he seemed too weak and clinging for her to marry. She then takes up the topic of her ideal man.

Pt.: All my life I had a clear picture of the kind of man I would like to marry. He is a tall, strong, clean-cut type, very successful and very intelligent. In my day-dreams I would meet him at a party, he would pay more attention to me than to any of the others, and eventually he would become completely devoted. I always liked the idea of a man doing all sorts of the little conventional things you see in the movies—bringing flowers, presents, surprise trips.

Ther.: Did you ever meet anyone who filled this ideal?

Pt.: Only once. About a year ago we met a couple at a bridge club we belong to. He seemed like a god to me, but he mostly ignored me. Somehow I always knew I'd never really get such a dream man.

Ther.: You wanted a strong man, but you always wound up with weak ones.

A comparison interpretation contrasting her wish-fantasy with her reality behavior.

Pt.: Yes, that's right. I know it can't be coincidental. I must attract weak ones. I know that I feel sure of myself with men like my husband when I first meet them. Maybe I can tell that they are drawn to me. Or maybe that I can run them around. That's a horrible way to be. I used to laugh at women who nagged their men, but I guess I'm just as bad. (*Weeps.*)

The therapist waits for her to regain control of her feelings. When she is able to speak again, he asks a question designed to elucidate the marital relationship.

Ther.: When you first met your husband, was he immediately drawn to you?

Pt.: In a way. He worked in the same office I did. We started having lunch together. . . .

It develops that at first the patient did not feel her future husband to be the child he seems now. He was a witty, lively sort of person who amused her greatly. Once sexual intercourse began, she found it more pleasurable than she had ever experienced before. This to her was proof that it would be a happy marriage.

Pt.: In the past year all that has disappeared. We haven't had any sexual relations for six months and before that only about once a month.

Ther.: Does your husband object to this?

Looking to see if she controls him in this respect also.

Pt.: No. It seems to suit him. He doesn't say anything about it.

Ther.: And does such a period of abstinence bother you at all?

Pt.: No. I seem to have lost my sexual interest. Even during my periods which used to be the time I was most excited, I don't feel it any more. Once in awhile I do feel affectionate toward John. Then I hug him or hold him in bed. But that's usually when I feel sorry for him, when I know he's sick emotionally and can't help himself. It's pity I feel, and you can't feel sexually toward someone you have only pity for.

Ther.: Nor toward a sick child. We must stop there for today, our time is up.

The therapist ends the hour with a repetition of the mother-child interpretation, proposing the absence of intercourse as further evidence for this concept.

Interview 17

The patient begins this hour by speaking of one of her friends at work. Together they criticize various aspects of the way the company office is operated. Also they confide in one another about their personal problems. The friend is unmarried and gets an allowance from her parents. Thus she is able to spend quite a bit of money on her clothes and personal belongings. She often gives the patient gifts of perfume or jewelry. Not only does this embarrass the patient, who cannot reciprocate, but it angers her in that the friend's largesse emphasizes her own limited funds, most of which are spent on rent, food, and household needs.

All this the therapist listens to without interposition or interpretation, waiting for an opportunity to take up the thread of the previous interview. It comes in connection with a dream.

Pt.: I had a dream last night that I can remember clearly. Usually I can't remember them the next day. It was about dogs. I was standing in a large field. Across the field I could see a dog—an Irish setter—coming through the grass. When he got closer I could see that he, or I guess it must be she, was carrying a little puppy in her mouth. It was a mother dog and her puppy. The puppy was sick I imagined, because his nose was running and he was being carried. Otherwise he could have walked.

Dreams are used in psychotherapy but not fully *interpreted* in the manner characteristic of psychoanalysis. For example, in psychoanalysis the analyst would attempt to get associations to as many elements in this dream as possible, i.e., track down the detailed thought connection of why it is an *Irish* setter, what a field means, etc. But in psychotherapy the therapist uses the dream as if it were any other type of material presented by the patient. He tries to sort out a theme or pattern in it which relates to the past, present, or transference and then, if the patient's learning state (resistance) is suitable, points out the theme for further discussion.

The technique used here at this moment is a typical one.

Ther.: So the dream is about a mother dog and her sick child.

Pt.: Of course it must refer to me and John. We've talked about my being a mother and he a child.

Ther.: And he gets a lot of colds with a running nose?

Pt.: Yes. I wonder why I dreamed about dogs. We don't have a dog. I was thinking of getting one, but then there's no one home in the daytime to take care of him. A dog is like a child. Maybe the dream is about that, too. I always wanted to have children, but now I'm not so sure. I'd never try to raise a child with John the way he is now.

Ther.: How is it that you haven't become pregnant?

Pt.: I was pregnant once before I was married and had an abortion. But you mean with John. At first we didn't even talk about having children. I don't know why. When I got to know him better, I got the feeling that he didn't want to have children. When I brought the subject up, he'd say we couldn't afford it or we didn't have enough room in the apartment. But I could tell that he really didn't like children. Sometimes we visit a neighbor who has children, and John ignores them. He won't play with them or talk to them. Says they're noisy brats who don't know their place.

Ther.: So you haven't tried to get pregnant?

Pt.: No. Now, of course, I'm not even sure I want to stay with John. This would be no time to have a baby. Maybe I've always sensed that. I think I know what it is. He would be jealous of a baby. A baby would take away some of the attention I give him.

Ther.: A baby would be a rival for your motherly care.

Here a working-through is taking place. Repeated consideration and interpretation of a central mechanism help to fix it in the patient's consciousness. The dream has served its purpose in reopening the mother-child topic. Its relationship to the patient's pregnancy wishes and concepts is left unexamined.

Pt.: I'm sure that's what he feels underneath. And he's right. I couldn't spend as much time with him.

Ther.: You say you always thought of yourself as having children?

Exploring the strength of her need to have a child or a child substitute.

Pt.: I began to think of having children when I was about fourteen. All my girl friends would spend hours talking about how many children we would have and what kind. I wanted three, two boys and a girl. I imagined just what they'd look like, where they would go to school, what they would become, and so forth.

Ther.: And your imagined husband was the ideal man?

Pt.: That's odd. I never even thought what their father would be like. My picture of an ideal man came later when I was about sixteen or seventeen.

How the adolescent idea of children without a father might relate to the pregnancy and abortion mentioned in passing is not explored. Such interesting by-paths must often remain untrod.

Interview 18

After only a few minutes have gone by, the therapist is aware of the presence of an intercurrent resistance. Instead of speaking freely and evenly on a specific topic, the patient appears uncertain and backward. She meanders from subject to subject, and her comments are punctuated with silences of atypical length. She overelaborates minutiae and makes no mention of her presenting problems or the material of the preceding interviews.

Pt.: I don't know what to talk about today. (*Pause.*) The other day I learned something interesting. I always like to learn new things. A friend and I were talking about baking. I brought up the fact that I've never learned how to make a pie. She offered to show me, so we went to her place. It's really very simple. First you make the dough. . . .

She gives in detail each step of pie-making. The therapist attempts to circumvent the resistance with a leading question but he is unsuccessful.

Pt.: . . . it came out pretty well. I'm going to try it at home my next day off.

Ther.: Does your husband like pies?

Pt.: Not especially. He doesn't pay much attention to what he eats. (*Pause.*) Then I saw my other girl friend, the one at work. She and I plan to go to a lecture together on psychology. She was the one who first became interested in psychology and psychiatry. She went to a lecture series and then began doing some reading. One day I saw a book on psychiatry on her desk. From then on it was our favorite topic of conversation. (*Long silence.*)

Ther.: What are you thinking about?

Pt. (*uneasy*): Something I read in one of the books. I can't remember which one. I liked the one by S. the best. It made a lot of sense to me. (*Silence.*)

Ther.: You seem to have some trouble talking today.

Pt.: I know. I was sure you'd notice it. I don't hide it very well when there's something I find hard to talk about.

Ther.: Why is it hard?

Pt.: I don't know. It just is.

Meeting a resistance, the therapist wonders first about its motive and content in terms of the transference. A further clue is that it has some association with her reading in psychiatry, an activity bound to have bearing on the therapeutic relationship. Hence the therapist gently shakes the transference tree to see what falls.

Ther.: Maybe it's hard because it has something to do with me.

Pt.: You're right. I read that in psychotherapy the patient has to tell all her feelings, even those toward the therapist. At the time I didn't think much about it. But when I began coming here I soon found out how hard that is. Lately, maybe because we've been talking about my treating a man as if he were a child, I've noticed that I have that tendency toward you. Actually I have two separate feelings about you. One is that you are some sort of superman, perfect, always right. But the other is opposite to it. Not that you are really a child, but I feel motherly toward you. Days when you look tired I wonder if you are getting enough rest. Or when you cough I think maybe you are getting a cold and shouldn't sit in this cold room.

Illustrating a mixture of transferences. Her image of the therapist contains elements of powerful-authority, ideal-model, and favorite-child transference. Noteworthy is the fact that her view of the therapist represents a composite of the two men in her life, the fantasied ideal and the reality weakling. That the patient is talking at her normal pace again and is developing a topic, indicates the diminution of the particular resistance. Since the patient, by herself, is coming closer to an understanding of the parallel between therapist and husband, the therapist does not interrupt.

Pt.: Of course my feeling that you should take better care of yourself is maternal. And, as you pointed out once, this is how I react toward John. I'm always worrying about his health. There's no reason I should worry about you. A doctor certainly knows how to take care of himself.

Ther.: Especially if he is a superman.

Pt.: (laughs): I almost forgot that. It's a funny

mixture. How can a superman be a child who needs a mother? Maybe I think that underneath all men are children.

To himself the therapist thinks of the possibility that she wishes to make men children, reduce a superman to the status of a child. Obviously it is no time to interpret such an impulse. The evidence is still scanty, and it must gradually be approached from the standpoint of defense rather than wish. In the next interview a chance for a wish-defense interpretation presents itself.

Interview 19

Pt.: After the last time I gave a lot of thought to that point about how men are children to me. . . .

The extra-interview working through of reflection.

Pt.: . . . I had a good example happen to me yesterday. One of the men where I work was trying to look up something in the files. He looked as if he didn't know what he was doing. To me, anyway, he looked puzzled. As I went over to help him I said laughingly to one of the other girls, "It's all too complicated for the poor boy." When I got there I found out he knew as much about the files as I did. He had found a mistake in them and that's why he was having trouble. But I thought of him as a confused little boy whom I would have to help. That was my first reaction, so it must be a strong desire in me to think of men as children who need me.

The patient goes on to another example involving a young man she was briefly engaged to. Again she is able now to see many of the mother-child aspects of this relationship. Then she begins to talk about her husband in terms of this theme.

Pt.: Two more things came to me about treating John as a child, a little boy. The first is not just treating him as one but in a way keeping him one. A few months ago he wanted to enlist in the Army. He thinks a war is coming and he would be drafted anyway. If he enlists he'd have a better job. But I thought of all sorts of reasons to talk him out of it. All the time I knew he wanted to be a soldier to see if he could be more of a man, a man among men and not a weakling doing women's work like clerking. (*Pause.*)

Ther.: You said there were two things in this regard. What was the other?

An interposition to keep the patient going.

Pt.: The other was when he wanted to grow a moustache. I had heard other women protesting about their husbands' growing a moustache and I laughed at them because I knew that they didn't like their husbands to assert their masculinity. But when John started it I was the same way. I poked fun at him for trying to be something he wasn't. I shamed him out of it. I kept him a boy, wouldn't let him do what men like to do.

Ther.: Why are you afraid of letting him be a man, more assertive?

A wish-defense interpretation made from the defense side. The therapist does not begin by pointing to her wish to weaken, fetter, and hamstring her husband but to her anxiety over his becoming strong and indomitable. Later the wish will be approached.

Pt.: I'm not sure. Maybe I want to be the boss. Or maybe I'm afraid he would give me a bad time.

Ther.: In what way?

Pt.: Leave me? I don't know.

As yet the childhood derivation of her relationship to men is unknown. The roles of the younger brother, father, and mother in determining her outlook during her formative years await discussion. Eventually the most effective interpretation of her behavior will show her the repetition of a childhood motif in her orientation to both husband and therapist.

NEO-FREUDIAN CONCEPTS

Psychoanalysis came into being about ninety years ago when Freud began to work with a distinguished Viennese physician named Joseph Breuer. Breuer was treating a young woman with bodily symptoms that at first seemed neurologically caused (Breuer and Freud, 1957). She complained of loss of sensation in her arm and leg, and seemed to suffer also from some visual defects. As she expressed otherwise hidden feelings under hypnosis, these symptoms disappeared, but they reappeared when she returned to the waking state. The pattern suggested a psychological rather than neurological disturbance, and this led Freud to the development of the "talking cure" of psychoanalysis and to his lifelong struggle to understand the psychodynamics of such neurotic disturbances. All through this period, psychoanalytic formulations and procedures evolved and changed in keeping with Freud's own observations with patients, his dissatisfactions about their adequacy at various stages in their development, and the inputs of colleagues with whom Freud worked.

In the early days of the evolution of psychoanalysis, some of Freud's own associates began to adopt views divergent from those of Freud, leading to a number of offshoots of Freudian psychoanalysis. They are referred to as neo-Freudian or new-Freudian because their deviations from the orthodox formulations were basically "variations on a theme by Freud," as Korchin (in press) refers to them. Alfred Adler and Carl Jung were the first to depart from the Freudian inner circle.

Adler (see Ansbacher and Ansbacher, 1956) was a Viennese physician who was critical of Freud's emphasis on the sexual drives as the mainspring of neurosis and of the emphasis on the discharge of and blockage of instinctual drives in the formation of the personality. He broke with Freud in 1911. In his early writings, Adler emphasized the inevitable helplessness of the child and the feelings of inferiority that were fostered by this helplessness. As seen by Adler, the neurotic solution was to compensate for the inferiority feelings by striving for power. In order to be healthy, the person had to give up this neurotic tendency by developing the inherent human need to involve oneself unselfishly with others, to identify with the group, in effect, to express healthy *social interest.* Adler believed that the person normally has the urge to grow and to strive for perfection through social identification. This is the antidote to the neurotic search for power. In Adler's psychotherapy more attention is given to the person's conscious intentions and sense of the future than to the past and to unconscious forces emphasized by Freud; individuals are encouraged to give up their neurotic style of life for one that is oriented to less selfish pursuits.

Carl Jung terminated his relationship with Freud in 1913 and formulated his own theoretical approach. Jung (1916, 1953) agreed with Freud that human beings' animal instincts had to be discharged or gratified for psychological health, but like Adler he emphasized much more than Freud the struggle of the individual to develop in a positive direction, to become *self-actualized,* by which Jung meant achieving a harmonious integration of all the conflicting and diverse aspects of the personality. As people grew older and more mature, their energies are redirected toward the spiritual meaning of life, their approaching death, and efforts to integrate their conflicting animal instincts with their spiritual needs. Jung also emphasized the unconscious fantasies, myths, and symbols (for example, Jung, 1965) that are ever-present in our thought, art, and religion and that express not only our unique

social history during life but universal biological tendencies in the human race as well.

Another influential neo-Freudian, originally part of the Freudian inner circle, was *Otto Rank,* the only nonphysician in the group. In common with Adler and Jung, Rank (1945, 1952) emphasized the constructive strivings of the person to grow, to break with the past in order to live independently in the present. For Rank, human life from its beginning is a struggle between two basic opposing tendencies, on the one hand to be in safe union with the protective mother (and hence the crowd or social system) and on the other hand to become a separate and distinct individual. Gratification of one of these tends to thwart the other. People have different ways of resolving this struggle; some are successful in coping with the anxiety of *separation* by remaining always bound and dependent, by never moving toward *individuation*—by remaining like a contented cow, so to speak. A few succeed in integrating both trends, experiencing both union and security, yet becoming a distinctive individual. Some strive to separate, yet are frightened and lonely in consequence, remaining constantly in conflict, in effect, neurotic. Rank made this struggle the central theme of psychotherapy and set a time limit for therapy to be completed in order to force the patient to face up to the inevitable separation.

Erich Fromm can also be regarded as a neo-Freudian, although he was not part of the intimate group that revolved around Freud in the early days of psychoanalysis. He began his career within the orthodox Freudian tradition then departed from it, becoming influential in his own right. Fromm obtained his Ph.D. from Heidelberg in 1922 and was trained in psychoanalysis in Chicago. In 1941 he wrote one of his best-known works, *Escape from Freedom,* in which he gave early evidence of departure from Freudian ideas and showed interest in the role of society in facilitating or undermining healthy personality development. Unlike most other psychoanalytically oriented writers, Fromm gave less emphasis in his writings to the individual character of the person and more to his or her *social character,* that is, the values and behavior patterns that are shared by most of the members of a society. Social character is a product of the culture in which people live.

In *Escape from Freedom,* Fromm expressed, along with other neo-Freudians, the struggle of the individual *to grow,* and to synthesize the need to feel secure and a part of the social environment with the need to be independent of that environment. As children develop, they become free to express their individuality, which is a strong inherent need, but in the process they feel isolated and helpless, a situation that Fromm saw as distinctively human. One inadequate solution to this conflict is to try to escape from the frightening condition of freedom and to submit to social authority. This is what happened in Nazi Germany, says Fromm, where the population subjected themselves to a totalitarian society in order to escape from the loneliness and anxiety of freedom (Fig. 13-2).

In later writings, Fromm (1947, 1955) added to this basic formulation, identifying a number of socially based needs in addition to *belonging* and *identity,* such as *transcendence* or seeking creatively to rise above one's animal nature, and having a stable *frame of reference* with which to perceive and understand the world in which one lives. Fromm sees failure of adjustment as largely

FIGURE 13-2 Search for belonging in Nazi Germany; search for belonging in an American religious revival meeting. (Top: Wide World Photos; bottom: James Holland, from Black Star.)

a result of the *failure of society* in meeting basic human needs, though he is optimistic that a more successful society can be created, one in which people are rooted in bonds of fellow-feeling yet able to transcend nature by achieving a sense of self-identity.

The above brief vignettes of some of the main neo-Freudian views do not exhaust the post-Freudian contributions to thought about the nature of human beings and their problems which have influenced psychodynamic therapy theory and practice. One can see too in the above descriptions that there is much in common among the neo-Freudians. Chief among these is the great emphasis on the *social forces* that shape the person and his or her problems, in contrast with Freud's emphasis on the *biological instincts* of sex and aggression in the causation of adjustive failure.

Neo-Freudian views have permeated the practice of psychotherapy even though most of them no longer exist as active therapeutic schools. Thus, if one goes to a psychodynamically oriented psychotherapist, one may no longer be able readily to find orthodox representatives of Adlerian, Rankian, or Frommian therapeutic systems, but their ideas have widely penetrated the therapeutic context. An exception seems to be the Freudian view, which still has fairly orthodox representatives; there are some Jungian therapists too, several of them located in the San Francisco Bay Area. The neo-Freudians have been as influential on our ideas about personality dynamics as on systematic therapeutic practice. Today the greater part of psychoanalytic-type practice exists in briefer treatment approaches which are much more oriented to the person's present functioning than to attempts to reconstruct his or her past. In typical current practice, one finds few couches for a patient to lie on, relatively little traditional free association or dream analysis, and relatively little formal emphasis on transference and its interpretation.

HUMANISTIC-EXISTENTIAL APPROACHES

The neo-Freudian movement contained within it some of the seeds of a later outlook that began to flourish about fifteen years ago in American psychology and is usually referred to as *humanistic psychology*. Adler, Jung, Rank, and Fromm, for example, all spoke of a *force for growth* in humans, an idea that was picked up and extended by psychologists such as Carl Rogers (1942, 1951), Abraham Maslow (1954), and others. These writers thought of people not so much as dominated by biological urges and events of their past, but more as heavily oriented to immediate social influences, future growth, and the actualization of their human potentialities.

Along with existential-phenomenological philosophical influences, the neo-Freudian outlook spawned what is referred to today as the *humanistic-existential* approach to psychology and psychotherapy. This approach rejects the more traditional psychoanalytic and behavioristic view in which people are seen as mechanistic systems (like machines), controlled both by external forces and internal biological urges. Humanistic-existential psychology sees a person as having the capacity for self-determination and growth, having purposes, options, and values, rather than being merely a victim of biological urges, environmental demands, and unconscious forces. In its therapeutic versions, this viewpoint focuses on the person's self-concepts and world view; it fosters awareness of one's private experience, acceptance and affirmation of one's unique self, and the freedom and responsibility to act so that one's full potential can be actualized. This emphasis on one's subjective, personal experience gives the humanistic-existential attitude a strongly *phenomenological* cast in contrast with psychology's traditional emphasis on observable behavior or action and the stimuli that activate such behavior. Phenomenology involves an emphasis on the psychological experience of events rather than on action or behavior and its external governance. This is also an outgrowth of existential philosophy, which is an orientation toward understanding nature and the meaning of human existence by emphasizing the interdependency of persons, their concern with the meaning of free choice, death and life, the human capability of growth, and the human problems of alienation, loneliness, and detachment in the modern world.

In humanistic-existential forms of psychotherapy, as in all insight therapies, it is necessary for patients to discover and grapple with the nature of their life patterns and the personal and situational factors that block them from using their potential creatively with satisfaction and forward movement. An essential key to growth and self-actualization is *awareness of oneself* and one's nature. Thus, as in the psychoanalytic and neo-Freudian forms of treatment, humanistic-existential psychotherapy is also psychodynamically or insight-oriented, and there is much overlap between these approaches.

Many specific varieties of therapy could be said to be humanistic-existential in outlook, and it is not possible here to review all of them or to give the theoretical-philosophical history of each. I shall briefly describe four well-known versions—Carl Rogers's client-centered therapy, the existential therapy of Rollo May, the logotherapy of Viktor Frankl, and Fritz Perls's gestalt therapy.

CARL ROGERS'S CLIENT-CENTERED THERAPY

In consequence of the Freudian depth view of neurotic symptoms with its concepts of defense mechanism and resistance, psychodynamic therapies took on certain insight-oriented patterns distinguishing them from early periods in which therapists advised, entreated, encouraged, prescribed for, and directed the troubled patient. The newer view was that the patient had to lead rather than the therapist, since it was the patient's own inaccessible or unconscious conflicts and feelings that were responsible for his or her

problem, and these had to be uncovered without frightening the patient away. In 1942 Rogers published a book that introduced what he called "non-directive therapy." This work not only abandoned the demeaning term (in Rogers's view) "patient" and substituted "client," but more importantly it strongly emphasized certain features of the therapist-client relationship that favored the honest exploration of the client's feelings. In this book and in a later one (1951) in which the term "client-centered therapy" is used, Rogers became an early exponent of the humanistic-existential outlook.

Rogers argued that for therapeutic change to take place, the client had to grow by discovering what was blocking him or her from self-actualization. In contrast with others (such as Freud) who had characterized human beings as essentially depraved because of destructive animal instincts, Rogers saw people as constantly striving toward the realization of their highest potentials and toward wholeness and integration if only they were free to become what they really were. The task of therapy, he believed, was to release this potential, and to do so required certain conditions that the therapist could create and which the client could perceive and respond to. These conditions included genuineness, an unconditional positive regard for the client as a person, and an accurate empathic understanding of the client's world of personal meanings and feelings.

By being *genuine,* the therapist shows respect for the client and an attitude of caring. He (or she) must not be deceitful, put up a façade, or play games. Although the therapist does not normally seek to introduce his own feelings into the therapeutic dialog, he is willing to share them when necessary. In short, he must be a real person with his client.

The proper therapeutic attitude toward the client includes *unconditional positive regard, acceptance,* and *warmth.* The therapist shows no disapproving reactions to what the client says; by accepting all statements at face value, he encourages the client to express his or her true feelings without fear of criticism. Rogers thought that this unconditional positive regard and support might well be the key factor in permitting the client to probe more deeply into his or her own feelings and to express them. Previously the client will no doubt have complained to, or sought help from, friends, associates, or family, but these persons have been only too willing to offer advice, to criticize the client's actions and feelings, or even to encourage some course of action. The therapist's attitude, however, is something new to the client. He listens, seems attentive, understands, is concerned, and, most importantly, he accepts whatever is said without evaluation, even the most reprehensible things which most clients would be ashamed to tell others or to express to themselves. Through all this the client finds that it is possible to talk freely without losing the positive regard and support of the therapist.

Clients are also helped to progress because the therapist *accurately senses* their inner world. He communicates this empathic understanding by showing that he is following, by restating what the client has said about his feelings, by reflecting their meaning back to the patient so that he can grasp it himself. In a typical interchange, for example, the client may say, "It bothers me when other people get ahead and I don't," and the therapist may respond, "You are troubled when others are successful and you are not." In this way, the therapist has shown he "hears" what is being said and accepts it, all in the same response. He could have responded instead, "You resent other people's success," and this might indeed have captured the underlying feeling even better since the statement is being interpreted by the addition of the word "resent," but the client may not be able at that point to accept the inference about resentment, and indeed he did not state it explicitly. The latter rejoinder by the therapist could readily lead to defensiveness on the part of the client ("No, I don't resent it").

The task of the Rogerian therapist is to provide an atmosphere of such complete acceptance that the client is freed from his defensiveness and allowed to move forward toward fuller insight.

In his later work, beginning around 1964 when he became a resident fellow at the Western Behavioral Science Institute in La Jolla, California, Rogers (1967) began to shift his attention from individual therapy to group therapy, developing his own version of the "encounter group" out of his earlier thinking about the therapist-client relationship and the tasks of therapy. This new development was facilitated when he shifted four years later to the newly formed Center for the Whole Person (Rogers, 1970), where he was free to expand his humanistic approach to the expansion of human consciousness.

The encounter group format permits a very intense group experience designed to get persons who are normally alienated from themselves, other persons, and society into closer emotional contact via encounters with self, with others, and with the world of sense and feeling. Rogers brings three basic themes to his encounter group work, themes that will seem familiar from his nondirective or client-centered therapy:

First, he assumes that experience with the group can affect permanent changes within the individual, and thus no distinction need be made between the general goal of personal development or growth and the specific goals of therapy itself. They are one and the same.

Second, honest confrontations are to be valued, even if the response to an individual group member seems negative and potentially damaging. An honest expression of negative feelings is helpful in the long run. Where a confrontation takes on the character of outright sadism, one of the group members or the group leader can verbalize this impression, thus bringing the hostile motive out into the open, where it can be dealt with by the target individual.

Third, Rogers is not particularly interested in the group process itself, as is true of many group workers. His primary emphasis remains on the awareness, expression, and acceptance of feelings by individual group members. The basic encounter situation requires for its therapeutic value a trusting and cohesive group, and in his own role as group leader Rogers prefers to facilitate the group process through minimal interventions, as was the case in nondirective or client-centered therapy.

ROLLO MAY'S EXISTENTIAL THERAPY

Existential psychotherapy appears to represent a "union [of psychoanalysis] with a form of European metaphysics called existential philosophy, and the resulting mixture has been appropriately termed "existential analysis" (Harper, 1959, p. 76). The philosophical roots are in the writings of older existentialist philosophers such as Kierkegaard, Nietzsche, and Schopenhauer and in some modern philosophical writers such as Martin Heidegger, Martin Buber, and Jean-Paul Sartre. One of the most articulate representatives of the existential point of view in the United States has been Rollo May (1967; May et al., 1958).

May is critical of traditional scientific approaches to the understanding of the human race because, like Sartre (1956), he believes that analysis destroys or loses sight of true human nature. Explanations on the basis of present mechanisms, past experience, evolutionary sequences, or environmental forces fail to permit us to understand an individual's "being" and the choices he or she makes. Thus, new scientific methods must be found which will be more adequate for revealing human nature.

May (1958, p. 37) begins one of his discussions of existential psychotherapy in the following fashion:

The fundamental contribution of existential therapy is its understanding of man as *being*. It does not deny the validity of dynamisms and the study of specific behavior patterns in their rightful places. But it holds that drives or dynamics, by whatever name one calls them, can be understood only in the context of the structure of the existence of the person we are dealing with. The distinctive character of existential analysis is, thus, that it is concerned with *ontology,* the science of being. . . .

The chief problem facing persons in our society, as May views it, is the closing or narrowing of their minds to experience as a result of anxiety, with the consequent reduction of the opportunities for them to actualize themselves as individual beings. As May puts it (1967, p. 41): "Neurotic anxiety . . . consists of the shrinking of consciousness, the blocking off of awareness; and when it is prolonged it leads to a feeling of depersonalization and apathy. Anxiety is losing the sense of one's self in relation to the objective world." The anxiety occurs because the core values that a person identifies with his or her existence as a self have been threatened. Thus, people's "sickness" is the method by which they attempt to preserve their threatened being. May sees modern society as having created in its young people particular vulnerability to anxiety. On this he writes (1967, p. 70):

First, I wish to submit a hypothesis, namely, that when the presuppositions, the unconscious assumptions of values, in a society are generally accepted, the individual can meet threats on the basis of these presuppositions. He then reacts to threats with fear, not anxiety. But when the presuppositions in a society are themselves threatened, the individual has no basis on which to orient himself when he is confronted with a specific threat. Since the *inner citadel of society itself is in a state of confusion and traumatic change during such periods,* the individual has no solid ground on which to meet the specific threats which confront him. The result for the individual is profound disorientation, psychological confusion, and hence chronic or acute panic and anxiety. Now is this not the state of our culture in the twentieth century? It is my belief, in other words, that the disintegration of the presuppositions of our historical culture . . . is intimately related to the widespread anxiety in the twentieth century. And it is also related to the particular difficulties of the human dilemma we must confront in our time.

In the absence of accepted external guideposts, individuals must find within themselves a basis for being oriented, and this in May's view is what stimulated the growth of psychoanalysis and, later, of existentialism. The "human dilemma" May refers to is our simultaneous capacity to experience self as a *subject*—for example, wanting, wishing, feeling—and as an *object* (which we can observe) oriented to external demands and having to do something rather than choosing to do so. Theories of human behavior which exclusively emphasize external forces, as well as those which in opposite fashion emphasize internal determinants of human behavior, must inevitably be incomplete and fail to comprehend humanity. In actuality, both categories are necessary features of psychological science, of meaningful living, and of psychotherapy. To discover oneself and to be open to experience means to recognize both sets of forces, one's inner experience as it is and the external culture and pressures to which one must respond. The goals of therapy are (1) to reverse the narrowing or closing of consciousness that has occurred under threat and anxiety and (2) to open up one's "being" to awareness.

Concerning the goal of the therapeutic encounter, May (1967, p. 109) writes:

Our chief concern in therapy is with the potentiality of the human being. The goal of therapy is to help the patient actualize his potentialities. The joy of the process of actualizing becomes more important than the pleasure of discharged energy—though that itself, in its own context, obviously has pleasurable aspects too. The goal of therapy is not the absence of anxiety, but rather the changing of neurotic anxiety into normal anxiety, and the development of the capacity to live with and use normal anxiety. The patient after therapy may well bear more anxiety than he had before, but it will be conscious anxiety and he will be able to use it constructively. Nor is the goal the absence of guilt feeling, but rather the transformation of neurotic guilt, together with the development of the capacity to use this normal guilt creatively.

No special technique of psychotherapy is advocated. According to May, existential analysis should not be regarded as a special school or system of psychotherapy, but rather as a set of *attitudes* about people and how to study them. That is, it is characterized best by the suppositions it makes about human beings, rather than by techniques. Such a statement is naturally quite confusing to one who wishes to understand the therapy, since it is what the therapist does, somehow, not what he or she privately thinks, that distinguishes one treatment from another. Yet technique and abstract analysis is, for the existentialist, an inappropriate concern, since presumably "being" cannot be analyzed without destroying it. The existential psychotherapist has had extensive training and experience in psychoanalysis, or some other form of insight therapy. May identifies himself, for example, as a psychologist trained in psychoanalysis in the neo-Freudian, interpersonal school (1958, pp. 76–77):

Existential analysis is a way of understanding human existence, and its representatives believe that one of the chief (if not *the* chief) blocks to the understanding of human beings in Western culture is precisely the overemphasis on technique, an overemphasis which goes along with the tendency to see the human being as an object to be calculated, managed, "analyzed." Our Western tendency has been to believe that *understanding follows technique;* if we get the right technique, then we can penetrate the riddle of the patient, or, as said popularly with amazing perspicacity, we can "get the other person's number." The existential approach holds the exact opposite; namely, that *technique follows understanding.* . . .

When editing this volume, therefore, we had difficulty piecing together information about what an existential therapist would actually *do* in given situations in therapy, but we kept asking the question, for we knew American readers would be particularly concerned with this area. It is clear at the outset that what distinguishes existential therapy is not what the therapist would specifically do, say, in meeting anxiety or confronting resistance, or getting life history and so forth, but rather the *context* of his therapy. . . . The context is the patient not as a set of psychic dynamisms but as a human being who is choosing, committing, and pointing himself toward something right now; the context is dynamic, immediately real, and present.

The traditions of existential psychotherapy are more European (where it has flourished) than American, although there appears to be increasing interest in it in this country, especially among those who decry the American mechanistic, functionalistic, and pragmatic point of view, which in the tradition of Darwin and Dewey evaluates actions in terms of their adjustive value. Existential psychotherapy is quite clearly an *insight therapy,* militantly *phenomenological* in orientation, critical of, yet with close ties to, psychoanalytic and neoanalytic approaches.

VIKTOR FRANKL'S LOGOTHERAPY

Frankl was initially trained in psychoanalysis, but three years in German concentration camps, including Auschwitz, pushed him toward existen-tialism and served as the personal backdrop for the development of logotherapy. The Greek word "logos" is translated as "meaning," and Frankl's psychotherapy (1963, 1965)—a version of existential analysis—emphasizes the person's search for meaning. For Frankl, the "will to meaning" is the most fundamental of all human motives. Without it one experiences an "existential vacuum." Along with May, Frankl feels that this is widespread in today's complex and confused times. Psychotherapy deals with problems of human adjustment, and logotherapy, which is concerned with the spiritual aspects of life, complements but does not substitute for psychotherapy. It is designed to help patients find an aim and purpose in life, to help them cope with existential crises. Thus, its emphasis is on value conflicts. It pushes the idea that the person has responsibility for his or her own beliefs and actions. Attention is directed not toward the past history of the person, but the present and future.

In one technique, called "paradoxical intention," Frankl encourages patients to wish for precisely what they fear will happen, and to do so with as much humor and self-detachment as possible. He gives an example of a young medical student who would tremble when the instructor approached her, and who as part of the treatment said to herself whenever he entered, "Oh, here is the instructor! Now I'll show him what a good trembler I am—I'll really show him how to tremble." But whenever she deliberately tried to tremble, she was unable to do so! Another technique, "de-reflection," requires patients to ignore rather than attend to what is troubling them and to concentrate on some more positive striving in its place. As shall be seen in the next chapter, these techniques are surprisingly similar to procedures used by behavior therapists. However, Frankl uses these and other techniques to lead patients toward awareness of their own values, to feel a sense of control over and responsibility for their actions and reactions, and to learn to deal with the existential problems of meaning that are troubling them.

FRITZ PERLS'S GESTALT THERAPY

Fritz Perls was also educated in psychoanalysis and was an escapee from the Hitler years in Germany, moving to the United States in 1951 and writing *Gestalt Therapy* in that year with two collaborators. Gestalt therapy, which for many years has been used at the Esalen Institute at Big Sur, California, is better geared to group therapy than individual, although there is growing interest in it for individuals as well. Gestalt means *whole* or totality, and it expresses the outlook of a number of influential and dissident psychologists in the 1920s that the whole was more than the sum of its parts, and that analysis of its elements or components destroys it. Perls draws on this outlook in psychotherapy, emphasizing balance and the integration of part functions in the total person. He also incorporates psychoanalytic and existential concepts into his system as well, focusing greatly on immediate experience as in the case of other existential therapies (see also Perls, 1967, 1969).

The goal of gestalt therapy is to restore the person's inherent capacity for growth by helping him or her get in touch with unrecognized needs and by encountering the environment creatively. The patient is urged to become "what he really is," to see through his facades, games, and defenses, and to be aware of and live in the "now," which is all that exists. He is encouraged to communicate in the present tense, rather than reminiscing about the past or dreaming of the future.

The focus on the awareness of *now* in gestalt therapy is nicely illustrated in the following brief therapeutic excerpt (Levitsky and Perls, 1970, p. 143). In the dialog, "T" stands for therapist and "P" for patient:

T.: What are you aware of now?

P.: Now I am aware of talking to you. I see the others in the room. I'm aware of John squirming. I can feel the tension in my shoul-

ders. I'm aware that I get anxious as I say this.

T.: How do you experience the anxiety?

ON A SUNNY EVENING

On a purple, sun-shot evening
Under wide-flowering chestnut trees
Upon the threshold full of dust
Yesterday, today, the days are all like these.

Trees flower forth in beauty,
Lovely too their very wood all gnarled and old
That I am half afraid to peer
Into their crowns of green and gold.

The sun has made a veil of gold
So lovely that my body aches.
Above, the heavens shriek with blue
Convinced I've smiled by some mistake.
The world's abloom and seems to smile.
I want to fly but where, how high?
If in barbed wire, things can bloom
Why couldn't I? I will not die!

1944   Anonymous
Written by the children in Barracks L 318 and L 417,
ages 10–16 years.

FIGURE 13-3 Anonymous, 1944. Written by children in the Terezin concentration camp. Of the 15,000 children confined there, about 100 came back. (From *I Never Saw Another Butterfly*, McGraw-Hill, 1964.)

P.: I hear my voice quiver. My mouth feels dry. I talk in a very halting way.

T.: Are you aware of what your eyes are doing?

P.: Well, now I realize that my eyes keep looking away—

T.: Can you take responsibility for that?

P.: —that I keep looking away from you.

T.: Can you be your eyes now? Write the dialogue for them.

P.: I am Mary's eyes. I find it hard to gaze steadily. I keep jumping and darting about. . . .

The awareness continuum has inexhaustible applications. Primarily, however, it is an effective way of guiding the individual to the firm bedrock of his experiences and away from the endless verbalizations, explanations, interpretations. Awareness of body feelings and of sensations and perceptions constitutes our most certain—perhaps our only certain—knowledge. Relying on information provided in awareness is the best method of implementing Perls's dictum to "lose your mind and come to your senses."

The use of the awareness continuum is the Gestalt therapist's best means of leading the patient away from the emphasis on the *why* of behavior (psychoanalytic interpretation) and toward the *what* and the *how* of behavior (experiential psychotherapy):

P.: I feel afraid.

T.: How do you experience the fear?

P.: I can't see you clearly. My hands are perspiring. . . .

As we help the patient rely on his senses ("return to his senses"), we also help him distinguish between the reality *out there* and the frightening goblins he manufactures in his own fantasies:

P.: I'm sure people will despise me for what I just said.

T.: Go around the room and look at us carefully. Tell me what you *see,* what your eyes—not your imaginings—tell you.

P.: (*after some moments of exploration and discovery*) Well, actually people don't *look* so rejecting! Some of you even look warm and friendly!

T.: What do you experience now?

P.: I'm more relaxed now.

The flow of communication is that among equals in the group, including between the patient and therapist. The patient's language must also reflect his or her own responsibility for feelings and actions, rather than conveying the sense of being a passive recipient of experience. Patients must focus on the content of their immediate experience and seek awareness of what is happening; dreams are used in this process of seeking awareness. Korchin (in press) has aptly summarized some of the procedures of gestalt therapy in the following passage:

Characteristic of Gestalt therapy are the numerous "games" or exercises developed by Perls and his colleagues. There are *role-playing games,* in which the patient has to enact different roles or parts of himself. Thus, where there seems to be a conflict between the "top-dog" (i.e., superego or "should") and the "underdog" (the depreciated self), the patient has to act out each portion in turn, presenting the top-dog's then the underdog's point of view. Other "splits" in the personality, as for example between masculine and feminine components, are similarly externalized and dramatized. In the game of *"I take responsibility"* the patient must keep adding the phrase "and I take responsibility for it" after comments on facets of his behavior. Thus, "I am aware that my arm is moving . . . and I take responsibility for it." In *"Exaggeration"* the patient amplifies and exaggerates a minor, perhaps incomplete or abortive, movement so that he can feel its full import. Related is a game in which the patient is asked to repeat over and over and often louder and louder a comment the therapist identifies as significant. In *"I have a secret"* each member of a group thinks of a personal secret and then tries to imagine how others would react to knowing it. Still without revealing it, members may then be asked to boast about how terrible their secrets are. In this fashion, Perls proposes, feelings of guilt and shame can be explored. These and comparable games are discussed by Levitsky and Perls (1970).

GROUP PSYCHOTHERAPY

Nowadays a considerable proportion of psychodynamically oriented or insight therapy is practiced in groups (of about five to fifteen patients) rather than with individuals, and, as noted earlier, gestalt therapy is most often offered in this form. There are many theoretical and procedural variations (see, for example, Shaffer and Galinsky, 1974).

The main advantage of the group therapeutic situation is that a patient interacts with other persons who have similar or diverse problems, and this interaction itself has certain values that individual psychotherapy lacks. For example, the simple exposure of a person to the problems and experiences of others can lead to the recognition that others are similarly unhappy or disturbed and can increase the confidence of a person who feels inadequate in the face of life's problems. The group situation also offers opportunities for a person to improve his or her relationship with others by learning how to relate to them better. Moreover, patients can and often do support one another, giving friendship, tolerance, and so on. When support comes from a fellow patient, it can mean more than when it comes from the therapist, since the other patients are not paid to give it.

A second advantage is that group therapy offers the therapist the opportunity to see a fairly considerable number of patients in a therapeutic situation at the same time. In mental hospitals, a single ward can be divided into several groups and seen by a therapist for an hour or so every week, thus spreading professional services much more widely among patients. Individual therapy is so time-consuming and demanding of therapeutic resources that there is an increasing tendency to utilize group therapeutic situations more and more as a treatment method.

A third advantage is that the therapist and patient have a superior chance to observe in action the patient's neurotic ways of relating to others. In individual therapy, all knowledge about interpersonal styles comes either from the patient's report, filtered through his or her blind spots, or from the patient-therapist interaction. However, this is a relationship which is difficult for therapists to observe accurately, since they are themselves involved in it. It is also a relationship which is unlikely to include the patient's entire repertoire of social behaviors, since the therapist is the only other person involved. The therapist thus has the opportunity to observe directly the interaction of all the members and to learn much about their characteristic social roles or styles of life. This information can be utilized later in individual contacts with the patients.

The therapist in the group situation commonly remains in the background, as in insight therapy in general, permitting and encouraging a free flow of interpersonal relationships between the members of the group. As a patient discusses his or her problems or symptoms, others offer their points of view or present some of their own experiences. Discussions ensue which include interpretations and criticisms of each other's attitudes. The therapist may enter the discussion to clarify or summarize some of the important issues or may draw out those who are not actively participating.

A comparatively new version of group therapy—"family group therapy"—involves treatment of family members as a group, usually husband, wife, and children (see Bell, 1975). The most important rationale for the simultaneous treatment of all or several family members is that the adjustmental problems of each individual member are usually related to interdependencies with other members. A husband's problems are likely to be bound up in his relationship with his wife and children; similarly for the wife. Furthermore, as therapists who have worked with children have long attested, treatment of the child alone is rarely as effective as simultaneous treatment of the adults on whom the child is dependent. The advantage gained by the therapist in seeing the emotional interactions of the various family members at first hand is most striking in family group therapy in which all interact together and with the therapist. Moreover, if one of the main functions of group therapy is to promote greater ability on the part of the individuals comprising the group to relate effectively to each other, this function is precisely the reason why group therapy with members of a family is so useful; each individual family member stands to gain greatly from more satisfactory interpersonal relations among the family as a whole.

Group therapy might be distinguished from one of its interesting offshoots, the Sensitivity Training Group (or *T-group*), whose purposes are not, strictly speaking, treatment of personal disorders but, rather, the acquisition of better awareness and understanding of the dynamics of interpersonal relationships and the cultivation of interpersonal skills. In the T-group, students, the executives of a company, the teachers in a school, professionals seeking understanding of themselves and others, for example, are brought together to interact and to learn from this interaction. The leader should be an experienced professional who can stimulate the members to react and can effectively control the reaction. In the usual group situation, oblique and guarded reference to feelings is the typical currency of interaction. In the T-group, the effort is made to get the members to express how they actually feel about things and toward each other and to interact on this emotional level, which is usually below the surface.

The T-group specialist assumes that such exploration of implicit emotional forces to make them explicit makes possible more awareness, not only of how groups function, but of how individuals relate to others and others to them. The T-group is an object lesson in interpersonal relations. The danger is that interpersonal threats may get out of hand and leave scars, or that special vulnerabilities of the person will be exposed without there being an opportunity to work them out. The mere exposure of feelings cannot be, in itself, desirable, unless such feelings can be explored fully and successfully managed. Therefore, in the hands of an ineffective leader, T-groups engender considerable psychological risks to the individual and to the natural group. When such groups are skillfully handled, members are thought to grow from the experience and to become capable of relating better to others.

Shaffer and Galinsky (1974) give a realistic though fictitious example of a group therapy session conducted from a humanistic-existential point of view. The group consists of four men, three women, and Dr. R, the therapist; they have been meeting for 2½ years. Five of the patients have been steady members of the group, and the other two joined it during the previous ten months. Part of the authors' very instructive account of the session proceeds as follows (pp. 94–98):

The group begins without any structuring from Dr. R, who is silent. Ruth, a "hippie"-type girl in her early twenties, is talking about the fact that Bob, the man with whom she is living, is probably having an affair with her best friend, Terry. She knows he is attracted to Terry, and each of them has recently, in talking to her about the other, made some ambiguous and erotically-tinged remarks. Ruth doesn't know what to do about this. She is annoyed with herself for being jealous, for she knows that whatever Bob has going with Terry is a purely "physical" thing. He made it clear to her when they decided to live together that he did not feel sexually bound by conventional notions of a monogamous relationship; yet she feels hurt and betrayed by Terry. Then at other times, she feels that she is being old-fashioned, that it is obviously just a sex thing for Terry, who is basically interested in another, unavailable man.

Mort, a brunette man in his middle thirties, razzes her. He says: That's right, Ruthie, Bob just has too much love in him to share with just one woman; besides, you love both of them so much this is really just an act of generosity on your part—you're giving two people you love to one another!

Ruth reacts with a slight giggle, and continues to discuss the problem. Mort continues to bait her. Felicia interrupts at this point, saying that it makes her uncomfortable to see the way Mort is baiting Ruth and the way she allows him to do it.

Ruth interrupts, saying: But what difference does it make? I'm used to Mort's sarcasm. What I'm worried about is Bob. Felicia says: Yes, but you take the same crap from both of them. Mort joins in, saying: Yes, she's so goddamned dumb with those rose-colored glasses on; doesn't she know what the world is like? Boy, she really asks for it.

Ralph then joins in for a moment: She may ask for it, Mort, but I notice you're always there firstest with the mostest to give it to her.

Felicia says in a quiet voice: Ruth isn't happy until she has something to make her really miserable.

Ruth then says: Would everyone stop talking about me as though I weren't here?

Felicia expresses pleasure at Ruth's ability to speak up. Dr. R then wonders when Felicia is going to start talking up for herself. Felicia at first reacts with defensiveness and confusion, saying: I *am* speaking up.

Dr. R replies: Yes, but on behalf of Ruth, which is your usual way of participating. Perhaps this is partly your way of testing out what you're learning as a social work student. Look, it's okay with me, I like having a co-therapist, but I find myself wishing that you'd find a way to take as well as give; sometimes I sense that underneath that competent, supportive exterior there's a needy, bewildered little girl looking for comfort.

Felicia responds: Yes, I know what you mean, and there are day-to-day problems that I could bring up and at times would like to bring up; but they always seem so insignificant alongside what the others introduce; I guess I'm not ready yet.

Dr. R replies: Okay—I just thought I'd give you a little nudge.

For a few moments everyone is silent. Dr. R asks the group members what they are experiencing. Alice speaks up and says she was thinking about Ruth's problem, and wondering why Ruth was suddenly quiet. Ruth speaks up, saying: I felt criticized by Al in a way—when he pointed out how rarely Felicia brought up her problems, I thought maybe he was also saying that I do the opposite—always take up the group's time.

Dr. R: No, Ruth, I don't feel that way; I feel you have the right to ask for as much from the group as you can.

Ruth: Well, anyway, I don't know what to do about Bob. I guess I should just wait and let this affair between him and Terry blow over—that is, if there *is* an affair; probably if I wasn't so insecure I'd just accept it for what it is.

Nelson: I don't know, Ruth—I could see being plenty jealous. I know I would be if Harriet (i.e., his current girl friend) was making it with some guy.

Mort, with heavy-handed sarcasm, says: But

Nelson, you're so square, so bourgeois; you have this monogamy hang-up; both she and Bob have complete sexual freedom—the only difference between them being that he can act on his while she can't act on hers; besides, she's supposed to understand that he loves her more than any other woman he screws because he's living with her—so what does she have to be worried about?

Ruth answers Mort: I'm not sure that the idea you ridicule is so crazy, Mort; Bob is a very unusual guy—he's able to love more than one woman at once, and he's made it clear that in many ways I'm very special to him—that's why I get annoyed with myself for being jealous.

Mort becomes angrier and raises his voice, shouting at Ruth: Bob has one helluva good deal with you because you're so fucking blind: he can ball anybody he wants and still be welcomed home by your bleeding heart!

Ralph says: Lay off her, Morty—do you want to help her or destroy her? Ruth then says to Ralph: I don't mind his tone—I just want to figure out if he's right.

Dr. R says: Mort and Ralph both seem to sense the same thing about you, Ruth—that without realizing it you let other people abuse you; Morty is concentrating on how you get it from Bob and Ralph is bothered by how Morty is talking to you.

Ruth asks: But if Mort is right, how is he abusing me?

Alice answers: By speaking to you with contempt!

Ruth says: I think he feels that's the only way he can get through to me; and if he's right—if I *am* being naive with Bob—I want to find out, and I don't care *how* I find out.

Dr. R says: Ruth, you keep so busy trying to figure out what is right and what is fair that you don't instinctively notice that Bob and Mort don't give two damns about whether or not they hurt you. But what impresses me is the irritation and impatience that I am beginning to feel. For just a second now I had the strong impulse to really start yelling at you, to tell you to stop letting everyone treat you like dirt—but then I would have in a sense been doing the same thing myself. So my hunch is that you have some kind of need to provoke anger.

Ruth, seemingly bewildered, asks: But why would I want to provoke you? Dr. R replies: I feel you continuing in the same vein; the innocent young girl, with a perplexed, almost eager expression on your face, still trying to figure it all out.

Ruth asks: But what's wrong with that? Aren't I supposed to discover the reasons for what I do?

Dr. R answers Ruth: Again I'm finding myself starting to become irritated; until you get in touch with what you're feeling right now I don't think we're going to get anywhere.

Ruth is quiet for a minute, while the rest of the group seem attentive. Then she says: I don't know—I guess I feel sad more than anything else, and somehow inadequate; I feel like you're all mad at me, and like you're probably right to be, but I can't figure out just why—mainly that I'm being stupid about something; if I could only figure it out, then I could stop doing it and you'd all stop being so impatient with me.

Dr R intervenes: So you mainly are aware of our anger with you—not yours with us, right? Ruth answers in the affirmative. Dr. R says: And what you're mainly aware of is your intense need to reason it all out, so you can then find a way to get us to stop being irritated with you.

Ruth says: That's right; and this feels like the story of my life; since I was very young I somehow was doing things wrong enough for my mother to get very mad at me—but somehow I could never be sure why.

At this point Felicia speaks up and says: I can understand that feeling: it's like: I'll be any way you want, so long as you love me. Mort then speaks up, saying: That's very good, Felicia, very empathic. I think we should give you A+ in Casework Methods II for that particular remark.

Alice quickly says: You know, Mort, when you get nasty like that I really feel like killing you. Mort is silent, and no one talks for a minute. Alice suddenly says: So why don't you turn your hostility on me? I'm waiting—my heart is pounding. Mort asks her what she means. She answers: I mean that when I say something like what I just said I expect to get some of your venom, and I imagine some of it would reach its mark and really get to me; so when I don't get it—like Felicia and Ruth seem to—I wonder why am I so lucky? When will my turn come?—and then I resent being so damned afraid of you.

Mort comments: There you all go again; because I say what I think and remind people of the kind of crap that passes for brilliant insight around here and don't play your love-in game, I become some kind of hostile monster who everybody is terrified of.

Dr. R breaks in, saying: Maybe if you allowed yourself to believe that people could be scared of you you'd have to start getting in touch with your own terror. Mort responds: Gee, Doc, you're getting more profound than Felicia—are the two of you in some sort of competition?

Dr. R says: Mort, level with me—do you believe the group when they say they're afraid of you? Mort answers: No. Dr. R rejoins: Well, I don't know how to convince you that they are; I know that *I'm* feeling it right now—as I often do when I start to tangle with you.

Mort says to him: You're just saying that to make your theoretical point. Dr. R answers: Bullshit! I don't tell you I'm feeling something if I'm not! Mort asks him: But what are you scared of? Dr. R: Probably of what you'll do if your rage gets great enough; I don't feel it right now, but I remember asking myself that same question last session—what *am* I afraid of in

you?—and my immediate fantasy was of your going really berserk and wrecking the office— but *completely* wrecking it, and of us standing by helplessly letting you do it.

Mort says to him: I still have the feeling you're putting me on. Dr. R replies: But isn't that your mistrust of everyone? Who does level with you completely as far as you're concerned? Mort answers: I don't know for sure—I'm never sure. Dr. R says: My guess is that if you had to admit that others are terrified, you might have to begin wondering why you never get frightened; you're very comfortable with your anger, but you don't ever express fear.

Dr. R then adds: By the way, Mort, I think my fear of your physical destructiveness is irrational, and probably has something to do with some uncomfortableness I still have with my own anger. But I also know that Alice's feeling of being intimidated by you is real.

At this point Mort doesn't say anything; he seems a bit red in the face, as though caught off guard. After a few seconds, Felicia says to Dr. R: I don't think you should have told him your fantasy—it probably will make Mort that much more afraid of his rage. And it sounds a bit pat to me—the same thing as what Mort likes to make fun of you for when you overplay the part of the "for-real," experiential therapist, letting us know just where you "are at" with everything.

Dr. R says: Well, Felicia, I invite you to become your own kind of therapist in your own style real soon—I sure as hell don't have a monopoly on technique; I do know that I felt quite genuine in saying what I did to Mort, and that it also felt great to hear you criticize me like that just now.

Felicia says: I can't imagine ever feeling that way about somebody's criticism of me. Dr. R rejoins: Well, I didn't get there overnight; I can remember in my earlier days not liking it one bit when my patients had something negative to say about me—or when anybody else did for that matter, but I was a rather different person then.

And so the session continues. As was the case in our illustrative psychoanalytic session which concerned essentially the same group . . . interaction in the present situation remains reasonably lively, and by the end of the meeting all participants have spoken up spontaneously, although a few have been considerably more active than others. While the analyst, Dr. M, remained silent for periods as long as seven or eight minutes in the psychoanalytic group, Dr. R, our existential-experiential therapist, is more active; for example, from the beginning of the session from which we drew an illustrative segment to its end, the longest period of time during which he said nothing lasted about five minutes.

SUMMING UP

In this chapter I have reviewed a highly diverse set of psychodynamic or insight-centered approaches to psychotherapy. We began with the orthodox Freudian outlook and approach—the grandfather of them all—then briefly considered the neo-Freudian concepts of Adler, Jung, Rank, and Fromm, and finally proceeded to the humanistic-existential approaches of Rogers, May, Frankl, and Perls. The group approach to psychodynamic therapy has also been discussed and illustrated. Such a review does not nearly exhaust the existing variety of psychodynamic approaches, but it illustrates some of the main themes. Much more elaborate accounts can be found in Korchin (in press) and in Shaffer and Galinsky (1974), who have reviewed eleven models of group therapy.

Not only do the techniques of treatment sometimes differ among the various approaches (though this has not been detailed here), perhaps even more importantly, their theoretical or philosophical outlooks concerning human nature diverge greatly as well. They have all been put together into the same chapter because of what they have in common. All are insight-oriented, or psychodynamic in outlook, even though the precise nature of the desired insight need not be the same. All presuppose that adequate adjustment and functioning at one's full potential has been blocked by forces of which the person is unaware or only dimly aware. And whether the focus is on the person's past history (as in Freudian psychoanalysis) or on the person's present ways of relating to his or her world (as in Perls's approach), the key therapeutic task is for individuals to discover themselves and to use their new insights to change their ways of managing or experiencing life.

CHAPTER 14 BEHAVIOR THERAPY

Behavior therapy arose as a protest against the psychoanalytic viewpoint on which most psychodynamic or insight psychotherapy is based today. In contrast with the insight therapy view, which emphasizes that hidden, unconscious forces underlie disturbed behavior, the philosophical origins of behavior therapy lie in the tradition of academic learning theory. To state it in oversimplified terms, personality is seen primarily as a function of outside environmental stimuli, social interactions, and social roles, rather than of inner forces. In its most militant form, subjective feelings, unconscious processes, or internal psychological events are totally rejected as scientific concepts and objects of inquiry; they are seen as incapable of verification and of no value in formulating the observable rules of behavior. Instead, the center of interest lies in observable behavior and the environmental conditions that shape it. Emphasis on the principles of learning is illustrated by a recent statement by one of the protagonists of behavior therapy, L. J. Reyna (1964, p. 169), who writes:

In the last fifteen years, growing both out of skepticism toward the claims of psychoanalytic theory and practice, and paradoxically, out of learning theory translations of analytic therapy accounts (e.g., Dollard and Miller, 1950), the influence of learning theory on therapeutic techniques has become more systematic and widespread. This is a logical development, since if therapy is viewed as a learning process, why not deliberately seek conditioning methods?

BASIC PRINCIPLES

Behavior therapists view neurosis or psychopathology in the following way: Neurosis is learned. What is learned is not some mysterious inner condition, but behavior, that is, words, actions, and emotional states that are unadaptive and undesirable and that the person would like to be rid of. These undesirable habits of response were acquired in the first place because some time in the past they succeeded in permitting the person to avoid painful experiences (aversive events). Now in the present they tend to be repeated, not only in the presence of the original aversive event, but also in a host of situations that are somehow similar to it. It is these undesirable responses that must be eliminated by psychotherapy.

Psychotherapy is not defined by the behavior therapist in terms of insight and as a reorganization of the personality, but as the *elimination of symptoms* and the learning of more adjustive responses. As Reyna puts it, "Psychotherapy can be viewed as a set of procedures designed to eliminate a variety of emotionally disturbing responses and useless, undesirable behaviors and to create more efficient behaviors for coping with designated everyday tasks, persons and situations" (Reyna, 1964, p. 169).

Another protagonist of the behavior therapy view, Leonard Krasner (1963, p. 60), puts it this way:

The key concepts in this new approach to psychotherapy are social reinforcement and behavior control. Social reinforcement refers to the use and manipulation of environmental stimuli to reward preselected classes of behavior in such a way as to increase the probability of their reoccurring. Psychotherapy is viewed as a lawful influence process within the broader context of studies of behavior controls, studies which investigate the conditions that change behavior.

HISTORICAL BACKGROUND

Actually, the concept of deconditioning as a therapeutic principle is not new. Even before learning theory became a significant enterprise within psychology, a technique called "negative practice" (Dunlap, 1917, 1932) was employed in the treatment of symptoms such as stammering, facial tics, and so on. It required the patient actually to practice the bad habit, presumably to place it under volitional control. Such procedures were referred to as "deconditioning," "desensitization," or "reeducation." One early textbook of abnormal psychology (Dorcus and Shaffer, 1945) gave considerable space to desensitization and reeducation.

However, such procedures did not have great impact on the practice of psychotherapy until the 1950s, when interest began to accelerate and an active professional movement of behavior therapists took shape. The use of behavior therapy in clinical practice has become so widespread in the last two decades that it can now be considered one of the major approaches to therapeutic practice.

The beginnings of the behavioristic ideology in psychology on which behavior therapy or behavior modification rests can best be traced to John Watson (1924), whose attack on psychoanalytic thought is illustrated in the quotation that follows:

I venture to predict that 10 years from now an analyst using Freudian concepts and Freudian terminology will be placed on the same plane as a phrenologist [one holding a long-discredited belief that bumps and depressions on the skull can be used to assess personality]. And yet analysis based on behavioristic principles is here to stay and is a necessary profession in society—to be placed on a par with internal medicine and surgery. By analysis I mean studying the cross section of personality in some such way as I have outlined it. This will be the equivalent of diagnosis. Combined with this will go unconditioning and then conditioning. These will constitute the curative side. Analysis as such has no virtue—no curative value. New habits, verbal, manual and visceral, of such and such kinds, will be the prescriptions the psychopathologist will write. [Parenthetical statement added.]

Behavior therapists are fond of citing a famous study by Watson and Rayner (1920) in which an eleven-month-old infant, Albert, was given a white rat to play with. Each time the rat was presented, a loud noise was also introduced. After five such simultaneous pairings of the rat and the noise, the rat—which had originally been a neutral stimulus—now evoked an emotional reaction of fear even when presented without the noise. In effect, the fear had been *conditioned* to the sights and sounds of the rat, and in time it generalized to other animals and furry objects, persisting even when the rat was presented to Albert four months later. Watson and Rayner even anticipated behavior therapy by suggesting that if the conditioned fear stimulus (the white rat) was presented in association with pleasant stimulation, the fear could be eliminated or, in effect, deconditioned. As we shall see, this is the sort of procedure, called reciprocal inhibition therapy, that was later used by Joseph Wolpe (1958, 1974), a psychiatrist and early pioneer of behavior therapy.

Watson and Rayner's vision of deconditioning was almost immediately realized in another classic experiment reported by developmental psychologist Mary Cover Jones (1924). Jones employed the behavior of eating to eliminate a child's fear of a rabbit. Presenting the rabbit first at a safe distance when the child was very hungry, she fed the child; at each additional feeding, Jones brought the rabbit a bit closer, so that eventually the rabbit failed to arouse fear even when the child was not eating.

Other interpretations of Jones's observation are possible. For example, the effects of the counterconditioning procedure may have nothing to do with "conditioning" as such. Rather, these effects might well depend on meanings and interpretations that the person derives from the experience. Thus, as the rabbit is brought closer, the child discovers that it does not act in the fashion anticipated. The trick has been to permit the child to *discover* that his fears that the rabbit

will jump on him or hurt him are really groundless. Or, as a patient imagines a frightening experience in the context of a safe and relaxing therapeutic situation, he or she begins to discover that the imagined experience is never followed by the harmful outcome that was always expected and that has always occasioned neurotic avoidance. In the treatment situation, the patient begins to think over what is happening, discriminating for the first time between real danger and his or her unreasonable fear. This interpretation emphasizes the *meanings* achieved by the patient through the experiences in therapy, rather than the concept of simple conditioning that is assumed by many behavior therapists. Many present-day behavior therapists are beginning to interpret the processes of conditioning employed in behavior therapy in this way (for example, Goldfried and Goldfried, 1975; Meichenbaum, 1974), an outlook which might be referred to as "cognitive behavior therapy." Such a position narrows the gap somewhat between psychodynamic therapies and behavior therapies.

The key distinction between psychodynamic and behavior therapies seems to lie in their respective *conceptions of the symptom.* The former, as noted earlier, consider the symptom to be comparatively unimportant, mainly as a superficial indication of a neurotic process of some kind. The neurotic process must be uncovered and overcome in order for the patient to become better adapted. To the behavior therapist this is mysticism and nonsense. The symptom does not symbolize some deeper problem: *it* itself is the problem, and it can and should be eliminated without changing other things. Since the symptom was acquired through learning, the therapeutic effort should be directed at unlearning it. Somehow the original learning process must be reversed, using the same principles that brought it into being in the first place. To the insight therapist, removing the symptom is not a cure. Such removal without altering the basic neurotic process is dangerous, because what is eliminated is not the basic problem but only the superficial expression of it. No such underlying problem exists as far as the behavior therapist is concerned. The purpose of psychotherapy is to unlearn maladjustive behaviors and replace them with adjustive ones.

The behavior therapists have tended to present their views as an attack on insight psychotherapy, probably because they have been the "outs" trying to get "in." London (1964, pp. 75–76) gives an admirable description of this polemic:

Their attack is mounted all at once on every level against insight therapy: They accuse it technically of producing insight when it should properly elicit action, theoretically of inferring motives when it should be observing behaviors, and philosophically of wallowing in sentimental humanism when it should be courting toughminded mechanism.

As for goals of therapy, the [behavior therapists] allege that insight therapists delude themselves and, at their worst, defraud society, by claiming to sell self-knowledge, for this is what practically nobody comes to them to buy. Even knowing that their clients seek relief, not information, they stock their bazaars with certificates that license dispensation of a balm they do not have. Face to face with customers, they then produce a diagram of illness and a blueprint for repair, both always the same—they say he suffers from illusions that must dissipate when once he knows himself. Chief among them, and most illusory of all—he thinks that what he thinks is his trouble really is his trouble. Almost by sleight of mind, the sufferer's surface troubles are made secondary, and the rationalization with which the therapist diverted his attention from them to begin with launches him on his introspective voyage, and perhaps keeps him there forever—for when does a man really know himself? Perhaps this could all be justified, says the [behavior therapist], if in the course of this tortuous trip,

the trouble went away, but mostly this is not the case except for random errors of the therapist in which he slips and, accidentally using [behavior] therapy, cures. The [behavior] therapies protest that they alone try to stop the endless spiral which extends the doctor's function by anchoring their efforts on the proximate source of trouble: the symptom. In this respect, they truly are reactionary, for they thus return to what was also once the goal of insight.

STRATEGIES

In contrast with psychodynamic therapists, behavior therapists take far more active responsibility in the therapy. They attempt to influence the patient very directly and explicitly. Their treatment involves confronting the patient with conditions designed to produce unlearning of the undesirable response (the symptom) and to substitute desirable responses.

Two main types of conditioning models are employed in behavior therapy. One is called *classical conditioning* and has its origins in the work of the Nobel prize–winning Russian physiologist Ivan Pavlov (1941); the other is referred to as *operant conditioning* and is stressed by a distinguished psychologist, B. F. Skinner (1938). We should review these briefly before describing some of the tactical procedures of behavior therapy.

Pavlov had placed a dog in a harness to study the nervous reflexes in salivation and digestion. Flow of saliva is brought about, of course, by the presence of food in the dog's mouth. This is an innate physiological reflex. But Pavlov also noticed something else: Just the sight of food was also capable of producing salivation, and Pavlov realized that some purely psychological process was taking place. The inborn physiological response to food in the mouth had been conditioned, as Pavlov put it, to the *sight* of the food, which was originally incapable of producing salivation. This conditioning depended on the pairing of a natural physiological response with some other stimulus, say the sight of the food, or any other originally neutral stimulus such as a noise, a light, or a tone, which when connected with the food eventually came to elicit the response. This is *classical conditioning.* A more cognitive way of viewing the "conditioned reflex" is to say that the sight of the food had become a *signal* for the coming of food, which is the reinforcement or reward for the expectation that was generated by the signal. The same elements are present in Watson and Rayner's experiment (cited previously) as in the Pavlovian situation with the dog. Albert's rat came to elicit fear when the natural fear-producing stimulus, noise, was regularly paired with it. The fear reaction had been conditioned to sight of the rat.

Skinner's *operant conditioning* also involves repeated presentation of stimuli that eventually come to elicit some given response with which they have been paired. However, the arrangement of the pairing is different. An operant re-

sponse is an action that the animal normally makes for some reason or other while "operating" on the environment, as it were. Only there is no natural or biological stimulus that will automatically evoke it, as in the case of the salivation response. If, whenever an operant response is made, it is repeatedly followed by some reinforcement or reward, or by the avoidance of pain, it can be connected with or attached to some signal or cue, which will then elicit it. This happens, for example, when an animal trainer gives a command, say to come or sit, and the animal responds appropriately. In this conditioning sequence, the animal first must make the response; then by using rewards and speaking the command or giving a suitable hand signal, the trainer eventually gets the animal to make the response whenever the command (cue) is given. By always rewarding the desired response and ignoring one that is undesired, the response can be changed or *shaped* systematically. For example, a pigeon can be "taught" to hold its head high as it walks by regularly rewarding it (say with food) whenever it lifts its head slightly above

FIGURE 14-1 Ivan Pavlov watching a 1934 experiment with a dog. (Sovfoto.)

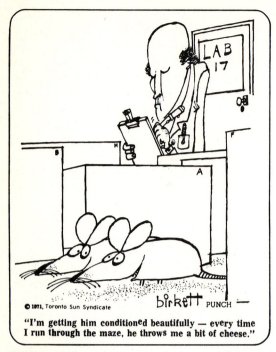

"I'm getting him conditioned beautifully — every time
I run through the maze, he throws me a bit of cheese."

FIGURE 14-2 Another way to look at conditioning.
(Drawing by Birkett, Punch Magazine; © 1971 Toronto
Sun Syndicate, Inc.)

with problems of living. The premise of behavior
therapy is that what has been learned or conditioned can be unlearned or deconditioned, so
that new responses can be acquired in its place.
Behavior therapy, then, seeks ways of helping the
person unlearn his maladjustive or undesirable
behaviors and replace them with more serviceable ones.

Consider, for example, the following use of the
Skinnerian concept of response shaping in a
troubled child (Wolf et al., 1964):

A three-year-old autistic (extremely withdrawn
and disturbed) boy lacked normal verbal and
social behavior. He did not eat properly, engaged in self-destructive behavior such as
banging his head and scratching his face, and
manifested ungovernable tantrums. He had
recently had a cataract operation, and required
glasses for the development of normal vision.
He refused to wear his glasses, however, and
broke pair after pair.

The technique of shaping was decided upon
to counteract the problem of glasses. Initially,
the boy was trained to expect a bit of candy or
fruit at the sound of a toy noisemaker. Then
training was begun with empty eyeglass
frames. First the boy was reinforced with the
candy or fruit for picking them up, then for
holding them, then for carrying them around,
then for bringing the frames closer to his eyes,
and then for putting the empty frames on his
head at any angle. Through successive approxi-
mations, he finally learned to wear his glasses
up to twelve hours a day. (See also Fig. 14-3.)

average and not rewarding it when its head is
held at a height lower than average. In this way
animal trainers can produce on command or
signal the remarkable repertoire of actions that
are often seen in circus acts.

Classical and operant or instrumental conditioning are both ways in which a response can be
learned or conditioned to a given stimulus, signal, or cue. Conditioning theorists see in these
models or patterns of conditioning basic ways in
which learning can take place in animals and in
humans. Fears can be conditioned in these ways,
along with any desirable or undesirable
(maladjustive) habits such as compulsions, sexual
inadequacies, debilitating social inhibitions, addictions, or any inept way of reacting or dealing

Procedures such as these involving systematically rewarding adjustive behaviors or punishing
maladjustive or undesirable ones have become
quite common in clinical work with disturbed
children, also with psychotic patients who have
been hospitalized for a long time. As we shall see
later, this basic pattern is being tried in "token
economy" programs in mental hospital wards.

The model for such programs is the operant conditioning and shaping procedures extensively employed by Skinner and his followers with pigeons, rats, and other animals in the laboratory.

The point was made earlier that it is possible to see the conditioning process (in which paired stimulus-response events become established as habits) in cognitive or meaning-centered terms. That is, such pairing or coupling of stimulus and response merely provides information about the environment which the person learns. Bandura (1974, p. 859) puts this as follows:

> Contrary to popular belief, the fabled reflexive conditioning in humans is largely a myth. *Conditioning* is simply a descriptive term for learning through paired experiences, not an explanation of how the changes come about. Originally, conditioning was assumed to occur automatically. On closer examination it turned out to be cognitively mediated. People do not learn despite repetitive paired experiences unless they recognize that events are correlated. . . . So-called conditioned reactions are largely self-activated on the basis of learned expectations rather than automatically evoked. The critical factor, therefore, is not that events occur together in time, but that people learn to predict them and to summon up appropriate anticipatory reactions.

TACTICS

In order to accomplish deconditioning and relearning, behavior therapists have developed a number of diverse tactics, all of which have in common the attempt to reverse what is presumed

FIGURE 14-3 These two autistic boys are shown receiving immediate positive reinforcement in the form of food for their social interactions in a play setting. (Allan Grant.)

to have been the original conditioning of the maladjustive response. Here we shall examine five such tactics or procedures: desensitization, aversion training, assertive training, the token economy, and modeling.

DESENSITIZATION (OR COUNTERCONDITIONING)

One could say that through conditioning certain normally neutral stimulus objects and events have been made "sensitive" in that the person becomes fearful in their presence. Moreover, because the person copes with this fear by *avoidance* of the fear-inducing or aversive stimulus, automatically acting to prevent confrontation with it, the maladjustive habit is never extinguished. In effect, the conditioned avoidance response prevents individuals from being in the presence of the fear stimulus without becoming fearful since they constantly avoid it at the first indication of its presence, thus narrowing the situations in which they can feel comfortable and participate. The conditioned fear or phobia and the habitual avoidance are troubling and maladjustive. The aversive stimulus must, therefore, be *desensitized,* that is, made incapable of generating the fear that produces the maladjustive avoidance response.

A version of this tactic has been used by Joseph Wolpe (1958, 1974) in which a desensitization procedure is coupled with relaxation training. Wolpe had been a practicing psychiatrist with a psychoanalytic orientation up until 1944, when he became interested in the writings of Pavlov and of Clark Hull, one of the American pioneers of learning theory. Out of this reading, he developed a therapeutic method which he called "reciprocal inhibition," a term borrowed from physiology. Physiologically speaking, activities of one muscle or nerve are sometimes antagonistic to those of others, so that when one responds, the other cannot. In the psychotherapeutic parallel, certain behavioral responses are considered antagonistic to others, and these can be substituted for the behavioral symptom which one wishes to eliminate.

Wolpe believes that all neurotic behaviors are consequences or expressions of *anxiety* and, therefore, that the response of anxiety must be eliminated. What is needed is to find responses that are inherently antagonistic to anxiety, that is, responses which reciprocally inhibit it. If, for any patient, the response that inhibits anxiety can be discovered, the unwanted symptom of the anxiety can then be controlled. If the anxiety-producing power of a stimulus is thus sufficiently weakened, the symptom produced by the anxiety need not then appear.

Wolpe usually employs one of a number of behaviors to inhibit anxiety. An example is the *conditioned verbal avoidance* response. The patient is given a series of harmless but painful electric shocks, but before being shocked he or she is instructed to say the word "calm" whenever the shocks become too strong. When the patient says "calm," Wolpe turns off the shock. The word "calm" eventually is associated in the therapeutic situation with relief from a painful experience. Therefore, whenever the patient subsequently experiences anxiety or tension in an everyday situation, he or she whispers the word "calm," which presumably reduces the anxiety just as saying the word gave protection in the therapeutic situation.

Another example is the use of sexual responses to cure sexual problems such as impotence. Wolpe assumes that the impotence is the result of anxiety, which results in sexual inhibition. Thus, the problem is to get the patient to attempt sex relations only when there is a *minimum of anxiety* (for example, in situations in which there is a clear desire), and to avoid those situations which are apt to be inhibiting. The patient might, for example, restrict himself or herself to a supportive sex partner who will cooperate by assisting in the freer performance of sexual acts without anxiety. In this way the reaction of anxiety to sexual experiences will be extinguished because it is never permitted to happen, and adequate sexual responses will in time be strengthened. This type of approach has been used widely with a variety of sexual dysfunctions.

Wolpe also uses *relaxation training* to inhibit anxiety, especially in cases where the predominant symptom is phobia, that is, the strong and unreasonable fear of common objects and places. The patient is first trained to relax all his muscles, as described by Jacobsen (1938). After training in muscular relaxation, the patient is asked to imagine vividly frightening experiences, starting from those that are only slightly or moderately frightening and working up to extremely frightening experiences. The motor relaxation is viewed by Wolpe as *antagonistic* to anxiety. The patient imagines the experience with little or no anxiety, and thus his or her sensitivity to the imagining of such experiences is *deconditioned.* The experiences can now occur presumably without the debilitating anxiety. If the image produces too much anxiety, the therapist goes back to a lower level on the hierarchy of anxiety-producing stimuli until the patient is again able to move upward.

In order to select the appropriate stimuli and procedures for the particular patient, Wolpe actually begins the therapy like the psychodynamic therapist, by listening to the patient describe his or her problems and symptoms and by taking a careful case history to find clues on which the strategy of treatment can be based. He then explains to the patient how neurotic symptoms develop, thereafter persuading the patient to extend the procedures that have been learned in treatment to the current life situation. Further details about the procedures of "systematic desensitization," as this procedure is typically called, and abundant case illustrations can be found in Wolpe (1974) and in A. A. Lazarus (1964, 1971). A brief example is offered below of Miss C, an art student suffering from severe anxiety at examinations which led to repeated failure.

Through systematic desensitization lasting four months, she was able to take her examinations and passed them. The illustration below describes the process of imagining successfully more distressing scenes in the course of a desensitization session (Wolpe, 1974, pp. 123–124):

Therapist: I am now going to ask you to imagine a number of scenes. You will imagine them clearly and they will generally interfere little, if at all, with your state of relaxation. If, however, at any time you feel disturbed or worried and want to draw my attention, you can tell me so. As soon as a scene is clear in your mind, indicate it by raising your left index finger about one inch. First, I want you to imagine that you are standing at a familiar street corner on a pleasant morning watching the traffic go by. You see cars, motorcycles, trucks, bicycles, people, and traffic lights; and you hear the sounds associated with all these things.

After a few seconds the patient raises her left index finger. The therapist pauses for five seconds.

Therapist: Stop imagining that scene. By how much did it raise your anxiety level while you imagined it?
Miss C.: Not at all.
Therapist: Now give your attention once again to relaxing.

There is again a pause of 20–30 seconds.

Therapist: Now imagine that you are home studying in the evening. It is the 20th May, exactly a month before your examination.

After about 15 seconds Miss C. raises her finger. Again she is left with the scene for 5 seconds.

Therapist: Stop that scene. By how much did it raise your anxiety?

Miss C.: About 15 units.

Therapist: Now imagine the same scene again—a month before your examination.

At this second presentation the rise in anxiety was five *suds* and at the third it was zero. The successive figures vary both with the individual and the scene. When the initial figure is over 30, repetition is unlikely to lower it. But there are exceptions. There are also occasional patients in whom an initial rise of 10 is too great to be diminished by repetition.

Having disposed of the first scene of the examination hierarchy, I could move on to the second. Alternatively, I could test Miss C.'s responses in another areas, such as the discord hierarchy—thus:

Therapist: Imagine you are sitting on a bench at a bus stop and across the road are two strange men whose voices are raised in argument.

This scene was given twice. After the patient reported on her response to the last presentation I terminated the desensitization session.

Therapist: Relax again. Now I am going to count up to 5 and you will open your eyes, feeling calm and refreshed.

Desensitization can be further illustrated by laboratory experiments relevant to it. One is a frequently cited experiment (Lang and Lazovik, 1963) which deals with the desensitization of a phobia. Twenty-four college students who volunteered for the experiment, including seven males and seventeen females, were selected on the basis of a questionnaire about fear of nonpoisonous snakes. The selected subjects had characterized themselves as having high fear, which had been confirmed in a follow-up interview. The subjects had reported habitually avoiding going anywhere near a live snake, refusing to enter the reptile section of a zoo, being unwilling to walk through an open field, becoming upset at seeing snakes in the movies or on television, and even being distressed at seeing pictures of snakes in magazines. The degree of their phobia for snakes was then measured more carefully in the laboratory by confronting the subjects with a five-foot black snake housed in a glass case. Each subject was persuaded to enter the room with the snake and describe his or her reactions. On entering with the subject, the experimenter walked to the case holding the snake, removed the wire grill covering the top, and assuring the subject that the snake was harmless, requested him or her to come over, look down at the snake, and perhaps touch it. The subject was encouraged to come as close to the snake as possible and later asked to rate the subjective anxiety that was felt on a 10-point "fear thermometer."

The experimental group, consisting of four males and nine females, was exposed to a desensitization treatment procedure, while a control group of three males and eight females was not given any treatment. The groups were chosen to be equal in degree of measured fear. Prior to desensitization, a series of twenty situations involving snakes (for example, writing the word "snake" or stepping on a dead snake accidentally) were described, and the subject graded each of them from most to least frightening. After the subject's rating of the anxiety-producing situations had been obtained, he or she was then given training in muscle *relaxation* and asked to practice this for ten to fifteen minutes at home every day.

Eleven 45-minute sessions of *systematic desensitization* followed. The subjects were first hypnotized and instructed to relax. They were then asked to imagine the situation with a snake that they had previously rated as least distressing. If the state of relaxation remained undisturbed, the next most distressing experience with snakes was imagined, and so on. If small amounts of anxiety were experienced with an item, that item was repeated under relaxation until the subject reported being undisturbed by imagining the

**TABLE 14–1   MEAN SNAKE-AVOIDANCE SCORES BEFORE AND AFTER
DESENSITIZATION THERAPY**

GROUP	PRE-THERAPY	POST-THERAPY	CHANGE SCORE*
Experimental	5.35	4.42	0.34
Control	6.51	7.73	−0.19

*Probability of the difference being the result of chance is less than 5 in 100.
SOURCE: Lang and Lazovik, 1963.

scene. In this way, the experimenter-therapist gradually proceeded up the scale as far as he could toward the items that were originally rated as most frightening, without disturbing the subject's relaxed state.

Following the desensitization treatment, both experimental and control subjects were then compared by Lang and Lazovik in the degree of snake fear. Although the two groups had been equally frightened initially, subjects treated with desensitization therapy were now more capable of approaching and touching the snake than the untreated subjects. After the desensitization procedure, seven experimental subjects held or touched the snake while only two control subjects did. The snake-avoidance scores, based on the distance ventured toward the snake, showed the same trend; the change from before to after therapy showed a lowering of phobic behavior in the treated group and a slight increase in the untreated group, as is shown in Table 14-1 above. The "fear thermometer" scores of the experimental group showed a slightly greater decrease after treatment than was true of the control. In a follow-up study of twenty subjects who were still available after six months, Lang and Lazovik also found that the therapeutic gains had been maintained and, in some instances, even increased. There was no evidence that other symptoms had been substituted for the snake phobia, an important point since such substitution might have been expected on the basis of the insight therapists' assumptions about the significance of symptoms. However, psychodynamic therapists would say they can make no assumptions about this experiment since it does not deal with "neurotic" behavior, as they understand it.

The Lang and Lazovik experiment is frequently cited because it was carefully designed and yielded findings quite consistent with the behavior therapists' contentions about the process of deconditioning or desensitization. However, it is not immune to criticism as an experimental analog or model of behavior therapy. The main issues that remain unresolved are: (1) It is not certain that the fears dealt with by Lang and Lazovik are comparable to the phobic reactions that are frequently seen in clinics. Lang and Lazovik *call* the fears expressed by their subjects "phobias." However, phobias seen clinically have led the patient to seek professional assistance. This was not the case with the subjects studied by Lang and Lazovik.

The key question is whether or not the fear of snakes in the experimental subjects is a manifestation of a *neurotic* difficulty or was a realistic (nonneurotic) fear which had little significance for the individual's adjustment in general. If such fears were not comparable to "neurotic phobias," it could be argued that desensitization might work for the experimental subjects but not for phobic neurotic patients. Behavior therapists have presented frequent reports suggesting the successful use of their techniques with "phobic" patients seen clinically. However, the unresolved issue concerns their definition and conception of neurosis. This issue applies particularly to the experiment reported by Lang and Lazovik. Certainly Lang and Lazovik conceive of neurosis in a way quite different from the way it is viewed by the psychodynamic therapists. The reader will recall the point made at the beginning of this chapter that the definition of neurosis made by psychodynamic therapists is quite different from that of behavior therapists.

(2) In the Lang and Lazovik experiment, it is possible that once the subject has reported a fear of snakes in the questionnaire, he or she may feel it necessary to behave in front of the experimenter in a fashion consistent with the earlier claim of fearfulness. Thus, it may be that the subject's degree of fear was really quite mild but appeared to be stronger. If so, the degree of accomplishment of experimental fear reduction could have been considerably less than assumed by behavior therapy protagonists.

(3) It is not entirely clear from the Lang and Lazovik experiment whether the unreasonable fear of snakes had actually been reduced, or whether the results mean merely that the subjects had been trained to *tolerate* the fear better and to engage in less evident avoidance behavior. For some behavior therapists, these two things, reduced fear and less avoidance behavior, are one and the same thing. From the author's viewpoint, these are not the same, and states of fear must somehow be distinguished from efforts to cope with fear. In any case, in spite of these difficult and unresolved issues, the experiment of Lang and Lazovik deserves serious attention by clinical workers because it serves as an experimental prototype of behavior therapy and, indeed, is so regarded by behavior therapists.

An experiment reported by Folkins, Lawson, Opton, and Lazarus (1968) has also recently supported the therapeutic value of desensitization procedures and raised some question about which elements of those procedures are really effective in reducing stress reactions. College students were exposed to a disturbing motion-picture film showing three wood-shop accidents, each of which usually produced substantial stress

reactions when watched. Skin conductance and heart rate, for example, normally rise sharply during the disturbing scenes, and subjects report considerable subjective distress. The subjects were given several different treatments prior to viewing the film. In one group, only training in relaxation was given. Another group of subjects were given "cognitive rehearsal," that is, in the fashion of Wolpe and of Lang and Lazovik they were told about the film and asked to imagine the scenes vividly. A third group was given both the relaxation training and the cognitive rehearsal, such as might be done in desensitization therapy. Then, following these diverse types of prophylactic experiences, the film was shown and the degree of subjective and physiological stress reaction measured while the subjects watched the accident scenes and applied their previous prophylactic treatment (for example, relaxation) to the experience.

Folkins et al. found that all the treatment procedures lowered the degree of stress reactions compared with a control group which did not receive any. The most effective treatment procedure (lowest stress reaction during the disturbing movie) appeared to be cognitive rehearsal, as illustrated in Figure 14-4. Combining this with the relaxation procedure, as is usually the case with desensitization therapy, appeared to be less effective, possible because the effort at relaxation interfered with the effort to prepare cognitively for the threatening experience. In any case, it was clear that the treatments did have a beneficial effect in reducing the level of stress reaction to the experience of watching the movie.

The experiment suggests that it might be possible to separate experimentally the various components in desensitization therapy and evaluate their comparative therapeutic value. Such experiments are helpful to our understanding of psychotherapy to the degree that the dynamics of the behavior of the experimental subjects are similar to those of neurotic patients in treatment. The validity of this latter assumption is typically

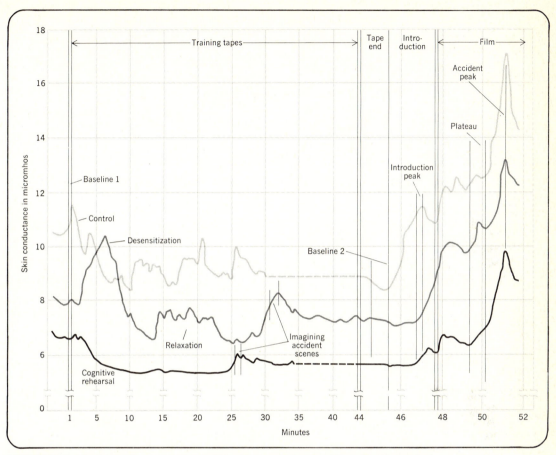

FIGURE 14-4 Stress reactions as measured by skin conductance while subjects watched movie accidents, following three experimental treatments, relaxation training, cognitive preparation, and desensitization. Increased skin conductance is an autonomic nervous system reaction to threatening or arousing experiences. Notice that the cognitive rehearsal condition produces the lowest level of skin conductance (the least stress reaction), while the control condition (no treatment) results in the highest levels during the film (highest stress reaction). (From Folkins, Lawson, Opton, and Lazarus, 1968.)

the basis of present controversy. However, as in the Lang and Lazovik experiment, it is possible to question whether the laboratory manipulations in this case too make a suitable analog to the real-life treatment of stress disturbances.

Systematic desensitization (or "reciprocal inhibition") in which the patient deals with fear- or

anxiety-inducing stimuli by gradually moving from low-sensitive stimuli to high-sensitive stimuli under conditions of simultaneous relaxation is only one of several forms of desensitization therapy. *Implosive therapy* (Stampfl and Levis, 1967), for example, offers quite a different tactic designed to accomplish the same result. In implosive therapy, the task of desensitization is handled by creating a massive flood of anxiety, rather than by minimizing the anxiety, but doing so in a safe and supportive clinical setting. The principle behind this procedure is that when harm is not forthcoming, the anxiety-producing or aversive stimulus will lose its power to generate anxiety, permitting extinction of the damaging avoidance behavior. One could say the patient is taught that what is dreaded will not happen. Instead of beginning with the mildest stimulus as in systematic desensitization, the therapist starts with the most frightening event the patient can conceive, imagining vividly the worst possible consequences of the experience in order to generate intense anxiety. Such a procedure is repeated for a number of sessions, and the patient is also encouraged to visualize these situations at home as well as in the therapeutic context. As Korchin (in press) observes, the approach is reminiscent of the abreaction or catharsis process in Freud's early work with hysteria, with the key difference that the patient is not encouraged to recover repressed memories reflecting the childhood origins of the phobic reaction, or to gain insight into its hidden psychodynamics.

AVERSION TRAINING

This tactic is designed to deal with problems of impulse control, that is, control over temptations which the person is having difficulty overcoming, as in alcoholism, overeating, smoking, drug dependence, and gambling. Its mode of operation is immediate punishment. The person cooperates in accepting or self-administering punishment (hence the term "aversion," which means things we are averse to) to extinguish or stamp out the unwanted behavior. In one version of aversion therapy, a drug (antabuse) is taken by the alcoholic. This produces severe nausea whenever the person takes a drink. In other versions painful electric shocks are used whenever the unwanted behavior occurs.

Such punishment can be given by the therapist or self-inflicted outside the therapist's office. For example, a patient may be given a portable shock generator that is activated by a timing device whenever his or her cigarette case is opened. In one laboratory study (Feldman and MacCulloch, 1965), slides of partially or fully nude men and women were shown to male homosexuals and the subject had to signal quickly to get another slide when a male picture was on the screen in order to avoid a painful electric shock. A. A. Lazarus has reported treating a male clinically who was having an extramarital affair but who wished to return to his wife. Whenever the "other woman's" photo was presented, it was followed by a shock which did not terminate until he looked at the photo of his wife. It is reported that his positive feelings toward the other woman waned sharply and his affection for his wife increased following a number of treatment sessions. Some behavior therapists have preferred to use noxious imagery rather than shock as the punishment (cf. Cautela, 1966). The patient is required, for example vividly to imagine the possible painful consequences of the actions to be controlled. If the problem is drinking, he or she would visualize being drunk, stumbling around, becoming nauseous, and being ridiculed.

It is noteworthy that aversion therapy inspired the portrayal of the treatment of Alex in *A Clockwork Orange,* the dystopian novel (and motion picture) that vigorously attacks the specter of thought control by the state. Alex is made to feel nauseous every time he has the impulse to engage in violence or sex. Similar ideologically based disapproval of "thought control" has been directed at experimental prison programs involving aversive techniques to produce more socialized behavior. It should be noted that in the usual clinical use of aversion therapy the patient is a willing accomplice in the use of punishment. The prison situation, however, generates legitimate doubt about freedom of choice of the inmate who accepts the treatment, and this is quite different from situations in which the person freely chooses to undergo aversive conditioning procedures. Nevertheless, aversion therapy has somehow gained unfavorable public attention because of its association with the idea of forcible control of the mind by the systematic manipulation of rewards and punishments. As Bandura (1974) has observed, moreover, people interpret what is happening to them and learn from the information derived from rewards and punishments meted out by the environment, and they are not easily controlled except insofar as they choose to be. Bandura (p. 859) notes:

> [There is] growing concern over manipulation and control by psychological methods. Some of these fears arise from expectations that improved means of influence will inevitably be misused. Other apprehensions are aroused by exaggerated claims of psychological power couched in the language of manipulation and authoritarian control. But most fears stem from views of behaviorism, articulated by popular writers and by theorists themselves, that are disputed by the empirical facts of human behavior.

ASSERTIVE TRAINING

People often seek therapeutic help in overcoming anxieties and inhibitions which impair their social functioning. The behavior therapy approach to this is to encourage systematic development of greater interpersonal skills. The person practices assertiveness in situations that normally elicited debilitating anxiety, inhibition, and avoidance. The first task is to discuss the situations that threaten the person and to suggest reactions that are more serviceable than those he or she has typically employed. Usually this is begun in mildly distressing situations in which the patient is encouraged to try out new ways of acting, and gradually the emphasis shifts to more intense and fearful situations. Patients may keep

notes of how they acted and what happened. In this way they are made more aware of and attentive to their inept reactions and to alternative ways of handling the situation. They may also be encouraged to rehearse how they will handle upcoming situations and to try them out to obtain feedback about how they work. Each success helps the patient see himself or herself in a more favorable light and to gain a greater sense of self-esteem and competence in handling social encounters.

THE TOKEN ECONOMY

As noted earlier, operant conditioning techniques have been employed to improve the behavior of psychotic patients who have been institutionalized for a long time and who have evidently not profited from other therapeutic approaches (cf. Ayllon and Azrin, 1965; Atthowe and Krasner, 1968). The tactic is to control totally the environmental reinforcement contingencies, thus systematically administering rewards for desirable behaviors and punishments for undesirable ones. After first designating patient behaviors to be encouraged and discouraged, a medium of exchange is established by the therapist, using a set of tokens such as poker chips, small cards, imitation coins, and so on. These may be used by the patient to trade for special privileges or pleasures such as weekend passes home, movie shows, the chance to watch TV, specially attractive food, or a private room. Each privilege has a particular price, that is, a given number of tokens that it takes to buy it, and good behavior is accorded some given amount of "wages" (number of tokens) which the patient can spend on the privileges. Let's assume a female patient this time: if she takes on a job, makes her bed, sweeps the floor, or whatever, she receives a specified number of tokens, along with indications of approval by the staff. She is told that because she did this or that (say, got to lunch on time) she is receiving the tokens. Writing about such token economies, Krasner (1971, p. 637) states:

> The goals of a token program are to develop behaviors that will lead to social reinforcement from others, to enhance the skills necessary for the individual to take a responsible social role in the institution and, eventually, to live successfully outside the institution. Basically, the individual learns that he can control his own environment in such a way that he will elicit positive reinforcement from others.

Typically, reinforced behaviors are increased and strengthened in the token economy as long as the tokens are given, and they decline when the tokens are withdrawn. In some studies, patients come to display a livelier interest in their environment than previously even after years of apathy and withdrawal, and they engage in more responsible behavior on the ward. It is too early to say that such effects are enduring and extend into the real world, where reinforcement patterns can be quite unpredictable. This is, of course, the *key practical issue* in all forms of treatment,

namely, whether and to what extent any improvements observed in the patient's state of mind and behavior *generalize* to the setting in which he or she lives outside the clinic, therapist's office, or institution.

MODELING

Learning not only depends on direct reinforcement of a person's actions, but it also comes about through watching and imitating others (Bandura, 1969, 1971). For example, a small boy who observes an adult acting aggressively is more likely to act aggressively himself. He has used the adult as a model for his own behavior. This principle can be extended to the therapeutic context, with the goal of learning new social skills or reducing fears and inhibitions, though it has been applied mainly in the laboratory. Thus, a phobic individual can be asked to watch someone who without fear touches a snake, holds it, and finally allows it to crawl over him. The therapist then encourages the patient to try out the same graded sequence, being guided physically in this by the therapist and praised for his or her efforts. The process of modeling is quite analogous to the tactic of desensitization, except that it first makes use of having patients observe a model doing what they are being encouraged to try, thus strengthening their resolve and helping them recognize that it can be done without harm.

CONTRASTS WITH INSIGHT THERAPY

We have already touched upon some of the contrasts between the behavior therapy approach and that of psychodynamic or insight therapy. It would be of great value at this point to be able to pull together the traditional contrasts in summary fashion. Fortunately, Korchin (in press) has already provided an excellent summary in tabular form, analyzing a series of issues on which psychoanalysis, humanistic-existential therapy

FIGURE 14-5 Coupons used at a day treatment center to reward patients for participating in therapeutic activities. (Oxnard Community Health Center, California, courtesy of Dr. Robert P. Liberman.)

(which Korchin treats separately from psychoanalysis), and behavior therapy differ. Table 14-2 graphically illustrates the way these issues are treated by the three approaches and offers a way to learn and hold in mind the comparisons that can be drawn.

RECONCILING BEHAVIOR THERAPY WITH PSYCHODYNAMIC THERAPY

As pointed out at the beginning of this chapter, behavior therapy began as a protest against psychodynamic therapy. Its early days have been filled more with ideological attack rather than thoughtful examination of the similarities and differences that exist between the two approaches. There are now beginning to be signs that clinical psychologists who think of themselves as behaviorally oriented are asking more enlightened questions, reducing some of the fruitless rhetoric, and finding some common causes with more psychodynamically oriented therapists.

In the author's opinion, Arnold Lazarus (1971) is the most flexible, thoughtful, and broadly based representative of this growing reconciliation between behavior and psychodynamic therapy. Lazarus (not a relative) persuasively argues that the therapeutic approach must be tailored to the characteristics of the patient and that often a complaint such as a phobia is not the real problem, although it can reflect a much more complex problem of living. Therapists must not rigidly apply their favorite behavior therapy technique; rather, they need to have on hand a broad spectrum of approaches, and they must begin with a careful examination of the patient's problem to decide which is the most suitable. Lazarus gives an example of what seems at first to be primarily a phobia about crossing bridges. The patient believes that his fear prevents him from having an effective adjustment, but later it emerges as something quite different. If the behavior therapist at this point undertook a traditional

desensitization tactic in order to permit him to overcome the "bridge phobia," he would have missed (as a previous therapist did) a great many other problems of living that should be dealt with in treatment. Lazarus (1971, pp. 33–36, parenthetical statements added) presents the following problem-focused interview with this patient:

Patient: I have a fear of crossing bridges.

Therapist: Do you have any other fears or difficulties?

Patient: Only the complications arising from my fear of bridges.

Therapist: Well, in what way has it affected your life?

Patient: I had to quit an excellent job in Berkeley.

Therapist: Where do you live?

Patient: San Francisco.

Therapist: So why didn't you move to Berkeley?

Patient: I prefer living in the city.

Therapist: To get to this institute, you had to cross the Golden Gate.

Patient: Yes, I was seeing a doctor in San Francisco. He tried to desensitize me but it didn't help, so he said I should see you because you know more about this kind of treatment. It's not so bad when I have my wife and kids with me. But even then, the Golden Gate, which is about one mile long, is my upper limit. I was wondering whether you ever consult in the city?

Therapist: No, but tell me, how long have you had this problem?

Patient: Oh, about four years, I'd say. It just happened suddenly. I was coming home from work and the Bay Bridge was awfully slow. I just suddenly panicked for no reason at all. I mean, nothing like this had ever happened to me before. I felt that I would crash into the other cars. Once I even had a feeling that the bridge would cave in.

Therapist: Let's get back to that first panic

TABLE 14-2 COMPARISON OF PSYCHONALYTIC, BEHAVIORAL AND HUMANISTIC-EXISTENTIAL APPROACHES TO PSYCHOTHERAPY

ISSUE	PSYCHOANALYSIS	BEHAVIOR THERAPY	HUMANISTIC-EXISTENTIAL THERAPY
Basic human nature	Biological instincts, primarily sexual and aggressive, press for immediate release, bringing man into conflict with social reality.	Like other animals, man is born only with the capacity for learning, which develops in terms of the same basic principles in all species.	Man has free will, choice, and purpose; he has the capacity for self-determination and self-actualization.
Normal human development	Growth occurs through resolution of conflicts during successive developmental crises and psychosexual stages. Through identification and internalization, more mature ego controls and character structures emerge.	Adaptive behaviors are learned through reinforcement and imitation.	A unique self system develops from birth on. The individual develops his personally characteristic modes of perceiving, feeling, etc.
Nature of psychopathology	Pathology reflects inadequate conflict resolutions and fixations in earlier development, which leave overly strong impulses and/or weak controls. Symptoms are partial adaptations or substitute gratifications, defensive responses to anxiety.	Symptomatic behavior derives from faulty learning of maladaptive behaviors. The symptom *is* the problem; there is no "underlying disease."	Incongruence exists between the depreciated self and the potential desired self. The person is over dependent on others for gratification and self-esteem. There is a sense of purposelessness and meaninglessness.
Goal of therapy	Attainment of psychosexual maturity, strengthened ego functions, reduced control by unconscious and repressed impulses.	Relieving symptomatic behavior by suppressing or replacing maladaptive behaviors.	Fostering self-determination, authenticity, and integration by releasing human potential and expanding awareness.
Role of therapist	An *investigator*, searching out root conflicts and resistances; detached, neutral, and non-directive, to facilitate transference reactions.	A *trainer*, helping patient unlearn old behaviors and/or learn new ones. Control of reinforcement is important; interpersonal relation is of minor concern.	An authentic person in true encounter with patient, sharing experience. Facilitates patient's growth potential. Transference discounted or minimized.
Necessary qualifications and skills	Highly trained in theory and supervised practice; much technical and professional knowledge. Must have firm self-knowledge, to avert dangers of counter-transference.	Knowledge of learning principles primary; understanding of personality theory and psychopathology secondary; no concern with self-knowledge. Actual interventions can be done by nonprofessional assistant.	Personal integrity and empathy valued over professional training and formal knowledge.

Time orientation	Oriented to discovering and interpreting past conflicts and repressed feelings, to examine them in light of present situation.	Little or no concern with past history or etiology. Present behavior is examined and treated.	Focus on present phenomenal experience; the here and now.
Role of unconscious material	Primary in classical psychoanalysis, less emphasized by neo-Freudians and ego psychologists. To all, of great conceptual importance.	No concern with unconscious processes or, indeed, with subjective experience even in conscious realm. Subjective experience shunned as unscientific.	Though recognized by some, emphasis is on conscious experience.
Psychological realm emphasized.	Motives and feelings, fantasies and cognitions; minimum concern with motor behavior and action outside of therapy.	Behavior and observable feelings and actions. Emphasis on extratherapeutic actions.	Perceptions, meanings, values. For some, sensory and motor processes.
Role of insight	Central, though conceived not just as intellectual understanding but as it emerges in "corrective emotional experiences."	Irrelevant and/or unnecessary.	More emphasis on awareness, the "how" and "what" questions rather than the "why."

SOURCE: S. J. Korchin. 1976.

experience about four years ago. You said that you were coming home from work. Had anything happened at work?

Patient: Nothing unusual.

Therapist: Were you happy at work?

Patient: Sure! Huh! I was even due for promotion.

Therapist: What would that have entailed?

Patient: An extra $3,000 a year.

Therapist: I mean in the way of having to do different work.

Patient: Well, I would have been a supervisor. I would have had more than fifty men working under me.

Therapist: How did you feel about that?

Patient: What do you mean?

Therapist: I mean how did you feel about the added responsibility? Did you feel that you were up to it, that you could cope with it?

Patient: Gee! My wife was expecting our first kid. We both welcomed the extra money.

Therapist: So round about the time that you were about to become a father, you were to be promoted to supervisor. So you would face two new and challenging roles. You'd be a daddy at home and also a big daddy at work. And this was when you began to panic on the bridge, and I guess you never did wind up as a supervisor.

Patient: No. I had to ask for a transfer to the city.

Therapist: Now, please think very carefully about this question. Have you ever been involved in any accident on or near the bridge, or have you ever witnessed any serious accident on or near a bridge?

Patient: Not that I can think of.

Therapist: Do you still work for the same company?

Patient: No. I got a better offer, more money, from another company in the city. I've been with them for almost 1½ years now.

Therapist: Are you earning more money or less money than you would have gotten in Berkeley?

Patient: About the same. But prices have gone up, so it adds up to less.

Therapist: If you hadn't developed the bridge phobia and had become a foreman in Berkeley at $3,000 more, where do you think you would be today?

Patient: Still in Berkeley.

Therapist: Still supervisor? More money?

Patient: Oh, hell! Who knows? (*laughs*) Maybe I would have been vice-president.

Therapist: And what would that have entailed?

Patient: I'm only kidding. But actually it could have happened.

Therapy in this case was deflected away from his bridge phobia toward unraveling a history in which the patient, the youngest of five siblings, tended to accept his mother's evaluation that, unlike his brilliant older brothers, he would never amount to anything. Desensitization was in fact employed, but not in relation to bridges. A hierarchy of his mother's real or imagined pejorative statements was constructed, and the patient was immunized to these hurtful allegations. He was also trained to assertive behavior. As he gained confidence in his own capabilities, his bridge phobia vanished as suddenly as it had appeared.

Perhaps it can be argued that the patient's bridge phobia developed through a process of conditioning, which (many behavior therapists regard) as the basis of all phobias. A behaviorist with whom I discussed the case contended that the man was apprehensive about his future and that his anxieties *just happened by chance* to erupt while traveling on a bridge. He added that bridges thereupon became invested with high anxiety potential and that the patient's avoidance of bridges blocked the extinction of his fears. But what was he really avoiding? Bridges per se? And was the first anxiety attack on the bridge fortuitous? Did not his bridge phobia serve the function of preventing the full impact of his own uncertainties and shortcomings vis-à-vis his work, competence, obligations, and achievements? Why did the phobia disappear as soon as these basic anxieties were overcome? These questions reflect the inadequacies of peripheral (stimulus-response) theories of learning. . . .

Notice here that Lazarus, a behavior therapist, has in this particular example moved pretty close to the psychodynamic position. It is not that he regards all phobias or problem reactions as having deep-lying dynamics that must be uncovered, but only that it is incorrect to force a dichotomy between a simple conditioning-deconditioning view of psychotherapy and a psychodynamic view. Rather, both extremes, behavioristic and mentalistic, should be avoided, and the tactics of treatment should be matched to the individual patient. Lazarus probably got a clue about this particular patient from the fact that desensitization concerning the bridge phobia had been tried and failed, and so he kept pressing in his interview for information that might suggest the nature of the real problem of which the bridge phobia was merely a symptom; it was necessary to tailor the desensitization process to the real fears and concerns underlying the surface fear of bridges. In this case description and explanation we see that treatment cannot be rigid but often should fall somewhere along the continuum between a behavioristic and a psychodynamic model.

One forum for this potential reconciliation is in the growing interest in the principles of self-control or self-regulation. For diverse and complex reasons, the individual can be seen as coming for help because he or she has failed in some area of self-control; for example, bodily tension cannot be managed, apprehensive thoughts abound, the patient cannot stop eating, smoking, feeling angry, or whatever, or the sex act cannot be completed, and the main task of behavior therapy is to restore control over such reactions, or gain it for the first time. The tactics of behavior therapy described earlier in this chapter (for

example, desensitization, aversion training, assertive training, the token economy, and modeling) all tend to focus on environmental manipulations by the therapist, although—as we saw—aversion training can also be self-administered once a plan has been established, and assertive training involves getting the person to rehearse and try out more serviceable patterns of conduct that could help him acquire undeveloped or inhibited social skills.

The extreme behavioral position is that such control of human behavior (including unwanted behavior) lies entirely in the external environment. Accordingly, it is fruitless and unscientific to refer to events within the person. On the other hand, the less philosophically doctrinaire behavior therapist can acknowledge that what takes place within the person—for example, intentions, thoughts, expectations, plans, commitments, threats—can be very important, even though these internal events are shaped and influenced by environmental rewards and punishments. The important problem then is determining the mechanisms of self-control and the links between them and the environmental contingencies. From this more flexible standpoint, then, people can be trained or helped to acquire self-control over impulses, reaction patterns, bodily states, and social behaviors; this can be done by manipulating the factors, both internal and external, that facilitate such self-control. The question of internal or external is less important than the rules by which self-control can be ac--complished.

Goldfried and Merbaum (1973, pp. 11–12) address the above point in giving a "working definition of self-control":

Self-control can be viewed as a process through which an individual becomes the principal agent in guiding, directing, and regulating those features of his own behavior that might eventually lead to desired positive consequences. Typically, the emphasis in self-control is placed on those variables *beneath the skin* which determine the motivation for change. It is equally important to realize, however, that environmental influences have played a vital role in developing the unique behavioral properties of the self-control sequence. Thus, we assume that self-control is a skill learned through various social contacts, and the repertoire of effective self-control is gradually built up through increased experimentation with a complex environment. . . . *Self-control represents a personal decision arrived at through conscious deliberation for the purpose of integrating action which is designed to achieve certain desired outcomes or goals as determined by the individual himself. . . .*

We conceive of the act of self-control as being mediated by cognitive processes which are available to conscious recognition. . . . (This) leans heavily on the importance of thought and language in delaying impulsive action, and for introducing a competing cognitive alternative into the self-regulatory sequence.

Notice that while the main focus above is on the external environment in facilitating or impairing self-control, it also allows for and makes use of psychological processes such as thoughts taking place inside the person. Training in self-control should thus require knowledge of the mechanisms of self-control (including thoughts) and how these might be influenced to help the person gain control over undesirable and wayward reactions.

Viewed in this somewhat broader light (see also Thoreson and Mahoney, 1974; and Williams and Long, 1975), the range of things that can be done by a patient being trained in self-control is greatly enlarged. Some of these include daily exercises in *relaxation* to gain self-control over tense muscles, an old technique you will recall being used by Wolpe in desensitization therapy. *Autosuggestion* is another related procedure for gaining self-control over negative emotional reactions, especially anxiety. The person may be

encouraged to think about or imagine something pleasant when such reactions become troublesome. Sometimes patients are trained to *give themselves certain instructions* about what to think or do every time they get the unwanted feeling or reaction.

Still another approach involves what might be called *cognitive redefinition* or relabeling. Ellis (1958, 1962) has been experimenting for some time with a procedure called "rational psychotherapy" which makes use of this principle. In essence, patients are taught that many of their negative emotions, such as anxiety or anger, arise because they have misjudged or misunderstood a social situation. For Ellis the task of therapy is to discover the incorrect interpretation or cognitive label the patient has applied to what is happening, then to substitute a more accurate and serviceable one. For example, a woman who operates on the assumption that "everyone must love me" or "I must be perfect" must learn that this is irrational and gets into self-defeating emotional patterns; she must learn to substitute a more rational premise.

Ellis (1959, pp. 340–343) gives an example of rational psychotherapy with a male patient, Caleb, who had a history of sixteen years of homosexual activity, though he had never actively approached a male himself during this period. On the basis of information about the patient, it was believed that the primary motive for the homosexuality was his strong fear of being rejected by all women and most males. Ellis illustrates the treatment approach and comments on it below:

Rather than spend much time belaboring the point that Caleb's fear of rejection probably stemmed from his childhood, the therapist convinced him, on purely logical grounds, that this was so since he had apparently feared being rejected by girls when he was in his early teens, and his fear must have originated sometime prior to that time. The therapist, instead, tried to get as quickly as possible to the source of his fear of rejection: namely, his illogical *belief* that being rejected by a girl (or a fellow) was a terrible thing. Said the therapist:

T: Suppose, for the sake of discussion, you had, back in your high school days, tried, really tried, to make some sexual passes at a girl, and suppose you had been unequivocally rejected by her. Why would that be terrible?

C (stands for client): Well—uh—it just would be.

T: But *why* would it be?

C: Because—uh—I—I just thought the world would come to an end if that would have happened.

T: But *why?* Would the world *really* have come to an end?

C: No, of course not.

T: Would the girl have slapped your face, or called a cop, or induced all the other girls to ostracize you?

C: No, I guess she wouldn't.

T: Then what *would* she have done? How would you—*really*—have been hurt?

C: Well, I guess, in the way you mean, I wouldn't.

T: Then why did you think that you would?

C: That's a good question. Why did I?

T: The answer, alas, is so obvious that you probably won't believe it.

C: What is it?

T: Simply that you thought you would be terribly hurt by a girl's rejecting you merely because you were *taught* that you would be. You were raised, literally raised, to believe that if anyone, especially a girl, rejects you, tells you she doesn't like you, that this is terrible, awful, frightful. It isn't, of course: it isn't in any manner, shape, or form awful if someone rejects you, refuses to accede to your wishes. But you *think* it is, because you were *told* it is.

C: Told?

T: Yes—literally and figuratively told. Told literally by your parents, who warned you, time and again, did they not, that if you did wrong, made the wrong approaches to people, they wouldn't love you, wouldn't accept you—*and that would be awful, that would be terrible.*

C: Yes, you're right about that. That's just what they told me.

T: Yes—and not only they. Indirectly, figuratively, symbolically, in the books you read, the plays you saw, the films you went to—weren't you told the same thing there, time and again, over and over—that if anyone, the hero of the book, you, or anyone else, got rejected, got rebuffed, got turned down, they *should* think it terrible, should be hurt?

C: I guess I was. Yes, that's what the books and films really say, isn't it?

T: It sure is. All right, then, so you *were* taught that being rejected is awful, frightful. Now let's go back to my original question. Suppose you actually did ask a girl for a kiss, or something else; and suppose she did reject you. What would you *really* lose thereby, by being so rejected?

C: Really lose? Actually, I guess, very little.

T: Right: damned little. In fact, you'd actually gain a great deal.

C: How so?

T: Very simply: you'd gain experience. For if you tried and were rejected, you'd know not to try it with that girl, or in that way, again. Then you would go on to try again with some other girl, or with the same girl in a different way, and so on.

C: Maybe you've got something there.

T: Maybe I have. Whenever you get rejected—as you do, incidentally, every time you put a coin in a slot machine and no gum or candy comes out—you are merely learning that this girl or that technique or this gum machine doesn't work; but a trial with some other girl, technique, or machine may well lead to success. Indeed, in the long run, it's almost certain to.

C: You're probably right.

T: O.K. then. So it isn't the rejection by girls that *really* hurts, is it? It's your *idea,* your *belief,* your *assumption* that rejection is hurtful, is awful. *That's* what's really doing you in; and that's what we're going to have to change to get you over this silly homosexual neurosis.

Thus, the therapist kept pointing out, in session after session, the illogical fears behind the client's fixed homosexual pattern of behavior—and *why* these fears were illogical, *how* they were merely learned and absorbed from Caleb's early associates, and, especially how *he* now kept re-indoctrinating himself with these fears by parroting them unthinkingly, telling himself over and over that they were based on proven evidence, when obviously they were completely arbitrary and ungrounded in fact. His fear of rejection, of losing approval, or having others laugh at him or criticize him, was examined in scores of its aspects, and revealed to him again and again. It was not only revealed, but scornfully, forcefully *attacked* by the therapist, who kept showing Caleb that it is necessarily silly and self-defeating for anyone to care too much about what *others* think, since then one is regulating one's life by and for these others, rather than for oneself; and, moreover, one is setting up a set of conditions for one's own happiness which make it virtually impossible that one ever will be happy. . . .

One of the most interesting aspects of this case is that some basic issues in Caleb's life were virtually never discussed during the entire therapeutic procedure—partly because the therapist thought that some of them would be analyzed in more detail later, and partly because he thought that some of the issues were largely irrelevant to Caleb's basic problems. Thus, the therapist felt that Caleb's homosexual pattern of behavior was, at least in part, caused by his over-attachment to his mother. . . . In the entire course of therapy, however, relatively little reference was made to Caleb's relations with his mother, and no detailed analysis of this relationship was effected. Nonetheless, Caleb's deviated pattern of ho-

mosexuality completely changed in the course of therapy—largely, in all probability, because the *main* cause of this homosexuality was *not* his Oedipal attachment to his mother but his severe feelings of inadequacy and fear of rejection—which *were* thoroughly analyzed and attacked in the course of therapy.

The possibilities of self-control have recently received a major boost from a fairly new area of research and clinical application called *biofeedback training*. Its focus is on the self-regulation of bodily states and symptoms associated with the stress emotions; examples are hypertension (high blood pressure), muscle tension, migraine and tension headaches, and excessive stomach motility. Although it was once believed that bodily or visceral states were outside of voluntary control (hence the term "autonomic"—see Chapter 5), the apparent ability of experienced yogas to control somatic reactions, along with the findings of recent psychophysiological research on such control, have led to the growing realization that these activities can, to some extent, be regulated by the person. It is not clear how such self-regulation is accomplished, and there is still much controversy about the degree of control, how long it can be sustained, and in what situations it can operate. However, if people can indeed be taught to gain some control over many of their bodily functions, including brain wave patterns and gastric motility, it may be of great therapeutic value in psychosomatic disorders and in the management of bodily disturbances and tensions that interfere with effective adjustment and the enjoyment of life.

For this reason, a very active new research area using biofeedback techniques has emerged. Biofeedback is merely the use of the ability (through modern electrophysiological technology) to measure and display visually a person's bodily reactions. When these data are fed back to the subject, he or she obtains information that can be used to gain a degree of control over the reactions. When the subject is successful in, say, lowering blood pressure, the biofeedback display communicates this; when he or she is unsuccessful, the machine shows it. The information thus gained assists the person to create the psychological (thoughts, distractions, and so on) or physical (posture, muscle relaxation, or whatever) conditions favoring the decrease in blood pressure. Biofeedback training procedures might help patients to learn techniques of self-regulation of the undesirable bodily products of stress emotion. This fits within the general area of self-control or self-regulation, although our knowledge of the processes underlying such control is still in its infancy (see Schwartz and Beatty, in press; Lazarus, 1975).

Some of the differences in outlook between psychodynamic therapy and behavior therapy may be irreconcilable—for example, their ideas about the origins and functions of the symptom, the goals of therapy, the basic definition of the neurosis, or the former's emphasis on unconscous processes. However, the growing emphasis within behavior therapy on self-control processes and their cognitive and other mechanisms suggests that these differences could ultimately become matters of shifting emphasis rather than extreme polarities. Psychodynamicists might come to acknowledge the important role of environmental stimulus factors in shaping maladjustive reactions, and behavior therapists might find ways of incorporating internal psychological processes, perhaps even unconscious ones, into their therapeutic programs to help troubled individuals gain control over their reactions. Goldfried and Merbaum (1973, p. 32, parenthetical comment added) give us a fitting ending to this discussion with the following balanced and non-polemical summary statement:

> While in no way underestimating the powerful impact of environmental contingencies, the emphasis on covert processes (what takes place inside the person) has merely enlarged

the picture. Interestingly enough, the shift in emphasis now being introduced by behavioral theorists is anything but original to the dynamicist, who has always considered internal states as his primary targets for treatment. What is original, we believe, is the concerted effort to integrate, objectify, and specify the (causal) antecedents of self-regulatory processes in scientifically meaningful terms. . . .

SUMMING UP

We have examined a number of behavior therapy approaches, all of which have in common an ideological rejection of the psychodynamic position that maladjustive behavior can best be understood as unresolved, unconscious conflicts which plague the person in his or her current affairs and into which the patient must gain insight if help is to be given. The behavior therapy emphasis is the *deconditioning* of unserviceable habits and the learning of more serviceable ones.

The *tactics* of treatment consist of various ways of manipulating the conditions of reward and punishment in such a way that the undesirable habit can be deconditioned, that is, by reversing the learning process that brought it into being in the first place. There is a wide variety of therapeutic tactics designed to accomplish this goal of deconditioning and the learning of more serviceable habits in the place of the maladjustive or undesirable ones. These include desensitization, which takes a number of divergent forms, aversion training, assertive training, the token economy, and modeling. Except in the case of aversion therapy, the behavior or emotion must be made to occur under aversive conditions in which the dreaded outcome fails to occur, thus detaching the aversive stimulus conditions from the maladjustive reaction. The *strategies* of behavior therapy are thus outgrowths of the principles of *classical* and *operant conditioning*.

Recent interest in the mechanisms of *self-control* and in training in self-control seems to offer possibilities of reconciliation between the psychodynamic therapies and the behavior therapies. The early arguments and rhetoric appear to have diminished, and in their place seems to be a great willingness on the part of behavior therapists to acknowledge the role of internal psychological processes as (psychodynamic) factors in self-control, while still conceiving the primary issue as that of external environmental influences and how these can be manipulated, either by the therapist or the patient, in facilitating greater self-control over one's reactions.

Our remaining task is to look at societal and institutional approaches to treatment. In addition we must evaluate psychodynamic therapy and behavior therapy and consider the success of all forms of treatment in general in meeting the mental health needs of individuals and the larger society. These tasks will be undertaken in Chapter 15.

CHAPTER 15 PSYCHOTHERAPY EVALUATED: ALTERNATIVE SOCIETAL APPROACHES

Having reviewed the main approaches to psychotherapy, we must now address two final matters: first, the evaluation of how well psychotherapy works, and second, the examination of other alternative types of treatment, including the physical therapies and institutional attempts to tackle the mental health problem.

HOW WELL DOES PSYCHOTHERAPY WORK?

The aggressive, movement-like qualities of behavior therapy have stimulated controversy and even polemics among professional workers (for example, Eysenck, 1952, 1961; Breger and McGaugh, 1965; Weitzman, 1967). Psychodynamic therapists tend to regard behavior therapy as superficial and suitable only for very limited types of cases. If so, the major neuroses, character problems, and psychoses, which may be the predominant forms of adjustive failure, cannot be dealt with by behavior therapy. The fact that the insight therapies tend to be somewhat vague about their procedures and results has made them more subject to attack. Behavior therapists such as Wolpe invite inspection of their procedures, and aside from their theories, which may well be excess baggage and wrong-headed, they are somewhat clearer about what they do to their patients than psychodynamic therapists.

The dialog stimulated by behavior therapists such as Wolpe has forced a reexamination by professionals of the assumptions and procedures of psychodynamic therapy. This is probably a general gain for the field of psychotherapy as a whole. The challenge has been laid down. Whether or not it turns out in the long run that the behavior therapists are correct, in part or in whole, they have drawn attention to issues that have been given much too little attention in the past. And they are certainly correct in arguing that the only possible test of therapeutic value is in the *effectiveness* with which the various approaches ameliorate the difficulties for which patients come to therapists for help.

Controversy usually means that the evidence in favor of one or another point of view is equivocal. If it could be certain that the claims of insight therapists were unjustified, most psychotherapists would probably abandon the concepts and procedures they now employ, leaving the field of therapy to the unscrupulous and the quack. Similarly, if one could be sure that behavior therapy offered the best prospects for the amelioration of the major forms of adjustive failure, this approach would undoubtedly take over the field, and the traditional approaches would dry up. In point of fact, the evidence about the outcomes of various kinds of psychotherapy, or, for that matter, of any kind of psychotherapy, is extremely meager, and what there is of it is highly ambiguous (see Korchin, in press).

The issue of the successfulness of therapy has generated much more heat than light. Although there has always been skepticism about what is accomplished by psychotherapy, especially among those who are not engaged in professional practice, an extremely vigorous and intemperate dissent was first expressed in 1952 by the British psychologist Hans Eysenck. He argued then (and again later, in 1960) that the available evidence failed to prove the value of psychotherapy, and he implied that insight therapies had little or no value in the treatment of psychopathology. In an interchange with Hans Strupp

(1963) Eysenck's (1964) strong bias is reflected in sympathetic and unqualified quotes from a number of respected but equally intemperate psychiatrists and a leading psychologist claiming the failure of insight psychotherapy. Eysenck (1964, p. 99) shows himself to be a fervent protagonist of behavior therapy in the following comment:

It is well known that theories and methods of therapy are not usually overcome by criticisms, however bad the theories, however useless the treatments, and however reasonable the criticisms. Theories and treatments only yield to better theories and treatments, and I realized fully that my 1952 review would not by itself have much effect on the theory or practice of psychotherapy without the provision of something else to take its place. Fortunately, we now have an alternative method of treatment rationally based on scientific concepts developed in psychological laboratories, and deriving its methods from modern learning theory. Behavior therapy . . . has already been shown to be a much shorter, and for many neurotic disorders a much more effective, method of treatment than psychotherapy, whether eclectic or psychoanalytic. . . . It is to be hoped that in the near future . . . psychologists will set up clinical trials to evaluate the adequacy of these two methods of therapy against each other.

Eysenck's conviction that insight therapies are valueless was also clear in an earlier statement (1961, p. 697) in which he quotes a sarcastic comment of the Roman physician Galen, implying that it also applied to psychotherapy: "All who drink this remedy recover in a short time, except those whom it does not help, who all die and have no relief from any other medicine. Therefore it is obvious that it fails only in incurable cases." For Eysenck there is thus no question about the ineffectiveness of insight therapy; he is certain that it does not work. However, for most knowledgeable workers in this field, the effectiveness of insight therapy is an important and unsettled question. As Bergin (1963, p. 244) points out: "For the rest of us who require more persuasive evidence before believing that a null hypothesis has been thoroughly confirmed, there remain questions regarding the validity of this challenging, but seemingly unrefuted assertion." On the basis of the current evidence about the alternative of behavior therapy, it is cavalier to claim its superiority without adequate comparative data concerning the kinds of adjustive difficulties for which either approach is or is not helpful.

Eysenck's casual treatment of evidence and his simplistic and polemical outlook in the face of the complexity of the problem is so striking that his reviews cannot be regarded as carrying any authority. His attack is cited here because he is so well known and his remarks illustrate the biases characteristic of the current controversy. By the same token, psychodynamic therapists have responded with considerable defensiveness. They argue that the evidence demonstrates the value of insight psychotherapy, though such evidence is quite meager and equivocal.

Why, after so long, are we unable to say with confidence how effective insight and behavior therapy are in ameliorating maladjustment? Is it not fairly simple to evaluate changes in patients after a treatment program as compared with the changes that might be observed in untreated patients? Such research is really enormously complicated, so complicated in fact that few studies have been performed with completely adequate methodology. It will be instructive to consider some of the main difficulties in doing adequate research on the outcomes of therapy. There are two main classes of difficulty. One concerns the specification of the treatment variables; the other has to do with the assessment of personality change.

SPECIFYING THE TREATMENT VARIABLES

Suppose that a research worker is attempting to compare the effectiveness of two or more types of treatment programs, and in order to minimize the idiosyncratic differences among individual therapists, each program is represented by several different therapists. Unless what each therapist does and says is carefully recorded and described, it is extremely difficult to say what it is about the therapist's actions that influenced the patient. We cannot depend on what the therapist *says* he or she is doing; we need to know what is actually done. The first difficulty then is that merely labeling a therapist as a Freudian or Jungian does not permit us to identify the *key actions* among many different schools which actually influence the patient.

A second difficulty concerns variations in the *aims of therapy* adopted for each patient and, hence, in the criteria of successful treatment. In some cases, the aim may be limited to giving the patient some support to tide him or her over a temporary crisis. In others, the objective may be to produce extensive changes in the patient's life pattern. The existential therapies are concerned with the problem of meaning and goal in life, surely a large and complex undertaking, while the behavior therapists have the more limited and concrete goal of relieving the patient of a symptom such as an incapacitating fear, a sexual hang-up, or ineptness of some kind in handling social situations. In some cases the treatment program may be brief, in others extensive and lengthy. How can therapies with such diverse objectives be compared? It would be a little like comparing apples and oranges. Since variations in aim are important, they cannot be dismissed casually.

A third difficulty is that a form of treatment may be more *effective with some patients* than with others. Patients often shop around to find the sort of therapist they think suits them best. Whether or not this matching of patient (or type of disturbance) and therapist (or type of treatment) makes any difference is a question that needs to be answered. If researchers ignore such matching, they may easily draw the wrong conclusions. They may "discover" erroneously that there is no difference in effectiveness between

FIGURE 15-1 Hebephrenic schizophrenic. (Benyas, from Black Star.)

two treatment programs when, in reality, one of them has considerable success with a certain type of patient and the other works well with a different type. If the match between patient and therapist is poor, no measurable gain may be observed over that observed for untreated controls.

There are also a large number of *patient characteristics* which clearly limit what any form of psychotherapy can do to facilitate solution to their adjustive problems. These characteristics include limited intelligence, physical illness, economic and occupational inadequacies, and poor family or societal supports. To evaluate the effectiveness of psychotherapy in general, or of a particular kind, such patient chacteristics must be taken into account. Moreover, adventitious circumstances in the life of the patient while therapy is taking place may make it appear that the therapy is helping or hurting when, actually, any improvement or deterioration may be the result of such circumstances. The termination of a destructive marriage, an unexpected inheritance, a

new and supportive job or romance are some of the events taking place during treatment which might have a favorable impact on the patient. To prevent erroneously assigning responsibility for the improvement or decline to the therapy itself, *control groups* must be employed in therapy-outcome research in which the influence of these adventitious circumstances could be evaluated (see Rubenstein and Parloff, 1959).

Recent research on the outcomes of therapy has brought out a fourth difficulty in the specification of treatment variables, that is, variations in the *adequacy of therapists.* In at least two studies the results have suggested that, even among experienced professionals, not only does therapeutic effectiveness vary, but some therapists seem to help their patients and others appear to make them worse (Bergin, 1963). If a given treatment method is represented by both effective and ineffective therapists, their positive and negative influences may well cancel each other out when the results are compared with an untreated control group. The adequacy of the therapists may be a crucial factor in whether positive, negative, or negligible effects of the treatment method they represent are observed.

Finally, one must also consider certain *advantages and disadvantages* inherent in the two major approaches to psychotherapy in making an evaluation of them. For example, behavior therapy clearly has the great advantage of simplicity, ease, and economy. It is brief, and if there is progress it will be visible. On the other hand, behavior therapy is most applicable to certain kinds of adjustive difficulties (which, by the way, turn out to be those in which it seems to have had the greatest success)—for example, mild phobias, sexual dysfunctions, and problems of impulse control. It has also been argued that behavior therapy with the therapist strongly and actively in charge is better suited to the poor and uneducated, because the latter can rarely accommodate to the introspective, existential concerns of psychodynamic therapy. It also seems particularly well suited in situations where psychologists have substantial control of the person's life, as in hospital wards and classrooms, and with behaviorally troubled children still young enough to be in the formative years. On the other hand, the psychodynamic approaches appear more attuned to existential neuroses, identity crises, depressions, vague disabling and long-standing anxieties, and moral or value dilemmas. As Arnold Lazarus (1971, pp. 218–219) puts it:

> The achievement of profound insights will frequently fail to eliminate tics, phobias, compulsions, or perversions, whereas operant conditioning, desensitization, or straightforward hypnotic suggestion may often quell these "symptoms" with neither relapse nor substitution. Should we then abandon the quest for self-knowledge in favor of conditioning techniques? Indeed, if one's goal is to overcome enuresis or to teach an autistic child to speak, or to instigate prosocial behaviors among schizophrenic inmates, the clinical and research evidence suggests that it would be foolhardy to bypass direct behavior approaches. . . . Since it is not always so easy to determine when limited problems of function or dysfunction become entangled with far-reaching problems of meaning, therapists should try to determine what they are dealing with before plunging ahead with deconditioning or reconditioning techniques. The basic question to be asked is whether one is dealing with a problem or a symptom. To desensitize a phobic patient, for instance, without first establishing whether his phobia is a straightforward avoidance response, or a psychotic manifestation, or a symbolic retreat, or a face-saving or attention-seeking device, or a weapon in family or marital strife violates the cardinal rule—"diagnosis before therapy." It may seem ridiculous to keep asserting the obvious. After all, what self-respecting therapist would apply desensitization (or any other technique) without first con-

ducting a thorough evaluation of the patient's problem? The answer, regrettably, is all too many.

It is evident that the problem of evaluating therapeutic outcomes is more complicated than is often assumed. Therefore, the question of whether or not a given treatment method is effective cannot be settled by casual statistical comparisons. Such casualness characterizes many of the attacks on psychodynamic therapy and, for that matter, attacks on behavior therapies as well. Debunkers of insight therapy overlook in their polemics the very sticky problems discussed here because they have already made up their minds and are trying to prove what they believe rather than to evaluate evidence. They do no service to the field, since only sophisticated research effectively encompassing the issues in question will ever settle the matter.

ASSESSING PERSONALITY CHANGE

Here we are thrust again directly into the unresolved difficulty, discussed in Chapter 7, that is, defining mental health. In the present context the question becomes, "How should improvement be defined?" Behavior therapists stress the disappearance of the symptom. Psychodynamic therapists seek more complicated and extensive changes in the patient's interpersonal relations and internal psychological economy. The arguments about the value of therapy, or the comparative value of different therapies, cannot be resolved merely by making objective observations of behavior change. They require some resolution of differences in values concerning mental health and illness.

The reader can get some idea below of some of the typical criteria of improvement that have been proposed by insight therapists (for example, Knight, 1941, p. 456). They include:

1 *Disappearance of presenting symptoms.*

2 *Real improvement in mental functioning:*

   a The acquisition of insight, intellectual and emotional, into the childhood sources of conflict, the part played by precipitating and other reality factors, and the methods of defense against anxiety which have produced the type of personality and the specific character of the morbid process;

   b Development of tolerance, without anxiety, of the instinctual drives;

   c Development of ability to accept one's self objectively, with a good appraisal of elements of strength and weakness;

   d Attainment of relative freedom from enervating tensions and talent-crippling inhibitions;

   e Release of the aggressive energies needed for self-preservation, achievement, competition, and protection of one's rights.

3 *Improved reality adjustment:*

   a More consistent and loyal interpersonal relationships with well-chosen objects;

   b Free functioning of abilities in productive work;

   c Improved sublimation in recreation and avocations;

   d Full heterosexual functioning with potency and pleasure.

If the implication of improvement or change in response to treatment were to be removed from the preceding criteria, what remains is merely a list of criteria of positive mental health. This illustrates the point that the two problems, the evaluation of therapeutic improvement and the definition of mental health, are really one and the same.

Still another difficulty now emerges: How are these various criteria of improvement to be measured? There is not so much difficulty when it comes to the criterion of disappearance of the symptom. This is more or less a clear-cut criterion, as behavior therapists themselves have pointed out. However, being clear-cut does not make

it, of necessity, the best criterion. On the other hand, how are other criteria, such as tolerance of instinctual drives, self-acceptance, or better interpersonal relations, to be measured? The adequate evaluation of psychotherapy requires solutions to assessment problems that have not yet been solved. Comparative research on the outcomes of psychotherapy requires that the investigator utilize tentative and not fully validated procedures of personality assessment. This limitation, perhaps as much as any other, accounts for the unsatisfactory state of research on therapeutic outcomes. It is disingenuous for critics of insight therapy to criticize in one breath the assessment procedures on which psychologists must presently rely and, in another breath, to attack the absence of clear research evidence about psychotherapeutic effectiveness, which itself depends on good assessment. Only oversimple answers to questions about psychotherapeutic effectiveness can be forthcoming until the many intermediate problems of personality assessment have also been solved.

LIMITATIONS OF PSYCHOTHERAPY

There are some evident limitations concerning what psychotherapy, as it is practiced today, can do to alleviate the individual and social problem of adjustive failure. These are twofold: (1) Not all patients appear to be equally suitable for psychotherapy, and (2) psychotherapy is not readily available to all.

SUITABILITY OF PATIENTS

Many personal qualities are relevant to whether or not a person can be treated by psychotherapy; these include intelligence and verbal skills, attitudes toward therapy, the nature of the problem, and the age of the person. *Lack of intelligence* and *the absence of verbal skills* pose severe handicaps for psychodynamic therapy because such therapy, as it is generally practiced, requires abstract communication and subtle understanding on the part of the patient. Persons who are not intellectually competent or capable of expressing themselves verbally can make little progress. Furthermore, people differ greatly in their values and *attitudes* relevant to therapy. Those who lack enthusiasm for introspection and verbal communication are handicapped with respect to participating in insight psychotherapy. The reader will recall from Chapter 10, for example, that lower-class, uneducated patients tend not to view psychotherapy favorably. They are thus usually deprived of this treatment method both by their own inclination and by the tendency of the educated therapist to find them less promising as candidates for the hours, months, and years of verbal interaction required by psychodynamic therapy.

Likewise, the *nature of the disturbance* is a highly relevant factor. For example, the *severely disturbed patient* with bizarre modes of thought or, even worse, the stuporous catatonic schizophrenic who has withdrawn from all human psychological contact offer poor prospects for traditional psychodynamic therapy; frequently they will not communicate verbally, and their interaction with the therapist remains at a very primitive level. The extremely fragile neurotic person who is presumed to be very vulnerable to further breakdown will usually be offered supportive treatment rather than risk exposure of hidden material that might overwhelm him or her and endanger an already precarious level of adjustment. Comparable psychotherapeutic restrictions apply to the patient with a *personality problem,* such as the criminal and the passive-dependent personality. It is believed that working psychotherapeutically with such individuals is very difficult. Frequently they do not want help with their problems of living, and what brings them to treatment is the concern of others about their behavior. Another example is the paranoid patient who has a distorted, persecutory concep-

tion of the world and is likely to assume that the therapist too harbors hostile impulses.

Advanced age severely limits the flexibility and motivation of the patient to reorganize his or her way of thinking and acting and to think ahead to the future, also making the elderly patient an uncertain candidate for psychotherapy.

These limitations apply especially to the psychodynamic therapies, which are the most ambitious regarding the changes they aim to produce. They are *logically* less fatal to the behavior therapies, which seek mainly to produce a minimum of relearning to alleviate symptoms. It is probable that the behavior therapies too suffer from limitations in regard to the kinds of patients who can be helped. However, too little evidence about their success with various types of patients is as yet available.

If psychotherapy is not effective with the types of persons mentioned, a very large troubled population remains for which the available methods of psychotherapeutic treatment are not applicable. This fact has had a sobering influence on those professional workers who were once inclined to see in psychotherapy a basic solution to most difficulties in human adjustment.

AVAILABILITY

The recognition that many people cannot be treated by traditional methods leads us logically to the second major limitation of psychotherapy; that is, it is a very costly procedure available to only a *very small fraction of the population.* Unlike an antitoxin injection or the removal of a diseased appendix, psychotherapy is largely a one-to-one relationship between patient and therapist, taking place over weeks at the very least, and commonly months and years. The professional training required to perform this kind of treatment can be obtained by only a small percentage of people. It has been justly estimated that we can never have sufficient numbers of trained people to perform enough psychotherapy to service the needs of more than a small fraction of our population. Actually, this number could be increased if psychotherapy training were not restricted to physicians (M.D.s) and psychologists (Ph.D.s). It is being proposed with increasing frequency these days that the population eligible to carry out psychotherapy professionally could be broadened substantially to include those with M.A.s, for example, and that fewer educational restrictions on such practice should be required. As it is now, only a small percentage of the patients in our mental hospitals, or of the many more who live outside institutions, can get attention from professionals. If society were to depend on psychotherapy by itself to deal with failures of adjustment, the mental health situation would indeed be quite hopeless. There could never be sufficient numbers of psychotherapists to even scratch the surface of the problem.

The issue of cost is by no means a simple one. For example, therapy which is "cheap" but inadequate may be, in a very real sense, costly, and therapy which is "costly" but effective might be in the long run the most economical. Thus, the issue of cost must be seen in relative rather than absolute terms. The point is well illustrated in a personal communication by one of the author's psychoanalytically oriented associates, who stated:

I have a relative who has suffered from psychotic depression for twenty-five years and has spent a good deal of time in mental hospitals during this period. The disruption of her own life and of the lives of her children has been considerable. She has cost the taxpayers a small fortune for her hospitalizations. She has had a number of courses of electroshock therapy—a "cheap" therapy. She has had various drugs. These too are "cheap." She is still prone to depression. She may return to the hospital any month, any year. On the other hand, I know of people who have been successfully and permanently treated for psychotic depres-

sion by psychoanalysis. The psychoanalysis cost perhaps $14,000. It was cheaper than the "cheap" therapies that failed to help my cousin permanently.

OTHER KINDS OF TREATMENT

Obviously, then, the sobering fact that psychotherapy is too limited to deal fully with the mental health problem, although it may be a valuable approach in many instances, must lead us in other directions.

There are a number of alternatives to psychotherapy as it is characterized in Chapters 13 and 14. Some of these, such as the physical therapies, are themselves not new and are losing favor. Others, such as community mental health centers, reflect newer ideas about the best way to get treatment to people who have not had access to it. Still another, namely hospitalization, is perhaps the oldest societal approach to adjustive failure, and it tends today to be seen as a last resort. Finally, there is an approach that is primarily directed at prevention and involves the restructuring of the social institutions fostering maladjustment in the developing child and in the adult.

HOSPITALIZATION

For many decades, the predominant approach to the treatment of severe failures of adjustment has been incarceration of the patient in a mental hospital. Institutionalizing people is an extreme solution for many reasons: (1) They are removed, often forcibly, from the settings and social supports with which they are familiar and deprived of the work responsibilities and prerogatives that help make them self-respecting persons. (2) The costs of hospitalization are exceedingly high. If the community must carry this economic burden, and few individuals can afford such care on a private basis, the cost is bound to be substantial.

Keeping the person in the community by means of community mental health centers would be easier and cheaper (for the community, not the family) than removing him or her to an institution. Moreover, the longer the patient remains in the mental hospital, the dimmer become his or her prospects of ever returning to a productive life in the community. (3) The action of hospitalizing the psychotic patient may encourage the patient's family to believe that the "sick" member is entirely responsible for the difficulties of the whole family, whereas in reality the whole family may constitute a disordered social system (see, for example, Boszormenyi-Nagy, 1965). All this argues against using institutionalization except as a last resort, and in favor of reluctance to hospitalize patients if there are other alternatives for helping them.

The main formal reasons (or rationalizations, perhaps) for institutionalizing patients concern the *danger* they pose to themselves and the community and the possibilities of *treating* them more effectively in a setting devoted to treatment. The trouble with this is that the reasons do not fit the facts very well. Only a very small percentage of patients are actually dangerous to anyone at any given time. Also, a very small percentage of patients are actually dangerous to themselves because of the prospects of suicide. Certainly, then, this would seem to be a poor excuse for locking up hundreds of thousands of people and isolating them from their families and communities. Moreover, a considerable proportion of those not hospitalized could be considered dangers to the community, as is evidenced by the shocking episodes of mass killings, homicides, and assassinations that are accomplished by individuals who have never been hospitalized or seen professionally. It is likely that people who end up in mental institutions are mainly those who *cannot take care of themselves* and have *no one willing to do so*, except perhaps the state. Since the state has to, it does so in the most stingy way it can. The book *Asylums*, by Erving

Goffman (1961), has made this point most effectively.

The second reason, that better treatment is available in an institution, is patently false. The most striking complaint about the typical mental hospital is that it provides mainly *custodial* care rather than treatment, largely because the community provides little in the way of funds for personnel who can provide treatment. Although this complaint does not apply to all hospitals, it is generally applicable even in the best institutions mostly because of the shortage of trained personnel. The key problem with mental institutions is thus *economic,* that is, the shortage of funds and the shortage of personnel who are qualified. Things seem to have improved somewhat in the past several decades (many of the pestholes have been cleaned up), but the situation is far from attractive, and the mental hospital, on the whole,

FIGURE 15-2   A psychiatric ward. (A. E. Woolley.)

is still an embarrassment to our society. The public is still suspicious and frightened of mental patients, one of the marginal groups of our society, and still thinks of them as "loonies" just as medieval people did. Society still punishes deviant individuals and is reluctant to forgive them their economic and social failure.

Because people can be committed to a mental hospital with comparative ease, this gives rise to concern that it is possible to "eliminate" someone by this device for political or other reasons. The greatest danger is probably in borderline cases of senility. Here the issue becomes one of how senile a person who is a financial burden or who has a large estate has to be to be declared incompetent or be institutionalized. Because of the importance of protecting the rights of individuals against unwarranted "seizure," the field of *forensic psychiatry* has emerged to deal with the legal aspects of commitment. Although the situation is far from ideal, particularly in backward communities, there are strong legal safeguards against unreasonable commitment, and the procedures followed in advanced societies today are overwhelmingly superior to those practiced in the Middle Ages.

In all states of the United States, for example, only a judge can commit a patient, and in most states, at least one of the physicians recommending commitment must not be on the staff of the hospital to which the commitment is made. A relative may petition to have the person committed, as may a police officer or community official. Typically, two medical signatures must be obtained, based on direct examination of the person. Commitment in most states (though not all) is made following a court hearing in which the physician presents the justification.

Davidson (1959, pp. 1902, 1905–1906), in the *American Handbook of Psychiatry*, has recently described the commitment process as follows:

Commitment is a process whereby one or, more usually, two doctors explain to the civil authorities why a patient should be placed in a mental hospital. The physicians *certify* that the patient is mentally ill. The judge *commits*. The process is started by someone—usually a relative—who thinks that the patient needs hospital care. The person who initiates the process is called an applicant or petitioner. . . .

The psychiatrist is often impatient with the legal details necessary to effect an involuntary commitment. He reasons that a psychosis is a disease, and that it should no more need formal legal adjudication than does pneumonia or appendicitis. . . .

To physicians, one of the most infuriating aspects of commitment is the requirement that "notice" be given to the patient. Certainly a paranoiac, given formal notice that he is about to be committed, will either seek to flee or will be prompted to violence. A person in a depression may commit suicide on receiving this notice.

The system in most communities is designed to lean over backward to protect the individual against unreasonable seizure. Nevertheless, the possibilities of railroading a person into a mental hospital lie not in the theory of the system but in its administration. When its administration occurs under sloppy or hasty conditions (as it sometimes does), the chances of unwarranted seizure are increased. In general, railroading is probably very uncommon, largely because of the honesty and impartiality of most doctors and judges who carry the responsibility for commitment. However, because of large hospital caseloads, the shortage of professional personnel, and the automatic presumption by most people that the seized person must be mentally incompetent, important legal rights of people can rather easily be violated, often quite unintentionally. This latter issue has been a major concern of some psychiatrists (for example, Szasz, 1963). Voluntary commitment, naturally, is easier to effect.

PHYSICAL THERAPY

Physical therapies are used for two reasons: First, as we say in Chapter 9, many professional workers believe that "mental illness" is the result of biochemical or neurological defects and that the ultimate treatment will be physical rather than psychological or social; second, other approaches often fail with highly disturbed persons, for example, those who have been in mental hospitals for a long time. Indeed, the use of modern drugs has resulted in quieter mental hospital wards and has sharply reduced the numbers of people who must be kept indefinitely under hospital care because they cannot function in the community.

The reader should not assume that the lines are always sharply drawn between these psychosocial and physiological positions, or that the use of physical therapies necessarily means that the user adopts a purely physiological stance about the causes of mental disorder. Many physicians employ drugs primarily as ways of calming the excited patient so that he or she can be reached more readily by psychological means. The bias of the author tends to be in the direction of social learning. However, if the reader is to be fully acquainted with actual therapeutic practice, *physical therapies* must be reviewed also. The physical therapies (especially drugs) probably represent the *most common* treatment approach to mental illness as it is practiced in mental hospitals throughout the United States today.

It should also be said that psychotherapy, in contrast with physical therapy, is rather rarely used nowadays in the treatment of hospitalized psychotic patients. Rather, psychotherapy tends to be the treatment of choice in the neuroses and milder difficulties of adjustment. With psychotic patients, drugs are the physical therapy in most common use. They are relatively inexpensive and easy to use. And as we saw in Chapter 10, social class has much to do with the kinds of treatment available to patients. For this reason, white middle- and upper-class persons are more apt to receive one or another form of psychotherapy, often before an adjustive difficulty escalates into a major adjustive failure, while lower-class persons (the poor and uneducated, including a large proportion of ethnic minorities such as blacks and Latinos) are more apt to be hospitalized and receive physical therapies such as electric shock and antipsychotic drugs.

There are four main forms of physical treatment in use: *insulin shock,* electric or *convulsive shock, psychosurgery,* and *drugs.* The last named is the most frequent. Miscellaneous treatments, such as baths and massages, are also used but are not important enough to deal with here.

Insulin shock In the *American Handbook of Psychiatry,* William A. Horwitz opens his chapter on insulin treatment (1959, p. 1485) with the statement, "Insulin shock therapy is considered the most accepted somatic treatment for schizophrenia." He goes on to say (p. 1486) that although its use has decreased in recent years and it has even been discontinued in some hospitals as a result of the introduction of tranquilizing drugs, "in a recent symposium at the International Psychiatric Congress, July, 1957, clinicians from many countries came to the conclusion that, for the time being, insulin is still an important tool in our therapeutic armamentarium for the schizophrenic patient." Horwitz's cautious enthusiasm is probably quite excessive, since insulin shock therapy now represents a comparatively minor method of treatment.

In insulin shock therapy, insulin is injected before breakfast, after which a hypoglycemic coma occurs. The treatment is usually ended with an injection of glucose or by forcing glucose in solution into the mouth. The dosage is increased each session until the point where the patient regularly goes into coma about two or three hours after the insulin injection. The treatments are given about five or six days a week until about fifty comas have occurred. As the treatment continues, the comas are gradually lengthened in duration up to a period of about one hour.

Coma is produced because insulin (a hormone) results in the withdrawal of sugar from the blood and, therefore, from the cells of the brain which, in consequence, are starved for metabolic activity. Insulin secretion is a natural process of the body which helps in the homeostatic regulation of blood sugar. The sugar is kept at proper levels in the blood by being stored in the liver and released when needed by the action of the insulin. In certain metabolic diseases, too much insulin is secreted, and the individual suffers from attacks of hypoglycemia, or else too little is available, and the individual suffers from diabetes. Insulin coma is thus a hypoglycemic attack, and if too severe it can produce convulsions and death. For this reason, careful nursing care is required while the patient is being treated to prevent the hypoglycemia from progressing too far before it is terminated. This makes the treatment **dangerous** and expensive to administer, facts that **have** probably contributed to the decline in **the use** of insulin treatment in favor of the tranquilizing drugs, which are cheaper, simpler to use, and safer. Insulin shock therapy is employed in practice without great concern about the possible mechanisms of its therapeutic action, as well as with questionable scientific evidence of its effectiveness.

Convulsive shock The originator of convulsive shock therapy, Meduna (1935), first tried camphor in oil injected intramuscularly, but later shifted to another camphor-based substance called "metrazol" which produced convulsions immediately and reliably. He believed that convulsions and schizophrenia were antagonistic. These seizures proved dangerous; there was a high probability of severe fractures. Moreover, with repeated use, patients became terribly frightened of the treatment, and metrazol was rapidly abandoned in favor of a convulsion-producing technique employing *electric shock*,

introduced by two Italians, Cerletti and Bini, in 1938. Electroconvulsive shock treatment became, for a time, the most widely used physical therapy in mental hospital psychiatry. It was cheap, comparatively safe, and reliable. It was not the method of induction of the convulsion that appeared therapeutically important to professional workers, but the *convulsion* itself (see Kalinowsky, 1959).

In the procedure used by Cerletti and Bini, which is still extensively employed, an alternating current of between 70 and 150 volts with a frequency of 50 or 60 cycles is passed through the head by electrodes placed on the temples. The duration of the shock is about .01 to 1 second. Patients vary greatly in the readiness with which they convulse, and the electrical current necessary to produce a seizure varies accordingly. By and large, the precise current characteristics are not well standardized, nor are they of great interest to clinicians employing electric shock treatment.

The patient is placed on a table, and mouth gags are used to prevent tongue bites and to protect the teeth. Drugs are often used also to reduce postconvulsive disturbances and reduce the danger of bone fractures. The treatment is usually given about three times a week, sometimes hundreds of times altogether. Electroconvulsive shock treatment has been widely used in the physician's office, as well as in the hospital. There is usually some impairment of immediate memory following the convulsion. Although research has not revealed evidence of much organic tissue damage following convulsions, the memory effects and evidence of alteration of electroencephalographic patterns make it certain that organic changes in the brain must be produced, perhaps temporarily, by the treatment. As with insulin shock therapy, evidence on the effectiveness of electroconvulsive shock treatment is ambiguous and controversial, although there is a substantial medical lore about the most suitable type of patient. The disorders for which electroconvulsive shock treatment is considered most appropriate are the affective disorders, that is, depressions and manic states. The immediate outlook for such patients is good with or without treatment, but the treatment is presumed to speed up the recovery. However, with these disorders, further attacks of depression or mania are very likely, and no one really claims that the treatment is a cure (Fig. 15-3).

While electroconvulsive shock treatment remains one of the most frequent of the physical types of therapy in mental hospitals, it too has suffered considerable decline with the introduction of tranquilizing drugs. Some psychiatrists believe that electroconvulsive shock is a highly effective method of treatment with mental patients, even the more mildly disturbed neurotic, and that psychotherapy has rather dubious value in comparison with it. A very different opinion would be expected from psychiatrists of a social-learning persuasion. In some communities (for example, San Francisco), attempts are being made to ban the use of electric shock treatment as dangerous and destructive and as a violation of the patient's civil rights. In any case, the therapeutic value of electroconvulsive treatment has not been proved unequivocally any more than is the mechanism of its effects clear to those who use it.

Psychosurgery Surgical operations on the intact brain of patients to relieve symptoms of mental illness came formally into being in psychiatry at about the same time as insulin coma and convulsive shock treatments. The approach was first conceived by Egas Moniz of Lisbon in 1933. In 1936 Moniz reported on twenty cases in which psychosurgery had been attempted by means of a technique called "prefrontal lobotomy." This technique was described in the United States by Freeman and Watts (1937), who amplified Moniz's theory that abnormal cellular connections among certain neurons of the brain were destroyed by the drastic brain surgery, presumably freeing the

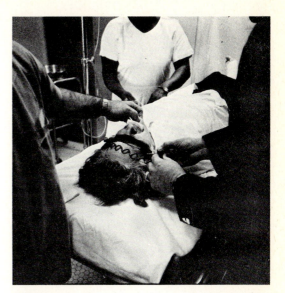

FIGURE 15-3 Electroshock therapy. (Paul Fusco, from Magnum.)

patient of his or her fixed abnormal ideas (see also Freeman, 1959). Freeman and Watts also noted that patients so treated could be relieved of the unbearable pain associated with fatal conditions such as cancer. Although the pain was still perceived by the patient, the suffering connected with it was much reduced.

Psychosurgery subsequently went through a period of wide usage, especially with severely disturbed patients of long standing. As with other physical treatments, psychosurgery declined with the advent of the tranquilizing drugs. In recent years, it has been restricted generally to terminal patients in severe pain and to severe, chronic psychotics who have not responded to other physical or psychological therapies. Because of the extensive destruction of brain tissue, psychosurgery is a more drastic procedure than the other methods we have considered. And as with all physical therapies, any theoretical rationale for psychosurgery is difficult to support, largely because the brain is an organ about whose structure and function as yet only very little is known.

Drugs The use of drugs in the treatment of mental illness has a very long history, and the chemicals used for this purpose have come and gone in fads, the so-called tranquilizing drugs being a fairly recent vogue. Drugs to produce sedation of excited mental patients, of which the *bromides* were one of the earliest forms, were once considered to be the greatest hope of medical psychiatry. However, enthusiasm for bromide treatment waned, especially with evidence of harmful toxic side effects, and these drugs are no longer extensively used. *Barbituric sedatives,* such as phenobarbital, sodium amytal, or seconal, have also had their day and are still used.

Drugs in psychiatry are generally considered to be of three main types related to their function: sedative, antidepressant, and antipsychotic.

1 The barbiturates and mild tranquilizers such as meprobamate are in the *sedative* group. When they are used as adjuncts to standard insight therapy, such use has sometimes been called ''narcoanalysis'' or ''narcosynthesis,'' a form of psychoanalytic-like therapy in which sedative drugs (for example, sodium amytal) are used to create a hypnotic state, in the same way that hypnosis has been used to facilitate the uncovering of unconscious mental activity (Wolberg, 1945). Sedative drugs have also been used to produce a deep narcotic sleep which may be prolonged for many days. The patient is kept asleep for eighteen to twenty-two hours a day over a period of several weeks being awakened only to provide for nutrition and other necessary functions.

2 The *antidepressants* include the amphetamines (dexedrine and benzedrine) and some newer drugs which usually have an activating effect and help bring the patient out of the doldrums. One of the newer drugs is a substance known as lithium (lithium carbonate) which is being used with enthusiasm in some clinical centers for depression, particularly a type of depression that is believed to be a stage of a cyclical pattern of reaction called manic-depressive psychosis. Clinicians using this drug see episodes of depression and manic excitement in a patient as expressions of a genetically based biochemical disturbance in the brain rather than as a problem of living arising from psychological stress and faulty social learning. In some presently unknown way, the lithium is thought to counteract this biochemical disturbance in patients with an organically based depression (Johnson, 1974). Drugs are also used by people who are not hospitalized, to perk up their spirits, to help them remain awake for long periods, or to gain a sense of excitement.

3 The *antipsychotic* drugs (for example, chlorpromazine and reserpine) are used particularly in the treatment of schizophrenia. It has been mainly the latter drugs which have so drastically altered the patient care practices of the modern mental hospital.

The list of chemical therapies used for mental patients is very extensive and need not be reviewed here. A rather thorough survey of non-tranquilizer chemical therapies is available (cf. McGraw and Oliven, 1959; and Redlich and Freedman, 1966). Included are such esoteric procedures as carbon dioxide therapy (in which the patient inhales mixtures of carbon dioxide and oxygen), chloral hydrate (the oldest hypnotic drug in modern medicine), and nitrous oxide (which was tried and abandoned as having too fleeting an effect and which frequently produces nausea). None of these substances compete today with the use of chemical agents commonly referred to as the ''tranquilizers.''

Many so-called tranquilizing drugs have come into being in recent years, the most common of which in mental hospital use are chlorpromazine, or variations of it, and reserpine, which is a preparation derived from rauwolfia, a substance found growing naturally. New compounds keep getting introduced because they are profitable and are used very widely in their milder forms outside hospitals. For example, meprobamate (commercial names for this include Miltown and Equanil) is a mild muscle relaxant that is sold freely and distributed widely. Librium and Valium are also heavily used nowadays. Different tranquilizers may be prescribed for different conditions. Many of the drugs produce some side effects which are themselves undesirable, a fact which should discourage indiscriminate or careless usage.

Perhaps the most promising effort in the field of psychopharmacology is the laboratory study of the effects of these substances on the brain and behavior. The tranquilizing drugs are thought to affect mainly the midbrain and the reticular formation, portions of the brain heavily involved in emotional states (see Chapter 5). There is evidence that some of the drugs block or alter the action of the chemical transmitters secreted at nerve endings and thus influence subcortical centers which control homeostasis. Comparatively little is presently known about their action or their effectiveness as a treatment agent, in spite of the fact that they are so heavily used. Active research efforts, however, are presently producing rapidly increasing knowledge. In his review of drug therapy in the *American Handbook of Psychiatry,* Hoch (1959, p. 1549) commented as follows on the way in which so-called tranquilizing drugs appear to work:

> A great deal of exploration has been going on in the last few years to elucidate the action of the tranquilizing drugs, but we still are not able to state how they influence mental disorders. The clinical-action radius of the tranquilizing drugs is fairly well known. What we do not know is how they influence central-nervous-system function and where. Clinical observations indicate that they relieve excitation and tension and make a person more calm. Therefore, they have a sedative action but lack some of the features of sedatives such as barbitu-

rates. The tranquilizing drugs have no uniform action on the psyche. Not all functions are reduced, but many productive symptoms in a mental disorder, such as hallucinations, delusions, etc., are influenced to a considerable degree. Emotional overcharge is also reduced. The tranquilizing drugs, as far as we know today, suppress symptoms, but they do not eliminate the basic structure of the psychosis. In many patients the symptoms can return rather quickly, even after successful treatment and when the drugs have been withdrawn.

An enthusiastic, readable, and informative discussion of the expanding field of psychopharmacology may be found in an article by Jarvik (1967). Jarvik regards the discovery of tranquilizing drugs as a real breakthrough in the treatment of the psychoses, particularly because such drugs, even if not producing cures of the disorder, make possible the humane management of disturbed patients. On this Jarvik (p. 51) writes sanguinely:

> Until it was discovered that drugs could help the severely disturbed, almost the only recourse in the management of such patients was physical restraint. Philippe Pinel, the famous French psychiatrist, campaigning for humane treatment of the insane at the end of the 18th century, freed the inmates of the grim Bicêtre mental hospital from their iron chains. Unfortunately, other physical restraints had to be substituted when patients became assaultive or destructive, and though the padded cell and the camisole, or straitjacket, may have been softer than chains, they allowed no greater freedom. Not until the mid-1950's did drugs finally promise total emancipation from physical restraint for most patients. Despite the fears of some psychiatrists, psychologists, and social workers that the social and psychological factors contributing to mental illness would be ignored, the use of psychopharmaceuticals radically improved the treatment of the mental-

ly ill within and without the hospital. Indeed, only with their use has it been possible for some families to be held together, for some individuals to be gainfully employed, and for some patients to be reached by psychotherapy.

The modern discipline of psychopharmacology is only about twenty-five years old. However, interest in the psychological effects of drugs is ancient, and occasional research in the area may be found over the past hundred years. Reference to the psychological effects of drugs may be found in the cuneiform tablets of ancient Assyria. The Chinese have used the herb Ma Huang (yellow astringent), which contains ephedrine, for more than 5,000 years. In the first century B.C., Horace was enthusiastic about alcohol. The use of opium goes back to the times of Homer in ancient Greece. Marijuana, the dried leaves of the hemp plant, *Cannabis sativa,* was apparently brought to the West from the Orient by Marco Polo, and as everyone knows, it is widely used today. About the middle of the nineteenth century, Moreau de Tours made the modern-sounding suggestion that physicians take hashish (derived from Cannabis) to experience mental illness so they could understand it better. This is precisely what has been proposed more recently for LSD. Other drugs with long histories include morphine, cocaine, mescaline (or peyote), and psilocybin. All these drugs are derived from plants. With the advances in chemistry during the first half of the nineteenth century and thereafter, many artificial drugs have been produced.

The belief that adjustive failure (even when it is mild) is the result of a biochemical defect or malfunction has also stimulated enthusiastic use of and experimentation with many other types of chemical treatments in growing numbers. One example is megavitamin therapy, which consists mainly of administering large daily quantities of vitamin substances. It is much too early to assess the value or potential dangers of such treatment,

though this has hardly dampened the current enthusiasm of its protagonists—often communicated to a receptive public in the mass media. Another interesting and controversial example is the use of amphetamines for hyperactive children. The fact that such drugs, which are activating in adults, are used to calm hyperactive children and to help make them more attentive in school reflects one of the paradoxical qualities of many drugs—that they can have opposite effects on different people or under different conditions. There have also been many criticisms of drug therapy with hyperactive children. For example, psychologists with a social science bias are skeptical that an organic disorder underlies most instances of overactivity and agitation in children (though this could be true in some), believing instead that such behavioral disturbances usually reflect psychosocial problems; moreover, many educators and observers feel that the drugs are used indiscriminately, and that although a comparatively small number of hyperactive children might have an organic defect, the drugs are given to large numbers of children merely to quiet them and keep them from creating classroom disturbances rather than to help them cope with their problems. This often bitter argument reflects at least two things: first, an ideological polarity about the causes and mechanisms of adjustive failure, and second, a lack of adequate research to evaluate the effectiveness of chemical (and other) treatments and to differentiate the conditions under which they do or do not work.

Widespread controversy exists over the value of drugs, even tranquilizers, in the treatment of mental illness. One of the difficult problems with drug research is the absence of adequate methods for evaluating the psychological and behavioral effects. New drugs (many of them basically the same as the old but with a new name) are repeatedly marketed with labels and descriptions of effects that are insufficiently established. For example, it is often taken on faith by the patient and physician that a drug will reduce apprehensiveness or depression. Absence of adequate methods of evaluation, and commercial disinterest in doing so, discourage precise knowledge in a field that has grown rapidly.

An even greater difficulty is the readiness with which psychological effects can be suggested to the person using them, even when such effects are not actually produced by physiological action. This is usually referred to as the "placebo effect." It has been shown over and over, for example, that when people expect a drug to produce depression, they are likely to report feeling depressed; conversely, if they expect to be excited, excitement tends to be reported. Not only is the effect reported, but physiological changes in accordance with the aroused psychological state are likely to occur as well, although the actual depressant or excitatory action of the drug may make the reaction even greater. The problem of disentangling the effects of suggestion or expectation from the actual physiological effects of the drug is crucial to psychopharmacological study, and much of the research that is performed fails to guard against this (Fig. 15-4).

There is an old saying in psychiatry that any new technique will achieve good results until the initial enthusiasm for it wears off; therefore, one had better take full advantage of it before it ceases to work. Surgical removal of foci of infection, thought once to be the toxic cause of mental illness, produced favorable reports of many cures (Cotton, 1921, 1922), until Kopeloff and Cheney (1922) did a controlled experiment which disproved the theory of focal infection. Similarly, bromides were once enthusiastically received just as tranquilizing drugs are today. Just the expectation on the part of the patient that a new curative drug has been found will produce evidence of improvement, as long as the doctors and nurses communicate positive expectations when they prescribe and administer the drug. Only when control patients are made to think

"This pill should make you feel better."

"I already do."

FIGURE 15-4 The placebo effect.

they are getting the same beneficial treatment can a suitable test of the genuine efficacy of the therapeutic procedure, sans suggestion, be made. The use of drugs is particularly vulnerable to this difficulty.

We have emphasized some of the difficulties inherent in evaluating the psychological effects of drugs acting presumably by virtue of their chemical effects on the nervous system. Nevertheless, although these problems are far from having been solved to date, it is better to allow an enthusiastic and qualified spokesman to express his optimistic view of the future of psychopharmacology. For example, Jarvik (1967, p. 59) writes:

In the future it should be possible to say in what ways each important psychopharmaceutical influences behavior, and thus to characterize it by a behavioral profile, just as we can now describe a chemical in terms of its chromatographic pattern. Ultimately, it ought to be possible to look at the chemical structure of any new drug and predict whether it will be useful as an antipsychotic, an antifatigue agent, an appetite stimulant, and so forth. By the same token, the physiological determinants of behavior will be so well worked out that we will understand why a drug which causes alertness also depresses hunger, or why one that causes difficulty in doing arithmetic also causes peculiar sensations in the skin. One can envisage the day when drugs may be employed not only to treat pathological conditions (reduce pain, suffering, agitation, and anxiety), but also to enhance the normal state of man—increase pleasure, facilitate learning and memory, reduce jealousy and aggressiveness. Hopefully such pharmacological developments will come about as an accompaniment of, and not as a substitute for, a more ideal society.

THE COMMUNITY MENTAL HEALTH CENTER

Still another modern approach to the mental health problem is the *community mental health center.* In such centers an effort is made to bring the professional to the people in the setting in which they live, rather than the other way around. This·is precisely the opposite direction from that taken when mental hospitals were first established; patients were removed from their homes and communities to institutions located in isolated areas, often miles from the nearest town, where they would be less of a nuisance. The express purpose was to create a barrier between the patient and the community. This barrier often could not be bridged after the patient had been away for a time. By making the mental health center a *part* of the local community, the psychological isolation typically produced by mental illness could be somewhat reduced.

M. Brewster Smith has forcefully pointed out recently that adjustive failure must be viewed as embedded in the contemporaneous society. In his view, its presence reflects a failure of the social structure as much as of the individual. In speaking of the community approach to mental health, Smith writes (1969, pp. 252–254):

The first mental-health revolution unshackled the insane. By calling them sick, it managed to treat them as humans. Its monuments and symbols are the great, usually isolated, state mental hospitals. The second revolution came from the spread of dynamic psychiatry (mainly Freud's) and was characterized by individual, one-to-one psychotherapy. Now the third revolution throws off the constraints of the doctor-patient medical model—the idea that mental disorder is a *private* misery—and relates the trouble, and the cure, to the entire web of social and personal relationships in which the individual is caught. . . .

Mental illness usually grows out of and contributes to the breakdown of a person's normal sources of support and understanding, especially in his family. It is part of a vicious circle. Not only has he himself faltered, but the social systems on which he depends have failed to sustain him—family, school, job, church, friendship, and the like. The task is not to cure an ailment inside his skin, but to strengthen him to the point where he can once again participate in the interactions that make up the warp and woof of life. . . .

The first big step in the third mental-health revolution has been to bring the treatment of the seriously disturbed back from the remote state hospital into the community. That means, among other things, taking patients away from the dehumanizing damage done by the old state hospitals with their isolation, their locked doors and back wards. We must keep patients in their home communities even if they go to hospitals there—this first of all.

The idea of the community mental health center also makes possible a new role for professionals in the mental health field, namely, going into the life situations of people in the community at strategic points where problems of adjustment are likely to arise. Clinical psychologists, for example, are entering school systems, not so much with the idea of doing individual psycho- therapy with disturbed children, but to consult with teachers about classroom and organizational practices that are germane to successful adjust- ment in school. They are also entering the homes of families who are in trouble, at their request, to assist in working out the difficulties. In this way the clinician is no longer merely waiting in his or her office for the disturbed person to appear, but entering the community social structures direct- ly. Therapists are getting to know community resources such as hospitals, police, and social service agencies. And they are also giving lec- tures and seminars on mental health to members of the community who are interested.

This is, of course, more of an ideal than a full-fledged reality. Although more than 400 com- munity health centers have been established all over the United States through the passage of the Community Mental Health Services Centers Act of 1963, which provides funds for short-term hospital care, day or night partial hospitalization for persons able to come either evenings or mornings, treatment while the patient lives at home and carries on normal activities (called outpatient therapy), emergency care around the clock, and professional consultation on request, the situation is far from happy. Such centers are plagued by inadequate funding and withdrawal of funding and by old-fashioned models of treat- ment; they have been widely criticized as seri- ously inadequate to deal with the scope of the problem faced by communities. Yet the basic idea of having professionals play a more active and diversified role right in the community is difficult to fault, and it may indeed represent the beginning of a new and more effective approach to mental health.

Within this concept of the community mental health center a new type of therapeutic unit is also proliferating called the *crisis intervention center* (cf. Caplan, 1964). Some of these remain open and staffed twenty-four hours a day and are often located right in the troubled and impover- ished ghettos of the inner city. Troubled persons can drop in or be brought by families, police, and other public employees with responsibility for those in trouble. Some of the patients of such centers are experiencing a highly disturbed, psy- chotic state; if need be, they can be referred immediately to admitting wards of hospitals able to care for people who at the moment are not in touch with reality, or who might be suicidal risks if allowed to return to the streets or homes where they live. Others are experiencing a transient personal crisis brought on by family difficulties, bereavement, loss of job, illness, or drug depen- dence. Still others come in to talk over a personal difficulty which has not yet gotten out of hand, and they may be seen over a limited time period in order to aid them in working out the difficulty before it becomes unmanageable. In such clinics professional workers must be extremely skillful in distinguishing among those patients who can manage without hospitalization and those who cannot be permitted to remain at large because they live alone without family support or are so disturbed that protective, intensive, and immedi- ate attention is required.

Some centers operate telephone "hot lines" with someone manning the telephone at all times to receive calls from persons feeling desperately lonely or at the verge of suicide. When such a center specializes in suicidal crises, it is usually called a *suicide prevention center*. In all of these crisis-oriented clinics the emphasis is on maxi- mizing the accessibility of qualified professionals or trained lay persons to anyone in need of help, including those who ordinarily would not have access because of limited financial ability, lack of knowledge, or a suspiciousness of institutional authority. Here too, the emphasis on providing help for those in need is more an ideal than a reality in that the centers usually fail to reach a high percentage of those who need mental health services or could benefit from them (Fig. 15-5).

Although the staff of the crisis clinic and other types of community mental health centers is usually professional, one recent development has been the more extensive use of less fully trained persons in working with the troubled individual, in which case the highly trained professional shifts to a more supervisory and consultative role. Even in the mental hospital, there is a growing recognition that the nursing and attendant staff are heavily involved in a therapeutic role; often they are even more important to patient welfare because of their frequent daily contacts with patients. Some institutions have also been experimenting with young college students as part-time ward personnel. These students play a therapeutic role with the patients, and many telephone hot lines are staffed by such young persons (cf. Cowen et al., 1967; Matarazzo, 1971; Rioch et al., 1963). There promises to be greater use of this approach in future years.

PREVENTION

There is another alternative to psychotherapy, namely, an effort to prevent adjustive failure before it happens. This requires restructuring the social and physical environments which have major pathology-producing potential. It is an approach frequently called "social engineering" or "social planning," and it focuses on such matters as the availability of jobs, the quality of and approach to education, the ways in which people can obtain self- and social respect, the easing of ethnic and racial tensions, making a suitable response to early warnings that individuals or groups are in trouble, and the like. The implicit assumption that lies behind this approach is that people become neurotic, psychotic, criminal, alcoholic, suicidal, and so forth because their lives are evidently deficient in the social conditions that nourish mental health. If these social conditions can be improved early enough in the person's development, there is a better chance that he or she will grow into a socially healthy and effective human being.

Nearly everyone connected with the mental health disciplines of psychiatry, psychology, and social work agrees that theoretically it is more difficult to correct maladjustment, once established, than to prevent it in the first place. This assumes, of course, that the difference between the well-adapted and the poorly adapted individual depends mainly on past learning rather than the adult conditions of life. Such an assumption is surely too simple, since some individuals live under more difficult conditions than others. But differences in adaptability to life conditions no doubt do exist among individuals. To the extent that adjustive failure results from such differences rather than from contemporary pathogenic conditions, prevention makes more sense than treatment, since it should be harder to change the personality once it is formed than to shape its development. What it has taken a good part of a lifetime to establish is not easily transformed by a few interviews, a chemical injection, a series of fifty insulin comas, or the sanguinity of attitude of a therapist. This shifts one's perspective from the treatment process to the processes of personality development and the conditions that influence it.

Two approaches to prevention can be taken. On the one hand, if we believe that the problem lies in physiological defects within the person, the possible solutions lie in controlling genetics through *eugenics,* or in somehow *correcting physical defects* that begin to appear very early in the life of the person. On the other hand, if it is believed that social experience is the main culprit, then the kinds of *experience* leading to inadequate modes of existence must be *discovered and changed.* We do not yet know what these experiences are, although there are many guesses.

A parallel might be drawn between the effort to produce mental health through social engineering and the effort of the traffic engineer to move people from one part of a megalopolis to another. Although they are on a very different scale of grandness—the former seeking to engineer the whole of living, the latter dealing only with transportation—the problems faced by both have much in common. For example, when a road becomes congested, one solution is to widen it or build a new highway to carry more traffic; however, the new road now attracts even more travelers to the area because of its increased capacity. Soon it becomes as congested as the original, or even more so, and the original disease, after treatment, may now be worse than it ever was. Traffic engineering as specific corrective must thus be accomplished within a much larger framework of social planning because the movement of people is linked to many other aspects of living in addition to road capacity.

The same dictum undoubtedly applies to social engineering. It is evidently impossible to do anything significant about the community structure without producing many other changes that were not anticipated. In spite of the best intentions, the principles of social engineering are as yet too limited to provide the necessary predictability and control over the problems of how people live and function, although there is no shortage of "expert" opinion in such matters. Nonetheless, the problems of social blight and adjustive failure are so urgent that it may not be possible to wait until the necessary knowledge is acquired to initiate programs of social engineering.

There is a further parallel in the cases of highway engineers and social engineers. Both kinds of engineers are likely to feel frustrated much of the time because society usually does not give them the power to implement their decisions. Instead, the decisions are based on political power struggles, with the engineers' recommendations being only one item of consideration in the decision process. Because, as has been pointed out, the decisions often produce unexpected effects and must be taken in the larger context of other decisions and values, this limitation is probably a good thing for the society. No one specialized group, not even an elite, is apt to

FIGURE 15-5 At suicide prevention and crisis intervention centers, experienced staff members handle "hot line" calls from desperate people. (National-Save-A-Life League, Inc.)

know what society needs or wants as well as the society as a whole, as expressed through the political process. This is not to say that social engineering is not desirable. Rather, the "experts" should not be allowed to *make* the decisions, but should serve as *consultants* to those who do.

The philosophy of social engineering has begun to filter into the mental hospital too, where it is much easier to manage because the hospital community is much smaller and simpler. In recent years, a number of studies of the mental hospital community have been published (for example, Goffman, 1961; Stanton and Schwartz, 1954; Fairweather, 1964; Ullmann, 1967; Spitzer and Denzin, 1968). These studies demonstrate the impact of the social organization of the hospital on the psychological state of the individual patients; the manner in which the hospital staff lives and works and their attitudes toward patients and toward mental illness play highly significant roles in patient behavior. Interest in the role of the social structure of the hospital turns the focus of attention somewhat away from the traditional concerns of clinical psychology and psychiatry with the inner psychological struggles of the patient and toward the patient's present *social* circumstances of living. Thus, social psychology is playing an increasing role in the mental health field.

Social engineering, either within the hospital or in the larger society, is not yet a burgeoning field. At the moment only weak beginnings may be found, noticeable stirrings which, however, are also being strongly resisted. The social engineering view of the hospital, for example, threatens traditional medical-clinical conceptions of the patient-doctor relationship and endangers traditional authority patterns among the staff. There is no sudden and widespread rush toward revising the hospital as a social community, and proposals to do this remain anathema to the typical hospital administration. Moreover, at the community level, social engineering implies to many a costly social-welfare approach to human problems. Important and emotional value systems touching on state planning and control are involved in this view, and it is questionable whether our society is presently prepared to see such programs through, however sensible they might be.

The most important force, however, which restrains the development of social engineering programs for the community is uncertainty and ignorance about the community changes that would be desirable and feasible and about the results they would actually accomplish. Any plan would affect many people in a multitude of ways, and one cannot be sure either that the desired effects would be produced, or that other more undesirable effects would not be produced. Yet it is abundantly clear to increasing numbers of professional workers that the massive mental health problem cannot be solved or even dented

by the traditional treatment approaches, and that engineered changes in the social conditions of life provide the ultimate answer. The difficulty is over whose dream of the good society, or whether any dream at all, is to win the day. Today's student will undoubtedly live through increasing controversy in the social sciences and in the community concerning these problems and ideas.

SUMMING UP

It is much easier to evaluate the effectiveness of behavior therapy than psychodynamic therapy because the former has the more concrete and limited aim of removing the symptom of which the patient complains, while the latter seeks ambitiously to produce a major alteration of the person's life-style so that he or she can live more effectively and happily. This is also a much more vague objective.

The major obstacles in the way of satisfactory research evaluation of the outcomes of therapy are twofold: First, it is often very difficult to identify exactly what the therapist is doing, in short, to specify the *treatment variables.* This is particularly so in the psychodynamic therapies. Thus, there is great variation in treatment aims in different therapies or with different patients. Some treatment approaches may also be more effective with certain kinds of patients or adjustive problems than with others, so that suitable comparisons of different therapeutic approaches require a proper matching of patient and treatment. Finally, there appears to be substantial variation in the skill or adequacy of therapists, so that research comparing one therapy with another would, of necessity, have to match the quality of the therapist in each.

Second, evaluating the outcomes of therapy requires that we be able accurately to *assess personality change* brought about by treatment. This is essential in the psychodynamic therapies, which aim at personality change rather than merely elimination of a specific symptom. Thus, research on therapeutic outcome depends on the science of personality assessment, which itself is still in its infancy.

Psychotherapy as it is practiced today has two major limitations in what it can accomplish toward amelioration of adjustive failure. First, many patients are simply not suitable for therapy, especially psychodynamic therapy. People who are lacking in intelligence and verbal skills, severely disturbed, suffering from personality disorders, or of advanced age are especially unsuited. Second, for many reasons—including economic and attitudinal ones as well as the shortage of qualified personnel—psychotherapy can be available to only a small fraction of the population that could benefit from it. Therefore, as the sole approach to society's mental health problem, psychotherapy is inadequate, and we must look to other approaches.

There are several alternatives to psychotherapy including hospitalization, physical therapy, and community mental health programs. *Hospitalization* has a number of highly undesirable features, such as high cost and the removal of patients from the settings with which they are familiar. This can result in loss of habits of work, responsibility, and social involvement. Patients can easily adopt a "sick role" from which it may be increasingly difficult to escape the longer they remain in the hospital. Moreover, most often hospitals fail to provide any real treatment and serve mainly as custodial institutions for troubled or deviant persons.

Physical therapy is used especially by those who see mental illness in medical-biological terms, and because other more psychological approaches have failed. There are four main types of physical therapy now in use: insulin shock, electroconvulsive shock, psychosurgery, and drugs. The first three have lost favor in recent decades, and except for electric shock are not so widely used, though they still have their devo-

tees. Controversy tends to surround their use, and there is some concern that extensive damage to the brain can be an unwanted outcome. Psychosurgery is especially vulnerable to this, since it involves deliberate destruction of brain tissues.

Of the physical therapies, *drugs* are by far the most common, and their use has indeed quieted mental hospital wards and sent many persons home who otherwise might have been doomed to permanent incapacity and hospitalization. In modern use there are three main types of drugs, the barbiturates and mild tranquilizers. the antidepressants, and the antipsychotic drugs. Drugs, as well as the other physical therapies, are generally not considered to be a cure for mental disorder. They serve mainly as a *palliative,* easing the patients' emotional turbulence and making them more manageable and accessible. Their mode of action on the brain and behavior is still somewhat unclear, though much research is being performed to discover how they affect the brain and behavior.

Community mental health centers have sprung up all over the country since passage of the Community Mental Health Services Act of 1963. In theory, such centers ought to provide many services for the members of the community, including partial hospitalization when needed, outpatient treatment, emergency care round the clock, consultation, and education. Its professional workers should be reaching out into the community with various services. In practice, however, limitations of funds (and in some cases old-fashioned ideas about mental health services) have resulted in a large gap between the ideal and the actual. Such innovations as *crisis intervention centers* and telephone *hot lines* for persons in trouble or considering suicide, most community mental health programs to date have been unable to fulfill adequately the mental health needs of their area.

Professional workers in the field of mental health generally feel that *prevention* of severe mental disorder is a more practical possibility than successfully treating it after it has developed. This means restructuring the environments within which people live to remove some of the most pathogenic conditions and providing services when an emotional problem emerges before it becomes more serious. Prevention in the form of *social engineering,* however, requires knowledge of the social causation of adjustive failure as well as of the ways in which innovative social programs involving change can be brought about.

This is by no means a simple matter, since our knowledge is more limited than we would like, and efforts to create changes often boomerang by producing unexpected and unwanted outcomes. Nevertheless if we are ultimately to have a major impact on the huge problem of mental health, this is the direction in which we must go. We must learn more about how adjustive failure is brought about and how its most severe forms can be prevented.

REFERENCES

Adams, H. B. Mental illness: Or interpersonal behavior. *American Psychologist,* 1964, **19,** 191–197.

Adler, N. The antinomian personality: The hippie character type. *Psychiatry,* 1968, **31,** 325–338.

Adler, N. Kicks, drugs and politics. *Psychoanalytic Review,* 1970, **57,** 432–441.

Albee, G. W. President's Message. *The Clinical Psychologist,* 1966, **20,** 7–9.

Aldrin, E., and Warga, W. *Return to earth.* New York: Random House, 1973 (paper).

Alexander, F., and French, T. M. *Psychoanalytic therapy: Principles and application.* New York: Ronald Press, 1946.

Alexander, F. G., and Selesnick, S. T. *The history of psychiatry.* New York: Harper & Row, 1966.

Allport, G. W. *Personality.* New York: Holt, 1937.

Allport, G. W. Personality: Normal and abnormal. In *Personality and Social Encounter.* Boston: Beacon Press, 1960. Pp. 155–168.

Allport, G. W. *Pattern and growth in personality.* New York: Holt, 1961.

Allport, G. W. The general and the unique in psychological science. *Journal of Personality,* 1962, **30,** 405–422.

Allport, G. W., and Vernon, P. E. *Studies in expressive movement.* New York: Macmillan, 1933.

American Psychiatric Association. *Diagnostic statistical manual: Mental disorders.* Washington, D.C.: APA, 1952. Latest edition, 1968.

Ansbacher, H. L., and Ansbacher, Rowena R. (eds.) *The individual-psychology of Alfred Adler.* New York: Basic Books, 1956.

Anthony, E. J. The mutative impact of serious mental disorder and physical illness in a parent on family life. *Canadian Psychiatric Association Journal,* 1969, **14,** 433–453.

Anthony, E. J. A risk-vulnerability-prevention program for children of psychotic parents. In E. J. Anthony and C. Koupernik (eds.), *Children at psychiatric risk.* New York: Wiley, in press, cited in Garmezy, 1974.

Ash, P. The reliability of psychiatric diagnosis. *Journal of Abnormal and Social Psychology,* 1949, **44,** 272–276.

Atthowe, J. M., Jr., and Krasner, L. A preliminary report on the application of contingent reinforcement procedures (token economy) on a "chronic" psychiatric ward. *Journal of Abnormal Psychology,* 1968, **73,** 37–48.

Ausubel, D. P. Personality disorder *is* disease. *American Psychologist,* 1961, **16,** 69–74.

Ax, A. The physiological differentiation between fear and anger in humans. *Psychosomatic Medicine,* 1953, **15,** 433–442.

Ayllon, T., and Azrin, N. H. The measurement and reinforcement of behavior of psychotics. *Journal of the Experimental Analysis of Behavior,* 1965, **8,** 357–383.

Baker, G. W., and Chapman, D. W. (eds.) *Man and society in disaster.* New York: Basic Books, 1962.

Baldwin, A. L., Kalhorn, Joan, and Breese, F. H. Patterns of parent behavior. *Psychological Monographs: General and Applied,* 1945, **58,** No. 3.

Bandura, A. *Principles of behavior modification.* New York: Holt, 1969.

Bandura, A. Psychotherapy based upon modeling principles. In A. E. Bergin and S. L. Garfield (eds.), *Handbook of psychotherapy and behavior change: An empirical analysis.* New York: Wiley, 1971. Pp. 653–708.

Bandura, A. Behavior theory and the models of man. *American Psychologist,* 1974, **29,** 859–869.

Bannerjee, S. and Agarwal, P. S. Tryptophan-nicotinic acid metabolism in schizophrenia. *Proceedings of the Society of Experimental Biology and Medicine,* 1958, **97,** 657–659.

Barron, F. *Creativity and psychological health.* Princeton, N.J.: Van Nostrand, 1963.

Bateson, G., Jackson, D. D., Haley, J., and Weakland, J. H. Toward a theory of schizophrenia. *Behavioral Science,* 1956, **1,** 251–264.

Baumrind, D. *Early socialization and the discipline controversy.* Morristown, N.J.: General Learning Press, 1975.

Bayley, Nancy, and Schaefer, E. S. Maternal behavior and personality development: Data from the Berkeley Growth Study. In C. Shagass and B. Pasamanick (eds.), *Child Development Research Reports of the American Psychiatric Association,* Vol. 13, 1960, 155–173.

Beers, C. W. *A mind that found itself. An autobiography.* New York: Longmans, 1908. (25th Anniversary ed.: Doubleday, 1935.)

Bell, J. E. *Family therapy.* New York: Jason Aronson, 1975.

Bem, S. L. Psychology looks at sex roles: Where have all the androgynous people gone? Paper presented at UCLA Symposium on Women, May, 1972.

Benedict, R. *The chrysanthemum and the sword.* Boston: Houghton Mifflin, 1946.

Bergin, A. E. The effects of psychotherapy: Negative results revisited. *Journal of Counseling Psychology,* 1963, **10,** 244–250.

Berne, E. *Games people play.* New York: Grove Press, 1964.

Bettelheim, B. *The informed heart.* New York: Free Press, 1960.

Bettelheim, B. *Obsolete youth: Towards a psychogram of adolescent rebellion.* San Francisco: San Francisco Press, 1969.

Bleuler, E. *Dementia praecox.* New York: International Universities Press, 1950.

Block, J. A study of affective responsiveness in a lie-detection situation. *Journal of Abnormal and Social Psychology,* 1957, **55,** 11–15.

Block, J. *Lives through time.* Berkeley, Calif.: Bancroft, 1971.

Born, W. Artistic behavior of the mentally deranged; and great artists who suffered from mental disorders. *Ciba Symposium,* 1946, **8,** 207–216; 225–232.

Boszormenyi-Nagy, Ivan (ed.). *Intensive family therapy: theoretical and practical aspects by 15 authors.* Vol. 1. Boszormenyi-Nagy and J. L. Framo (eds.). New York: Hoeber-Harper, 1965.

Brady, J. V. Ulcers in "executive monkeys". *Scientific American,* 1958, **199,** 95–100.

Brady, J. V., Porter, R. W., Conrad, D. G., and Mason, J. W. Avoidance behavior and the development of gastroduodenal ulcers. *Journal of the experimental analysis of behavior,* 1958, **1,** 69–72.

Braines, C. H. (ed.) *Collected papers in experimental pathology.* Moscow: Academy of Medical Sciences, 1959 (as cited in Maher, 1966).

Bramel, D. A dissonance theory approach to defensive projection. *Journal of Abnormal and Social Psychology,* 1962, **64,** 121–129.

Breger, L., and McGaugh, J. L. Critique and reformulation of "learning theory" approaches to psychotherapy and neurosis. *Psychological Bulletin,* 1965, **63,** 338–358.

Breuer, J., and Freud, S. *Studies in hysteria.* New York: Basic Books, 1957. (Also published as case histories, trans. by J. Strachey (ed.), The standard edition of the complete psychological works of Sigmund Freud. Vol. 2, London: Hogarth, 1955. Pp. 19–181. First published in 1895.)

Bridger, W. H. Sensory habituation and discrimination in the human neonate. *American Journal of Psychiatry,* 1961, **117,** 991–996.

Brown, R. *Social psychology.* New York: Free Press, 1965.

Campbell, D., Sanderson, R. E., and Laverty, S. G. Characteristics of a conditioned response in human subjects during extinction trials following a single traumatic conditioning trial. *Journal of Abnormal and Social Psychology,* 1964, **68,** 627–639.

Cannon, W. B. The James-Lange theory of emotions: A critical examination and an alternative theory. *American Journal of Psychology,* 1927, **39,** 106–124.

Cannon, W. B. *Bodily changes in hunger, pain, fear, and rage.* New York: Appleton-Century-Crofts, 1928.

Cantril, H., with the assistance of H. Gaudet and H. Herzog. *The invasion from Mars.* Princeton, N.J.: Princeton Univ. Press, 1947.

Caplan, G. *Principles of preventive psychiatry.* New York: Basic Books, 1964.

Casey, R. G., and Masuda, M., and Holmes, T. H. Quantitative study of recall of life events. *Journal of Psychosomatic Research,* 1967, **11,** 239–247.

Caudill, W. Observations on the cultural context of Japanese psychiatry. In M. K.

Opler (ed.), *Culture and mental health.* New York: Macmillan, 1959. Pp. 213–242.

Caudill, W., and Doi, L. T. Interrelations of psychiatry, culture and emotion in Japan. In I. Galdston (ed.), *Man's image in medicine and anthropology. New York: International Univ. Press, 1963.*

Cautela, J. R. Treatment of compulsive behavior by covert sensitization. *Psychological Record,* 1966, **16,** 33–41.

Cerletti, V., and Bini, L. L'elettroshock. *Archivis di psicologia neurologia e psichiatria.* 1938, **19,** 266–268.

Christian, J. J., and Davis, D. E. Endocrines, behavior, and population. *Science,* 1964, **146,** 1550–1560.

Clausen, J. A. Mental disorders. In R. K. Merton and R. A. Nisbet (eds.), *Contemporary social problems.* New York: Harcourt, 1966. Pp. 26–83.(b)

Coelho, G. V., Hamburg, D. A., and Murphy, Elizabeth B. Coping strategies in a new learning environment: A study of American college freshmen. *Archives of General Psychiatry,* 1963, **9**(5), 433–443.

Cohen, L. H., Hilgard, E. R., and Wendt, G. R. Sensitivity to light in a case of hysterical blindness studied by reinforcement, inhibition and conditioning methods. *Yale Journal of Biological Medicine,* 1933, **6,** 61–67.

Colby, K. M. *A primer for psychotherapists.* New York: Ronald Press, 1951.

Coleman, J. C. *Abnormal psychology and modern life.* (Rev. ed.) New York: Scott, Foresman, 1972.

Cortés, J. B., and Gatti, F. M. Physique and propensity. *Psychology Today,* 1970, **4,** 42–44, 82, 84.

Costa, E. Effects of hallucinogenic and tranquilizing drugs on serotonin-evoked uterine contractions. *Proceedings of the Society of Experimental Biology and Medicine,* 1956, **91,** 39–41.

Cotton, H. A. *The defective, delinquent and insane.* Princeton: Princeton Univ. Press, 1921.

Cotton, H. A. The etiology and treatment of the so-called functional psychoses. *American Journal of Psychiatry,* 1922, **2,** 157–210.

Cowen, E. L., Gardner, L. A., and Zax, M. (eds.) *Emergent approaches to mental health problems.* New York: Appleton-Century-Crofts, 1967.

Damon, A., and Polednak, A. P. Physique and serum pepsinogen. *Human Biology,* 1967, **39,** 355–367.

Darwin, C. *The origin of species.* London: J. Murray, 1859.

Darwin, C. *Expression of the emotions in man and animals.* New York: D. Appleton Company, 1873. (Reprinted by courtesy of Appleton-Century-Crofts, Inc.)

Davids, A. Alienation, social apperception, and ego structure. *Journal of Consulting Psychology,* 1955, **19,** 21–27.

Davidson, H. A. The commitment procedures and their legal implications. In S. Arieti (ed.), *American Handbook of Psychiatry.* New York: Basic Books, 1959. Pp. 1902–1922.

Davidson, M. A., McInnes, R. G., and Parnell, R. W. The distribution of personality traits in seven-year-old children. *British Journal of Education Psychology,* 1957, **27,** 48–61.

de Klerk, D. Magnetic properties below one degree K. *Physics Today,* 1953, **6** (2), 4.

Deutsch, A. *The shame of the states.* New York: Harcourt, 1948.

Diggory, J. C., and Rothman, Doreen Z. Values destroyed by death. *Journal of Abnormal and Social Psychology,* 1961, **63,** 205–209.

Dobzhansky, T. *Mankind evolving.* New Haven, Conn.: Yale Univ. Press, 1962.

Dobzhansky, T. Changing man. *Science,* 1967, **155,** 409–415.

Dobzhansky, T. Of flies and men. *American Psychologist,* 1967, **22**(1), 41–48.

Dohrenwend, B. P., Chin-Song, E. T., Egri, G., Mendelsohn, P. S., and Stokes, J. Measures of psychiatric disorder in contrasting class and ethnic groups. In E. H. Hare and J. K. Wing (eds.), *Psychiatric epidemiology.* London: Oxford Univ. Press, 1970. Pp. 159–202.

Doi, L. T. Some thoughts on helplessness and the desire to be loved. *Psychiatry,* 1963, **26,** 266–272.

Dollard, J., and Miller, N. E. *Personality and psychotherapy.* New York: McGraw-Hill, 1950.

Dorcus, R. M., and Shaffer, G. W. *Textbook of abnormal psychology* (3d ed.) Baltimore: Williams & Wilkins, 1945.

Duffy, Elizabeth. *Activation and behavior.* New York: Wiley, 1962.

Dukes, W. F. N = 1. *Psychological Bulletin,* 1965, **64,** 74–79.

Dunlap, K. The stuttering boy. *Journal of Abnormal and Social Psychology,* 1917, **12,** 44–48.

Dunlap, K. *Habits, their making and unmaking.* New York: Liveright, 1932.

Ebbinhaus, H. *Uber das Gedächtnis.* Berlin: Duncker & Humblot, 1885.

Ekman, P. Communication through nonverbal behavior: A source of information about an interpersonal relationship. In S. S. Tomkins and C. E. Izzard (eds.), *Affect, cognition and personality.* New York: Springer, 1965. Pp. 390–422.

Elkins, S. Slavery and personality. In B. Kaplan (ed.), *Studying personality cross-culturally.* New York: Harper & Row, 1961. Pp. 243–270.

Ellis, A. *Reason and emotion in psychotherapy.* New York: Lyle Stuart, 1962.

Ellis, A. A homosexual treated with rational psychotherapy. *Journal of Clinical Psychology,* 1959, **15,** 338–343.

Ellis, A. Rational psychotherapy. *Journal of General Psychology,* 1958, **59,** 35–49.

Epstein, S. The measurement of drive and conflict in humans: Theory and experiment. In M. R. Jones (ed.), *Nebraska symposium on motivation.* Lincoln, Nebr.: Univ. Nebraska Press, 1962. Pp. 127–209.

Erikson, E. H. *Childhood and society.* New York: Norton, 1963.

Erikson, E. H. Growth and crises of the healthy personality. In M. J. E. Senn (ed.), *Symposium on the healthy personality.* New York: Josiah Macy, Jr., 1950. Pp. 91–146.

Erikson, E. H. A healthy personality for every child: A fact-finding report: A digest. *Midcentury White House Conference on Children and Youth*. Raleigh, N.C.: Health Publications Institute, 1951. Pp. 8–25.

Etzioni, A. Working life and stress in the post-modern era. Paper given at symposium organized by L. Levi, "Society, Stress and Disease: Working Life," in Stockholm, June 11, 1974.

Eysenck, H. J. The effects of psychotherapy: An evaluation. *Journal of Consulting Psychology,* 1952, **16,** 319–324.

Eysenck, H. J. (ed.) *Behavior therapy and the neuroses.* New York: Pergamon Press, 1960. (a)

Eysenck, H. J. The effects of psychotherapy. In H. J. Eysenck (ed.), *Handbook of abnormal psychology.* New York: Basic Books, 1961. Pp. 697–725.(b)

Eysenck, H. J. The outcome problem in psychotherapy: A reply. *Psychotherapy,* 1964, **1,** 97–100. (b)

Fairweather, G. W. *Social psychology in treating mental illness: An experimental approach.* New York: Wiley, 1964.

Faris, R. E. L., and Dunham, H. W. *Mental disorders in urban areas.* Chicago: Univ. of Chicago Press, 1939.

Feifel, H. Introduction. In H. Feifel (ed.), *The meaning of death.* New York: McGraw-Hill, 1959. Pp. 13–18.

Feifel, H., and Branscomb, A. B. Who's afraid of death? *Journal of Abnormal Psychology.* 1973, **81,** 282–288.

Feldman, M. P., and MacCulloch, M. J. The application of anticipatory avoidance learning to the treatment of homosexuality. I. Theory, technique and preliminary results. *Behavior Research and Therapy,* 1965, **2,** 165–183.

Fenichel, O. *The psychoanalytic theory of neurosis.* New York: Norton, 1945.

Fenz, W. D. Strategies for coping with stress. Paper presented at symposium "Coping with stress and anxiety" at a conference on "Dimensions of Anxiety and Stress," held in Oslo, Norway, June 1975.

Fenz, W. D., and Epstein, S. Changes in gradients of skin conductance, heart rate and respiration rate as a function of experience. *Psychosomatic Medicine,* 1967, **29,** 33–51.

Ferster, C. B. Classification of behavioral pathology. In L. Krasner and L. P. Ullmann (eds.), *Research in behavior modifications.* New York: Holt, 1965. Pp. 6–26.

Folkins, C. H. Temporal factors and the cognitive mediators of stress reaction. *Journal of Personality and Social Psychology,* 1970, **14,** 173–184.

Folkins, C. H., Lawson, Karen K., Opton, E. M., Jr., and Lazarus, R. S. Desensitization and the experimental reduction of threat. *Journal of Abnormal Psychology,* 1968, **73,** 100–113.

Foote, N. N., and Cottrell, L. *Identity and interpersonal competence.* Chicago: Univ. Chicago Press, 1955.

Frank, G. H. The role of the family in the development of psychopathology. *Psychological Bulletin,* 1965, **64,** 191–205.

Frank, J. D. *Persuasion and healing.* New York: Schocken Books, 1963.

Frankenhaeuser, M. Experimental approaches to the study of catecholamines and emotion. In L. Levi (ed.), *Emotions: Their parameters and measurement.* New York: Raven Press, 1975, pp. 209–234.

Frankl, V. E. *Man's search for meaning: An introduction to logotherapy.* New York: Washington Square Press, 1963 (paper).

Frankl, V. E. *The doctor and the soul.* New York: Bantam Books, 1965 (paper).

Freeman, W. *Psychosurgery.* In S. Arieti (ed.), *American Handbook of Psychiatry,* Vol. II. New York: Basic Books, 1959. Pp. 1521–1540.

Freeman, W., and Watts, J. W. Prefrontal lobotomy in treatment of mental disorders. *Southern Medical Journal,* 1937, **30,** 23–31.

French, J. D., Hernández-Péon, R., and Livingston, R. B. Projections from cortex to cephalic brain stem (reticular formation) in monkeys. *Journal of Neurophysiology,* 1955, **18,** 44–55, 74–95.

Freud, Anna. *The ego and the mechanisms of defense.* New York: International Univ. Press, 1946.

Freud, S. The dynamics of the transference. *Collected papers,* XXVIII. International Psychoanalytical Library, No. 8. London: Hogarth, 1921, Vol. 2, Pp. 312–322. (First published in 1912.)

Freud, S. *Collected papers.* Vol. II. London: Hogarth, 1924.

Freud, S. Psychoanalytic notes upon an autobiographical account of a case of paranoia (dementia paranoides). In *Collected papers.* Vol. III. London: Hogarth, 1933. Pp. 390–472. (First published in German, 1911.)

Freud, S. *Autobiography.* Trans. by J. Strachey. New York: Norton, 1935.

Freud, S. *A general introduction to psychoanalysis.* Garden City, N.Y.: Garden City Books, 1943. (First German ed., 1917.)

Freud, S. *The ego and the id.* In *The complete psychological works of Sigmund Freud.* Vol. XIX. London: Hogarth, 1961. (First published in 1923.)

Friedman, M., and Rosenman, R. H. *Type A behavior and your heart.* New York: Knopf, 1974.

Friedman, S. B., Chodoff, P., Mason, J. W., and Hamburg, D. A. Behavioral observations on parents anticipating the death of a child. *Pediatrics,* 1963, **32,** 610–625.

Fries, M. E., and Lewi, B. Interrelated factors in development: A study of pregnancy, labor, delivery, lying-in period, and childhood. *American Journal of Orthopsychiatry,* 1938, **8,** 726–752.

Fromm, E. *Escape from freedom.* New York: Rinehart, 1941.

Fromm, E. Psychoanalytic characterology and its application to understanding of culture. In S. S. Sargent and Marian W. Smith (eds.), *Culture and personality.* New York: Basic Books, 1949. Pp. 1–12.

Fromm, E. *Man for himself.* New York: Rinehart, 1947.

Funkenstein, D. H., King, S. H., and Drolette, Margaret. *Mastery of stress.* Cambridge, Mass.: Harvard Univ. Press, 1957.

Galton, F. *Hereditary genius.* London: Macmillan, 1869.

Ganzfried, Solomon. *Code of Jewish Law.* Trans. by Hyman E. Goldin. New York: Star Hebrew, 1928.

Gardner, R. W., Holzman, P. S., Klein, G. S., Linton, Harriet B., and Spence, D. P.

Cognitive control, a study of individual consistencies in cognitive behavior. *Psychological Issues,* 1959, **1,** No. 4.

Garmezy, N. (with Streitman, S.) Children at risk: The search for the antecedents of schizophrenia. Part I. Conceptual models and research methods. *Schizophrenia Bulletin,* 1974a, No. 8. National Institute of Mental Health. Pp. 14–90.

Garmezy, N. Children at risk: The search for the antecedents of schizophrenia. Part II. Ongoing research programs, issues, and intervention. *Schizophrenia Bulletin,* 1974b, No. 9. National Institute of Mental Health. Pp. 55–125.

Gellhorn, E. *Principles of autonomic-somatic integrations.* Minneapolis: Univ. of Minnesota Press, 1967.

Gillin, J. Magical fright. *Psychiatry,* 1948, **11,** 387–400.

Ginsburg, S. W. The mental health movement: Its theoretical assumptions. In Ruth Kotinsky and Helen Witmer (eds.), *Community programs for mental health.* Cambridge, Mass.: Harvard Univ. Press, 1955. Pp. 1–29.

Glickstein, M., Chevalier, J. A., Korchin, S. J., Basowitz, H., Sabshin, M., Hamburg, D. A., and Grinker, R. R. Temporal heart rate patterns in anxious patients. *American Medical Association Archives of Neurological Psychiatry,* 1957, **78,** 101–106.

Glueck, S., and Glueck, E. Family environment and delinquency. Boston: Houghton Mifflin, 1962.

Goffman, E. *The presentation of self in everyday life.* Garden City, N.Y.: Doubleday, 1959.

Goffman, E. *Asylums.* Garden City, N.Y.: Doubleday, 1961.

Goldfried, M., and Goldfried, A. Cognitive change methods. In F. Kanfer and A. Goldstein (eds.), *Helping people change.* New York: Pergamon Press, 1975.

Goldfried, M. R., and Merbaum, M. A perspective on self-control. In M. R. Goldfried and M. Merbaum (eds.), *Behavior change through self-control.* New York: Holt, 1973. Pp. 3–34.

Goltz, F. Der Hund ohne Grosshirn. *Archiv für die gesamte psychologie,* 1892, **51,** 570–614. Not seen.

Gottesman, I. I., and Shields, J. Schizophrenia in twins: 16 years' consecutive admissions to a psychiatric clinc. *British Journal of Psychiatry,* 1966, **112,** 809–818.

Graham, D. T. Some research on psychophysiological specificity and its relation to psychosomatic disease. In R. Roessler and N. S. Greenfield (eds.), *Physiological correlates of psychological disorder.* Madison, Wis.: Univ. of Wisconsin Press, 1962. Pp. 221–238.

Grinker, R. R. "Mentally healthy" young males (homoclites). *Archives of General Psychiatry,* 1962, **6,** 405–453.

Grinker, R. R., and Spiegel, J. P. *Men under stress.* New York: McGraw-Hill, 1945.

Gurin, G., Veroff, J., and Feld, Sheila. *Americans view their mental health.* New York: Basic Books, 1960.

Hallowell, A. I. Psychic stresses and culture patterns. *American Journal of Psychiatry,* 1936, **92,** 1291–1310.

Hamburg, D. A., and Adams, J. E. A perspective on coping: Seeking and utilizing information in major transitions. *Archives of General Psychiatry,* 1967, **17,** 277–284.

Hamburg, D. A., Hamburg, Beatrix, and deGoza, S. Adaptive problems and mechanisms in severely burned patients. *Psychiatry,* 1953, **16,** 1–20.

Hargreaves, W. A., Starkweather, J. A., and Blacker, K. N. Voice quality in depression. *Journal of Abnormal and Social Psychology,* 1965, **70,** 218–220.

Harlow, H. F. The nature of love. *American Journal of Psychology,* 1958, **13,** 673–685.

Harlow, H. F., and Harlow, Margaret. Social deprivation in monkeys. *Scientific American,* 1962, **207,** 136–146.

Harlow, H. F., and Zimmerman, R. R. Affectional responses in the infant monkey. *Science,* 1959, **130** (3373), 421–432.

Harper, R. A. *Psychoanalysis and psychotherapy.* Englewood Cliffs, N.J.: Prentice-Hall, 1959.

Hartshorne, H., and May, M. A. *Studies in the nature of character.* Vol. 1, *Studies in deceit.* New York: Macmillan, 1928.

Hartshorne, H., May, M. A., and Maller, J. B. *Studies in the nature of character.* Vol. 2. *Studies in service and self-control.* New York: Macmillan, 1929.

Hartshorne, H., May, M. A., Maller, J. B., and Shuttleworth, F. K. *Studies in the nature of character.* Vol. 3. *Studies in the organization of character.* New York: Macmillan, 1930.

Hay, D. H., and Oken, D. The psychological stresses of intensive care unit nursing. *Psychosomatic Medicine,* 1972, **34,** 109–118.

Heath, R. G. A biochemical hypothesis on the etiology of schizophrenia. In D. D. Jackson (ed.), *The etiology of schizophrenia.* New York: Basic Books, 1960.

Heath, R. G., Martens, S., Leach, B. E., Cohen, M., and Angel, C. Effect on behavior in humans with the administration of taraxein. *American Journal of Psychiatry,* 1957, **114,** 14–24.

Hemmendinger, L. Developmental theory and the Rorschach method. In Maria A. Rickers Ovsiankina (ed.), *Rorschach psychology.* New York: Wiley, 1960. Pp. 58–79.

Hendrick, I. *Facts and theories of psychoanalysis.* New York: Knopf, 1939.

Hilgard, E. R., and Wendt, G. R. The problem of reflex sensitivity to light studied in a case of hemianopsia. *Yale Journal of Biological Medicine,* 1933, **5,** 373–385.

Hirsch, J. (ed.) *Behavior-genetic analysis.* New York: McGraw-Hill, 1967.

Hirsch, J. Jensenism: The bankruptcy of "science" without scholarship. *Educational Theory,* 1975, **25,** 3–28.

Hoch, P. H. Drug therapy. In S. Arieti (ed.), *American Handbook of Psychiatry.* Volume II. New York: Basic Books, 1959. Pp. 1541–1551.

Hofer, M. A., Wolff, C. T., Friedman, S. B., and Mason, J. W. A psychoendocrine study of bereavement: Part I. 17-hydroxycorticosteroid excretion rates of parents following death of their children from leukemia. *Psychosomatic Medicine,* 1972, **34,** 481–491.

Holland, R., Cohen, G., Goldenberg, M., Sha, J., and Lefier, A. I. Adrenaline and noradrenalin in the urine and plasma of schizophrenics. *Federal Proceedings,* 1958, **17,** 378.

Hollingshead, A. B., and Redlich, F. C. *Social class and mental illness.* New York: Wiley, 1958.

Holmes, T. H., and Rahe, R. H. The social readjustment rating scale. *Journal of Psychosomatic Research,* 1967, **11,** 213–218.

Holt, R. R. Individuality and generality in the psychology of personality. *Journal of Personality,* 1962, **30,** 377–404.

Holzman, P. S., and Gardner, R. W. Leveling and repression. *Journal of Abnormal and Social Psychology,* 1959, **59,** 151–155.

Horney, Karen, *Neurotic personality of our times.* New York: Norton, 1937.

Hornick, E. J., and Myles, C. L. Teenage drinking. *Psychiatric Opinion,* 1975, **12,** 12–16.

Horwitz, W. A. Insulin shock therapy. In S. Arieti (ed.), *American Handbook of Psychiatry.* Vol. II. New York: Basic Books, 1959. Pp. 1485–1498.

Irwin, O. C. The amount and nature of activities of newborn infants under constant external stimulating conditions during the first ten days of life. *Genetic Psychology Monographs,* 1930, **8,** 1–92.

Jackson, D. D. A critique of the literature of the genetics of schizophrenia. In D. D. Jackson (ed.), *The etiology of schizophrenia.* New York: Basic Books, 1960.

Jacobson, E. *Progressive relaxation.* Chicago: Univ. Chicago Press, 1938.

Jahoda, Marie. Toward a social psychology of mental health. In Ruth Kotinsky and Helen Witmer (eds.), *Community programs for mental health.* Cambridge, Mass.: Harvard Univ. Press, 1955. Pp. 296–322.

Jahoda, Marie. *Current conceptions of positive mental health.* New York: Basic Books, 1958.

James, W. *Principles of psychology.* Vol. 1. New York: Holt, 1890. Chap. 10.

Janis, I. L. *Psychological stress.* New York: Wiley, 1958.

Janis, I. L. Psychological effects of warnings. In G. W. Baker and D. W. Chapman (eds.), *Man and society in disaster.* New York: Basic Books, Inc., 1962. Pp. 55–92.

Jarvik, M. E. The psychopharmacological revolution. *Psychology Today,* 1967, **1,** 51–59.

Jensen, A. R. How much can we boost IQ and scholastic achievement? *Harvard Educational Review,* 1969, **39,** 1–123.

Jensen, A. R. Input: Arthur Jensen replies. *Psychology Today,* 1969, **3,** 4–6.

Jervis, G. A. Introductory study of fifty cases of mental deficiency associated with excretion of phenylpyruvic acid. *Archives of Neurology and Psychiatry,* 1937, **38,** 944–963.

Jervis, G. A Studies of phenylpyruvic oligophrenia. The position of the metabolic error. *Journal of Biological Chemistry,* 1947, **169,** 651–656.

Jervis, G. A. Phenylpyruvic oligophrenia: Deficiency of phenylalanine oxidizing system. *Proceedings of the Society for Experimental Biology,* New York, 1953, **82,** 514–515.

Johnson, F. N. *Lithium research and therapy.* New York: Academic Press, 1974.

Jones, H. E. The Longitudinal Method in the Study of Personality. In I. Iscoe and H. W. Stevenson (eds.), *Personality Development in Children.* Austin, Tex.: Univ. Texas Press, 1960. Pp. 3–27.

Jones, Mary C. The elimination of children's fears. *Journal of Experimental Psychology,* 1924, **7,** 382–390.

Jung, C. G. *Analytical psychology.* New York: Moffat, Yard, 1916.

Jung, C. G. *Collected works.* Vol. 7. *Two essays on analytical psychology.* New York: Pantheon, 1953.

Jung, C. G. Symbol formation. In G. Lindzey and C. S. Hall (eds.), *Theories of personality: Primary sources and research.* New York: Wiley, 1965. Pp. 77–85.

Kagan, J. American longitudinal research on psychological development. *Child Development,* 1964, **35,** 1–32.

Kagan, J., and Moss, H. A. *Birth to maturity: A study in psychological development.* New York: Wiley, 1962.

Kalinowsky, L. B. Convulsive shock treatment. In S. Arieti (ed.), *American Handbook of Psychiatry.* Vol. II. New York: Basic Books, 1959. Pp. 1499–1520.

Kallmann, F. J. Genetic aspects of psychoses. In *Biology and Mental Health and Disease.* New York: Hoeber–Harper, 1952. Pp. 283–298.

Kallmann, F. J. *Heredity in health and mental disorder.* New York: Norton, 1953.

Kallmann, F. J. The genetics of human behavior. *American Journal of Psychiatry,* 1956, **113,** 496–501.

Kant, I. *The classification of mental disorders.* Doylestown, Pa.: Doylestown Foundation, 1964.

Katz, J. L., Weiner, H., Gallagher, T. F., and Hellman, L. Stress, distress, and ego defenses. *Archives of General Psychiatry.* 1970, **23,** 131–142.

Kenniston, K. *The uncommitted: Alienated youth in American society.* New York: Delta (Dell), 1965.

Kenniston, K. *The Young radicals: Notes on committed youth.* New York: Harcourt, 1968.

Kety, S. Biochemical theories of schizophrenia. *Science,* 1959, **129,** 1520, 1590, 3362.

Knight, R. P. Evaluation of the results of psychoanalytic therapy. *American Journal of Psychiatry,* 1941, **98,** 434–446.

Knutson, A. L. New perspectives regarding positive mental health. *American Journal of Psychology,* 1963, **18,** 300–306.

Kohn, M. L. Social class and schizophrenia: A critical review. In D. Rosenthal and S. S. Kety (eds.), *The transmission of schizophrenia.* Oxford: Pergamon Press, 1968. Pp. 155–173.

Kopeloff, N., and Cheney, C. O. Studies in focal infection: Its presence and elimination in the functional psychoses. *American Journal of Psychiatry,* 1922, **2,** 139–159.

Kopin, I. J. Tryptophan loading and excretion of 5-hydroxyindoleacetic acid in normal and schizophrenic subjects. *Science,* 1959, **129,** 835.

Korchin, S. J. *Modern Clinical Psychology.* New York: Basic Books, 1976.

Korchin, S. J., and Herz, M. Differential effects of "shame" and "disintegrative" threats on emotional and adrenocortical functioning. *Archives of General Psychiatry,* 1960, **2,** 640–651.

Korchin, S. J., and Ruff, G. E. Personality characteristics of the Mercury astronauts. In G. H. Grosser, H. Wechsler, and M. Greenblatt (eds.), *The threat of impending disaster.* Cambridge, Mass.: M.I.T. Press, 1964. Pp. 197–207.

Kraepelin, E. *Clinical psychiatry.* Trans. by A. R. Diefendorf (ed.). New York: Macmillan, 1907.

Krasner, L. Reinforcement, verbal behavior and psychotherapy. *American Journal of Orthopsychiatry,* 1963, **33,** 601–613.

Krasner, L. The operant approach in behavior therapy. In A. E. Bergin and S. L. Garfield (eds.), *Handbook of psychotherapy and behavior change: An empirical analysis.* New York: Wiley, 1971. Pp. 612–652.

Krasner, L., and Ullmann, L. P. (eds.) *Research in behavior modification.* New York: Holt, 1965.

Krech, D., and Crutchfield, R. S. *Elements of psychology.* New York: Knopf, 1958.

Kretschmer, E. *Physique and character.* New York: Harcourt, 1925, 1926.

Lacey, J. I. Somatic response patterning and stress: some revisions of activation theory. In M. H. Appley and R. Trumbull (eds.), *Psychological stress,* New York: Appleton-Century-Crofts, 1967. Pp. 14–37.

Lancaster, E., and Poling, J. *Final face of Eve.* New York: McGraw-Hill, 1958.

Lang, P. J., and Lazovik, A. D. Experimental desensitization of a phobia. *Journal of Abnormal and Social Psychology,* 1963, **66,** 519–525.

Langner, T. S., and Michael, S. T. *Life stress and mental health.* Glencoe, Ill.: Free Press, 1963.

Lauer, J. W., Inskip, W. M., Bernsohn, J., and Zeller, E. A. Observations of schizophrenic patients after iproniazid and tryptophan. *Archives of Neurology and Psychiatry,* 1958, **80,** 122–130.

Lazarus, A. A. Crucial procedural factors in desensitization therapy. *Behavior Research and therapy,* 1964, **2,** 65–70.

Lazarus, A. A. *Behavior therapy and beyond.* New York: McGraw-Hill, 1971.

Lazarus, R. S. *Psychological stress and the coping process.* New York: McGraw-Hill, 1966.

Lazarus, R. S. Psychological stress and coping in adaptation and illness. *Psychosomatic Medicine,* 1974.

Lazarus, R. S. A cognitively oriented psychologist looks at biofeedback. *American Psychologist,* 1975.

Lazarus, R. S., and Eriksen, C. W. Effects of failure stress upon skilled performance. *Journal of Experimental Psychology,* 1952, **43,** 100–105.

Lazarus, R. S., and Longo, N. The consistency of psychological defenses against threat. *Journal of Abnormal and Social Psychology,* 1953, **48,** 495–499.

Lazarus, R. S., and Opton, E. M., Jr. *Readings in personality.* Middlesex, England: Penguin, 1967.

Lazarus, R. S., Speisman, J. C., Mordkoff, A. M., and Davison, L. A. A laboratory study of psychological stress produced by a motion picture film. *Psychological*

Monographs: General and Applied, 1962, **76** (34, Whole No. 553).

Lea, A. J. Adrenochrome as the cause of schizophrenia: Investigation of some deductions from this hypothesis. *Journal of Mental Science,* 1955, **101,** 538–547.

Lerner, I. M. *Heredity, evolution and society.* San Francisco: Freeman, 1968.

Levi, L. The urinary output of adrenalin and noradrenalin during pleasant and unpleasant emotional states: A preliminary report. *Psychosomatic Medicine.* 1965, **27,** 80–85.

Levitsky, A., and Perls, F. S. The rules and games of Gestalt therapy. In J. Fagin and I. L. Shepard (eds.), *Gestalt therapy now.* Palo Alto, Calif.: Science and Behavior Books, 1970. Pp. 140–149.

Levy, D. M. *Maternal overprotection.* New York: Columbia Univ. Press, 1943.

Lewis, O. The culture of poverty. *Scientific American,* 1966, **215,** 19–25.

Lidz, T. *The origin and treatment of schizophrenic disorders.* New York: Basic Books, 1973.

Lidz, T., Fleck, S., and Cornelison, A. *Schizophrenia and the family.* New York: International Universities Press, 1965.

Lindemann, E. Symptomatology and management of acute grief. *American Journal of Psychiatry,* 1944, **101,** 141–148.

Lindemann, E. Psychosocial factors as stressor agents. In J. M. Tanner (ed.), *Stress and psychiatric disorder.* Oxford: Basil Blackwell & Mott, 1960.

Lindsley, D. B. Emotion. In S. S. Stevens (ed.), *Handbook of experimental psychology.* New York: Wiley, 1951. Pp. 473–516.

London, P. *The modes and morals of psychotherapy.* New York: Holt, 1964.

Lorenz, K. On aggression. Wien: Dr. G. Borotha-Schoerler Verlag, 1963. English translation by K. Lorenz. New York: Harcourt, Brace & World, 1966.

Lucas, U. A. *Men in crisis: A study of a mine disaster.* New York: Basic Books, 1969.

Maas, H. S., and Kuypers, J. A. *From thirty to seventy.* San Francisco: Jossey-Bass, 1974.

MacFarlane, Jean W., Allen, L., and Honzik, Marjorie P. A developmental study of the behavior problems of normal children between twenty-one months and fourteen years. Univ. of Calif. Publications in Child Development. Vol. II. Berkeley, Calif.: Univ. California Press, 1954.

MacLean, P. D. Psychosomatic disease and the "visceral brain": Recent developments bearing on the Papez theory of emotion. *Psychosomatic Medicine,* 1949, **11,** 338–353.

MacLean, P. D. The limbic systems with respect to self-preservation and the preservation of the species. *Journal of Nervous and Mental Disorders,* 1958, **127,** 1–11.

Madison, P. *Personality development in college.* New York: Addison-Wesley, 1969.

Madison, P. The campus: Coming of age at college. *Psychology Today,* 1971, **5,** 71–74, 104–108.

Magoun, H. W. *The waking brain.* (2d ed.) Springfield, Ill.: Charles C Thomas, 1963.

Magoun, H. W. *The ascending reticular system and wakefulness.* Springfield, Ill.: Charles C Thomas, 1954.

Maher, B. A. *Principles of psychopathology.* New York: McGraw-Hill, 1966.

Mahl, G. F. Anxiety, HCL secretion, and peptic ulcer etiology. *Psychosomatic Medicine,* 1949, **11,** 30–44.

Mahl, G. F. Physiological changes during chronic fear. *Annals of the New York Academy of Sciences,* 1953, **56,** 240–249.

Mahl, G. F. Relationship between acute and chronic fear and the gastric acidity and blood sugar levels in macaca mulatta monkeys. *Psychosomatic Medicine,* 1953, **14,** 182–210.

Malmo, R. B. Activation: A neuropsychological dimension. *Psychological Review,* 1959, **66,** 367–386.

Malmo, R. B. Studies of anxiety: Some clinical origins of the activation concept. In C. D. Spielberger (ed.), *Anxiety and behavior.* New York: Academic Press, 1966. Pp. 157–177.

Malzberg, B. Important statistical data about mental illness. In S. Arieti (ed.), *American Handbook of Psychiatry.* New York: Basic Books, 1959. Pp. 161–174.

Marshall, S. L. A. *Men against fire.* Washington, D. C.: *The Infantry Journal:* New York: Morrow, 1947. (As cited in Smelser, 1963.)

Martin, B. *Anxiety and neurotic disorders.* New York: Wiley, 1971.

Maslow, A. H. *Motivation and personality.* New York: Harper & Row, 1954.

Mason, J. W. Strategy in psychosomatic research. *Psychosomatic Medicine,* 1970, **32,** 427–439.

Mason, J. W. A re-evaluation of the concept of "non-specificity" in stress theory. *Journal of Psychiatric Research,* 1971, **8,** 323–333.

Masserman, J. H. *Behavior and neurosis.* Chicago: Univ. Chicago Press, 1949.

Masserman, J. H. *Principles of dynamic psychiatry.* 2d ed. Philadelphia: W. B. Saunders Co., 1961.

Masuda, M., and Holmes, T. H. The social readjustment rating scale: A cross-cultural study of Japanese and Americans. *Journal of Psychosomatic Research,* 1967, **11,** 227–237.

Matarazzo, J. D. Some national developments in the utilization of nontraditional mental health manpower. *American Psychologist,* 1971, **26,** 363–372.

May, R. Contributions of existential psychotherapy. In R. May, E. Angel, and H. F. Ellenberger (eds.), *Existence: A new dimension in psychiatry and psychology.* New York: Basic Books, 1958. Pp. 37–91.

May, R. *Psychology and the human dilemma.* Princeton, N.J.: Van Nostrand, 1967.

McClearn, G. E. The inheritance of behavior. In L. J. Postman (ed.), *Psychology in the making.* New York: Knopf, 1962. Pp. 144–252.

McClearn, G. E. *Genetics and behavior development.* Review of Child Development Research. Vol. 1. New York: Russell Sage, 1964.

McGraw, R. B., and Oliven, J. F. Miscellaneous therapies. In S. Arieti (ed.), *American Handbook of Psychiatry,* Vol. II. New York: Basic Books, 1959. Pp. 1552–1582.

McNeil, E. B. *The quiet furies: Man and disorder.* Englewood Cliffs, N.J.: Prentice-Hall, 1967.

Mechanic, D. *Students under stress.* New York: Free Press, 1962.

Mechanic, D. Religion, religiosity, and illness behavior: The special case of the Jews. *Human Organization,* 1963, **22,** 202–208.

Mechanic, D. *Medical sociology.* New York: Free Press, 1968.

Meduna, L. V. Treatment of schizophrenia with induced convulsions. *Zeitschrift für Geschichte, Neurologie und Psychiatry,* 1935, **152,** 235–262.

Meehl, P. E. Schizotaxia, schizotypy, schizophrenia. *American Psychologist,* 1962, **17,** 827–838.

Mehrabian, A. Attitudes in relation to the forms of communicator-object relationship in spoken communications. *Journal of Personality,* 1966, **34,** 80–93.

Mehrabian, A., and Wiener, M. Non-immediacy between communicatory and object of communication in a verbal message: Application to the inference of attitudes. *Journal of Consulting Psychology,* 1966, **30,** 420–425.

Meichenbaum, D. *Cognitive behavior modification.* Morristown, N.J.: General Learning Press, 1974.

Menninger, K. A. Regulatory devices of the ego under major stress. *International Journal of Psychoanalysis,* 1954, **35,** 412–420.

Miller, D. R., and Swanson, G. E. *Inner conflict and defense.* New York: Holt, 1960.

Mintz, A. Non-adaptive group behavior. *Journal of Abnormal and Social Psychology,* 1951, **46,** 150–159.

Moniz, E. *Tentatives operatoires dans le traitement de certaines psychoses.* Paris: Masson, 1936.

Moore, H. E. *Tornadoes over Texas.* Austin, Tex.: Univ. of Texas Press, 1958.

Morris, G. O., and Wynne, L. C. Schizophrenic offspring and parental styles of communication. *Psychiatry,* 1965, **28,** 19–44.

Murphy, Lois B., et al. *The widening world of childhood: Paths toward mastery.* New York: Basic Books, 1962.

Netter, F. H. *The Ciba collection of medical illustrations.* Vol. 1. New York: Ciba, 1958.

Newsweek. The heroin plague: What can be done? July 5, 1971, 27–32.

Nomikos, M. S., Opton, E. Jr., Averill, J. R., and Lazarus, R.S. Surprise and suspense in the production of stress reaction. *Journal of Personality and Social Psychology,* 1968, **8,** 204–208.

Opler, M. K. Cultural differences in mental disorders: An Italian and Irish contrast in the schizophrenias—U.S.A. In M. K. Opler (ed.), *Culture and mental health.* New York: Macmillan, 1959. Pp. 425–442. (a)

Opler, M. K. *Culture and mental health.* New York: Macmillan, 1959. (b)

Osmund, H., and Smithies, J. Schizophrenia: A new approach. *Journal of Mental Science,* 1952, **98,** 309–315.

Ottenberg, D. J. Teenage alcohol abuse: Focusing our concern. *Psychiatric Opinion,* 1975, **12,** 6–11.

Papez, J. W. A proposed mechanism of emotion. *Archives of Neurology and Psychiatry,* 1937, **38,** 725–745. As cited in Magoun, 1963.

Parkes, C. M. *Bereavement.* New York: International Universities Press, 1972.

Pastore, N. *The nature-nurture controversy.* New York: King's Crown, 1949.

Pavlov, I. P. *Lectures on conditioned reflexes.* Vol. 2. W. H. Gantt (ed. and tr.), New York: International Publ., 1941.

Penrose, L. S. Inheritance of phenylpyruvic amentia (phenylketonuria). *Lancet,* 1935, **2,** 192–194.

Perls, F. S. Group vs. individual therapy. *ETC,* 1967, **34,** 306–312.

Perls, F. S. *Gestalt therapy verbatim.* Lafayette, Calif.: Real People Press, 1969.

Perls, F. S., Hefferline, R. F., and Goodman, P. *Gestalt therapy.* New York: Julian Press, 1951.

Pervin, L. A., and Yatko, R. J. Cigarette smoking and alternative methods of reducing dissonance. *Journal of Personal and Social Psychology,* 1965, **2,** 30–36.

Pettigrew, T. F. *Profile of the Negro American.* Princeton, N.J.: Van Nostrand, 1964.

Phillips, B. N., Martin, R. P., and Meyers, J. Interventions in relation to anxiety in school. In C. D. Spielberger (ed.), *Anxiety: Current trends in theory and research.* New York: Academic Press, 1972, Vol. II, pp. 409–464.

Piaget, J. *The origins of intelligence in children.* New York: International Univ. Press, 1952.

Porter, R. W., Brady, J. V., Conrad, D., Mason, J. W., Galambos, R., and Rioch, D. Some experimental observations on gastrointestinal lesions in behaviorally conditioned monkeys. *Psychosomatic Medicine,* 1958, **20,** 379–394.

Prince, M. *The dissociation of personality.* New York: Longmans, 1905.

Prince, M. Miss Beauchamp—The theory of the psychogenesis of multiple personality. *Journal of Abnormal and Social Psychology,* 1920, **15,** 82–85, 87–91, 96–98, 102–104, 135.

Pugh, W., Erickson, J. M., Rubin, R. T., Gunderson, E. K. E., and Rahe, R. H. Cluster analysis of life changes. II. Method and replication in Navy subpopulations. *Archives of General Psychiatry.* 1971, **25,** 333–339.

Rado, S., Buchenholz, B., Dunton, H., Karlin, S. H., and Senescu, R. A. Schizoptypal organization: A preliminary report on a clinical study of schizophrenia. In S. Rado, and G. Daniels (eds.), *Changing concepts in psychoanalytic medicine.* New York: Grune and Stratton, 1956.

Raimy, V. *Misunderstandings of the self.* San Francisco: Jossey-Bass, 1975.

Rank, O. *Will therapy.* Trans. by Julia Taft. New York: Knopf, 1945.

Rank, O. *The trauma of birth.* New York: Bruner, 1952.

Rapoport, A. *House form and culture.* Englewood Cliffs, N.J.: Prentice-Hall, 1969 (paper).

Redlich, F., and Freedman, D. X. *Theory and practice of psychiatry.* New York: Basic Books, 1966.

Reich, W. *Character analysis.* Trans. by J. P. Wolfe, (3d ed.) New York: Orgone Institute Press, 1949.

Reiff, R. The ideological and technological implications of clinical psychology. In *Community Psychology*. Boston, Mass.: Report of the Boston Conference on the Education of Psychologists for Community Mental Health, 1966.

Reik, T. *Listening with the third ear.* New York: Farrar, Straus & Co., 1948.

Reyna, L. J. Conditioning therapies, learning theory, and research. In J. Wolpe, A. Salter, and L. J. Reyna (eds.), *The conditioning therapies.* New York: Holt, 1964. Pp. 169–179.

Ricks, D. F., and Berry, J. C. Family and symptom patterns that precede schizophrenia. In M. Roff and D. F. Ricks (eds.), *Life history research and psychopathology.* Minneapolis: Univ. of Minnesota Press, 1970. Pp. 31–50.

Rimland, B. The differentiation of childhood psychoses: An analysis of checklists for 2,218 psychotic children. *Journal of Autism and Childhood Schizophrenia,* 1971, **1,** 161–174.

Rioch, M. J., Elkes, C., Flint, A. A., Usdansky, B. S., Newman, R. G., and Silber, E. National Institute of Mental Health pilot study in training mental health counselors. *American Journal of Orthopsychiatry,* 1963, **33,** 678–689.

Robins, L. N. *Deviant children grown up.* Baltimore: Williams & Wilkins, 1966.

Rogers, C. R. *Counseling and psychotherapy.* Boston: Houghton Mifflin, 1942.

Rogers, C. R. *Client-centered therapy.* Boston: Houghton Mifflin, 1951.

Rogers, C. R. The process of the basic encounter group. In J. F. T. Bugenthal (ed.), *Challenges of humanistic psychology.* New York: McGraw-Hill, 1967.

Rogers, C. R. *Carl Rogers on encounter groups.* New York: Harper & Row, 1970.

Rokeach, M. (ed.) *The open and the closed mind.* New York: Basic Books, 1960.

Rosenfeld, H. M. Instrumental affiliative functions of facial and gestural expressions. *Journal of Personality and Social Psychology,* 1966, **4,** 65–72.

Rosenhan, D. L. On being sane in insane places. *Science,* 1973, **179,** 250–258.

Rosenthal, D. *Genetic theory and abnormal behavior.* New York: McGraw-Hill, 1970.

Rosenthal, D. Three adoption studies of heredity in the schizophrenia disorders. *International Journal of Mental Health,* 1972, **1,** 63–75.

Rosenthal, D. Issues in high risk studies of schizophrenia. In D. F. Ricks, A. Thomas, and M. Roff (eds.), *Life history research in psychopathology.* Vol. III. Minneapolis: Univ. of Minnesota Press, 1974. Pp. 25–41.

Rubenstein, E. A., and Parloff, M. B. (eds.), *Research in psychotherapy.* Washington, D.C.: American Psychological Association, 1959. (Proceedings of conference on April 9–12, 1958.)

Ruff, G. E., and Korchin, S. J. Psychological responses of the Mercury astronauts to stress. In G. H. Grosser, H. Wechsler, and M. Greenblatt (eds.), *The threat of impending disaster.* Cambridge, Mass.: M.I.T. Press, 1964. Pp. 208–220.

Sachar, E. J., Mackenzie, J. M., Binstock, W. A., and Mack, J. E. Corticosteroid responses to the psychotherapy of reactive depressions: II. Further clinical and physiological implications. *Psychosomatic Medicine,* 1968, **30,** 23–44.

Sarason, I. G. Experimental approaches to test anxiety: Attention and the uses of information. In C. D. Spielberger (ed.), *Anxiety: Current trends in theory and research*. New York: Academic Press, 1972, Vo. II. Pp. 383–403.

Sarbin, T. R. Notes on the transformation of social identity. In N. S. Greenfield, M. H. Miller, and L. M. Roberts (eds.), *Comprehensive mental health: The challenge of evaluation*. Madison, Wis.: Univ. of Wisconsin Press, 1967.

Sarbin, T. R., and Juhasz, J. B. The historical background of the concept of hallucinations. Unpublished manuscript, Univ. of California, Berkeley, 1966.

Sarbin, T. R., and Mancuso, J. C. Failure of a moral enterprise: Attitudes of the public toward mental illness. *Journal of Clinical and Consulting Psychology*. 1970, **35,** 159–173.

Sargent, S. S. Reactions to frustration—A critique and hypothesis. *Psychological Review,* 1948, **55,** 108–114.

Sartre, J. P. *Being and nothingness.* Trans. by Hazel Barnes. New York: Philosophical Library, 1956. Particularly that part entitled "Existential Psychoanalysis."

Schmidt, H. O., and Fonda, C. P. The reliability of psychiatric diagnosis: A new look. *Journal of Abnormal and Social Psychology,* 1956, **52,** 262–267.

Schofield, W., and Balian, Lucy. A comparative study of the personal histories of schizophrenic and non-psychiatric patients. *Journal of Abnormal and Social Psychology,* 1959, **59,** 216–225.

Schreiber, F. R. *Sybil.* New York: Warner, 1974 (paper).

Schwartz, G., and Beatty, J. *Biofeedback: Theory and research.* New York: Academic Press, in press.

Schwarz, B. E., Hakim, K. B., Bickford, R. G., and Lichtenheld, F. R. Behavioral and electroencephalographic effects of hallucinogenic drugs. *Archives of Neurology and Psychiatry,* 1956, **7,** 83–90.

Scott, W. A. Social psychological correlates of mental illness and mental health. *Psychological Bulletin,* 1958, **55,** 65–87.

Selye, H. *The stress of life.* New York: McGraw-Hill, 1956.

Selye, H. *Stress without distress.* Philadelphia: Lippincott, 1974.

Shaffer, J. B. P., and Galinsky, M. D. *Models of group therapy and sensitivity training.* Englewood Cliffs, N. J.: Prentice-Hall, 1974.

Shannon, I. L., and Isbell, G. M. Stress in dental patients: Effect of local anesthetic procedures. Technical Report No. SAM-TDR-63–29. USAF School of Aerospace Medicine, Brooks Air Force Base, Texas, May, 1963.

Shapiro, D., Tursky, B., and Schwartz, G. E. Differentiation of heart rate and blood pressure in man by operant conditioning. *Psychosomatic Medicine,* 1970, **32,** 417–423.

Shaw, E., and Woolley, D. W. Some serotonin-like activities in lysergic acid diethylamide. *Science,* 1956, **124,** 121–122.

Sheldon, W. H. (with the collaboration of S. S. Stevens). *The varieties of temperament: A psychology of constitutional differences.* New York: Harper & Row, 1942.

Sheldon, W. H. (with the collaboration of C. W. Dupertuis and E. McDermott).

Atlas of men. New York: Harper, 1954.

Shneidman, E. S. Orientations toward death: A vital aspect of the study of lives. In R. W. White (ed.), *The study of lives.* New York: Atherton Press, 1963. Pp. 201–227.

Shoben, E. J., Jr. Toward a concept of the normal personality. *American Psychologist,* 1957, **12,** 183–189.

Silber, E., Hamburg, D. A., Coelho, G. V., Murphy, Elizabeth B., Rosenberg, M., and Pearlin, L. I. Adaptive behavior in competent adolescents. *Archives of General Psychiatry,* 1961, **5,** 354–365.

Simpson, M. T., Olewine, D. A., Jenkins, C. D., Ramsey, F. H., Zyzanski, S. J., Thomas, G. T., and Hames, C. G. Exercise-induced catecholamines and platelet aggregation in the coronary-prone behavior pattern. *Psychosomatic Medicine,* 1974, **36,** 476–487.

Singer, J. L., and Opler, M. K. Contrasting patterns of fantasy and motility in Irish and Italian schizophrenics. *Journal of Abnormal and Social Psychology,* 1956, **53,** 42–47.

Singer, M. T., and Wynne, L. C. Stylistic variables in family research. Unpublished paper presented at a symposium sponsored by Marquette University and Milwaukee Psychiatric Hospital, October, 1964.

Singer, M. T., and Wynne, L. C. Communication styles in parents of normals, neurotics and schizophrenics: Some findings using a new Rorschach scoring manual. *American Psychiatric Association Research Report No. 20,* Washington, D. C.: American Psychiatric Association, 1966. Pp. 24–38.

Skinner, B. F. *The behavior of organisms.* New York: Appleton, 1938.

Smelser, N. J. *Theory of collective behavior.* New York: Free Press, 1963.

Smelser, N. J., and Smelser, W. T. (eds.), *Personality and social systems (2nd ed.).* New York: Wiley, 1970.

Smith, M. B. "Mental health" reconsidered: A special case of the problem of values in psychology. *American Psychologist,* 1961, **16,** 299–306.

Smith, M. B. The revolution in mental health care—"A bold new approach"? In M. B. Smith (ed.), *Social psychology and human values: Selected essays by M. Brewster Smith.* Chicago: Aldine, 1969. Pp. 252–260. Also appeared in *Transaction Magazine,* St. Louis: Washington University, 1968.

Spiro, M. E. Cultural heritage, personal tensions, and mental illness in a South Sea culture. In M. K. Opler (ed.), *Culture and mental health.* New York: Macmillan, 1959. Pp. 141–172.

Spitzer, S. P. and Denzin, N. K. (eds.) *The mental patient: Studies in the sociology of deviance.* New York: McGraw-Hill, 1968.

Sprenger, J., and Kraemer, H. *Institoris, H. Malleus Maleficarum.* Trans. by Rev. Montague Summers. London: Pushkin, 1928.

Srole, L., Langner, T., Michael, S., Stanley, T., Opler, M. K., and Rennie, T. A. C. *Mental health in the metropolis: The midtown Manhattan study.* New York: McGraw-Hill, 1962.

Stampfl, T. G., and Levis, D. J. Essentials of implosive therapy: A learning-theory-based psychodynamic behavioral therapy. *Journal of Abnormal Psychology,* 1967, **72,** 496–503.

Stanton, A. H., and Schwartz, M. S. *The mental hospital.* New York: Basic Books, 1954.

Stern, C. *Principles of human genetics.* San Francisco: Freeman, 1960.

Sternbach, R. A. *Principles of psychophysiology.* New York: Academic Press, 1966.

Strupp, H. H. The outcome in psychotherapy revisited. *Psychotherapy,* 1963, **1,** 1–13.

Symington, T., Currie, A. R., Curran, R. S., and Davidson, J. N. The reaction of the adrenal cortex in conditions of stress. In Ciba Foundations Colloquia on Endocrinology, Vol. VIII, *The human adrenal cortex.* Boston: Little, Brown, 1955. Pp. 70–91.

Szara, S., Axelrod, J., and Perlin, S. Is adrenochrome present in the blood? *American Journal of Psychiatry,* 1958, **115,** 162–163.

Szasz, T. S. The myth of mental illness. *American Psychologist,* 1960, **15,** 113–118.

Szasz, T. S. *The myth of mental illness.* New York: Norton, 1961.

Szasz, T. S. *Law, Liberty and psychiatry.* New York: Macmillan, 1963.

Thigpen, C. H., and Kleckley, H. M. *The three faces of Eve.* New York: Harper, 1949.

Thompson, W. R. Behavior genetics. In *McGraw-Hill Yearbook of Science and Technology.* New York: McGraw-Hill, 1965. Pp. 27–35.

Thoreson, C. E., and Mahoney, M. J. *Behavioral self-control.* New York: Holt, 1974.

Tinbergen, N. *The study of instincts.* New York: Oxford Univ. Press, 1961.

Tinbergen, N. Ethology and stress diseases. *Science,* 1974, **185,** 20–27.

Toch, H. *Violent men.* Chicago: Aldine, 1969.

Toffler, A. *Future shock.* New York: Random House, 1970.

Tompkins, V. H. Stress in aviation. In J. Hambling (ed.), *The nature of stress disorder.* Springfield, Ill.: Charles C Thomas, 1959. Pp. 73–80.

Trevor-Roper, H. R. Witches and witchcraft. *Encounter,* May, 1967, **28**(5), 3–25; June, 13–34.

Tyler, Leona, E. *Tests and measurements.* 2d ed. Englewood Cliffs, N.J.: Prentice-Hall, 1971.

Ullmann, L. P. *Institution and outcome: A comparative study of psychiatric hospitals.* London: Pergamon Press, 1967.

U.S. Department of Health, Education and Welfare. NIMH reports continued drop in patient population. *Psychiatric News,* 1969, **4,** 16.

U.S. Department of Health, Education and Welfare. Population dip in institutions cited in report. *Psychiatric News,* 1970, **5,** 28.

Visotsky, H. M., Hamburg, D. A., Goss, Mary E., and Lebovits, B. Z. Coping behavior under extreme stress. *Archives of General Psychiatry,* 1961, **5,** 423–448.

von Kugelgen, E. R. Psychological determinants of the delay in decision to seek aid in cases of myocardial infarction. Ph.D. dissertation, Univ. of California, Berkeley, 1975.

Ward, Mary J. *The snake pit.* New York: Knopf, 1946.

Watson, J. B. *Behaviorism,* New York: People's Institute Publ., 1924.

Watson, J. B., and Rayner, R. Conditioned emotional reactions. *Journal of Experimental Psychology,* 1920, **3,** 1–14.

Watt, N. F. Longitudinal changes in the social behavior of children hospitalized for schizophrenia as adults. *Journal of Nervous and Mental Disease,* 1972, **155,** 42–54.

Watt, N. F. Childhood roots of schizophrenia. In D. F. Ricks, A. Thomas, and M. Roff (eds.), *Life history research in psychopathology.* Vol. III. Minneapolis: Univ. of Minnesota Press (in press; cited in Garmezy, 1974).

Watt, N. F., Tolorow, R. D., Lubensky, A. W., and McClelland, D. C. School adjustment and behavior of children hospitalized for schizophrenia as adults. *American Journal of Orthopsychiatry,* 1970, **40,** 637–657.

Weiss, J. M. *Effects of coping behavior on development of gastrointestinal lesions in rats.* Proceedings of the 75th Annual Convention, American Psychological Association, 1967. Pp. 135–136.

Weitzman, B. Behavior therapy and psychotherapy. *Psychological Review,* 1967, **74,** 300–317.

Wenger, M. A., Jones, F. N., and Jones, M. H. Physiological psychology. New York: Holt, 1956.

White, R. W. Motivation reconsidered: The concept of competence. *Psychological Review,* 1959, **66,** 297–333.

Whiting, J. W. M., and Child, I. L. *Child training and personality: A cross-cultural study.* New Haven, Conn.: Yale Univ. Press, 1953.

Whorf, B. L. Science and linguistics. In T. M. Newcomb and E. L. Hartley (eds.), *Readings in social psychology.* New York: Holt, 1947, pp. 210–218.

Wile, I. S. What constitues abnormality. *American Journal of Orthopsychiatry,* 1940, **10,** 216–228.

Wilbairs, R. J. *Biochemical individuality.* New York: Wiley, 1956.

Williams, R. L., and Long, J. D. *Toward a self-managed life style.* Boston: Houghton Mifflin, 1975.

Withey, S. B. Reaction to uncertain threat. In G. W. Baker and D. W. Chapman (eds.), *Man and society in disaster.* New York: Basic Books, 1962. Pp. 93–123.

Witkin, H. A. Psychological differentiation and forms of pathology. *Journal of Abnormal and Social Psychology,* 1965, **70,** 317–336.

Witkin, H. A., Dyk, R. B., Faterson, H. F., Goodenough, D. R., and Karp, S. A. *Psychological differentiation.* New York: Wiley, 1962.

Witkin, H. A., Lewis, Helen, B., Machover, Karen, Meissner, P. B., and Wapner, S. *Personality through perception.* New York: Harper & Row, 1954.

Wittenborn, J. R. Symptom patterns in a group of mental hospital patients. *Journal of Consulting Psychology,* 1951, **15,** 290–302.

Wittenborn, J. R., and Holzberg, J. D. The generality of psychiatric syndromes.

Journal of Consulting Psychology, 1951, **15,** 372–380.

Wittkower, E. D., and Fried, J. Some problems of transcultural psychiatry. *International Journal of Social Psychiatry,* 1958, **3,** 245–252.

Wolberg, L. R. *Hypoanalysis.* New York: Grune & Stratton, 1945.

Wolf, M., Risley, T., and Mees, H. Application of operant conditioning procedures to the behavior problems of an autistic child. *Behavior Research and Therapy,* 1964, **1,** 305–312.

Wolf, S., and Wolff, H. G. *Human gastric function.* Oxford Univ. Press, 1947.

Wolff, C. T., Friedman, S. B., Hofer, M. A., and Mason, J. W. Relationship between psychological defenses and mean urinary 17-hydroxycorticosteroid excretion rates: I. A predictive study of parents of fatally ill children. *Psychosomatic Medicine,* 1964, **26,** 576–591.

Wolff, P. H. Observations on newborn infants. *Psychosomatic Medicine,* 1959, **21,** 110–118.

Wolpe, J. *Psychotherapy by reciprocal inhibition.* Stanford, Calif.: Stanford Univ. Press, 1958.

Wolpe, J. *The practice of behavior therapy.* 2d ed. New York: Pergamon, 1974.

Woolley, L. F. Experimental factors essential to the development of schizophrenia. In P. Hoch and J. Zubin (eds.), *Current problems in psychiatric diagnosis.* New York: Grune & Stratton, 1953.

Wynne, L. C., Ryckoff, I., Day, J., and Hirsch, S. Pseudomutuality in the family relations of schizophrenics. *Psychiatry,* 1958, **21,** 205–220.

Wynne, L. C., and Singer, M. T. Thought disorder and family relations of schizophrenics: I. A research strategy. *Archives of General Psychiatry,* 1963, **9,** 191–198.

Yolles, S. Patient release hits peak. *Science News,* 1967, **92,** 107.

Yolles, S. F., and Kramer, M. Vital statistics. In L. Bellak and L. Loeb (eds.), *The schizophrenic syndrome.* New York: Grune & Stratton, 1969. Pp. 66–113.

Zborowski, M. Cultural components in response to pain. In E. G. Jaco (ed.), *Patients, physicians, and illness.* New York: Free Press, 1958. Pp. 256–268.

Zigler, E. Familial mental retardation: A continuing dilemma. *Science,* 1967, **155,** 292–298,

Zigler, E., and Phillips, L. Psychiatric diagnosis: A critique. *Journal of Abnormal and Social Psychology,* 1961, **63,** 607–618.

Zilboorg, G., with G. W. Henry. *A history of medical psychology.* New York: Norton, 1941.

Zola, I. K. Culture and symptoms—An analysis of patients' presenting complaints. *American Sociological Review,* 1966, **31,** 615–630.

ACKNOWLEDGMENTS

p. 28, Figure 2-3. From *On Aggression* by Konrad Lorenz, copyright © 1963 by Dr. G. Borotha-Schoeler Verlag, Vien; English translation copyright © 1966 by Konrad Lorenz. Reproduced by permission of Harcourt-Brace-Jovanovich, Inc.

p. 50, Figure 3-1. Nomikos, M. S., Opton, E. Jr., Averill, J. R., and Lazarus, R. S. Surprise and suspense in the production of stress reaction, *Journal of Personality and Social Psychology*, 1968, 8, 206. Copyright 1968 by the American Psychological Association. Reprinted by permission.

p. 51, Table 3-1. From Tompkins, V. H. Stress in aviation, in J. Hambling (ed.), *The Nature of Stress Disorder*, 1959, p. 76. Courtesy of Charles C Thomas, Publisher, Springfield, Illinois.

pp. 53, 66. Hamburg, David A., Hamburg, B., and DeGoya, S. Adaptive problems and mechanisms in severely burned patients, *Psychiatry*, 1953, 16: 2–4, 19. Reprinted by special permission of The William Alanson White Psychiatric Foundation, Inc.

pp. 58, 63, 77, 95—Table 4-1. Mechanic, D. *Students Under Stress*. New York: Free Press, 1962, pp. 37, 121, 142, and 158. Copyright 1962 by The Free Press of Glencoe, a division of the Macmillan Company.

p. 58. Friedman, S. B., Urodoff, P., Mason, J. W., and Hamburg, D. A. Behavioral observations on parents anticipating the death of a child, *Pediatrics*, 1963, 32, 618–619.

p. 61, Table 3-6. Epstein, S. The measurement of drive and conflict in humans: Theory and experiment, in M. R. Jones (ed.), *Nebraska Symposium on Motivation*. Lincoln, University of Nebraska Press, 1962, p. 179.

p. 68, Table 3-9. Glickstein, M., *et al.*, Temporal heart rate patterns in anxious patients, *Archives of Neurological Psychiatry*, 1957, 78: 101–106.

p. 76. "She Begged and Wept for Son's Treatment," San Francisco *Examiner*, February 9, 1975, p. 22.

p. 103, Figure 5-3A. From Magoun, H. W. *The Ascending Reticular System and Wakefulness*, 1954. Courtesy of Charles C Thomas, Publisher, Springfield, Illinois.

p. 103, Figure 5-3B. French, J. D., Hernandez Peon, R., and Livingston, R. B. Projections from cortex to cephalic brain stem (reticular formation) in monkey, *Journal of Neurophysiology*, 1955, 18, 74–95.

p. 106, Figure 5-4. Krech, D., and Crutchfield, R. S., *Elements of Psychology*. New York: Alfred A. Knopf, 1969.

p. 107, Table 5-1. Wenger, M. A., Jones, F. N., and Jones, M. H. *Physiological Psychology*. New York: Holt, Rinehart, and Winston, 1956.

p. 108. Sternbach, R. A. *Principles of Psychophysiology*, New York: Academic Press, 1966, pp. 23–24.

p. 112, Figure 5-6. Mason, J. W. Strategy in psychosomatic research, *Psychosomatic Medicine*, 1970, 32, 436.

p. 113, Figure 5-7. Adapted from an original painting by Frank H. Netter, M.D. from THE CIBA COLLECTION OF MEDICAL ILLUSTRATIONS. Copyright by CIBA Pharmaceutical Company, Division of CIBA-GEIGY Corporation. All rights reserved.

p. 115, Figure 5-9. From *Stress Without Distress* by Hans Selye, M.D. Copyright © 1974 by Hans Selye, M.D. Reprinted by permission of J. B. Lippincott Company.

p. 121, Table 5-2. Holmes, T. H., and Rahe, R. H. The social readjustment rating scale. *Journal of Psychosomatic Research*, 1967, 11, 216.

pp. 130, 136. From *Abnormal Psychology and Modern Life*, Fourth Edition by James C. Coleman. Copyright © 1972 by Scott, Foresman and Company. Reprinted by permission of the publisher.

p. 142. Mahrer, B. A. *Principles of Psychopathology*. New York: McGraw-Hill, 1966, p. 3

p. 143. Masserman, J. H. *Behavior and Neurosis*. Chicago: University of Chicago Press, 1949, p. 43.

p. 148. Hornick, E. J., and Myles, C. L. Teenage drinking, *Psychiatric Opinion*, 1975, 12, 13–14.

pp. 148–149. McNeil, E. B. *The Quiet Furies: Man and Disorder*. Englewood Cliffs, N.J.: Prentice-Hall, 1967, pp. 185–186.

p. 158, Reprinted from G. H. Grosser, H. Wechsler, and M. Greenblatt (eds.) *The Threat of Impending Disaster* by permission of the M.I.T. Press, Cambridge, Massachusetts.

pp. 154–156. Grinker, R. R. "Mentally healthy" young males (homoclites), *Archives of General Psychiatry*, 1962, 6, 405. Copyright 1962, American Medical Association.

p. 164. Madison, P. *Personality Developments in College*, 1969, Addison-Wesley, Reading, Mass.

p. 165. Madison, P. The campus: coming of age at college. Reprinted from *Psychology Today* Magazine, October 1971. Copyright © 1971 Ziff-Davis Publishing Company. All rights reserved.

pp. 167–169. Barron, F. *Creativity and Psychological Health*. Princeton N.J.: Van Nostrand, 1963, p. 144.

pp. 167–168. "SLA Woman's Last Letter," San Francisco *Chronicle*. © Chronicle Publishing Company, 1974.

pp. 169, 181. Smith, M. B., "Mental health" reconsidered, *American Psychologist*, 1961, 16, 299–306. Copyright 1961 by the American Psychological Association. Reprinted by permission.

pp. 175. Knutson, A. L. New perspectives regarding positive mental health, *American Psychologist*, 1963, 18, 300–306. Copyright 1963 by the American Psychological Association. Reprinted by permission.

pp. 190–192. Frank, J. D. *Persuasion and Healing*. New York: Schocken Books, 1963, pp. 46–49.

pp. 196–197. "From Charity to Bloodshed—An Overview of Medieval Contributions," (pp. 68–70) in *The History of Psychiatry* by Franz G. Alexander, M.D. and Sheldon T. Selesnick, M.D. Copyright © 1966 by The Estate of Franz Alexander and Sheldon Selesnick. By permission of Harper & Row, Publishers.

p. 208, Figure 9-2. Lerner, J. M. *Heredity, Evolution, and Society*. San Francisco: W. H. Freeman and Co., 1968, p. 240.

p. 209, Table 9-1. Reprinted from *Heredity in Health and Mental Disorder* by Franz J. Kallman, M.D. By permission of W. W. Norton & Company, Inc.

p. 210, text, and Table 9-2. Thompson, W. R. Behavior genetics in *McGraw-Hill Yearbook of Science and Technology*. New York: McGraw-Hill, 1965, pp. 27–35.

p. 213, Figure 9-3. Maher, B. A. *Principles of Psychopathology*. New York: McGraw-Hill, 1966, p. 332.

p. 221, Figure 9-5. Lerner, I. M. *Heredity, Evolution, and Society*, San Francisco, W. H. Freeman and Co., 1968, p. 285.

p. 231. Opler, M. K. *Culture and Mental Health*. New York: Macmillan, 1959, p. 437.

p. 246, Table 11-1. Singer, M. T., and Wynne, L. C. Communication styles in parents of normals, neurotics, and schizophrenics, *American Psychiatric Association Research Report #20*. Washington, D.C.: American Psychiatric Association, 1966, p. 32.

pp. 259–260, 264, 266–267. Zigler, E., and Phillips, L. Psychiatric diagnosis: a critique, *Journal of Abnormal and Social Psychology*, 1961, 63, 607–618. Copyright 1961 by The American Psychological Association. Reprinted by permission.

pp. 261–262. From "Mental Disorders" by John A. Clausen, which appears in

Contemporary Social Problems by Robert K. Merton and Robert Nisbet, Copyright 1961, 1966 by Harcourt Brace Jovanovich, Inc. and reprinted with their permission.

p. 263, Table 12-1. Wittenborn, J. R., and Holzberg, J. D. The generality of psychiatric syndromes, *Journal of Consulting Psychology*, 1951, 15, 372–380. Copyright 1951 by The American Psychological Association. Reprinted by permission.

pp. 277–279. Anthony, E. J. A risk-vulnerability-prevention program for children of psychotic parents, E. J. Anthony and C. Koupernik (eds.), *Children at Psychiatric Risk*. New York, John Wiley and Sons, in press.

pp. 288, 293–302. Kenneth Mark Colby, *A Primer for Psychotherapists*. Copyright 1951, The Ronald Press Company, New York.

pp. 291–292. Franz, Alexander, and Thomas M. French, *Psychoanalytic Therapy-Principles and Applications*. Copyright 1946, renewed © 1974, The Ronald Press Company, New York.

pp. 308–310. From *Existence: A New Dimension in Psychiatry and Psychology*, by Rollo May, Ernest Angel, Henri F. Ellenberger, Editors, © 1958 by Basic Books, Inc., Publishers, New York.

pp. 308–309. May, R. *Psychology and the Human Dilemma*. Princeton, N.J.: Van Nostrand, 1967, pp. 70, 109.

pp. 311–312. Reprinted by permission of the editor and the publisher from A. Levitsky and F. Perls, The rules and games of Gestalt Therapy, J. Fagan and J. L. Shepard (Eds.), *Gestalt Therapy Now*. Palo Alto, Calif.: Science and Behavior Books, 1970.

pp. 314–318. John B. P. Shaffer and M. David Galinsky, *Models of Group Therapy and Sensitivity Training*, © 1974, pp. 94–98. Reprinted by permission of Prentice-Hall, Inc., Englewood Cliffs, New Jersey.

p. 322. London, P. *The Modes and Morals of Psychotherapy*. New York: Holt, Rinehart, and Winston, 1964, pp. 75–76.

pp. 327–328. Reprinted with permission from Joseph Wolpe, *The Practice of Behavior Therapy*, 1974, Pergamon Press, Inc., pp. 123–124.

p. 329, Table 14-1. Lang, P. J., and Lazorik, A. D. Experimental desensitization and the experimental reduction of threat, *Journal of Abnormal Psychology*, 1968, 73, 106. Copyright 1968 by the American Psychological Association. Reprinted by permission.

p. 331, Figure 14-4. Folkins, C. H., Lawson, K. D., Opton, E. M. Jr., and Lazarus, R. S. Desensitization and the experimental reduction of threat, *Journal of Abnormal Psychology*, 1968, 73, 106. Copyright 1968 by The American Psychological Association. Reprinted by permission.

p. 335, 338, 349. Lazarus, A. A. *Behavior Therapy and Beyond*. New York: McGraw-Hill, 1971, pp. 33–36, 218–219.

pp. 336–337, Table 14-2. Korchin, S. J. *Psychology and Mental Health*. New York: Basic Books, in press.

pp. 340–342. Ellis, A. A. A homosexual treated with rational psychotherapy, *Journal of Clinical Psychology*, 1959, 15, 340–343.

pp. 359–362. Jarvik, M. E. The psychopharmacological revolution. Reprinted from *Psychology Today* Magazine, May 1967. Copyright © 1967. Ziff-Davis Publishing Company. All rights reserved.

INDEX

Page numbers in *italic* refer to Reference section.